Coalition Strategies of
Marxist Parties

Coalition Strategies of Marxist Parties

Edited by Trond Gilberg

Duke University Press   Duke Press Policy Studies

Durham and London 1989

© 1989 Duke University Press
All rights reserved
Printed in the United States of America
on acid-free paper ∞
Library of Congress Cataloging-in-Publication Data
Coalition strategies of Marxist parties / Trond Gilberg, editor.
p.   cm. — (Duke Press policy studies)
Bibliography: p.
Includes index.
ISBN 0-8223-0849-5
1. Communist strategy.   2. Communist parties   3. Coalition
governments.   I. Gilberg, Trond, 1940-   . II. Series.
HX518.S8C55 1989   88-9579
324.2—dc19

Contents

Editor's Preface   vii

Acknowledgments   ix

1 Introduction   *Trond Gilberg*   1

2 Coalition Strategies and Tactics in Marxist Thought
Jiri Valenta   29

PART 1   Regional Studies: Europe

Overview   *Trond Gilberg*   59

3 Marxists and Coalitions in Western Europe   *Trond Gilberg*   62

4 Communists in the Postwar All-Party Coalitions of
Eastern Europe   *Charles Gati*   106

PART 2   Regional Studies: Developing Countries

Overview   *Trond Gilberg*   133

5 Marxists and Coalitions in Latin America   *John D. Martz*   135

6 Vietnamese Communism and the Strategy of the United Front
William J. Duiker   173

7 The Coalition Strategies and Tactics of Indian Communism
Stanley A. Kochanek   202

8 Coalition Strategies and Tactics of Marxist Parties in Africa
David E. Albright   238

9 The Coalition Strategies and Tactics of the Indonesian Communist
Party: A Prelude to Destruction   *Frank Cibulka*   284

10 Conclusion   *Trond Gilberg*   304

Notes   325

Index   355

Contributors   377

Editor's Preface

During the early part of this decade, many individuals, both policy makers and scholars, wondered about the "new look" of some communist parties as they billed themselves as potential participants in the pluralistic game of politics in many parts of the world. This image was certainly different from the old notion of dedicated revolutionaries who scornfully rejected the existing order and plotted its overthrow. How genuine was the new look? Were the communists sincere when they discussed coalitions and alliances? What were their long-range strategic goals of interaction with other elements of the political order in which they operated? What were their tactical policies in pursuit of these strategic goals? Some of us began to examine these questions more systematically. We ran a panel at an academic conference, enjoyed the feedback from our colleagues, and began the process of writing this book. Now, several years later, it is a finished product, after many full-scale revisions and updates. The topic is still very relevant, and that shows the enduring importance of the questions we asked a number of years ago. Scholars will need to return to this question in the future; perhaps the best strategy is a continuous examination of this crucial subject.

Acknowledgments

Many individuals have played an important part in the making of this book. There are, first of all, the contributors, without whom there naturally would have been no book. They endured my repeated calls for revisions in stolid perseverance and responded with excellent analyses. Professor William Riker of the University of Rochester provided invaluable commentary, both directly and indirectly through his pioneering work on coalitions. Professor Vernon V. Aspaturian of The Pennsylvania State University supplied much valuable criticism and, as usual, offered many brilliant suggestions on this and other topics. Richard Rowson particularly guided me through the many drafts of the manuscript. Susan Eberly did a superb job of editing, and Linda Verbeck endured my handwriting and competently typed the various versions. My family endured my long hours at the office and put up with my occasional preoccupation with coalition strategies and tactics. The reviewers of the manuscript provided many useful suggestions. I owe all of these individuals much gratitude for their efforts. I hope they enjoyed the project as much as I did.

1

Introduction
Trond Gilberg

One of the dominant issues of politics worldwide during the last century has been the question of how political organizations that call themselves "Marxist" conduct relations with other structures in the domestic political system and how they relate to the self-appointed "centers" of the "world communist movement," whether such a center is located in Moscow, Beijing, Belgrade, or Havana. Karl Marx is partly responsible for this confusion, because there were a number of personifications of this remarkable thinker: first, Marx the humanist, concerned with human alienation and its remedy, human freedom; then, Marx the revolutionary, who wrote endlessly about the injustices of capitalist society as he saw it and the ways in which this form of socioeconomic and political system could be destroyed and a better world built upon its ruins; finally, the older "mature" Marx (and his successor Friedrich Engels) who examined societies from the vantage point of their capacity for peaceful change—reform rather than revolution. An individual can claim any or all of these three heritages of Marx, and the many variations create the extraordinarily rich tapestry of concepts known as "Marxist." This variety (and the ensuing confusion) has been responsible for some of the fiercest infighting among disciples of the original mentor, as we shall see below.

The conceptual diversity created by Marx and Engels was further complicated by the rise of many individuals who claimed to be disciples of the masters but in fact proceeded to change some basic tenets of "Marxism" or to add to them in such a way that the new conceptual package bore only *some* resemblance to the original. Throughout Europe there emerged syndicalists, anarchists, and anarcho-syndicalists. There were revisionists and Bakuninists, and many who simply entertained vague notions about the injustices of the societies in which they lived and the need to do something about it. Some of these individuals called themselves "socialists," and we should remember that "socialists" of all shades until very recently paid homage to Karl Marx and Friedrich Engels even as they rather consistently produced programs and policies that deviated significantly, in spirit and execution, from any or all of the "Marxes" known in their time. It was a sine qua non for anyone on the left to call himself or herself a "Marxist" and to adopt the trappings of this complex creed, be they slogans, symbols, or expected acts.

The most important of these "latecomers" were the individuals who struggled for leadership of the Russian Social Democratic party in the late 1800s, not because they were more profound thinkers than others but because some of them went on to capture power in a very large country, thus assuring for themselves the right to add their notions of "Marxism" to the hopper. Furthermore, the fact that these individuals ended up in power, while others who also considered themselves Marxists did not, established as a political fact the notion that the Russians would end up as leaders of the international movement that based itself upon Marxist thought, thus indelibly influencing the very notion of Marxism and, in fact, producing a separate brand, "Marxism-Leninism." This brand, in turn, changed over time, both in theory and in practice, thus further confounding the efforts of those who would like to try to bring some analytical sense to this welter of concepts.

The fact of acquired political power helped establish a particular version of one aspect of Marxism as the dominant creed, both theoretically and in practical policy, after the Russian Revolution. The same fact of acquired power also produced the greatest challenge to Russian (or Soviet) supremacy in interpretations of Marx, because it was Maoism *in power* that gave rise to the *ideological* debates between Moscow and Beijing and the Maoist challenge, which in turn had significant organizational ramifications on the left of the political spectrum throughout the world. Some of the bitterest political struggles fought anywhere during the last century have been the ideological battles between "Russian" and "Chinese" Marxists. This is not really surprising; after all, civil wars tend to be more brutal and fundamental than regular warfare. (This statement, of course, implies that all Marxists have something in common, no matter how furious their protestations to the contrary; more about this later.)

In between the establishment of Russian ideological supremacy and the rise of the Chinese challenge there developed a great many varieties of Marxism, produced by regional, cultural, and individual differences and proclivities. Each movement had its own thinkers, poets, songwriters, speechwriters, orators, and bureaucrats. Some of these thinkers were more sophisticated than Lenin, more "Marxist" (whether "early," "middle," or "mature") than Zinoviev, more exciting writers than Stalin (which actually did not require a great deal of writing capability). Nevertheless, they were "Marxists," too. But the Soviets ran a country, and they became more important for that reason. Thus we must all pay attention to the "Marxist-Leninists" every day, and particularly those who run the Soviet Union itself. No other fact of political life has had a more profound effect upon "Marxism" than the exercise of power by alleged "Marxists."

Marx and Engels were Europeans (and *West* Europeans at that). Lenin, Trotsky, and even Stalin had (or acquired) a European orientation. It therefore stands to reason that the early ideological debates of Marxist doctrine focused on themes that were familiar to Europeans, at least in part. The Russians were, of course, "hybrid" Europeans, and many of their ideas carry important overtones of a historical and cultural background that is quite different from that of Central or Western Europe or Scandinavia. But there were others, elsewhere, who also considered themselves Marxists, often because they had lived in Europe and had become acquainted with the tenets and the debates of European leftists; others had simply read the works of the great mentors and felt a kindred spirit. This was true of individuals in parts of Asia and Latin America. These individuals either subordinated themselves to the European-based doctrine and tried to apply it to their own conditions, or they interpreted it creatively in their own setting, even producing themes and ideologies that competed with important aspects of Karl Marx's work. No matter; even in the latter case these individuals considered themselves Marxist, and were proud of it. Such was the amazing pull of this multifaceted doctrine everywhere.

Africa was rather different. Most of the continent was divided among colonial powers, and the inspiration for "Marxists" therefore came mostly from Europeans who happened to be in Africa. As time passed, indigenous thinkers also developed a connection between the European Marx and their own ideas about politics, economics, and society. Particularly in Africa, but also in those parts of Asia which were under colonial rule, the basic ideas of "Marxism" were fundamentally tied in with the crucial question of how one relates to these Europeans, whether as thinkers, colonial administrators, revolutionaries, or economic exploiters. Hence the inextricable link between the alleged *internationalist* doctrine of Marxism, on the one hand, and national independence, on the other hand. This is a connection that Marx may not have wanted (although that, too, is an assumption that may be repudiated by some of his writing); but no matter, in the 1980s the conflict between nationalism and internationalism is *the* most important question for all "Marxists," and thus for all of us, directly or indirectly.

At this point one must ask about *commonalities* in this rich and confusing doctrine that is called Marxism by scholars who study it, individuals and groups who allegedly practice it, and masses of people who fear it. What, if anything, do *all* "Marxists" have in common? I would venture to suggest that they *do* have a number of characteristics in common, and that these characteristics are so important that we can justifiably speak of Marxists as definable political entities and thence proceed to examine them.

First of all, Marxists of all kinds share a sense of outrage at the existing political and socioeconomic order, be it "feudal" or "capitalist." It is seen as exploitative, unjust, favoring the few at the expense of the many, inefficient and wasteful, and only marginally contributing to the fulfillment of the human potential. There is a great deal of the early Marx in this view of the presocialist society, and this may indeed account for the power of persuasion that Marxism has for so many people, for it pinpoints fundamental human needs and their shortcomings while stating most forcefully that *it* stands for justice, fairness, and humanity. It is not difficult to understand that such a doctrine can appeal to an unemployed steel worker whose children cannot go on to higher education, the desk clerk laboring under a tyrannical master for measly wages, the coolie in the rice fields who must always worry about his next meal, the marginal farmer eking out a living on substandard soil, or the day laborer at the mercy of the union boss in the hiring hall. The Marxist emphasis on justice and the good society also appeals to the intellectual and the dreamer, the theorist and the utopian. Marxism is, in a fundamental sense, a powerful doctrine of protest in an imperfect world. In a way, it is so broadly based in the matters it protests and the solutions it offers that we are all in some measure, however small, Marxists.

Second, "Marxists" believe, at least doctrinally and officially, that human beings are perfectible, that they are "good" at the core. The injustices against which all "Marxists" inveigh are caused by mistakes in the way that humans have organized themselves into societies, and not by basic flaws in the nature of man and woman. There are, no doubt, many careerists and fellow travelers who disregard this philosophical notion for narrow personal purposes, and Marxism in practice also tends to dent this belief most severely, because there is often a great deal of distance between the *theory* of the good society and the *practice* of Marxist regimes. This discrepancy does not invalidate the drawing power of the dream of human perfectibility, however; it simply leads Marxists toward searches for new ways to make manifest the doctrine of human goodness. Thus, for every individual who succumbs to cynicism because practical Marxism is a betrayal of Marx the theorist and believer, there is another who is attracted to precisely those aspects of the dream that can be called idealistic.

Third, "Marxists" claim that they know *how* to create the conditions necessary for the fulfillment of human potential, thus creating the good society. Specifically, Marxism claims that exploitation, alienation, and the injustice that humans perpetrate upon each other can be removed by rearranging the political and economic relationships in society and establishing a new societal order. Specifics may differ on how this is accomplished, but the notion of fundamental political and socioeconomic change as a prerequisite for the new society is common to all "Marxists." For example, the exploiters who must be dethroned, the "expropriators" who must be "expropriated"—be they the bankers, the industrialists, the military-industrial complex, the comprador bourgeoisie, the feudal landlords, the absentee landowners, or the lackeys of foreign imperialism —must be thrown aside in favor of something new, this "something" being rule based, first, upon a revolutionary class, and, subsequently, upon the "whole people." This "revolutionary class" may be the urban proletariat, the poor peasantry, or the rural day laborers; there may be combinations of these elements, and the combination may vary over time. The common theme is the notion that it is the *exploited* who will become the rulers, and these new rulers will exercise more justice, understanding, and humanity than their predecessors, precisely because the new leaders have experienced exploitation and thus know what it is and how to avoid it. Again, there are undoubtedly untold numbers of careerists and cynics who extol these ideas for their own personal, parochial purposes. But the *doctrine* is still attractive on this point and ensures that Marxism has an appeal beyond that of mere careerism.

Fourth, Marxism continues to claim historical necessity, determinism, the inevitability that the promised land will be reached *some day*. This notion has become rather shopworn over time, and it is possible that few of those who now rule in the name of Karl Marx actually believe this. But the early attraction of the doctrine surely had something to do with this claim to certainty, and out of this early attractiveness came the mass movement, which produced organization, hierarchy, power—the main sources of attraction today. The notion that Marxism in theory and practice will, in fact, be around for a very long time also has a great deal to do with more practical notions of planning, redistribution of wealth, and the accumulation of wealth, socialist style.

Fifth, "Marxists" of all hues believe or practice the notion that the new and superior political and socioeconomic order is based on *public* and *communal* needs, organization, and practice, thus eschewing *personal, parochial,* and *egotistical* views and practices. There are many specific organizational forms of Marxism in the world today, along with thousands of books and articles that proclaim to be correct doctrine, but they all emphasize the idea that the common good is superior to the private good, and that Marxism is the way to ensure this ideal.

All of this is important and would have at least temporary attraction for a large number of people who could be expected to organize themselves politically in pursuit of such ideas and ideals. Ultimately, of course, Marxism, like any doctrine, will survive only if it offers a prospect of eventually capturing power and implementing the doctrine through the exercise of such power. The greatest attraction of Marxism, then, is that it works when it comes down to this fundamental political question, because, over time, Marxists have captured power, they have held it, and they have implemented it. They have been so successful in this endeavor, in fact, that today a very substantial part of the world's territory and population is ruled by Marxists. Political success over time is the most important element that Marxists have in common. And this success inspires those who have yet to succeed. The *dream* lives on because it is attractive; the *reality* of power beckons because it is there, in the form of regimes and states that claim to be Marxist, exercising power over society according to the formula of Marx as they see it.

The commonalities end here. There is no universal agreement among Marxists on *how* one captures power. There is no such consistency even in Marx himself. The *revolutionary* Marx professed to know how this was done, how it *must* be done in accordance with historical necessity: a revolution, arms in hand, by the exploited classes under the leadership of the communist party, then a period of the dictatorship of the proletariat, under which regime the old order would be smashed; then, as the exploiters were thrown on the dustbin of history, the new, socialist, and ultimately communist, order could be constructed. But the *older* or *mature* Marx discussed the *peaceful* road to power through organization, the ballot box, reform, and a slower pace of change. These themes in fact became very important in Marx's late works and in the works of Engels. Many scholars, believers, and practitioners have demanded that the *real* Marx stand up on these and related issues. In fact, Marx argued for both revolution *and* revisionism, and advocated both the gun barrel and the ballot box as the proper vehicle for the acquisition of power. That is why so many people can disagree on the *methods* of capturing and maintaining power and still call themselves Marxist. All things to all men — not quite, but many things to many men, on the tactical issue of *how* one acquires power. And that is ultimately what this book is about.

A number of other areas of disagreement stem directly or indirectly from this ambiguity on the ways and means of capturing power. For example, the nature of the "vanguard of the proletariat," the communist party, varies, depending upon the road to power that one chooses. In other words, the armed struggle of the proletariat (or any other class in a class war) requires one kind of leadership and party organization, and the peaceful road through elections and mass participation demands another. Here, too, Marx vacillated, and his disciples vacillated even more. In the end, the successful "disciple" Lenin advocated and established a certain kind of party which did the job in tsarist Russia, but then proceeded to set itself up as a model in other countries with vastly different conditions. This became one of the great sources of contention among Marxists, to the detriment of the cause championed by Lenin and certainly to the detriment of indigenous labor movements in areas such as Western Europe and North America. The controversies resulting from that policy issue in turn reverberate throughout the Marxist movement everywhere today. Add to that the fact that the Chinese have *their* ideas about party organization and cadre policy, and the picture becomes even much more complicated, with little prospect of commonality. Organizational diversity, therefore, is added on to the other differences that permeate this "movement."

Two other issues have always been of great importance to Marxists, namely, the question of religion and the problem of nationalism. The latter has dominated much of Marxist political life since the so-called Bolshevization of the Comintern after 1923, when, as the CPSU emerged as the effective leader of the international organization, the Comintern and its member parties became little more than instruments of Soviet *state* foreign policy. The issue was joined again after World War II, when other parties, too, achieved their goal of capturing power in their respective political systems, but the *manner* in which they came to power still indicated Soviet supremacy in the movement, because, by and large, it was the Red Army that put these parties into power in the first place. In those cases where the local party came to power on its own, as was the case in countries such as Albania, Yugoslavia, and China, the Kremlin has experienced a great deal of trouble over the issue of "national roads" to socialism and communism, indicating once again that there is no such thing as a common Marxist position on this issue, either.

In the 1980s those regimes in Eastern Europe that were established by means of Soviet power claim their own autonomy as they emerge as *national* communist-ruled political and socioeconomic systems. It is this fact of life that has resulted in altered relationships within the erstwhile Soviet "bloc" and has sent the current Kremlin leadership in search of a new international order of the "socialist commonwealth."

Religion, as a universal manifestation among humans, produced an insurmountable problem for all "Marxists," both in theory and in practice. It is one thing to discuss the nefarious effects of the "opium of the people" upon the downtrodden masses, but quite another to eradicate it from human consciousness, or even to control its manifestations, and *practical* policy by Marxist regimes has varied greatly as well, depending upon the nature, doctrine, and strength of religious feelings and organizations in the systems ruled by such Marxist parties.

The upshot of a discussion such as this is the realization that "Marxism" is a very diverse set of *concepts*, in which there are enough commonalities to talk about a discernible core, but barely so, while in fact diversity in conceptualization is a prime characteristic. The differences become even more startling when one begins to examine "Marxism" in practice. Here, the vagaries of historical traditions, cultural peculiarities, and personal proclivities are such that the analyst must step very carefully indeed, lest his or her generalizations become subject to very serious questions of "exceptions to the rule." Still, it is one of the most important facts of life in this century that there are many, many individuals and groups who call themselves Marxist that seek power (and quite a few have obtained it) while yet others in this category are likely to obtain it in one form or another in our lifetime. The question of how they have done this in the past and how they might conduct themselves on this dimension in the future is of prime importance to our understanding of one of the most important and persistent political phenomena of our time. And for some of us it may have a direct impact upon the way we live, or perhaps on whether or not we live at all.

No individual or political organization operates in a political vacuum. This is a truism that must nevertheless be stated, because it is of fundamental importance if one wishes to examine the methods utilized by Marxist parties (or any other political organization) to capture political power. The political conditions existing at any one time in any national setting are, in turn, influenced by conditions in other areas of societal activity, such as economics, cultural life, and mores and customs. Furthermore, all of these elements are influenced by history and the traditions that have been established over long periods of time, as well as the formal structures and institutions that have evolved with their procedures and rules of conduct. In short, even Marxist parties, ostensibly dedicated to the remaking of the existing societal order, are part of that order in some way, and must be studied in that context. This is of particular importance as the party in question examines the options available to it as it attempts to expand its influence *prior* to the attainment of full political power at the national center. It is one thing to impose one's ideological beliefs upon society when power has been achieved, but quite another to operate in a setting where others have equal or greater power. This book, by and large, examines the policies of Marxist parties *prior* to the achievement of full political power or, alternatively, policies utilized to maintain and consolidate such power afterwards. One of the most commonly used methods is that of coalition building, maintenance, and termination.

Coalitions, as pointed out by Professor William Riker, are constellations of "players" in various forms designed to maximize the power and influence of each of the participants. Throughout the history of Marxist parties, participation in coalitions has been a major feature of the policy output of such parties, primarily in the process of obtaining and consolidating power, but also occasionally after such an initial period, and for some duration thereafter. Thus Marxist parties seem to have long-range coalition *strategies*, but also short-range coalition *tactics*, designed to maximize chances and capitalize on opportunities as they arise. Given the bewildering array of national, country-specific conditions in which such parties operate, and given the ambiguities in Marxist doctrine itself about society, the state, the goals of power, and the road to power, the variations in practical policies are endless. The scholar must either simplify the sample of parties to be examined or he must undertake case studies; in fact, he must do both. This book does do both as it explores this important theme.

One way to simplify the examination is to distinguish between the broader category of "Marxist" parties, and the more restrictive (but still extensive) category of "Marxist-Leninist" or *communist* parties. The latter are those parties that model themselves on the CPSU in terms of organizational structure and adhere to Leninist concepts of power and the way to obtain it and hold it, and subsequently, the way in which society and polity are to be organized. Leninist parties are centrally organized, with a strict hierarchy; the party program emphasizes centralized power, the transformation of society through planning and supervision. Externally, Leninist parties remain dedicated to the Soviet Union and the CPSU (even though the last two decades have seen increasing emphasis among such parties on political autonomy and national sovereignty). The path to power is characterized by extreme tactical flexibility, in which a variety of methods are employed to reach the "commanding heights," but the strategic goal is always the establishment of communist power to the exclusion of all others. Marxists-Leninists, therefore, are more easily definable, both in terms of ideological outlooks and also in policy terms, than are other Marxists. For the scholar, it is important to remember that "Marxist" is the broader category, and "Marxist-Leninist" a subcategory thereof. But the latter has become more important, because it is the Marxist-Leninists who have captured power in a number of countries. Only the future will tell if other Marxists will experience the same success.

For Marxist and Marxist-Leninist parties alike, coalitions become vehicles of power enhancement, or, in difficult times, political survival. Such an approach requires both flexibility and a thorough analysis by each party leader of the circumstances in which the party finds itself at any one time, including the opportunities that may exist for coalition building or coalition termination. Specifically, the following questions must be addressed:

a. Who is the main political enemy?
b. Is this enemy a permanent or a temporary adversary? If temporary, what circumstances will change its status?
c. Who is the main ally?
d. Is this a temporary or permanent ally? What causes the respective status of this player?
e. What kinds of policies should be developed to deal with permanent allies and permanent enemies?
f. What kinds of issues can be utilized to form temporary alliances with short-term friends?
g. What is the declared policy toward "others" in the system if political power is obtained? If we are analyzing ruling parties, what is the record of honoring such declarations?

Since Marxist parties are, by definition, organizations of the political left, a number of questions should be asked about relations with the rest of the political spectrum "left of center." For most of these parties, relations with the rest of the political left do constitute the most important political questions. Specifically:

a. What are the relations between avowedly Marxist parties and other parties which have only a tangential relationship with Marxism or have rejected this heritage?
b. What is the status of relations between Marxist parties, such as communist (or Leninist), Trotskyist, Maoist, and anarcho-syndicalist groups? Furthermore, many political systems contain "liberal" parties which share some of the attachments of Marxists to social and economic justice but reject the notion of public ownership of the

means of production and furthermore eschew the revolutionary road to change in favor of evolution and piecemeal development. What is the relationship between Marxist parties and these "bourgeois-liberal" groups?

These questions can be extended to an examination of the relationships between Marxist parties and the right wing of the "bourgeoisie," the landowning class, and the established church. Finally, Marxist parties and groups must decide how to relate to the phenomena of nationalism, ethnic particularism, and regional differences. All of these issues demand specific policies from Marxist parties, and these policies are either long-range, "strategic" in nature, or shorter-range "tactical" policies. In some cases tactical changes are so abrupt that they must be classified as instant adjustments even to tactical policies. All three of these categories, taken together, constitute the policy sets of Marxist parties in their own environments.

As discussed above, Marxist parties claim to be part of an international movement, even though many of them spend a good deal of time and energy castigating each other or some alleged international center for violations of ideology or unwarranted interference in the internal affairs of each party. In the contemporary era crucial problems of this international dimension revolve around the question of relations with at least three would-be "centers," namely the Soviet Union, China, and Cuba. Which Marxist parties have permanent or temporary alliances with one or more of these centers, and which do not? What are the circumstances under which such alliances are made and unmade? In addition, how do Marxist parties relate to other internationalist movements and organizations such as pan-Slavism, pan-Islamic tendencies, and alleged pan-Europeanism? How do such parties deal with other internationalist manifestations such as the Catholic Church or other religious movements and organizations of an ecumenical nature? How are *those* relations correlated and coordinated with the *political* international relations of Marxists? The answers to these questions, I would submit, go a long way toward explaining the success or failure of each Marxist party in its local environment.

After the split in the international working-class movement, which had developed during the last few years of the nineteenth century and was formalized by the meetings at Kienthal and Zimmerwald and then the Russian Revolution itself, many countries had several Marxist factions inside the parties of the left. After the establishment of the Comintern in 1919, factionalism turned into formal organizational splits, which produced four basic categories: (a) Marxist-Leninist parties, adhering to Moscow and the tactical and strategic guidelines emanating from that center;

(b) more moderate parties, which still adamantly clung to the notions of Marxism, as they were seen in any particular national setting, but eschewing the subordination to the Comintern and the CPSU; (c) leftist parties, which called themselves Marxist but utilized only some of the tenets of the great inspirer (e.g., parties which considered themselves to the *left* of the newly established communist or Marxist-Leninist groups, such as the Communist Workers' Party of Germany, KAPD, and the left wing of the Norwegian Labor party, DNA); (d) finally, assorted anarchist, syndicalist, and anarcho-syndicalist parties. In some countries all of these groups existed, while in others only two or three survived the fraternal verbal bloodletting that followed the splits in the international movement. It was clear, then, that the question of coalitions became even more complicated after 1919, since all Marxist organizations had to figure out ways to deal with each other in addition to establishing relationships with assorted other parties at the center or to the right on the ideological scale.

The establishment of the Comintern soon gave rise to CPSU dominance over the formal structures of the international movement, with an ensuing tendency for policy to be determined in Moscow, with expectations that the local parties would loyally and effectively implement those policies in their national settings. For each communist party the tasks of political maneuvering now became excruciatingly difficult. From the Moscow center came directions about policy and policy changes, often communicated late or in a confusing fashion, increasingly designed to serve the needs of the Soviet state as it tried to deal with a hostile international environment. At the same time, the communists had to deal with the complex situation inside the labor movement itself, where other parties and groups existed under the mantle of "Marxism," competing for much the same clientele. This was just the beginning of the communists' problems, however. In addition, they must also relate to various shades of the "bourgeoisie" and *their* organizations and parties, all the while dealing with issues that cut across class lines and ideological divisions, such as religion, nationalism, national sovereignty, and animosities between states and peoples (some of which predated Marx by centuries). It is no wonder that policy at times became confused, and that communist parties, by and large, failed in their quest for power until the prevailing conditions at home changed drastically through such cataclysmic events as war and defeat and the rise of anticolonialism.

Throughout most of the history of Marxist parties, the CPSU and the Soviet Union played a key role in the formulation of the coalition strategies and tactics utilized by these groups. This was so particularly for Marxist-Leninist or communist parties, and that stands to reason, given their commitment to Moscow on all major ideological, political, and organizational matters. But it was also true, at least indirectly, for other Marxists, because they had to react to the policies emanating from the Kremlin and from the local communists on this issue. Under such circumstances the vagaries and vicissitudes of Soviet domestic politics inserted themselves decisively into the political life of every Marxist organization everywhere, sooner or later. The impact of this Soviet dominance was greatest in Europe, because of Europe's proximity to Moscow and the fact that communications were better, and also because the Soviets focused on this part of the world as the area of greatest revolutionary potential and greatest threat of hostile state action. But the Comintern sections in Asian affairs were also very active, indicating the understanding in the Kremlin that here, too, was an area that carried considerable revolutionary potential. By contrast, Africa was considered a colonial backwater in which it would take time to develop revolutionary consciousness and potential, and Latin America, with some exceptions, was under the influence of Yankee imperialism, thus providing potential for the future but hardly constituting the front line of revolutionary activity and opportunity.

This early emphasis on Europe and Asia was maintained for a considerable time; in fact, the Soviet leadership did not begin a serious and sustained approach to the colonial territories of Africa until the last years of Stalin's rule. Attention was focused on the leftist organizations of the independent states on that continent, but a major Soviet effort had to await the rash of decolonization of the 1960s and 1970s. As for Latin America, the Comintern paid rather little attention to it even though a few attempts at coordination of policy were made prior to the dismantling of the Third International in 1943. Again, it was the onset of national liberation movements that pinpointed this region and some of the countries in it as an area of concern and opportunity, in which skillful use of coalition strategies and tactics could be promoted.

Thus the early history of Marxist parties and their coalition strategies and tactics is focused in Europe, and particularly Western and Northern Europe. By the same token, the more contemporary era demands greater attention to the Third World and the policies of Marxists there. This book does both. It also describes and analyzes this sweep of historical change, from the origins of Marxist doctrine and the various movements in Europe that called themselves Marxist, through the momentous events in war-torn Russia and the feedback of Russian-style communism upon the Marxists of Western Europe and North America; then, later, the erroneous Soviet attempt to impose their own conceptions about society and revolution in the case of China. The focus then shifts to the sweep of Soviet *state* power over a good part of the European continent and the establishment of communist, Marxist-Leninist regimes in those countries that were located close to the Soviet Union itself. And then, as the colonial empires of the West began to break up after World War II, the political upheaval that ensued produced new opportunities for power in Asia and Africa, albeit in conditions that varied greatly from the European (and Russian) experience. In a way, the fact that individuals and groups that consider themselves Marxist have managed to operate with considerable stamina and success in such greatly varying circumstances over time is a tribute to their political skill.

As the tale begins, there were rumblings of revolution over much of Europe during the 1830s and particularly in that fateful year 1848. The 1848 revolutions reflected the ideas of freedom that swept the bourgeoisie and the intellectuals of societies in the throes of rapid socioeconomic change, mostly caused by the industrial revolution. Many of the ideas of the enlightenment had also been embraced for a period of time, though festering in the rigid, hierarchical, and authoritarian political systems of the first half of the nineteenth century. This was a formidable set of ingredients, indeed, and it was bound to have repercussions in many social strata, including the emerging industrial proletariat and its organizations. As the century unfolded economic development accelerated, producing a teeming proletariat and lumpenproletariat, especially in Great Britain, but also in Germany, France, the Low Countries, and somewhat later, the Scandinavian countries. Karl Marx was profoundly influenced by both of these trends —the revolutionary movement among the bourgeoisie, particularly the liberal part of it, and also the emergence of a huge substratum of society, the wretched workers and their families. Out of this combination emerged the fundamental rage at socioeconomic and political injustice and the need to do something about it. This is really the essence of Marxism before power, and it is an essence that had a great deal of fascination for the workers as they watched their own lives being transformed by the juggernaut of industrialization, urbanization, and pauperization. It was not difficult to be a Marxist as long as a Marxist railed against social injustice, economic exploitation, and political emasculation. It was also comforting to know that history itself demanded rectification of these great injustices. Like religion, Marxism promised a better life hereafter, except that the political ideology held out the vision that it would be here on Earth, perhaps in one's own generation, but surely in one's children's lives, that the good society would be established.

On the basis of these few but fundamentally important political tenets many flocked to the banner of Marxism; after all, it is difficult to be against social justice and economic fairness, personal freedom and individual happiness. But there were other aspects of Marxism that were not emphasized, perhaps even ignored, by the leaders of the European working class movements and their followers alike, and these became the great bones of contention later. For example, the rigid, centralizing tendencies of political and social organization that could be found in Marx (particularly the "revolutionary" Marx) were strange to many in parts of Western Europe, where the social and economic history of regions and countries had fostered localism and autonomy. In addition, there were elements in Marx (later to be highlighted by Lenin) of class animosity and indeed hatred that were hard to fathom in societies in which there surely was exploitation but also compassionate rule. The notion of noblesse oblige, for example, and the fact that the ruling class in Britain (and particularly the Conservatives) *themselves* reformed the societal order to alleviate the plight of the masses did not fit in the scheme of things as envisioned by the revolutionary Marx. The introduction of extensive social legislation in Bismarck's Germany did not fit the bill either. Throughout Northern Europe, relationships between ruler and ruled quite simply did not reflect the unrestrained greed of the former, but rather demonstrated a considerable amount of paternalism and concern for fellow human beings, regardless of social standing. These are all historical facts that need no further elaboration here, except to make the point that revolutionary Marxism was unrealistic in terms of the experiences of the West European working class itself. This was even more the case in the question of religion. Intellectuals in Western Europe might be atheists, but the workers were not. And as thousands upon thousands of farmers' sons and daughters left the countryside and poured into the cities, the elements of traditional thought that included religion, paternalism, and a certain level of concern for others went with them.

Given this discrepancy between the demand for change, which was shared by so many, and the restraining values and behavior patterns that injected a humanizing touch even to nineteenth-century society in Western Europe, Marxism in practice was clearly in for a rough time. And the political cynicism, the penchant for cold violence, and the tactical flexibility later exhibited by the Marxist-Leninists in the making and unmaking of coalitions simply turned away many good West European revolutionaries and seekers of justice. This was particularly the case with the Leninist notion of using class brothers for limited purposes and limited periods of time. In Western Europe this extreme tactical flexibility on the issue of coalitions was a distinct disadvantage, and it helped alienate the masses of the workers, the intellectuals, and smallholders, thus turning the communist parties into small bands of true believers who executed the most dizzying coalition turns and twists before ever-shrinking audiences. Only when the communists turned back to alliances that reflected fundamental values and attitudes in their respective societies did they experience meaningful success in terms of mass support or support of significant political actors (which, after all, is the goal of coalition formations).

"The great betrayal." This was the characterization made by one old Scandinavian revolutionary describing the imposition of Marxist-Leninist norms and behavior upon the local labor movement and its organizations after the Russian Revolution. The old activist had been enthusiastic about the Revolution itself. He believed in the stirring statements of the "Internationale" about the final struggle, human freedom, and happiness. He, like countless others, had looked to the east which, after November 1918, seemed to represent the dawn, politically as well as physically. But he had soon been disappointed. In 1921 the twenty-one conditions for Comintern membership had imposed conditions of political behavior that were meaningless in Scandinavia; he particularly opposed the idea of clandestine activity, the ban on religion, and the idea of violence which permeated the conditions. He also resented the idea that, for tactical reasons, he must help make alliances with individuals and groups whom he had earlier opposed as "class enemies." He was part of a group that was expelled from the Comintern in 1923 because of "deviationism"; in fact, he maintained that it was the Russians who deviated. Throughout the 1920s he watched the tactical maneuverings of the "loyal" communists with disgust. When the communists approached his party in the 1930s about the need for a "people's front" he was distrustful. Communist collaborations with the Nazi occupiers up to June 22, 1941, confirmed his suspicions. The fact that the communists were active in the anti-Nazi underground after June 1941 was appreciated, but he always asked himself: "What's the catch?" He was one of the leaders who weeded communists out of the trade unions and other mass movements on the left after the schism of 1947 and establishment of the theory of the two camps. And when the news of the anti-Stalin speech of 1956 burst upon the world, he stated, "I knew it since 1921 or 1923." The individual in question has since passed on, but to his dying day he was convinced that the communists had betrayed the Revolution, had played games with it, and ultimately only wanted power for themselves, not for the workers, and not for the Cause.

The experience of this old activist illustrates one of the main reasons for the lack of Marxist success in obtaining political power in Western and Northern Europe. The revolutionary practices of the communists ran counter to the inclinations of many who considered themselves both Marxist and revolutionary. At the other end of the ideological spectrum, the revolutionary messages of Marxism were simply alien to many, both because of class interests and also because of deeply held values and attitudes. In between, the masses of smallholders, workers, and landless laborers were ambivalent, caught between nationalism and internationalism, religious beliefs and atheism, societal values and class values. Thus, Marxism was irrelevant for some, troublesome for many others. Marxism-Leninism, on the other hand, became too cynical, too power hungry, and too manipulative for all but a few ambitious individuals and a relatively small band of true believers. Tactical flexibility and long-range power enhancement goals, as expressed through coalition policies, became detrimental to the success of Marxism and Marxism-Leninism in Western and Northern Europe.

The situation was rather different in Eastern Europe. With the exception of East Germany and Czechoslovakia, there was no real tradition of participatory democracy in this region (even in East Germany that tradition was rather shaky), and the organizational infrastructure so common to Western and Northern Europe was largely lacking. Thus, the mechanisms for social and political integration by the working class were insufficient to provide participatory channels for this social stratum, thus producing a sense of alienation. Much of the urban proletariat was first generation, exhibiting many of the traditional attitudes and values commonly associated with the peasantry. The autocratic tradition of the political systems in the region precluded real political participation for most citizens, especially the workers, smallholders, peasants, and landless laborers, and this in turn reduced or eliminated the possibilities for the creation of Marxist parties or any real room for political maneuvering in the form of coalition strategies and tactics. At the same time the systems of the region were exploitative and hierarchical and created political apathy, privatism, fervent rejection, or complete withdrawal from commitment to the existing political order among many. These individuals either attached themselves to various movements, such as native fascism, or they believed in a mystical form of nationalism, quite often coupled with fervent religiosity, or they became atomized and "available" for political mobilization by radical movements of the left or the right. In any case, the exploitative nature of the domestic political order made the conspiratorial and hierarchical elements of Marxism-Leninism more germane to the local political culture than the cultures of Western and Northern Europe. When Marxism-Leninism was finally imposed on these systems, it seemed less alien and inappropriate than similar developments would have in the West or the North.

The favorable elements for the establishment of Marxist parties and other organizations in Eastern Europe were, by and large, overshadowed by other factors that militated against such developments. The most important of these were the continued grip of traditional attitudes and values on the masses of the population, primarily because of the rural nature of most of the region. Furthermore, religion and the organized churches were adamantly anticommunist, and in populations with considerable religiosity this was a major factor. Finally, anti-Russianism pervaded the populations of the region, with a few exceptions, and the fact that Marxism-Leninism at the end of World War II was a Soviet (or Russian) political export item further reduced its mass appeal, and even its appeal to most elements of the political and socioeconomic elite.

In the end, communist power succeeded in Eastern Europe for two basic reasons. First of all, and certainly most importantly, the presence of Soviet troops in the region after the defeat of Nazi Germany ensured a considerable amount of Soviet influence there, regardless of the nature of the domestic political order. In addition to this, the great powers had already "allocated" much of the region to the Soviets in terms of political influence, so there was no real opportunity for anti-Moscow and anticommunist elements to appeal to outside authority. Secondly, the local communist parties showed considerable skill in their political maneuverings in the fluid situation that developed after the defeat of Nazi Germany and the dismantling of the local fascist regimes. These skills were displayed in a variety of ways, not least in the area of coalition formation, development, and exploitation.

The coalition policies of the East European Marxist parties soon came to be dominated by the communists, who were better organized than the others, and also had the support of Moscow in many subtle and more overt ways. Many of the local communist leaders also exhibited a much better understanding of local conditions than their counterparts in Western and Northern Europe in the 1920s and 1930s. Furthermore, the Soviets had learned a great deal from the failures of the Comintern and were more willing to consider variations in approach and local peculiarities. And, as stated above, the nature of East European society was much closer to the basic tenets of Marxism-Leninism than were the democratic and developed societies in the West and the North. All of these factors produced at least some favorable preconditions for political maneuverings in coalitions and alliances.

Perhaps the most important domestic factor aiding the communists' quest for power was the obvious need for change, and drastic change at that, throughout most of the region. The political and socioeconomic regimes of the area were outmoded, in some cases even semifeudal in nature, and in all cases lacking in the area of innovation, which was now sorely needed. There was indeed widespread agreement on the need for reform in a variety of fields, and most of these demands for change corresponded with the action program established or developed by the local communists. These widely demanded changes would include land reform and the redistribution of land, especially the dismantling of the latifundia system in existence in several countries; further development of industry; the removal of control of the banking system from the hands of elements who had maintained close contacts with the Germans and the local fascists; and, in the political realm, punishment of collaborators, fellow travelers, and Nazi elements and their organizations, with corresponding acceptance of the political left, which had been banned and persecuted in some countries and barely tolerated in others. Given this correlation between communist goals and general goals, the influence of the former was bound to be enhanced. And so the political systems of the region gradually moved toward greater communist influence, and, in the period 1947–1948, they ended up under communist *rule*. Communist rule, in turn, resulted in the dismantling of coalitions and the establishment of political monopoly by the communists, for all intents and purposes. In this respect Eastern Europe followed in the footsteps of the Soviet Union itself and, in turn, helped set the stage for subsequent patterns of power acquisitions in Asia and Latin America.

While the communist demand for reform struck a note of wide acceptance in post–World War II Eastern Europe, the attempt by local leaders of these parties to emphasize nationalism and the notion of "national roads to socialism and communism" added further to their credibility, because they could now claim that they were national leaders and not mere lackeys of the Kremlin. It is impossible to determine the relative weight of Soviet influence, the popularity of communist demands for change, and the credibility added by the communists' national stance, but all three were important elements, and they added to the success of the coalition strategies and tactics as practiced by Lenin's local successors. In contrast, the communists of Western and Northern Europe lacked all these assets two decades earlier as *they* maneuvered in coalitions. There was little direct Soviet influence; the local noncommunist and nonsocialist regimes had already undertaken political and socioeconomic reform and continued on this path; the communists themselves were seen as "Vaterlandslose Gesellen" whose constituency was the Kremlin, not their own countries. Thus, in Eastern Europe the package of factors spelled success, and in Western and Northern Europe dismal failure.

Asia, Africa, and Latin America represented yet other problems and other opportunities. In Asia the teeming cities, some of which were under virtual foreign economic control, seemingly provided excellent possibilities for the expansion of Marxist influence and perhaps even the establishment of actual power for communists in a number of areas. Still, the region was so vast, so populous, and so diverse that no common strategy could be meaningfully established for the whole region (even though the Comintern proceeded to do just that). Instead, the huge political systems of China and India required separate approaches (as indeed India requires a separate chapter in this book). After the debacle of 1927 in China, the local communists recognized this and proceeded to establish their own theoretical framework, their own path to power, and their own system of rule, which in turn had a profound effect upon doctrine and practice among Marxists everywhere. The interplay of Marxism-Leninism, Soviet-style, and Maoism, coupled with local organizational capabilities and a keen eye for organizational possibilities, in turn propelled the Vietnamese communists to power after successful confrontations with two of the most powerful Western states at the time, and with ramifications for political life in both of those Western states well beyond the importance of Vietnam itself. This in its own right deserves a separate chapter in this volume. As for the Indonesian communists, they exhibited enormous capabilities of political organization in a predominantly rural system, thus running directly counter to Soviet experience but also differing significantly from the Chinese model, which was based on military power and not on organizational prowess. The Indonesian case prior to the blood bath of 1965 is a fascinating case of skills in organizing a network of party groups, front organizations, and infiltration of other political structures; it is also an example of enormous skills and successes in coalition building, maintenance, and maximization. The Indonesian case cannot be subsumed under a more general "Asian" category, but must be examined in its own right, in a separate chapter.

The diversities of Marxism in Asia, then, are enormous. There were nevertheless certain elements which existed throughout this enormous continent, producing similar conditions in the political, socioeconomic, and cultural realms and thus establishing common opportunities and obstacles for Marxists of all kinds. Asia was a continent dominated by colonial powers. Thus anticolonialism became a major rallying point for countless individuals who had never heard of Karl Marx but opposed foreign rule. This foreign rule was administered by individuals who were racially, culturally, and linguistically different; thus anticolonialism also meant anti-Europeanism (and its subforms of anti-British, anti-French, anti-Dutch). The masses of the population lived and died in abject poverty—hence the real class element of the Asian societies examined here. And that class distinction was a factor both in the cities and in the countryside, thus making it possible for revolutionaries to utilize opportunities in both the city and the village. There was also a local hierarchy of individuals who prospered by their relations with the colonial powers. These individuals and groups could be classified as traitors ("compradors") and thus targeted for political and even physical action.

There were other common factors as well. Most of the leaders of Asian Marxist organizations were intellectuals who had spent a considerable amount of time in the West and had become acquainted with Marxism and some of the European interpretations of the great master. In some cases the Asian Marxists, upon returning to their homelands, began to implement the doctrine slavishly, without deviation, but many others adapted it to existing conditions at home. Without fail, the adaptors were more successful in terms of capturing and maintaining power, once again proving the correctness of the adage that *all* political parties, even the Marxists, must exist inside a national environment, with its cultural and historical antecedents and peculiarities.

These peculiarities were massive indeed. In China, an inefficient system of imperial rule gave way to Chiang Kai-shek and his Nationalists, but the Marshal failed to extend his rule over the entire country, thus leaving the door open for regionalism and the emergence of warlords, who ruled their fiefdoms with cruel control. The central authorities were corrupt and inefficient; economic conditions were wretched for the overwhelming majority of the population; socioeconomic conditions, therefore, were favorable for coalition approaches by the most successful and best organized Marxists, the communists. A great deal has been written on this topic, and this book will not focus specifically upon the Chinese experience. The successful revolution in that country nevertheless meant the establishment of a major communist power which provided some Marxists with a new model for political action and socioeconomic development, thus further complicating the coalition strategies and tactics of other Marxist parties.

The three Asian systems examined in this book were colonial systems, and the Marxist parties therein were forced to operate at a double disadvantage until the end of World War II. First of all, they had to deal with the leaderships of other domestic political movements, many of whom were hostile to any kind of Marxism (and representing a political culture whose main values often were drastically different from those espoused by Marxists of all stripes). Secondly, the Marxists had to contend with the colonial administration, which was British in India, French in Indochina, and Dutch in Indonesia. This dual challenge of political hierarchies backed by the military power of the colonial masters made it very difficult for Marxists to operate inside coalitions or out.

The rural nature of much of Indian, Indonesian, and Vietnamese society demanded Marxist policies that dealt with the question of land reform, land redistribution, and forms and methods of production in the countryside. The colonial states of all three societies made anticolonialism and national independence the most important political issue of the day. The Marxists, no matter what their particular ideological bent, were obliged to face these issues with some understanding of the local political culture. Those who did not were bound to end up on the "dustbin of history."

Marxists like to argue that history marches inexorably forward, and that revolutions are as inevitable as the final outcome of this historical process, "communist society." It is unlikely that too many of them actually *believe* in this argument. And an equally valid point has been made by many analysts and observers that politics is "accident"; that without World War I there would have been no Russian Revolution, and without World War II the colonial empires in Asia and Africa would have lasted longer, thus denying revolutionaries of all kinds the opportunity to utilize the chaos that always follows the withdrawal of established power. This is an interesting controversy which is not likely to be settled soon, but it is also not necessary to settle it for the purpose of this book. The historical fact is that in a period of five to ten years from the end of World War II colonial rule had been dismantled in India, Indochina, and Indonesia, and this had produced new and unexpected possibilities for coalition politics by Marxist parties in all three countries. These opportunities were utilized very differently in the three systems, and the results were, predictably, very different as well. If history marches inexorably toward a common goal, it has taken very tortuous paths indeed in Asia.

The successes and failures of the Marxists in these three former colonial systems stemmed, in large measure, from the differences in the political order left behind by the British, French, and Dutch as they sailed away from their Asian empires of the past. In India, there was a powerful primary political force in the country which dominated the issues of national sovereignty and economic development; and this force, the Congress party, left little room for others to maneuver, particularly Marxists. The second most important political force on the Indian subcontinent rallied around the Muslim faith, always one of the most effective roadblocks against Marxist power. In addition, the British left behind a rather efficient and relatively capable civil service which managed to create some semblance of order in a chaotic situation in a short time (at least compared to the duration of decolonization). The political environment of India was therefore rather unfriendly for Marxist parties.

Indochina was very different. The vacuum left by the departing French was ably filled by Marxist groups whose leadership knew about organization, coalition politics, and military discipline. On the opposing side of the political spectrum were inefficient, corrupt, and squabbling leaders who presented no real challenge to the likes of Ho Chi Minh. Thus, after years of armed warfare and coalition building in the entire territory of Indochina, the communists got the chance to establish full power in the North. North Vietnam, in turn, became a base from which coalitions could be managed south of the border. The rest of the story is painful history for Americans but an instructive lesson in the powerful combination of nationalism, anticolonialism (and anti-Westernism), and military power that was crafted and exercised, much of it through coalition strategies and tactics.

Indonesia represents yet another case. Here too the issues of national independence and economic reform dominated the political scene for decades prior to the Dutch departure. Here too nationalist forces, with no particular attachment to Marxist doctrine, emerged as the dominant political force early. Thus there was no "reason" why one branch of the Indonesian Marxists should become as successful as a mass movement as actually did occur. Once again the observer is struck by the importance of personality, circumstances, and individual political skills, rather than the "inexorable march of history." Some of the Indonesian Marxists were very good at understanding the key issues of their society and their time. They were superb at organization, especially mass mobilization in the countryside, a fact not normally attributed to Marxists. But they were also lucky, because individuals among the nationalists, and particularly the president, Sukarno, were ideologically friendly to some aspects of leftism and chose to make alliances with the communists against their rivals. Thus the endemic factionalism of the Indonesian political elite redounded to the benefit of men such as Aidit, who served ably under the red banner.

The astonishing success of mass organization had a great deal to do with the ferocity and thoroughness of retaliation once the non-Marxist elements in the military felt compelled to act. The execution of a few nationally prominent communists simply would not do, because the network of organizations would survive and cast up other leaders. The generals therefore embarked upon the process of completely uprooting Marxism from the Indonesian political system. The resulting bloodbath was major, even by the standards of the twentieth century.

Vietnam, Indonesia, and India represent success, total destruction, and survival with mixed results, in terms of the quest for power and the stakes of the game. These drastically different stories in considerable measure hinge upon the successes and failures of coalition strategies and tactics in Asian history.

Africa exhibited some conditions that were similar to Asia, but on the whole the "dark continent" was sui generis on most dimensions pertaining to Marxism and coalitions. The similarities with Asia are clear: Africa, too, was a continent dominated by colonial masters, and it remained in that condition much longer than other parts of the world. This meant that there were white rulers and black fellow travelers and compradors, and eventually it also meant that the issues of national independence and economic development became predominant. But the continent of Africa is so diversified in terms of political and socioeconomic development that generalizations are hazardous at best. It is necessary to divide this enormous land mass in a number of ways for analytical purposes; for example, North Africa is vastly different on almost all political dimensions from the sub-Saharan part of the continent. Furthermore, Arab Africa must be distinguished from "black" Africa on a number of dimensions. The careful analyst will also inquire about differences between the political cultures left behind by the British, the French, the Belgians, the Spaniards, the Portuguese, and the Italians, on the assumption that these colonial powers all had their peculiarities in terms of administration, the exercise of power, and achievements in the socioeconomic realm. And we must, of course, attempt to factor in such complexities as religious heterogeneity, tribal animosity and warfare, and ethnic and racial diversity, which are endemic to Africa. The confusing picture that emerges illustrates both the opportunities and the pitfalls for Marxist coalition politics in Africa.

On balance, the disadvantages outweighed the advantages, at least until the decolonization process was well under way. Throughout sub-Saharan Africa the level of political consciousness was low, not least because the colonial masters had considered this state of affairs as an advantage, conducive to stability. Few people had heard of Karl Marx, and for those who did the notions of a proletarian revolution seemed inappropriate for agrarian societies with little urbanization. The Maoist version of Marxism was appropriate for Asia (or parts thereof) but did not fit tribal societies and political cultures in which parochialism was the order of the day rather than the exception. In those areas where the level of political consciousness and social mobilization were higher, nationalists basing their appeal on Islam blocked the path to power, even to opportunity, because many Marxist groups were simply banned and persecuted.

As the decolonization process marched across the "dark continent," African versions of socialist thought and practice emerged, tailored to local conditions, themselves products of local cultures and traditions. These ideologies, while emphasizing collectivism and public ownership of the means of production (and thus having some important elements in common with Marxist thought), also emphasized "Africanism" and tended to regard *all* European-based doctrines with considerable skepticism if not outright animosity. The importance of Marxist or "Marxist-like" parties and organizations in Africa increased only when the indigenous socialists and nationalists needed Soviet (and Cuban) aid to get power and to hold it. And then many local Marxists found that the Kremlin was quite prepared to sacrifice the fortunes of "fraternal" parties if it served the interests of the Soviet *state*. There is certainly nothing new in this, but it nevertheless reduced the influence and the opportunities for all Marxists in Africa.

Despite these severe liabilities, there *are* people who call themselves "Marxists" in power in Africa today. These individuals preside over ruling parties and have engaged in coalition building, maintenance, and termination. Since they are still in power, their policies must be considered successful. But at the same time it should be pointed out that their success, at least in part, is due more to outside assistance than to their own political capabilities. This is clearly a factor of major importance as we examine coalition politics in these systems.

The final area of concern for this book is Latin America. Today this area of the world provides examples of successes by Marxists (or individuals who adopted a version of Marxism *after* they came to power) as well as spectacular failures by the political left to hang on to power once obtained. It is also a region which today seems to provide the greatest potential for further expansion of power by Marxists. Inevitably, the old question resurfaces: What *kinds* of Marxists are these? Are they the servants of Moscow, or are they indigenous revolutionaries attempting to deal with the explosive problems of poverty, overpopulation, social and economic injustice, excessive dependence on others (particularly in terms of foreign debt), and a legacy of autocratic regimes (still dedicated to the maintenance of the old order)? The analyst is confronted by the fact that both kinds of Marxists can be found in this troubled region. Furthermore, the Marxist-Leninists are not necessarily the most radical and thus the predictable "troublemakers"; indeed, there are groups that call themselves socialist who have exhibited a greater penchant for drastic change, while the communists have been more cautious. And there have emerged, in recent years, groups that stand in a class by themselves when it comes to methods of class struggle and the goals of society *after* the revolution has been successful. Finally, there are urban and rural guerrillas or even simple bandits who attempt to topple the existing order for purposes of their own, some of them adopting certain Marxist slogans without any evidence that they understand those parts of it that call for *building* a new society after the old has been torn down.

A distinction should be made here between South America and Central

America. In South America, national independence was established early for most states, and this issue, so potent in Asia and Africa (and even in parts of Europe prior to World War I) did not provide much of an opportunity for revolutionaries. In Central America, on the other hand, the issue of colonialism or excessive dependence upon external powers (and particularly the United States) has remained very potent until the present time. It is symptomatic that the successful case of "Marxist" power in Latin America came from the central part of the region, and not from the vast areas of South America, with all its many political and socioeconomic problems. In Central America it was (and is) possible to claim that full national independence has not been achieved, that the local leaders are lackeys of Yanqui imperialism, that the misery of the people is the result of Wall Street interference, and that only the communists (the local version thereof) can provide solutions. And it is of course in Central America that the example of Cuba has the greatest impact on revolutionaries and their opponents alike.

This is not to argue that South America is devoid of revolutionary potential and opportunities for coalition maneuvering by Marxists and others. There are enormous problems in the region, both socioeconomic and political. The tradition of autocracy and military dictatorships has produced systems which only now are beginning to establish vehicles for popular participation in the political process. Overpopulation, unemployment, and mass poverty continue to be the order of the day. A tradition of coercion, lawlessness, and terrorism helps create endemic instability that usually establishes the preconditions for revolt and successful coalition strategies and tactics by revolutionaries. Despite these favorable circumstances, "classical" Marxism as preached by the urban intellectuals of South America prior to the advent of national liberation movements after World War II was sectarian and ineffective in its quest for power and influence. This was so partly because the rural masses of the region distrusted the city and all that emerged from it. The early South American Marxists also hewed close to the Comintern line in a political setting that did not fit Moscow's perception, with the inevitable result that these followers of Marx and Engels remained isolated and ineffective.

Another major reason for Marxist failures south of the Panama Canal was the strength of the Catholic Church and its fear and hatred of Marxism. This enormous handicap in profoundly religious populations could only be broken when radical priests began to demand changes that resembled the Marxist program. And even when this happened, the impact was greater in Central America than in the southern part of this hemisphere.

This, in turn, had a profound effect upon the coalition possibilities of Marxists everywhere in the region.

As one examines the political behavior of Marxist parties, one is struck by a number of facts which clearly are of paramount importance in the systematic analysis of their coalition strategies and tactics. First is the variety of such parties in the world today. Whatever the merits of "Marxism" as a doctrine for power, it certainly is a *popular* doctrine in much of the world, at least for the believers and professors. Secondly, these parties operate under all kinds of conditions, with all kinds of possibilities and all manner of restrictions. Their tactical flexibility is infinite, and at times it becomes just a tactical game which threatens to remove any strategic goal, such as capturing power or remaking society. One of the most astonishing capabilities of these parties is the coalition-making skills that they have exhibited. Marxist parties have made coalitions with other leftists, with nationalists of all kinds, with military dictators, landlords, landless peasants, workers, urban intellectuals, rural bandits, and the terrorists of the city. The bourgeoisie (and the petty bourgeoisie) has been frequently wooed. Coalitions have been made from above and from below; they have been terminated and remade with dizzying speed and bewildering variety. No one can seriously question Marxists' capabilities of making and unmaking coalitions. It is not so clear that they know how to make *winning* coalitions.

The systematic study of coalitions, which this book provides, shows that Marxists are not likely to make winning coalitions (in the sense that these coalitions lead to power) unless they can deal with the issues of nationalism and national independence, religion, and prevailing values in society in a manner that puts them in part of the mainstream of the local political culture. Furthermore, they must be able to deal with nationalists, religious leaders, and those who express the prevailing values of the time. Thus coalitions are made with issues, values, *and* people. All of this makes a great deal of common political sense. It is stated here because Marxists have often forgotten it in their coalition tactics, and sometimes in their strategies.

Since Marxists are often determined to *change* the political mainstream of the societies in which they operate, they may not wish to operate in it, as described above. Under such circumstances they need protectors and promoters, preferably close by, but not necessarily so. Thus the communists in Eastern Europe were in a minority in the coalitions in which they participated, but the proximity of the Soviet Union helped them tip the balance in their favor. Similarly, Soviet aid (and the aid of Soviet allies) helped other Marxists prevail in their coalitions, against odds that seemed rather formidable at the time.

Capturing power is of no value unless one can hold on to it. All rulers (and most good political scientists) know that the exercise of power is the making and unmaking of coalitions, so that scarce resources can be distributed with minimum conflict. This certainly has been the experience of ruling Marxist parties, as they confront the scarcities of the societies they have captured and, increasingly, the scarcities they themselves have created. All Marxist rulers must deal with nationalism, because they rule in a finite area, exercising power over people who consider themselves Germans, Czechoslovakians, Romanians, Cubans, or other nationalities. In fact, those Marxist leaders who wish to continue to rule have become nationalists too. This coalition between nationalism and alleged internationalism is matched by a similar relationship with religion and its organized manifestations. Unless one believes Albanian claims, ruling-Marxists have not been able to eradicate religion and must coexist with it in some fashion, even cooperating with it, occasionally or consistently.

Ultimately ruling Marxists must make a coalition with their own society, the society they inherited when they came to power and the society they produced through their policies. The fact that all Marxist rulers try to complete this balancing act through political adjustment to societal reality is a testimony to the fact that they, too, know the crucial value of the coalition between society and polity.

One of the most important political phenomena of the last century is the rise of "Marxism" as a doctrine and "Marxist" parties as political players virtually everywhere in the world. The story of their political behavior patterns, of which coalition strategies and tactics constitute an important part, will now be pursued in more detailed case studies, encompassing Marx's thought on coalitions and Marxist approaches to them in Western Europe, Eastern Europe, Africa, Latin America, and the three major Asian cases of India, Indonesia, and Vietnam.

2

Coalition Strategies and Tactics in Marxist Thought
Jiri Valenta

All I know is that I am not a Marxist. —Karl Marx

A coalition, as defined in Webster's Third New International Dictionary, is "a temporary alliance of distinct parties, persons or states for joint action or to achieve a common purpose." This view of coalitions has been considerably enriched during the last two decades by various political scientists in the West. The concept of coalition building is crucial in theories developed by William H. Riker, Robert Axelrod, William A. Gamson, Michael A. Leiserson, and others.[1] Their critics argue that these theories do not make the prediciton of political behavior any easier and that some important features of these theories, such as Riker's famous "size principle" and "winning coalition," are in most cases irrelevant.[2] In my opinion, however, these theories have been very helpful in elucidating the processes of bargaining and decision making which occur in Western pluralistic political systems. Coalition theory is basic not only to these political processes but to politics which, as David Easton has defined it, is the authoritative allocation of values.[3] This allocation, as Riker has suggested, is the process of coalition formation.[4]

My intention herein is to critically assess the meaning and role of the political coalition as defined in Marxist theories. What has been the thinking of Marxist theoreticians regarding political power and politics, the notion of revolution, the dictatorship of the proletariat, and parliamentary government? How have they viewed alliances, coalitions, and coalition formation? Have the basic premises of Marxist theories on political power and politics and coalition building undergone changes in the 130 years since the publication of Marx's famous *Communist Manifesto*? If this is true, how has it been so? Can the hypotheses of Riker, Axelrod, and others, even though they focus on Western political systems, be useful for the study of political coalitions in communist theories?[5]

In my discussion I shall attempt whenever possible, conceptually and analytically, to distinguish the several levels of coalitions and to relate some specific Marxist-type jargon such as "alliance from below," "alliance from above," etc., to general coalition theory. I shall address the "why," "when," "where," "what," "who," and "how"' of coalitions; in other words: 1. (*why*) goals and purposes of coalitions, payoffs for joining, problems of compatibility, consensus, conflicts, and harmony; 2. (*when*) timing and duration of coalitions; conditions or circumstances for beginning and ending coalitions; 3. (*where*) level at which coalitions should be made (international, national, regional, local); 4. (*what*) forms coalitions should assume and choice of arena (government coalitions, party coalitions, parliamentary coalitions, electoral coalitions, penetrative coalitions, class coalitions, group coalitions); 5. (*who*) possible coalition partners, reasons for choice, conditions, and circumstances; relationships of goals to coalition partners (cooperative coalitions of hegemonic coalitions); 6. (*how*) degree of commitment to coalition partners; intensity of association, problems of size.

I shall focus on theoretical Marxist writings ranging from the classic works of Marx, Engels, and Lenin to those of Mao Tse-tung and other thinkers including the so-called Eurocommunists and their precursors. I shall also discuss coalition theories as practiced by Marxist and Leninist parties, particularly their materialization in the popular fronts of the 1930s and the coalition governments of the 1940s, and their influence on the policies of West European communist parties in the 1970s.

Interpretations of Marx's and Engels' Theories

Marx and Engels were not political scientists. They did not deal extensively with the issues of political institutions and political coalitions. As a result, their work is of little relevance to the analysis of political processes. The various interpretations stemming from their theoretical works are very relevant, however, and should be highlighted before proceeding to a discussion of their thoughts on political coalitions.

As pointed out by Vernon Aspaturian, Robert Tucker, Adam Ulam, and other scholars, for Marx's followers and interpreters Marxist theory has conveyed at least two, if not three, distinct, even contradictory, interpretations of revolutionary theory.[6] The first is a product of the early, humanistic Marx of pre-1848; the second, of the middle, revolutionary Marx of the late 1840s and 1850s, a proponent of the theories of violent revolution and dictatorship of the proletariat—the precursor of Lenin; the third, of the mature, evolutionary Marx, advocate of universal suffrage, an organized labor movement, and emancipation of the proletariat (in some developed capitalist countries) through democratic rather than revolutionary means—harbinger of the social democrats and, as some would argue, the "Eurocommunists." The trajectory of Engels' thought is much the same.

Upon careful study of Marx and Engels, one is impressed by their ambiguity on the matters of violent revolution, the dictatorship of the proletariat, and democratic change through parliamentary procedure. Their brilliant, although ambivalent and somewhat inconsistent theories on the proletarian revolution allow differing interpretations. Of these, revolutionary Leninism and evolutionary social democracy are primary interpretations, while Eurocommunism is a secondary derivative of both the revolutionary and evolutionary interpretations. Marx's theoretical equivocalness on the development of capitalism and its transformation and on the role of the working class in this transformation are reflections of socioeconomic and political changes taking place during his own lifetime. Neither Marx nor Engels has much to say about the practical politics of the proletariat or coalition politics. Because they leave many questions unanswered, various interpretations have arisen regarding these crucial questions.

Marx and Engels:
A Revolutionary Interpretation

Marx and Engels' political writings, particularly until 1848, were strongly influenced by the experience of the 1789 and 1830 French revolutions. Marx's most revolutionary work, *The Communist Manifesto*, was written after his departure from Germany and during the prerevolutionary situation of 1848 in Paris. It suggests the necessity of the revolutionary overthrow of existing capitalist societies. "Political power, properly so called, is merely the organized power of one class for oppressing another,"[7] and the immediate aim of the communists (as his followers were now known) is the formation of the proletariat into a *political* class, the overthrow of bourgeois supremacy, the conquest of political power by the proletariat, and "despotic inroads on the rights of property" by this organized class.[8] The state is seen as a bourgeois dictatorship, deserving as such to be overthrown.[9] At the writing of the *Manifesto* there was no universal suffrage anywhere in monarchial Europe, or even in England, and the franchise was restricted by high property qualifications. Thus one does not encounter a great deal of discussion on "parliamentary democracy" and parliamentary work in Marx's early writings. For Marx, parliament in mid-nineteenth-century Europe was the very antithesis of universal suffrage. The state, as it existed in most European countries, was doomed to disappear and to be replaced, as Marx pointed out in *The Class Struggle in France, 1848–1850*, by "the class dictatorship of the proletariat—a necessary transition point along the road to the abolition of class distinctions."[10] In a letter to his friend J. Weydemeyer in 1852 Marx again stated that "the class struggle necessarily leads to the dictatorship of the proletariat."[11] Twenty-five years later, after the failure of a short-lived experiment with the Paris Commune, Marx again elaborated on the dictatorship of the proletariat in the marginal notes to the program for the German Workers' party (the Socialist Workers' Party of Germany), known as *The Critique of the Gotha Program* (written in 1875): "Between capitalist and communist society lies the period of the revolutionary transformation of the one into the other. There corresponds to this also a political transition period in which the state can be nothing but *the revolutionary dictatorship of the proletariat.*"[12] Here Marx's references to the dictatorship of the proletariat can be intrepreted again as being an advocacy of rule by a minority based on violence.

The only lengthy discussion of coalitions in the earlier theoretical works of Marx and Engels is found in the fourth and final chapter of the *Manifesto*, "Position of the Communists in Relation to the Various Existing Opposition Parties." Here Marx addresses, if only very briefly, the questions of why and what kinds of coalitions should be formed by a communist party. He portrays some of the socialist and bourgeois parties as being tactical allies of the communists. As perceived by the communists, the main political payoff for building coalitions with other revolutionary parties was "the attainment of immediate aims for the enforcement of the momentary interests of the working class." But in the long run, as Marx said, the communists "also represent and take care of the future of that movement."

As to the level on which and with whom coalitions should be undertaken, the *Manifesto* dictates that the communists ally themselves on a national level in various European countries with partners who, of course, would differ according to each country. As to the choice of coalition partners and the reasons and conditions surrounding this choice, the communists could consider other socialist parties and even bourgeois parties as allies, but only on a temporary basis and during the early, prerevolutionary part of the struggle. In France they would coalesce with the social democrats against the conservative and radical bourgeoisie, reserving the right to take up critical positions against the social democrats. In Switzerland they would support the radicals without losing sight of the fact that the Swiss party consisted of antagonistic elements. In Poland they would support the party that insisted on agrarian revolution as the prime condition for national emancipation. In England and in America the communists would work with existing working class parties. Finally, in Germany they would work and fight alongside the bourgeoisie whenever it acted in a revolutionary way against the absolute monarchy, the feudal hierarchy, or the petty bourgeoisie. These coalitions, which were not democratic in nature, would be class-oriented and temporary. The communists would preserve a critical attitude toward their temporary coalition partners and instill into the working class the clearest possible recognition of the incompatibility and hostile conflict of interests between bourgeoisie and proletariat. The final goal of the communists would be "the forcible overthrow of all existing social conditions."[13]

It was Marx's belief that such other social classes as the middle class and the peasants (with the exception of the rural proletariat) and their political parties were doubtful allies who would tend to behave in a reactionary manner. Marx saw their role as being only a transitory one which would disintegrate under the impact of the evolution of capitalism. Nevertheless, on several occasions after 1848, Marx and Engels discussed briefly the possibility of alliances of the proletariat with the peasant and middle classes.[14]

In Marx's and Engels' revolutionary writings, the nature and purpose of alliances with various other political parties and classes are tactical. Such coalitions should not be mistaken for democratic, electoral, or parliamentarian alliances such as those existing in pluralistic systems. There is a basic class antagonism that makes a genuine coalition of the proletarian and bourgeois parties unlikely. In revolutionary circumstances the existing political institutions, meaning also the alliance partners, must be abolished. The theories of the revolutionary Marx, articulated particularly durign the period from 1848 to 1850, form a genetic link to the writings of Lenin and his followers.

Marx and Engels: Humanist and Evolutionary Interpretations

Some of Marx's works, particularly some of his pre-1848 writings, such as the *Economic and Philosophical Manuscripts of 1844* and even *The*

German Ideology, offer another, quite different, interpretation.[15] Careful study of these works, to which the concepts of self-alienated man and alienation (*Entfremdung*) are central, suggests that Marx was heir not only to the French Revolution but also to the Enlightenment and its accompanying humanism, in which totalitarianism played no part. As some scholars argue, there is even a certain congruence of thought between at least some tenets of Marx's political and philosophical theories and J. J. Rousseau's concepts of direct democracy and general will and perhaps even a few similarities with J. S. Mill's classical liberalism.[16]

In his early works and even in some later works Marx refers only a few times to the "dictatorship of the proletariat," placing more emphasis on the idea of *Aufhebung des Staates* whereby the state, whose functions become increasingly irrelevant and unnecessary, is finally abolished and transcended. As pointed out by Shlomo Avineri, *Aufhebung*, a philosophical term, refers to a kind of "dialectical abolition" of the state through revolutionization of the mode of production and self-emancipation of the proletariat by way of universal suffrage. The classless society of the future will no longer require a state.[17]

It is clear, even in such revolutionary works as the *Manifesto*, that the communist party as envisioned by Marx was not a conspiratorial group or a minority sect imposing a revolutionary dictatorship of the proletariat, but a leader and educator. Even in this work self-alienation and emancipation are key terms. Indeed, in the *Manifesto* Marx did not write solely about the need for a "proletarian revolution" with "despotic inroads on the rights of property." He also wrote about the need to "raise the proletariat to the position of ruling class *to win the battle for democracy (die Erkämpfung der Demokratie)*." He called for general suffrage as one of the first objectives of the proletariat and looked forward to lengthy organizational work rather than toward an immediate revolution.[18] Already in 1850 Marx maintained that at least fifteen or twenty, if not fifty years were needed for the workers to become capable of assuming power.[19] The phrase "dictatorship of the proletariat," which would later become one of the main tenets of Lenin's theoretical paradigm, is nowhere to be found in the *Manifesto*. In fact, it was mentioned only once in his work and twice in his private correspondence (1850 and 1852, each time in a different context and sense), and again only in 1871 and 1875 after the demise of the short-lived experiment with the Paris Commune. In none of these instances was a substantial explanation given. But the phrase could be interpreted as, among other things, being synonymous with majority rule of the workers' representatives in parliament.

Although in the late 1840s and 1850s Marx doubted the effectiveness of the democratic process, later in 1860 to 1880, when an independent working class movement had come into existence throughout most of Europe and universal suffrage was extended to workers in England, France, and parts of Germany, he began to think, as argued most persuasively by George Lichtheim and other scholars, that democratic institutional processes, at least in a few developed European countries, could serve the real interests of the proletariat.[20] Marx had always believed that, unlike in continental Europe, the British working class needed universal suffrage to obtain political power, and that England would not need to undergo a violent revolution. Although parliament was downplayed in Marx's writing, and parliamentary politics were never discussed in detail, the usefulness of parliament for the working class did not go unrecognized.

In fact, in the writings of the mature Marx and Engels there is growing acceptance of the possibility of peaceful change by working within democratic institutions. Already in the 1852 essay "The Chartists" Marx noted that the socioeconomic and political conditions in England at that time differed markedly from those on the Continent. Marx concluded that "the carrying of Universal Suffrage in England would, therefore, be a far more socialist measure than anything which has been honoured with that name on the Continent. Its inevitable result, here, is the *political supremacy of the working class.*"[21]

In *Critique of the Gotha Program* Marx does more than simply recognize the necessity of the state's being the "revolutionary dictatorship of the proletariat" during the period of revolutionary transformation. He also describes it as a form of state "*democratic republic*" where democratic forms, such as the demand for universal suffrage, will be realized.[22] Indeed, the growth of universal suffrage in Europe in 1860 to 1880 and the failure of the Paris Commune in 1871 were factors which were instrumental in further developing Marx's and Engels' thought on revolution and politics. Marx would not explicitly admit the possibility of a nonviolent seizure of power in two or three of the more developed countries of the West. Addressing the First International in Amsterdam in 1872, he pointed out that:

> The workers must one day conquer political supremacy in order to establish the new organization of labour. . . . But we do not assert that the attainment of this end requires identical means. We know that one has to take into consideration the institutions, mores, and traditions of the different countries, and we do not deny that there are countries like England and America and, if I am familiar with your institutions, Holland, where labour may attain its goal by peaceful means. But if this is true we also must

recognize that in most countries of the continent, violence must be the lever of revolution.[23]

The option of a peaceful, democratic means for achieving communist goals is also strongly suggested in Marx's private correspondence to the English socialist H. M. Hyndman in 1880:

> If you say that you do not share the views of my party for England I can only reply that that party considers an English revolution not necessary, but—according to the historical precedents —possible. If the unavoidable evolution turns into a revolution, it would not only be the fault of the ruling classes, but also of the working classes.[24]

After the death of Marx, Engels would add France to the list of advanced industrialized countries where revolutionary change might occur through parliament in a peaceful, constitutional manner.[25] Engels, who had the good fortune to live into the 1890s, tended after Marx's death to adopt a gradualistic, evolutionary concept of political change (albeit with qualifications) that surpassed that of his closest associate and coauthor.

Engels, even more than Marx, took seriously the possibility of arriving at pluralistic communism through the democratic processes of parliament. Confronted with the parliamentary success of the German Social Democratic party (after the repeal of antisocialist laws in Germany in the 1880s and 1890s, during a period of growing political strength for the party), Engels recognized that the ballot could indeed replace the bullet. He argued that the attainment of universal suffrage and democracy as predicted in the *Manifesto* had proven to be one of the most powerful weapons of the proletariat. He also admitted that some of his and Marx's revolutionary ideas from the years 1848 to 1850 had been illusory and obsolete. The socioeconomic and political conditions had changed drastically since that time. Parliamentarian tactics had come to be viewed as a means for achieving the peaceful transition to a proletarian state, not only in Germany but perhaps also in other developed capitalist countries of the continent. The German workers had done a great service to their comrades in the rest of Europe by showing them how to make use of universal suffrage, transforming the franchise from a tool of deception into "an instrument of emancipation."[26] As Engels stated in 1893, "We have no ultimate aim. We are *evolutionists*. We have no intentions of dictating laws to mankind."[27]

In their later writings Marx and Engels acknowledged that violent struggle tuned to the mode of 1848 had become obsolete. The implicit message of the mature, evolutionary Marx and Engels is that the extension of liberal democracy, at least in some developed European countries, might enable the workers to gradually build, in a parliamentary fashion (and, by implications, within parliamentary coalitions), a socialist society.

It is important to note that at the time of Marx's death his early humanist writings were mostly unpublished and unknown, indicating that perhaps Engels and Marx himself had forgotten about them. The middle, revolutionary Marx was largely of historical interest in tracing the evolution of Marx's intellectual ideas rather than his political behavior. It was the mature, evolutionary Marx that was bequeathed directly to Engels and his camp followers in the late nineteenth century. All Marxist parties at the end of the nineteenth century were offshoots of evolutionary Marxism, which was already being proliferated by K. Kautsky and others into national socialist and social democratic parties at the same time that it was being revised and modified by E. Bernstein in a more evolutionary direction. The revolutionary Marx had been forgotten by Marx, Engels, and almost everybody else.

Lenin: Coalitions as Tactical Alliances

It has been pointed out that the political writings of Marx and Engels, saying little as they do about the practical conduct of communist parties, have not produced a political theory or a coalition theory. The communist theoretician who did write explicitly about these subjects was Lenin. However, Lenin based the bulk of his work on the elaboration and revision of selected writings of Marx and Engels, their earlier revolutionary work much more than their later writings. Lenin in a sense rescued the revolutionary Marx from oblivion, but he came on the scene after Engels and Marx had both died. Given the circumstances of Russian political life, he felt that social democracy had little relevance for Russia and that Marx's revolutionary ideas made more sense. Yet it is important to note that Lenin also was influenced for a short period of time by evolutionary Marxism via the Russian Social Democratic party, particularly the work of a founder of Russian Marxism, G. Plekhanov. There is a school of thought that argues that Lenin did not and could not have known the "young" Marx since such humanistic works as *Economic and Philosophical Manuscripts of 1844* and *The German Ideology* had been forgotten by Lenin's time and were published in full only after Lenin's death.[28]

Lenin's major philosophical work, *Materialism and Empirico-Criticism*

(1909), does not reflect the philosophical dialectic of Marx's message on the emancipation of the proletariat. At the center of Lenin's thought and writings and certainly one of his most original contributions is his theory on revolution outlining the strategy to be used by the avant garde proletarian communist party during prerevolutionary and revolutionary situations. Whereas in the latter part of their lives Marx and Engels came to appreciate the efficacy of the ballot, Lenin ignored many of the possibilities made available by democratic methods. He went beyond the evolutionary Marx and Engels by denying the possibility of a peaceful seizure of power by the proletariat. A careful study of Lenin's major work, *The State and Revolution: The Marxist Theory of State and the Tasks of the Proletariat in the Revolution*, written while Lenin was in hiding in August-September 1917, and subsequently *The Proletarian Revolution and The Renegade Kautsky* (written in response to Kautsky's critical study of the Bolshevik Revolution, *The Dictatorship of the Proletariat*) reveal Lenin's reinterpretation of Marx and Engels. Lenin's main objective herein was to revive Marx's and Engels' thought on the state and revolution while refuting Kautsky, who stressed an evolutionary interpretation of their works. In so doing Lenin explicates only those passages which speak of the proletariat's violent revolution and dictatorship.

Lenin also revised Marx's and Engels' views on the possibility of a peaceful seizure of power in England, the United States, and Holland (Marx), and France and Germany (Engels). According to Lenin violent revolution was necessary not only in the less developed countries but also, because conditions had changed since Marx's death, in all developed capitalist countries. Since imperialism, as the highest state of capitalism, had permitted the development of an even more repressive state apparatus, England, the United States, Holland, France, and Germany were no longer exceptions.[29] Whereas Marx and, even more so, Engels, thought that the number of countries in which the proletariat participated in parliamentary work to assure a peaceful transition was increasing, Lenin thought the reverse was true. Whereas Engels spoke of universal suffrage as a great achievement of the proletariat and of the "democratic republic" as the special form for the dictatorship of the proletariat, Lenin, interpreting Engels' words in his own fashion, argued that what Engels had meant was that the democratic republic inevitably leads to such an extension, development, unfolding, and intensification of the struggle as to bring about the dictatorship of the proletariat.[30]

Drawing on sporadic quotations and references from Marx and Engels, Lenin had developed a notion of the necessity for the socialist revolution and the dictatorship of the proletariat introduced by an elite party and based on violence, which he summed up in his famous dictum "*kto kogo?* (Who-whom?)." The application of violence is at the very heart of his concept of the proletarian dictatorship. As Lenin wrote in 1916, "whoever expects that socialism will be achieved *without* a socialist revolution and the dictatorship of the proletariat is not a socialist. Dictatorship is state power based directly on *violence*. And in the twentieth century—as in the age of civilization generally—violence means neither a fist nor a club, but troops."[31] Lenin addressed in great detail the question of coalitions, particularly the kinds of coalitions that should be formed and the reasons for their formations. His very concept of dictatorship of the proletariat is related to the concept of class coalition of social forces in a revolutionary situation, which would occur sooner or later in all capitalistic societies. The dictatorship of the proletariat is:

> a specific form of class alliance between the proletariat, the vanguard of the working people, and the numerous non-proletarian strata of the working people (petty bourgeoisie, small proprietors, the peasantry, the intelligentsia, etc.), or the majority of these strata, an alliance against capital, an alliance whose aim is the complete overthrow of capital, complete suppression of the resistance offered by the bourgeoisie as well as of attempts at restoration on its part, an alliance for the final establishment and consolidation of socialism.[32]

Lenin's ideas on the strategy for a dictatorship of the proletariat, his concept on the necessity of forming an "alliance of workers and peasants" is his major contribution to communist theory. Lenin's advocacy of a workers' coalition with the peasants also had important political implications in that it enabled the Bolsheviks to win the support of this stratum and thereby to identify themselves with the majority of the Russian people and win the civil war.

In addition to his ideas on coalitions of classes and social groups, Lenin developed theories on the role of political parties, parliament, and coalitions among political parties. Like the "revolutionary" Marx of 1848, Lenin described the political parties and parliaments as essentially reactionary institutions of oppression representing class interests and dominated by financial capital. They should be abolished and replaced by proletarian democracy.[33] Lenin's ideas on the abolishment of parliament were also embodied in the program of the Bolshevik party in 1919.

While having a basically negative view of parliament and alliances with bourgeois political parties, Lenin did not deny that these institutions and structures could be used to the Communist party's advantage during preparation for the proletarian revolution. Parliamentary opposition and working within the parliament through coalition building and often coalition manipulation were tactics that corresponded to a prerevolutionary situation and were now encouraged. Parliament could be used as an arena for building tactical alliances with other political parties as long as it was possible thereby to achieve concrete cases of tactical compromise and results on behalf of the proletariat. As Lenin had already realized in his work *What Is to Be Done* (1902)—a guide of sorts for those who wish to build a professional, centrally organized, revolutionary party—"Only those who are not sure of themselves can fear to enter into *temporary alliances even with unreliable people*; *not a single political party could exist without such alliances*."[34] In building these coalitions the Communist party, according to Lenin, must agree to tactical compromises and even concessions in order to achieve its final strategic goal—the dictatorship of the proletariat. Because of these beliefs, Lenin opposed the boycott of the Third Duma (the Russian parliament, which was far from being a true parliament in the Western sense) in 1907 and later criticized the Bolshevik boycott of the First and Second Duma (1905–1906). In 1908 he would support the expulsion from the party of those who were in favor of boycotting the Duma, the *Otzovisty*.[35] The first Bolshevik government led by Lenin after the October Revolution in 1917 was at least for several months a coalition government with the Left Socialist revolutionaries.

Lenin's similar thoughts on coalitions were well developed in his pamphlet *Can the Bolsheviks Maintain State Power?* and in his essay *On Compromises*, both written in September 1917 shortly before the October Revolution.[36] His most authoritative treatment of coalition politics can be found in the important and very powerful essay *"Left-Wing" Communism: An Infantile Disorder*, which was published in June 1920 and became the basis for mature Leninist theory on questions of political coalitions. Lenin's aim in writing this work was to give other communist parties the benefit of the Bolshevik political experience and at the same time warn against the "left-wing" error of exaggerating its significance. Its publication was related to the important theoretical debate on the question of revolution and political coalitions which took place in the Communist International (or Comintern) in 1919–1921, particularly prior to and during the Third Congress in June 1921. Lenin's main thesis was that parliamentarianism and tactical alliances with other parties had not become "historically obsolete" with the advent of the Soviet example, as was maintained at that time by some German, Italian, Dutch, and Austrian left-wing communists. In response to their allegations, Lenin argued that since these parties lack the strength to do away with bourgeois parliaments and every other type of reactionary institution, they must work within them and learn how to work legally in the most reactionary parliaments.[37] In building parliamentary coalitions the communist parties have to exploit every opportunity to win allies by compromise and concession and learn how to manipulate coalitions by exploiting the "conflicts of interests" among the bourgeois parties.

In *"Left-Wing" Communism* Lenin basically restated the practical need in politics for coalition building as a *tactical means* to be employed by communist parties under the conditions of a prerevolutionary situation. He also argued sharply against those who viewed the Soviet case as being the "single model" for building socialism and their mechanical application of the Soviet experience. In Lenin's view these attitudes were "leftist stupidities." As he explained at the Third Congress of the Communist International, "The revolution in Italy will run a different course from that in Russia. It will start in a different way. . . . The Communist International would not expect the Italian Party to slavishly copy the Russian Revolution."[38]

Yet in its entirety *"Left-Wing" Communism* does not imply that Lenin believed parliamentarianism to be a goal or that political coalitions should become truly democratic, electoral, parliamentarian, or government coalitions in which communist parties would participate to assure the peaceful transition of capitalist society. Lenin did not give up or revise his basic rationale for coalition building—preparation of the proletarian revolution and the dictatorship of the proletariat. Western communist parties were urged and obliged to seek parliamentary alliances because of their weakness and the lack of a revolutionary situation in Europe at that time. But they were also urged to do so as a means for preparing a revolutionary situation through constitutional methods. When the situation became ripe for revolution, they would be ready to act.

The Debate over Coalitions
in the Comintern

Lenin died in 1924, being the last great Soviet theoretician for some time to come to creatively interpret the revolutionary Marx and Engels. The work of his successor, Josef Stalin, can hardly be considered an original contribution to Marxism. In his book *Problems of Leninism* (1924), Stalin's ideas on the dictatorship of the proletariat and political power are basically a restatement, in catechistic form and dialectical crudity,[39] of ideas already formulated by Lenin. Despite this occurrence, during Stalin's rule in the 1920s and 1930s debate in the Comintern was continuous on the question of political coalitions, although it focused more often on coalition manipulation than on coalition building, particularly the coalition tactics of the so-called "united front from below" versus the so-called "united front from above."

Both terms originate in Lenin's writings and refer to the building of temporary, tactical coalitions. The "united front from below," also called in communist theoretical language "left-wing tactics," refers to demonstrational or penetrative coalitions of the communists with the rank and file of socialist parties and trade unions and other leftist groups. It does not refer to electoral, parliamentary, or government coalitions with the political leaders of socialist parties nor imply the coalition's participation in parliament or the government. It rather implies the penetration, subversion, and absorption of the rank-and-file social democrats as allies in the struggle against social democratic leaders—the chief enemies. The ultimate strategic goal of these coalitions is to prepare for the proletarian revolution.

The "united front from above," also called "right-wing tactics," refers to coalitions with leaders of political parties, trade unions, and ancillaries which occupy a position to the right of the communist party. Although these are preferably coalitions with socialist parties, they can also include bourgeois parties. "Right-wing tactics" provide for communist participation in electoral, parliamentary, and even government coalitions. Although there was disagreement among communist leaders about the duration of these coalitions, the payoffs of coalition building were both short-term and long-term: defeat of right-wing parties in the elections and gains in prestige and electoral strength.

The Comintern's thesis and instructions on coalition politics in the 1920s and 1930s should not be viewed as solely the work of Stalin but rather as the product of prolonged debates (certainly continuing until 1929, and even occasionally into the 1930s) among competing groups within the Soviet leadership and also representatives of other parties and Comintern officials. The important point, however, is that the Comintern's strategies following Lenin's death were not so much the result of new theoretical work as they were logical steps taken from the vantage point of political practice and experience. The main theoretical work on the subject continued to be Lenin's *"Left-Wing" Communism*. Only its practical implementation differed.

Following a theoretical debate influenced by the failure of the revolution in Europe in 1919–1921 and the impact of Lenin's work *"Left-Wing" Communism*, the Comintern in 1921 adopted an official policy aimed at establishing coalitions with socialist parties. These coalitions, which were supposed to be from "below"—class and penetrative coalitions—had their roots in Lenin's thesis that the proletariat, not yet "strong enough to overthrow" parliament, must "utilize" an alternative means in the struggle. "Anti-parliamentarianism" was declared "naive."[40]

This strategy was abandoned after Stalin emerged as Lenin's successor in 1924–1929. Already at the Fifth Congress of 1924, after repudiating Marx's and Engels' evolutionary views and even some of Lenin's ideas, the Comintern decided to entirely abandon the policy of electoral and parliamentary coalitions and to replace it with a policy favoring only class or penetrative coalitions. This meant that the communist parties had to view coalitions with the socialist rank and file as tactical manipulative coalitions in the communists' struggle to achieve the dictatorship of the proletariat. The political payoff for those members of the socialist parties who were asked to join coalitions with the communists was supposed to be the defeat of their own party leaders. The coalitions thereby formed were not "democratic" but rather employed "revolutionary strategic maneuvers of the communist van-guard." Electoral coalitions were "categorically rejected by the Communist International." This policy and the process of so-called Bolshevization in the late 1920s and early 1930s brought the communist parties into a state of increasing isolation within their own countries. Comintern leaders such as N. Bukharin and others who advocated electoral alliances were purged.[41] Overall the strategy of class, penetrative coalitions failed to bear fruit. It actually proved to be disastrous, contributing as it did to heavy losses at the polls, to a decline in active Party membership, and in 1933 to the victory of fascism in Germany, where the communists, blindly following the Comintern line, refused to cooperate with the Social Democratic party.

Electoral Coalitions

The Comintern shift in favor of electoral coalitions—the so-called popular fronts—occurred in 1934–1935. The theoretical basis and justification for such strategy are again found in Lenin's *"Left-Wing" Communism*. This reversal came about not only as the result of another debate in the Comintern, but also because of new political developments. The main catalyst was the increasing power of fascism in Europe. In 1934 the Spanish and French republics had come under attack by fascist groups, and it was feared they were heading in the same direction as Germany. Then, in spite of orders to the contrary, French party members began to violate Comintern theses in coalition politics in response to the challenge from the right. As a result, the French Communist party, after an internal

debate, was forced into a sudden reversal of its policies, in which cooperation with other parties was favored although the policy of accepting electoral coalitions had not yet been officially sanctioned by the Comintern.
Around that time there ensued a debate among Comintern and Soviet
officials about the strategy of coalition politics.[42]

It is still difficult to determine to what extent policies favoring electoral coalitions were the independent creation of some of the West European parties (particularly the French and Spanish) and to what extent they
were instigated by the Comintern apparatus and the Soviet leadership.[43]
Although Stalin must have had the last word in any debate (at least from
1929 on), the changing political reality was the main factor which brought
about the Comintern's new approach to coalition building. The resolution
of the Seventh Comintern Congress of August 1, 1935, on the report of the
ECCI (Executive Committee of the Communist International) acknowledged the validity of electoral coalitions as a response to new realities,
noting the historic "significance of the fact that the social-democratic
workers and a number of social-democratic organizations are already struggling hand-in-hand with the communists against fascism and for the interests of the toiling masses." It asked the communist parties "to strive in the
future by every means to establish the united front on a national as well as
international scale." This resolution, echoing Lenin's *"Left-Wing" Communism*, declared that antifascist popular electoral alliances were a policy to be
pursued by communist parties. "Election campaigns must be utilized" by
the communists to "declare for a common platform and a common ticket
with the anti-fascist front, depending on the growth and success of the
united front movement, and on the electoral system in operation."[44]

The result of this shift was a complete reversal in the policy of the
Communist International and a total abandonment of the previous strategy
on coalition. Abandoned also, at least temporarily, were the notions of
dictatorship of the proletariat and violent revolution. The uniqueness of
the new strategy (the popular front) in terms of coalition building was that
for the first time it included the communist parties in electoral and parliamentarian majorities. Originally the size of the popular front coalitions
was limited by the number of members belonging to the workers' parties,
e.g., communists and socialists. However, later in 1935 the coalition size
was enlarged, under the name of popular front, to include such bourgeois
parties as the Radical party in France and the Republican party in Spain.
The enlargement of the coalition ensured their ability to win. In 1936
popular front governments, supported by the working class, the peasants,
and sections of the middle class, were elected to office in France and Spain.

Although the popular fronts did not have a long life, the local parties benefited from their brief existence, perhaps even more than the U.S.S.R. For the Soviet leadership, the main payoffs for these alliances were on an international level: a temporary slowdown in the growth of fascism in Europe, and because of the containment of pro-Hitler fascist groups, support for a temporary Franco-Soviet alliance and a Spanish-Soviet alliance. For the local parties, the main payoffs of the popular fronts were on a national level: electoral victories over fascist and right-wing parties. There were additional related payoffs in that the popular fronts provided a means for establishing electoral strength, moving their parties from a sectarian position to a position wherein they were recognized as the respected supporters of national governments and the defenders of parliamentarian democracy. Although for the local parties the popular front policies of the 1930s were still mainly tactical and manipulative in the Leninist sense, they were also the product of West European political realities. Thus they were important for the local parties in terms of experience and tradition and represented in their temporary break with Stalinism the application of a truly "Marxist" analysis to specific circumstances in their countries. Some European communist leaders such as Santiago Carrillo believe they were "antecedents" of the Eurocommunist-type democratic coalitions of the 1970s.[45]

Government Coalitions

The coalition governments of 1944–1947, known as "national fronts," "patriotic fronts," "fatherland fronts," "leftist blocs," and "committees for national liberation," offer another example of coalition politics as it has existed in communist theory and practice. In some respects these post–World War II government coalitions are reminiscent of the electoral coalitions of the 1930s. In both cases the communists decided to work within the system by using democratic institutions and building coalitions with other parties.

The coalitions of the postwar period were substantially different, however, in that they were not geared primarily to achieving the strength in numbers necessary to ensure electoral victory. Formed under the influence of the power equilibrium in Europe following World War II, they were rather coalitions of national unity including representatives of the communist parties and several other major parties. In 1947–48 these coalition governments disintegrated: In the East the noncommunist parties were excluded, whereas in the West the casualties were the communist parties. According to prevailing interpretations, this process was facilitated by a long-term program of communist takeover, following Marx and Lenin's revolutionary dictum of proletarian dictatorship exemplified in the Bolshevik takeover in 1917.[46] Old evidence and recent findings suggest that the trajectory of coalition governments in 1944–1947 was somewhat more complex. There was actually a great deal of uncertainty and debate among Soviet and also other communist leaders as to how to proceed with government coalition politics.[47] There were probably some communist leaders who even believed that the purpose of these coalitions was to achieve consensus and harmony more than an irreversible class conflict leading to the proletarian revolution and that the transition to socialism could occur by peaceful means, without a dictatorship of the proletariat. If only for tactical reasons, the Soviet leadership in 1944 fully approved of the coalition governments and seemed to believe that their duration should be prolonged for several years in some cases. What was certain, as pointed out by Carrillo, was that in 1944–1947 no one, including the Soviet leaders, among them Stalin himself, described these coalition governments as being dictatorships of the proletariat or as being modeled according to Lenin's dictum. Indeed they differed significantly from the Soviet model. After all, it was the Soviet government which dissolved the Comintern in 1943 to facilitate the work of the national alliances in Europe (composed of patriotic forces of every persuasion) in the struggle against fascism. "The dissolution of the Communist International," as Stalin himself explained, "facilitates the work of patriots in freedom-loving countries, regardless of party or religious faith, into a single camp of national liberation—for unfolding the struggle against fascism."[48]

Such coalitions were also desirable since the communist parties in general, despite the growth of their membership during the war, were still minor political parties in most European countries. The Soviets were initially concerned that imposition of a Leninist-type proletarian dictatorship in various European countries could threaten wartime alliances, invoke an undesirable American response, and strengthen Western unity. The Soviets' payoff for a coalition government with noncommunist participation in Eastern Europe was to gain time in which to gradually consolidate their political gains in that area. Although the coalition governments seemed to be encouraged and tolerated, particularly in the more developed countries of Central Europe (Czechoslovakia and Hungary), here as elsewhere the communist party played what Riker would call a pivotal position in these coalitions. The Soviets' payoff for coalition governments in Western Europe (Italy, France) was to ensure a degree of Soviet influence in the alliance parties and leave open the way for future communist party gains.

Again there appeared to be some debate and controversy (if not confusion) among communist theoreticians about the nature of coalition governments in general and in Eastern Europe in particular. Some, such as the Hungarian-born Soviet academician E. Varga, recognized the stabilizing and organizing function of the contemporary capitalist state and believed that coalition governments in Eastern Europe should be of a transitional nature, assuming a middle position between the old bourgeois states and the Soviet state. This would allow for some of the institutions of these governments to be creatively reshaped without complete destruction of the old state.[49] The only really coherent and authoritative theoretical contribution to communist coalition theory in the 1940s is that of Chinese leader Mao Zedong, *On Coalition Government*, published in April 1945. Having dealt seriously with the question of coalition government since 1935 during the popular front era, Mao, like Lenin, viewed coalitions as being only temporary class alliances which would gradually usher in the dictatorship of the proletariat. However, seeing coalitions in the light of China's agrarian, semifeudal society, Mao assigned the peasants an even greater role than Lenin in the art of building class coalitions with the workers. Among the proletariat's coalition partners he also included the national bourgeoisie and even such feudal groups as the patriotic princes. According to Mao, these classes would all participate in a government coalition wherein the communists would take up pivotal positions. The main objective of this coalition strategy was to build a "new democratic state system," which, as specified by Mao, would differ from the Soviet model. Mao's theories, however, had little if any impact on other communist thinkers or on the communist movement, not only in Europe but in China as well. In practice, Mao, like Tito, resisted Soviet pressure to build a coalition government with bourgeois elements. After his 1949 ascension to power, he revised his coalition government theory to accommodate the Leninist theory of the dictatorship of the proletariat and the communist party in the 1949 theoretical work *On the People's Democratic Dictatorship*.[50]

Although the building of coalition governments in 1944–1947 lacked a precise theoretical elaboration, it nevertheless came about as the result of a coherent, pragmatic plan. The evidence is scattered, but we know from available sources that after the abolition of the Comintern of 1943–1944 a plan was devised for a gradualist strategy of "broad coalitions." The chief protagonists were the Soviet leadership and two former Comintern leaders, G. Dimitrov and D. Manuilskii, as well as other European communist leaders living at that time in Moscow. In fact, the Soviets and East European leaders, while advocating considerable compromises with the middle class and peasantry, discouraged any form of radicalism after the liberation of the West as well as the East European countries, particularly any attempt on the part of radical elements to establish a proletarian dictatorship. East European leaders like the Hungarian M. Rákosi again drew the attention of their radical comrades to Lenin's warning in *"Left-Wing" Communism*, arguing that the duration of a coalition government could be a decade or more. Those who, like the Yugoslavs, did deviate in 1944–1945 from the coalition formula were pressured (unsuccessfully) to compromise and follow the established coalition pattern. Even in the Balkan states of Bulgaria and Romania, agrarian countries without democratic traditions, caution was originally exercised against radicalism. In Czechoslovakia, the Soviets supported Gottwald's "specific path toward socialism," and in both Czechoslovakia and Hungary genuinely free and democratic elections were held. In East Germany the Soviets originally confirmed and supported the East German leader A. Ackerman's thesis of 1946 about "einen besonderen deutschen Weg zum Sozialismus" (a special German path to socialism) based on coalition politics. According to this thesis Germany should advance toward a type of middle democracy situated "between bourgeois and socialist democracy." Ackerman himself justified his thesis while evoking an evolutionary interpretation of Marx's views about the possibility of a peaceful, democratic way toward socialism in the most developed capitalist countries.[51]

In Western Europe the Soviets also discouraged any radicalism within the communist parties during and shortly after the war. Thus party leaders M. Thorez and P. Togliatti were not allowed to return to France and Italy during the war to lead the resistance because of fears that by doing so they might spoil relations with the Western allies. The Soviets rather encouraged the participation of both parties in the Committees of National Liberation which formed the provisional coalition governments of France and Italy in 1944. Togliatti returned to Italy in 1944, bringing with him the concept of "a new Party," and, with Soviet blessings (albeit temporary), began to substitute the Leninist notion of dictatorship of the proletariat with A. Gramsci's notion of "working class hegemony." (Gramsci's ideas on coalitions will be discussed later.)

With the establishment of Cominform in 1947 there was again a sharp reversal in the thinking and practice regarding communist coalitions. The revolutionary ideas of Marx and Lenin again took precedence over the evolutionary Marx. The reasons for this shift are varied. First, the international and regional equilibrium of power upon which the large post–World War II coalitions of political parties was based began to change drastically in 1947. Europe was gradually transformed into a cold-war battlefield. The government coalitions became too large to satisfy the many conflicting interests in internal and international politics, and the Soviet leaders began to view the payoffs for tolerating coalition governments as not sufficient to warrant their existence. They discovered to their surprise that the West, while being enormously concerned about communist participation in coalition governments in Western Europe, exhibited no particular concern over events in Eastern Europe. Finally, the Soviet leaders noticed that the dissolution of Comintern and communist participation in democratic coalitions were leading to the isolation, inadequate coordination, and increasing independence of some of the parties. Radical elements in the communist parties, particularly in the East (who disagreed with those leaders who believed in an evolutionary path toward socialism) pressed for a speedier implementation of the ultimate goal of the dictatorship of the proletariat. Those communist leaders who favored "specific paths toward socialism" were obstructed by the new Soviet line which maintained that government coalitions were in fact "democratic dictatorships of worker and peasants" which, by promoting "class struggle" from "above and below," were heading toward socialist revolution.

Overall, it seems that the coalitions of 1944–1947 were not an indispensable tool for the seizure of power either by the Soviets or the European communist leaders. For such communist theoreticians as Varga and some East and West European leaders they were seen as useful (albeit temporary) alliances of political and social forces. In Eastern Europe they provided the Soviet leadership with a convenient institution that could be abolished in a Leninist fashion at any time Stalin should see fit. The experience of coalition governments in 1944–1947 did not have a uniform impact in both parts of Europe. In Eastern Europe coalition governments would generally be viewed as a negative example for communist takeovers, to be used particularly in countries with democratic traditions and democratic political cultures such as Czechoslovakia. On the other hand, for the Italian party participation in coalition governments would be viewed as having provided it with valuable payoffs. As before in the 1930s, coalition participation helped it to temporarily regain popularity, prestige, electoral votes, and legitimacy.

Democratic Coalitions: "Eurocommunism"

So far, the democratic form of communism called Eurocommunism, having been born of political practice, has shown itself to be rather weak in theory. In essence, it is a derivative concept of Marx's early humanist, revolutionary, and late evolutionary thought reinforced by various thinkers such as Gramsci, R. Luxemburg, and perhaps Kautsky. However, it still carries much Leninist legacy. The term *Eurocommunism* as used here does not mean to designate a concept or condition but rather the trend toward democratic, pluralistic, and independent communism in advanced, industrial countries.

Some of the ideas are not new. Insofar as Eurocommunist theory stands for democratic communism and a permanent commitment to the values of Western humanism, some of its intellectual origins lie in Marx's early humanistic works, particularly his *Economic and Philosophical Manuscripts of 1844*. Insofar as Eurocommunist theory represents a commitment to democratic values and an evolutionary development of society characterized by respect for democratic institutions, free and universal suffrage, and other democratic rights, its theoretical roots are also to be found in Marx's political writings and in the evolutionist thoughts which he and Engels to an even greater degree expressed in the later part of their lives. The ambiguities inherent in their works notwithstanding, the Eurocommunists can claim, as Kautsky but also Lenin and their followers have done, a truly, albeit derivative, Marxist heritage. As it has emerged in the last several decades, pluralistic communism or Eurocommunism in the 1970s stands in contrast to the one-dimensional revolutionary interpretation of Marx put forth by Lenin. Thus Kautsky, a disciple of Engels, was actually the first Marxist to attempt a synthesis of the revolutionary and evolutionary views of Marx and Engels by harmoniously integrating socialist ideas and democratic principles. He might be considered the proto-Eurocommunist. Carrillo claims that in Kautsky's critique of Lenin, *The Dictatorship of the Proletariat*, "there are certain arguments that seem rather reasonable." The French Eurocommunist theoretician Jean Elleinstein goes even further. He says that Kautsky was wrong about the political situation in Russia, but that he was right about political democracy, while Lenin was wrong on this score.[52]

The "Eurocommunists" Carrillo, Elleinstein, and others can and do claim as part of their heritage the writings of the brilliant theoretician and leader of the German and Polish communist parties, Rosa Luxemburg. Luxemburg did not treat Marx's theories as did Lenin, seeking out the quirks in Marx's work to support her own interpretations and theoretical framework. For Luxemburg, Marx was a great theoretician but also a fallible one, and his hypotheses and theoretical conclusions were limited to the times in which he lived. She was one of the first communist theoreticians to point out the inherent danger of Leninism, of confusing the dictatorship of the proletariat with the dictatorship of the vanguard minority party. She viewed Lenin's dictatorship as the Eurocommunists do today—as being a product of the backward socioeconomic and political conditions in Russian society, which mitigated against the effective operation of Western democratic institutions such as parliament. "The dictatorship of the proletariat," Luxemburg argued, "consists in the *manner of applying democracy*, not in its *elimination*." Although Luxemburg viewed the nature of democratic institutions as far from being satisfactory, she pointed out that "it is a well-known and indisputable fact that without a free and untrammeled press, without the unlimited right of association and assemblage, the rule of the broad mass of the people is entirely unthinkable."[53] Luxemburg opposed Lenin's conspiratorial tactics and adhered to the democratic character of the socialist movement. Her thinking did not pivot exclusively on revolution (as did that of Lenin) or exclusively on evolution (as did the thinking of social democrats like Bernstein). At the heart of her theories and practical positions were both the revolution and evolution. In synthesizing the revolutionary views of Marx and Engels, she emphasized the necessity of mass action along with parliamentary action.[54]

Insofar as Eurocommunism specifically advocated the undertaking of coalitions with other political and social forces as a strategy to be utilized by the working class, the main theoretical work which can be viewed as proto-Eurocommunist is that of Gramsci. Gramsci, like Luxemburg, was inspired by the Bolshevik example but refused to consider it as a model to be followed in the socially, economically, and culturally more advanced West European countries. Gramsci, however, attached importance not only to Marx and Lenin but also to Machiavelli and the overall tradition of Western political thinking since the Renaissance. Gramsci's eleven-year sojourn in Mussolini's prisons (1926–1937), where he also died, gave him time during which to reflect on communist theories and to make his own contribution. He in turn inspired other European communist thinkers in their writing and their search for a road to socialism different from that being followed in Soviet Russia.

Unlike Lenin, who made some observations similar to those of Gramsci shortly before his death in his final work, *"Left-Wing" Communism*, Gramsci was the first communist theoretician to initiate the search for genuinely democratic political coalitions. The first ever Marxist theorist of culture and of political superstructure asked the questions not only if and why coalitions should be formed, but what kinds should be undertaken and with whom and, most importantly, how. He addressed the important questions of equilibrium and disequilibrium, compatibility of interests of coalition partners, and the size of coalitions as important factors in the strategy of coalition building. His major theme was the concept of "working class hegemony," which Gramsci (without directly admitting it) wanted to substitute for Lenin's revolutionary reinterpretation of Marx's dictatorship of the proletariat. In contrast to the tactics successful in the feudal aristocracy of tsarist Russia, the concept of "hegemony," designed to suit the different circumstances of the parliamentary bourgeois democracy of Europe, is described by Gramsci as leading to equilibrium among the various heterogeneous forces in society. Gramsci's equilibrium, like hegemony itself, can only be achieved by a changing consensus, by seeking "allies," and not by violent coercion. When such equilibrium exists, a "homogenous politico-economic-historical bloc"—another crucial Gramsci concept—can be inaugurated. A historical bloc can be formed within a coalition of the basic forces in (Italian) society such as the workers and the middle class, the peasant masses and the Catholic Church. Gramsci emphasized the need for studying coalition building as the means for forging consensus as a prerequisite for "hegemony" and the victory of "a historical bloc." His theories were to be recognized after World War II as a great contribution not only to Italian Marxism but also to the development of communist thought in Europe in general.

The development of Eurocommunist theory of alliances has corresponded with the practical politics of some West European parties, particularly the Italian (PCI), and gradually such others as the Spanish Communist party (PCE). The 1947 Comintern criticism of the strategy of coalition politics was only formally accepted by the PCI. The PCI did not give up but rather continued to develop coalition strategies, endeavoring since the mid-1950s to form a broad electoral and parliamentarian coalition of Italian political and social forces, including socialists and Catholics, and the middle class and peasantry. The Italian leader P. Togliatti's 1956 concept of "polycentrism" of autonomous communism merged with Gramsci's legacy of "hegemonic bloc" and manifested itself in the program of the PCI which culminated in the 1970s with E. Berlinguer's concept of "historic compromise" with the Christian Democratic party. Gramsci's legacy and the Italian communist example were also followed since the mid-1950s by the PCE, which under Carrillo's leadership began to advocate and work toward a *frente nacional antifranquista*, while expanding the scope of alliance partners to include Catholics and other social forces in the 1960s. A similar road was followed by several other West European parties.

Eurocommunist theory was further developed in Carrillo's book *Eurocommunism and the State*, published in 1977. Carrillo is not a political theoretician but rather a politician. Thus his arguments are not entirely smooth on the theoretical level. His book, however, is a powerful and important one, as suggested by the vitriolic Soviet and East European criticism it has stimulated. The main thesis of Carrillo's work is that socialism will be achieved in the developed countries of the advanced West by using democratic means to form a genuinely democratic coalition described as a "new political formation." Carrillo's main arguments have their inspiration in the ideas of Marx and Engels and some of Lenin's and Kautsky's ideas, but also those of Luxemburg and Gramsci. He repeats the point made in Marx's *Manifesto* about the need to *"raise the proletariat to the position of ruling class, to win the battle of democracy."*[55] He maintains that the work of Marx and Engels (albeit Marx was wrong about certain things) is basically "valid" for communists who want "to transform present-day capitalist society by democratic means." Lenin, in Carrillo's view, was only "half-right" when he declared that despite "an immense abundance and diversity of political . . . forms all communist governments in their essence will necessarily be a single one: *the dictatorship of the proletariat.*" According to Carrillo, this is no longer true.

As Carrillo says, restating the evolutionary views of Marx in counterpoint to Lenin, today *"the diversity and abundance of political forms* likewise entails the possibility of *the dictatorship of the proletariat not being* necessary."[56] According to Carrillo's restatement of Luxemburg's argument, Lenin and his followers, including Carrillo himself, underestimated and belittled the value of democracy. Struggle against "bourgeois democracy" became an "obsession" within the communist movement. The dictatorship of the proletariat and violence were an "unavoidable historic necessity," but only in the underdeveloped countries where the workers "were completely ignorant of democracy." This is true in all present socialist countries, with the exception of Czechoslovakia. Dictatorship might still be necessary in the underdeveloped countries. In the developed countries of the West, however, as Carrillo states, the peaceful transformation of society can occur.

As to coalition politics in the developed countries of the West, Carrillo views class or penetrative coalitions as obsolete. Coalition building, defined as genuine democratic political coalitions, which he calls "the new political formation," acquires decisive importance. It is "linked" to "the new historic bloc," and to "the question of "anti-monopolistic alliances."[57] As to what kinds of coalitions should be formed, particularly their size, and how they should come into existence, Carrillo's vision goes beyond the purely electoral coalition. Temporary coalitions may become genuine democratic alliances of several parties and social organizations based on consensus.

Doubtless, Eurocommunist theory, though weak and untested, presents an ideological challenge to Leninist thought and its interpretation. This is particularly true of the PCE's platform. The 1978 congress of this party set a precedent by symbolically dropping the Leninist label and changing the party's designation from "Marxist-Leninist" to "Marxist revolutionary and democratic." As the continuous Soviet polemic with the Eurocommunist thinkers reveals, Soviet and also some East European ideologists still view the bullet as more reliable than the ballot. In Leninist fashion, they argue that the communist parties must not abide by the will of the electorate. This can create only an "arithmetic" and not a "political" majority. The Eurocommunist criticism of Leninism, forcefully stated by Carrillo and other Eurocommunist leaders and theoreticians such as M. Azcárate and J. Elleinstein, has brought them into collision with conservative ideologists in the USSR and Eastern Europe who have accused them of reviving Kautsky and Bernstein. By virtue of the Eurocommunists' refusal to entirely deny the validity of Lenin's thought, emphasizing instead the humanistic and evolutionary interpretation of Marx freed of the baggage of Russian Byzantian heritage, Eurocommunism, although not a unified concept or strategy, may potentially represent an alternative to Leninism.

Conclusion

Despite continuous theoretical search by contemporary Western Marxists (not included in this essay) there is still no coherent theory on political coalitions of direct political value. Political theoreticians in the West, accepting the fact that democratic coalitions simply exist (and not questioning their existence) have developed their theories basically by asking *how* and *when* coalitions are built, *what* payoffs they afford, and what size they should be. Many communist theoreticians, on the other hand, have debated for at least one hundred years, and still continue to debate, *why* and *if* democratic coalitions should be pursued. Frequently debated has been the issue of what kinds of coalitions should be formed, and occasionally who should be able to join, but the crucial questions of *how* and *when* coalitions should be formed have been touched on only very briefly and only by theoreticians more closely associated with theories of democratic communism or so-called Eurocommunism.

Thus some generalizations advanced in Western theories on political coalitions, such as Riker's thoughts on political payoffs and Axelrod's notion of compatibility and conflicting interests, can be useful in the study of communist theories on coalitions. Usually the hypotheses advanced by the students of coalition behavior in Western political systems are, so far, only peripheral to the understanding of communist coalition theories.

This state of affairs occurs primarily because Marx's and Engels' theoretical work has produced little theory on the subject of politics and political alliances. They touched on this important subject casually and only very seldom. The ambiguities and unresolved contradictions in their theories make at least three different interpretations of their work possible. Besides the humanistic interpretations of the early works of Marx, there can be found two additional contradictory interpretations: revolutionary and evolutionary. The first is genetically linked to Lenin, particularly his concept of the communist party as a vanguard of the revolution, and what is ambiguously defined as Leninism. The second is linked to social democracy.

Lenin's theories, basically, as strategy and tactics for revolution by the elite party, focus on politics in general and on coalition politics in particular. The twists in his theories notwithstanding, it is obvious that he favored the communists working within political coalitions, but only for tactical and manipulative reasons. Lenin's envisaged tactical alliances were groupings basically intended as a means for the abolition, by revolutionary steps, of democratic institutions and the establishment of the dictatorship of the proletariat. Nevertheless, Lenin does provide some important thoughts on coalition building, compromise, and concessions but also coalition manipulation and the destruction of democratic coalitions, ideas which have been of major theoretical importance to communist parties both during Lenin's lifetime and thereafter.

There were some debates in the Comintern in the 1920s and 1930s on the issue of coalitions, coalition building, and coalition manipulation. Coalition manipulation and infiltration of socialist parties had to be radically changed in 1934–1935 for a policy of electoral and parliamentarian coalitions. In this shift, more important than theory was practice. Events themselves were the guide. After World War II there was a short-lived experiment with coalition governments. Again, coalition building was not so much the result of theoretical debate as of practical experience amidst theoretical confusion. Only in the last few decades did communist theoreticians and leaders begin to discuss democratic coalitions and question how and when coalitions should be formed and the serious degree of commitment to coalition partners.

Pluralistic communism, or Eurocommunism, is in many respects the antithesis of Leninism and the very negation of Stalinism. It makes Marxism synonymous with democratic socialism, if not social democracy. Themselves products of a different political culture, the Eurocommunists see Lenin's thought on coalitions as unfit for the advanced, developed countries of the West. As the Eurocommunists profess, it is not the tactical alliance leading to the overthrow of democratic institutions and to the establishment of the dictatorship of the proletariat, but rather the communist parties working within democratic systems by building genuine democratic coalitions, such as the "historical bloc" or the "new political formation," that can enable the communists in the West to facilitate a peaceful transition toward socialism. The prime motivating factor in the formation of such coalitions does not necessarily have to do with ideological considerations. More important is the calculation of expected political payoffs in the attempt to minimize conflicts of interests and ideological incompatibility.

As to the body of Eurocommunist thought, some of it is utopian, while some of it now (1988) is regarded as a bit passé in non-Eurocommunist Western Marxism and exists in hypothetical form awaiting empirical validation. But even in this untested form it presents the only attempt for Marxists today to follow Marx's favorite motto—*De omnibus dubitandum* (All things are subject to doubt).

PART 1

Regional Studies: Europe

Overview

Trond Gilberg

As indicated by the chapter by Jiri Valenta, Marxist thought, as exemplified by the writings of Marx, Engels, and Lenin, contributed little to the systematic study of coalitions because Lenin considered such arrangements necessary *tactical* devices which were mere preliminaries to the establishment of the dictatorship of the proletariat, while the two German thinkers tended to promote the idea of coalitions as reactions to existing situations and developments rather than strategic devices for socioeconomic and political change. The dearth of systematic Marxist thought about coalitions does not preclude the possibility that practitioners of Marxism may have behaved in ways which were analyzable or predictable from the vantage point of coalition theory. The individual contributions of the rest of this book will address this possibility, thus providing insights into likely coalition behavior by Marxists in the future.

The fact that the first Marxist-inspired revolution in the world occurred in a country which was, at least in part, European, with revolutionary leaders drawing their inspiration from the Germans Karl Marx and Friedrich Engels, produced a predilection for interpreting this political doctrine from the vantage point of European realities and contexts. The fact that the Russians were the only successful Marxist revolutionaries for a considerable period of time ensured the dominance of the Kremlin in the international communist movement. This predilection for a European bias in interpreting political relationships obscured the possibilities of coalition strategies and tactics based on different cultural, socioeconomic, and political realities, and it took another successful revolution under Marxist auspices to broaden the perspective on this question. The Chinese Revolution, based upon Mao's thought, reestablished the notion that coalition strategies and tactics are appropriate in agrarian and non-Western societies as well; the context and players differ, but the "rules of the game" may indeed apply to very different socioeconomic, cultural, or political contexts. But it is also clear that the specific manifestations of coalition behavior among Marxists are likely to depend upon those specific circumstances of region and of country. These circumstances will provide the context in which any political organization—whether such an organization is system supportive or dedicated to the destruction of that system in all or part of its manifestations—must operate.

The existing political and socioeconomic order and the cultural traditions of society provide more than a framework within which political organizations operate; they help establish the mindset of its citizenry, the screen of perception through which reality is seen by all practitioners. Thus it is likely that European Marxists think like Europeans, and not like Middle Easterners or Africans. A study of European Marxism, then, must focus on those specifically European aspects of life that are likely to exercise a crucial influence upon thinking and perceptions among political practitioners in that context.

The European political and socioeconomic context in the second half of the nineteenth century and the beginning of the twentieth had a number of characteristics which were common to the region, while others existed in the western but not in the eastern part of the continent. Throughout Europe the period in question was characterized by institution building and the establishment of political processes and procedures which attempted to regularize political behavior. Institutionalization was fairly advanced. In the economic sector, modernization had begun, characterized by the development of industry and attendant urbanization. Educational institutions were established and expanded. There developed an industrial proletariat and an urban bourgeoisie, and various programs and institutions were established to deal with the social problems of the area. Throughout the region, then, a process of political development was under way; differences between east and west and among specific contexts had to do with *degrees* of political development.

Other aspects of politics and social life in Europe varied greatly from east to west and north to south. In western and northwestern Europe, political development had already advanced considerably beyond institutionalization and the regularization of political processes by the turn of the century. Here the birth pangs of mass political participation were already over; groups and parties formed and political pluralization had taken place. This was particularly important in terms of the new industrial proletariat, which had formed its trade unions, youth organizations, self-help societies, and political parties. In some cases the labor parties were already among the largest in the domestic political context; in others they had a long way to go, but there was steady expansion. In some countries, and notably Germany, the regime refused to accept full political citizenship for the burgeoning mass movement of the working class; in others, like England and Scandinavia, these parties and organizations were all on their way to political respectability. The political context in which local leftist parties operated thus differed even in this subregion. But, on the whole, "politicization" here meant not merely institution building but also mass participation and group formation.

In southern and eastern Europe, on the other hand, mass participation was not as highly developed and certainly not accepted by the local political elites. Participation, when it occurred, tended to be anomic and sporadic rather than organized. Marxists, therefore, operated in a fundamentally different context here, and could be expected to develop different behavior patterns and organizational forms.

These regional differences were compounded by different degrees of socioeconomic development and also values and attitudes on such fundamental political issues as individual rights versus collective needs, religious preferences and the political posture of the churches, and the rights of assembly and petition. No political practitioner could escape these constraints and opportunities of time and place.

The following two chapters examine the coalition strategies and tactics of Marxist parties and organizations in Western and Eastern Europe, recognizing the important differences between these two regions, while also keeping in mind the similarities that existed (and will continue to exist). Subsequent chapters will examine Marxist behavior in other regions of the world.

3

Marxists and Coalitions in Western Europe
Trond Gilberg

As pointed out by Jiri Valenta, Marxist thinkers from Marx and Engels to the contemporary political leaders of the Soviet Union, Eastern Europe, and China have grappled with the problem of relations between Marxist organizations and other structures, particularly parties and other political entities of the domestic political order. In addition, Marxists, as avowed internationalists, have attempted to put these relationships in the context of the internationalistic tendencies and outlooks that generate the ideological "package" we know as "Marxism." Since Western Europe produced the earliest Marxists and also appeared to be the region most likely to experience a successful revolution under Marxist auspices, the dividing lines between various factions, all of which claimed the heritage of Karl Marx and Friedrich Engels, were drawn most sharply there in the late nineteenth century and during the first two decades of the twentieth. After the Russian Revolution this change was primarily between the communists ("Marxists-Leninists") and the "others"; since the communist parties had acquired a powerful patron in the ruling Soviet party, they became the primary focus of analysis and policy by the non-Marxist forces of West European politics. This does not mean that other Marxist parties were unimportant; rather, these structures became themselves the object of communist policies since the latter utilized the former as elements of coalition strategy and tactics in the communists' broader quest for power in the societies of Western Europe. The primary focus of this chapter is therefore those parties of the region which called themselves "communist," adhered to "Marxism-Leninism" as defined in the Kremlin, and maintained a special relationship with the CPSU. The coalition strategies and tactics of these parties were (and are) a mixture of ideological preconditions, pragmatic assessments of political opportunities and liabilities, and the personality traits of party leaders.

The Communist Weltanschauung

Proletarian Internationalism

Communists and their organizations exist in a curious relationship to their socioeconomic and political environments. One of the most fundamental aspects of communist life has always been the existence of *proletarian internationalism*, a special relationship based on *international* solidarity. This solidarity presumably supersedes attachments to the local environment and the political manifestations therein. Communists are, presumably, obliged to consider this international relationship before their local policies are established. This does not mean that all strategies and tactics of communist parties are determined by proletarian internationalism; Lenin and all other subsequent leaders of the Soviet party have emphasized the need for proper concern with the local environment, and tactical flexibility has always been stressed. But it is also true that there is a doctrinal core of communism which cannot be jettisoned, even if such an act would be beneficial in the local situation and for a short period of time. Communist parties may occasionally behave like "normal" parties, but they are definitely different, both because of proletarian internationalism and because of their doctrinal basis.[1]

Relationships with Other Forces and Organizations of the Left

Because of its claim to doctrinal purity and the "one right way," organized communism is profoundly ambivalent about other forces and organizations on the political left. On the one hand, the existence of socialists, social democrats, Trotskyists, and even leftist "bourgeois" parties is detrimental to the "unity" of this side of the political spectrum, and the communists have always been dedicated to this unity as a final theoretical goal. On the other hand, history has decisively denied the communists the unity which they craved in theory, and this has meant that practical steps must be made to regulate relations with those other leftist organizations. These relations have varied greatly over time, partly because of policies established in Moscow, and partly because of local considerations.

Relationships with "Bourgeois"
Organizations and Parties

Because of the pluralization of the political party systems in Western Europe, local communist parties, from the very inception of their existence, faced the vexing problem of a great many parties and organizations which could not be described as "leftist" or "progressive," but rather represented all kinds of ideological variations, ranging from "left-leaning" liberals to arch-conservative nationalists (and, of course, fascists in many countries during the interwar period). As much as the European communists rejected the doctrines of these parties, they remained a fact of political life throughout the entire period since the Russian Revolution, and practical relations had to be established. These relations, too, varied greatly over time, depending on the often bewildering change on the local political scene.

While policies toward local leftists and "bourgeois" elements (under the auspices of the prevailing policy line from Moscow) have remained the primary strategic and tactical concerns of West European communists for sixty years, the line followed vis-à-vis each subset of actors was profoundly determined by the doctrinal core of organized communism and political events in each system at any one time. Since entire libraries have been filled with discussions of communist doctrine, I shall be brief on this subject, concentrating on those elements which had the greatest impact upon communist coalition behavior. Among these points, the following are decisive.

The communist commitment to public ownership of the means of production in banking, industry, commerce, and trade. Since the splits between West European parties traditionally can be traced to differences in economic doctrine, the communist emphasis on nationalization in many sectors helped establish its negative relationship with a multitude of parties and organizations doctrinally and operationally dedicated to free enterprise and capitalism. Occasional attempts by local communists to cooperate with these ideological counterparts in economic doctrine were therefore interpreted as mere "maneuvers," which must be dismissed, at least until a truly desperate situation arose.

The emphasis on eventual destruction of private agriculture and the achievement of collectivization. Even though many "adjustments" have been made by communist parties and mass organizations in the field of agrarian policy, the fact remains that doctrinally the demise of private agriculture is established as both inevitable and beneficial—inevitable because of the unstoppable march of history to its predetermined end, and beneficial because public ownership in this sector is, presumably, the key to higher production in "postcapitalist" agriculture. Such a doctrine is diametrically opposed to one of the most durable political and socioeconomic phenomena in European politics, namely the peasantry's commitment to private ownership of the land and the rights to the production emerging from it. Given the innate conservatism of the peasantry, the issue of land ownership was key to one of the most fundamental hostilities in West European history, namely the struggle between communist and agrarian parties.

The communist rejection of political pluralism. If the political history of Western Europe in the twentieth century can be said to have produced a fundamental principle, then political pluralism, as manifested by the development of many parties and interest organizations, may be said to be the one most important such principle. Furthermore, the existence of such a great variety of political actors was based on wide cultural acceptance of the right to choose one's own group and to compete for political power through this organization. Despite diversity and competition, several of the countries in Western Europe developed a broadly based agreement on the fundamentals of the system, which made it possible to stress unity in diversity. The communist penchant for *organic government*, in which the individual citizen stands in direct relationship with the political elites through the mechanisms of *political mobilization*, is in strong contrast to this pluralist principle. Thus, whereas the ruling party in Great Britain accepts as a matter of course, indeed of necessity, the existence of "Her Majesty's Loyal Opposition," communists look with great skepticism upon such manifestations and are wont to mutter threateningly about "factionalism" and "antiparty behavior." These manifestations are more than mere semantics—they indicate the fundamental difference between pluralism and political mobilization, between individualism and collectivism. In a pluralistic political culture the relationship between the communists and other participants was bound to be strained and difficult.

The communist penchant for monopolizing "the truth" in the form of an exclusivist ideology. Countless analysts have stressed the extent to which Marxist ideology has stood in the way of any meaningful cooperation and collaboration between communists and others in a pluralistic political setting. It has also been argued that we should not overemphasize the exclusivist aspects of the ideology; Marxism, it has been said, never precluded communist maneuverability. Both of these points are, paradoxically, correct. Communist parties in Western Europe have often shown extreme maneuverability, and have been wont to change alliances practically overnight, but this facility did not enhance their credibility; on the contrary, most other participants in the political system considered such communist policies as mere maneuvers which would be discarded as soon as the tactical advantages had been reaped. It is this legacy of skepticism and mistrust that is now haunting the so-called Eurocommunist parties in Western Europe as they attempt to convince a doubting electorate about their *real* commitment to political pluralism.

The extreme *tactical* flexibility of the communists, coupled with their *strategic* commitment to the eventual capture of political power and the exclusion of all other political elements, also forced numerous splits in the ranks of the old Marxist parties of Western Europe. There had been significant policy differences between factions of the old socialist organizations of the region even in Marx's time, and the progenitor of international revolution was himself a dedicated ideological infighter, but by and large these organizations remained intact until the beginning of the twentieth century, when the frictions between revolutionary and reformist tendencies boiled over into open splits. This trend was accelerated by the advent of World War I. The Zimmerwald conference marks the turning point in this development. After that crucial event, the idea of a unified international movement, based on Karl Marx's thought, was no longer valid. From that time on, various groups and political parties, all claiming adherence to the master's thought, struggled for power and influence in the political left in Western Europe. The policy line of the communist parties in the region illustrated this tactical jockeying for advantage as well as the persistent quest of these parties for local power while at the same time maintaining strong (and subservient) ties with Moscow.

The Changing Policy Line of International Communism

Throughout the decades of international communism in Europe, the problems of relations with other political manifestations in the local environment and with Moscow have produced periods of different policy lines for the communist parties of the region. During such periods the fundamental tenets of the ideology were modified, but not basically changed; it was always understood that at some point, and given the right circumstances, these basic tenets would once again be operationalized. Since the Russian Revolution, the following time periods can be distinguished.

The Movement in Hiatus: 1917–1919

In the months immediately following the Russian Revolution pressing domestic concerns prevented the leaders of the Bolshevik party from actively seeking a firm role in the international communist movement. This was therefore a period in which each communist party in Western Europe was basically left to its own devices; in many countries the leftist factions in existing socialist and social democratic parties began to organize their eventual split from the mother organization and the formation of their own separate parties. Policy lines were therefore often confused and contradictory. Common to all these diffuse leftist groups were revolutionary enthusiasm and the expectation that the world revolution was just around the corner. For this reason relations with the "bourgeois" parties were strained and coalitions were rejected, while relations with the left remained murky and unfocused as the Bolshevik groups (many without a clear-cut notion of the meaning of *Leninist* bolshevism) sought to establish themselves. Economic policy lines were not firm, especially in regard to agriculture, but many of the leftist optimists of the day dismissed these problems in favor of the grand goal of power and societal transformation. As for religion, it was clear that any real leftist must reject such foolish nonsense, which had been used for the purpose of keeping the working people in subjugation for centuries. Permeating all of this was a diffuse optimism, both about the inevitable result of current political upheavals and the solution to the many practical problems confronting the would-be builders of a new society and a new world.[2]

*The Formation of the Comintern and
the Crest of the Revolutionary Wave: 1919–1921*

Early in 1919 the Communist International (Comintern) was formed. Power had been consolidated in Bolshevik hands in the core of Russia, and it was time to turn attention to international communism and the achievement of the world revolution by means of strict organization and coordination of political activities in Europe and elsewhere. The Executive Committee of the Communist International (ECCI) was conceived as "the general staff of world revolution," and its headquarters in Hotel Lux in Moscow (the city where the entire Bolshevik government moved in late 1918) began to coordinate the activities of all communist parties abroad. Gone was the acceptance and diffuse revolutionary optimism and local initiative; now the ECCI, in typical Leninist fashion, set about the task of establishing the one correct line in all fields of communist policy. This was to have profound effects upon the latitude accorded local communist parties in the field of coalitions and coalition strategies.

Since 1919 represented the height of revolutionary optimism, the ECCI declared that relations with other political actors in the local environment was a secondary question, and that the primary concern of all communists must be the revolutionary offensive, which would manifest itself in strikes, mass demonstrations, organizational expansion, and even clandestine operations, if such were needed to topple the seemingly feeble "bourgeois" governments of Western Europe. Social democrats and socialists must be dealt with ruthlessly for what they were—errand boys of capitalism and the bourgeoisie. The strategy of *united fronts from below* must be utilized; in this strategy, the communist parties must mercilessly "unmask" the activities of class treason in which the social democrats were engaged, while the masses of these organizations must be won over for the communist cause. This, then, became the first wave of splitting efforts in the mass organizations of the working class, notably the trade unions and the cooperative movement, as well as in the leftist parties themselves.

In 1920, at the second congress of the Comintern, the centralization of the organization was formally established in the famous (or infamous) twenty-one points, which spelled out the preconditions for membership in the world organizaton. These points basically represented the Russian revolutionary experience and contained many elements which were alien to the political environments of much of Western Europe, and this fact spurred a vigorous period of controversy within the Comintern, in which several parties refused to succumb to some of the twenty-one points. This conflict, which culminated in the "bolshevization" of West European communist parties in 1923–1924 (see below) represented the "shaking down" of the organization after a period of organizational uncertainty.[3]

With the promulgation of the twenty-one points and the emergence of the Russian party as the predominant force in the Comintern, a powerful incentive for endless conflict had emerged inside the international organization, indeed in the working class movement as a whole. The twenty-one points established rigid organizational rules which offended those groups that adhered to Marxism (or elements thereof) but refused to establish strict internal discipline and a hierarchial organization. Chief among these groups were the anarchists and anarcho-syndicalists, who constituted small factions in some leftist parties, especially in Northern and Central Europe, but carried much greater influence south of the Alps.[4] The social democrats and moderate socialists, while theoretical adherents of Marxism, criticized the autocratic elements of the twenty-one points and especially rejected the rules of clandestine organization and the ban on religion, which, they claimed, reflected the Russian experience, not the West European tradition.[5] The seeds of future splits between allegedly Marxist parties and groups were sown.

The Period of United Fronts and the Final Bolshevization of West European Communist Parties: 1921–1928

The second congress had established the internal prerequisites for the world organization; the third redefined the relationship between communists and others in the local political environment, and therefore effected a major change in communist coalition strategies. Basically the third congress took note of the fact that the revolutionary wave, which had produced significant unrest in Europe but failed to establish another Soviet regime, had crested, and that the bourgeoisie had begun a counteroffensive to consolidate its power. Under these circumstances communist parties must be prepared to take such measures as would be necessary for survival in a defensive period. In relations with the social democrats and socialists, united fronts from above were encouraged; basically a front would involve cooperation between the party leaderships involved, and would thus represent a form of coalition. At the same time, united fronts from below remained a favorite tactic of the ECCI; in effect this meant that local communists were expected to continue their efforts to undermine the mass base of the very parties with whom they negotiated and cooperated at the leadership level. Small wonder that subsequent communist coalition efforts were spurned or seen with a great deal of skepticism among social democrats and socialists.

The new coalition strategy involved limited cooperation also with the "progressive bourgeoisie," which in practice meant that, under certain circumstances, nonsocialist parties in the center or center-left of the ideological spectrum could be approached for limited cooperation and limited coalitions. This was the first time that the ECCI had crossed the line between socialism and capitalism in its coalition strategy, and the moves produced some heated debates in the Comintern and its associated forums. Thus the Norwegian Labor party (DNA) protested strenuously through its leader, Martin Tranmael, who accused the Comintern of "right-wing deviationism." This was a particularly severe criticism for the ECCI, because the DNA was one of the few West European parties in which the majority had decided *for* the Comintern, while a smaller, right-wing group broke out and formed the Norwegian Social Democratic party in 1921. The ECCI had consistently nurtured high hopes for the DNA, at times even hinting that the revolution was next on the agenda in Norway. Now the undisputed leader of that party had defied a number of credos in the Comintern by criticizing the leadership of that organization on a crucial question of coalition strategies. It was time for the "bolshevization" of the DNA (see below).[6]

In 1926 another form of coalition strategy was sponsored by the ECCI. This was the so-called Labor Party approach, in which all left-wing parties would join forces in an umbrella organization, which would have a joint leadership, while each participating member would retain its own organizational machinery and considerable political autonomy. This was a rather obvious strategy for parties unable to generate much support on their own; it allowed for united fronts from above and below at the same time and enhanced the power of the small communist parties by establishing their political equality with the much larger social democratic parties. (Almost all the communist parties were small in Western Europe at this point, due to the successful process of "bolshevization.") This line was so transparent that it had little practical success, but virtually all West European communist parties tried it. There were no Tranmaels in these parties and thus no accusations of Comintern deviations this time. The intervening event preventing such heresy was the "bolshevization" of the communist parties, which occurred in 1923–1924.[7]

Bolshevization was a seemingly necessary result of the twenty-one conditions and their implementation. The synchronization of political tactics, strategies, even basic outlooks which was envisioned in the conditions could not be implemented without "administrative measures," since elements in many West European communist parties resisted some or all of the conditions. Throughout the period 1921–1924, and culminating in the latter year, the Soviet elements within the ECCI leadership consolidated their position and then set about the task of reducing recalcitrant communist parties to submission. This goal was reached by means of a series of purges and splits in most West European communist parties, in which "autonomist" elements were politically eliminated, while safe "yes-men" were installed in the respective leadership organs. By the middle of the decade the Comintern had become a "lean" organization, in which extreme centralization and discipline prevailed. This centralization was purchased at the expense of domestic influence, however, as large numbers of communist party members voted for "bolshevization" with their feet, away from their erstwhile comrades. Many of the prominent leaders from the period 1918–1923 also chose to refuse this form of synchronization and rejoined the social democrats and the socialists. The result of this process was inevitable: the Comintern proclaimed external flexibility in coalition strategies while practicing extreme control in its own organization. This discrepancy was not lost on observers in Western Europe. The coalition efforts of 1921–1928 were, by and large, dismal failures.[8]

In many ways the period 1920–1928 was crucial in determining the fate of the international working class movement in Western Europe. During this period the Soviet party became predominant in the Comintern, and the last vestiges of real internationalism were rubbed out in the CPSU, so that the ECCI became just another instrument of Soviet state foreign policy. This transformation of the Comintern required the final subjugation of all of the organization's member parties to the central leadership, now firmly in the hands of the Soviets. And since the Soviet state must of necessity deal with other states, all of them controlled by "bourgeois" elites, there was an increased need for local communist parties to show greater flexibility in their respective environments, for the purpose of securing short-term Soviet state interests. This increased flexibility on the part of the communist parties in Western Europe at times produced policies which were directly detrimental to other Marxist organizations while at the same time benefiting non-Marxist groups and parties in various countries.

This extreme tactical flexibility enraged those elements of the left who had cooperated with the communists when the latter were still advocating revolution. The DNA's criticism of the Comintern in 1920–1921 was just a forerunner of the leftist barrage which emerged during the 1921–1928 period. For many it was clear that the concept of international revolution had been betrayed and that the great vision of a just society, with workers' power achieved through the dictatorship of the proletariat, had been abandoned. Criticism was also voiced about the extreme hierarchical nature of the Comintern, which effectively removed any kind of autonomy and revolutionary élan for local parties. These critical voices harked back to the statements of the rebels at Kronstadt as well as the leading spokesmen of the Workers' Opposition in the Soviet party. The bureaucratization of the CPSU itself was criticized by many even in the Soviet Union. Leon Trotsky's prophetic words on this score would later become a rallying point for the Fourth International.[9]

The practical results of all this were reflected in numerous splits in existing Marxist parties, with attendant conflicts, and lack of cooperation on the political left in Western Europe. The maverick DNA was expelled from the Comintern in November 1923 and promptly declared that it would carry on the revolutionary process in Norway despite the rightist deviation of the ECCI and its loyal Norwegian affiliate, the NKP (Norwegian Communist party—Norges Kommunistiske Parti).[10] In Germany the Communist Workers' party (KAPD—Kommunistische Arbeiter-Partei Deutschlands) likewise criticized the Comintern and the loyal German section. Anarcho-syndicalist tendencies further consolidated themselves in Latin Europe, and a number of smaller communist parties elsewhere experienced similar splits.[11]

These conflicts over ideology, programs, and outlooks had a profound effect on the coalition strategies and tactics of the Marxist parties in Western Europe. While the communist parties exhibited considerable flexibility in relations with the non-Marxist left and even the "bourgeois" parties, the rest of the Marxists decried such policies as betrayal of the revolution and cynical tactical maneuvers dedicated to the interests of the Kremlin, but not to the ideal of the international revolution. Thus was born the idea of a revolutionary left *in spite of* the Soviet Union and the CPSU. This was to become a very important element later, during the "New Left" period and the Sino-Soviet split during the 1960s and 1970s.

The Struggle against the "Social Fascists" and the "Clear Line" against Coalitions: 1927–1934

Just as the Comintern line had changed rather abruptly in 1921, it changed again in the period late 1927 to early or mid-1928, and the policy differences were every bit as profound as they had been six years earlier. This major policy change was related to the existing political conditions in the Soviet Union and represented a return to ideolological orthodoxy in many ways in the Comintern.

Basically, then, the new line, which was determined at a meeting of the ECCI in the fall of 1927, represented a denial of much of the policy sponsored by the same organization since 1921. The social democrats, who had been wooed as coalition partners and esteemed colleagues in the Labor party scheme, were now castigated as "social fascists" who only differed from the real fascists in terms of the color of their shirts. All thought of cooperation with these elements was now dropped, and instead local communists were enjoined to engage in "merciless struggle" against these traitors to the working class, be it in the unions, in the cooperatives, in elections, or even in the streets, if need be. Such an approach was considered indispensable, since the "social fascists" merely represented the left wing of the bourgeoisie, and the communists were now engaged in a merciless struggle against these forces as well. The communists now encapsulated themselves in a frenzy of internal purges, ideological orthodoxy, and unmitigated hostility against any other political manifestation. Since most communist parties were small and insignificant in their own systems, this turnabout in policy was of no political consequence, and only served to strengthen the outlook among noncommunists that the disciples of Moscow were totally alien elements without any relevance to the local situation. Thus a major opportunity was lost for the communists as the depression swelled the ranks of the unemployed and created a mass of discontented elements. Because of the utter irrelevance of communism, these hordes mostly joined the ranks of the social democrats, who alone on the left seemed to have meaningful and practical programs designed to combat the economic crisis.[12]

So profound was the aversion to political cooperation now enforced by the Comintern that the West European communists refused to recognize the emerging danger of fascism. Thus a concerted and cooperative policy on this issue by the left was not forthcoming, and a major chance to stop the new totalitarian movement was lost. For this reason communists were to suffer greatly, but paradoxically out of this mistake arose the greatest opportunity for coalition building and enhanced political influence up to the present time, namely, World War II. It is doubtful, however, that many communists in the early 1930s took such a long view of history; they were steeped in the momentary fulfillment of the policy line, which required political exclusion, not cooperation and coalition building.

The policies of the West European communist parties during this period by and large decried the whole idea of coalitions with anybody, for tactical or stategic reasons. This kind of approach helped produce the final alienation of the social democrats and moderate socialists, who gradually abandoned much of their Marxist heritage (in deed if not in words) and thus removed themselves from the ranks of the Marxist parties. The Trotskyists, anarchists, and anarcho-syndicalists remained small, sectarian in outlook, and incapable of acting meaningfully in their local environments, except for countries such as Spain, where the anarchists remained relatively strong. The gradual alienation of the real revolutionaries from the Moscow-controlled international movement was now finalized; subsequent cooperation between the various elements of the left was based upon shared pragmatic interests, not a common ideological foundation.[13]

The Period of Popular Fronts: 1934–1939

The emergence of fascism in Germany and the consolidation of the Hitler regime, despite Stalin's predictions of the former's demise, resulted in a fundamental reevaluation of Soviet policies in Europe and elsewhere. Since the West European communist parties had become reliable (if ineffective) instruments of Moscow's foreign policy after bolshevization, this also meant a drastic revision of *their* policies. Beginning in 1934, and culminating in the decisions of the seventh Comintern congress in 1935, Moscow now sponsored a policy of united fronts of *all* antifascist forces, regardless of ideological preferences; this, then, was the era of the popular (or people's) front. The "people's front" was indeed the broadest coalition effort ever undertaken by the communists in Europe. It superseded in scope and effort anything undertaken during the united front period of 1921–1927, since the latter period merely included "progressive" bourgeois parties as possible coalition partners, whereas the people's front accepted anyone who was antifascist.

Communists all over Europe now began an extraordinary activity in formal and informal coalitions. In some countries, notably France, they cooperated with the socialists and became one of the mainstays of the popular front government in that country. Elsewhere communists occasionally withdrew their electoral lists from the competition and threw their support behind the socialists and social democrats, both in national and local elections. Communists rubbed shoulders with other leftists, indeed many rather conservative "bourgeois," on a variety of action committees designed to alleviate the problems of the great depression and widespread unemployment. The obstructionist policies of splitting the trade unions and other mass organizations were discarded for more cooperative activities. The European communists became the staunchest supporters of their local political cultures and of nationalism, and their dedication to collective security was boundless. Great Britain and France, those arch-reactionary powers of the period 1928–1934, were now discovered as valuable, indeed indispensable, defenders of democracy, in which camp the Soviet Union and all West European communists could also be found. The world watched in wonder and some bewilderment as this transformation took place, and the inevitable question was asked: Is this a fundamental political change, or merely tactics necessitated by the immediate situation and the needs of the Soviet Union?[14] The German-Soviet nonaggression pact of August 1939 answered that question as clearly as could be wished, and ushered in a period of serious decline for the West European communists.

While the communists exhibited extreme flexibility in coalition formation during this period, other left-of-center elements also cooperated against the common enemy, the fascists. The Spanish Civil War represented a high water mark of such leftist unity; communists, anarchists, syndicalists, socialists, and social democrats rallied around the Spanish Republic, and many others, without specific party affiliation, volunteered to serve on the battlefield and in the newspaper columns in the cause of progressivism. In retrospect it seems clear that this great outpouring of common wishes and hopes on the left had little to do with real ideological affinity, but rather depended upon the identification of a common enemy. Nevertheless, almost all leftists, party members or not, were willing to forget old differences, at least temporarily, and to engage in coalition formation for the purpose of defeating the fascist forces. While such coalitions were by definition short-term, there were also many who hoped that the shared experiences on the battlefield would make it possible to restore "working class unity" on a more fundamental level after the conflict.[15]

These hopes were clearly illusory. During much of the civil war, Soviet advisors in Spain spent a good deal of their time and energy in the liquidation of the local anarchists and syndicalists, and communist cadres made it clear that whatever coalitions they formed would be controlled by their cells and regional organizations. Thus even the Spanish Civil War was a period of *controlled* coalitions.[16]

The "Collaborationist" Phase: August 1939–June 22, 1941

The signing of the so-called Hitler-Stalin pact came as a bombshell for many West European communists. It is clear that many of those who had been active in the antifascist period had believed in the cause, and the sudden revelation that Stalin and Hitler, behind their backs, and in violation of all concepts of "internationalism," had negotiated a treaty which ran counter to most of the cherished tenets of the people's democracy period caused a most serious conflict of conscience. This conflict raged between those who blindly followed the signals issued in the Kremlin and those who had sought to combine the larger ideals of social justice and equality in Marxism with their own profound loathing of fascism and everything represented by that Austrian corporal, Hitler. Hence began the defections from the party, and the hemorrhage became even more serious after the German occupation of much of Western Europe, as the local communists entered their least honorable role, the collaborationist phase.

During the period from August 1939 through April and May of 1940, West European communists were required to undertake yet another tortuous revolution in policy. All of a sudden the defenders of democracy, Great Britain and France, were warmongers on a par with Germany, or oftentimes worse. Since almost all organized political groups in Western Europe were anti-Nazi and clearly expressed their opinions on this point, these erstwhile allies in the popular front were now castigated as the most nefarious of warmongers. The trade union hierarchy in Western Europe, which was almost exclusively in the hands of the social democrats, reacted strongly against this kind of policy by excluding communists from those positions which they had obtained in the popular front period. The reaction of the nationalistic and moderate bourgeoisie was even more ferocious, thus further isolating the followers of Moscow in each local environment.[17]

Three major events completed the transition of the West European communists from the status of a somewhat curious but nevertheless welcome fighter for democracy to a pariah of the political system. There was, first of all, the German attack on Poland, which came shortly after the conclusion of the Hitler-Stalin pact and thus established a sense of cause and effect among many in Western Europe. Secondly, the Soviet attack on Finland in November 1939 enraged public opinion even further, while the leaderships of West European communist parties demonstrated their slavish dedication to Moscow by parroting TASS on the "progressive" and "peace-loving" nature of the action. Thirdly, the attacks on, and subsequent subjugation of, Denmark, Norway, Belgium, the Netherlands, Luxemburg, and France ushered in a period in which the communists in occupied countries actually collaborated with the German military administration in an effort to take over the leadership of the working class organizations, whose leaders had been forced to go underground, or had been arrested. The spectre of the local communists cooperating with the hated Germans became indelibly established in the minds of many, both left and right, and prevented a stable mass following of the communists when they did become nationally minded. This image could not be erased by the fact that throughout the second half of 1940 the communists were also outlawed, their organizations disbanded, their members arrested. In the public mind, communists had collaborated, and that was all that mattered.[18]

The nonaggression pact between Nazi Germany and the Soviet Union was seen as the great betrayal by many Marxists who were not members of a communist party, and indeed it was so perceived by many of the card-carrying communists as well. Thousands upon thousands of communists left their respective parties; some of them joined groups in the extreme left wing, many more entered the socialist and social democratic parties, and a few turned to the other extreme of the ideological spectrum and became fascists. For all of these Marxists, communist or not, the pact demonstrated once again that the coalition tactics of the communist parties merely aimed at satisfying the interests of Moscow, while their strategies looked for the eventual establishment of Soviet power in Europe, in which all Marxist groups and parties would be subjected to communist control, up to and including liquidation. No cooperation would be possible with such traitors. Thus the extreme coalition skills of the CPSU on the right, attempted by the West European communist parties, precluded coalitions on the left in this period.[19]

Then came June 22, 1941, and the great transformation of the West European communists.

The Second World War and People's Coalitions

As was discussed in the Introduction, communist coalition strategies, by and large, were unsuccessful in the interwar period insofar as they did not produce increased power and influence for the communists in the local environment; on the contrary, it can be argued that the extreme facility with which the communists switched coalitions almost overnight had a profoundly negative effect upon their chances in the local electorate and in public opinion. The problem was essentially that the communists changed their allies and their tactics, but not their basic policy commitments and their fundamental strategies. Thus there was no attempt by the communist parties to accept the existing system of political pluralism and relatively open competition; the communists only coexisted with pluralism as long as necessary, without recognition of its basic value. Similarly, the concepts of "societal revolution" and "dictatorship of the proletariat" were never abandoned in this period—their *application* was merely denied by circumstances. While it was possible for many communist parties to make temporary alliances with capitalists and agrarians, the dedication of the former parties to eventual destruction of the capitalist economy and the collectivization of agriculture remained firm as doctrine throughout the entire period. Communist coalition behavior was therefore always tactical, or at least perceived by others as merely tactical, while the doctrine remained firm—a most undesirable phenomenon for the potential coalition partners of the communists. Furthermore, after the mid-1920s West European communists were widely perceived as mere lackeys of Moscow, and therefore not trustworthy. These phenomena, taken together, largely explain the severe problems encountered by West European communists during the interwar period.

This tactical flexibility on the part of the communists was particularly galling to the other Marxist parties of the region. The latter organizations were either dedicated to revolution as a principle (the Trotskyists, for example), or at least they had a program which established both the methods of achieving power and the end result of this power, and they attempted to maintain some cohesion between the two; this was essentially the case of the social democrats. The extreme tactical flexibility of the communists was disturbing to such parties and served to reinforce the notion that one simply could not trust the "lackeys of Moscow." And in the social democratic and socialist parties there were strong elements who still felt that cooperation with the "bourgeoisie" must remain very limited lest one forget the requirements of class solidarity and class cohesion. To all of these individuals and groups there was something suspect about the coalition tactics of the communists.

The Great Fatherland War and
the Emergence of Communist Patriotism

The German attack on the Soviet Union on June 22, 1941, changed the political situation and the fortunes of the West European communists drastically. For the first time since the establishment of the Soviet Union, the interests of Moscow and the interests of most West European states coincided in the common struggle against the establishment of a fascist order in Europe. From the very beginning of their desperate struggle, the Soviet leaders realized, in turn, that their survival now was inextricably tied to that of the West European democracies. Hence loyal communists could best serve the needs of internationalism by becoming patriots in their own countries; such a position would help divert part of the German might from the Eastern front and would mobilize valuable allies for Moscow. Furthermore, here was a situation where the "objective" interests of the world movement (read: the interests of world communism as defined by the CPSU leadership) could be married to the elemental force of nationalism and resistance to the German occupier. From the very beginning of the "Great Fatherland War" Moscow encouraged forceful actions on the part of local communists in defense of national independence and sovereignty. Such actions could be most effective in the context of a broader coalition effort of all anti-Nazi forces in the respective West European countries.[20]

The story of communist underground activity is well known and need not be repeated here. Suffice it to say that the communists everywhere threw themselves into the struggle against the Germans, and there is little doubt that their activities often represented the most important military resistance found in occupied Europe. At times this resistance was undertaken in cooperation with the underground organizations of other parties and groups, thus realizing again (as in the popular front period) the "grand coalition" of all anti-Nazi forces, regardless of ideological preference and socioeconomic background. In other cases the noncommunist underground stood aloof from the overtures and approaches of "Moscow's boys," with the result that some of the most spectacular feats of sabotage were carried out by the communists alone. Whatever the specific scenario, the communists benefited from these developments. If they were admitted to the broader anti-Nazi groups, their enthusiasm for daring actions and forceful defense of national interests impressed many of the others, whose leaders were often committed to limited actions, passive resistance, and damage limitation. If the communist cadres undertook actions of their own, the word rapidly spread among the general population who these daring patriots were. After all, communists were dying for the national cause. What more of a demonstration of patriotism could one require? Add to this the fact that the Comintern emphasis on clandestine organizations, so out of place in many countries when it was introduced in 1920, now paid off in better organization and better security, with resulting effectiveness. The local communists were building successful coalitions from above whenever they were admitted to the broader resistance, and they consistently built coalitions from below by means of their mind-captivating sabotage activities.[21]

While the spectacular resistance activities of the local communists and the heroic struggle of the Soviet Union against the common enemy produced a great deal of goodwill in the populations of Western Europe, a certain transformation also took place inside the communist parties themselves. In their efforts to broaden their base and expand their activities, the communist parties of Western Europe began to admit many individuals whose enthusiasm for military resistance vastly exceeded their Marxist credentials. Inside leadership circles in many countries the opinion began to take hold that the war represented a fundamental dividing line even for communists, so that the postwar era would be a period of national reconstruction and goodwill which would make it possible for *all* progressive forces in West European society to cooperate for the common, national good. This tendency was immeasurably strengthened by the announcement from Moscow in 1943 that the Comintern had been abolished, thus enabling all communists and associated forces to further the national cause without undue memories of the erstwhile bitter enemy of nationalism, the "general staff of world revolution." This decision in Moscow made it possible even for dyed-in-the-wool apparatchiki to broaden their horizons in the national setting.[22]

The nationalistic tactics of the West European communist parties after June 22, 1941, were effective because, to a considerable extent, they were genuine. The communist leaders may have been able to divorce themselves from national feeling and attitudes to some extent, but their followers were not, and they relished the notion that they could fight the common enemy shoulder to shoulder with other patriots. The socialists and social democrats, in turn, appreciated this genuine approach by the communist rank and file, even if their leaders remained rather skeptical. The notion of the unity of the working class was still very much alive in the generation of the 1940s working class, whose fathers had been involved in the heady experience of revolution and great internationalist expectations after the first world war; it now appeared that this unity could be reestablished after two decades of painful separation. In retrospect it is clear that the Marxist-Leninist vision of society, polity, and the revolutionary struggle was simply too different from the version accepted by most other West European Marxists to allow for real class unity. But that was not so clear during the dangerous, but exhilarating, days of the Resistance.

Victory, Reconstruction, and the Grand Coalition

After the German capitulation in Europe, conditions were favorable for a new relationship between the local communists and the other political actors in their environment. That primary reference point for all communists, the CPSU, had officially dismantled the Comintern and encouraged broad coalitions of all anti-Nazi forces in Western Europe. The same policy was seemingly pursued in Eastern Europe as well, where the Red Army was in force. In the local environment of Western Europe, a great deal of goodwill had developed for both the Soviet Union and the domestic communist parties, due to the heroic struggle of the former on the battlefronts and the daring underground activity of the latter, in which many had lost their lives in the struggle for national freedom. This sympathy extended from the conservatives through the ranks of the social democrats but was, naturally enough, strongest in the latter groups. Inside the communist parties themselves, important elements had come to the fore during the war when primary commitment was to national reconstruction; these elements were clearly dedicated to a broad progressive front, which could affect the national reconciliation that had already largely taken place among those who had been active in the underground. Even the more orthodox elements in most communist parties had accepted basic aspects of the broad front approach, primarily because of Moscow's sponsorship of this cause. On the whole, then, the circumstances seemed very appropriate for a new approach to coalitions, the more so since new elections were soon to be held—the first since the German occupation.

In several West European countries the scenario now unfolding was essentially the same. First, the communists emerged as one of the strongest and most cohesive elements of the national front, parading proudly in the streets with national armbands and showing their dedication to the cause of the grand coalition, consisting of all anti-Nazi and anti-collaborationist forces, regardless of ideology and social origin. Secondly, the local communist parties, in congresses, manifestos, and slogans in the press dedicated their efforts to national reconciliation and especially the political unification congress or some other vehicle which could produce a united party—a goal, it was said, which was tragically postponed for two decades because of a series of "misunderstandings." Third, there were proposals for joint electoral lists between communists, socialists, and social democrats in the forthcoming national elections. Fourth, the communists asked for an end to the prewar schism in the mass organizations of the labor movement, especially in the trade unions.[23]

This policy had immediate payoffs in a number of countries even before elections were held. In Denmark and Norway communists were included in the interim governments which were established upon the return of the royal family and the wartime government in exile to London. In Sweden the communists had cooperated with the unity government which was formed during the war, and this cooperation continued in 1945. Similar arrangements were made in Belgium, the Netherlands, France, and Italy; in the two latter countries, all indications were that the communists had acquired a massive following and would become forces of considerable importance, perhaps even crucial to the postwar political systems of these countries. On the other hand, in Great Britain the Labour party maintained its control over the British left; in Germany the occupation regimes in the three Western zones took their time accrediting political parties, and in Spain and Portugal extreme right-wing dictatorships survived the end of the war, thus preventing any communist resurgence. Thus the fortunes of the West European communists were mixed, but on the whole they had greatly improved, thanks to fortunate circumstances and changes in their policies. In a few countries, the communists appeared to be on the verge of coming to power as members of a grand coalition.[24]

The first postwar elections, which were held in many countries in the fall of 1945, tended to confirm the soundness of the new coalition tactics employed by the communists since 1941. In country after country, the communist party scored impressive gains which lifted them up to a much more impressive electoral position than had ever been the case. In Denmark and Norway, for example, the communist share of total votes was 12.4 percent and 11.9 percent, respectively. In Belgium, the Netherlands, and France, the first elections yielded 12.7 percent, 10.6 percent, and 26.1 percent respectively. In Italy the communists obtained 18.9 percent and in Sweden 6.3 percent (1948). Clearly the general electorate had accepted the communist claim that they were now an integral part of the local political environment.[25]

Successful as the elections had been for the communists, they nevertheless sent some disconcerting signals. First of all, the prewar party system had basically been restored. The conservatives suffered some losses in a few countries, but clearly intended to remain as a political force to be reckoned with. The agrarians had likewise survived the war, basically intact. And, most important of all, the social democrats quickly reasserted their sway over the left-of-center electorate in a number of countries, while also reestablishing their control over the mass organizations of the labor movement, especially the trade unions. For the local communists, then, there developed the need for coalition tactics which would essentially deal with the familiar scenario of multiparty systems whose players derived their support from traditional sources of socioeconomic class, and, in a few countries, regional configurations.

Most West European communist parties now developed tactics which lasted until late 1946, in some cases until 1947. The most important elements of these strategies were the following.

United fronts from above combined with united fronts from below. Beginning in the spring of 1945 and continuing past the elections which were held in the fall or early the following year, the West European communist parties attempted to forge an organizational link with the socialists and social democrats, which would in essence leave the communist organization intact, while achieving access to important decision-making structures. Coupled with this approach was an attempt to gain more influence in the trade unions and other mass organizations by means of communist membership in the top bodies of these structures, under the auspices of "working class unity." As time wore on, the communist parties began to emphasize the need for unity on a "real class basis," not merely unity for the sake of unity; this, then, was the beginning of a more clear-cut ideological stance, which was to become more prominent in 1946 and into 1947. During this period of a gradual hardening of the line in ideological matters, the communists also began selectively to intimate that "elements" in the socialist and social-democrat parties had been too "passive" during the war—a further hint that "working class unity" had its price, even though it remained high on the agenda.

Devotion to the "grand coalition" of all anti-Nazi forces, regardless of ideology and social origin. As a continuation of the wartime alliance of all anti-Nazi and antifascist forces, the West European communists advocated a form of cooperation which ensured the continued existence of their own organizational structures while providing access to important coordinating committees and boards. It was clear that the communist parties envisioned such cooperation within the framework of existing party structures, and thus the coalitions established would be primarily tactical rather than long-range and structural. In this field, too, there was a development toward more "exclusive" interpretations of the concept of "grand coalition," as many communist spokesmen began to hint darkly at extensive passivism or perhaps even collaboration in the ranks of the bourgeoisie during the war, especially among rightist elements.

Downplaying of the fundamental tenets of communist ideology and a concomitant stress on reform rather than revolution. As a natural concomitant of the conciliatory policy conducted toward the socialists, social democrats, and part of the bourgeoisie, the West European communists downplayed the revolutionary elements of their party programs, but refused to jettison these platforms; the emphasis was now on land reform rather than collectivization and the establishment of state farms; there was talk of limited nationalization of banks and private enterprises, rather than the establishment of full public ownership of the means of production. By the same token, there was acceptance (at least for the time being) of political pluralism and genuine political competition, rather than stress on the need for revolution, the dictatorship of the proletariat, and political synchronization under communist auspices.

These moderate tendencies began to fade somewhat during 1946, as the communist parties of the area began to reevaluate their coalition tactics toward the rest of the political left and the bourgeoisie as well. The need for "principled class policies" was emphasized more frequently; there were occasional discussions of the dictatorship of the proletariat, and the main platforms of the classical economic program of Marxism-Leninism appeared occasionally. More frequent mention was made of the Soviet experience and its relevance for other countries. On the whole, however, West European communists modified their ideological emphasis (without basically changing it) to serve the coalition needs as they were perceived at the time.

Emphasis on national needs and national coalitions and a corresponding deemphasis on internationalist tenets and aspects. One of the most troublesome aspects of communist policies during the interwar period had been the tendency to follow the interests of the Soviet Union and the CPSU rather than the needs of each individual party. In the immediate postwar period, and lasting into late 1946 or early 1947, each party instead stressed the need for national roads of reconstruction and development—an integral part of the coalition tactics of West European communism during this period. Here too, however, the latter part of the period saw a tendency to discuss national peculiarities within the concept of socialism and communism; it was not so much that national conditions took precedence over historically determined development patterns (which would have led to a denial of the inevitability of socialism and communism) but rather the argument emphasized national roads to that goal. For those who had believed in the possibility of fundamental changes in communist policies, these were disquieting notes indeed.[26]

The first two years after the conclusion of World War II are critical for an understanding of communist coalition strategies and tactics. For the first time many of the preconditions for basic change were present. The CPSU and the Soviet Union had given the green light, directly or indirectly, through the abolition of the Comintern. Because of the activities of local communists in the wartime underground, there was widespread acceptance of them and their organizations in the local political environments, and especially among those groups which still considered themselves Marxist. There were nationally minded elements inside the leadership of most of these parties. As a result of these favorable circumstances, both communists' coalition policies and their political ideology seemed to come into harmony as many of the revolutionary and exclusionist doctrines were downplayed, while flexible and relatively reasonable relationships were worked out with the rest of the left and even the bourgeoisie. This strategy was nevertheless modified (and later abandoned, as will be discussed below) for a variety of reasons. First of all, the first postwar elections, successful as they were in terms of lifting most West European communist parties to a level of public support hitherto unknown, had not transformed the political system but had rather reproduced the parties and their traditional support groups along prewar lines. Most troublesome of all was the reestablishment of unquestioned socialist and social democratic control over the organizations of the labor movement. This relative success, which nevertheless left the local communist parties frustrated, resulted in serious internal debates, especially at the leadership level, where the "nationalists" came under increasing fire from the "orthodox," the latter arguing that the coalition strategies being utilized had presented the radicalized masses with no choice between communists and social democrats, thus paving the way for reconstruction of the latter's dominance of the left. Examples of such debates (which took place in virtually all parties) are the quarrels between Peder Furubotn, who led the Norwegian Communist party (NKP) in its wartime resistance activities, and Emil Løvlien, prewar head of the party; in France a similar debate between Jacques Duclos and some of the communist resistance leaders shook that party.[27]

Secondly, the "honeymoon" between the allies began to sour a bit in 1946, and the Soviet Union began to exercise closer control over political life in the East European countries, where the so-called progressive coalition had hitherto been in vogue. This cooling of East-West relations and the hardening of Moscow's line in Eastern Europe had an effect west of the Elbe as well: old-time apparatchiki, well schooled in the phenomenon of anticipatory behavior, began to take cues from Moscow once again and interpreted the need for more "class conscious" utterances and policies. This kind of policy had the effect of undermining public confidence in the depth of change undergone by the communists in Western Europe, and electoral and organizational support began to drop off again. Thus in those countries which had local or national elections in 1946 and 1947, a perceptible reduction of the communist vote could be observed. In Italy and France forceful communist policies in the trade unions and in strike leadership consolidated opposition against them in otherwise fragmented political systems. The "communist wave" had crested and begun to recede in Western Europe, and once this retreat had started, the various factors discussed above fed on each other, hastening the demise of the broad coalition approach and returning the communists of this region to relative isolation and irrelevance, but with ideological orthodoxy vastly strengthened.

The Period of Two Camps and
Orthodox Synchronization

Much has been written about the establishment of the two-camp theory at a meeting of the Communist Information Bureau (Cominform) in the summer of 1947, and details will not be repeated here. Suffice it to say that this event ushered in a period of orthodox synchronization in the entire communist movement, be it Eastern or Western Europe, and the tactics and strategies of the "grand" or "progressive" coalition could no longer be employed. The three preconditions for such a strategy all vanished rapidly in this period. The Soviet Union and the CPSU began to demand a more clear-cut "class policy" in Western Europe as well as in the eastern part of the continent; the hardliners in the local party leaderships were thereby encouraged to move against their "nationalist" colleagues; and the hardening of the ideological line, both externally and internally, alienated much of the hitherto sympathetic public. This was especially dangerous in the labor movement, where the social democrats began a veritable purge of communists wherever they could, and many embarrassing questions were asked concerning the collaborationist phase of communist policy in the period August 1939 to June 22, 1941. Such forceful methods of scathing rhetoric of the communist press, which now regularly castigated leading social democrats as "passivists" and "collaborators" during the war, could accomplish little other than a steady escalation of the political warfare of the left, with the inevitable result of further communist impotence. This time, both domestic and external factors served to remove the rationale for any broad communist coalition strategy or tactics just as effectively as the same conditions had helped expand them during the immediate postwar period. It was time for ideological stocktaking, both internally and externally.

This ideological stocktaking came with the ouster of Tito's Yugoslavia from the Cominform in 1948. The spectre of Titoism was now born, and it meant that almost all of the policies which had been applauded and encouraged during the war and in the immediate postwar period were scrutinized and rejected. Policies designed to attract a mass following were castigated as ideologically dangerous, leading to an unacceptably low level of ideological consciousness in the masses. Attempts to broaden local communist influence by means of the "grand coalition" approach were denounced as unwarranted dealings with the class enemy and their errand boys, the social democrats. Deemphasis on the economic goals of nationalization and collectivization of agriculture was criticized as "obscurantism" which reduced the profile of the party and failed to present a clear choice for the masses. Above all, there were broad hints that those who had perpetrated such policies might be guilty of "domesticism," "nationalism," and perhaps also "Titoism."

In terms of coalition tactics, the new policy line had the effect of dramatically reducing the breadth and scope of such effort emanating from the West European communist parties. Just as the two-camp theory of the world effectively sealed the Soviet bloc off from the rest of Europe, indeed the rest of the world, so did the new policy line isolate the local communist parties from the rest of their political environments. Gone was the attempt to enter into even limited cooperation with any part of the bourgeoisie. The only coalition attempts by West European communist parties in this period were to be found under the rubric of united fronts from below, and this concept described the ceaseless attempt by the communists of the region to wean the masses away from the socialist and social democratic leaderships, who had retained their unshakable hold on the mass organizations of the labor movement in Western and Northwestern Europe. In France and Italy, the communists quickly established themselves as the dominant force in the trade unions, a fact which led to an early three-way split between socialists, communists, and "Christian" forces in the union movement in those countries. From this vantage point of strength in the two large countries, the communist unions could occasionally establish "action unity" in the form of strikes under their leadership. Elsewhere in Europe, the drab cloak of uniformity settled over the communist parties and reduced their coalition efforts (as well as their tactics) to a minimum.[28] This situation remained, with few deviations, until the end of the Stalin era in early 1953.

The Exceptions to the Rule:
Finland and Iceland

Even though the developments described above had general validity throughout most of Western Europe, there were two noteworthy exceptions. In Finland, the serious splits and weaknesses among the socialists and social democrats created move favorable conditions for the communist party, and this resulted in considerable influence for the Finnish communists even at a time of general decline for much of the rest of West European communism. The special foreign policy situation of Finland and the close Soviet scrutiny over Finnish politics in this period also contributed to gains for the SKP (Suomen Kommunistinen Puolue). The SKP participated (as a dominant member) in a coalition of leftist organizations in the SKDL (Suomen Kansan Demokraattinen Liitto), which gained membership in the first postwar government in Finland. The SKP succeeded in maintaining its support base in the industrial proletariat and also parts of the rural smallholders and lumberjacks of central and northern Finland, despite the continued emphasis on Marxist-Leninist orthodoxy exhibited by the party. Considerable evidence exists that the Finnish party was viewed by large segments of the population as primarily a protest party; the ideological fine points were of lesser concern. The SKP has retained some of its position throughout the period up to the present time, despite occasional setbacks.[29]

Iceland represented yet another exception to the rule of general communist isolation and relapse into stale ideological orthodoxy in the period 1947–1953. The communist party was itself a coalition of leftist forces, which had been founded in 1930. In 1938 this loose confederation was consolidated in the Althydubandalagid, or AB, in which the communist faction was the most important. Throughout the entire period since 1938, however, the AB had lacked the internal cohesion of its European counterparts, and it also lacked the ideological commitment which had characterized the communists on the Continent. As a faraway place, Iceland attracted little attention from Moscow during the years of the Comintern, and the result was a considerable ideological diffuseness in the AB, coupled with a strong nationalist bent which made the party palatable to many in a culture imbued with native radicalism and egalitarianism. In addition, the AB became an important factor in the struggle for Icelandic independence from the union with Denmark, and this strong element of nationalism was never abandoned by the party. Thus, when the rest of the West European communists began to abandon the broad coalition strategy in 1946–1947, the AB expanded its efforts in this area and participated in a coalition government under the leadership of the Progressive party in 1944–1947. Even though the AB went back into opposition in the subsequent period until the end of the Stalin era, it continued to garner considerable numbers of votes in each subsequent election. Throughout the entire period the main emphasis of the party's policy was nationalism and an ability to cooperate with all political parties in the local political environment, just as it had during the heyday of the broad coalition in Europe proper. Here, then, was a party which remained basically untouched by the vicissitudes of policy changes in Moscow and the charges of "domesticism," "nationalism," and "Titoism" emanating from virtually every party headquarters in Western Europe. The leaders of the AB were "domesticists," and "nationalists"; they were proud of it, successful at it, and entertained no idea of ceasing such a policy.[30]

The ideological orthodoxy of the West European parties during this period, coupled with the increasing bureaucratization and rigidity of party structures and the witch hunts of "Titoists," "domesticists," and "nationalists" alienated those elements of the West European left that wanted revolution but abhorred bureaucratism. Elements of the "New Left," which were to become such an important factor in West European politics in the 1960s and 1970s, could even now be found among the leftist intellectuals and some of the workers of the region. Their arguments harked back to the workers' opposition of Shliapnikov and Kollontai, and indeed went back to those aspects of Marx which had attributed revolutionary *spontaneity* to the industrial proletariat—a notion which had always been denied and ridiculed by Lenin and his successors. This quest continues today, in various forms, in the West European left.[31]

The Post-Stalinist Era, Polycentrism, and "Eurocommunism"

The death of Stalin was a watershed in the history of communism, as has been pointed out by virtually every serious student of the matter. The movement was never again to reach the kind of unity it had had under the old dictator, but more than that, the right of the Soviet Union and the CPSU to decisively influence events in the West European communist parties was never again to be unquestioningly upheld. From now on, "national roads" became the rule rather than the exception to the rule. Furthermore, after the succession crisis in the Soviet Union in the period 1953–1955, the twentieth CPSU congress and Khruschev's scathing attack on Stalin and Stalinism, and the Polish and Hungarian events of 1956, followed by the unsuccessful attempt by the Soviet leadership "to reestablish the center" (in Zbigniew K. Brzezinski's term), there emerged a direct challenge to Soviet leadership of the camp in the form of China. During the last two decades the Sino-Soviet dispute has been the single most important factor in the international communist movement, with a profound impact upon the political strategies and tactics of the West European communist parties.

The Sino-Soviet split represented a threat to the Soviet claim to be the chief model for international communism, but it did more. It produced a countermodel and thus set the stage for a series of splits which divided the West European communist parties into a pro-Moscow and a pro-Peking faction, often with a "centrist" group in between. During the 1960s the fractious tendencies of the West European communist parties resulted in the development of a plethora of groups and parties to the left of the local communists. In two countries, Denmark and Norway, there were established leftist socialist parties (Socialist People's parties, or SF, in both countries) which drew support from both the social democrats and the communists. The SF youth organizations made serious inroads into the corresponding structures serving the Danish Communist party (DKP) and the NKP in Norway. Elsewhere, similar situations developed. This bewildering set of developments presented the communist parties in Western Europe with entirely new problems. Increasingly they responded to these developments with policies based on local needs and perceptions rather than on signals emanating from Moscow.[32]

During the post-Stalinist era, therefore, any attempt at generalization for all West European communist parties and their coalition strategies and tactics is an exercise in futility. Instead, one may outline several tactics which were followed at one point or another by different parties, and for different reasons. The most important of these are the following.

Occasional cooperation with other parties of the left, determined on the basis of ad hoc arrangements and usually of limited duration. This approach was utilized on occasion in parliamentary and local elections primarily by the NKP in Norway, the DKP in Denmark, and the French Communist party (PCF). In Denmark and Norway the fragmentation of the left, represented by the formation of the two left socialist parties and the establishment of several small splinter groups to the left of the communists, represented special problems. The NKP and the DKP generally had only scorn for the extreme left; on one occasion the main press organ of the DKP characterized them as "sandbox radicals."[33] The two SF parties, on the other hand, represented a much more formidable competition, and more meaningful relations had to be developed with these parties. On several occasions both the NKP and the DKP lamented the unnecessary fragmentation of the left which had been brought about by the establishment of the SF and their youth organizations, but in several elections the communists and left socialists entered the race on a joint list, or informally supported each other. There was also a tendency for "action unity" among these parties in a number of policy issues, especially related to foreign policy neutrality, their position on the U.S. involvement in Vietnam, domestic budgetary and fiscal matters, and in economic policy questions generally. The debate over Danish and Norwegian membership in the Common Market (EEC) provided a golden opportunity for the two Nordic communist parties to become members of a larger coalition of parties and groups opposing such membership.[34] This anti-EEC coalition lost in Denmark, but was successful in Norway, thus giving the NKP a chance to expand its influence way beyond its actual numbers. During the EEC debate the NKP took an extreme nationalist stance and managed to reach elements of the population which had been lost to the party since 1945–1946. The anti-EEC bloc, in which the NKP was one of the most active members, counted in its ranks the SF, elements of the Labor party (DNA), the Agrarians (SP), and large numbers of trade unionists (even though the trade union leadership at the national level supported Norwegian membership, as did the DNA leadership); furthermore, fishermen, smallholders, and a significant part of the Liberals were included. This was indeed the most successful broad coalition in which the NKP had been engaged, and there were party leaders who confidently predicted a new beginning for the party, which had been reduced to less than 1 percent of the electorate in the 1960s. This led to further efforts designed to actually merge the NKP with other parties (see below).[35]

The DKP also succeeded in breaking out of its isolation by means of a broad anti-EEC coalition. In Denmark, however, the agrarian interests associated themselves firmly with the EEC, while in Norway the same elements opposed it; Danish labor, more closely associated with West German markets, generally supported membership, as did the fishing industry, and most of the city intellectuals displayed a marked leaning toward the Continent, whereas many of their colleagues in Norway were nationalistic and semi-isolationistic; all of these elements helped uphold Danish membership, and the DKP could therefore claim less of a success than could the NKP in Norway. In both countries, however, communist influence was limited by the fact that the SF and their youth organizations (SUF in both countries) took the lead in the movement on the left, and in Norway, the agrarians were extremely active in the EEC question. Thus even this spectacular example of a broad issue-oriented coalition was only a limited success.[36]

In France electoral cooperation between the PCF and the Socialists (under Mitterrand) became a standard feature of the coalition strategies utilized by the French communists during the 1960s and 1970s, especially during the latter decade. On at least two occasions the leftist bloc came close in its quest for parliamentary majorities, but ultimately failed because of the mutual distrust between the two coalition partners and the eventual retreat from *actually* putting communists into the government by significant elements of the French working class and petite bourgeoisie. After each defeat the coalition partners quarreled extensively, accusing each other of virtual treason, thereby rekindling the old flames of rivalry and distrust. In the PCF, the defeat of the coalition in elections in the 1970s resulted in a considerable internal debate as well, in which the entire question of relations with the rest of society came up for reappraisal. It seemed clear that the PCF was headed for a significant move to the left, once again adopting a "principled" stand of opposition against "bourgeois society." This development represented a departure from the French version of "Eurocommunism." (For a discussion of this latter point, see below).[37]

Informal support of the ruling noncommunist party (or parties) determined by issue-by-issue evaluations. During the 1960s and 1970s the Left Party of Communists of Sweden (VPK), the NKP in Norway, and the Italian Communist party (PCI) have been the most prominent proponents of a policy which shies away from actual coalition arrangements with the ruling party or party coalitions, but nevertheless provides crucial support for such ruling parties on an ad hoc basis. This possibility increased communist influence beyond any independent strength which could be mustered by the three parties, especially the NKP and the VKP. In all three cases such a policy was made possible by the decline of the dominant party, the Social Democrats in Norway and Sweden, and the Christian Democrats in Italy.

The VKP played the role of crucial informal support party for the Swedish Social Democratic party (SD) throughout the 1960s and into the 1970s, as the thirty years of SD dominance in Swedish politics began to ebb. During part of this period the SD was clearly dependent upon communist support, since the nonsocialist bloc had achieved parity with the left of center. Because of this crucial position the VPK became an influence on the SD, steadily pulling it to the left in economic, social, and foreign policy. This kind of dependence in turn helped polarize Swedish politics, eventually setting the stage for the social democratic defeat in the parliamentary elections in 1976. The VPK has repeatedly voiced its position as primary support group for the SD, provided the Social Democrats' leader Olof Palme continue his "principled socialist policies." It is clear that such a position of continuous support for the strongest competitor of Swedish communism generated considerable controversy during the 1970s, resulting in a split in the VPK in which the pro-Moscow, hard-line faction around Hilding Hagberg in the northern province of Norbotten formed their own party, the SKP (Swedish Communist party). The SKP severely castigated the VPK and its leaders, Carl-Henrik Hermansson and Lars Werner, for their tendency to support the "bourgeoisie" instead of the Soviet Union, thus opting for a policy of opportunism rather than principled class politics.[38]

The Norwegian Labor party (DNA) also suffered several setbacks in its electoral fortunes and lost power in 1963, for the first time since 1935. After a brief interregnum, in which a nonsocialist coalition held power, the DNA came back, but in a considerably weakened position. For a period of time the party had to rely upon the support of the SF and the NKP in parliament and outside of it, with the result that the Norwegian social democrats, too, were pulled considerably to the left in policy terms. This did not have any long-range benefits for the communists, however; during much of the 1960s and 1970s a government of nonsocialist coalition parties held power. And most important of all, the support provided by the NKP did not seem to have any lasting effects on the DNA, which soon recovered from its leftist tendencies in the early 1960s and continued its policy of broadly acceptable welfare state output.[39]

The most extensive support function in recent West European history has been that of the PCI vis-à-vis the Christian Democratic party (DC) in Italy during the 1970s. During much of this decade, and especially in the period 1976–1979, the Italian communists helped maintain a minority government of the DC. Without this support the government would have fallen, as was indeed demonstrated during 1979, when the withdrawal of PCI support resulted in a governmental crisis, the resignation of the DC government, and subsequent elections in which the PCI suffered meaningful setbacks. The long-range goal of the Italian communists was the establishment of "Il Compromisso Istorico," in which the DC and the PCI would rule together. Had this policy been successful, Berlinguer and his colleagues could in fact have claimed a most definite achievement by means of coalition strategies, and it would have produced direct PCI membership in the ruling coalition for the first time since the mid-1940s, with unforeseeable effects in the Italian political system, perhaps the entire Western alliance. The failure to achieve this goal, and the subsequent defeat of the PCI in the elections, have resulted in a serious internal debate, somewhat similar to the controversy which practically dismantled the Spanish party (PCE). Berlinguer, head of the PCI and the chief architect of this coalition strategy, was forced to admit certain mistakes, and the Italian party also appeared to be moving to the left, into "principled opposition" once more.[40]

Actual efforts to establish a broadly based party on the left by means of full organizational unification between communists and others. During the post-Stalinist era, only the NKP in Norway had seriously considered carrying its coalition strategy to the final and logical end, namely the organizational dismantling of the party structure and the formal merging of the NKP with other political forces. This startling development was the result of a process which began in the 1970s with ad hoc electoral arrangements with the SF; toward the end of the decade, the emergence of a broad coalition dedicated to preventing Norwegian membership in the EEC had accelerated the trend toward nationalism and "cooperationism" in the NKP, and the party agreed to join in a Leftist Electoral Alliance (SV) in the parliamentary elections of 1973, after the successful completion of the anti-EEC campaign, which had resulted in a resounding defeat in a national referendum for those who advocated membership. The SV, which consisted of the NKP, SF, and assorted other left-of-center groups, scored a startling success, obtaining over 16 percent of the vote, and thus became a crucial group on the left in the Storting (Parliament). This success further accelerated the trends toward more organized cooperation among the members of the SV in the postelection period. During 1974 and early 1975 the members of the coalition held numerous meetings to effect the merger; at a unification congress in early 1975 both the SF and the NKP leaderships accepted organizational union, subject to ratification by their respective party bodies. The SF in fact did accept the merger agreement and formally dismantled their party structure. In the NKP, however, a furious debate rocked the party to its foundations. The NKP leadership under Reidar Larsen had staked its continued political fortunes on the merger, but "orthodox" groups, headed by Martin Gunnar Knudsen, refused to accept the actual dismantling of the party apparat and the "subjugation" of the NKP to a joint structure, in which former SF elements would constitute by far the most important faction. In the end, Larsen was deposed and left the NKP to join the SV, of which he subsequently became parliamentary leader. Knudsen took over the leadership of a decimated NKP which has been reduced to near oblivion in Norwegian politics.[41]

"Eurocommunism" as a Coalition Strategy

The often bewildering coalition strategies and tactics utilized by West European communists in the post-Stalin era have met with some success, certainly more so than at any time since the immediate postwar period, and infinitely more than during most of the interwar era. What accounts for this relative level of success during the 1960s and 1970s? As discussed above, one of the most damaging aspects of West European communist approaches to coalitions during earlier periods was the discrepancy between tactical maneuverability on one hand and fixed adherence to a set of ideological dogmas on the other hand—dogmas which, if implemented, would lead to the political and perhaps physical destruction of these very coalition partners. This discrepancy produced a yawning gap in credibility which could not be overcome by the West European communists until the 1960s. With the emergence of the Sino-Soviet split, however, the communist parties outside the direct reach of the CPSU could afford to examine their relationships with Moscow in a new light. The concept of polycentrism, which had been introduced by the Italian communist leader Palmiro Togliatti in 1954, gained credence, especially since Soviet authority was weakened by a series of events culminating in the Polish and Hungarian uprisings of 1956 and the frantic Soviet efforts to reestablish their hegemony—efforts which largely failed by 1960. By the early 1960s, serious questions were asked in virtually all communist parties in Western Europe concerning the Stalin era in the Soviet Union and the subjugation of Eastern Europe in the late 1940s and early 1950s; furthermore, most party leaders now reasserted the right for each party to choose its own path to socialism and communism. Thus one of the primary dogmas of earlier international communism had been effectively weakened—namely the dogma of international solidarity as defined by the Kremlin.

The Soviet invasion of Czechoslovakia further weakened the remnants of this pro-Moscow solidarity. The communist parties of Norway, Sweden, Iceland, Great Britain, Italy, and the Benelux countries condemned the invasion in sharp terms, while the Danish and French parties (as well as the totally dependent German Communist party—DKP), after tortuous reasoning and many qualifications, accepted the Soviet explanations for the invasion. Basically, however, the West European communist reaction to Czechoslovakia was sufficiently anti-Soviet to increase the credibility of almost all the local communist parties in the area. This, then, was the beginning of Eurocommunism as a contemporary phenomenon.

During the early to mid-1970s, the West European deviance from the Soviet model developed further. By now the PCI and the Spanish Communist party (PCE) had been joined by the PCF as the three big parties advocating a major policy shift for "developed" communist parties (the CPSU was indirectly, and sometimes directly, castigated as a "primitive" party appropriate for a society at a lower level of development). The majority of the other West European communist parties joined in the chorus of "Eurocommunism." The combination of policy points which comprised this package proved to be well suited for the greater maneuverability of local communist parties in this period, because it questioned a sufficiently large number of earlier ideological tenets to make "the new line" credible. Basically, "Eurocommunism" emphasized the following points.

a. National conditions determine the path taken to socialism and communism; the CPSU cannot claim to be a model for other parties or the Soviet Union a model for other countries (nor can any other model be established with validity for all parties).

b. Eurocommunism accepts political and limited socioeconomic pluralism and is willing to abide by the decisions of the electorate, even if this would mean that communist parties in power would have to leave office.

c. Civil rights are absolute and not relative—i.e., they exist regardless of political systems. This was a significant admission for a political movement which had always emphasized that the relationship between the individual and the collectivity, the citizen and public authority, was different in socialist and communist systems than in capitalist states; Eurocommunism was willing to submit to the same standards of human rights as any other political group, and did in fact criticize the performance of the Soviet Union on this score.

d. Eurocommunists expressed their willingness to cooperate with other political groups even beyond the social democrats. The broad coalition was thus reestablished, at least in theory.[42]

These major points of ideological reevaluation, plus a series of fortuitous political circumstances, made Eurocommunism a more palatable package for many in Western Europe. The development of détente set the stage for an analysis of communist programs on their own merits in a less charged atmosphere than had existed during earlier decades. The clear appeal by the West European communists to "modern" public opinion in "developed" political systems stood in sharp contrast to the "primitivism" of the CPSU and the Soviet Union and appealed to the sense of cultural superiority still felt by many in Western Europe when considering the eastern part of the continent. All in all, the confluence of maneuverability and a more flexible ideological program helped the West European communists out of their isolation in the 1960s and 1970s.

Two Exceptional Cases Revisited:
Iceland and Finland

The vicissitudes of West European communists did not prevent the two maverick parties in Finland and Iceland from continuing their relative success story. The Finnish party, despite its considerable internal factionalism, continued to play a major part in domestic politics through coalition government membership or in important support positions during the 1960s and 1970s. It was the Icelandic party, however, which scored the biggest successes during this period. The AB participated in coalition governments in 1971–1974, and from 1978 on. In addition, it controlled the trade union association and various other mass organizations. During the elections of 1978, the gains for the AB were of such a magnitude that it seemed possible that the party would actually take over the leadership of the coalition. In the end the AB did not reach this goal, but became a major member of the government.[43] There were setbacks in 1979, which reduced these chances. The AB remained a member of the coalition, but did not get the premiership.[44]

While the relative success of the Finnish party was produced by the serious splits in the party system as well as the foreign policy position of Finland, the AB in Iceland made its own successes by means of a continued emphasis on nationalism and staunch independence vis-à-vis the CPSU and the Soviet Union. The most dramatic example of this was the AB's denunciation of the Czechoslovak invasion in 1968. The Icelandic comrades sharply condemned this action as "imperialism," and the party even went so far as to publish a resolution which threatened with expulsion anyone who engaged in any kind of relationship with the "imperialist forces" led by the Red Army.[45] Throughout the rest of the 1960s and up to the present time the Icelandic party has continued its nationalistic policy to such an extent that the communists became the most vocal voices in defense of Icelandic interests in the so-called "cod war" with Great Britain (in which the main issue was the extent of Icelandic territorial waters and the rights of British fishermen to harvest in disputed areas). The AB also scored considerable points in public opinion on the issue of continued American presence on the island (the air force base at Keflavik). Furthermore, the AB led the Icelanders in a dispute with Norway over fishing rights at Jan Mayen Island.[46] The anti-American stance of the AB undoubtedly correlates quite well with the feelings of major sectors of the Icelandic population. Its policy positions also represented the political "mainstream" in such fields as fiscal control, regulation of economic activity, and the emphasis on socioeconomic equality through welfare-state mechanisms.

The results of these policies were renewed political successes in recent elections. In the parliamentary elections of 1978, the AB obtained 22.9 percent of the vote (whereas the leading nonsocialist party, the Independence party, dropped to 32.7 percent from a high of 42.7 percent in 1974). Since the AB emerged as one of the major victors of the election, it appeared possible that the party might be asked to head the new coalition government. In the end this possibility was averted by rather concerted action on the part of the other political organizations in Iceland, but the AB obtained several important ministerial posts. Subsequent electoral setbacks for the AB could not remove it from a major share of power in Iceland.[47]

In Finland, the SKP experienced a considerable amount of success during the 1970s. Because of the instability of the Finnish political system, and especially the left, the SKP became a major political factor, despite its own internal splits and factionalisms. Thus in the period 1975–1976 the SKP participated in a coalition government. In 1978 the SKDL (electoral front dominated by the SKP) held three governmental posts in the coalition government headed by the Social Democrats.[48]

The sources of strength for Finnish communism continued to vary from those of the Icelandic comrades. A faction in the SKP did take a fairly nationalistic stance on a number of issues, but the foreign policy position of Finland generally precluded the kind of policy exhibited in Iceland or even Norway and Sweden by the local communists. The main appeal of the SKP was predominantly its economic program, which emphasized a considerable amount of nationalization and leveling, and also the party's ability to appeal to both urban and rural radicalism and the strong elements of protest and rejection of authority found in much of Finnish society. Coupled with real economic difficulties during much of the 1970s, these policies represented a rather potent political package in contemporary Finland. As stated above, this resulted in full-fledged SKP participation in a coalition government in 1975–1976 and 1978 and continued important political influence since that time.

Other Marxist Parties in the 1960s and 1970s:
The Impact of the Sino-Soviet Dispute and the "New Left"

Many of the West European leftists had expressed their misgivings with the direction of the international communist movement since the "bolshevization" of communist parties in the Comintern in 1923. Put briefly and bluntly, it was felt that the interests of the movement were submerged under the foreign policy needs of the Soviet state, to the benefit of the latter but to the detriment of the former. Certain dramatic events confirmed this suspicion; chief among them were the pact between Hitler and Stalin in 1939, the anti-Tito campaign in the period 1948–1955, and the revelation of the twentieth CPSU congress in early 1956. But these problems were still debated in the context of Soviet supremacy in the international movement. This supremacy was rudely shattered by the well-documented Sino-Soviet dispute. After this momentous dispute broke in 1959–1960, it was possible for Marxist individuals and groups to criticize the Soviet Union and the CPSU while at the same time maintaining the notion that one's credentials as a real Marxist were intact. This development spawned a great many splits in West European communist parties; in almost all of them, there developed a pro-Chinese faction which copied Peking's criticism of Moscow as an established power of "state capitalism." Other elements, which were not particularly pro-Chinese, likewise castigated the Soviet Union for its "revisionist" policies and inclinations.[49]

The Maoist groups which developed all over Western Europe in this period tended to reject the notion of political cooperation with other party leaderships, but they were firm believers in and practitioners of the notions of "action unity" and "coalitions from below," in which they attempted to rally the rank and file of workers, farmers, and intellectuals behind various action committees established to fight a particular policy of their respective governments. Many issues presented themselves for such "action unity" during the 1960s and 1970s; the most important were efforts to get the United States out of Vietnam, the campaign against nuclear weapons and U.S. troops in Europe, membership in the Common Market (particularly important in countries which were not among the original founders of the EEC), and nuclear power plants. Here smaller Marxist parties exhibited considerable skill in garnering support and influence well beyond their numerical strength in the electorate or in party membership.[50]

This disenchantment with the Soviet Union and the CPSU as revolutionary forces also inspired the so-called "New Left" of the 1960s and 1970s. Having determined that the "fatherland of socialism" was no longer interested in revolution, but rather played the part of a global power which would at best *use* revolutionary movements for their own purposes, the amorphous mass of radicals, many of them youngsters, formed their own groups and organizations, which succeeded in gathering support from large segments of the population, including industrial workers normally under the control of social democrats and communists. The revolutionary firebrands of the 1960s and early 1970s were the Rudi Dutschkes and the Cohn-Bendits, not the established leaders of the local communists, Maoists, or even Trotskyists.[51]

It may be argued that it was these movement leaders that exhibited the greatest capability for coalition building, because they possessed no real organizational structures of their own but depended upon their ability to produce action unity with others of like mind. On the other hand, this very lack of organizational structure doomed the New Left to a temporary existence, dependent upon the emergence of certain explosive issues and dissatisfactions in important segments of the general populace. Some of these issues included frustration with insensitive bureaucracies, dissatisfaction with the policies of the superpowers, and the general life-style of materialistic societies. But these issues were in part generationally dependent; the youngsters who rebelled against bureaucracy obtained an education and became civil servants, and their families needed food and shelter, thus preempting the radicals' criticism of materialism. The issue of U.S. involvement in Vietnam ceased with the events of 1975. By the end of the decade, the New Left, with its remarkable capabilities of coalition formation, had largely spent itself.

The New Left should have been highly vulnerable to takeover tactics by the Marxist and Marxist-Leninist parties, given the latter's organizational capabilities and financial means (some of which originated in Moscow). It is a measure of the contempt in which many truly radical individuals held the communists and the others on the organized left that this did not happen to any great extent. The extreme flexibility of the coalition tactics of the Marxist parties, and especially the communists, had finally alienated the real revolutionaries—the final, ironic result of the Russian Revolution in the international perspective.

The 1980s: The Shock Therapy of Crises

The 1980s so far have produced a number of political shocks for all Marxists, regardless of their relationship to the Soviet Union, the CPSU, CCP, or other international "centers" of Marxism. There was, first of all, the Soviet invasion of Afghanistan; then followed the war between China and Vietnam and Vietnam's continued occupation of Kampuchea, and finally, the imposition of martial law in Poland. All of these issues tended to divide the Marxists even further than had been the case in previous decades.

Basically the splits were rather predictable. The so-called Eurocommunist parties denounced the Afghan venture, deplored the Sino-Vietnam war, and rejected the Soviet-sponsored imposition of martial law. This position was exhibited by the Swedish VPK, the PCI, the PCE, and the British communists, for example. The PCF, on the other hand, accepted the Soviet position on these issues, and the French communists moved perceptibly closer to Moscow in this decade. The Finnish party touched the issue of Afghanistan gingerly, due to its own internal factionalism, and tried to blame the West for this debacle. The AB in Iceland was, as usual, outspoken against such imperialism.[52]

A number of communist parties remained true to the CPSU on these issues, as they had in the past. This was true, for example, of the DKP and the West German communists.[53]

The Maoists and Trotskyists also reacted predictably to the invasion and the martial law regime in Poland. This was seen as a further example of the imperialist policies of the Soviet Union and the CPSU. This line was also propounded by those in Western Europe who had begun to associate themselves with the Albanians (and thereby proclaimed a plague on both Moscow and Peking).

The important issues of the 1980s in the international communist movement illustrated the fundamental (or "strategic") differences between the various groups and parties that called themselves Marxist, and thus pointed out the near impossibility of any strategic coalitions being formed among these entities. On the other hand, there was still the possibility that even these structures could join hands for temporary, tactical purposes. This indeed happened on issues such as the stationing of U.S. missiles on European soil, the use of nuclear power in energy production, and the policies of the United States in Central America. On these issues there were more commonalities, for limited time spans, than divisions. But the very unwillingness of the various Marxist parties to establish any lasting relationships with their alleged Marxist colleagues illustrated the distance traveled since the revolutionary and internationalist optimism of the early years of the "Great October."

The dilemmas facing the West European communists during the 1980s were many and fundamental. Electoral reverses continued throughout the decade, removing the Icelandic, Finnish, and French parties from coalitions and reducing their proportion of the total electorate's allegiances further. Most of the other communist parties in this region also experienced reverses at the polls, particularly the Spanish party, which also underwent a split as a result of these developments. In some cases, such as Belgium, communist representation in parliament disappeared altogether as a result of the electorate's rejection of policies and programs advocated by the party. It was clear that the communists of Western Europe were unable to generate mass support in the region.

Other Marxist parties fared better. In a number of countries, and notably in Scandinavia, leftist parties with Marxist-oriented political platforms continued to obtain a combined vote of up to 10 or 12 percent. In Finland the Communist party (SKP) split in 1985–1986, and the moderate faction, which still espoused important Marxist ideological tenets, did reasonably well in mass support. In other countries such as Belgium and The Netherlands there was also some support for Marxist parties other than the communists themselves.[54]

The inability of the communists to attract popular support and the failure of other Marxist organizations to gain significant advances in this area led to internal debates in both sets of parties and emphasis on a number of action programs and activities designed to overcome these deficiencies.

Internally, the Marxist parties (communists included) hotly debated issues which have always been crucial to their existence, namely relations with the U.S.S.R. and the CPSU, relations with each other, and relations with the noncommunist, and non-Marxist left—all issues pertaining to coalition strategies and tactics. Throughout most of the decade both sets of parties advocated the need for action unity on the left, i.e., common activity on issues such as peace, disarmament, the placement of U.S. missiles on European soil, and alleged U.S. imperialism. This action unity was to include the socialists and social democrats of Western Europe, who continued to dominate the political left throughout the decade. But despite a great deal of effort on behalf of issues which had considerable mass appeal, the Marxists and communists continued to lack direct support. One of the fundamental reasons for this was the issue of Marxist relations with the Soviet Union, as well as skepticism about the allegiance of these parties to real democracy, their rhetoric notwithstanding.[55]

The relationship between West European Marxists, on the one hand, and the Soviet Union and the CPSU, on the other, remained a key issue throughout the decade. The West European public remained skeptical about the Kremlin's intentions, despite the statements emanating from the Soviet capital concerning peace, disarmament, and the culpability of the United States in the arms race. The actions of the post-Brezhnev leadership simply did not bear out the verbal and written contentions of Soviet propaganda. Thus the efforts of West European Marxists to hail the "progressive" and "peace-loving" policies of the Soviet Union by and large failed to convince the masses of Western Europe. Instead the peace and disarmament movements of the decade focused on *both* global powers and laid the blame for the arms race at both Washington's and Moscow's door.[56]

The debate over relations with Moscow further illustrated the quandary in which all Marxist organizations in Western Europe found themselves in the 1980s. Electoral logic would dictate abandonment of Marxism as an ideological lodestar; the relationship with the Soviet mentor would then automatically come into question. Throughout the decade a spirited debate about the nature of Marxist parties took place across the continent, and an integral part of this debate was the question of coalition strategies and tactics. Toward the end of the decade, this debate has produced no definitive answers, but rather a number of splits between "traditionalists," emphasizing the need for clear, class-based, and pro-Soviet policies, and the "reformists," who want national approaches to socialism and a clear commitment to political democracy and economic pluralism, with a corresponding reduction in traditional political and socioeconomic tenets and the relationship with the Soviets. The most severe splits took place in Spain and Finland, with the most precise and incisive debate in the French and Italian communist parties. As the decade wore on there was in fact a trend toward more orthodoxy in a number of parties—a tendency that boded ill for the fortunes of West European Marxists in their own societies.[57]

It may be melodramatic to argue that West European Marxism and Marxism-Leninism stand "at the crossroads"; such arguments have been made before, with little resulting effect upon the behavior or fortunes of groups operating under this rubric. But during the 1980s the West European public, particularly the moderate left, showed that it did not accept the platforms or coalition tactics of the Marxists on any of the issues which they had in common. The Marxists were shunted aside in the leadership of the peace movement, the ecological movement, and in the discussion of economic problems. This is particularly significant because the 1980s produced a number of economic problems that should have lent themselves to the overtures of the Marxists, notably in the dabate over inflation, unemployment, and the decline of the European industrial base. The peace and ecological debates carried a number of possibilities for influence enhancement, but the mass support was not forthcoming. It seems clear that, once again, the Marxists and Marxist-Leninists foundered on their liabilities of ideologism, relations with the centers of communist power, especially Moscow, and competition from other leftists with a more meaningful program. Once again, Marxist coalition *tactics* failed; in the 1990s the *strategies* must be debated. But in the next decade, as in the years past, the Marxist parties will have to confront the fundamental fact that restructuring their coalition strategies and tactics will mean altering the basic nature of their parties. Such fundamental change seems unlikely indeed.

Conclusion:
Marxist Coalition Strategies and Tactics
and Political Realities

The survey of coalition strategies and tactics presented above has pointed to a number of fundamental problems besetting Marxist parties as they attempt to relate to the local environment in which they function. There is, first of all, the dichotomy between a fundamentalist, revolutionary ideology and the need to coexist with other participants in the political system, at least until the revolution can be engineered. Secondly, Marxist parties during the last decade or so have had to face the crucial question of whether or not they represent a fundamentally different political organization, which is indeed stressed in the ideological tenets of Marxism-Leninism, or "just another party," another political line. This crisis of identity has not been solved, as is clearly seen in the contemporary controversy in most West European communist parties over "Eurocommunism" and the *real* meaning of this theme. Thirdly, West European communist parties must still live with the legacy of erstwhile dependence upon, and subservience to, the CPSU and the Soviet Union; the question of "proletarian internationalism" still haunts party headquarters almost everywhere. Fourthly, each West European communist party must live with the fact that they face a credibility gap in the genuinely pluralistic societies of Western Europe, insofar as their coalition *strategies* have often been perceived as mere *tactics* dictated by Moscow, or some short-term perception of advantage. In short, local communists may wish to appear as "just another party," but considerable segments of West European public opinion are not willing to accept this image. This fact has kept communists out of national executive power in all but a few West European countries, and in those exceptions special circumstances prevail to a very large degree. Even in France, where the PCF participated in a coalition government with the Socialists, the former were in a distinctly subordinate position, and many analysts actually considered them little more than "hostages" whom the Socialists "held" to ensure the proper behavior of the PCF in national politics.

These problems loom large as the present generation of communist leaders in Western Europe survey the opportunities and liabilities for their movement. On the "opportunities" side of the ledger, the still recent energy crisis, sluggish economic performance, continued high unemployment and inflation, and a dawning realization that the future is not likely to lead to ever greater achievements and prosperity all appear to present a political movement dedicated to fundamental change with considerable opportunities. The "liabilities" side is nevertheless even more impressive, thus contributing to a considerable amount of soul searching and reassessment in contemporary West European communism. The energy crisis may produce opportunities, but the communists are not the only ones to propose answers, and the current problems in this field in the Soviet Union and Eastern Europe clearly show that "communist" solutions are no better than "capitalist" ones. Despite mediocre economic performance in a number of Western countries during the second half of the 1970s, these systems are still way ahead of the countries of Eastern Europe in a number of fields, and the gap is actually widening in some areas of activity. Pessimism about the future has led to a nostalgia for the past and a massive conservative trend (which is also reflected in increased resistance to the "welfare state" in Western Europe) rather than belief in a brave new world of communism. Above all, the West European communists are up against a great deal of competition, be it from assorted groups to their left, the socialist or social democrats on their immediate right, or even nonsocialist parties dedicated to policies which compete (sometimes rather successfully) with the programs of the left in a variety of fields. On the whole, therefore, there is little reason for West European communists to assess their prospects for the immediate (and even medium-range) future with a great deal of optimism. By and large their coalition tactics have failed in Western Europe; successes have been rare, and have only been obtained in countries where the local communists significantly deviated from the "model" (e.g., Iceland), or where external factors have proven especially favorable (e.g., Finland). Even societies occasionally in deep socioeconomic and political crisis, such as Italy, have so far avoided a step which would give the communist party an unequivocal part of *national* political power. The basic assessment of West European communists must therefore be that their coalition *strategies* (as devices for long-range gain) have not worked, even as their coalition *tactics* (dedicated to short-term gains) have occasionally been successful. An obvious policy would therefore be to adopt successful tactical policies as future strategies (especially in terms of nationalism and the need to emphasize local rather than international conditions) for maximization of opportunities. The current reassessment of Eurocommunism, which is under way in the French, Italian, and assorted other West European communist parties, shows the difficulty with which European communism confronts the question of nationalism versus internationalism. At the present time it appears likely that much of West European communism will return to "principled" (i.e., ideologically based) opposition and relative isolation rather than further cooperation and integration into the local political environment. If that happens, future scholars will assess our era as yet another failure in terms of communist coalition policies in Western Europe.

These problems are further magnified for the other Marxist parties of Western Europe. The socialists and social democrats have by and large jettisoned their ideological ballast already (even though most of these parties have been less explicit about it than the German Social Democrats at Bad Godesberg in 1959). What remains is a rather confusing collection of groups and parties that claim the Marxist heritage and criticize the CPSU and the local communists for having abandoned it. These structures are even less likely to achieve lasting gains from their coalition efforts, because they are more radical than the local communists and thereby even less accepting of the existing order than the adherents of Leninism. As long as the basic aspects of West European society remain, the prospects for any kind of success in electoral or mass support terms remain extremely slim. Faced with this prospect, most of these groups and parties tend to retreat into their ideological shell, in which the faithful constitute the relevant audience, and the political game becomes the sophistry of arguing the fine points of ideology in an empty hall. In such circumstances Marxism, the movement for the masses, has become the ideology devoid of mass appeal. That, too, is part of the legacy of the "Great October."

In the final analysis, the lack of strategic (or long-range) success of Marxist coalition policies in Western Europe is ascribable to the widely held notion that the strategies of the Marxists (whichever group they may belong to) have never changed, while the tactics are infinitely malleable; in other words, the Marxists are perceived as ultimately dedicated to the capture of full political power for the purpose of fundamental societal transformation, in which scheme any tactical adjustment is permissible. As long as public actors are capable of dealing with such fundamental problems as unemployment, welfare, and defense, the Marxists of that region will score only fleeting and modest gain.

4

Communists in the Postwar All-Party Coalitions of Eastern Europe
Charles Gati

In the years following World War II, between 1945 and 1948, most parliamentary governments in Europe, East and West, were composed of representatives of different political parties. They were "coalition governments" in the broad sense of the term; to wit, the several political parties participating in the activities of such governments agreed to coordinate their policies in the pursuit of certain immediate objectives.[1] Partners and competitors at the same time, these parties formed coalitions primarily because under prevailing external and internal conditions none of them could effectively govern alone. At least formally, then, the postwar coalitions resembled both some of the prewar European coalitions as well as those in existence in Western Europe, Latin America, and elsewhere at the present time.[2]

The basic similarity notwithstanding, the postwar European governments still differed from other coalitions in the following respects. First, they came into being under the influence of international agreements and great-power pressure, backed by the presence of foreign troops. Elections only followed the formation of the first, provisional governments, and the distribution of cabinet portfolios reflected international expectations as much as internal (or eventually electoral) preferences. Second, the other source of postwar coalitions was a genuine domestic socioeconomic consensus within the European polities, including opposition to the reemergence of the old order and the affirmation of such objectives as economic reconstruction and the fostering of social mobility. Third, the postwar coalitions were almost invariably all-party formations,[3] governments of "national unity," with the real or potential opposition co-opted—at times successfully, at times unsuccessfully—into an all-inclusive political framework. Fourth, and paradoxically, the all-party coalitions nevertheless did not prevent—on the contrary, they soon encouraged—political fragmentation. Despite unity statements, interparty antagonisms flourished, as well as intraparty feuds and highly contentious factionalism within each of the parties. Such political fragmentation became an important source of the eventual demise of the all-party governments. Fifth, most postwar coalitions for the first time included representatives of communist parties (CPs), partly because of the new Soviet role in Europe after the war and partly because of the role these communist parties had played in the anti-Nazi, antifascist resistance during the war. Communist participation in the governments invariably became the primary political issue within the coalition. Some of the noncommunist parties and leaders—uncertain of the proper evaluation of, and reaction to, communist goals—pursued a policy of reasonable accommodation with their CPs (often in order to gain time), while others pursued a policy of firm resistance from the beginning because of the long ideological distance between the communists and themselves. Marxist parties of the left viewed this communist participation with a mixture of apprehension and hope for reunification of the working class movement.

Although these five features characterized the coalition governments of both Eastern and Western Europe, the ultimate political outcome in the two halves of Europe turned out to be very different indeed. By 1947 or 1948, the noncommunist parties of Eastern Europe were altogether prevented from meaningful political competition, while in Western Europe the CPs—debarred from the coalitions—still actively continued to compete for power and influence. Put another way, the East European all-party coalitions gave way to de facto communist one-party hegemony just as the all-party coalitions of Western Europe gave way to competitive coalitions without communist participation. The difference between one-party hegemony in Eastern Europe and competitive coalitions in Western Europe thus reflected the difference between Soviet political values on the one hand and those of the United States and its European allies on the other. It furthermore reflected the fact that the pluralistic societies contained Marxist-oriented parties (such as some of the left-wing socialist organizations of Western Europe) which competed for political power, while in the eastern half of the continent, such competition was anathema for the local *communist* leaders and their Soviet members alike.

The purpose of this chapter is not to document once again or analyze the process of takeovers, or discuss the eventual demise of the European all-party coalitions as manifested by 1947–1948. Rather, the main purpose here is to explore the five characteristics of the all-party coalitions in Eastern Europe, with some emphasis on the role of the CP's in these coalitions. In addition, the question will also be raised whether the East European coalitions may tell us something about the nature of such all-party coalitions in which there are considerable ideological distances between the participating parties. Given the widespread tendency now to press for "coalition governments of reconciliation" in rapidly changing and politically unstable countries—in Afghanistan, for example—do the postwar all-party coalitions of Eastern Europe offer any guidance about the durability of all-party coalitions in other polities?

International Influences

Knowing as we now do what happened in Eastern Europe by 1947 or 1948, we can look back and assign a high degree of foresight, certainty, and consistency to Soviet planning and policy. After all, there is the conspicuous evidence of the seemingly methodical process of takeovers, beginning with the era of "genuine coalition," followed by the era of "bogus coalition," and ending in "monolithic control" by the communist parties. Or, according to another interpretation, the process included the phase of "liberation" (1944–1945), then the phases of "retribution" (1945–1946), and "engineered disruption" (1946–1947), culminating in communist "monolithic control."[4] There is also the oft-quoted evidence, reported by Milovan Djilas, of Stalin's statement with respect to the political map of postwar Europe: "This war is not as in the past; whoever occupies a territory also imposes on it his own social system. Everyone imposes his own system as far as his army can reach. It cannot be otherwise."[5] In retrospect, to repeat, the evidence points to a highly purposeful and determined Soviet commitment to one-party hegemony at any price.[6]

This account, accurate as it may well be, leaves a few perplexing questions unanswered. As of 1944 or 1945, or even later, how come hundreds of noncommunist politicians failed to see the sign on the wall? How could they assume, as did many Western leaders as well, that the nature of the Soviet interest varied from country to country—that while the eventual Soviet domination of, say, Bulgaria was likely, the same certainly could not be said about Czechoslovakia? Indeed, how could they assume—as did most of them—that the Soviet Union would miss its historic opportunity and support broadly based coalition governments in the region for some time to come, perhaps for decades?

The answers to these difficult questions must acknowledge the prevalence of wishful thinking both about Soviet goals and Western interests. It must also acknowledge the political skill of some of the East European communists—of Gottwald in Czechoslovakia, Bierut and Gomulka in Poland, Rakosi in Hungary. Yet, in order to understand and appreciate noncommunists' perceptions *at that time*, the answer should also acknowledge the apparent lack of an early, all-encompassing Soviet grand design for East Europe as well as a genuine Soviet commitment to broad coalition governments.

More tentative and flexible than often assumed, the Soviet Union simply did not have a single policy toward all of Eastern or East Central Europe.[7] Divided Germany was a special case, of course. Given its extraordinary geopolitical significance, combined with considerable U.S. interest, so was Poland. Yugoslavia was different mainly because it was not liberated by Soviet forces. As for Romania and Bulgaria, it was self-evident—at least by late 1944—that Moscow was determined to impose its system of values on them; yet it was not self-evident at all at the time that the same fate would await Hungary and Czechoslovakia as well. In short, Adam Ulam has observed, "Soviet policies responded to specific circumstances and to the wider repercussions of Soviet thrusts in this or that area."[8]

As for the Soviet commitment to coalition governments, the fact is that Moscow could have installed communist governments at once; after all, the Red Army liberated most of Czechoslovakia and all of Poland, Hungary, Romania, and Bulgaria. Why the Soviet Union shied away from doing so and instead supported all-party governments is at least partly explained by the revealing record of a series of secret planning conferences held in the Soviet capital in the fall of 1944.[9] Attended by all the prominent Hungarian communist political émigrés—who received their guidance from the Soviet leadership, including Stalin himself, and from such Comintern leaders as Dimitrov and Manuilski—these meetings focused on the nature of the postwar political order in Hungary and on the role of the CP in it. The probably incomplete list of participants identifies twenty-four top party leaders, all of whom agreed that the new postwar government would have to be broadly based. Some wondered if the CP would or could enter the government at all. Most of them assumed that it would even include those leaders of the authoritarian prewar regime of Admiral Miklos Horthy, who near the end of the war had finally turned against Hitler—including Horthy himself and Count Istvan Bethlen, one-time conservative prime minister and the admiral's most trusted and influential advisor throughout the interwar period. Significantly, just as the Moscow meetings concluded, Horthy—having been kidnapped by the Germans from Budapest on October 15, 1944—signed a document transferring power to the extremist pro-Nazi Arrow Cross leader, Ferenc Szalasi. Noting that development, Stalin told one of the Hungarian CP leaders, Ernö Gerö, in late October,

"We would have accepted Horthy. But the Germans took him away. They forced him to sign the document. Once there is a document, it doesn't matter how it was obtained. Horthy is morally dead."[10] And so, in contrast to the earlier plan—which had aimed at keeping Horthy in power in order to provide for continuity and lend legitimacy to the new regime—the Russians now told the Hungarian CP leaders in Moscow that the new government would have to be without Horthy, after all.

Thus, in the apparently typical Hungarian case, the substance of Soviet planning included the imperative of forming coalition governments of national unity and continuity. Beyond that, Soviet policy was flexible and given to improvisation. Of course Stalin did hope to increase Soviet influence in Europe; there is no reason to dismiss his remarks to Djilas. All the same, Stalin's hopes were not identical with his expectations. As a calculating man of realpolitik, he could not assume that the United States and especially England would tolerate the forceful sovietization of Eastern Europe. As a Marxist, he could not assume that prevailing social and economic conditions everywhere in the eastern half of Europe were then, or would soon be, conducive to, or "ripe" for, radical transformation. Whatever the ultimate objectives, then, *the only clearly identifiable, specific, immediate Soviet commitment was to the formation of broadly based coalition governments in Eastern Europe*. As Stalin's comrade, Czechoslovak CP leader Klement Gottwald explained at a closed meeting of Slovak CP functionaries after his return from Moscow: "We cannot govern on our own, and neither can they (noncommunists). They cannot govern without us, and neither can we without them."[11]

The apparent tentativeness that marked Soviet goals was by far the most pronounced feature of official thinking in Washington and London.[12] As early as 1942 several subcommittees of the U.S. Advisory Committee on Postwar Foreign Policy addressed themselves to the issue of the postwar European political order. It appears that one of Washington's concerns was the question of postwar boundaries between the Soviet Union and its European neighbors. The Advisory Committee also considered the creation of an Eastern European federation (presumably in order to mitigate the age-old problem of nationality conflicts after the war), and there were several discussions about the role of exiled governments in the postwar era. As far as can be determined, however, none of these issues was resolved. As Lynn Etheridge Davis concludes, members of the Advisory Committee did not have

> a clear idea of what post-war Eastern Europe would look like, politically, territorially, or economically. *They hoped that the Atlan-*

tic Charter principles would be implemented, but they came to no definition of possible alternative futures for Eastern Europe. Implicitly, at least, they seemed ready to await Soviet initiatives and then respond. They never determined what would and would not be acceptable in terms of Soviet initiatives. They certainly never considered the promotion by the United States of its own solution for the future of Eastern Europe whether it be United States enforcement of the holding of free elections or United States imposition of nonaligned or buffer states in this region of the world.[13]

It seems, therefore, that what the United States was interested in—though cannot be said to have been committed to—was the implementation of the Atlantic Charter and the ideal of self-determination, i.e., representative government through free elections. In practice, given chaotic conditions after the war and hence the impossibility of holding elections right away, the U.S. interest thus also amounted to the promotion of broad coalition governments.

The British—and Prime Minister Churchill in particular—were obviously more skeptical of Soviet objectives. Unlike President Roosevelt, they not only thought in balance-of-power terms but negotiated with Moscow accordingly as well. Yet even the British

> did not realize quite how powerless they were in the face of the Red Army's advance westwards and Stalin's determination to establish total political monopoly in all areas conquered by the Red Army. In this failure to understand Stalin the British can be charged with naiveté, blindness, even arrogance. But the pressing needs of war-time alliance and lingering fears of a second Soviet-German deal were powerful impulses to wishful thinking and to the ignoring of danger signals.
>
> The British hoped that, while the Soviet Union's security requirements would prevail in countries near its borders, *there would be some kind of Anglo-Soviet influence-sharing inside those countries between liberals and the Left, between peasant parties, social democrats and communists*. This idea turned out to be a pipe dream, but it was not shameful.[14]

In the famous "percentage agreement" with Stalin,[15] Churchill sought to translate this general "idea" into a specific deal. At his October 9, 1944, meeting with Stalin in the Kremlin, he proposed—and the Soviet leaders accepted—the following distribution of influence in Eastern Europe between England (and, as far as Stalin was concerned, the United States) on the one hand and the Soviet Union on the other:

Greece	Western influence: 90%	Soviet: 10%
Yugoslavia	Western influence: 50%	Soviet: 50%
Hungary	Western influence: 50%	Soviet: 50%
Bulgaria	Western influence: 25%	Soviet: 75%
Romania	Western influence: 10%	Soviet: 90%

Although "influence" was never defined and hence the agreement lacked specificity, Stalin (as well as Churchill, of course) assigned some importance to it. For in less than twenty-four hours—on October 10, 1944, and then on October 11—the Russians raised the issue again at two high-level meetings in the Kremlin.[16] The apparent result of these two long, petty, and rather disjointed sessions between the two foreign ministers, Eden and Molotov, was to make no change for Greece, Yugoslavia, and Romania, but to increase the allocation of Soviet influence in Hungary from 50 percent to 80 percent and in Bulgaria from 75 percent to 80 percent.

At none of the three meetings was any reference made to the other three countries of Eastern Europe: Poland, Yugoslavia, and Czechoslovakia. However, a few months later, at the February 1945 Yalta conference of the "Big Three" (Roosevelt, Churchill, and Stalin), there was considerable discussion about Poland and some about Yugoslavia. The agreement on Poland called for the establishment of a "Polish Provisional Government of National Unity," organized on a broad "democratic basis with the inclusion of democratic leaders from Poland itself and from Poles abroad." "This Polish Provisional Government of National Unity," the Big Three declared, "shall be pledged to the holding of free and unfettered elections as soon as possible on the basis of universal suffrage and secret ballot. In these elections all democratic and anti-Nazi parties shall have the right to take part and to put forward candidates."[17]

As for Yugoslavia, which was liberated largely by its own effort, the Big Three could only "recommend" that "the Tito-Šubăsić Agreement [of November and December 1944] should immediately be put into effect and a new Government formed on the basis of the Agreement." In addition, the new government so created "should declare" that the country's legislative body (AVNOJ) "will be extended to include members of the last Yugoslav Skupstina [prewar Serbian assembly] who have not compromised themselves by collaboration with the enemy."[18] The Big Three's endorsement of such a very broad Yugoslav coalition government was thus based on the agreements between Marshal Tito, leader of the communist partisan forces, and Dr. Šubašić, prime minister of the Royal Yugoslav government-in-exile in London. The most specific part of the agreement had to do with the composition of the postwar cabinet, which was to include six members of the Šubašić government and twelve members of Tito's so-called National Committee.[19]

Czechoslovakia's was a different story altogether. Unlike Šubašić, who was clearly London's man in Yugoslavia, the head of the Czechoslovak government-in-exile, Dr. Edvard Beneš, was able to maintain excellent relations with London, Washington, and Moscow as well. Distinguished and clever, Beneš also benefited from the fact that Czechoslovakia had had a truly representative form of democracy in the interwar period and that it was liberated by both the Soviet and American armies. Although the country's political future was hardly ever mentioned at formal allied conferences (because it was so self-evident that Czechoslovakia, under Beneš, would continue to have a multiparty political order after the war), Beneš had held extensive discussions with all three allied leaders.[20] Indeed, the first provisional government established in the Slovak city of Košice in the spring of 1945 was a coalition government composed of representatives of several political parties—as informally approved by the three allies.

Thus the interim governments which came into being in Eastern Europe after World War II invariably responded to and at least formally reflected international agreements and pressures. As specified by the Yalta "Declaration on Liberated Europe," they were expected to be "broadly representative of all democratic elements in the population." In practice, some of them were more representative (i.e., Czechoslovakia) than others (i.e., Yugoslavia), but as Table 1 shows, noncommunists dominated East European cabinets everywhere except in Yugoslavia. Although the West and Moscow had different interpretations of the meaning of "representative government" in general and of the Yalta Declaration in particular, all three allies, for reasons of their own, found it quite convenient for now to either directly impose or recommend the establishment of broadly based coalition governments. The coalition formula was the classical "easy solution": The United States was satisfied by the emphasis on "representative" governments; the British thought the "percentage government" and Yalta might give them more influence, especially in the Balkans, than their military position in the area would have justified; and the Russians, who, in the best Stalinist tradition, were suspicious of the British and hence circumspect, obtained the stamp of Western approval for the legitimate inclusion of communists in the coalition governments. Strange bedfellows as the allies were, they now gave birth to governments of even stranger bedfellows in Eastern Europe.

Table 1
Formal Distribution of Portfolios in
Eastern Coalition Governments 1944–1948

Country	Period	CP/Others	Number of Government Portfolios (Percent of Total)	
Bulgaria	9/9/44–	Communist party	4	(25%)
	3/31/46	Others	12	(75%)
	3/31/46–	Communist party	4	(25%)
	11/22/46	Others	12	(75%)
	11/22/46–	Communist party	10	(50%)
	12/11/47	Others	10	(50%)
	12/11/47–	Communist party	12	(60%)
	7/20/49	Others	8	(40%)
Czechoslovakia	4/4/45–	Czech and Slovak CPs	8	(32%)
	7/8/46	Others	17	(68%)
	7/8/46–	Czech and Slovak CPs	9	(41%)
	2/25/48	Others	13	(59%)
	2/25/48–	Czech and Slovak CPs	11	(58%)
		Others	8	(42%)
Hungary	12/22/44–	Communist party	3	(25%)
	11/15/45	Others	9	(75%)
	11/15/45–	Communist party	4	(22%)
	2/1/46	Others	14	(78%)
	2/1/46–	Communist party	4	(21%)
	5/31/47	Others	15	(79%)
	5/31/47–	Communist party	4	(24%)
	9/24/47	Others	13	(76%)
	9/24/47–	Communist party	6	(38%)
	12/10/48	Others	10	(62%)
Poland	7/21/44–	Workers' party	5	(33%)
	12/31/44	Others	10	(67%)
	12/31/44–	Workers' party	5	(29%)
	6/28/45	Others	12	(71%)
	6/28/45–	Lublin Committee	16	(76%)
	2/6/47	Others	5	(24%)
Romania	8/23/44–	Communist party	1	(8%)
	11/4/44	Others	12	(92%)
	11/4/44–	National Democratic Front	11	(85%)
	3/6/45	Others	2	(15%)
	3/6/45–	Communist party	3	(20%)
	3/29/46	Others	12	(80%)

Table 1
(continued)

Country	Period	CP/Others	Number of Government Portfolios (Percent of Total)	
	3/29/46–	Communist party	4	(25%)
	11/29/46	Others	12	(75%)
	11/29/46–	Communist party	4	(33%)
	4/13/48	Others	8	(67%)
	4/13/48–	Workers' party	12	(67%)
	12/24/48	Others	6	(33%)
Yugoslavia	3/7/45–	National Committee (Tito)	23	(82%)
	9/45	Others	5	(18%)

Domestic Consensus

No doubt unwittingly, a classified ad appearing in the January 5, 1945, issue of the Hungarian newspaper *Szentesi Lap* alluded to the major source of the initial political consensus in Eastern Europe. "Attention!" a high school art teacher advertised, "I can teach you to write, read, and speak Russian, using such an easy method that everyone can learn how to write, read, and speak Russian in three months." To learn Russian, and learn it fast, was sound enough advice to all East Europeans. They knew —politicians of all persuasions certainly knew—that the region's fate was going to be strongly influenced, if not determined, by the Soviet Union. What they did not know for sure was how long Moscow would support the earlier, wartime coalition agreements which were to be implemented after the war.

Back in December 1943 such a cooperative agreement had been concluded in Moscow between Czechoslovak political figures, including President Beneš and representatives of the Czech Communist party. In Hungary, the tiny CP reached an accord in the fall of 1944 with the Smallholders party and the Social Democrats. Unrealistic as it may have been, there was the Tito-Šubăsić deal in Yugoslavia. Also in 1944, as the war was coming to an end, a common program and subsequently an antifascist coalition surfaced in Romania and Bulgaria. Only in Poland was it impossible to bring together the two major contending forces during the war—the Soviet-backed "Lublin Committee" and the London-based government-in-exile; but, by June 1945, foreign pressure eventually produced a "government

Table 2
Communist Party Membership in
Eastern Europe 1944–1948

Party's Name	Date	Number of Members	As Percent of Population
Bulgarian CP	9/1944	25,000	
	10/1944	50,000	
	1/1945	254,140	
	12/1946	490,000	
	6/1947	510,000	7.1%
	12/1948	496,000	6.9%
Czech CP	6/1945	597,500	
	7/1945	712,776	
	3/1946	930,214	
	11–12/1947	1,070,909	
Slovak CP	9/1945	200,866	
	12/1945	197,227	
	3/1946	151,330	
	11/1945	210,222	
Czech & Slovak CPs	3/1946	1,081,544	
	9/1947	1,172,000	9.4%
	12/1947	1,281,131	
	2/1948	1,400,000	
	5/1948	2,150,000	
Polish Workers' party	7/1944	20,000	
	12/1944	32,000	
	4/1945	301,695	
	12/1945	235,300	
	6/1946	347,105	
	12/1946	555,888	
	5/1947	823,340	3.3%
	12/1947	820,786	
	6/1948	997,024	
	9/1948	1,006,873	
Hungarian CP	12/1944	2,500	
	2/1945	30,000	
	5/1945	150,000	
	7/1945	508,801	5.7%
	1/1946	608,728	
	1/1946	653,300	
	1/1947	670,818	
	3/1947	708,646	

Table 2
(continued)

Party's Name	Date	Number of Members	As Percent of Population
	12/1947	864,000	
	6/1948	887,472	9.6%
Romanian CP	8/1944	2,000	
	10/1945	256,000	
	9/1947	710,000	4.4%
	2/1948	806,000	5.0%

of national unity" even for that deeply divided country.

The agreements were based on the political reality of the moment. As Soviet forces were liberating much of Europe, there could be no question about the key role the various communist parties were to play in the political life of the several East European countries. It was also apparent, however, that these parties could not govern alone, for with the exception of Czechoslovakia, as Table 2 shows, they lacked popular appeal. In addition, the Soviet Union, sensitive to its Western allies' perception of the legitimacy of the emerging political order in Eastern Europe, still sought inclusion of noncommunists in the various governments.

If geopolitical necessity was thus an important source of the initial tendency toward limited cooperation, so was the prevailing domestic socio-economic consensus about the immediate tasks ahead. Although—because of the subsequent disintegration of the coalition governments and the establishment of communist political hegemony—the generally cooperative spirit of 1944–1945 has been deemphasized, such a domestic-programmatic consensus did exist in Czechoslovakia, Hungary, and to a lesser extent in Bulgaria, Romania, and perhaps even Poland and Yugoslavia as well. That consensus rested on the disintegration of the old order and on the opportunity to build a new one. Accordingly, there was a unanimous commitm ..nt to the primacy of reconstruction on the basis of united, concerted action. In the countries where it had not been done (especially Hungary and Poland), there was no opposition to the implementation of land reform, which was both long overdue and immensely popular. There was agreement in principle that the privileges of the past should be erased, educational opportunity be made available to all, and, generally speaking, social mobility fostered. There was, for now, a shared view about building a "mixed" economy along agrarian-socialist or social-democratic lines. Finally, it was widely recognized that the coming transformation of society from primarily agrarian to a primarily industrial pattern, would necessitate radical, if not revolutionary measures.

To that extent, it was also widely recognized that such socioeconomic transformation would require a political order different from Western-style pluralistic democracy. Seldom defined in precise terms, the "new democracy," "people's democracy," or "popular democracy" labels implied a political system devoted mainly to *substantive*, i.e., socioeconomic, concerns. True, there was consensus about such political matters as the punishment of "war criminals," and the populist-agrarians as much as the social-democrats and the communists paid lip service to political liberties and the benefits of free and competitive political processes. But, under chaotic conditions, all parties—apprehensive as some of them were about communism—sought to focus on what united them: the burning socioeconomic issues of food supply, housing, health care, transportation, and public order.

Thus the immediate task of reconstruction, combined with the ever-present background of international pressures, produced an uneasy domestic consensus during the last months of, and immediately after, the war. Certainly, the consensus was short-lived; it barely, if ever, existed in Yugoslavia or Poland, and it managed to survive for only a year or two in Czechoslovakia and Hungary. Where it did last, however, both communists and noncommunists supported it because they hoped to gain time and eventually improve their relative power positions. Those noncommunists who helped uphold the domestic consensus—and hence the coalition —did so in the expectation of forthcoming changes in international alignments leading to the withdrawal of Soviet armed forces from Eastern Europe. The communists, in turn, also needed time, in order to make themselves palatable to their own people and thus avoid the possibility of defeat by a premature move toward hegemony.

Call it deception, temporary abnegation, or political tactics, the communists' professed noncommunist platform was an additional circumstance behind the domestic consensus. "We do not want in any way to limit the sovereignty of other parties but . . . to cooperate with them," said the Polish CP leader, Wladyslaw Gomulka, in February 1945 (although in July, he identified the popular Peasant party leader, Stanislaw Mikolajczyk, as "a symbol of all anti-democratic elements, all of which is the enemy of democracy and the Soviet Union").[21] In December 1944 the Hungarian CP spokesman, József Révai, declared, "We do not regard national collaboration as a passing, political coalition, as a tactical chess move, but rather as a long-lasting alliance. We will stand by our given word."[22] The Bulgarian Georgi Dimitrov, stated—at the November 7, 1945, anniversary celebration of the Russian Revolution in Moscow, of all places—that the "assertion that the communists allegedly want to seize full power . . . is a malicious legend and slander. It is not true that the communists want to have a single-party government."[23]

Whether these professions of "national collaboration" were sincere and whether they were really meant to apply to *some* of the countries in the region are controversial questions beyond the scope of this chapter. What should be stressed here is that although some of the prominent noncommunist political leaders in the area, such as Mikolajczyk in Poland, considered these statements purposefully deceptive, equally prominent noncommunists such as Beneš in Czechoslovakia and Tildy in Hungary seemed to view communist goals as tentative and communist tactics as flexible. Wrong as they turned out to be later on, their perception, then, was not based on wishful thinking alone. For, as the previously described Moscow meeting of Hungarian communists in the fall of 1944 illustrates, contemporary evidence pointed to the absence of a definitive Soviet grand design for the region as a whole.[24] (After all, as late as March 1946 the authoritative Soviet journal, *Bolshevik*, conspicuously failed to include Czechoslovakia, Hungary, and even Poland among the new "people's democracies.") Most importantly, however, the majority of noncommunist parties and politicians could forge an alliance with the CPs not only because they knew that reconstruction and rebirth required Soviet backing and communist participation, but because by and large they shared the communists' avowed socioeconomic objectives.

The All-Party Coalition

With respect to immediate socioeconomic objectives, then, the initial differences between the CPs and such noncommunists as the agrarians, social democrats and liberals were quite minimal, which made the formation of all-party coalitions all but inevitable; yet, soon enough, political differences turned out to be so substantial as to make the eventual demise of all-party coalitions a foregone conclusion.

Strictly speaking, the new governments were all-inclusive in Romania, Hungary, Bulgaria, and Czechoslovakia. In the three former cases, high-ranking military officers who had turned against Hitler's Germany at the last minute were co-opted into the new governments.[25] Indeed, the

Table 3
Parliamentary Elections
in Eastern Europe 1944–1948

Country	Date	Parties/"Fronts"	Number of Seats (Percent of Total)	
Bulgaria	11/18/1945	Fatherland Front	279	(all)
	10/17/1946	Fatherland Front	364	(79%)
	[competitive]	Agrarians (Petkov)	92	(20%)
		Social Dem. (Lulchev)	6	(1%)
Czechoslovakia	5/16/1946	Czech & Slovak CPs	114	(18%)
	[free]	Czech National Socialists	55	(16%)
		People's party	47	(16%)
		Slovak Democrats	43	(14%)
		Social Democrats	38	(13%)
		Others	3	(1%)
Hungary	11/4/1945	Smallholders	245	(60%)
	[free]	Communist party	70	(17%)
		Social Democrats	69	(17%)
		National Peasants	23	(6%)
		Bourgeois Democrats	2	—
	8/31/1947	Communist party	100	(24%)
	[competitive]	Smallholders	68	(17%)
		Social Democrats	67	(16%)
		Nat. Peasant Govt. Front	36	(9%)
		Total	271	(66%)
		Democratic People's party (Barankovics)	60	(15%)
		Hungarian Independent party (Pfieffer)	49	(12%)
		Indep. Hung. Dem. party (Balogh)	18	(4%)
		Others	13	(3%)
		Opposition Total	140	(34%)
Poland	1/19/1946	Government Front	394	(89%)
		Other pro-bloc parties	22	(5%)
		Polish Peasant party (Mikolajczyk)	28	(6%)
Romania	11/19/1946	Government Front	377	(91%)
		National Peasant party (Maniu)	32	(8%)
		Others	5	(1%)

Table 3
(continued)

Country	Date	Parties/"Fronts"	Number of Seats (Percent of Total)	
	3/28/1948	Government Front	405	(98%)
		Liberals (Brantianu)	7	(2%)
		National Peasants (Maniu)	2	—

first Romanian cabinet under General Sănătescu (August 23–November 2, 1944) was dominated by generals, with the leader of each of the so-called "Historical Parties" (National Peasant, Liberal, and Social Democrat) as well as the CP in the government as ministers without portfolio. The second Sănătescu cabinet (November 4–December 2, 1944), in which the four party leaders continued to serve as ministers without portfolio, was made up of eleven representatives of the three "Historical Parties" and one communist, as well as General Sănătescu as premier. When Sănătescu was replaced by another general, R. Rădescu, the composition of the cabinet remained more or less unchanged until March 1945, when the sham or bogus coalition under the premiership of Petru Groza took over. But from August 1944 to March 1945, a Moscow-approved all-party government had existed in Romania, even as both the Russians and the Romanian CP concurrently worked hard to undermine it, both from within and from without.

In Hungary, the Provisional Government—whose long tenure lasted from December 11, 1944, to November 15, 1945—was also headed by a general (Béla Dálnoki Miklós), and there were two other military officers in the cabinet; all three had served the old regime. The Miklós government included three communists, two social democrats, two smallholders, one national peasant, and one unaffiliated (Count Géza Teleki as minister of religion and public education). After the relatively free elections held in November 1945 (see Table 3), the two smallholders-led governments under the premierships of Zoltán Tildy and Ferenc Nagy (November 15, 1945, to May 31, 1947) no longer included the generals or Count Teleki, but with nine (later on ten) smallholders, four social democrats, one national peasant, and four communist ministers, they reflected the results of the election. Once again, the CP sought to undermine the government it repeatedly pledged itself to support, eventually succeeding in the summer of 1947 when a bogus coalition assumed power.

In Bulgaria, a link with the past was provided by the inclusion of four leaders of the semimilitary "Zveno" ("The Link") group in the new government formed in September 1944. Authoritarian by temperament, skeptical of parliamentary institutions and party politics, but not unfriendly toward the Soviet Union, Zveno was useful in organizing Bulgaria's reentry into the war on the Allies' side and in giving an impression of continuity and legitimacy. Its nominal leader, Kimon Georgiev, was premier—until September 1946—of the coalition government in which, formally at least, noncommunists outnumbered CP ministers by a margin of three to one. As elsewhere in Eastern Europe, Zveno, agrarian, and social democratic representation in the cabinet was gradually assumed by leaders more willing to accommodate the CP as Velchez was replaced by Georgiev as head of Zveno, Petkov by Obbov as leader of the Agrarian Union, and the three prominent social democrats (Pastukhov, the centrist Cheshmedzhiev, and Lulchev) by the pro-communist Neikov. All in all, the Bulgarian government was an all-party formation more in name than substance—as in Romania and as it developed somewhat later in Hungary.

In Czechoslovakia, the "old regime" had consisted of genuine democrats—rather than military leaders with an authoritarian or semifascist past—as well as the only large and legal CP in Eastern Europe. In 1945 they became the "new regime," with the venerable Beneš as president. Although there were (free) elections in the late spring of 1946, the distribution of cabinet portfolios remained essentially unchanged between April 1945 and the February 1948 coup d'état (see Table 1). No significant elements were left out of the government, which, in Beneš' words, rejected the "purely political conception of democracy in a liberalistic sense" and instead understood it "as a system in the economic and social sense also."[26] Despite the apparent continuity in party representation in the prewar and postwar governments, Beneš declared in 1945, "Our house must be rebuilt both politically and socially, with a new content, new people, and often with new institutions" and that "political democracy will have to develop systematically and consistently into a so-called economic and social democracy."[27] This general orientation, which was intended to make Czechoslovakia a "bridge" between East and West, was supported not only by Beneš' own National Socialists, but by the social democrats, the Slovak Democratic party, and the initially very soft-spoken leaders of the CP as well.

Thus, following Seton-Watson's schema, the era of "genuine" coalition may be said to have existed in Czechoslovakia for about three years, in Hungary for about two and one-half years, in Romania for six months, and in Bulgaria perhaps for only four months. There followed the period of

Table 4
Seton-Watson's "Stages" of East European Politics
After World War II

Country	Genuine Coalition	Bogus Coalition	Monolithic CP Rule
Romania	August 1944– March 1945	March 1945– November 1947	November 1947–
Bulgaria	September 1944– January 1945	January 1945– July 1948	July 1948–
Hungary	December 1944– May 1947	May 1947– December 1948	December 1948–
Czechoslovakia	April 1945– February 1948		February 1948–
Yugoslavia		March 1945– September 1945	September 1945–
Poland		June 1945– October 1947	October 1947–

"bogus" coalition with more accommodating noncommunists still in the government—lasting for two and one-half years in Bulgaria and Romania (until the fall of 1947) and for about one year in Hungary (until late 1948). Czechoslovakia, as Seton-Watson notes, "leaped" from the "genuine coalition" phase to monolithic CP rule after the 1948 coup (see Table 4).[28]

As for Yugoslavia, the few noncommunist members of the government formed in March 1945 were altogether left out of the decision-making process and never allowed to have their parties properly organized. Even the short period of "bogus" coalition—heavily dominated by Tito's forces —came to a predictable end in September 1945 with the resignation of Foreign Minister Šubašić. It seems that Tito, who came to power on his own, did not feel obliged to provide for continuity with the past; rightly or wrongly, he felt his rule was legitimate. The inclusion of Šubašić, Grol, and a few others from London was no more than a polite gesture to the British, who assisted him during the war, and to the Russians, who thought that a one-party government in Yugoslavia would needlessly exacerbate their relations with the British and the Americans.

Finally, Poland was sui generis. On the one hand—as in Romania, Hungary, Bulgaria, and Czechoslovakia—the Polish government formed in June 1945 was at least nominally inclusive, with several of the political parties of the past represented in it. Although the National Democratic party, which had been one of the major parties before the war, was excluded, the coalition was composed of five parties: Mikolajczyk's People's (Peasant) party, the Polish Socialist party, the Democratic party, the Christian

Labor party, and the Polish Workers' (Communist) party. On the other hand, however, the CP—as in Yugoslavia—thoroughly dominated the government from the beginning; indeed, the actual division in the government was not between communists and noncommunists, but between "Lublin" Poles, who were both pro-Soviet and pro-CP, on the one hand, and the "London" Poles on the other. With sixteen of the twenty-one ministries held by members of the Lublin group, the government was a bogus coalition from the start—with Mikolajczyk, almost single-handedly, putting forth a noncommunist point of view for two years. This "coalition," in turn, was to give way to the establishment of monolithic CP rule in the fall of 1947.[29]

All in all, the all-party governments of Eastern Europe—with the notable exceptions of Yugoslavia and Poland—began as genuine coalitions. During this phase they were characterized as follows:

> Several political parties, differing in social basis, ideology and long-term programme, and possessing each its own party organizations, combined on a common short-term programme, which nominally included a purge of fascists, fairly radical social reforms, political freedom and a foreign policy friendly to both the U.S.S.R. and the Western Powers. Real freedom of speech and meeting existed, and there was little political censorship except on the one subject—the U.S.S.R. Not only might Soviet policy not be criticized, but it was hardly possible to write anything about any aspect of Russia which did not coincide with the official Soviet line. But this seemed a small price to pay. Apart from this, a wide variety of opinions, representing various political views and social categories, could be freely expressed. Nevertheless, already during the first stage, the communists seized control of most of the "levers of power"—in particular the security police, the army general staff and the publicity machine.[30]

The phase of bogus coalition was aptly summarized by Seton-Watson as follows:

> The governments still contain non-communist parties, but these are represented by men chosen no longer by party membership but by the communists. The essential feature of this stage is that the peasant parties, and any bourgeois parties who may have been tolerated at the beginning, are driven into opposition. In this stage opposition is still tolerated but becomes increasingly difficult. Opposition newspapers may be published, but their

distribution becomes dangerous in the capital and almost impossible outside it. Censorship is exercised not only by the government but also by the communist-controlled printers' trade unions, which "indignantly refuse to print reactionary calumnies against the people's authorities." Opposition meetings are broken up by lorryloads of communist toughs, while the police "objectively" take no action against aggressors or aggressed.[31]

Political Fragmentation

The postwar East European coalitions of either variety did not last long—whether by comparison to the durability of the coalition in neighboring Austria, which lasted over two decades, or by absolute European standards.[32] The reason for their demise, it is generally acknowledged, had to do with external factors: with ever-increasing Soviet pressure and—until 1947 when it was too late—with the lack of Western support to noncommunists. It is also acknowledged that early control by the CPs of key ministries—particularly those of internal affairs and defense, was the major domestic factor determining the ultimate political outcome.

For analytical purposes, it may be useful to separate the issue into (1) the decay of the coalition per se and (2) the eventual communist victory.

The coalitions' decay was inherent in their oversized quality. Dodd identifies three general types of coalition status: first, the greater than minimum winning status (i.e., "oversized" coalitions from which "at least one party could be subtracted" and yet "the cabinet's majority status [is still] sustained"); second, the minimum winning status (i.e., surely the most durable coalitions, which "do not contain any party that could be subtracted" without losing their winning status); and third, the less than minimum winning status (i.e., "undersized" coalitions with no "reliable parliamentary majority").[33] Clearly, the all-party governments of postwar Eastern Europe had far greater than minimum winning status. They were oversized and thus nondurable, primarily because the coalitions included parties, or factions within parties, which were expendable. "If this [the expendable] party is omitted from the cabinet," Dodd explains, "some or all of the other coalition partners will gain in the sense that they will obtain new ministerial positions formerly controlled by the expendable party(ies). Realizing this, the various parties within the coalition act to reduce the size of the cabinet by removing at least one party."[34]

But which party or parties were expendable in the postwar East European all-party coalitions? Formally, the evidence points to the CPs. As

Table 3 shows, none of the communist parties of Eastern Europe could win parliamentary majority in an election, free or otherwise, and only the Czechoslovak CP could obtain a plurality of votes. Further analysis (implied by the composition of cabinets shown in Table 1) suggests that the communist parties were formally a minority even *within* their own creation, the all-encompassing "fronts" as well (i.e., the Fatherland Front in Bulgaria and the Government Front in Poland and Romania). Moreover, the CP was certainly "the odd man out" in East European politics, of course, as the ideological distance between the communists and others was considerably greater than it was among the noncommunist parties. Thus, had the cabinets reflected the ideological makeup of parliaments, the communists would have been expendable. As a matter of fact, in the unique case of Hungary where the Smallholders' party obtained 57 percent of the vote and 60 percent of the seats in 1945, it could have governed alone, without the communists, the social democrats, and the national peasants.

The reason it did not happen this way can be explained by two considerations. The obvious one is that, given the proximity of the Soviet Union and the presence of the Red Army, it was simply unrealistic and even unthinkable to exclude the communists from the coalition altogether. (In the one known case when the "unthinkable" almost happened—in Hungary after the 1945 elections—the second echelon of the smallholder leadership did urge the formation of an all-smallholder government, but the party's leaders rejected the idea not only because they assumed that Moscow would not accept it, but also because they did not want to share the burden of responsibility for the country's economic recovery and political fate all by themselves.)

The less obvious reason why the CPs were not expendable had to do with the extremely high level of dissension and factionalism within all noncommunist parties. Instead of uniting in the face of gradually increasing communist challenge to the status quo (as signified by the all-party coalition) and thus isolate or otherwise weaken the challenger, the noncommunist parties allowed their own political differences, personal rivalries, and petty jealousies to replace their common interests. Simply put, what was frequently thought to be expendable was *another* noncommunist party or *another* faction within a noncommunist party, not the CP. The inability of all the noncommunist parties of Eastern Europe to join forces in defense of the coalition status quo served to enhance the communists' "positional advantage" (as Paul Zinner put it) and sealed their own political fate. This is how it "worked" in Czechoslovakia, for example, where the CP shared power with four noncommunist parties:

Postwar Coalitions of Eastern Europe 127

The National Socialists were antagonistic toward the Slovak Democrats, because of their separatist tendencies. Obversely, the Slovak Democrats considered the National Socialists the foremost exponents of the hated policy of "Czechization." There was friction between the National Socialists and the People's Party, because of the former's outspoken anti-clerical attitude and because these parties vied for the favors of the same constituency. The National Socialists and Social Democrats were continually at loggerheads. Their traditional rivalry was exacerbated by post-war conditions. To some extent, they too were contending for the favors of the same constituency, and the National Socialists exerted great pressure to wean away the moderate wing of the Social Democratic Party. . . . The conflicts . . . prevented the formation of anything approaching a coherent anti-communist front.[35]

For an illustration of intraparty divisions, there is the *typical* case of the Polish Social Democrats (PPS) who joined the communists (RRP) and the Peasant party in the postwar coalition:

The PPS was the least homogeneous of the three main political parties. On the one hand, there was the core of founding members from the old RPPS, led by Osobka-Morawski, who could be counted on to collaborate with the Communists. On the other hand, there was the large number of recruits who joined the party after the Congress of September 1944, many of whom were influenced in doing so by the nationalist traditions of the old PPS and by the hope that a strong socialist party might provide an alternative to Communism. These new arrivals were divided roughly into three main groups. To the right were members of the old PPS from the underground, led by the veteran trade-unionist, Zygmunt Zulawski. They were fundamentally anti-Communist, realized the need for coming to an understanding with the PPR and the Soviet authorities, but hoped to maintain the identity of the PPS as a moderating influence. In October 1945 an attempt by Zulawski to found a separate Social Democratic party was frustrated by the Communists and the National Council. A compromise was reached in December, when the Zulawski group was given eleven seats on the executive council of the PPS. But within a year Zulawski himself, who rivalled Mikolajczyk in determination, had left the Party. In the centre was a large body of moderates who accepted the inevitability of collaboration with the Communists, considered a united front of left-wing parties desirable to prevent reaction, and trusted in the numerical strength of the socialists to make their influence felt. This group was the most variegated and fluid of the three and contained many opportunists. Finally, there was the left wing, which scarcely differed from the former members of the RPPS except in being newcomers. Chief amongst them was Jozef Cyrankiewicz, who had come under Communist influence while still in a concentration camp and who became secretary-general of the PPS in July 1945. A man of considerable intellectual ability, with a keen sense of his own interests, he played an important part in the process by which the PPS and the PPR were finally merged into one party.[36]

The more these interparty and intraparty antagonisms grew, the more the oversized coalition worked in favor of the communists, who on account of their "positional advantage" — and despite their minority standing — were the only ones who were not expendable; their participation in the coalition was predetermined. Moreover, since they needed non-CP allies to keep the appearance of a broadly based government, many noncommunists positioned themselves in such a way as to be kept by the ultimate winner — the CP. To the extent that the CPs continued to need non-CP participation in the cabinet, not all noncommunists were expendable, only almost all of them. This crucial piece of information made all too many non-CP parties, factions, or individuals turn against their own parties or colleagues in order to prove their utility to the communists.

Hence the "size principle" and the general notion that over-sized coalitions are nondurable were indeed operative in postwar Eastern Europe, except that the communist parties had two decisive advantages. The first was the external backing of the Soviet Union, of course, and the second was their internal cohesion.[37] Put another way, the breakup of the coalitions was made possible by the self-destruction of the noncommunist elements, as much as it was due to the considerable strength, determination, skill, and cohesion of the communist side. Because they were too divided and because of their fervent desire to avoid a civil war or direct Soviet military intervention, such eminent democrats as Beneš and Tildy — and of course opportunists like Groza and Cyrankiewicz — shied away from applying equally the coalition rules of conduct: in order to gain time and survive, they were reluctant to encroach on communist prerogatives, while the CPs could, and did, provoke internal turmoil in the other parties. Many noncommunist leaders came to believe that if they were to stay on, they could influence the political system from within. After all, their alternative was political exile or worse, and, given the way the oversized coalition worked, they knew that there would always be others to fill the quota of noncommunists in the emerging political order.

Implications and Conclusions

The East European coalition governments of national unity born after World War II contained the seeds of their own decay. They were given birth by an international alliance that was about to collapse. The initial domestic unity of purpose began to fade away as soon as, or even before, fascism was defeated and economic reconstruction achieved. The oversized coalitions were structurally conducive to easy CP manipulation. In the Balkans and in Poland, Moscow's commitment to sovietization was all but total, while in Czechoslovakia and Hungary the lack of effective counter-vailing power—domestic and international—gave the communist side a largely unexpected opportunity to get its way by 1947–1948.

Elsewhere in Europe, however, the CPs allowed themselves to be eased out of the broad postwar coalition governments soon after they had joined them—in France, Italy, Belgium, Luxemburg, Austria, Norway, Denmark, Iceland, Greece, and Finland. Later on, communists have participated in the management of municipal governments in hundreds of cities and towns throughout Western Europe. Of all these countries, only in Greece did one of these communist parties make an overt move toward political hegemony. That the others did not does not mean that they did not wish to or that they might not do so in the future; but it does mean that in the face of countervailing power—be that the strength of cohesive domestic forces or the fear of external reaction—they have quite consistently opted for a cautious course and for what seemed politically feasible under the circumstances, thus accepting either minority status in coalition governments or opposition within the rules of constitutional conduct.

Therefore, the entry of communists into coalition governments does not "lead" to CP takeovers. It is a mistake to overemphasize the communists' "ultimate" objectives; surely they, like others, seek more power. It is a mistake to assume that the CPs will emerge, more or less automatically, as the eventual victors of coalition infighting; winning does not happen "automatically" in politics. And it is a mistake to identify all those who enter into coalition agreements with the CPs as collaborators or fellow travelers; in Western Europe, they were the ones who succeeded in co-opting the communists rather than the other way around.

The lesson from the East European experience is that, given the ideological distance between the CPs and the democratic parties, communists can be very difficult, even deceitful, coalition partners. Their internal cohesion and self-discipline can—and in Eastern Europe did—give them a decisive edge over their competitors. Although it did not determine the ultimate outcome, the very nature of the all-party coalition certainly helped their cause as it fostered factionalism and dissension in the ranks of the other parties. Finally, the positional advantage they derived from international conditions provided the CPs with certain resources—material and psychological—that the West consistently denied to noncommunists. All in all, then, if the all-party coalitions of Eastern Europe eventually collapsed because they no longer reflected the political needs and alignments which were operative at the time of their birth, the lesson for other polities is that all-party coalitions with communist participation can only endure if the domestic and international circumstances which produced them in the first place endure as well.

PART 2

Regional Studies: Developing Countries

Overview

Trond Gilberg

The two preceding chapters have demonstrated the problems confronting Marxist parties as they interact with other, established organizations of the left, whose leaders also claim to represent the working class and true Marxism. Under these circumstances Marxist parties have vacillated between accommodation and confrontation, between coalition formation and the disruption of established ties with other political entities.

Many of these problems stem from the fact that in Eastern and Western Europe there was a labor movement of sorts *prior* to the formation of Marxist parties. This movement, while ostensibly adhering to the class analysis of Marx and Engels, contained a number of factions which, in reality, rejected the concepts of class struggle and violent revolution; their very existence inside the labor movement belied the notion of democratic centralism. In such a context, the Marxist parties found themselves as competitors with older, established entities, whose organizational networks often exceeded that of the organized Marxists. Only under special circumstances, such as severe economic crises or military occupation by a friendly power, could some of the alleged Marxist parties obtain power. For the others, much of the political reality and environment has been hostile, thus necessitating constant struggle for political survival, with little prospect of obtaining and maintaining power.

In the world of developing countries, by contrast, the situation would seem to be different. Here, state formation is a relatively recent phenomenon (with the exception of South America); the development of groups and organizations is in its infancy; many of these young political systems have a long tradition of rule by a colonial master. Economically, there is serious underdevelopment, producing conditions which would superficially seem to foster class conflict, and hence brighten the prospects of Marxist parties.

On the other hand, nationalism is a most potent force, at least among many of the political and socioeconomic elites. This clearly poses a problem for those who call themselves Marxists in these systems.

Furthermore, any political entity in a developing country is confronted with the fluid organizational networks of early development. Groups are formed and disbanded, factions split away, and many political behavior patterns are based upon family and kinship ties, tribal loyalties, and religious beliefs. In such an unsettled political environment, who is the main ally, and who could be classified as the chief enemy? The very nature of the organizational networks in a developing system creates enormous problems for the coalition strategies and tactics of Marxist parties. These problems compound the doctrinal difficulties mentioned above.

The chapters in this section focus on these and other problems confronting Marxist parties in Central and South America, Africa, Southeast and Southwest Asia, and India.

5

Marxists and Coalitions in Latin America
John D. Martz

Throughout its history Latin America's intellectual tapestry has consisted of many interwoven intellectual fabrics. The early heritage of Spanish monism was followed in due course by the belief in individual rights enshrined by Enlightenment thought. This in turn was subsequently joined by a radical tradition which emphasized problems of social inequality. As such concerns were communicated from the Old World to the New, theorists in the latter found the process of adoption and adaptation fraught with difficulties. First came an initial familiarity with vaguely socialist ideas which preceded contact with the writings of Marx. Early antecedents included the importation of European utopian socialism, with the ideas of such figures as Saint-Simon enjoying currency in literary circles. Not until the wave of European immigrants reaching the Plate River region at the turn of the century, however, was there more than a pallid drawing-room flirtation with Marx.

Indeed, there are few references to Latin America in Marx, Engels, Lenin, or Kautsky. For Marx himself, there was but a cursory knowledge of the works of Prescott on the Mexican and Peruvian conquests. He also commented journalistically on such events as the "guerrilla war" between Mexico and the United States in the 1840s and later the European occupation of Mexico in the 1860s. The fact remained, however, that his doctrinal formulations were not greatly instructive to those in Latin American who first looked to him for guidance.[1] Consequently, Latin Americans were confronted with the task of "constructing, without guidance, an original Marxist interpretation of Latin American reality, and then promoting its acceptance in countries where very few men were well-versed in philosophy, sociology, or economics—to say nothing of dialectical materialism."[2]

Such figures as the Argentine Juan B. Justo and Uruguay's Emilio

Frugoni epitomized early efforts to interpret Marxism. As the former wrote in 1896, it was necessary to "adopt all that is science: we will be revolutionary . . . but quite unlike those false revolutionaries . . . whose sole interest is in upsetting what exists."[3] Frugoni was among those to treat socialism as broader than pure Marxism. As he put it, "socialism" was a movement answering desires for social and human justice. Thus, "Marxism is a channel, and as such it acts as a guide, but certainly a channel is not the whole river."[4] Prior to the Russian Revolution, then, Latin American *pensadores* tended to see in Marx a rather remote figure. Some were more attracted to the anarchist themes of Bakunin; the Cuban José Marti, for one, spoke of Bakunin as "tender and radiant."[5]

Until the 1917 convulsion in Russia, Latin American Marxism was largely on its own. The early socialist political organizations in some cases dated back to the 1890s, while communist parties came into being only after the October Revolution. The first such organizations were largely indigenous, with only propagandistic inspiration from Russia. The first direct influence on Latin American Marxists came from the twenty-one conditions of V. I. Lenin, adopted at the Second Congress of the Comintern in 1920. These preached victory for the Russian Revolution; creation of communist parties in all capitalist nations; membership in international socialism; the elimination of colonialism; and the use of revolution to destroy capitalism and imperialism.[6] The role of the party in raising proletarian consciousness and constructing the vanguard of the revolution soon became recognized doctrine for the Latin Americans.

Within a few years, many of the original socialist parties proceeded to divide, with majority factions choosing to affiliate with the Soviet party. Socialist parties and trade union organizations were relegated to a peripheral role. The Marxist cause became the responsibility of the communist parties. The pattern which emerged would dominate the region throughout the pre-Castro years. As we have written elsewhere:

> The furtherance of Marxism rested in the hands of the emergent Communist parties . . . [which] regularly altered and adapted their tactics in accordance with the dictates of Moscow. Through the years they have been consistent in adhering to the requirements of international events. With but a few exceptions of any real importance, the Latin-American Communists have placed the interests of their own countries second to those perceived by their Soviet comrades.[7]

Such was the tradition which took shape from 1920 on.

The Pre-Castro Era:
Orthodoxy and Obedience

The Communist Parties and Bolshevization (1920–1935)

The Latin American Communist parties swiftly came under the influence and often the direction of the Communist International. Although concerted control from the Comintern did not occur until 1924 under Zinoviev, the linkage soon tightened. The earliest communist parties were generally in nations where industrialization and the labor movement had gone furthest. The Argentines from their 1919 founding regarded themselves as a loyal Comintern affiliate; the Mexicans organized in September 1919 and the Uruguayans in October 1920, soon to be followed by the Chileans and the Brazilians. The methods followed several different paths. In Argentina and Mexico a schism within socialist organizations led to the creation of a communist party, while in Chile and Uruguay existing socialist organizations simply altered their name while adhering to the Communist International.

During the decade of the 1920s the Third International was preoccupied with regions of greater importance to the Soviet Union. Two Swiss communists, Jules Humbert-Droz and Alfred Stirner, provided some supervision from headquarters in Moscow. Of greater relevance were the occasional agents sent to recruit, proselytize, and organize. The two most prominent at the very outset were Manabendra Nath Roy and Sen Katayama. The former, an Indian who helped to found his country's communist party, first went to Mexico in 1918 and two years later helped to unite several of its minuscule groups into what became Mexico's official communist party. He traveled extensively throughout Central America in recruiting sympathizers, although formal parties did not immediately result. In effect a moderate, oriented toward socialism, he was subsequently branded a "right-wing deviationist" at the time of Bukharin's expulsion and later became an angry critic of Stalinism. The Japanese Katayama traveled even more than Roy throughout the region, and cultivated a number of youths who became influential in the 1920s and 1930s.

The move toward "bolshevization" of the world's communist parties came with the Fifth Congress of the Comintern in 1924. The basic notion was to champion the reorganization of the parties in accordance with Soviet patterns and practices, and this provoked little serious objection in Latin America. Certainly the obedience of national parties to Comintern instructions was not seriously questioned. At the same time, Latin America received a particularly low priority from a generally unconcerned

Comintern. It was thus possible for the nascent parties to practice a degree of tactical flexibility. Various methods were employed to undertake the infiltration of workers' and intellectuals' organizations, and there was care in attempting to recognize and be guided by the conditions of individual countries.

Even so, the communist parties of the region almost from their inception viewed Moscow as the mecca from which all wisdom originated. In the words of one analyst:

> Well before the struggle for Soviet leadership broke into the open in the late 1920's, the Latin American parties had adopted the custom of parroting the line of the dominant faction in the Soviet Union. It was an ingrained habit before it became compulsory for Latin American Communists to look upon the Soviet-dominated Comintern as the final arbiter in ideological and other disputes within their organizations . . . . After 1929 those individuals unwilling to accept decisions reached in Moscow were purged, and the Latin American parties lost all semblance of independent existence.[8]

The trend toward bolshevization became far more pronounced at the Sixth Comintern Congress in 1928, at which representatives from eight Latin American countries were present.[9] The dominant attitude of Soviet authorities commanded a large degree of ideological and tactical rigidity which would mark the Latin American experience for years to come. While the as yet unpurged Bukharin, presiding over the meeting, declared that "Latin America now enters, for the first time, into the sphere of the Comintern's influence,"[10] Soviet interest was still limited. There was little discussion of Latin American affairs; rather, a commission was named to prepare a report. It subsequently stated that revolution in Latin America required communist parties, revolutionary labor organizations, and the incorporation of agricultural workers.

It was further assumed that the national bourgeoisies of Latin America were weak, serving as mere appendages of British and North American imperialism. Specific steps were prescribed for the strengthening of existing political parties. These included organizational emphasis on the party, the proselytizing of industrial and agricultural workers, and an intensification of ideological indoctrination. The result, it was held, would be bourgeois-democratic revolution throughout the hemisphere. In point of fact, no such revolutions were to follow. Nevertheless, bolshevization set in progressively, as strikingly illustrated by two important meetings held in 1929. First was a gathering of communist trade union representatives from across Latin America at Montevideo, Uruguay, in May of 1929. This was followed immediately by the First Conference of Latin American Communist Parties in Buenos Aires.

The first was viewed as recognition from Moscow that Latin America had some significance. Attended by assorted Comintern and European labor leaders, the Montevideo conference brought into being the Latin American Trade Union Confederation. While it later proved of negligible importance, the symbolic value in 1929 was undeniable. The Buenos Aires conference ran from June 1 to June 12, 1929, with twenty-eight delegates from fourteen Latin American parties. Extended discussions included such topics as recruitment problems among the urban middle classes; the need for unity regarding the peasantry; and the matter of race. This last was particularly contentious, with contradictory perspectives resulting in a failure to adopt specific theses. There were valiant if unconvincing efforts to conceal the weakness of the communist movement hemispherically. Delegates announced memberships which were far from realistic; e.g., the Mexicans claimed a membership of two thousand, when no more than four-hundred had been reported as marchers in the May Day parade.

Whereas the Latin American parties in their earliest years had been willing to seek political alliances—rarely with success, to be sure—after 1928 they were dominated increasingly by the tactical guidance of the Soviet Union. A greater degree of rigidity was accompanied by the doctrinal insistence that new governments would be based on so-called soviets of workers, peasants, and soldiers. Party discipline was given greater emphasis. Individual parties could pursue power either through electoral or insurrectionary methods, but never might they compromise in order to ally with non-Marxist organizations. The parties consequently found themselves isolated from national politics and riddled with their own internal dissension.

The aggressiveness of the communist parties was generally self-defeating. In Argentina, for instance, the communists attacked both the socialists and the Radical party government in 1929 and 1930 as imperialists and fascists, ultimately helping to destroy the constitutional system and usher in true fascism under military rule. In Mexico the communists, following Moscow's command, supported a military uprising in the northern region as a means of establishing soviets. Contrary to expectations, however, the government did not crumble; it responded by expelling party officials and suppressing the organization. Still another example of insensitive rigidity came in Cuba, where the 1924–1933 Machado dictatorship was overthrown. The Cuban communists condemned all the revolutionary forces as fascist and instruments of Yankee imperialism. "Thus the spectacle was offered of a revolutionary and nationalistic government, to which

Washington was refusing diplomatic recognition as a radical and communist government, being fought, at the same time, by the communists as a lackey of Yankee imperialism."[11]

One case in which greater flexibility was exercised came from Chile, where the party had gained some influence over the workers' Federación Obrera de Chile (FOCH). In the 1925 elections the party backed a reformist democratic candidate for president, in the process winning two senate and seven deputy seats. Within two years the growing repression of the government had been brought to bear, and by the close of the decade the Communist Party of Chile divided over tactical questions. The schism became public when the Ibáñez dictatorship was overthrown in July 1931. The proclamation on 4 June 1932 of a self-styled "socialist state" under Colonel Marmaduke Grove was opposed by the communists, who termed the short-lived movement sheer bourgeois demagoguery. In the final analysis, the anticoalition Comintern line, along with the fallout over the Stalinist-Trotskyite struggle, helped to assure yet another failure.

The Popular Front and World War II (1935–1945)

By 1935 the doctrinal and tactical poverty of bolshevization had become evident. Moscow replaced its previous emphasis on exclusivity with a collaborative approach designed to help deter the threat of European fascism. For the Latin Americans, problems were recognized by a self-critical report published in May of 1935. It cited communist parties' inadequacies in developing a mass movement and organizing the proletariat. Another failing to be cited was ideological immaturity and, in some instances, an inability to work with non-Marxist reformists. The communist parties had thereby: "underestimated the special importance of bourgeois national reformism, which has great influence over the petty bourgeoisie, peasantry, and even over the working class in Latin America. As a result of this, they frequently adopted a "neutral" position when big mass struggle took place, fell into a neutral attitude, and isolated themselves from the masses of the toilers at times when big political events took place."[12]

When the Seventh Comintern Congress met in Moscow in August of that same year, the tactic of the Popular Front was advanced, while it was proclaimed that "many of our comrades in Latin America have characterized nearly all the bourgeois and petty bourgeois parties as fascists, thus hindering the establishment of an anti-fascist Popular Front."[13] With the announcement of a new tactical approach, the Latin Americans were prompt to respond. Once again they looked to Soviet interpretations of Marxist dogma for guidance. Increasingly the more creative and imaginative Marxist thinkers in Latin America found themselves shunned or stigmatized for any challenge to the official ideology of international communism.

The tactic of the Popular Front stressed the need to work with other parties and organizations. The most striking instance was that of Chile, where Moscow dispatched the Peruvian Eudocio Ravines soon after the close of the Seventh Comintern Congress. Following official acceptance of the policy to seek accommodation with bourgeois parties, Chile's communists in March of 1936 joined with the socialists, dissident communists, the centrist Radical party, and the Democrats to constitute an official Popular Front. The communists also cooperated with non-Marxist and socialist labor organizations. In the 1937 congressional elections the Popular Front led its competition while the communists placed one senator and seven deputies. The next year they joined in support of the victorious presidential candidate, Pedro Aguirre Cerda. After having exerted major influence inside the Popular Front on behalf of the Aguirre Cerda candidacy, they shrewdly refused to join the government or to accept ministerial posts. Thus the communists laid claim to having elected the government while standing apart as a sharp critic. The party secretary-general, Carlos Contreras Labarca, provided the rationale for what proved a shrewd move politically:

> The Communist Party declares that its inviolable and exemplary fidelity to the Popular Front . . . has never been inspired by the wish to obtain any participation in the government. . . . The Communist Party considers that its responsibility in carrying out this program can be fulfilled outside the government. . . . Consequently, it leaves the Popular Front entirely free to decide, in the best interests of the people, what executive tasks may devolve upon the Communist Party.[14]

The communist position was an obvious contrast to that of Chile's socialists, whose electoral strength was greater. The two groups—whose competition has survived in one form or another to the present—amply illustrated the pragmatically based political judgments which helped to divide them. For the socialists, a major role in governmental responsibility, along with an opportunity to strengthen their electoral appeal, justified participation in the executive. The communists saw it differently, all the time challenging the socialists for hegemony in the labor movement. Additionally, their effort to remain true to the drastic shifts of Soviet policy —including the short-lived Hitler-Stalin pact from August 1939 to June 1941—further underlined the basis for their major policy decisions.

Chile's socialists, who gradually lost ground to the communists within the labor movement during this period, first sought to force the communists out of the Popular Front before themselves withdrawing from the administration in January 1941. Two months later the communists' tactics were rewarded when the party more than tripled its previous high in congressional elections, resulting in the addition of three senators and fourteen deputies. With Hitler's attack on the Soviet Union, Chile's communists shifted position swiftly while continuing to press the divided socialists. When the latter struggled over the relative ambitions of party founder Marmaduke Grove and the skillful Secretary-General Salvador Allende, the communists furthered their own interests, especially inside the labor movement. Strengthening their influence inside the leftist coalition, which was renamed the Democratic Alliance after the November 1941 death of President Aguirre Cerda, the communists increased both membership and political influence.

Their high-water mark was realized in the wake of the September 1946 presidential elections, wherein Gabriel González Videla assumed the presidency with a Radical/Liberal/Communist coalition. The socialists had for the time been eclipsed, while the Communist party received three posts in the nine-member cabinet. Within five months the cabinet fell and the communists went over into opposition. The onset of the cold war led in 1948 to adoption of the so-called Law for the Defense of Democracy, which outlawed the party and removed some forty thousand registered communist voters from the electoral lists. Nonetheless, the impact of the party during the Popular Front period was undeniable. Its tactical approach had served the party better than that of the socialists, although both had based their political decisions on short-term, opportunistic considerations rather than basic doctrinal teachings.

Cuba's Popular Front experience was also instructive. Having failed to work with antisystem elements during the uprisings of the early 1930s, the communists subsequently demonstrated their willingness to cooperate even with the political right. This was to produce an understanding with Fulgencio Batista, at that time the effective power behind the presidential chair. Their tacit alliance with Batista produced the legalization of the party in 1938, the first time in the party's thirteen-year history. The Popular Front outlook was suggested by the words of long-time party secretary-general Blas Roca at the January 1939 Third National Congress of the party.

> We fight for the unity of the people of Cuba, for the unity of the revolutionaries, and for a great united front, to realize immediately an urgent practical program; . . . for defense of the national

economy; for defense of our country from Nazi-fascist invasion; help for Spain and China; collaboration with the democratic countries, etc.[15]

With flexibility the order of the day, the party joined with a one-time renegade communist group to establish the Unión Revolucionaria Comunista (URC), which in due course competed in the 1940 elections for a Constituent Assembly.

This produced official party support for the presidential candidacy of Fulgencio Batista as a member of the misnamed Socialist Democratic Coalition. The communists gained ten seats in the Chamber of Deputies and over one hundred city councilmen throughout the island. More importantly, the party advanced its cause in the labor movement, and by the mid-1940s constituted the single most powerful influence within the national Confederación de Trabajadores de Cuba (CTC). The party also increased its membership from some 23,000 in 1934 to 122,000 by 1944. When Batista unexpectedly stood aside for the 1944 elections, his own handpicked successor was defeated by Ramón Grau San Martin. While this was a setback for the communists, the party soon recovered to negotiate a modus vivendi with Grau. The conciliatory attitude so effective with Batista was turned toward the new president. Cooperation between the communists and Grau's *auténticos* within the CTC was negotiated, and in the 1946 congressional elections the communists entered a coalition with the *auténticos*. The alliance also led to the selection of the communists' Juan Marinello as vice-president of the Senate.

The Popular Front attitude and mentality unquestionably registered throughout the hemisphere, and Argentina perhaps was typical in the extent to which it shaped communist activities, yet did not substantially alter the course of national political affairs. Consistent with the Popular Front line, the Argentine Communist party in 1937 backed the presidential candidacy of Marcelo T. de Alvear, a former president running for the traditionalistic Radical party. When he was defeated by the military-backed Roberto Ortiz, the party swiftly sought to mend its fences with the new chief executive. It praised his presumed commitment to a "moderate democratic government," while attacking his opponents as representatives of the oligarchy. Leaning heavily on antifascist declarations, the party under its hemispherically influenced Victorio Codovilla was weakened by the 1943 military coup, and then by the emergence of their bitter enemy, Juan Domingo Perón.

Even so, the communists improved their political standing and, with 1945 legalization for electoral purposes, increased its membership while polling over 150,000 votes in the February 1946 elections. Their later setbacks within the labor movement reflected less the communist political or doctrinal position than the skill of Perón. Elsewhere, the hemisphere reflected the fact that revolutionary and reformist forces had been stimulated by the experience of World War II and the championing of the Four Freedoms by pro-Allied propaganda. For the Marxist organizations, the looming potential for what would become the cold war between the Soviet Union and the United States underlined the strategic and tactical questions which lay ahead. The prospects for alliances and for coalition building—so widely and effectively employed during the Popular Front years—were to be dimmed by the frigidity of the cold war.

The Cold War Years (1945–1959)

Through the years of World War II, the communist parties had maintained the conciliatory attitude which had stemmed from the Popular Front experience. Earl Browder, the North American party leader, had been forceful in championing a willingness to work with capitalist governments. However, he was expelled in 1945 and the veritable honeymoon with the United States swiftly drew to a close. The Cominform was established in 1947, four years after the demise of the Comintern. Among its principles was a strong opposition to the United States and to democratic governments generally. For Latin America, the tactic to be adopted became known as "critical support," although the term ironically had been adopted by Latin American Trotskyites.

This notion permitted a pragmatism which was intended to recognize local conditions as an element in building organizational strength. Although some twenty communist parties existed at the close of World War II, several were so weak as to be moribund. "Critical support" was envisaged not as a re-creation of unwavering radicalism, but rather as a tactical approach to the cold war. Governments that opposed U.S. policies or supported even indirectly the Soviet Union in world affairs received encouragement without regard to their own ideological outlook. Local communist parties were also joined by renewed activity from such tactical allies as groups of students and intellectuals.

Orthodox communists attempted increasingly to work through intermediaries. Emphasis was placed on international "peace" movements and congresses, while propaganda efforts through Eastern European embassies were stepped up. There was greater attention toward pro-Soviet sentiment than toward pure Marxism; in similar fashion, the writings of Marx and Lenin were displaced in favor of tracts by Stalin. Of fundamental importance was a relentless anti-imperialism deliberately pointed toward the United States. Just as the latter reflected cold war rivalries in such accords as the Rio Treaty of 1947 and in anticommunist resolutions adopted by Inter-American Conferences, so did the Soviet Union shape its approach within the same context of international conflict.

If United States policy and the East-West rivalry were important in the shaping of communist strategy and tactics, the same could be said of the rising social and political fervor in postwar Latin America. The promising economic situation which existed in 1945 gradually gave way to pessimism and disillusionment, especially as North American priorities focused initially on the recovery of Europe, only to be redirected by 1950 to the Far East. As Aguilar wrote, Latin America was beset with familiar "agrarian, industrial, and social conflicts," which produced a feeling of neglect "by its great northern neighbor, whose sole preoccupation seemed to be to assure anti-Communist postures."[16] Economic debates over capitalism and world imperialism thereby accompanied the growing hemispheric discontent in the postwar period.

There was also a growing fragmentation of Marxist organization, with orthodox communist parties less hegemonic than in earlier years. In Mexico, for example, the eminent trade unionist Vicente Lombardo Toledano in 1947 established the Marxist Partido Popular, whose members numbered many of the most prominent intellectuals in the country. It differed from the communist party in its willingness to collaborate with the government; on international affairs, there was no significant difference between the two. During the same period in Venezuela, there was a manufactured division of the communist party into "black" and "red" factions. One collaborated with the military dictatorship inside the country, while the other opposed it from involuntary exile. Unsurprisingly, both opposed the nation's most popular organization, the outlawed social democratic party Acción Democrática (AD).

The rise of factionalism and doctrinal conflict also became increasingly evident during the cold war years. In addition to Machiavellian maneuvers such as the deliberate division of the Venezuelan party, many of the most respected and creative Marxists were intellectuals who rejected the classic obedience of the parties to the international communist movement. In addition, vestiges of Trotskyism further compounded the picture. Bolivia was a striking case, where three rival groups had taken shape by the decade of the 1950s. Not until December 1949 was an official communist party proclaimed. In the meantime the Partido de Izquierda Revolucionaria (PIR) had grown from a youth movement, also claiming the name Communist party. Amid this power struggle, The Trotskyite Partido

Obrero Revolucionario (POR) centered its efforts on the trade union movement. In 1954, two years after the moderate nationalist seizure of power by reformists, the POR itself divided into three groups.

For the Trotskyites in Bolivia and elsewhere—small in number but quite vocal prior to the Cuban Revolution—the orthodox communist parties were Stalinist deviationists existing for the benefit of the Soviet Union. As such they constituted an obstacle to proletarian revolution. Similar in these criticisms to many nonparty Marxists but more virulent in tone, they remained an annoyance to the larger, traditionalistic organizations. The venom of Trotskyite attacks were only to be matched in the 1960s by the language engendered by rival interpretations of the Cuban Revolution. Sample the words of a Bolivian published in 1961 by the Liga Socialista Revolucionaria:

> The Communist Party has established an unqualified reputation for servility, impudence, and political irresponsibility. In truth, no other result could be expected. . . .
>
> Neither the Fourth International nor Moscow will lead the world revolution—because they are worn-out instruments, incapable of taking over power, and in their hands the revolutionary movement is immobilized, impotent, and submits to the leadership of other classes—unless they change their tactics in the struggle, renew their cadres and eliminate their corrupt hierarchies, which would seem, frankly, to be even more difficult.[17]

These postwar years, then, were marked by doctrinal and personalistic divisions which generally weakened both the Marxist movement and, most particularly, the traditional communist parties. For the latter, the attacks by nonparty Marxists were accompanied by the sometimes flexible and customarily opportunistic tactics of the moment. In this sense a modicum of "Popular Frontism" had endured. It proved most effective in Guatemala, the prime instance of Marxist penetration into governing circles prior to Cuba. Traditionally the preserve of one or another repressive dictator, Guatemala had begun to experience political openness only after 1944. As the process unfolded, the small nascent group of young Marxists had formed a clandestine organization in September 1948. Three years passed until the creation of a so-called workers' party; a merger with other mini-parties produced the Partido Guatemalteco de Trabajadores (PGT) in late 1952. It joined with labor and peasant organizations in a "national democratic front" supporting the presidential candidacy of former army colonel Jacobo Arbenz Guzmán.

Following his victory in an uncontested election, the politically inexperienced and pliant Arbenz was influenced increasingly by both reformist and Marxist advisors. The PGT itself became the major political organization on the underdeveloped Guatemalan scene. It gradually extended its reach to a variety of front organizations, as well as government agencies. Alliances with non-Marxist groups were pursued vigorously, while personal friendships with Arbenz and his closest advisors were cemented. In addition, the controversial Agrarian Reform Law of 1953—in content no more extreme than its long-established Mexican counterpart—provided the opportunity for Communist loyalists to secure administrative positions in the Instituto Nacional de Reforma Agraria (INRA) and affiliated offices.

For the Guatemalan communists, who did not pursue appointment to ministerial-level positions, the goal was the encouragement of anti–United States policies. In the interests of maximizing anti-*yanqui* sentiment, they sought to shape the policies of a government brought into power by non-Marxist forces. The official party itself never surpassed some four thousand members, while the number to be politically active was even smaller. For a time there were such transitory successes as pro-Soviet votes in the United Nations, anti-imperialist pronouncements at OAS meetings, and vocal support for peace conferences which alleged U.S. bacteriological warfare in the Korean War. Nevertheless, international factors proved decisive. Both the regime and the political system were weak, and the United States action in 1954 to unleash the Central Intelligence Agency easily brought down what was always an indecisive and ineffective government.[18] The Guatemalan Communists paid a price, although the episode yielded propaganda benefits for the Soviet Union. Orthodoxy and obedience to the Soviet Union had been paramount. This was to change drastically with the coming of the Cuban Revolution.

The Post-Castro Era: Heresy and Conflict

The Impact of the Cuban Revolution

Latin America will never again be as it was prior to January 1959 and the ascendance of Fidel Castro and his Twenty-sixth of July Movement to power in Cuba. Neither will hemispheric Marxism be the same; communist party orthodoxy was shaken to its very roots. In Cuba itself, the Castro-led insurgency was not initially Marxist. Neither was there either cooperation or cordiality between Castro and the orthodox Cuban Communist party, which dated from 1924. Indeed, by the 1950s a comfortable understanding had been negotiated by the party and the long-time strongman Fulgencio Batista, whose corrupt dictatorship was the target of the Twenty-sixth of July Movement, among other opposition groups.

Juan Marinello, Blas Roca, and Carlos Rafael Rodríguez had been dominant party figures whose tacit acceptance of Batista's rule had been evident as early as 1938, when the latter stood behind the presidential chair. Marinello at one point was a Batista cabinet minister, and after 1952 the communist-influenced labor movement eschewed strikes or demonstrations against the regime. When Fidel Castro attempted to call down an urban strike against Batista in April 1958, the communists (then known as the Partido Socialista Popular—PSP) had refused. Rather, they reiterated doctrinal orthodoxy about the industrial proletariat as the revolutionary vanguard; Castro was a petty-bourgeois adventurer with no sense of class consciousness. Only late in 1958 did the PSP dispatch Rodríguez to the Sierra Maestra to establish contact with Castro. When the *fidelista* movement achieved power, it had done so without an important role having been played by the Cuban communists; neither had it in any meaningful sense been Marxist at the time.

This fact has been amply documented. A typical statement was that of Castro himself in May 1959, when he protested: "I don't know why the slanders against our revolution that it is Communist, that it is infiltrated with communism. Can anyone think that we conceal obscure designs?"[19] Whatever the later controversies over the origins of the Castro movement, it had not seized power under Marxist banners. The doctrinal evolution of subsequent years goes beyond our present scope. In terms of continental symbolism, however, the very nature of the Cuban revolutionary struggle produced widely varying interpretations by Marxists and non-Marxists alike. This inevitably provoked rather different approaches to the seizure of power, several variants of which are analyzed below in "Paths to Power."

For the moment, however, suffice it to note that hemispheric repercussions—magnified in the early 1960s through Cuban efforts to export revolution—ranged from unyielding admiration to sharply critical assessments which attacked the apparent deviation from traditional Marxist orthodoxy. Thus the Cubans and their followers called upon the seizure of power by violent means, rejecting a gradualistic approach as a defeatist ignoring of Latin American experience. For pro-Moscow loyalists, it was argued that the building of socialism required the existence of objective conditions and a patiently lengthy process whereby a peaceful transition would ultimately reward the faithful. For several years the powerful ideological dispute unleashed by the very fact of the revolution centered less on methods of governing, or of coalition building with other organizations, than upon the forcible mounting of guerrilla insurgency.

As the ideological apostle of the Cuban Revolution, Ernesto "Ché" Guevara scorned the traditional communist view favoring a peaceful transition in Latin America. He was similarly unpersuaded by contentions that so-called "objective" conditions were necessary. Rather, he focused on the presence of "subjective" factors, most basic of which was an awareness of the possibilities available via the road of violence. Certain about the outcome of revolutionary change, he contended that the degradation of individual and collective life in Latin America was an assurance of true revolutionary upheaval. Fundamentally, then, Guevara reinterpreted Marxism to emphasize the varying importance of prerevolutionary conditions.

Perhaps his best known and in some ways most lasting prescriptions are those dealing with armed conflict. These are largely spelled out in what constituted a detailed instructional guide to the tactical and technical aspects of guerrilla warfare.[20] Of special significance here, Guevara saw the hemispheric lessons of the Cuban Revolution as stressing two major points: first, the experience was but the first of many forthcoming anticolonialist, anti-imperialist movements and, second, it was illustrative of the proper road to meaningful revolution. The degree to which the Cuban Revolution provided a model for the hemisphere further occupied Guevara's concern, including a sometimes convoluted effort to stress the charisma of Castro and the idiosyncracies of the Cuban experience without denigrating the implications for revolutionaries across the continent.[21]

Ultimately the 1967 death of Guevara as he was leading a romantically quixotic and pragmatically impossible quest for revolution in Bolivia assured his place in the pantheon of Latin Americans who, whatever their ideology, protested the ills and injustices of the societies in which they lived. The idealistic strain in Guevara's intellectual and personal makeup also emerged in his discussions of the human goals of socialism. As he put it in a 1965 letter, the true revolutionary should be guided by sentiments of love:

> We can see the new man who begins to emerge in this period of the building of socialism. His image is as yet unfinished, since the process advances parallel to the development of new economic forms. . . .
>
> The vanguards have their eye on the future and its recompenses, but the latter are not envisioned as something individual; the reward is the new society, where human beings will have different characteristics; the new society of communist man.[22]

Whatever Guevara's theoretical strengths and weaknesses, he stands today as an opponent of Marxist sectarianism who recognized that the Cuban Revolution often diverged from classical Marxist theory. "He considered all of Latin America his native country and viewed the Cuban revolution as the first part of a larger struggle to eventually embrace and emancipate the entire region."[23] In both intellectual and practical terms, Guevara and his interpretation of the Cuban Revolution provided inspiration for what may be called the "New Left." While its antecedents included nineteenth-century socialism, idealism, and anarchism, the doctrinal breeze created in Cuba was to have an energizing effect on Latin American Marxism of the 1960s and thereafter.

The Rise of the New Left

Somewhat illogically, the leading follower of Guevara was the French Marxist Régis Debray, today an "establishment" advisor to François Mitterrand but twenty years ago an ambitiously adventurous soldier of fortune. None of his voluminous writings in recent years have captured an audience as did the singular if eminently naive *Revolution in the Revolution?* He was especially critical of Marxist orthodoxy linked to "Popular Frontism," as well as denouncing past failures of communist parties. His view of the Latin American organizations was scarcely gentle, as Debray made clear. "Each one [of the Latin American communist parties] may have its own history but they are alike in that they have not, since their founding, lived through the experience of winning power in the way the Chinese and Vietnamese parties have; they have not had the opportunity, existing as they do in countries possessing formal political independence, of leading a war of national liberation; and they have therefore not been able to achieve the worker-peasant alliance—an interrelated aggregation of limitations arising from shared historical conditions."[24]

Debray also took the occasion to denounce Trotskyism in Latin America, angrily dissecting notions of peasant self-defense. He depicted Trotskyite doctrine as unrealistically based on a presumably spontaneous awakening of consciousness, leading to uprisings in city and countryside. Peasant organizations would be attacking rural holdings while urban workers seized control of urban means of production. The Frenchman saw all of this as utopian in projecting a direct passage from union action to mass insurrection. Reliance on an insurrection of brief duration was equally unrealistic, producing a fragmentation of revolutionary forces. Trotskyism would lead to isolation from the masses. Bluntly, "The Trotskyist conception of insurrection resembles self-defense: both provocative, both acting in the name of the masses. . . . The masses are the scapegoats. These fine theoreticians lead them to suicide, singing hymns to their glory."[25]

Debray, despite his international notoriety, was neither experienced nor knowledgeable about Latin America. More sensitive and better informed declarations came from a host of Latin American Marxists, many of whom were outside the ranks of organized parties. Elsewhere we identified the characteristics which emerged from the writings of the New Left. Among the more important were: stress on broad-based popular movements rather than formal party organizations; reliance on armed struggle and violence rather than a peaceful transition to socialism; the inevitability of creating "revolutionary conditions" via guerilla activity; faith in peasant-supported rural movements; and an ideological independence from international communism.[26] In some instances, exponents had been reflective of the 1950s radicalism which actually predated the Cuban Revolution. Colombia's Luis Emiro Valencia and the Venezuelan Domingo Alberto Rangel were representative figures.

The first had penned impassioned nationalistic studies of the Colombian economy and social system and advocated a peasant-worker alliance, sweeping nationalization, and rural insurrection, accompanied by a united urban working class as prerequisites for the establishment of socialism. The Venezuelan Rangel, a former youth leader of the reformist party Acción Democrática, had written in 1958 that a capitalist alliance with the United States should be supplanted by a socialist regime. He maintained that the need for class struggle and a rejuvenated drive for worker domination had been diluted by the populism of centrist parties after the 1958 overthrow of the military dictatorship. In later years he became a widely read, muckraking iconoclast who to this day inveighs against the bourgeois democracy of his homeland. His role as a political and social critic has been accompanied by a weakening of Marxist purity in his writings.

The presumed model of Cuba as interpreted by the New Left also registered its impact on political actions. A case in point was Luis F. de la Puente Uceda of Peru, who accepted the thesis of creating subjective conditions. As he saw it, "we start from the idea that conditions are not fully ripe, but the beginning of the insurrectional process will be the triggering factor leading to their development in ways which no one can now foresee. Moreover, it must be stressed that if such subjective conditions have not attained their necessary ripeness, this is partly due to the inability of the leftist parties and groups to foster and cultivate the ground."[27] He proceeded to form his Movimiento de Izquierda Revolucionaria (MIR) as the tool for guerrilla warfare in the Andean highlands. This was designed to consolidate as a popular, anti-oligarchic and anti-imperialist movement which would lay the foundations for the building of socialism in Peru. The undertaking foundered when he was killed in December of 1965. Soon thereafter a rival group was defeated by army troops—one led by Hugo Blanco, an avowed Trotskyite.

In Colombia the priest Camilo Torres was prominent for a time. By training a sociologist who never fully embraced a Marxist vision of Colombian society, Torres initially advocated formation of a popular party which would pursue agricultural cooperatives, urban collectivism, the abolition of free enterprise, and worker ownership and participation in industry. Frustrated in the attempt, he took to the mountains in October 1965, declaring that "The Catholic who is not a revolutionary is living in mortal sin."[28] Killed in battle only four months later, he presaged the emergence of Liberation theologians in more recent years. As Sheldon Liss writes, "Camilo's thought and actions led other priests and theologians to the use of social science techniques and scientific Marxist methodology."[29]

Far more melodramatic was the fatal failure of Guevara himself in his Bolivian insurrectionary campaign. His difficulties, as chronicled in his diary, reflected a host of tactical and quasi-military problems which ran contrary to his writings on guerrilla warfare. A few days before his capture and killing, Guevara lamented that the Bolivian peasants had not provided the necessary support and assistance; the revolutionary zeal and morale of his forces—largely Cubans and hence alien to Bolivian highland Indians —had reached a low point. Yet Guevara believed to the end that, despite conditions, the insurrectionary *foco* could be created. As Jay Mallin remarked, Ché Guevara chose Bolivia and "set out to prove his theory, and he failed, and as a result of his failure, he died."[30]

Toward the close of the 1960s, with Guevara and Torres among those whose lives had been lost in guerrilla struggles, Latin American Marxists began turning once again toward an emphasis on electoral combat. Nonetheless, the writings of the New Left were not so easily extinguished, nor was tactical and strategic orthodoxy completely restored. In psychological terms, the symbolism of the Cuban Revolution had touched Latin American imaginations eager for presumably new and more efficacious means to rectify historical ills. Luis Aguilar put it eloquently: "The Latin American New Left is being taught that Castro's victory shows that extremism is no longer an infantile disease, that heroism and enthusiasm need no allies, that a small band of fighters is capable of creating the subjective conditions for revolutionary victory, that the leftist parties in the cities should not be trusted, that a ratio of one against five hundred makes the guerrilla invincible."[31]

Predictably, many of the sharpest critics of the New Left were old-line

Muscovites affiliated with the traditionalistic parties. For them, heresy had been committed in the eagerness to embrace the Cuban Revolution, which for them was a unique historical event not susceptible to repetition elsewhere. Conflicts, controversies, and venomous diatribes marked the dialogue. Rejection of the Cuban model as applicable elsewhere was challenged, for example, by the Peruvian Jorge del Prado. In his view the mass support necessary for revolution was absent in Peru, and a lengthy program of recruitment and proselytizing was required. The Guatemalan Alfredo Guerra Borges also praised the Cubans but insisted that conditions in his own country were not conducive to insurrection.

A striking exchange which effectively documents the nature of the ideological and tactical conflict was provided by events immediately after the 1967 meeting of the Cuban-sponsored Latin American Organization of Solidarity (OLAS). In response to *fidelista* declarations, the Colombian and Venezuelan communist parties issued a joint statement premised on the belief that it was "not possible to forge a single political line, a single tactic and method of struggle to be applied in every country." In their own cases it was necessary to collaborate with "democratic" movements in building broad, electorally oriented united fronts. Thus the two communist parties, "faithful to their revolutionary duties, believed that, working within the framework of the particular conditions existing in their respective countries, they should guide the struggle of their peoples against their enemies —imperialism and oligarchy." Finally, mutual respect and noninterference in the affairs of other parties were "rules which should be strictly followed."[32]

There were also thinkers who applied critical reasoning to both orthodox and New Left perspectives. Jorge Abelardo Ramos, an independent-minded Argentine who criticized Stalin and had praise for both Lenin and Trotsky, envisaged a popular workers' state as best serving revolutionary socialism. A member of the younger generation of Argentine Marxists, he advocated a combination of parliamentary politics with unionization and, if conditions were favorable, guerrilla activity. Denying the *guevarista* argument that revolutionary circumstances could be created if necessary, he insisted that the urban working class was no less crucial than the peasant. For Ramos, Cuba was to be admired, but constituted an exceptional rather than typical revolutionary model. Liberation of a semicolonial country such as Argentina required an understanding of its historic traditions: "Only the Latin American proletariat can become the guide and leader of the huge peasant masses or of the petty bourgeoisie in the struggle for economic independence, national unity and socialism."[33]

By the close of the decade the Soviet invasion of Czechoslovakia had further fragmented the unity of Latin American Marxism. More than a few of the communist parties divided over the issue, in most cases with the younger members departing to form their own organizations. Venezuela's Teodoro Petkoff, for example, denounced the Venezuelan party with the publication of an angry *Checoslovaquia, el socialismo como problems*. By 1970 he had led the formation of the new Movimiento al Socialismo (MAS). Petkoff's calls for nonviolent movement toward socialism has come to resemble Eurocommunism, adopting a Leninist expectation that revolution would first be democratic-bourgeois and only later become socialist. By the time Petkoff ran futilely as the MAS presidential candidate in 1983, his actions were more akin to democratic socialism than to the more rigorous doctrinal stance of his younger years. His repeat candidacy in 1988 underlined Petkoff's bourgeois proclivities.

The ideological and tactical heresies of the Cuban Revolution, in sum, gained respectability over time. The partial sovietization of the Castro regime further complicated the picture, as did other events of international communism. Tactics and strategy became more heterogeneous in Latin America, especially as the difficulties of armed rebellion were underscored by failures in Bolivia, Peru, Venezuela, and elsewhere. Both the orthodox and the less traditionalistic Marxist parties began to display greater flexibility, with a concomitant willingness to experiment as might seem suitable for their particular circumstances. The most intriguing case was that of the 1970–1973 Chilean government of Salvador Allende Gossens. Tactical and strategic issues concerning alliances, coalitions, and methods of seizing power appeared in stark contrast to the *fidelista*, New Left approach.

Electoral Tactics and the Lessons of Chile

Salvador Allende, a cofounder of Chile's Socialist party in 1933, spent much of his career pursuing its self-definition as revolutionary, anticapitalist, and class-oriented. He reiterated a belief that "revolutionary" denoted a radical change in the social order through a popular democratizing process. This rested upon his unflagging conviction in the feasibility of charting a nonviolent course to socialism. "We have said that we are going to create a democratic, national, revolutionary and popular Government which will open the road to socialism because socialism cannot be imposed by decree. All the measures . . . lead to the revolution."[34] Multiple approaches were feasible, depending upon national circumstances; for Chile, however, Allende never wavered.

First elected to the Chamber of Deputies in 1937 and later becoming minister of health for the Popular Front of President Aguirre Cerda in 1939, he came to believe that his party's support for Popular Front rule was a distraction from its ultimate goal. Viewing the democratizing influence of World War II as a fortuitous boost to socialism, he proceeded into the late 1950s with what he called the "Thesis of the Workers' Front." This forbade any accord with middle class or reformist political parties; only alliances with working-class parties were acceptable. As a consequence, the stance of the Chilean Socialist party in its early years hardened and narrowed. The need for indigenous doctrine and tactics was emphasized. The result was what Allende described as a "Chilean Road to Socialism"—a Marxist interpretation of history based upon the nation's historical traditions.[35]

In both the 1964 and 1970 presidential elections, then, Allende ran at the head of a multiparty Unidad Popular coalition which included the Socialists, Chile's Communist party, and several quasi-Marxist miniparties. Winning power with a narrow victory in 1970, he viewed the outcome as one more step along the path to socialism. Observing that Chile would be experimenting with new forms of political and socioeconomic organization, he directed greater attention to the tactics and techniques of solidifying authority during what was presumably a transitional period. With political freedom upheld as a prerequisite for social freedom, he underlined the importance of the unity of the masses. When the working class would gain control of the entire state—as always, using institutional means—the class struggle could be resolved. Coalition on the left was basic. Only in the final desperate days of summer 1973, however, did he return to an acceptance of informal accord with reformist parties.

Viewed in 1970 by many Marxists as a fallen idol who was little more than a disguised social democrat, Allende gambled on Chile's heritage of democracy and constitutional legitimacy. Not for Allende was the method to be one of arming the workers or turning a unified lower class against the establishment and its military defenders. In Marxist-Leninist terms, as Liss aptly writes, Allende's experiment was doomed from the outset:

> He tried to build socialism from above, beginning without a revolutionary situation or a vanguard capable of dealing with the reactionary forces. *Unidad Popular* had no ideological unity beyond the belief that it could gradually transfer power from the bourgeoisie to the workers by using the machinery of the state to alter the nation's infrastructure, thereby weakening the upper and middle-class hold on it.[36]

The tactics of the *Unidad Popular*, notwithstanding ultimate failure, were strongly shaped by the actions of the moderate Communist party, which constituted the backbone of both electoral coalitions. It sought internal unity, attempted to mobilize popular support, and defended constitutional practices, whether for opportunistic or doctrinal reasons. Far more than the disunited Socialist party—the left wing of which was largely beyond Allende's effective control—the communists urged caution and moderation rather than violence or radicalism which would alienate middle-class groups. Thus the communists shared with Allende the view that the welfare of the masses required a full and open quest for individual potential. In Allende's words:

> The building of the new social regime is based on the people, who are its protagonist and its judge. It is up to the State to guide, organize and direct but never to replace the will of the workers. In the economic as well as in the political field, the workers must retain the right to decide. To attain this means the triumph of the Revolution.[37]

The communists also more clearly backed his insistence upon moderation in the face of open defiance by the ultraleftist Movimiento de Izquierda Revolucionaria (MIR). Refusing to join the coalition but attempting to push it ever further to the left through such actions as illegal land seizures, the MIR demonstrated the tactical dispersion of Chilean Marxism while producing strong criticism from the pro-coalition communists. Cole Blasier quotes the Soviets as describing how "the Chilean Communist Party repeatedly unmasked the traitorous and provocative role of the MIR," and the latter imprudently facilitated "the fascist coup in the country."[38]

The communists had also attempted to deal with the Christian Democrats in Congress, as had Allende.[39] The eventual overthrow of the *Unidad Popular* government was later termed a consequence of a political inability, despite coalition efforts, to achieve popular support. "The key problem . . . was to achieve monolithic working class unity and gather round it . . . a strong alliance of the intermediate sections of the population, above all the peasants, and also the middle strata of the urban population."[40] It was the very absence of such unity on the left that contributed directly to the political weakness which Allende could not transcend. That the failure of coalition efforts was also a function of intransigence on the part of such non-Marxists as the Christian Democrats does not alter the fact that post-coup interpretations across the continent were profoundly influenced.

If the assorted failures of rural-based insurgency and/or urban terrorism in the 1960s had produced an upsurge of tactical reliance upon constitutional and electoral methods, the outcome of events in Chile similarly raised greater misgivings over such exercises in parliamentary and representative competition. Only a few Marxist observers—in most cases unaffiliated independents and intellectuals—focused on the logical explanation that individual conditions, once again, would best dictate both the methods of winning power and of building permanent power. The evident solidification of the Castro regime was not widely viewed as instructive, given the dependence upon the Soviet Union which had come with the passing of years. As political events in the late 1970s began to revive notions of armed insurrection, they also included a revival of efforts to merge with "progressive" if non-Marxist elements. The purported doctrinal and tactical hegemony of earlier years had long since become a forgotten artifact of Latin American Marxism.

Paths to Power: A Plurality of Approaches

Venezuela: From Insurgency to Eurocommunism

A prime example of shifting tactics and attitudes is that of Venezuela, especially in the decade following the Cuban Revolution. This essentially coincided with Venezuela's own ouster of military dictatorship in 1958 and the institution of an electoral, party-based regime in 1959. At that time the sole Marxist organization, the Partido Comunista de Venezuela (PCV), was eager to join a multiparty accord pledging cooperation in support of constitutional government. It was bluntly frozen out, and participated in elections as a minor supporter of a centrist presidential candidate, a retired navy admiral. The party lists polled 3.2 percent, producing two senators and seven deputies.

By early 1960 the party of President Rómulo Betancourt had suffered a schism, with its radical youth wing breaking away to form the quasi-Marxist Movimiento de Izquierda Revolucionaria (MIR). At least a few of its leaders were self-proclaimed Marxist-Leninists and, inspired by the example of Cuba, they took to the mountains shortly thereafter. The strategy was to emulate what they mistakenly termed a "peasant revolution" in Cuba, employing *foco* tactics. By early 1962 the senior leaders of the communist party were unable to restrain their own younger members and reluctantly proclaimed their support of violent efforts to overthrow the government. The resultant combined guerrilla forces became known as the Fuerzas Armadas de Liberación Nacional (FALN).

In the months to come the FALN learned only slowly that its ignorance of Venezuelan conditions condemned the rural approach to failure. They were attacking a popular, democratically elected regime headed by a party and president whose very core of national strength rested with the peasantry and small provincial towns. Only belatedly was this fact recognized, and the arena for violence shifted to Caracas and other major cities. Accepting their immediate inability to seize power, the young Marxists sought to spread a wave of terror which would decimate the legitimacy of the government, shatter civic order, and provoke a restless military into scuttling the constitutional system. This, it was reasoned, would ultimately degenerate into a repressive dictatorship; the eventual popular uprising would then be led by the Marxist faithful.

The urban effort included random bomb explosions in public buildings, indiscriminate machine-gunning, and similar acts. There were also shrewd propaganda strokes designed to shatter the international image of the government: a Spanish soccer star was kidnapped for a time; art exhibits loaned by the French to Venezuela were stolen, later to be returned; U.S. investors were singled out via arson and fire-bombing at local facilities of Sherwin-Williams and Sears. Even a freighter was hijacked—a novelty in the world of 1963. As elections scheduled for December of that year neared, the Betancourt government struggled to maintain constitutionality while protecting the dynamics of the campaign. An ill-considered attack on a trainful of holiday passengers resulted in seven deaths and prompted a major revulsion of public opinion. In defiance of FALN threats, over 90 percent of eligible voters went to the polls in December.

The consequences for the left were sharp. Both the MIR and the PCV were outlawed, with their congressional members stripped of parliamentary immunity and jailed. Meanwhile debate over tactics was renewed. Some argued for a return to rural activism; others wanted a rejuvenated urban campaign; still others, including orthodox senior PCV leaders, argued for a return to constitutionality via peaceful political action. By 1966 the PCV politburo withdrew from the FALN and, encouraged by a partial amnesty from the government, began to move back toward legality. This was eventually followed by 1968 electoral participation (although not under the communist rubric). By the time of the 1973 elections, Venezuelan Marxists had splintered further, although sharing in a commitment to electoral politics.

Two presidential candidates competed that year. The orthodox PCV ran separate congressional candidates but supported a non-Marxist candidate whose party had divided from Acción Democrática in 1968. His opponent came from the MAS, which as noted earlier had split from the PCV. In addition, the MIR also collaborated behind the MAS candidate. On election day in December 1973, the two presidential candidates polled a combined total of less than 10 percent. Only a handful of congressional seats were won. In 1978 there were no fewer than three presidential candidates competing for the left and together they won but 7 percent of the vote. Much the same occurred in 1983.[41]

By the early 1980s a clear pattern had been established. The path of violence, whether rural or urban-based, was discredited, and Venezuelan Marxists now work within the democratic system which has endured for more than a quarter-century. Organizationally and doctrinally, they remain divided. The PCV itself redivided under the two Machado brothers, who had founded the movement a half-century earlier. The MIR also broke in half, while the MAS suffered internal feuding over electoral policy and presidential candidacy. Several other miniparties competed as well, but without placing members in Congress. For the past decade it has indeed been within that body that both the communist party and its ideological rivals have centered their activity.

All of the Marxists have participated in legislative actions, and opportunism rather than principle has been the basic guide. Especially the MAS, with relatively larger delegations, frequently joined the centrist oppositions, whether Christian Democratic of Social Democratic. This was true in opposing the AD government on certain terms of petroleum nationalization in 1975–1976; opposing the Christian Democratic regime over its Central American policy in 1980–1982; and in criticizing the terms of debt renegotiation from another AD administration in 1984. Opposition for its own sake has been the hallmark, with short-term political advantage the order of the day. Informal coalitions were negotiated whenever convenient, but not in lasting fashion. Lip service to theoretical unity of the left has been paid by all, but a practical willingness to coalesce has been in short supply, especially for the MAS. It has succeeded narrowly in gaining more electoral support than its rivals, but by far too small a margin to bring about any meaningful collaboration. The Venezuelan electorate has demonstrated repeatedly its lack of enthusiasm for any and all Marxist parties and candidates; meanwhile, the parties expend their energies in constant if meaningless maneuvering.

Marxism in Nicaragua

The experience of the Nicaraguan Revolution, still being written, reflects several tactical and doctrinal shifts over time. The original Communist party (officially labeled the Partido Socialista Nicaraguense—PSN) was tolerated for some years by the original Somoza, Anastasio, the founder of the dynasty. By 1950, in response to U.S. sentiment, he outlawed the party and exiled its leaders. By 1959, although still illegal, the PSN epitomized a conservative, pro-Moscow orthodoxy which alienated its younger members and sympathizers. The latter broke away under Carlos Fonseca Amador to create a group committed to guerrilla activism—the Frente

Sandinista de Liberación Nacional (FSLN). It adopted *fidelista* military tactics while being attacked by the PSN, which hoped to organize the proletariat while awaiting the maturation of revolutionary conditions.

The PSN would later undergo a three-way division in the 1970s, leaving the small Partido Comunista de Nicaragua (PC de N) along with two personalistic groups which both claimed the old name PSN. Both the revolutionary anti-Somoza struggle and the Marxist cause, however, were to emerge from the evolution of the FSLN. For eighteen years from 1961, it continued armed struggle against the national guard. It was strongly informed by the Cuban model, and concentrated on building peasant support in rural areas. Fonseca, Tomas Borge, and Silvio Mayorga had rejected the original PSN approach in founding the FSLN, and expounded what was frequently termed the "strategy of popular revolutionary war." While it was forced by events to shift back and forth from offense to defense while moving about the countryside, its fortunes did not rise significantly until the early 1970s.

Following the December 1972 Managua earthquake, the disruption to the economy was further aggravated by the blatant confiscation of international emergency and relief funds and materials by the insatiable greed of the younger Anastasio Somoza. The growing revulsion against the regime naturally nourished the revolutionaries. In turn they initiated a series of highly public attacks not dissimilar to those of Venezuela's FALN during the latter's period of urban violence. In December 1974, for instance, an attack on a private party produced the capture of several high-ranking *somocistas*. Their release was obtained in exchange for the freeing of *sandinistas*, publication of FSLN communiqués, and related actions; the propaganda effect was great. In August 1978 twenty-five guerrillas headed by Edén Pastora (Comandante Cero) seized the National Palace with more than two thousand hostages. They escaped with the release of some sixty *sandinistas* and half a million dollars in ransom.

Such symbolic victories popularized and publicized the FSLN, although its own leadership was factionalized by tactical and doctrinal divisions. From 1975 the differences became important within the movement. The *proletarios* stemmed from the urban guerrilla movement and worked to organize and recruit support among the urban poor; they were closest to traditional Marxist thought, both in terms of revolutionary strategy and in the tactics of accepting temporary alliance with other groups. Members of the Guerra Popular Prolongada (GPP) had emerged from FSLN rural groups and argued for a lengthy campaign to amass popular support; their critics charged them with undue caution. There was also the *tercerista* group, several of whose leaders had been expelled from the GPP — the more prominent included the Ortega brothers and Edén Pastora. The most flexible and heterodox of the FSLN groups, they pursued cooperation and informal alliance with Christian Democratic and other centrist, bourgeois parties. They also conducted guerrilla activities with a boldness and vigor far greater than the others.

The rapid deterioration of the Somoza regime and the rising tempo of popular opposition helped to ameliorate the potential impact of such internal factionalism. Another crucial event was the January 1978 assassination of long-time publisher and Somoza critic Pedro Joaquín Chamorro. Spontaneous opposition continued, with each of the three FSLN factions finding new volunteers flooding to the anti-Somoza cause. The successful August attack on the National Palace further galvanized the populace, and the FSLN reunified its forces for the decisive campaign. Encouraged by Fidel Castro and swayed by the obvious value for unity at this juncture, an overarching Frente Patriótica Nacional (FPN) provided a structure for coherence in the final drive to oust the dynasty, which reached fruition on 17 July 1979.

Throughout the long period of armed struggle, the FSLN in ideological terms had referred back to the example of Augusto César Sandino, the guerrilla leader of the late 1920s and early 1930s. In point of fact, Sandino's ideology was more reformist than revolutionary, although blending anti-imperialism with a concern for the poor and the oppressed; FSLN views were more precise, following Leninist thinking as regarded national revolution. Carlos Fonseca Amador had been articulate in etching programmatic goals, and in this effort was followed by others who came to direct the revolutionary government after July 1979.[42] The influence of the *terceristas* exerted pressure in the direction of collaboration with disparate Marxists as well as with nonsocialist groups, and this was evident during the early period of government.

From the very beginning, there were both political and ideological tensions inside the revolutionary regime. The *sandinistas*, while clinging to a belief in the inevitability of class warfare, espoused two sometimes conflicting expressions of Marxist doctrine. Their broad programmatic commitment was toward "national reconstruction," and in this they reiterated a willingness to work within a pluralistic coalition of anti-Somoza Nicaraguans. At the same time, the *sandinistas* remained faithful to their "historic program" which envisaged a one-party state. Such contradictions were present from the very outset of the new regime. From 1979 to 1981 the Junta of National Reconstruction included reformists as well as Marxists. *Sandinista* ideology "expanded and evolved to encompass a broad program of reforms to redistribute income, wealth, power, and status and to alter foreign policy and the roles of the external actors. It has also, with certain necessary tensions with its populist origin and framework, pursued the somewhat contradictory goals of moderating popular redistributive demands while expanding support for the FSLN and for the revolution."[43]

As pressures gradually mounted both inside the country and from the United States, moderate non-Marxists were gradually driven from the junta. The National Directorate of the FSLN, chaired by Daniel Ortega Saavedra from 1981, assumed unchallenged domination. Further defections included the April 1982 departure of Pastora, who was soon to lead guerrilla forays from Costa Rican soil with aid from the CIA and other non-Nicaraguan sources. As Marxist control solidified, disputes over both strategic and tactical measures continued to characterize the revolutionary leadership. Controversy over the shape and form of national elections in November 1984 was typical. Although the *commandantes* of the FSLN concurred over the necessity of convening a nationwide vote, there were divisions over both the timing and the treatment of would-be opposition groups.

The dispute was not grounded in significant ideological issues, but rather upon international perceptions of and reactions to the details of the contest. With the jerry-built coalition Coordinadora Democratica Nicaraguense supporting former Junta member Arturo Cruz, there were other parties with Marxist loyalties which also sought to participate. These numbered among them the Partido Socialista Nicaraguense (PSN), which had initially cooperated with the government; the Partido Comunista de Nicaragua (PC de N); and the Movimiento Acción Popular-Marxista Leninista (MAP-MP). Each presented its own presidential candidate rather than joining the FSLN. None agreed to unite with the others in a nongoverning Marxist coalition. The *sandinista* victory with an announced two-thirds of the vote further consolidated efforts to institutionalize the revolution. It also brought Daniel Ortega and Sergio Ramirez to the presidency and vice-presidency respectively.

From 1985 forward the regime was plagued increasingly by administrative mismanagement, a progressive disintegration of the economy, and the external pressures of the U.S.-organized and supported counterrevolutionaries (the so-called *contras*). The struggle for survival encouraged greater ideological unity among the *commandantes*, as well as increasing harassment of domestic opposition. Press censorship, the suspension of constitutional guarantees, and the maintenance of a state of emergency were among the tools of repression which were called into play. The notion of political pluralism seemed but a dim memory from the past, and attention was directed more toward the long and tortuous process of discussion and negotiation undertaken by the presidents of Central America.

The Esquipulas initiative of Costa Rica's Oscar Arias Sanchez became the central focus in 1987 and beyond. The revolutionary government, seeking to keep alive the Central American negotiations as well as a cessation or diminution of *contra* activity, responded with a host of reforms. Late in 1987 the opposition press was permitted to reopen; exiled church critics reentered the country; and the state of emergency was lifted. By the time the U.S. House of Representatives voted down the Reagan administration's proposal for further assistance to the *contras* in February 1988, political opponents were experiencing relatively greater freedom than had existed for several years. Antigovernment marches were held, demonstrations challenged *sandinista* leadership, authors of political graffiti went unpunished by security forces, and sharp attacks in the press were permitted. What remained uncertain was the extent to which such measures were short-term opportunistic tactics, or represented instead a shift of outlook for the *sandinistas*.

There was reason to believe that the leadership itself was divided. President Ortega, whose personal authority had grown progressively since his 1984 election, personified the willingness for pragmatic adjustment which had marked the *terceristas*. However, the ideological hardliners were highly skeptical over concessions to opponents; headed by Interior Minister Tomas Borge, the only surviving founder of the FSLN, they clearly resisted the course of compromise. Thus, even as the revolutionary regime faced dire challenges in 1988, both tactical and doctrinal dissent remained inside the top leadership. At the same time, moreover, there were still Marxist organizations inside Nicaragua which were not in league with the *sandinistas*. Certainly the domestic critics of the FSLN policies were not limited to non-Marxists. Assuming the continued exercise of political authority by the *sandinistas*, it was unclear whether or not the once promised pluralism might be meaningfully resurrected. Neither could it be predicted that alliances or coalitions might be adopted as a mechanism to improve the chances for political survival.

Whatever their ultimate fate, the *sandinistas* provide a rare case study for Latin America. Only they and the Cubans have seized power by armed insurgency in the drive to establish Marxist control. This in itself is unusual. The Nicaraguan experience also diverges in many important particulars from the Cuban. Among other things, the sheer fact of Cuba shifted the context within which the Nicaraguans operated. And as these words are written, the Nicaraguan Revolution is still evolving. Close observers of the scene in Managua must await later events before venturing definitive judgments. This will be true whether or not the *sandinistas* survive, and whatever the shape of the regime as the decade of the nineties approaches. Thus far, however, there have been disputes over the role of international communism; the importance of electoral participation; the value of political pluralism; and possible collaboration via formal coalition with other organizations, be they Marxist or bourgeois reformist. The presence of tactical and doctrinal disagreement, then, is undeniable. In contrast to the Cuban experience, in addition, has been the absence of a single dominant personality about whom doctrine and policy might solidify. Neither Ortega nor Borge, let alone their colleagues, have demonstrated either the desire or capacity to assume such a position. In short, much remains to be written about the Nicaraguan Revolution and its place in the unfolding of Marxist political movements in Latin America.

Elections versus Anarchism in Peru

More than a half-century ago Peru was distinguished by two of the more striking political thinkers of the Latin American left—José Carlos Mariátegui and Victor Raúl Haya de la Torre. The former remains today as arguably the most original and imaginative Marxist theoretician to emerge in Latin America. Yet during his lifetime Mariátegui was embroiled in disputes with pro-Moscow figures. At the time of his premature death in 1930, he had been denounced by the country's communist leadership as a traitor to the cause, and even more damningly, as a Trotskyite. His sometimes friend and rival, Haya de la Torre, also broke from orthodox Marxism to found the famous Alianza Popular Revolucionaria Americana (APRA), which became Peru's major party. Haya's early writings upended orthodox Marxist thought in the effort to evolve a dogma applicable to the nonindustrialized, predominantly Indian context of Peruvian politics. His lifetime quest for the presidency contributed to Haya's subsequent shift to the center, and, at times, even to rightist positions. Yet he retained personal control of the APRA until his 1979 death at the age of eighty-four, when he was mounting yet another candidacy for the presidency. Curiously enough, he had been born the same year as Mariátegui.

While the APRA spent many years outlawed by military and civilian conservatives, the Peruvian Communist party was even more continuously illegal after its 1928 founding. When Peru returned to civilian rule in 1980 under President Fernando Belaúnde Terry after twelve years of military government, both the communists and a host of Marxist-Leninist organizations became active. It was estimated that between forty and fifty political parties existed. Of the thirty-four to take part in 1980 presidential and congressional elections, no fewer than two dozen presented a Marxist-Leninist orientation. Divisions centered on ideology, revolutionary tactics and strategy, personal rivalries, and disagreement over the role of violence. For the decade of the 1980s, Peru emerged as both a curious and important case, for alongside attempts to build an electorally powerful leftist coalition, there has been the emergence of a strangely quixotic if ruthless guerrilla band known as Sendero Luminoso (Shining Path).

In the electoral area, efforts to build a revolutionary alliance of the left secured no less than 34 percent of the vote for delegates to the 1978 Constituent Assembly. Two years later, however, similar unity proved elusive, and the entire left suffered in the process. Marxist-Leninist parties received 13.7 percent of 4.1 million votes for president, which was shared by five rival candidates. Ten of 60 Senate seats and 14 of 180 in the Chamber of Deputies went to their orientation. This provided impetus for construction of a common front for the November 1980 municipal elections. The Izquierda Unida (IU) polled 27 percent of the vote in Lima and won pluralities in six of twenty-three departmental capitals. With the internally divided APRA running poorly, the left found itself the nation's second electoral force behind the Acción Popular (AP) of Belaúnde.[44]

Recognizing anew the value of collective action, leftist parties began to treat the Izquierda Unida as a mass organization rather than electoral alliance. Alfonso Barrantes Lingán of the PCP became its president, and the IU by 1981 was seeking to strengthen its position as a meaningful opponent to the government. Twice during the year Barrantes and members of the coalition's executive committee met with President Belaúnde for extended discussions. Thereby gaining legitimacy while rejecting administration policies, they presented their own set of proposals. These reflected the pragmatic air of the IU, stressing such objectives as wage increases, a price freeze on basic commodities, salary adjustments being tied to inflation and the like. Although the Trotskyist parties stayed outside the IU, the latter represented the bulk of leftist political organizations in the country.[45]

The IU contemplated the possibility of a Popular Front alliance with the APRA, which was overcoming its internal divisions and returning to its more traditional reformist position. However, it was concluded that the IU should compete with the APRA for control of mass organizations. The PCP's Jorge del Prado promised that constant recruitment and proselytizing would produce a single party capable of further promoting a class struggle. Denouncing the Trotskyists' refusal to engage in dialogue with other groups, the IU began looking toward the 1983 municipal elections. This, it was believed, presented an opportunity to progress via electoral means. History was seen as running in its favor.

The 13 November 1983 vote gave some substance to IU optimism. While the government and Acción Popular suffered a resounding defeat throughout the country, the IU swept to victory in Lima as Barrantes became mayor with 35 percent of the vote. The *aprista* candidate followed with 28 percent and the AP received a mere 12 percent in finishing fourth. While the revived APRA won overall with some 34 percent of the vote nationwide, the IU recorded a strong second-place finish with 30 percent while triumphing in several departmental capitals. There was also a personalistic element in the Barrantes victory, in that his campaign program included improved child nutrition, health care, and free breakfasts for school children.

All of this left the coalition eager for national elections in 1985. With the massive unpopularity of the Belaúnde government presaging a crushing defeat for Acción Popular, the way was open for an APRA victory under its vigorous new leader, thirty-five-year-old Alan García. For Izquierda Unida, Alfonso Barrantes carried the coalition banner. The IU promised a hundred-day "people's survival program" with health, food, and new jobs —all to be financed by nonpayment of the foreign debt. Expropriations would include the copper industry and leading Peruvian banks. On 14 April 1985 the APRA won a major victory; Alan García and legislative slates both won 48 to 49 percent of the vote. Had spoiled and blank ballots not been tallied, García would have won the outright 50 percent necessary to avoid a presidential runoff.

Barrantes and the coalition easily came in second, although on balance its totals were somewhat lower than had been hoped by party leaders. Outpolled two to one by the APRA, the IU and its candidates won 24 percent of the vote. In Congress, the two slates dominated representation. Of the 60 Senate seats, the APRA received 31 and the IU 16. In the 180-seat Chamber of Deputies, the former gained 90 members and the IU 45. In both cases the conservative Partido Popular Cristiano was a distant third and Belaúnde's AP a devastating fourth with barely 6 percent of the vote. After initial hesitation, Barrantes opted out of a second-round runoff. There was disappointment that, seven years after a leftist alliance had won one-third of the votes in the 1978 Constituent Assembly race, it was unable to surpass 25 percent of the vote. With Barrantes's popularity having been a positive factor in 1985, there was further reason to question either the durability or long-range viability of the leftist coalition.

The municipal elections of November 1986 soon underlined the fragility of the Izquierda Unida. Confronted by a major *aprista* campaign spearheaded by the vigorous politicking of President García, the IU saw nine of Peru's largest cities select the APRA nominees. The Marxist coalition lost is mayoralties in Cuzco, Puno, and in Lima. In the last of these, Alfonso Barrantes was ousted by the *aprista* Jorge del Castillo; the margin was 31.6 to 34.5 percent. In the wake of his defeat Barrantes was ousted from the coalition leadership and charged with undue collaboration with the García government. Whereas he was likely to rebound politically, Barrantes's setback documented the internal weakness and doctrinal inconsistencies which mark the left in Peru. Furthermore, such sectors as the military remain unalterably opposed to Marxist influence in government.

It remains true that success by the left can provoke severe hostility from the armed forces. Furthermore, by the mid-1980s the army in particular was engaged in warfare with a very different Marxist-Leninist group, the Sendero Luminoso (Shining Path). Its origins come from the 1964 departure from the PCP of a small Maoist faction headed by the young philosophy professor Abimael Guzmán Reinoso. Criticizing the communist commitment to achieving socialism by peaceful means, this splinter group was first known as the Bandera Roja (Red Flag). It was in turn shattered through a division between *limeño* leaders and Guzmán in his provincial Ayacucho home. The latter first called itself the Peruvian Communist Party Shining Path, from which its present name derives.

A 1971 revolutionary leaflet presented Guzmán's ideas, according to which armed struggle was to be undertaken once conditions were ripe. An avowed admirer of José Carlos Mariátegui and of Chairman Mao with his "Gang of Four," Guzmán became a bitter critic of the current Chinese leadership, as well as Muscovite spokesmen. Adopting the title "Comrade Gonzalo," Guzmán established firm personal control of the movement. Other Peruvian Marxists came to view Guzmán as a messianic fanatic and a terrorist comparable to Iran's Ayatollah and to Pol Pot of Cambodia. By 1981 the Sendero Luminoso had become active in its terrorist attacks and both Belaúnde and the Peruvian military concluded that the expanding activism was a serious matter. Late in the year, the government declared a state of emergency in selected provinces and assigned the Guardia Civil—the national police—the responsibility of controlling Sendero.

Nonetheless, the "people's war" was intensified during 1982. Police barracks were attacked, public buildings were bombed, and in August attacks on electric pylons brought the conflict to Lima itself. In defiance of a far-reaching antiterrorist law decreed by Belaúnde, Sendero advanced its tactics to include assassinations in Ayacucho and its environs. Both political leaders and innocent citizens were targets. The Interior Ministry reported no fewer than 658 incidents between July 1981 and July 1982, recording 53 deaths. For the whole of 1982 there were 147 fatalities, 79 of whom were civilians.[46] In December of that year the cabinet resigned and the president declared a new state of emergency and militarized five Andean provinces.

For the first time since 1965 both police and army forces were unleashed to confront the rural guerrillas.

Modern antiguerrilla weapons were introduced, the army took authority over the militarized zone, and by mid-1983 the death toll approached one thousand. The violence escalated, while Sendero attacks in Lima and other urban centers continued. Although popular support for the SL was limited, the latter gave no appearance of doubting its tactics. International attention came from the death of eight journalists in January 1983, who had gone to investigate a reported incident of Sendero violence. They were killed in the community of Uchuraccay, the circumstances of which remain shrouded in controversy. An independent commission of prominent Peruvians headed by the novelist and essayist Mario Vargas Llosa conducted its own inquiry, with its report issued in March.[47] Included was a consideration of the tension between modernizing and traditional Peru, as described by Vargas Llosa in the world press.[48]

Sendero Luminoso continued to widen its zone of warfare, and violent attacks in Lima itself recurred. The frustrated Belaúnde government, determined to control the problem, instead found itself charged by Amnesty International with human rights violations. Moreover, its military efforts merely expanded the scope of the conflict and spotlighted the SL movement. It was estimated that no more than five hundred guerrillas were actively fighting for Sendero, although collaborators numbered in the thousands. At the same time, three steps in its five-part program has been achieved. As outlined by Guzmán, the first encompassed a conversion of "backward" areas into bases of revolutionary support. The second called for attacks on the bourgeoisie; third came a more generalized guerrilla war. This had followed a March 1982 Ayacucho jailbreak which freed a number of sympathizers.

Still lying in the future were the critical fourth and fifth stages. These began with the "conquest and expansion of bases of support," which implied expanded activism in other departments and provincial universities. Lastly came the projected siege of the cities and the ultimate collapse of the state, which were not expected until the 1990s.[49] Whatever the validity of the claim, Sendero Luminoso had presented a serious challenge to the government. While the survival of the latter was not in question, its tactical errors and military inability to curb the movement were damning. The capacity of Sendero to disrupt rural life and to produce at best questionable countermeasures from the regime was exceptional. Notwithstanding an increasingly anarchistic doctrinal stance which at one point denounced all but the Albanian Marxists — only to attack the latter in a subsequent manifesto — Sendero remained a manifestation of socioeconomic depredation and armed protest which would not be simply ignored.

As 1985 elections approached, Peru's dedicated but inept democratic government was being pressured from all sides. Its manifest unpopularity laid the way for political victory from the born-again reformism of the APRA. The Izquierdo Unida, notwithstanding the organizational insecurity of its coalition, constituted an important electoral force in which the Peruvian Communist party was paramount. Meanwhile, the quasi-anarchistic thrust of the Sendero Luminoso continued to bedevil portions of the Peruvian Andes while stimulating nonproductive violence on the part of the military. In the eyes of one close observer, "Peru's fragile democracy, restored with great enthusiasm in 1980, is caught in a deadly cross fire between the Shining Path and the Palace of Pizarro."[50]

All of this was occurring at a time when the economy was nearing the point of disintegration and the United States was labeling democratic Peru, owing to military purchases from the Soviet Union, "a target of Soviet influence." The Reagan administration was preoccupied with what it saw as a menacing Soviet presence; the Lima military mission of an alleged six hundred Russians, one hundred of whom were KGB agents, was seen as evidence of Marxist intrusion.[51] At the same time, both Fernando Belaúnde and his military had looked to Washington for sustenance. When Alan García assumed power, new impetus was directed toward populist reforms, and more varied methods were applied to the anti-Sendero campaign. By 1988, however, the guerrilla movement remained viable; several provinces were under martial law; and the IU was struggling to maintain itself as a relevant political actor. If the nation was no longer on the brink of disintegration, the impact of coalition politics was dwarfed by the Sendero-induced conflict.

Conclusions:
Marxism and Latin American Reality

There can be little denial of the diversity of tactics and of doctrine which have marked the Latin American experience with Marxism. The pre-1959 era was marked progressively by the domination of the Soviet Union and the international communist movement over Latin American dependencies. When the tactics of the Popular Front were dictated, local subsidiaries loyally and unblinkingly followed orders. The post–World War II era of the cold war produced new shifts, which in most cases gravitated away from collaboration with reformists bourgeois parties. Even cooperation between and among rival Marxist-Leninist organizations was uncommon. Circumstances were to be altered drastically as a result of Fidel Castro's rise to power and his ultimate embrace of the Soviet Union.

Especially since that time, vigorous debate has concerned alternate paths to power. Invariably, this is tied to basic strategic agreement over the goal of seizing power. The initial interpretation of the Cuban experience persuaded many that the path of violence would be decisive. Disagreements over a rural versus urban context for strife and confrontation drew upon competing notions as to the relative potential for success. This was sheer revolutionary pragmatism, with the later ideological trappings little more than a post facto justification. Where Salvador Allende and the Chilean communists—if not many of Allende's fellow socialists—opted for the peaceful road to socialism, it was with the conviction that nonviolence was more aptly suited to the nation's political experience. Allende's own shifting between support of and opposition toward coalition with non-Marxist groups was also an artifact of his practical assessment of political reality at a given point in time.

Especially during the last quarter-century, Latin American Marxism has also seen a greater fragmentation of its party organizations and proliferation of new ones. The general tendency has been to eschew alliance and coalition more often than not. Chile was something of an exception, although we have seen that even the victory of the first democratically elected Marxist chief of state was not sufficient to unify the left. In Venezuela a bedazzling burgeoning of Marxist party organizations has stimulated bitter internecine warfare which exhausts the energies of the left without focusing on the non-Marxist opposition. Peru's IU has demonstrated a greater proclivity and flexibility toward coalition building than has been customary, yet that too is far from solid.

Most fundamental to an understanding of the coalition tactics of Marxist parties in Latin America is an appreciation of the cultural and political reality of the region. Consider some important characteristics which obtain in the majority of countries: personalism and the role of the individual pervades life and society; the military penchant for direct intervention in politics has historic roots; parliaments are customarily subservient branches of government; multiparty systems are endemic, and a proliferation of parties is normal; the diverse versions of Marxism, Leninism, Trotskyism, and the like assure a rich variety of interpretations in the region; the high value given to intellectual and artistic achievement is remarkable; and there is a romanticism attached to strong populist leaders who take up arms in defense of personal freedom and in pursuit of social justice.

These are traits which one finds mirrored in Latin American Marxism. Thus, *caudillismo* and individualism often emerge from Marxists as well as other political figures, which discourages cooperation and collaboration with rivals. The role of the armed forces becomes a factor in any tactical planning which Marxists may undertake. The subsidiary nature of many parliaments makes the formation of legislative coalitions relatively unimportant in most countries; unlike Europe, the Latin American states are preeminently presidential (excepting recently independent ministates which came out of the British colonial system). The prevalence of party disunity and fragmentation affects the parties of the left no less than others in the region. Any communist or Marxist-Leninist organization is in danger of schism, provoked as often by personal ambition as by doctrinal dispute.

Unity of organization, thought, and action is also rendered improbable when Marxist writers, thinkers, and artists include such internationally famed and fiercely independent figures as the Mexican muralists Diego Rivera and David Alfaro Siqueiros; the Ecuadorean master Osvaldo Guayasamin; the poet Pablo Neruda; and such novelists and essayists as Carlos Fuentes and Gabriel García Márquez. Widely admired leaders of armed rebellion also act with relative freedom of thought and action, from Tupac Amaru and Padre Hidalgo against the Spaniards through Zapata and Sandino to Father Torres and Ché Guevara.

Latin America provides unmistakable justification for the Gilberg contention that "Marxist" is the all-inclusive category, with "communist" a subcategory which in turn can be divided into further groupings. In addition, more than a few contemporary centrist parties now regarded as social democratic had origins which were based in some part on elements of classical Marxist thought. In organizational terms, moreover, even some of the Christian Democratic parties appear attached to patterns of democratic centralism, although they would deny any allegiance to Leninist principles or teachings. Here, too, the pervasive presence of Marxist thought in university and intellectual circles inevitably reaches many budding young aspiring politicians, whatever their basic programmatic outlook.

Without extending unduly this line of argumentation, let it simply be recorded and recalled that Latin American Marxist parties cannot be understood apart from their environments. While long-range strategy agrees on the necessity of seizing power by one or another means, there are widely differing circumstances which affect tactical judgments as to the best and most pragmatic approach. The willingness to build either all-Marxist coalitions or to negotiate opportunistic alliances with bourgeois parties will reflect very practical Marxist perceptions. The lessons of the Nicaraguan Revolution in the overthrow of Somoza—whatever the eventual fate of the *sandinistas*—reiterate the Cuban experience of a broad national movement winning power without dominant communist participation. For these parties the picture is clear, as Blasier has written:

> The Communist Parties in Latin America are being forced to come to terms with the reality that such broad, loose, national fronts are leading and winning revolutions almost without them. Whereas they used to refer to such groups as "ultra-Leftists," "putschists," "petty bourgeois extremists," and the like, they must now accept them as effective revolutionary organizations. Put another way, if the Communists can't beat these radical nationalists, it is better to join them.[52]

For other Marxist-Leninist organizations as well, the nature of conditions in the country in question will be crucial. There may be collaboration with democratic reformists or even with military dictatorships. Flexibility will be the order of the day. The evaluation and assessment of individual conditions by the Marxist-Leninist parties will dictate the extent to which coalition tactics may be employed. The ultimate objective of total power will remain a given.

6

Vietnamese Communism and the Strategy of the United Front
William J. Duiker

An essential feature of Marxist parties' coalition strategies is the technique of the united front. This is also a cardinal element in Marxist-Leninist ideology. In the prerevolutionary period, communist parties have used united front tactics to broaden the base of the movement in preparation for the seizure of power. Once in command, they have turned to the united front as a means of consolidating their position in the decisive period of "who defeats whom" to prepare for the advance to socialism.

While virtually all communist parties have used a united front strategy to some degree, the concept has been particularly valuable in relatively backward preindustrial societies where the proletariat, through its vanguard party, lacks the strength and political consciousness to seize and retain power on its own. Nowhere is this more true than in the case of Vietnam. There the strategy of the united front was a crucial factor in the long communist struggle for power, first against the French and later against the United States and the Saigon regime in the South. Since victory in 1975, the Party has once again turned to the concept of the united front to carry out the task of national reunification and the construction of a socialist society.

Vietnam, then, makes a good case study for the investigation of the role of the united front in a preindustrial society. What are the major components of the front? What was the role of the Party in creating and directing the front? What were the major problems encountered in assembling the front, and how did Party leaders attempt to resolve them? Finally, how has the Party attempted to use the united front in achieving its objectives in the postrevolutionary period and how successful has it been in this task?

Origins of the United Front
in Vietnam

When the Vietnamese communist movement first began to material-
ize in the mid-1920s, the guiding strategic document for all communist
parties in Asia was Lenin's famous "Theses on the National and Colonial
Questions," first presented at the Second Congress of the Comintern held
in the summer of 1920. Lenin's objective was to relate Marxist revolutionary doctrine and strategy to the concrete conditions in precapitalist societies of Asia and Africa. Because the native bourgeoisie, repressed by the
imperialist presence and the remnants of reactionary feudalism, was too
weak to fulfill its historical mission of launching the capitalist revolution,
and because the working class lacked the strength and experience to seize
power on its own, the overthrow of the twin evils of imperialism and
feudalism could only take place by means of an alliance of several progressive classes in pursuit of the common objective. In such cases, the Communist party, the sole legitimate representative of the working class, was
instructed to cooperate with progressive elements within the peasantry and
the bourgeoisie in a common alliance against the sources of domestic
reaction and world imperialism. Since most societies in Asia and Africa
were under direct or indirect colonial domination, such an alliance in
practice meant that the Party should seek a common front with existing
bourgeois nationalist parties, so long as they were truly progressive, in a
joint effort to wrest independence from colonial rule. Only after the overthrow of the colonial regime and the remnants of the feudal order
—signifying the completion of the first, or bourgeois democratic stage of
the revolution—should the Party rally the more radical elements within
the alliance to wage the second or socialist stage of the revolution to topple
the bourgeoisie and lead the revolution into a proletarian stage.[1]

This approach became a major vehicle of policy for decades to come,
and it was primarily the *communists* who employed it, because there were
few other Marxist or leftist groups of any significance in Indochina. In its
broad outlines, Lenin's strategy of the united front was a tour de force,
providing Marxists with a doctrinal and strategic framework for analyzing
the course of historical change and promoting revolution in Asia. To Ho
Chi Minh, then a young Vietnamese patriot active in socialist circles in
Paris, the relevance of Lenin's ideas to conditions in his own country was
immediately apparent.[2] Vietnam in the early 1920s was a classical example
of a precapitalist society under colonial rule. Its working class was small
and politically unsophisticated. The peasantry, comprising well over 80
percent of the total population in the country, was brutally exploited and

politically restive, but lacked cohesion and leadership. Resistance to the French colonial regime was centered in a small but increasingly vocal urban middle class, composed of merchants, teachers, students, journalists, and petty functionaries. In the years immediately following the end of World War I, a number of political parties and factions had begun to form, but, lacking experience and a clear sense of purpose, they posed no serious threat to French rule.

In 1920, at the Congress of Tours, Ho Chi Minh became a founding member of the new French Communist party. Over the next four years, first in Paris and later in Moscow, he honed his skills in the theory and practice of Leninism. From the beginning he had an instinctive sense of the importance of the concept of the united front and of the issue of nationalism in societies such as Vietnam, where virtually all classes and religious and ethnic groups shared the common experience of colonial repression. At the same time, he was acutely conscious of the disarray in the Vietnamese anticolonial movement, and the need for organization and leadership. That leadership, he came to believe, could only be supplied by a party of the proletariat. Nor was he motivated simply by patriotism, for he saw the plight of his countrymen in global terms, as a reflection of the worldwide exploitation of colonial peoples by the imperialist nations of the West. This early commitment to the concept of class-based internationalism surfaced in Paris in the early 1920s, where he played a leading role in creating the Intercolonial Union, an organization composed of radical intellectuals from French colonies throughout Africa and Asia, and operating under the general sponsorship of the French Communist party.[3]

In 1924 Ho Chi Minh was assigned as a member of the Comintern delegation in Canton, China, with instructions to apply Lenin's strategy of the united front to the specific conditions in Vietnam. Operating from his base in South China, he immediately formed a set of organizations designed to enlist the support of the mass of the population in a collective effort to overthrow French rule and promote social revolution in Vietnam. The centerpiece of his strategy was the Vietnamese Revolutionary Youth League (*Viet Nam Cach Menh Thanh Nien Hoi*), a broad front organization dedicated to the dual objectives of national independence and social revolution. In deference to the political immaturity of the population, the primary appeal of the League was to anticolonial sentiment, but the demands of ideology were met by providing new recruits with lectures of Marxism-Leninism at the League's training institute in Canton. A second safeguard for the revolutionary character of the League was met by the creation of a small clandestine inner core—called the Communist Youth Group (*Thanh Nien Cong San Doan*)—which Ho viewed as the nucleus out of which a formal communist party would eventually be created. Finally, Ho attempted to link the young revolutionary movement in Vietnam with a broader coalition of radical parties and groups through the creation of a League of Oppressed Peoples of Asia (*Hoi Dan Toc Bi Ap Buc The Gioi*). Centered in Nanking, this organization had high-level support in Kuomintang circles and the Comintern, but achieved little and was eventually abandoned.[4]

For the next several years, the League concentrated its efforts on recruitment. By 1929 it had a membership of about one thousand members and had become one of the most prominent organizations opposed to French rule. In the process, however, the League leadership was faced with a number of decisions on issues relating to the future course of the united front in Vietnam. In the first place, how should relations with bourgeois nationalist parties be established? Should formal alliances be set up, and on what basis? To what degree should the League temper its support for social revolution in order to appeal to patriotic groups of moderate political persuasion? How much stress should be placed on the issue of national independence? Comintern advice on such issues was somewhat ambiguous and seemed to imply that the details should be worked out by individual communist parties in accordance with local conditions. Lenin had recognized that, at least in the initial stages, communist parties would often be smaller and weaker than their nationalist rivals, and had suggested that in such cases, the Party need not lead the alliance, so long as it retained its independence of action. This proviso was often difficult to put into practice, however, and had proved disastrous in China when the alliance between the Chinese Communist party (CCP) and the Kuomintang ended with the massacre of communist elements by Chiang Kai-shek's forces in Shanghai in 1927.

In Vietnam there was no Kuomintang to provide the League with a formidable rival for leadership over the anticolonial movement, but merely an assortment of regional parties and factions lacking cohesion or consensus on common objectives. Ho apparently viewed the League from the outset as the organization which could provide the leadership and sense of direction for all truly progressive forces within the anticolonial movement, and in its approach to rival parties the League consistently assumed a position of superiority and often tried to recruit members of such parties into its own ranks. This strategy had its pitfalls, for it led to resentment and distrust of communist intentions by the leaders of such groups. This became a permanent feature of the Vietnamese nationalist movement and in future years posed a serious obstacle to the Party's efforts to form "united front from above" alliances with nationalist groups against colonial rule.[5]

The problem of setting proper priorities was an equally difficult one and soon led to a growing split within the ranks of the League itself. During the first years of its existence, the League placed central importance on the issue of nationalism, and most of its members were petty bourgeois intellectuals attracted to the League less for its utopian doctrine than for its patriotic appeal for the overthrow of French rule. While the issue of class struggle was not entirely ignored, ideological issues were apparently not stressed and, according to one source, even those members given instruction at the training institute in Canton received only rudimentary exposure to Marxist-Leninist theory and practice.[6]

By 1928 the moderate and predominately patriotic character of the League's program and the flabby ideological foundations of many of its middle class members evoked criticism among radical elements, who demanded a higher level of recruitment among workers and poor peasants and the formation of a formal communist party. In response, the League leadership attempted to increase its efforts to recruit among the poor, but refused the radicals' demand for the creation of a communist party at the organization's first national congress, held in May 1929. The radicals bolted the congress and formed their own Communist Party of Indochina. The issue was referred to Moscow, where policy views had hardened in the aftermath of the collapse of the CCP-Kuomintang alliance in China. Alliances with bourgeois nationalist parties were to be abandoned in favor of concentration on the working class and poor peasantry in preparation for a predicted wave of social revolution to come.[7]

In Moscow, the split within the Vietnamese movement was resolved in favor of the radicals, and in 1930 a formal Indochinese Communist Party (ICP) was created out of the remnants of the rival factions. The programmatic documents of the new organization, as approved at the first session of the new Central Committee in October, reflected the sectarian attitude prevailing in Moscow. The revolution would be based on the worker-peasant alliance, but the Party was admonished to maintain a strongly proletarian character. While plans called for the formation of a united front (*phan de dong minh*, or anti-imperialist league), it, too, was defined on a narrow basis and included only workers, poor peasants, and the most radical members of the petty bourgeois intelligentsia. Finally, the emphasis on nationalism which had characterized the League's program was replaced by a new emphasis on class struggle.[8]

The new strategy not only pointed up the Comintern's growing distrust of the role of the bourgeoisie in the revolution of Asia, it also demonstrated Moscow's continued skepticism toward the revolutionary potential of the peasantry—an attitude which originated with Marx but continued to win adherents in the U.S.S.R., who envisaged primarily urban insurrections in Asia based on the Bolshevik model. Ho Chi Minh appeared to have some reservations about this attitude—some of his articles and speeches in the 1920s had asserted the potentially revolutionary character of rural unrest in colonial Indochina—but he apparently did not publicly register his disagreement with the new trend in Comintern thinking, although he was present at the formation of the ICP in 1930.[9]

In China, the attempt by the Comintern to force the Chinese revolution into the Procrustean mold of the Bolshevik model had led to near disaster for the CCP and, eventually, to the emergence of an independent party practicing a uniquely Chinese brand of communism. In Vietnam, Comintern guidance had equally tragic consequences when the young ICP, partly at the urging of Moscow, gave its active support to a peasant rebellion in the summer and fall of 1930. In the French suppression that followed nearly 90 percent of the Party leadership was imprisoned or executed.[10] Unlike the case of China, however, the debacle did not lead to an open split in the Party or the emergence of a purely independent form of "national communism." Indeed, the ICP leadership, which for the next few years consisted primarily of students returned from the Stalin School in Moscow, obediently followed the ultraleftist line adopted by the Comintern until it shifted with the inauguration of the Popular Front in 1935. Party theoretical journals fretted publicly over the insufficient number of workers within the Party and criticized the old League leadership, including Ho Chi Minh, for its reliance on outmoded policies of nationalism and alliance with the bourgeoisie.[11]

The strategy of the Popular Front, promulgated at the Comintern Seventh Congress in 1935, called on member parties to form alliances with all progressive and democratic forces against the common danger of world fascism. The new policy took the ICP by surprise, but after a short period of hesitation and some grumbling from hard-liners within the ranks, the ICP adapted its own strategy to conform to the new guidelines.[12] The primary consequences of the shift in Comintern strategy were a decline in official repression in Indochina and increased flexibility for the ICP to reconstruct its links with urban moderates and the peasants. During the next three years cautious efforts were made to establish alliances with bourgeois nationalist parties. Party activists also began to organize factory workers in so-called "mutual assistance associations" (an embryonic form of trade unions) while in rural areas Party cadres organized peasant associations to mobilize demonstrations against high taxes and official corruption.[13]

The Vietminh Front and the Struggle
for National Independence

The period of the Popular Front played a crucial role in bringing the ICP out of the wilderness and back into the mainstream of the Vietnamese revolution, and the recent comment by Party Secretary General Le Duan that the period of the Popular Front was the equivalent of that of the May Fourth Movement in China is not out of place.[14] But the major weakness of the Popular Front was that it prevented the ICP from proclaiming its leading role as a major force in the struggle for independence. Constrained by Comintern instructions from attacking the colonial regime directly, the Party had only limited success in winning the support of fervent nationalists.

That dilemma was resolved with the advent of World War II. The signing of the Nazi-Soviet pact in August 1939 put a dramatic end to the already disintegrating Popular Front. In Indochina the ICP was suppressed by the colonial regime and forced underground. The following year the French were compelled by force majeure to consent to the Japanese occupation of Indochina.

Released from the constraints of Popular Front strategy, the Party acted quickly to restore its credibility in the struggle for national independence. In November 1939 the Central Committee set up a new Indochinese united front of all progressive forces, regardless of class and religion, to oppose imperialism and fascism and prepare an armed uprising to seek independence. Two years later, at a Central Committee meeting chaired by Ho Chi Minh (for several years Ho had been absent from Party counsels while living in the Soviet Union and China), this strategy was given more concrete form with the establishment of the League for the Independence of Vietnam, commonly known as the Vietminh Front. The new front was described as a broad alliance of classes, political parties, religious groups, and patriotic individuals against the common enemies of Japanese fascism and French colonialism. Broader in its coverage than the Leninist four-class alliance, its program appealed to the tribal minorities living in the strategically crucial mountainous areas surrounding the Red River Delta, and to the progressive elements in Laos and Cambodia against the common enemy of French colonialism.[15]

The most visible feature of the new front was its clear focus on nationalism. Proclaiming that there were two central tasks in the Vietnamese revolution, that of anti-imperialism (national independence) and anti-feudalism (the land revolution), the Party declared that under present conditions the task of anti-imperialism must be given the highest priority. This was a bold bid for the support of all patriotic elements in Vietnamese society, including the landed gentry and the national bourgeoisie, who according to the resolution issued at the close of the plenum, were now suffering from the impact of imperialism and fascism and were sympathetic to the revolution, or were at least neutral.[16]

To win the support of such groups, however, the Party would obviously have to temper its traditional appeal to class struggle. Most important, it would have to moderate its land program, replacing a call for confiscation of the land of landlords with a more limited program calling for rent reduction and the seizure of land belonging to the colonial regime and traitorous elements. This was a gamble, for in the new revolutionary strategy adopted by the conference, calling for an escalating guerrilla struggle in rural areas leading to a general uprising in the cities, the support of the peasantry would be crucial. The Party did not shrink from the task, however. According to the resolution:

> In the present stage, the nation has prime importance, and all demands which are of benefit to a specific class, but which are harmful to the national interest must be subordinated to the survival of the race. At this moment, if we do not resolve the problem of national liberation, and do not demand independence and freedom for the entire people, then not only will the entire people of our nation continue to live the life of beasts, but also the interests of individual social classes will not be achieved, for thousands of years.[17]

To a certain extent the new front probably represented an imitation of the Maoist strategy of people's war recently adopted in China. Put another way, however, it could be viewed as a return to the program of the League, when Ho Chi Minh had singled out anti-imperialism and anti-feudalism as the twin pillars of the revolutionary movement. Now, as then, the primary appeal was to the cause of national independence. The League foundered on that issue, as radicals contended that the demands of patriotism had submerged those of ideology. Now the front would be under the firm direction of a disciplined and experienced Communist party. The guiding role of the Party, however, would be disguised in order to maximize the appeal to moderates.

Throughout the next four years the ICP attempted to mold the new Vietminh Front into a formidable weapon to turn against the French and the Japanese. Front work proceeded on two levels. At one level Ho Chi Minh, from his base in South China, attempted to persuade the leaders of rival nationalist parties to join with the Vietminh in a "united front from above" to create a broad anti-colonialist and antifascist alliance to seek independence at the close of the war. This effort was hindered by the legacy of bitterness between the nationalists and the ICP and had only modest success. Eventually the Party created its own puppet political parties, the Democratic party and the Socialist party, to attract progressive but noncommunist intellectuals into the movement.

In the meantime, the mass organizations set up during the Popular Front were renamed "national salvation associations" (*cuu quoc hoi*) and placed under the administrative direction of the Vietminh Front, where they were used to broaden the membership of the front at the base level. Success was greatest in rural areas of North and Central Vietnam, where poor economic conditions produced widespread hunger, but a small municipal apparatus was built in the major cities. Paradoxically, the front had less success in the Mekong Delta, where the Cao Dai and Hoa Hoa sect movements were largely resistant to outside influence, but did well in Saigon, where thousands of young Vietnamese were recruited into an ostensibly apolitical, but Party-directed, Vanguard Youth Movement under the communist organizer Pham Ngoc Thach.

The overall effectiveness of ICP strategy was strikingly demonstrated during the August Revolution of 1945, which brought the Vietminh briefly to power at the close of the war. Vietminh guerrillas, taking advantage of the vacuum left by the surrender of Japan, attacked villages and market towns throughout the northern and central regions of the country while Party operatives sparked general uprisings in the major cities. In Hanoi the forces of the front seized power almost without bloodshed and set up a provisional democratic republic with Ho Chi Minh as president. In the South, where the Vietminh organization faced stiffer competition from rival nationalist groups and the sects, it entered a coalition with other parties and factions to negotiate with the returning French. By October, however, they were driven from Saigon by arriving French military forces.

It was a measure of the ingenuity and tact of Ho Chi Minh that the new government in Hanoi was able to maintain itself in power during the next several months of political maneuvering and tortuous negotiations with the rival nationalists and the French. Popular support for the Vietminh was fairly broad, but it was also shallow, and based on such "mass line" issues as moderate social reform, ending the food crisis, and national independence, as well as the implied support of the allied powers. Now burdened with the responsibility of power, the Party had to adopt measures sufficiently progressive to appeal to poor peasants and workers yet sufficiently moderate to avoid alienating the patriotic landed gentry and the urban bourgeoisie. In negotiations with the French, Ho had to satisfy militant nationalists yet avoid a collapse of talks and the onset of war. For a few months he was able to maintain a delicate balance, negotiating a preliminary agreement with the French and bringing rival nationalist parties into a coalition cabinet. As a gesture of sincerity, the ICP dissolved itself, although it remained in fact the dominating force in both the government and the front. By the summer of 1946, however, the uneasy alliance with the nationalists began to break down, and the government was restructured in October, with key cabinet posts in the hands of the ICP and its sympathizers.[18] When the war with the French broke out in December, the government was strongly leftist in composition.

Front Strategy During the
First Indochina War

The Vietminh strategy of mobilizing a national coalition of classes, ethnic groups, and religious factions under Party leadership formed the basis for the Party's political program during the next several years of war against the French. The foundation of the front was the Leninist concept of the worker-peasant alliance, with the proletariat viewed as the leading force and the peasantry as the basic force of the revolution. This was not simply a ritualistic gesture of the need for proletarian leadership over a Maoist-style peasant war against French power in the cities. While Vietminh strategy was based on the need to carve out liberated base areas in the countryside, and while the vast majority of the military forces in the service of the revolution were of peasant origin, Party leaders viewed the cities as crucial to the struggle, not only as a source for leading cadres in the Party, but from a strategic point of view as well. Party planners were convinced that, unlike the Kuomintang in China, the French colonial regime could not be starved out by strangulation from the countryside, but must be overthrown from within, by a general uprising in urban areas. The Party's municipal apparatus was thus called upon to undermine support for the French in the cities, and, through workers' strikes and demonstrations, to destabilize the French regime.[19]

This carefully constructed image of a national struggle linking town and country, Catholics and Buddhists, ethnic Vietnamese and the national minorities became a set feature of Vietminh propaganda and was widely accepted as accurate. A closer look, however, reveals that the public image is somewhat misleading. In the first place the movement in the cities did not fully meet expectations. Recruitment for the Party's municipal apparatus was impeded by public apathy and French repression, and fell short of requirements. Mobilization of the urban population against the colonial regime had only sporadic success, and after an impressive series of popular demonstrations in Saigon in 1950, the movement declined for the remainder of the war. By 1952 Party leaders became resigned to the fact that the urban areas would not play an active role in the resistance struggle against the French.[20]

The Party's overall weakness in urban areas was accentuated by its failure to attract active support for the national liberation struggle from the leaders of rival nationalist parties. The Vietminh Front had been designed as a broad nationalist alliance in which the ICP was only one, and not in appearance as the dominant element. This image became crucially important by the late 1940s, when the French attempted to create a noncommunist alternative to the Vietminh in the form of an Associated State of Vietnam under the titular leadership of former emperor Bao Dai. Few nationalists were attracted to the "Bao Dai formula," convinced that it was simply a fig leaf for continued French domination. But many had been antagonized by the high-handed tactics used by the ICP in the summer and fall of 1946 and refused to respond to Vietminh appeals for cooperation. Party leaders had anticipated this problem and in late 1946 had created a new front, the League for the National Union of Vietnam, or *Lien Viet*, to attract support from independents and moderates. But the ruse was not particularly successful, and in 1951 the *Lien Viet* was merged with the Vietminh into a single Lien Viet Front. The appearance of this new organization coincided, however, with a perceptible turn to the left in the government's posture, and had little apparent effect in broadening the base of the movement.[21]

The relative weakness of the Party's urban program made recruitment in the rural areas doubly important. The peasants, although comparatively under-represented in the leading councils of the Party, were the foot soldiers of the revolution and the key to the success of people's war strategy. The victory in August 1945 had been based in considerable measure on the ability of the Front to mobilize peasants in the famine-raked areas of the Red River Delta and the central coast. During the war against the French, these areas continued to supply the bulk of the recruits to the revolutionary armed forces. Elsewhere, the Party ran into difficulties. In the South, efforts to establish an effective alliance with the sects foundered on mutual suspicion, and sect leaders turned to the French. In tribal minority areas, Party efforts to organize were blunted by a French strategy of granting autonomy to tribal groups under their own leaders.[22] Even in areas considered sympathetic to the revolution, difficulties arose as the need for recruits increased. By 1950 it became clear that the relatively moderate land reform program emphasizing rent reduction rather than land redistribution was having indifferent success in attracting support from the rural poor. Beginning in 1951, more emphasis was placed on confiscation of landlord land and on guaranteeing that local peasant associations were dominated by poor and landless peasants. Party sources assert that the stiffer policy, which culminated in a new land reform law in 1953, had a significant impact on recruitment efforts at the village level.[23]

It was at this time that the Party's long-projected but hitherto dormant strategy of linking the Vietnamese revolution with its counterparts in Laos and Cambodia first came into play. The world war had stimulated the growth of small but active nationalist movements in both protectorates. In 1951 radical elements within the nationalist movements in both countries were organized by the Party into separate revolutionary parties under the overall guidance of the ICP. This coincided with the increasing extension of Vietminh military operations throughout Indochina.[24]

After 1951, for a variety of reasons, the war became progressively more military in character, and the role of the united front became limited in practice to promoting the recruitment of the rural population into the revolutionary armed forces. The united front strategy followed during the First Indochina War had contributed in a number of ways to the successes achieved on the battlefield and, in the spring and summer of 1954, at the conference table. But it had also revealed that support for the Party and its programs was stronger in some areas than in others, and that its appeal was weakest in South Vietnam. It was no accident that the compromise settlement engineered at Geneva resulted in a divided Vietnam, with the communists represented by the Democratic Republic of Vietnam (D.R.V.) in the North, and the noncommunists in a new Republic of Vietnam in the South.

The National Liberation Front and the Second Indochina War

In the fall of 1954, the Party (renamed in 1951 the Vietnam Workers' party, *Dang Lao Dong Viet Nam*, or VWP) returned in triumph to Hanoi. For the next few years emphasis was placed on building a socialist society in the D.R.V., while seeking the reunification of North and South by political means. Under the new conditions the united front resumed the importance it had attained during the early period of the conflict against the French. The Party's initial political objective in South Vietnam was to consolidate and broaden its base among the diverse groups within the local population and the new U.S.-supported regime of Ngo Dinh Diem. At first, Party policy focused on compelling the Diem regime to carry out the provisions of the Geneva Accords which called for national elections throughout the country. Vietminh cadres (several thousand of whom had been left behind in the South after the signing of the Geneva agreement) and so-called "under the blanket" sympathizers (many of them intellectuals who had become involved in the movement through urban protests during the war against the French) formed "peace committees" whose aim it was to pressure the Saigon government to agree to hold national elections. The most prominent of such committees was set up in the Saigon metropolitan area, but similar bodies were established in provincial and district capitals and even in rural villages where the communists had established a presence during the Franco-Vietminh War.[25]

While overt activities were restricted to such legal or semilegal operations, Party activists in the South were also preparing for the possible resumption of revolutionary war. To that purpose, clandestine Vietminh organizers sought contacts with other groups hostile to the Diem regime, notably with the religious sects and tribal minority groups in the Central Highlands. As had been the case during the pre-Geneva period, this initiative had only moderate success, and despite Diem's efforts to suppress sect opposition to his centralizing efforts, only dissident elements agreed to coordinate their military activities with those of the communists.[26]

Hanoi's efforts to compel the Diem regime to hold national elections failed. Organizations such as the peace committees were shut down and their leaders were arrested, while roving tribunals went from village to village to hunt down and execute suspected communist sympathizers. It was apparently as a result of such setbacks that in September 1955 Hanoi established a new national front organization, the Fatherland Front (*Mat Tran To Quoc*), to achieve reunification. Successor to the Lien Viet Front, it was based in Hanoi, but designed to operate in the South as well. The new front was a broad one:

> ready to welcome into its ranks all those who are sincerely opposed to the U.S.-Diem scheme of dividing the country, and sincerely stand for national reunification. The front is ready to unite with all patriots whatever their political tendencies, religions, etc. Thus it will include all persons who now sincerely want to serve the Fatherland, whatever parties or groups they have belonged to in the past.[27]

For the next few years Hanoi attempted to promote the revolutionary movement in the South by primarily political means. But the repressive measures adopted by the Diem regime kept the Party's forces off balance, rooting out its infrastructure in the villages and arresting its operatives in Saigon and the big cities. In early 1959 the Central Committee decided to step up the pace of the revolutionary activity. While Party leaders appeared initially somewhat uncertain of the best strategy to adopt, it was clear from the outset that political struggle would play a significant, if not dominant, role in the revolutionary rise to power. The major weakness of the Diem regime was political—its lack of support among the population—while the primary strength of the communists was also political—their experience and organizational base, a legacy of the previous conflict against the French.

To deal with the changed situation, the Party decided to create a new united front that could appear to represent the legitimate aspirations of the southern population in its struggle against the Saigon regime. In line with the Vietminh model, direct links between the new front and the communists would be disguised in order to avoid frightening moderates; in order to appeal to autonomous sentiment in the South, no direct ties with the regime in the North would be visible. In short, the new front would appear as a broad, nonpartisan movement representing all progressive elements in South Vietnam against the Diem regime.

The new front, however, clearly owed its origins and existence to the Party. At the Third National Congress of the Vietnam Workers' party, held in 1960, several speakers alluded to the need for such as organization to provide the symbolic leadership for the national liberation struggle in the South. As described by Party veteran Ton Duc Thang, the new front should take the form of a Leninist four-class alliance. Its program would be general in nature and would emphasize such nonthreatening issues as national independence, peace, neutrality, and social reform. Its ultimate objective would be the creation of a peaceful, democratic government in South Vietnam which would discuss the issue of national reunification with the D.R.V. in due course.[28]

A few weeks later, at a conference held secretly in South Vietnam, the new front formally took shape. Delegates representing the various interest groups in South Vietnamese society joined a new organization called the National Front for the Liberation of South Vietnam, or the NLF. The nationalist component was emphasized by identifying the Diem administration with U.S. imperialism. The communist complexion of the organization was disguised by endowing leadership in individuals not heretofore identified with the Party, but from the elements that had been active in progressive circles in the 1950s.[29] The delicate issue of social revolution was handled with caution. Emphasis was on democratic freedoms, workers' rights, and "land to the tiller" programs, reflecting the declared goal of completing the national democratic rather than the socialist stage of the revolution.

Like its predecessor, the new front operated on various levels. On the one hand, it took the form of an alliance of formal political parties. The most prominent, of course, was the VWP itself, which, through the Central Committee and the Politburo, played the directing role in the Vietnamese revolution. In this instance, because the Party was anxious to mask its role in the revolutionary struggle in South Vietnam, an allegedly separate Marxist-Leninist party, called the Peoples' Revolutionary Party (PRP), was established in the South in 1962. In actuality, the PRP was directly subordinated to the VWP Central Committee in Hanoi. The other two political parties affiliated with the NLF were the Democratic Party of South Vietnam (*Dang Dan Chu Mien Nam Viet Nam*), which represented the interests of the urban bourgeoisie, and the Radical Socialist party (*Dang Xa Hoi Cap Tien*), which was formed to appeal to progressive intellectuals. Both were essentially puppet parties which were created to appeal to progressive and patriotic elements in the South who for one reason or another were not members of the VWP. They were apparently the southern counterparts of the two similar parties in the D.R.V., the Democratic party and the Socialist party, both of whom were now affiliated with the VWP-dominated Fatherland Front, and later in the Provisional Revolutionary Government (PRG) set up in 1969 as a shadow government to represent the South in negotiations. Neither, however, possessed the substance of power, and their positions on domestic and international issues were virtually indistinguishable from those of the VWP.[30]

For millions of ordinary Vietnamese the most visible manifestations of the new front were the functional mass organizations. Descendants of the national salvation associations of the 1940s, they represented the various interest groups in South Vietnamese society. The most prominent, because they reflected elements considered important to the overall success of the revolutionary struggle, were the Farmers' Liberation Association and the Youth Liberation Association. Others represented the prominent ethnic and religious groups in southern society, such as the Association for Vietnamese of Chinese Origin, the Patriotic Buddhist Believers' Association, the National Liaison Committee of Patriotic and Peace-Loving Catholics, and the Patriotic Khmer Monks' Solidarity Association.

Within a few years, membership in the NLF and its functional mass organizations reached into the millions. To countless observers in Vietnam and abroad the NLF and its affiliate organizations were identified with the rising level of domestic discontent against the Diem regime and its successors in South Vietnam. Although it was widely recognized that the NLF had the active support of the D.R.V. and included members of the Vietnamese communist movement in its ranks, it was at the same time widely viewed as an organization independent of Hanoi and largely representative of the aspirations of the South Vietnamese people.[31]

The role of the front in the struggle in the South was multifaceted, and reflected the flexible nature of the Party's revolutionary strategy. By 1963 Party strategists had come to realize that there were several possible scenarios by which victory in the South might be achieved, ranging from a negotiated settlement to an all-out military offensive based loosely on the Maoist model of people's war. In the latter case, the role of the NLF would be primarily to mobilize popular support and participation in the war effort. In the event of a diplomatic solution, the front could play an active political function as part of a coalition government in a transitional period between the end of hostilities and the rise of the communists to power. This option apparently first received serious consideration in 1962, when great power negotiations over Laos led to a tripartite coalition government including rightists, leftists, and neutralists under Souvanna Phouma, and briefly convinced party leaders that a similar arrangement was possible in Vietnam. Hanoi's demand that the Diem government be overthrown was replaced by an appeal for the formation of a coalition government including "all political parties, cliques, groups of all political tendencies, social strata, members of all religions." In preparation for a possible settlement on the Laotian formula, Hanoi began to approach neutralist figures in South Vietnam and exile groups in France on their possible interest in serving in such a coalition government with the NLF. To maximize communist influence, prospective "under the blanket" sympathizers who were considered acceptable to the United States were groomed as possible members of a neutralist "third force" in a future coalition government. This group would presumably have helped to usher in communist control.[32]

By late 1963, however, it became clear that the United States had little interest in pursuing a political settlement in Vietnam along the lines of the Laotian agreement. From that point Hanoi's attention shifted to a dual military-political approach which would combine a general offensive against Saigon's armed forces in the countryside with a popular uprising led by the Party's clandestine apparatus in the major cities. The new strategy reflected the Party's disillusionment with the primarily military people's war approach used against the French and a conviction that the August Revolution model of combined urban-rural, military and political struggle could work more effectively in the South. Overall, the new approach demonstrated the Party's confidence in its political organization in South Vietnam and the ability of the NLF to mobilize support in both urban and rural areas for the cause of the revolution.

Between 1963 and 1968 the Party's operatives in the South carried on front activities on several levels. In rural areas the primary task of the front was to recruit peasants into front organizations and the People's Liberation Armed Forces. Some groups, like the tribal minorities in the Central Highlands, received particular attention because of their strategic location. In general the "mass line" approach was adopted. Land reform in liberated areas, for example, was kept moderate in order to attract or at least neutralize middle and rich peasants. Where necessary, however, party units relied on the selective use of terrorism to achieve compliance and respect from the local population.

If the Party's rural policy was essentially an adaptation of techniques used in the war against the French, its urban strategy represented a deliberate, if qualified, return to the model of the August Revolution. While preparing for the possibility of protracted revolutionary war, Party leaders also considered the possibility of a collapse of the Saigon government or a political settlement. Hanoi's strategy reflected this duality. On the one hand, the clandestine apparatus, composed primarily of dedicated young workers and students, carried out terroristic activities to destabilize the Saigon regime and create conditions for the general uprising. In the meantime front operatives worked behind the scenes to undermine support for the government in the South and promote the growth of the NLF as a possible element in a coalition government.

On the whole, the Party's rural strategy was effective. Recruitment efforts attracted thousands of adherents into the various organizations of the movement, and by late 1964 the revolutionary forces reportedly controlled 90 percent of the territory and over half the population of South Vietnam. But the Party continued to encounter difficulties with a number of key religious and ethnic groups in South Vietnam, and with the middle class in the major cities. The Catholics, the sects, and the overseas Chinese were largely resistant to the appeal of the revolution, and the front was limited to allying itself with dissident elements in such groups. Most significant, perhaps, was the Party's failure to work effectively with the rising Buddhist movement in the South. During the Diem era, a number of Buddhist bonzes and lay intellectuals became actively involved in politics. Some, like the enigmatic Thich Tri Quang, were vocal in their opposition to the war and to the Diem regime, and many leading figures in the Diem government asserted that the movement as a whole was under direct communist influence.

In fact, however, the Party had relatively little success in penetrating the Buddhist movement. While higher echelons tended to place the blame on the local apparatus, captured Party documents suggest that the problem was rooted in Hanoi's overall perception of the movement. Party leaders viewed Tri Quang and his followers as nothing more than petty bourgeois intellectuals who at heart were unreliable allies and potentially counter-revolutionaries.[33] As in the case of the bourgeois nationalist parties, where the Party could not dominate, cooperation was difficult.

The Party's inability to construct an effective and cohesive alliance in the cities did not have a serious adverse effect on the growth of the movement as a whole, but it helps to explain why the Saigon government was able to survive during the chaotic period following the fall of the Diem regime. In 1965 the Party's southern leadership was slow to take advantage of the turmoil following the assassination of Ngo Dinh Diem, and unable to prevent the consolidation of power by generals Nguyen Van Thieu and Nguyen Cao Ky at mid-year. In 1966, when rebellion against the Saigon regime spread in the northern cities of Hue and Da Nang, Party units in the area were ineffective in seizing the opportunity to guide it to their advantage. In both instances, the Party's urban base was too weak to make full use of the opportunity.[34]

Such problems did not immediately deter Party strategists in Hanoi from pursuing their efforts to utilize their forces in the cities to bring down the Saigon regime. This was clearly demonstrated in the Tet Offensive in early 1968. Captured documents show that Party strategists had fairly high expectations that a general uprising could succeed in such major urban centers as Saigon and Hue. Sapper squads were called upon to attack key government installations to create an atmosphere of chaos, while Party activists circulated throughout the urban area, distributing leaflets and calling upon the populace to rise in support of the revolution. The collapse of the Saigon regime would lead to the formation of a coalition government which would arrange for the departure of U.S. forces and open negotiations for peaceful reunification with the North.[35] In order to maximize support for such an eventuality from heretofore uncommitted elements in the South, a new front organization, entitled the Alliance of National, Democratic, and Peace Forces (*Lien Mien Dan Toc Dan Chu Va Hoa Binh*, or ANDPF), was established. Its program focused specifically on the goal of ending the war, and called for the creation of a free, independent, peaceful, and neutral South Vietnam. Like the NLF, its economic and social program was moderate. Its membership consisted mainly of middle class progressives, of whom many were presumably among the so-called "under the blanket" elements who were secretly in sympathy with the revolution but, in the words of one communist source, "could not endure the hardship" of life with the resistance. The chairman was Trinh Dinh Thao, a lawyer who had first become involved with the movement during the resistance against the French.[36] Had the Tet uprising succeeded in forcing the collapse or resignation of the Saigon regime, the ANDPF might have surfaced in early February and played a formative role in the coalition government to arrange for a cease-fire and the departure of U.S. forces. But the response of urban residents in Saigon and Hue to the uprising was below the Party's expectations, and the Saigon regime survived. The ANDPF was not formally unveiled until April and never achieved the recognition level of the NLF.

The Tet Offensive is often described as a watershed event in the history of the Vietnam War, marking a shift in American policy from escalation to gradual withdrawal and the pursuit of negotiations. It may be that Tet had an equally significant impact in Hanoi, as Party leaders evaluated the wreckage of their urban apparatus in the South and the failure of their urban-rural strategy to achieve a decisive victory. What is clear is that after 1968 Hanoi's strategy in the South put less emphasis on the role of the front and on the urban uprising in the final seizure of power, and more on the military offensive. This was reflected in the increasing part played by regular units of the North Vietnamese armed forces in the final years of the war, a trend necessitated by the destruction of local forces during the Tet Offensive and growing difficulties encountered in the recruiting effort in the South.[37] It was also clearly demonstrated in the Easter Offensive of 1972 and in the final "Ho Chi Minh" campaign which resulted in the seizure of Saigon in the spring of 1975. Both offensives relied primarily on military attacks by North Vietnamese units in rural areas and did not, like Tet, include plans for a general uprising in the cities.[38]

In the end, then, history repeated itself. As in 1954, what had begun as a primarily political struggle, with a heavy emphasis on the role of the united front, had ended in a classical military confrontation. United front work in the rural areas was relatively effective, but disappointing in the cities, resulting in an abandonment of plans for a joint offensive and uprising. It is only fair to say, however, that the front had prepared the way for final victory, and had helped to undermine support for the Saigon regime from crucial elements within the urban middle class. Psychological factors were of considerable importance in the collapse of morale in South Vietnam during the 1975 offensive.

In another way, too, Hanoi's victory was not totally military in nature. Hanoi's success in promoting opposition to the war throughout the globe —what was sometimes described as its "global united front" uniting the socialist countries, the various national liberation movements in the Third World, and the working class and other progressive forces in capitalistic countries against the conflict in Vietnam—was of crucial significance in bringing about a diplomatic settlement and the withdrawal of U.S. forces from South Vietnam.[39]

The United Front in Revolutionary War: The Vietnamese Model

As presented in this chapter, the Vietnamese version of the united front can be described as an amalgam of Leninist and Maoist elements adapted over time to indigenous conditions in Vietnam. Structurally, there is little that is unique in the Vietnamese model. Like its Leninist and Maoist counterparts, it is based essentially on an alliance between the proletariat—through its vanguard party—and progressive elements within the peasantry and the bourgeoisie. At the core is the classical worker-peasant alliance. What is distinctive about the Vietnamese version lies primarily in emphasis and application. Party leadership over the front, for example, has been a key feature in the Vietnamese version from its inception, a consequence of Ho Chi Minh's conviction regarding the weakness of bourgeois nationalist parties in Vietnam.[40] The CCP, following Comintern advice to join with the stronger Kuomintang in a "bloc within," learned that lesson only through bitter experience. The Party's assertion of superiority within the front has been a constant source of irritation in its relations with other organized political forces in Vietnam society, and one reason for its persistent difficulties in urban areas. On the other hand, it enabled the party to claim a central position in the national liberation struggle, and to exercise firm control over revolutionary strategy. On balance, it was probably more an advantage than a handicap.

The emphasis on nationalism, of course, has been a salient characteristic of the united front in Vietnam since the emergence of the Vietminh in 1941. But Party leaders have long been sensitive to the dangers of what is termed "petty bourgeois nationalism" within the movement (this is one of the major criticisms made by Hanoi today about the communist leadership in China) and they are exceedingly proud of their loyal adherence to the basic tenets of Marxism-Leninism. As a matter of policy, the Party has attempted to achieve a balance between the claims of nationalism and ideology within the movement and to maintain proletarian hegemony within the Party (although statistically workers are in a distinct minority and intellectuals make up the majority in the leading echelons). As this chapter has shown, this balance has not always been easy to achieve. Significantly, however, it did not appear to present insuperable problems to Party operations during the war in the South.

A third idiosyncrasy of the Vietnamese model is its strong emphasis on the need for a dual urban-rural base. While the alliance of rural and urban forces has been given lip service in most communist-directed fronts, few have asserted so insistently the need to build the movement in both areas. Hanoi is particularly scornful of the "peasant communism" practiced by the Maoists in China, and ascribes many of the internal splits within the CCP to that factor. In actuality, as we have seen, the Vietnamese model is stronger in theory than in practice. Front efforts did not bring the cities over to the side of the revolution in either the First or Second Indochina conflicts. At best, as in China, it neutralized the strength of the enemy in his own stronghold, no mean feat in itself.

Finally, the Vietnamese model has an "international" flavor which is essentially absent from most other versions. This feature originated with Ho Chi Minh but has been maintained effectively since his death in 1969. It reflects the need for a small country beset by powerful enemies to seek allies abroad. Few communist parties have been as sensitive to this issue as the Vietnamese.

The United Front and the Construction of Socialism

As originally developed, the united front was seen as a tool to be used primarily during the period leading up to the communist seizure of power. One of Mao Zedong's most important contributions to the theory and practice of the united front was his innovative use of the front—under Party leadership—down to the final stage of communism. Mao's concept of Peoples' Democratic Dictatorship provided communist parties in the preindustrial societies with the means of broadening their base of support among the local population for the surge to socialism.

In October 1954, when the Vietnamese Party leadership returned to Hanoi after the Geneva Conference, it followed Chinese practice and announced the formation of a Peoples' Democratic Dictatorship based on the worker-peasant alliance and the vanguard role of the Party.[41] There were persuasive reasons for adopting such a course. Whereas the size of the Party had expanded rapidly during the conflict with France, its political base in the North was still shallow. Over 90 percent of the inhabitants resided in rural areas. While the countryside had provided solid support for the Vietminh struggle, the average peasant's understanding of Marxist doctrine was limited. The tribal minorities, who comprised a significant proportion of the total population, could be expected to resist efforts to integrate them into Vietnamese society. The Party's urban base was also weak. The proletariat, the communists' natural constituency, was diminutive in size, politically unsophisticated, and only partly under Party leadership. The economic and technological base was small and had been further weakened by the flight of refugees to the South.

There were good reasons, then, for the Party to adopt a moderate program designed to encourage economic growth and consolidate popular support prior to the advance of socialism. During the next few years the regime concentrated its efforts on realizing basic reforms which could win broad approval, while delaying the advance to socialist ownership. Toward the various national minority groups the D.R.V. was relatively solicitous. While there was some pressure among tribal peoples to practice settled agriculture, they were allowed to retain their cultural traditions and languages and guaranteed representation in the political system. The Chinese community, the basis of much of the manufacturing and commercial activity in the North, was allowed to retain its separate school system, and Chinese nationals were not forced to seek Vietnamese citizenship. Catholics were promised the freedom to practice their religion, and the traditional link between the local church and the Vatican was retained. The regime also made special efforts to enlist the support of the small but vital educated community, assuring "bourgeois specialists" that their talents would be welcome in the nation-building process. In a program reminiscent of the Hundred Flowers campaign in China, intellectuals were encouraged to speak out on national problems. Binding all such groups together would be the new Fatherland Front, established in September 1955, and its mass organizations.

In effect Party leaders hoped to adopt the Maoist strategy of building a broad constituency within society based on an attitude of mutual trust between the Party and the mass of the population, while at the same time carefully adhering to the Leninist principle of maintaining firm Party leadership over the course of the revolution.[42]

In practice, it was not always an easy balance to achieve, and the "mass line" strategy did not always work out smoothly. The land reform program, begun before the Geneva Conference and completed in 1956, resulted in a substantial redistribution of land to the poor and the destruction of the landlord class. But it was marred by controversy and ended in recrimination. The problem was rooted in the dilemmas of the united front concept, and reminiscent of the dispute between radicals and nationalists in the League thirty years before. Many leading Vietminh cadres during the war against the French had come from the patriotic landed gentry. On returning to their home villages after the cease-fire, such veterans were frequently attacked by local cadres responsible for carrying out the land reform program. Some were simply criticized for their class background, while others were even labeled reactionaries and accused of treason to the cause of the revolution. To what degree this represented official policy is a matter of debate. Eventually, however, the Party leadership criticized such "leftist excesses," and a number of leading figures in the government or the Party, including Secretary General Truong Chinh, were dismissed from their posts.[43]

Other aspects of the Party's front strategy encountered similar problems. The policy of encouraging urban intellectuals to speak out soon led to criticism of the Party itself and its domination over all spheres of life, and was hastily scrapped. Official pressure on nomadic peoples to take up settled agriculture led to some discontent in tribal areas, while restrictions on the power of the Church (viewed by the Party as an independent force potentially hostile to the revolution) alienated many Catholics.[44]

Such problems were an indication that the Party's efforts to enlist mass support for its program of political integration and socialist transformation would not be easily realized, and the Party's behavior in the immediate post-Geneva period demonstrated that when its power or its supreme position in society was threatened, it was prepared to take stern measures. But the effort to build a national consensus around the Party's program continued, and in general succeeded. The nationalization of industry and the collectivization of agriculture, begun in 1958, were carefully orchestrated to accommodate the sensitivities of key groups in the population, and encountered little public hostility. The war in the South, which began to affect northern society in the early 1960s, undoubtedly posed new problems for the regime, but it was a measure of the overall effectiveness of front strategy that the diverse groups in the population were mobilized in a common effort to achieve national reunification. Indeed, some observers have contended that the war served to heighten patriotic sentiment and accelerate national integration.[45] Throughout the conflict the regime handled the national minorities with care. Ethnic Chinese and tribal youths, for example, were apparently not subjected to military conscription, although enlistment drives were conducted among both groups. When inducted into military service, they were often placed in separate units.[46]

The United Front and
National Reunification

Throughout the war Hanoi had consistently declared that victory in the South would be followed by a transitional period of separate administration prior to the formal reunification of the two zones into a single state. This strategy was based on the premise that the war would probably come to an end as the result of a negotiated settlement, leading to a coalition government composed of both communist and noncommunist forces. In the event, Hanoi's triumph in South Vietnam in 1975 was more abrupt and complete than had been anticipated, and many supporters of the Saigon regime fled the country. After a brief period of hesitation during which Party leaders apparently considered a prolonged period of separation of the two zones, Hanoi announced in the fall that reunification would take place in 1976. The process began in April, with elections for a unified national assembly, and was completed with the creation of a single Socialist Republic of Vietnam (S.R.V.) in July. The southern-based Peoples' Revolutionary party, which had posed as a separate revolutionary party during the war, was merged with the VWP in a new Vietnamese Communist party (VCP), and the front organizations in the South, the NLF and ANDPF, were abolished and integrated into an enlarged Fatherland Front for the entire country. In December a National Party Congress announced that there would not be a prolonged period of delay before the socialist transformation in the southern provinces. Rather, after a short period of consolidation and reconstruction, the advance to socialism would begin in the late 1970s.

Hanoi's decision to move rapidly toward unification and socialist forms of ownership in South Vietnam represented a calculated risk. Although open resistance to the new revolutionary administration had been minimal, many southerners harbored a deep distrust of northern dominance. Moreover, much of the population in the South was imbued with what Party leaders viewed as "petty bourgeois" habits and attitudes, a legacy of two decades of capitalist administration and American presence. There was a numerous and relatively affluent middle class, and a substantial number of prosperous land-owning farmers in the Mekong Delta. The Catholics, the sects, and the overseas Chinese had a long tradition of hostility to communism and could be expected to resist centralized rule and economic transformation.

Party leaders were undoubtedly aware of such problems and counted on the trusted weapon of the united front to surmount them. Still convinced of the essential popularity of the revolutionary message among the mass of the population in the South, they opted to continue using the concept of the four-class alliance as the base of the front down to the final stage of communism. As in China after 1949, the "mass line" would lead gradually to socialist transformation. In accordance with this strategy, at first the regime moved with caution. Private businessmen were assured that their property would not be confiscated, and that their legitimate profits were guaranteed. Official policy called for an effort to rally the local bourgeoisie to the new regime, and only a handful of so-called "comprador bourgeoisie," most of whom were speculators, bankers, and owners of large commercial and manufacturing firms, were accused of serious economic crimes against the people and severely punished.[47] To reassure private farmers, the regime announced that land would remain in private hands for the time being, and that no land reform program would be necessary because of the destruction of the landlord class under the Thieu regime. Following the Chinese practice of using "bourgeois specialists," the new revolutionary administration in the South attempted to utilize local expertise whenever possible and encouraged individuals in professional and managerial positions to remain at their posts. This did not always work out in practice, for cadres sometimes adopted hostile attitudes toward such elements, leading to official warnings against applying an overly rigid "classist" approach in selecting individuals for responsible positions.[48] Through such a strategy, the regime hoped to rally patriotic and progressive elements behind the government programs until the next stage of the revolution.

One of the major challenges for the regime would be to overcome the legacy of suspicion in the South against northern domination. During the war regional sentiment had been one of the factors limiting support for the revolution in South Vietnam, and occasionally erupted even within the NLF itself. Now Hanoi hoped to disarm such criticisms in advance. The establishment of the new revolutionary administration was accompanied by assurances that there would be no "bloodbath" of recalcitrant elements, although many southerners suspected of loyalty to the old regime were sent to re-education camps. Party and government officials in the southern provinces were strictly warned against arrogance in their relations with the local population, and overzealous cadres who used harsh measures to root out any decadent practices such as Western dress and hairstyles were publicly chastised. To allay suspicions of northern "carpetbagging," members of the southern apparatus, and of the "third force," some of whom had been clandestine members of the Party, were given visible positions in the new revolutionary administration. A few, such as former NLF chairman Nguyen Huu Tho and PRG Minister of Foreign Affairs Nguyen Thi Binh, were given high positions in the central government. As a token gesture to southern sentiment, the "third force" Saigon journal *Tin Sang* was given permission to continue publication and to engage in mild criticism of regime policies.

Those elements of southern society who aroused the most anxiety among Party leaders in Hanoi were undoubtedly the members of religious and ethnic groups, such as the Catholics, the overseas Chinese, the tribal minorities, the Buddhist intellectuals, and the sects. While liberation associations representing such groups had been formed and affiliated with the NLF during the war, many were mere paper organizations and had relatively little active support. With the conflict at an end, the regime made conciliatory gestures to bring such groups into the national front. A decree issued by the new revolutionary government shortly after the fall of Saigon guaranteed freedom of religion, and even the sect organizations were permitted to continue in operation, although the central headquarters of the Hoa Hoa—considered a hotbed of counterrevolutionary sentiment—was disbanded. Relations with the Vatican were retained, and Catholics were permitted to practice their religion, while sect areas and the tribal minorities were given special treatment.

In actuality the regime was deeply suspicious of the political orientation and inner convictions of such groups and worked actively to undermine the relationship between leadership elements and the rank and file of the membership. This was particularly evident with the Buddhist intellectuals and the Catholics—both of whom Party leaders considered fundamentally hostile to the doctrines of Marx and Lenin. This attitude was graphically displayed in an inner-Party document written sometime in 1979 and describing the regime's attitude toward the Catholic Church. According to the document, the Church organization in Vietnam was fundamentally reactionary and allied to U.S. imperialism. The technique to be used to weaken and transform the Church into an organization supporting state policies was the classical united front approach of *divide et impera*. Progressive elements within the Church should be encouraged while differences among the other groups should be exploited in order that reactionary elements could be eliminated.[49]

The Party's confidence that its conciliatory approach would lessen public suspicion of its intentions in the South and prepare the way for socialist transformation throughout the entire country was soon disappointed. Despite efforts to place southerners in positions of high visibility, northerners were still prevalent in the administration, inspiring widespread local resentment, even among individuals who had served in the NLF. Despite official admonitions against insensitive handling of southern sensibilities, northerners were frequently arrogant in their behavior toward the local population. Such attitudes were aggravated by official fears of the spreading influence of "decadent" southern culture throughout the country. Signs of discontent were particularly evident among the ethnic and religious minorities. Dissident elements from among such groups became increasingly active toward the end of the decade and began secretly or actively to oppose the regime. Although few posed a serious security risk to public order, they were a constant and growing source of concern.

The Party's decision in early 1978 to strengthen its control over the economy in order to reverse the deteriorating conditions in that sector only compounded the problem. Prosperous farmers, many in sect areas, resisted the regime's efforts to herd them into low-level collective organizations.[50] The nationalization of private industry and commerce, announced in March, and rumors that the move signaled a decision by the regime to eliminate the economic power of the Chinese community in Vietnam, led to a massive exodus of ethnic Chinese to China and other countries in Southeast Asia.[51] Tribal minorities resented regime plans to resettle ethnic Vietnamese from coastal areas in the Central Highlands.

Faced with an impending crisis, the Party changed course once again. In the fall of 1979 a new policy was announced, granting profit incentives to encourage production increases, slowing the pace of collectivization in the South, and restoring a limited private commercial and manufacturing sector throughout the country. The regime conceded that the process of building socialism would not be completed "in the main" before the late 1980s. Under this more tolerant program the economy began gradually to recover and the approach was reaffirmed at the Party's Fifth National Congress held in the spring of 1982. But there were serious political and social implications inherent in the new policy. The class of landowning farmers in the Mekong Delta (only about 20 percent of all farm families in South Vietnam were enrolled in cooperative organizations in 1983) were considered generally hostile to collectivization. According to official press reports, there were more than twenty thousand members of the bourgeoisie in Vietnam (as compared with only two thousand in the North in 1954), and over half of all retail trade throughout the country was in private hands. Party sources frankly conceded that few members of the urban bourgeoisie were loyal to the regime and its policies. Some, like the overseas Chinese, were openly suspected of ties with international imperialist forces. All were viewed as a source of decadent culture which is eroding the foundations of socialism.[52]

It was probably because of this concern that the regime combined relatively liberal economic policies with a tough approach to the various minority elements in the South. Potential sources of dissidence, such as the United Front for the Liberation of Oppressed Races (UFLRO), an organization representing tribal groups in the Central Highlands which had been originally established under the Saigon regime), have been vigorously suppressed. The United Buddhist Church, formed by noncommunist Buddhist intellectuals in the 1960s, has been forcibly disbanded and several of its leading members arrested. A number of priests and nuns have been convicted of serious crimes against the state and, in an effort to undermine the authority of the church, a new pro-government front organization called the Committee for the Solidarity of Patriotic Catholics was set up in 1983. Even individuals previously considered sympathetic to the regime, such as the Catholic "third force" intellectual Chan Tin, have been officially attacked or forced to resign from responsible positions for having expressed views critical of regime policies. Such measures have effectively prevented such groups and individuals from posing a credible threat against the regime, but they have also made a shambles of the official policy of uniting all groups in the population within the bosom of the Fatherland Front.[53] Party leaders were aware of the problem and attempted to address the issue by incorporating specific provisions about the role of the Front in the new constitution, approved in December 1980. But more than lip service would be required to restore the link between the Party and the masses. As one prominent intellectual sympathetic to the regime observed in 1981, the Front and its organizations had become no more than a facade, and badly needed reform.[54]

Today the regime is facing serious challenges in its effort to transform into an advanced socialist society. One source of the problem is economic. Unless the economy can be significantly improved, popular support for the regime, already slipping, could further decline. But the measures required to promote economic growth and social tranquillity inevitably encouraged elements hostile to socialism and suspected of loyalty to world imperialism or "international reactionaries" (Hanoi's code name for China). In the view of many Party leaders, slackness in the struggle against such forces within Vietnam could seriously undermine the authority of the regime at a crucial moment in the Vietnamese revolution.[55] In recent years Hanoi has attempted to straddle the issue, granting limited incentives to encourage economic growth while waging a fierce struggle against Western influence and maintaining a steady pace of socialist transformation. The results have not been promising, and the new leadership which has begun to emerge since the Sixth Party Congress in December 1986 appears more sensitive to the need to reconcile the Party's long-term goals with the needs and aspirations of the general population.

A key issue to the success of this effort will lie in the ability of the regime to impose its will on the South. In retrospect, it seems clear that in the hubris of victory in 1975 Hanoi underestimated the problems it would face in integrating the two regions and bringing the entire country to socialism. Historically, the peoples of the southern provinces have been distinct in character and attitude from their northern compatriots, and more receptive to Western cultural influence. This divergence was strengthened by twenty years of separation and American presence. Powerful social forces, like the Catholics, the sects, and the overseas Chinese, have demonstrated strong resistance to the egalitarian and centralizing message from the North.

The situation poses a severe challenge to the concept of the united front, which has served the Party so effectively in the past. Indeed, there are signs that the regime has tacitly concluded that some elements in the population, such as the overseas Chinese, cannot be effectively integrated into the front and into the socialist society it is designed to bring about. Having drawn that conclusion, the regime is resigned, and perhaps even determined, to permit them to leave. It is not likely, however, that it will feel compelled to abandon the concept of the united front itself, which is, after all, an article of faith in Hanoi. The Leninist principle of the vanguard party is deeply rooted, and based on long historical experience. At the same time, Party leaders will not easily abandon the supreme conviction that the revolution, and the leadership of the Party, are deeply rooted in the minds of the Vietnamese masses. It is probable that the VCP will continue to apply its front policies with that combination of flexibility and tough-mindedness that has so often characterized its behavior in the past.

It will not be an easy task, for Hanoi is faced with the central dilemma of many ruling communist parties in developing societies. The fact is such parties are often the victims of their own success. Through the astute application of the techniques of party organization and the united front, they are often able to take advantage of the weakness of their rivals during a period of social disintegration to rise to power. But they are often less qualified in terms of experience and ideological orientation to preside over the difficult period of transition to an industrial and technologically advanced society. And they soon discover that it is easier to assemble a broad popular alliance to achieve national independence and unification than to carry that alliance through to the final stage of communism. For the Vietnamese, long a divided nation caught in the maelstrom of the cold war, the problems of peace, as of war, appear to be of unusual complexity. It would be folly to underestimate the capacity of the Party to resolve its current problems—it has, after all, a good record of rising to the occasion. But it will require all of the ingenuity and experience of the Party's veteran leadership to cope with the problems it faces today.

7

The Coalition Strategies and Tactics of Indian Communism
Stanley A. Kochanek

The communist movement in India has been in existence for over sixty years. There are few countries in Asia or Africa, however, where communist parties have become so divided over the ability to analyze the objective conditions and resulting coalition strategies and tactics which would lead to a successful communist revolution. As a result the Indian communist movement has been unable to translate its potential assets into a nationwide political force. The movement has become highly fragmented and remains primarily a regional phenomenon.[1]

Origins of Indian Communism

The character of the movement has been shaped by the social complexities of the environment within which it must function, as well as its own internal dynamics. The Communist Party of India (CPI) was founded in December 1925 as scattered groups of Indian communists drawn from the major urban industrial centers of the North were brought together by the combined efforts of the Communist Party of Great Britain (CPGB) and M. N. Roy, a Bengali Brahmin and Comintern representative charged with directing revolutionary activities in Asia.[2] From the very beginning this small band of urban intellectuals under the watchful guidance of the CPGB was confronted with the critical task of assessing the political character of the Indian National Congress, led by Mohandas K. Gandhi, and the appropriate coalition strategies and tactics to employ in its relationship with the nationalist movement. From 1925 to 1947 the CPI loyally followed the twists and turns of the Comintern line on coalition strategies, with mixed results. Indian independence in 1947 brought the Indian National Congress to power under the leadership of Jawaharlal Nehru and created a new set of conditions. The issues of the assessment of the class character of the Congress, the CPI's relationship with the Nehru government, and the correct path to revolution produced widely divergent views among Indian Communist leaders and sharp shifts in coalition strategies and tactics. Within a brief period of four years, from 1947 to 1951, the party experimented with a variety of strategies toward the Congress government, ranging from rightist collaboration to leftist urban revolt to Maoist armed guerrilla struggle. Divergent interpretations of the relative success and potential of each of these strategies ultimately led to a series of splits in the communist movement in 1964, 1969, and again in the 1980s.

Although the fragmentation of the Indian communist movement began in the 1960s over coalition strategies and tactics, the initial split had its origins in the regional character of the party, its diverse leadership, and the social complexities with which the party had to contend.[3] By the 1980s India had developed two major communist parties and a variety of smaller parties, factions, and splinter groups, each attempting to develop and experiment with its own indigenous path to revolution. The CPI, the pro-Soviet parent party of the 1920s, has come to represent the rightist and centrist factions of the movement. Its basic strategy calls for a revolution from above by developing a coalition with the progressive bourgeoisie to create a National Democratic Front composed of all patriotic forces including the nonmonopolist bourgeoisie, the intelligentsia, the peasantry, and the working class. The CPI accepts the 1956 Communist party of the Soviet Union's (CPSU) doctrine of the possible peaceful transition to socialism and therefore participates in the Indian electoral process.

The CPI's electoral strength has declined substantially as a result of the split and because of its past coalition tactics of cooperation with the Indian National Congress faction led by Indira Gandhi. As seen in Table 1, the CPI's all-India vote has dropped from 5.19 percent of the popular vote in 1967 to 2.60 percent in 1980. Although the party received 2.71 percent of the vote in 1984, it was able to win only six seats in the Lok Sabha, the lower house of the Indian Parliament. In its heyday of cooperation with the Congress, it had held twenty-three seats. Party membership was 459,513 in 1978, 466,488 in 1981, and 478,500 in 1984. Its various front organizations claimed a total membership of some five million. The largest front organization, the All-India Trade Union Congress, claims a membership of 2.6 million.[4]

The Communist Party of India, Marxist (CPM) came into existence in 1964 as a portion of the centrist faction joined leftist and Maoist groups in splitting off from the CPI to form their own party. The CPM seeks to create a

Table I
Electoral Strength of Indian Communism in
the Lok Sabha, 1952 to 1984

Year	Party	No. of Seats	Party Vote (%)	Total Communist Vote (%)
1952	CPI	16	—	3.30
1957	CPI	27	—	8.92
1962	CPI	29	—	9.96
1967	CPI	23	5.19	9.40
	CPM	19	4.21	
1971	CPI	23	4.73	9.85
	CPM	25	5.12	
1977	CPI	7	2.80	7.10
	CPM	22	4.30	
1980	CPI	12	2.60	8.63
	CPM	36	6.03	
1984	CPI	6	2.71	8.67
	CPM	22	5.96	

Source: Robert L. Hargrave, Jr., *India: Government and Politics in a Developing Nation* (New York: Harcourt Brace Jovanovich, 1980), 204–5, XV, and Walter Andersen, *India*, in Richard F. Staar, ed., *Yearbook on International Communist Affairs 1985* (Stanford: Hoover Institution, 1985), 179–86.

revolution from below and replace the existing bourgeois-landlord state led by the Indian National Congress with a People's Democracy composed of peasants, workers, and other antifeudal and anticapitalist forces led by the CPM. For some time the CPM claimed to follow a path of equidistance in the world communist movement and believed each country must develop its own independent path to socialism. By the 1980s, however, the party began to develop a decidedly pro-Moscow tilt. While the party generally accepts the possibility of a peaceful transition to socialism, it considers elections and participation in legislative institutions simply part of its larger strategy of mass struggle. Over the past decade the CPM has replaced the CPI as the strongest communist party in India.

Although the CPM has become India's most important communist party, its strength is regionally concentrated in three states—West Bengal, Tripura, and Kerala. The CPM increased its all-India vote from 4.21 percent in 1967 to 6.03 percent in 1980 and its total number of seats in the Lok Sabha from nineteen to thirty-six. It suffered a slight setback in the Rajiv Gandhi landslide in 1984, winning only 5.96 percent of the vote and twenty-two seats. It recovered its momentum in March 1987, however, when it swept the polls in the states of West Bengal and Kerala. The CPM claimed a party membership of 368,000 in 1986 and over eleven million members in its various front organizations, including the 1.7-million-member Center of Indian Trade Unions (CITU), its labor wing. Membership in its front organizations has been declining in recent years, however, and the CPM has been unable to translate its front support into an all-India power base.[5]

Since the 1964 split in the communist movement in India, a variety of smaller parties, factions, and groups have developed to the right and left of the two major parties. The Communist Party of India, Marxist-Leninist (CPML), an Andhra Maoist faction, and a variety of fluid formations on the left, came into existence in 1969 when extreme left-wing and Maoist factions of the CPM split off to form a variety of independent units. Today there are more than a dozen separate factions and groups which are collectively referred to as Naxalites. Naxalites are generally pro-Chinese.[6] These groups call for a mass revolutionary movement and armed struggle to overthrow the state power of the comprador bourgeoisie, landlords, and bureaucratic bourgeoisie. These diverse formations are experimenting with a wide variety of efforts to bring about an indigenously based revolution. They form and dissolve with amazing fluidity. Similar fragments have also begun to develop on the right.

Overall, communism has proven to be quite effective in enhancing mass mobilization, but has had considerable difficulty in translating its potential assets into political power. The communist movement in India has a large number of front organizations, considerable strength in the trade union field, and the best organized parties in the country. Yet after sixty years of existence, the CPI and CPM had a combined membership of about 850,000 and their all-India electoral support has been relatively stagnant at less than 10 percent of the popular vote.[7] The parties have difficulty retaining members, members lack ideological training, and the class composition of the parties remains relatively unchanged. Factionalism and lack of discipline are endemic, and the movement has had difficulty translating the strength of its mass organizations into party growth. Perhaps even more critical is the movement's inability to establish firm roots in the vast Hindi belt of North India which contains almost half the Indian population.[8] Both parties, moreover, are led by a gerontocracy that will soon pass from the scene.

Communism in India, in short, has become stagnant and remains a strategic but limited regional force which has had considerable difficulty in pushing out from its regional environments into new areas. Communism in India has developed in isolated pockets under special conditions and has had a limited impact. These characteristics have reduced their ability to develop an effective coalition strategy.

The Environment of Indian Communism

The growth of the communist movement in India has been inhibited by a variety of social and institutional factors. In the first place, India is a highly pluralistic and segmented society in which social conditions lack uniformity. Each of India's twenty-five states has its own distinctive cultural, linguistic, and social diversities which make them distinct political units requiring their own strategy and tactics. Moreover, this very segmented character of Indian society has tended to determine the focus of political competition among social groups and cultural communities based on languages, region, caste, and religion and not on class. These status groups cut across class lines and inhibit the development of class identities and mobilization based on class appeals.

These social and cultural diversities have played a significant role in the uneven development and class composition of the communist movement itself. The communist movement began among the urban intellectuals in the British port cities of Calcutta, Bombay, and Madras. The party did not even exist in the South until the 1930s, when it proved highly successful in infiltrating the nationalist government and building a party base in areas where the Congress was weak and where the party could identify with regional movements against local princes who survived under British tutelage. In states like Andhra and Kerala the communists succeeded in developing a strong rural base anchored in the complex caste structure of the region. In contrast, the development of the party in West Bengal drew upon alienated Bengali intellectuals whose traditional status had been challenged as a result of British rule and who, drawing upon Bengal's terrorist and anarchist past, saw communism as a way of restoring their previous status.[9] Only very recently have Bengali communists turned to the rural sector for support.[10]

The simultaneous development of both an urban and a rural base presents its own set of problems. India's urban-based class structure is small and embryonic. Industrial workers in the organized sector of the economy make up only 10 percent of the total work force of 180 million. Moreover, only 3 percent, or five million, are factory workers. Therefore, not only is the industrial work force small but its portion of the total labor force has remained remarkably stable over the past several decades.[11] Until very recently the communist movement in India focused most of its attention on the mobilization and organization of this small urban industrial sector, with mixed success. The largest trade union in India remains the Congress-dominated Indian National Trade Union Congress (INTUC). The CPI-led INTUC claims 2.6 million members, or 25 percent of the total work force in the organized sector. The CPM-controlled Center of Indian Trade Unions (CITU) claims 1.7 million members.[12]

Organizing the rural sector presents even greater problems. Rural India contains 80 percent of the population and 72 percent of the labor force. The land reforms introduced by the Nehru government shortly after independence essentially eliminated the old feudal landed class. In their place there emerged a new, powerful rural force composed of a mixed status-class group of middle peasant cultivators, most of whom belong to the backward classes. These middle peasants, whom the communists call India's Kulaks, own between 2.5 and 15 acres of land, control 51 percent of the land, and constitute 35 percent of the rural households and 25 percent of the total population of India. They have emerged as a powerful political force in the rural population of India and have come to challenge the formally dominant position of the older traditional notables and large landowners who own more than 15 acres of land, control 39 percent of the total land, but make up only 6 percent of the rural households.[13]

Although the landless and the small landowners constitute almost 60 percent of the rural households, they have low levels of political consciousness, lack a sense of solidarity, have proven to be difficult to mobilize and organize, and are unevenly distributed throughout the subcontinent. These tenants, small landholders, and landless are still largely under the influence of the traditional notables and large landowners. Mobilization of the rural poor represents a long-term prospect and it will take some time before they are reached by modern forms of political organization. Moreover, the landless and small landowners do not share a common interest. The small landowners, holding less than 2.5 acres of land and controlling 10 percent of the total land, do not identify with the needs and aspirations of the bottom 27 percent of the rural landless population.[14] Finally, the distribution of the landless population is very uneven. Landless laborers tend to comprise a higher proportion of the rural sector in three southern states of Kerala, Tamil Nadu, and Andhra and in the northeast province of West Bengal, where they constitute 34 to 37 percent of the rural population. In contrast, landless labor in the Hindi belt of north India in the states of Uttar Pradesh, Madhya Pradesh, Rajasthan, and Punjab and in the western state of Gujarat represent only 12 to 23 percent of the rural sector. There has generally been a high correlation between high proportions of landless labor and communist strength.[15]

Uneven social conditions are reinforced by institutional and structural factors of the Indian political system which combine to place additional burdens on communist development. The social diversities of India have resulted in a communist movement which is nationally weak but with major pockets of strength at the extreme ends of the subcontinent in the states of Kerala, West Bengal, and Tripura. A communist government first came to power in Kerala in 1957 and communist governments existed in Kerala, West Bengal, and Tripura in 1980. Under India's federal constitution, however, states are not sovereign or autonomous. The central government occupies a dominant position in the system. As a result, communist power in a state cannot be translated into federal power because of the degree to which Indian states are subject to central guidance. Moreover, given the strength of the Indian police, military, bureaucracy, and judiciary, electoral Yennans cannot easily be converted into revolutionary base camps. Communist pockets of strength can be very easily isolated and contained. Thus state governments have enough power to attract blame but not enough power to reshape society except in limited ways. While state communist governments may use this power to bring about reform and build a stronger party base, their opportunities are still limited. Local outbreaks have been contained by central government intervention.[16] Thus structural factors reinforce cultural factors to prevent a breakout and make it difficult to translate local outbursts into mass all-India movements.

Another institutional feature of the Indian political system that raises problems for the communist movement is the single-member district plurality or winner-take-all electoral system. This system makes electoral coalition essential for capturing power and even for survival. The dominance of the Congress party from 1951 to 1977, the Janata victory of 1977–1980, and the return to power of Indira Gandhi in 1980 were all based on the relative success or failure of forging opposition united fronts. From 1951 to 1977 an all-India vote of 40 to 45 percent was easily translated by the Congress party into an absolute majority and parliamentary supremacy against a divided opposition which was able to secure a combined vote of 55 to 60 percent. The ability of major opposition parties to forge a united front in 1977 and a corresponding split in the Congress party resulted in a Janata victory. The breakup of the Janata coalition was a critical factor in Indira Gandhi's massive parliamentary victory in 1980.[17] A fragmented opposition also contributed to Rajiv Gandhi's landslide victory in 1984.

Coalition strategies have not only played a determining role in national politics but in state politics as well. The ability of the CPM to forge coalitions with other leftist parties and regional parties has contributed to its electoral successes even in its strongholds of Kerala and West Bengal, where initially the party by itself was in an electoral minority.[18] The CPM has been able to remain more ideologically principled than the CPI in selecting coalition partners primarily because rightist parties happen to be weak in these states and its chief competitor is the Congress.

In short, the weaknesses and fragmentation of the communist movement, combined with the social and structural features of the Indian political system, make coalition strategies and tactics essential to electoral success at both state and national levels. Yet the formation of coalitions is more difficult for communist parties because of the need to justify these actions in terms of a complex ideological analysis of conditions and objectives. Moreover, given the intellectual character of the communist leadership, the development of a correct line acquires a special significance and has become the basis of numerous factional conflicts. The class character of the state, the composition of the ruling party, and the permissible coalitions that may be formed all combine to determine the correct coalition strategies and tactics to employ at any given point in time and become subjects of intense debates and factional conflicts.

The coalition strategies and tactics pursued by Indian communism can be divided into roughly five distinct phases: the Comintern line from 1925 to 1947, the period of revolutionary transition from 1947 to 1951, the era of uneasy constitutionalism from 1951 to 1964, the period of fragmentation and competition from 1964 to 1978, and the attempt at forging left and democratic unity which began in 1978.

The Comintern Line, 1925–1947

From the time of its creation in December 1925 to 1947, the CPI basically followed the Comintern line. At the same time, however, factional differences within the party, even during this early period, resulted in the existence of an alternate strategy that commanded considerable support, created delays in implementation, and led to temporary deviations and departures from the official line by local units. Factional infighting was contained by the umpire role performed by the Comintern and the CPGB.[19] Thus from the very beginning, as Gene Overstreet observed, the CPI "was characterized by a higher degree of undiscipline" than most communist parties in the world.[20]

The implementation of Comintern policy by the CPI was carried out largely under the guidance of the CPGB. At the time of the CPI's creation in 1925 Comintern policy called for the forging of a united front with bourgeois nationalist movements. This policy was developed by Lenin in the wake of the failure of the long anticipated revolution in Western Europe following World War I. Lenin was convinced that the stalled communist advances in Europe could be revived by weakening Western imperialist influence in colonial areas and transforming European colonial empires into a burden rather than a blessing. This could be accomplished by fomenting and encouraging nationalist revolt. Thus Lenin saw the immediate task of the Comintern line in Asia not in terms of promoting communism but as a strategy for furthering the cause of revolution in Europe.[21]

Implementing the Comintern line of united front in India required a detailed assessment of the political character of Gandhi and the India National Congress. The Congress, established in 1885, had become the focal point of Indian nationalist aspirations. The CPI assessed the Congress fight for independence from Great Britain as the embodiment of a progressive international class alliance led by the bourgeoisie. The CPI's role was to further radicalize the movement by cooperating with radical nationalists within the Congress and developing a strong left wing within the movement. Since the CPI at the time was composed of literally a handful of members, its leverage was clearly limited.

Lenin's death in 1924, the failure of the Comintern united front strategy in China in 1927, and the consolidation of power by Stalin as leader of the CPSU brought a major shift in Comintern policy to the left. The New Left strategy was laid down by the Sixth World Congress of the Comintern in 1928 and called for ruthless struggle rather than cooperation with the nationalist bourgeoisie. The nationalist bourgeoisie were now declared to be a collaborationist and reactionary force and the CPI was instructed to break its ties with the Congress. The new antibourgeois nationalist line included attacks on all sections of the Congress, even its progressive left wing led by Jawaharlal Nehru.[22] This shift marked the first of several unsuccessful attempts to develop an independent communist base and had the negative effect of isolating the CPI from the mainstream of the nationalist movement. The CPI did not participate in the Gandhian civil disobedience movement which began in 1930, and its attempt to establish a base in the trade union movement so alarmed the British that most top communist leaders were arrested and tried for conspiracy.[23]

The immediate impact of Stalin's new line was to badly weaken the movement not only in India but elsewhere as well. The strategy did, however, have two significant unintended consequences for the CPI. First, the British conspiracy case against the communists created sympathy within India toward the arrested communists, especially among the youth of the country. Second, the jails were transformed into Marxist universities as many young congressmen arrested in the Gandhian civil disobedience movement became converted to communism while incarcerated as a result of their encounters with the CPI activists.[24]

The rise of Hitler in Europe and Stalin's fear of Germany led the U.S.S.R. to seek allies in an effort to enhance Soviet security. The result was a shift in Comintern policy to the right. The Seventh World Congress of the Comintern in 1935 declared it was necessary for communists to reconcile the interests of socioeconomic reform and world revolution with the bourgeois-democratic sentiments of nationalist leaders.[25] In effect the new line called for a return to the united front policy of Lenin and cooperation with bourgeois nationalism. The Comintern united front strategy proved to be critical to the establishment and development of the CPI in India. The new strategy roughly coincided with the formation of the Congress Socialist party (CSP), the first major Socialist party in India. The CSP was formed in 1934 as a group within the Indian National Congress with the objective of pressing for a Congress commitment to social and economic reform. The creation of the CSP enabled CPI members to infiltrate the Congress by joining the new party. The communists became the most active and influential group within the CSP, gained legal cover for their party which had been banned by the British, and were able to identify themselves with the nationalist cause. The strategy proved so successful that communist membership increased from fifty in 1935 to five thousand by 1942.[26] In addition, the communists succeeded in capturing control of CPS units in areas of the South and in the North Indian state of Bihar. As a result, by the time CPS leaders realized what was happening and decided to expel the communists, they found to their shock and amazement that the latter were able to take the entire state party organization with them in most of the South. These areas along with West Bengal remain the center of communist strength in India to this day.[27]

The twists and turns of the Comintern during the war years from 1939 to 1947, like Stalin's ultraleft tactics of 1928 to 1935, proved to be a disaster for the CPI and prevented the party from capitalizing on its gains of the united front period. The CPI's sudden volte face of first denouncing the war as the great imperialist war and then embracing the war effort as part of the great people's struggle against fascism following the Nazi attack on the U.S.S.R. alienated many of its potential supporters. More significantly, however, the CPI's refusal to support the Gandhian Quit Indian Movement of 1942 totally isolated the communists from the nationalist mainstream and stigmatized them in Indian eyes as an antinational force.

The antinational stigma of the CPI's pro-British policy of the war years was reinforced especially in the vast Hindi belt of North India by the party's support for the Muslim League and its demand for the creation of

Pakistan.[28] Thus, while the united front of 1935–1939 had helped develop a communist base in the South, the Comintern policy of the war years so alienated Indian nationalist sentiments in the critical Hindi belt that the communists to this day are a weak or nonexistent force in the region which contains over half the population in the country. Overall, Comintern policy of the war years proved to be a disaster for the CPI. Its only gains during the period came when the British restored the legal status of the party which it had lost in 1929 and thus allowed the party to function in the open during a period when most congressmen were in British jails.

Despite the problems created by shifts in Comintern policy from 1925 to 1947, the CPI by the time of independence had succeeded in establishing itself as an embryonic force on the Indian subcontinent. At the same time, however, its development had been extremely uneven. Regionally, the party had established a base in the southern states of Tamil Nadu, Kerala, and Andhra, the northeast corner in the state of West Bengal, and to a lesser extent in the North Indian state of Bihar. Functionally, the CPI had created a trade union wing, a student organization, and a small peasant front. This peculiar pattern of development was to have a profound effect on the ability of the CPI to develop a unified line for independent India.

The Years of Revolutionary Transition, 1947—1951

The uneven development of the communist base and the diverse social structure in each of these regions made it extremely difficult for the communist leadership to agree upon a single interpretation of objective conditions and an appropriate postindependence all-India strategy. The CPI leadership differed in its analysis of the basic class character of the state, the relationship of the party to the bourgeois nationalist movement led by Nehru, and the appropriate tactics of armed struggle or peaceful cooperation. These differences produced four distinct lines, each with its own support base and each competing for acceptance and legitimacy as the correct analysis of the path to revolution.[29] These internal differences were compounded by the changing global patterns of the world communist movement which was itself attempting to develop an appropriate line to cope with the emergence of the cold war, decolonization, and the creation of communist states in Eastern Europe and China. Identifying with the international line was an essential part of establishing the legitimacy of any given domestic line. Domestic and international forces combined to produce frequent and sharp shifts in CPI strategy and tactics from 1947 to 1951 and laid the foundations for the later splits in the party.

A rightist group led by P. C. Joshi, S. A. Dange, and the British communist Rajani Palme Dutt saw the Congress as a government of the big bourgeoisie in alliance with feudal elements. However, this group considered Nehru, India's first prime minister and Congress leader, as a progressive force who could be encouraged to support progressive policies with the help of the left. In these circumstances, they argued, the CPI should follow a nonviolent, anti-imperialist strategy based on a four-class coalition composed of the proletariat, the peasantry, the petty bourgeoisie, and the middle bourgeoisie in opposition to the proimperialist and reactionary tendencies in the Congress but in support of the anti-imperialist tendencies of Nehru.

The rightist analysis was totally rejected by a powerful leftist faction in the CPI led by B. T. Ranadive. The left saw the Nehru government as a bourgeois-capitalist government representing the big and middle bourgeoisie. They therefore advanced a three-class anticapitalist revolutionary strategy composed of the proletariat, the peasantry, and the petty bourgeoisie based on urban violence and armed insurrection in the countryside. This strategy was designed to overthrow the bourgeois government of Nehru and the Congress.

Between the right and the left there existed a strong centrist faction led by Ajoy Ghosh, who tried to act as a peacemaker and at the same time ensure a uniformity between the CPI and the CPSU line.

A fourth faction, led by C. Rajeshwar Rao, offered a totally different line which attempted to draw upon the experience of India's first agrarian revolt in the Telengana areas of the state of Andhra. The Andhra or Maoist line saw the Nehru government as a colonial government dominated by the big bourgeoisie. They therefore called for an anti-imperialist, antifeudal national liberation movement based on a unity of all classes except the big bourgeoisie and the feudal landlords. This united front would develop an agrarian revolution that would spread throughout India.

In the four years from 1947 to 1951 the CPI changed its line four times as each faction succeeded briefly in establishing the supremacy of its respective strategy. The rightist strategy of cooperation with the new Indian government and the British in the war effort continued into the early months of independence. The national executive committee of the CPI rallied to the support of the Nehru government in 1947 and moved toward a policy of alliance with the progressive wing of the Congress. Behind the scenes, however, the war, independence, and partition had sparked a major internal debate over the correct line. The West Bengal unit of the party which had traditionally been anti-Gandhi and anti-Congress pressed for a policy of insurrection. The Bengali leadership saw the chaos caused by the war and partition in the province of West Bengal and especially its capital city of Calcutta as creating conditions which were ripe for revolution. They succeeded in shifting the headquarters of the CPI from Bombay to Calcutta, and at the second party congress in March 1948, they secured the adoption of a resolution calling for a mass insurrection to overthrow the newly established bourgeois national government of Nehru. Support for this line was legitimized by reference to the CPSU's endorsement of the Zhdanov line, which had been aimed largely at Western Europe and had called for a leftist insurrection. The Bengali communists saw themselves as part of a great worldwide movement of revolution which would catapult the CPI to power in India. As a result, the party embarked upon an eighteen-month campaign from October 1948 to March 1950 of urban and rural uprisings supported by the CPSU. Although the line included rural uprisings, the tactics of leftist line were largely based on urban insurrection and general strike. It called for a united front from below and a class alliance of the working class, peasantry, and revolutionary intelligentsia to bring about a one-stage people's democratic revolution through violent means.[30]

The line advocated by the Bengali urban intellectuals was not, however, shared by the more rural-oriented leadership in the CPI in the province of Andhra. Just as the Bengalis saw the chaos in Calcutta as creating revolutionary conditions throughout India, the Andhra communists saw a new revolutionary line for India based on their successful revolt in the rural Andhra regions known as Telengana. The early communists in the largely rural state of Andhra had been influenced by Bengali terrorists in British jails during the 1930s. Unlike the Bengalis, they were drawn largely from the educated children of aristocratic landlords. Since Andhra had no industrial proletariat worth the name, the Andhra communists were among the first to organize and seek support of the rural-based agricultural laborers. The communist movement in Andhra was able to strike especially strong roots in the Telengana area of Andhra, which at the time was controlled by the Nizam of Hyderabad, one of the over five hundred princely rulers that survived as part of the British raj. The Congress movement had confined its activities largely to the areas of India under direct control of the British and thus was almost nonexistent in Telengana. The Andhra communists therefore had a relatively free hand in organizing the poor peasantry and landless laborers in Telengana in the context of a regional nationalism which took the form of a national liberation movement to free the people of Telengana from the rule of the nizam. A mass struggle was begun as early as 1946[31] and had become well established by the time of Indian independence.

The Andhra communists saw their successful experience in Telengana as applicable to the rest of India and pressed their line in the form of what became known as the Andhra Thesis. The Andhra Thesis drew upon Mao Zedong's New Democracy. It identified feudalism and imperialism as the main enemy and called for a two-stage revolution with a four-class alliance of the peasantry, middle bourgeoisie, and petty bourgeoisie under the leadership of the working class. Guerrilla warfare based on the peasantry would be the instrument for struggle rather than urban insurrection and general strike advocated by the Bengalis.[32]

Encouraged by the success of the Maoist-led communists in China in October 1949 and preoccupied with the intensification of the cold war, the CPSU came out in support of the Andhra Thesis. In January 1950 the Cominform called upon all colonial and dependent countries to follow the Chinese way. Soviet endorsement helped legitimize the Andhra line and enabled C. Rajeshwar Rao, the Andhra communist leader, to replace B. T. Ranadive as General Secretary of the CPI. India was launched on the road to peasant revolt.[33]

The Andhra line of rural insurrection proved to be no more successful in bringing about a communist revolution in India than the leftist Ranadive line of urban uprising. Both were severely crushed by the newly established government of the Congress under Nehru. The CPI was banned, some three thousand communists were imprisoned, and party membership was seriously depleted.[34] Moreover, for the third time in its short history, the CPI became stigmatized as an antinational force for attempting to disrupt the first government of free India. After three years of violent struggle, the CPI stood close to paralysis and disintegration.

The Era of Uneasy
Constitutionalism, 1951–1964

On June 1, 1951, Ajoy Ghosh was selected general secretary of the CPI with the support of the CPSU and the CPGB. The rightists, under the ideological guidance of Rajani Palme Dutt of the CPGB, succeeded in regaining control of the CPI and the party haltingly moved from insurrection to an era of constitutional communism. Dutt argued that revolution in India was premature and the Congress too strong and established to enable a CPI-led revolution to succeed in the near term. The first task, he insisted, was to build a strong party and strengthen the anti-imperialist forces in India. Dutt acknowledged that the Nehru government was composed of representatives of the big bourgeoisie but saw the Congress divided and vacillating between a pro-British and an anti-British group. It was the duty of the CPI to strengthen the anti-British, anti-imperialist sectors of the Congress and form a united front against the Western imperialist powers.[35]

Dutt's analysis produced an uneasy compromise, and Ajoy Ghosh presided over a badly divided party. Ghosh's strength lay in his ability to serve as a peacemaker between the right, left, center, and Maoist factions, and unity was restored at the price of a weak central leadership and considerable regional independence. The CPI became a loose collection of regional units held together by Ghosh and the mediating influence of the CPSU and CPGB.

The shift in the CPI line from insurrection to united front came on the eve of India's first general elections. Nehru released the jailed members of the CPI and the party pulled itself together in time to participate in the Indian elections. Given its past history, the CPI did remarkably well. Although it won only sixteen seats in India's Lok Sabha, the lower house of the national parliament, and 3.30 percent of the popular vote, the party showed considerable electoral strength in Andhra, Kerala, and West Bengal. The CPI's success at the polls strengthened the position of the rightists, and yet also sparked a major debate over the forces responsible for this electoral performance. The right considered the election results to be proof of the success of its noninsurrectionalist line. The leftists and Maoists, on the other hand, saw in the results a strong justification of their line in the sense that the party did well in precisely those areas where mass mobilization and agitation by the CPI had been the most intense.[36]

Despite differences over the causes of its electoral successes, the rightists were able to further strengthen their position within the CPI as a result of a major shift in the Soviet line toward India. Nehru's consolidation of control over the Congress and the government following the elections, his efforts toward creating a planned, democratic, socialist model of development, and the increasing acceptability of his global policy of nonalignment began to attract Soviet approval. The U.S.S.R. ended its public attacks against the Nehru government and began to encourage the CPI to support his progressive policies. The rightists in the CPI came increasingly to argue that the communists should support not only Nehru's progressive anti-imperialist foreign policy but also his progressive domestic policies of planned economic development. They therefore pressed for a united front with the Congress and Nehru.

The leftists and Maoists continued to view India from a different perspective. These factions were firmly entrenched in the major base areas of the CPI in the states of Andhra, West Bengal, and Kerala. They saw the Congress party in these states as their major adversary rather than as a potential ally. They therefore pressed for a more militant anti-Congress line.[37] As a result the CPI became plagued by the conflicting pulls of a national strategy based on an essentially weak all-India position and a regional strategy based on building key pockets of strength. National weakness called for cooperation with Nehru and the Congress in an effort to influence Indian foreign and domestic policy. Regional pockets of strength, on the other hand, called for opposition to the Congress, which acted as the chief barrier to local communist success.

From 1951 to 1964 the CPI succeeded in working out a series of tentative compromises and the party appeared to be moving in the direction of constitutional communism under the doctrine of peaceful transition to socialism.[38] The three party conferences held during the 1950s at Madurai (1953), Palghat (1956), and Amritsar (1958) accepted a strategy which gradually moved the party toward a rightist, united front line of cooperation with the Nehru government and peaceful transition to socialism.[39] At Madurai the CPI succeeded in reaching an uneasy compromise among its divided factions in the form of a tactical line which called for opposition to the Nehru government as a whole but support for specific progressive acts. By 1956 at Palghat the right moved into a position of increasing dominance, reinforced by the legitimizing line developed by the twentieth party congress of the CPSU, which laid down the line of peaceful coexistence and the possible peaceful transition to socialism. By 1958, with the election of the first communist government in history in the state of Kerala, the CPI meeting at Amritsar officially declared itself committed to the principle of constitutional communism and victory through the parliamentary path. The CPI had now become the largest opposition force in India and had seen its electoral strength almost triple from 3.31 percent in 1952 to 8.92 percent in 1957. Substantial growth in support was also reflected at the state level in Kerala, West Bengal, Andhra, and the Punjab.

The consensus that appeared to be developing within the CPI on the correct strategy and tactics for the movement was shattered by a series of events from 1959 to 1962 which were to end in the first of the series of splits in the party. Although the first split in 1964 coincided with the development of a major schism within the world communist movement itself, the causes of the Indian split were largely indigenous. Three major developments in the late 1950s combined to reopen debates over the character of the Indian government, the relationships of the CPI to Nehru and the Congress, and the appropriate strategy and tactics to be pursued in the future. The first major event which was to help destroy the painfully constructed consensus of the 1950s was the Sino-Soviet split. The split had the effect of removing the single, authoritative mediator and the ability to legitimize competing domestic lines by identifying them with the world movement as a whole. The second event that shattered consensus was the Tibetan revolt and the India-China border dispute which became public in 1959. The territorial dispute between India and a communist government created serious problems for the CPI by forcing it to choose between Indian nationalism and proletarian internationalism. Finally, the removal of the communist government in Kerala by the central government controlled by Nehru and the development of a major food crisis in the communist stronghold of West Bengal reopened all the old issues of the 1947 to 1951 period.

The CPI's sixth party congress, which met at Vijayawada in 1961, reflected the divisions within the party as dozens of draft resolutions were submitted for adoption. Ajoy Ghosh succeeded in averting a split by establishing a tenuous consensus. The compromise, however, proved to be short lived. The death of Ajoy Ghosh in January 1962, the Indian elections of February 1962, and the India-China border war of October 1962 combined to destroy the consensus of the 1950s and resulted in the first of a series of splits in the Indian communist movement.

The most difficult problem faced by the CPI was the party's response to the India-China border war. The rightists who controlled the central party leadership led a stampede to identify with Indian nationalist sentiment and condemned the Chinese action. The Congress government accepted the rightist leadership of the CPI as an indigenous national force. Leftists, however, were much more reluctant to condemn the actions of a socialist state and were arrested by the government of India as Chinese agents and traitors. The rightist leadership at the center immediately moved to establish their control of the state party units decimated by the arrests of the leftists. They captured control of these local units and reorganized the state parties to place themselves in firm control. When the border crisis eased and the left communists were released from jail in 1963, the left moved immediately to recapture control of their state parties and the CPI headed toward an unavoidable split.

The split in the CPI became final when each faction held its own seventh party congress toward the end of 1964, one in Calcutta and the other in Bombay. The split reflected two totally divergent views of revolutionary strategy and tactics and these differences became clearly outlined in the respective party gatherings of the two CPIs. At the same time, however, the split did not completely resolve the internal differences within the two successor parties. The four original factions split two ways, with the rightist and some centrists remaining in the CPI and the leftists, Maoists, and the remaining centrists joining the new CPM. This heterogeneity was to lead to a further split in the CPM in 1969 and in the CPI in 1980.

The documents that emerged from the seventh party congresses of the CPI and CPM provide a comprehensive picture of the issues which had plagued the party for over a decade.[40] Although the CPI blamed the split on the Chinese, at the heart of the dispute lay the fundamental issue of coalition strategy and tactics toward the Indian National Congress and its government led by Nehru. The CPI saw India as ruled by the national bourgeoisie following a capitalist path of development, which it felt had strengthened the base of nationalism and represented a historical advance from the former imperialist bureaucratic state of the colonial era. The national bourgeoisie, however, was not a monolithic entity but was subject to a process of increasing differentiation between the upper bourgeoisie and the rest of the bourgeoisie. It was the upper bourgeoisie composed of the monopolists and feudalists which represented the main antidemocratic and reactionary force. They were in fact in opposition to the more progressive elements in the national bourgeoisie. It was therefore essential for the CPI to align with these progressive elements to transform the existing national bourgeois state into a national democratic state by forming a coalition from above and developing a national democratic front. This national democratic front would bring together all patriotic forces, including the working class, the peasantry, the intelligentsia, and the nonmonopolist segment of the national bourgeoisie. The national democratic front would be a transition stage in which power would be jointly exercised by all classes toward eradicating imperialist interest, semifeudal elements, and monopoly capital. Gradually, however, the working class would come to occupy a leading position in the alliance under the leadership of the CPI. The national democratic state could therefore advance through the parliamentary process accompanied by mass struggle to prevent a reversal of progressive policies and to isolate the reactionaries. The combination of peaceful mass struggle and the isolation of the ruling class would ultimately result in their surrender. If, however, the ruling class were to strike back with the armed might of the state, then armed struggle might be necessary. In order to accomplish these long-term objectives, the immediate strategy for the CPI was to cooperate with the progressive leaders of the Congress and oppose the right reactionaries represented by the rightist opposition parties.

The CPM's analysis reflected a totally different set of coalition strategies and tactics. The CPM saw the Indian state controlled by the big bourgeoisie in alliance with the big landlords. This bourgeoisie-landlord state was following a capitalist path of development which, instead of strengthening the national base of the state, was leading to the strengthening of monopolists, increasing the penetration of foreign capital, and making

India dependent upon imperialist foreign aid. This development path therefore threatened national independence and the growth of imperialism. Since the Indian revolution was still in its agrarian stage, however, the CPM must focus its attack not only against the landlords and the imperialists, but against the Indian bourgeoisie as well. The CPM must work toward replacing the joint control of the bourgeois-landlord class by a people's democracy built on a revolution from below based on mass struggle. People's democracy would consist of a coalition of all democratic, antifeudal and anticapitalist forces composed of the peasants and workers brought to power through a process of mass struggle of trade unions, peasants, and other mass organizations. This revolution from below based on a people's democratic front would use elections and the parlimentary process as a tactical weapon of struggle. Fighting elections and forging alliances with the left based on a common program would not be expected to produce fundamental change but would result in limited tactical objectives of helping solve local problems and enhancing the morale of the democratic movement. Although the CPM would strive for a peaceful transition to socialism, it must be prepared for the fact that the ruling class might resist. To accomplish this long-term objective, the CPM must work to build a people's democratic front, form a worker-peasant alliance, and establish working-class hegemony over popular forces. Coalitions would be forged only with parties of the left, and cooperation with the bourgeois-landlord dominated Congress party was out of the question.

In short, the split in the CPI in 1964 represented a classic difference between two strategies of communist revolution. The CPI, with a uniformly distributed but weak national support base, wanted a revolution from above through a national united front. The CPM, with strong regional pockets of support, wanted a revolution from below to destroy the bourgeois-landlord state.

The Period of Fragmentation and Competition

Following the split in the CPI in 1964, the communist movement in India faced a period of fragmentation followed by a decade of intense competition based on divergent ideological lines. From 1964 to 1969 the CPI and CPM fought bitterly over the claim to legitimacy as the only true vanguard party in India. The CPI condemned the CPM as Chinese splitters while the CPM accused the CPI of class collaboration. Within the CPM itself the party leadership fought to maintain party cohesion in a desperate effort to control its ultraleft and Maoist wings. The delicate balance that existed within the CPM at the time of the split was soon shattered, however, by the party's unexpected successes in the 1967 Indian elections. The CPM suddenly found itself as the dominant partner in a broad-based leftist coalition which controlled governments in the states of Kerala and West Bengal. Shortly following the election, tensions within the CPM reached the breaking point when a local peasant uprising led by CPM extremists erupted among the tribal peoples of the Naxalbari area of West Bengal. The uprising was immediately hailed by the Chinese as the start of a true revolution in India based on Maoist principles of armed struggle. After initial hesitation, the embarrassed CPM leadership condemned the revolt as a left-sectarian deviation. However, the uprising had a electrifying affect on the CPM membership, and Naxalite groups emerged in various parts of the country attempting to duplicate the Naxalbari success. The stage was set for the second major split in the communist movement in five years.

Naxalite factions throughout India came together on April 22, 1969, to form a third communist party, the Communist Party of India, Marxist-Leninist (CPML). An Andhra Maoist faction, however, considering the designation "Marxist-Leninist" to be redundant, refused to join the new party, and established its own independent unit. Within a decade Naxalite splinter groups began to spring up throughout India like wild mushrooms. By 1979 a CPI journal was able to identify eleven separate factions.[41] Naxalites tended to be pro-Chinese, favored agrarian revolution, opposed formation of alliances or coalitions with the national bourgeoisie, and rejected electoral and parliamentary paths to socialism. They differed in their assessment of the class character of the state, appropriate strategy and tactics, open versus underground revolutionary activity, and the exact characterization of China and its competing leadership groups.[42] They have been able to attract support especially among younger people and students, but generally the movement spawned more leaders than followers.

As a result of the splits of the 1964–1969 period, Indian communism acquired a fluid character in which no single faction could claim legitimacy as the recognized vanguard party. Three major formations emerged which in turn began to spin off a bewildering array of splinter groups and factions of all types which have tended to form and dissolve with amazing speed in a desperate search for a correct indigenous path to communist revolution in India. The experimentation of the Naxalites with armed struggle, however, has been largely on the fringe of the Indian political spectrum and has had limited success. The major competition for supremacy has been between the CPI and CPM, each pursuing its own line in its effort to expand its base of support and its claim to legitimacy. The CPI committed itself to a strategy of revolution from above in the form of a coalition with the progressive bourgeoisie in the Congress. The CPM attempted a revolution from below while simultaneously attempting to wreck the political system from within. Both employed electoral and parliamentary arenas for purposes of mass struggle and mutual competition.

The fragmentation of the communist movement reached its high point at a time when the Indian National Congress was itself undergoing the first of a series of major splits over the issue of Indira Gandhi's leadership of the party. The Congress split in 1969 widened the gap between the two major communist parties as each party interpreted the split and its implication in very different ways. The CPI saw the split in the Congress as offering a historic opportunity for the application of the CPI line. The split was seen as a sign of a division in the national bourgeoisie between its progressive and reactionary sectors. It therefore called for an alliance with the progressive wing led by Indira Gandhi as the first step toward the establishment of its long sought national democratic front in which the CPI would ultimately play the dominant role.

In the early years of the Congress split, from 1969 to 1971, Indira Gandhi led a minority government, and the support provided by the CPI gave the party considerable leverage in pressing for the adoption of its program. The creation of a national democratic front appeared to the CPI to be imminent. The CPI succeeded in establishing a coalition government with the Congress in the state of Kerala at the expense of the CPM and came to see the Kerala example as the first phase of its national democratic front which would eventually extend to the center. As a result, Congress-CPI cooperation moved gradually from alliance with the progressive wing of the Congress to embracing the entire Congress as progressive. To the CPI leadership the validity of their line seemed self evident. To the CPM, the CPI-Congress alliance smacked of tailism and class collaboration.

The CPI-Congress alliance was further bolstered by communist pressure from within the Indira Congress. As early as 1967 a group of former communists led by Mohan Kumaramangalam, a South Indian communist, allowed its membership in the CPI to lapse and joined the Congress party. Their objective was to pursue the strategy of national democratic front from within the Congress itself. The author of this strategy was Kumaramangalam. Kumaramangalam argued that the support enjoyed by the Congress among peasants, workers, and sections of the petty bourgeoisie was based on the attraction of these groups to the Congress promise to build socialism in India. Any anti-Congress attacks only enabled the reactionary elements within the Congress to rally support in the name of these progressive programs. The most effective strategy therefore was to build a powerful movement within the Congress to act as a pressure group to insist on immediate implementation of publicly declared progressive Congress policies.[43]

The former communists who joined the Congress found a ready instrument through which they could press their case, called the Congress Forum for Socialist Action (CFSA). The Forum had existed within the Congress for some time and acted as a loose discussion group for debates on Nehru's socialist ideas. Just as the communists had used the CSP in the 1930s as a mechanism for infiltrating the Congress, so by the late 1960s the CSFA came to play a similar role. The former communists infiltrated and captured control of the Forum and used it as a lever to radicalize the Congress and press for the implementation of Congress declarations, including the nationalization of major private sector banks, control of monopoly, and the abolition of princely purses and privileges. At the time of the Congress split in 1969, Forum members were in a strategic position within the Congress and were able to exert considerable leverage on Indira Gandhi and her government.[44] Thus communist pressure from without was reinforced by communist pressure from within the Congress and the long sought national democratic front demanded by the CPI seemed to be near at hand.

The entire strategy of the CPI was thwarted, however, as a result of the Congress election victories of 1971 and 1972. Following the Indira wave which restored Congress dominance in the parliamentary election of 1971, the Congress was faced by a massive influx of former members anxious to take advantage of Indira's coattails to restore them to power in the state elections of 1972. As a result, the relatively small communist faction within the Congress was simply inundated by the mad dash of former congressmen to join the Indira Congress. The strategic position of the former CPI members within the Congress was destroyed and the Congress no longer had to depend on CPI support.[45] Although several former communists succeeded in gaining positions in Indira Gandhi's government,[46] a counterattack by old-guard congressmen succeeded in reducing their impact. By mid-1973 the CFSA was forced to dissolve, Kumaramangalam died in an airplane crash, and the Congress under Indira began to drift to the right. The CPI advance was stopped.

A new but unexpected crisis developed in the Congress in June 1975 which was to have an even more devastating impact on the CPI's pro-Congress line. Indira Gandhi's government had come under increasing attack in the mid-1970s for its apparent inaction and seeming inability to cope with a growing domestic economic crisis touched off in part by the 1973 global oil crisis. The noncommunist opposition, under the leadership of Jayaprakash Narayan, a highly respected Gandhian, began to galvanize an all-India mass movement into a potentially potent coalition capable of challenging the continued dominance of the Indira Congress. In the midst of the opposition challenge, the legitimacy of Indira Gandhi's position as prime minister was called into question when Justice Jagmohan Lal Sinha of the Allahabad high court ruled that Mrs. Gandhi had committed "corrupt practices" under the Representative of the Peoples Act (1951) during her 1971 election campaign.[47] Faced by an increasingly unified, electorally potent opposition movement and a court threat which called into question the legitimacy of her power, Indira Gandhi declared an internal national emergency beginning at midnight on June 25, 1975. All major opposition leaders were rounded up and arrested under the Maintenance of Internal Security Act (MISA), civil liberties were suspended, and Indira entered a twenty-month period of emergency rule.[48]

The CPI openly welcomed the declaration of the emergency as necessary to combat the fascist movement led by Jayaprakash Narayan and the parties of right reaction. CPI leaders believed they could turn the emergency into a communist revolution. Almost a decade of close cooperation with Indira Gandhi and the Congress seemed to be on the verge of bringing about a massive revolutionary breakthrough for the CPI. The CPI's image of a national democratic government dominated by their party seemed near.

Instead of looking to the CPI for support in her period of political isolation, Indira Gandhi turned to her younger son Sanjay Gandhi for political advice and moral support. The CPI became increasingly upset by the rise of Sanjay as a political force within the Congress and began attacking him as a reactionary. As part of their campaign against Sanjay, the CPI warned Indira to beware of the growing influence of right reactionaries within her party. The continued attacks against Sanjay finally resulted in a blistering backlash from Indira Gandhi in defense of her son. In a public speech before a group of congressmen in late December 1976, Mrs. Gandhi lashed out at the CPI for its attacks against Sanjay and condemned the communists for their past antinational behavior. Since her son played no political role, she declared, the attacks against Sanjay were really aimed at her personally. She found the charges of reactionary influence on her government to be insulting and accused the communists of collaboration with the British during the freedom movement and launching similar attacks against her father.[49] Mrs. Gandhi's open attack against the CPI and her swing to the right threatened a decade of Congress-CPI cooperation.

Despite increased strain between the CPI and Mrs. Gandhi, the CPI continued its policy of alliance with the Congress through the 1977 election. The surprising defeat of Indira Gandhi and the end of thirty years of

Congress rule by a coalition of largely rightist opposition parties called the Janata delivered a crushing blow to the entire CPI line.[50] The CPI suffered heavy losses at the polls as a result of its support of the emergency and its alliance with the Congress. Its popular vote dropped from 4.73 percent in 1971 to 2.8 percent in 1977, and the size of its parliamentary group was cut from twenty-three to a mere seven. As one of the few parties to support the emergency, the CPI was attacked by the opposition parties for its support of Indira and was accused of tailism by the CPM. Despite strong opposition from a pro-Indira faction led by S. A. Dange, the eleventh party congress of the CPI in March 1978 openly repudiated its support of the emergency and called for a new policy line of left unity.

Unlike the CPI, the CPM never considered the split in the Congress in 1969 as anything more than a crisis within the ruling party having little class significance. They rejected the CPI's analysis of the class implications of the split and the coalition strategy which followed from that analysis. Instead they characterized the CPI policy as one of class collaboration and tailism. In addition they saw the Indira victory of 1971–72 as setting the stage for one-party rule and authoritarianism. The CPI dismissed CPM attacks as blind anti-Congressism and they joined Indira Gandhi in bringing down CPM governments in West Bengal and Kerala and actively helped the Congress suppress the CPM. As a result the CPM was forced to lead a semiclandestine existence throughout most of the 1970s and was especially hard hit during the period of the emergency, when it was subjected to systematic repression by the government.[51]

However, the CPM proved to be remarkably resilient. Its well developed regional organization, dedicated cadre, and deeply implanted support base not only enabled the party to survive but also limited the impact of the Janata wave in its base areas. Although its performance at the national level was not impressive and declined slightly from 5.12 percent in 1971 to 4.3 percent in 1977, the party, in coalition with other leftist parties, succeeded in gaining control of the governments in the strategically located northeast states of West Bengal and Tripura.[52]

Post-1978 Convergence:
Attempts at Left and Democratic Unity

The results of the March 1977 elections were a severe shock to the communist movement and the entire left. The end of thirty years of Congress rule was brought about not by the left but by a coalition of largely rightist political parties. In fact the left was reduced to an almost irrelevant national force. The communists turned in their worst performance since 1952 as their combined vote dropped from 9.85 percent in 1971 to 7.1 percent in 1977 and the size of their parliamentary group dropped from forty-eight seats in 1971 to twenty-nine in 1977. Within the communist movement, however, the CPM almost held its own and succeeded in establishing a stronger foothold in its base areas in the northeast. The CPI, in contrast, was electorally and politically humiliated. The entire CPI line of alliance and coalition with the Congress which it had pursued for almost a decade was in shambles and the party hovered on the verge of a split.

The victory of the right and the defeat of the left touched off a wave of deep soul searching among Indian leftists. The left was suddenly presented with the possibility of the emergence of a two-party system in which two bourgeois parties would compete for power to the total exclusion of the left. This prospect sparked a major debate among leftist intellectuals and raised demands for the immediate creation of a left and democratic alternative based on CPI-CPM cooperation and unity.[53] The left, it was argued, must learn a lesson from the bourgeois parties and unite to form a third force in Indian politics or face the prospect of a total loss of influence in the Indian political system.

Given the drastically altered political environment, both the eleventh party congress of the CPI at Bhatinda and the tenth party congress of the CPM at Jullundur, meeting in the spring of 1978, endorsed the principle of left and democratic unity.[54] However, it was quite clear that each party had a very different concept of precisely what left and democratic unity would entail. This became painfully clear when the leaders of the two communist parties met on April 13, 1978, in New Delhi for the first time since the 1964 split to discuss the possibility of left unity. Despite the repeated calls for unity of the left by supporters and sympathizers, the unity talks produced very limited results. The fundamental issues which had produced the split in 1964 now combined with mutual suspicion and uneven party development to prevent unity in 1978.

The CPI and CPM differed fundamentally over their respective definitions of which parties were democratic and the appropriate coalitions, strategies, and tactics to pursue in light of changed political circumstances. Despite repudiation of its support of the emergency, the CPI was not prepared to change its overall assessment of the Congress. The Congress, it was argued, continued to contain left and democratic forces which could serve as allies and could be won over to help create a left and democratic alternative.[55] For this reason, continued cooperation between the Congress and the CPI in the Kerala united front government was essential. The chief enemy at this particular stage, according to the CPI, was the newly elected Janata government, which represented parties of right reaction in league with imperialism. The Janata was incapable of playing a democratic role, and the unity of the left must be designed to prevent the Janata from consolidating its control and ultimately bringing an end to Janata rule. Left unity would be brought about, therefore, only if the CPM repudiated its negative and opportunistic line of supporting the Janata party and agreed to join a mass struggle to end its rule.

The CPM, on the other hand, saw the CPI as unregenerate and harboring a desire to continue to cooperate with the bourgeois-landlord Congress led by Indira Gandhi.[56] The CPI's repudiation of the emergency was seen as half-hearted and its entire policy was symbolized by the party's continued support of the Kerala united front government. The CPM saw the authoritarian character of Indira Gandhi and the Congress as the principal enemy and insisted on building left unity to prevent a return of authoritarianism. Despite its class character and its many failures, the CPM saw the Janata as a major positive anti-authoritarian force which had played a historic role in restoring democracy to India following twenty months of emergency rule. Left and democratic unity must be based on support of the Janata government as an essential element in the struggle for democracy and against authoritarianism. It was necessary therefore for the CPI to end all cooperation with the Congress, including its continued support for the Kerala united front government. In short, the CPM saw left and democratic unity as support for the Janata against the Congress while the CPI saw left and democratic unity in terms of a unified struggle against the Janata and forces of right reaction.

Although the assessment and coalition strategies toward the dominant bourgeois parties represented the major stumbling bloc to unity, a variety of other divisive issues which had led to the 1964 split also persisted. The CPI resented the alleged anti-Soviet, pro-Chinese positions of the CPM in international affairs and its failure to endorse Soviet positions on key global foreign policy issues. In addition the CPI remained committed to its national strategy of a revolution from above designed to create a national democratic front dominated by the CPI. In contrast, the CPM claimed it was committed to an independent strategy which opposed any interference by either the U.S.S.R. or China in domestic affairs and a policy of equidistance which rejected any leading center in the international communist movement. Domestically, the CPM remained committed to strong states, decentralized federalism, and a revolution from below designed to bring about a people's democracy.[57]

Given these totally different assessments of strategy and tactics, the CPI-CPM unity talks of April 1978 were able to produce agreement only on a limited program of unity in action on specific antipeople policies of the Janata government and not on a mass struggle against Janata rule. The ideological differences of the past now became complicated by demands that each party not only acknowledge its past mistakes but openly repudiate them through a process of self criticism. Thus, despite widespread pressures for the unity of the left, the CPI and CPM continued their polemics in their respective party journals and public statements.

Despite their continued ideological differences, however, a series of domestic and foreign policy events during the period from April 1978 to the elections of January 1980 helped to gradually narrow the gap between the two parties. The disintegration of the Janata government and its collapse in the summer of 1979 eliminated a major source of conflict. The two parties also developed a series of similar views on Chinese intervention in Vietnam, Vietnamese intervention in Cambodia, and Soviet intervention in Afghanistan.[58] As a result the ideological gap between the two parties began to narrow and, except in a few local instances, the CPI and CPM fought the 1980 election together for the first time since 1964. In the wake of Indira Gandhi's surprising comeback victory, the unity of the left and disintegration of the Janata enabled the communists to emerge from the elections as the only coherent opposition. The communists succeeded in restoring some of their previous losses as the total communist vote increased from 7.1 percent in the Janata debacle of 1977 to 8.63 percent in 1980. As a result the strength of the communist legislative contingent was almost restored to pre-emergency levels as its total number of seats increased from twenty-nine in 1977 to forty-six in 1980. The relative success of the two communist parties, however, was quite marked. The CPM gained substantial popularity among the liberal intelligentsia because of its nationalist, anti-authoritarian, and federalist stance and established itself as the dominant force on the left. The party increased its vote from 4.3 percent to 6.03 percent and the size of its parliamentary group from twenty-two to thirty-six seats. In addition the party regained control of the government of Kerala for the first time in eleven years. The CPI, in contrast, suffered a second major defeat. Its total vote dropped to its lowest point in history from 2.8 percent to 2.6 percent, but its parliamentary group increased marginally from seven to eleven seats despite the fact that the party contested forty-one fewer seats than in 1977.[59]

The unexpected victory of Indira Gandhi, however, reawakened old divisions and suspicions within the communist movement. The CPM saw the victory of Indira as a threat to its tenuous hold over coalition governments in West Bengal, Tripura, and Kerala and prepared to defend its electoral Yennans. The CPI, on the other hand, was confronted by a resurgence of Dangeism and demands for a restoration of the CPI-Congress alliance. Although Dange had resigned from the chairmanship of the CPI in early 1977 on the grounds of ill health, his moves were clearly tactical. Dange had repeatedly resisted any CPI repudiation of its pro-Congress line and its support for the emergency. He considered support for the emergency essential to prevent the danger of a reactionary destabilization launched by the forces of right reaction. The excesses committed during the emergency, he argued, were not due to Mrs. Gandhi but to the existence of an alternate power center focusing on Sanjay Gandhi, Indira Gandhi's son, and several ministers backed by United States imperialism. The communist movement in India, he insisted, was simply too weak to go it alone, and as for the CPM, they had no meaningful understanding of Marxism-Leninism.[60]

Despite the defeat of the Dange line at Bhatinda, Dange bided his time by withdrawing from the party leadership. As Mrs. Gandhi began to stage a comeback, he openly challenged the Bhatinda line and called for a policy of coalition with the Indira Congress in the 1980 elections. When the CPI leadership refused, Dange and his supporters worked openly and covertly on behalf of Congress candidates.[61] Shortly after Indira Gandhi's electoral victory, Roza Deshpande, Dange's daughter, quit the CPI and formed a fourth communist party called the All India Communist party.[62]

The restoration of Congress dominance and the split in the CPI resulted in a de facto return to the communist strategy and tactics of the 1950s. The close relationship between Indira Gandhi and the U.S.S.R. enabled Mrs. Gandhi to secure the support of the communists for her progressive foreign policy. Her domestic policies, however, were characterized as reactionary and the two communist parties joined a group of splinter leftist parties to form a small sixty-seat leftist bloc in the Indian parliament. At the same time, however, the two communist parties continued to reflect divergent attitudes toward the Congress and Indira. The CPM saw Indira Gandhi as a threat to its base areas of Kerala, West Bengal, and Tripura, while the CPI still harbored forces sympathetic to a restoration of the CPI-Congress alliance. The death of Sanjay Gandhi in an airplane accident in the summer of 1980 removed a major barrier to CPI-Congress cooperation and the party faced increased pressure from its rank and file to patch up with Indira.[63]

The future of the strategy of left and democratic unity, therefore, remained uncertain and tenuous. The new line enunciated by both major communist parties in 1978 represented the beginning of a complex process of trying to reconcile a classic Marxist split between two divergent approaches to revolution in the context of a highly segmented and pluralist social and political environment. Although the two parties developed an increasing convergence of understanding on a variety of domestic and foreign policies, the fundamental ideological conflict between a strategy of revolution from above based on a national democratic front versus a revolution from below based on people's democracy persisted. Given this deep-seated cleavage, complete unity within the communist movement remained highly unlikely.

While the basic difference over strategy and tactics between India's two major communist parties made merger remote, the 1980s witnessed a period of increased cooperation and convergence in the name of left and democratic unity. The CPI was invited to join the CPM-dominated government of West Bengal in September 1981 and cooperation between the two parties reached its highest level since the 1964 split. The new relationship was greatly facilitated when the CPM appeared to abandon its long-standing policy of equidistance in its attitude toward China and the Soviet Union. The CPM began to increasingly tilt toward the U.S.S.R. on a whole array of foreign policy issues.[64]

The movement toward left and democratic unity received a major boost when it was reaffirmed by the CPM's eleventh congress at Vijayawada, Andhra Pradesh, in January 1982 and the twelfth congress of the CPI at Varanasi, Uttar Pradesh, in March 1982. Leaders of the CPI even went as far as to talk about a complete merger of the two parties. However, all suggestions for merger were quickly rejected by the CPM. Despite the movement toward convergence, a variety of issues made merger difficult. First, the two parties had become increasingly unequal in size, support base, and power. Following the split it was the CPM which had emerged as India's premier communist party and therefore claimed the mantle of legitimacy. Its popular vote was double that of the CPI, it held a larger block of seats in the Lok Sabha, and it dominated left-front coalitions in its base areas. In addition, its front organizations claimed a size twice as large as those dominated by the CPI. Its chief weakness, however, was its inability to develop a base outside its regional strongholds. The CPI, on the other hand, had a much broader national base. These differences created tensions between the regional outlook of the CPM and the more national outlook of the CPI and made agreement on coalition strategies very difficult.[65]

A second major difference was even more fundamental. The CPM still saw the Indian state and government as a bourgeois landlord state requiring a coalition of all democratic, antifeudal and anticapitalist forces. The CPI, in contrast, argued that India was controlled by a national bourgeoisie requiring a coalition of progressive forces in a national democratic front. This basic difference created disputes over which of the bourgeois parties were suitable coalition partners and which party was to lead the coalition.

A third issue that divided the CPI and the CPM focused on the fundamental cause for the 1964 split itself. Each of the parties had become dominated by a gerontocracy whose members were in their seventies and eighties. They had all been comrades together and had all been involved in the disputes leading up to the split. Old hostilities, widespread suspicions, and lingering doubts persisted. True cooperation could occur only if past errors were acknowledged and repudiated. Confession of error was not enough; past policies must also be disavowed. This clearly could not happen since the CPI still contained elements that wanted to restore cooperation with the Indira Congress and the CPM still harbored a strong pro-China lobby. Thus past and present intermingled as the old-guard leadership of each party blamed the other for the original split.

The assassination of Indira Gandhi on October 31, 1984, the succession of Rajiv Gandhi, her son, to the prime ministership and the sweeping victory of the Congress party at the polls in December 1984 threw the communist movement into turmoil. The strategy of left and democratic unity was in a shambles as both communist parties were swept aside in the Rajiv landslide. The size of the communist bloc in the Lok Sabha dropped 40 percent, from forty-eight seats to twenty-eight seats, while their popular vote remained stagnant at 8.67 percent.[66]

The election defeat touched off an unprecedented attack against the leadership of both parties at their quadrennial party conferences. The CPM held its twelfth party congress in Calcutta in December 1985. The thirteenth party congress of the CPI was held at Patna in March 1986. A small group of young ideologically centrist CPM members from West Bengal demanded the building of a stronger regional base in West Bengal, less cooperation with the CPI, and a return to equidistance in relations with China and the Soviet Union. Within the CPI, Rajiv's victory fueled a desire for a return to cooperation with the Congress.[67]

At the state level the CPM experienced yet another split in July 1986, when a group of CPM rebels in the state of Kerala was expelled and formed yet another Communist party called the Communist Marxist party. The rebels differed with the CPM central leadership over the application of the concept of left and democratic unity. They insisted on an alliance with the Kerala Muslim League as part of the party's left and anti-authoritarian front. The central leadership disagreed and accused the rebels of succumbing to communal politics and parliamentary infatuation which threatened Indian unity.[68]

As in the past the CPM and CPI had a difficult time coping with the dominant Congress party. On the one hand, both parties found Rajiv's foreign policy to be progressive because of its pro-Soviet tilt and non-aligned rhetoric. On the other hand, they found his domestic policies to be a disaster. Rajiv was accused of denigrating the public sector, allowing domestic monopolies and foreign multinationals to expand, and undermining national self-reliance.[69]

At the same time, however, the CPI found the CPM's criticism of Rajiv's economic policies to be hypocritical. At the very time that the CPM was criticizing Rajiv's economic policies, the party was encouraging greater multinational and monopoly investment in West Bengal.[70] Thus parochial and sectarian attitudes continued to divide India's communists as they attempted to implement their recent line of left and democratic unity.

Although the electoral defeats of 1984 and the rise of Rajiv Gandhi accentuated tensions among India's competing communists, Rajiv's triumph, like Indira Gandhi's in 1971 and the Janata in 1977, proved to be short lived. Within two years of his election as prime minister and leader of the Congress party, Rajiv's support began to erode. The cumulative effects of his leadership style, a series of corruption scandals, and failed performance called into question his competence, credibility, and moral authority. These problems were compounded by a series of electoral defeats in several Indian states. Among the most stunning defeats for Rajiv were the victories of CPM-led left front coalitions in the states of West Bengal and Kerala in March 1986. The CPM-dominated left front government which had ruled West Bengal for ten years was returned to power with a massive two-thirds majority. At the same time, in the state of Kerala a CPM-led left front defeated a Congress-led coalition and eliminated the last Congress toehold in the South. Since Rajiv had campaigned vigorously in both states, the defeats were seen as a reflection of his declining popularity and galvanized greater cooperation among India's diverse opposition parties.[71]

Although the communists came to Rajiv's rescue by blocking the reelection of Zail Singh as president of India, they have since decided to join an emerging anti-Rajiv opposition coalition.[72] Despite strong Soviet support for Rajiv, the communist movement has decided to form a broad united front designed to oust Rajiv and the Congress. Fearful of repeating their error in 1977 when they failed to cash in on the Janata revolution, the communists have decided to lend their full support to the anti-Rajiv movement. The ultimate survival and success of this movement is yet to be tested, but in the past India's communists have prospered most when they have employed a united front approach.

Communist Coalition Strategies in India

Despite over sixty years of devoted effort, the fact is that uneven patterns of social and party development, the structural features of the political system, and the diversities and rigidities of Indian communism have combined to make the movement weak, divided, and primarily a regional rather than a national force. Communism has emerged as a force in India only under limited and ideal conditions as in Kerala, West Bengal, and Tripura. There is little likelihood of a major breakout from these strategic zones at the opposite ends of the subcontinent in the near future that would transform these electoral Yennans into a national political force. Despite forty years of electoral politics, a combination of cultural and political factors have prevented the Communist movement from securing even 10 percent of the national vote and they remain an electoral minority even in some of their regional strongholds. This electoral weakness and limited geographic spread have made coalition strategies and tactics critical to communist success and survival. Unless and until the communists are able to penetrate the vast Hindi belt and achieve a national threshold of 25 to 30 percent of the vote like communists in Italy, the movement's impact will be limited and dependent upon successful coalition politics.

The limited impact of the communist movement in India compared to other parts of Asia such as China, Vietnam, and North Korea has touched off a major debate among Indian leftists.[73] Critics attribute the lack of progress to poor leadership and the inflexible and unimaginative application of Marxist-Leninist principles to the complex Indian scene. Leftist critics have charged Indian communist leaders with failing to take into account the significant changes in economic and political development in India since independence. The development of political democracy, they argue, has created conditions in India which are more like those that existed in Western Europe in the early twentieth century than the more backward and primitive conditions in Russia or China at the time of the revolution. In view of India's higher stage of development, communist leaders must cease trying to apply their orthodox and rigid Leninist style of communism to the India scene. This rigid orthodoxy, for example, is reflected in the fact that the CPM has yet to even criticize Stalinism. If communism is to be successful in India, it must look to the more flexible variations of Eurocommunism which are being developed by European communists and not to the rigid Marxism-Leninism of the past.

Indian communist leaders dismiss these alleged subjective judgments of their critics, totally reject Eurocommunism as a pernicious, reformist, and divisionist ideology, and attribute their limited but significant success to unfavorable objective conditions.[74] The problems facing the communist movement, they argue, have little to do with the quality of leadership but must be understood in terms of objective conditions. Unlike China, India was controlled by a single imperialist power which succeeded in building a strong centralized state. The centralized character of the British raj led to the development of a centralized ruling class which was able to bring together all sections of society under the organizational and ideological influence of the Indian National Congress. The communist movement has had a difficult time breaking the monopoly control of the Congress and its influence over the masses. Despite mistakes in strategy and tactics, the communist movement has proven to be successful in India. It has performed a revolutionary role, has survived as an independent entity, and has established significant pockets of strength under difficult objective conditions.

The future progress of Indian communism, argue both CPI and CPM leaders, can only be made by the faithful application of traditional Marxist-Leninist principles to Indian conditions and not through revisionist doctrines like Eurocommunism. "Euro-Communism," according to Mohit Sen, chief idealogue of the pro-Soviet CPI, "needs not only to be rejected but criticized and relentlessly combatted. All efforts have to be made to see that it does not become the Maoism of advanced capitalist countries and repeat the damage and disaster of that pernicious ideology."[75] E. M. S. Namboodiripad of the CPM is equally adamant toward the reformist doctrines of Eurocommunism. "The doctrines of proletarian dictatorship, proletarian internationalism, [and] hegemony of the working class in the democratic struggle," he declared, "are the logical culmination of the doctrine of class struggle and the reality of imperialism's ferocious attacks. That is why CPI(M) adheres to these basic tenets of Marxism-Leninism and do not propose to abandon them."[76]

Despite its concentration on the ideological superstructure and its stress on the need for appropriate objective conditions, the Indian communist movement is faced by a variety of internal problems which have played a major role in limiting its success. Poor leadership, a limited social base, factionalism, and parochialism have combined to weaken and fragment the movement. Indian communism is still under the direction of middle class urban intellectuals and has developed very few mass leaders. Most communist leaders in India are still founder members of the original CPI, are aging rapidly, and have built their entire life around being party functionaries. They are totally preoccupied with the intricacies of Marxist-Leninist ideology, which they tend to apply in a form that borders on scholasticism. As a result internal conflicts take on a highly personal and factionalized form which is reinforced by the highly factionalized social environment. Changes in line are usually accompanied by changes in leadership and deviant lines become identified with individuals. The CPI-Congress alliance, for example, has become identified as Dangeism, and S. A. Dange resigned as general secretary of the party when the line was changed. Thus internal disputes are quickly translated into ideological conflicts and differences of interpretation are immediately labeled reformism, sectarianism, deviationism, or revisionism. This tendency has been especially prevalent on the left fringe of the movement among Naxalites. For example, Naxalite factions are labeled the pro-Charu Mazumdar CPI(ML), the Satyanarayan Singh, or SNS-led CPI(ML), the anti-Lin Piao faction, or the pro-Lin Piao faction.[77] In short, Indian communism has yet to produce a national charismatic figure like Lenin, Mao, or Ho Chi Minh capable of transcending local parochialism, uniting regional leaders, appealing to the masses, and creatively applying Marxist ideology to Indian conditions.

In the absence of an all-India charismatic leader, Indian communist leadership has been far from free of personality clashes, and its regional leaders tend to be highly parochial. Both leaders and followers, moreover, continue to be drawn from a limited social base. As a result communism in India suffers from powerful federalist tendencies in which the central party organization is weak and the state, district, and mass front organizations are strong and independent of central control. A 1978 organizational report of the CPM, for example, accused state leaders of ignoring their Politbureau duties in favor of provincial party affairs. Provincial party organizations, in turn, were criticized for failing to file appropriate reports with the center, making decisions without consulting the central leadership, and persistently deviating from national policy in the name of special local conditions. Within state parties, the report continued, party cadres function independently of state leaders and were developing a pattern of cadre bossism centered on control of the local party secretariat. This pattern of bossism affected the party's ability to recruit and hold new members.[78] As a result the party was faced by a stagnation of membership and an inability to bring about a material change in its basic middle class composition.[79]

The combination of unfavorable objective conditions of the Indian environment and problems of internal cohesion, therefore, have weakened and fragmented the communist government in India. This weakness in turn enhances the need for an effective coalition strategy. Because of the special needs of communist ideology, however, the development of coalition strategy and tactics becomes a double-edged sword. They are essential to success and yet divisive because of their ideological content. In general the communist movement in India has prospered most during periods of united front. It was during the united front period of 1935 to 1939 that the communists were able to establish an effective base in India and enabled the party to identify with nationalist aspirations. The era of constitutionalism of the 1950s was also highly successful and witnessed the gradual and steady growth of communist support. Even Dangeism might have proven to be more successful had it been pursued in a more flexible way, especially during the period of the emergency from 1975 to 1977.

In contrast, periods of independent action and revolutionary upheaval have isolated the party and have created the risk of a nationalist backlash. The leftist strategies of 1928 to 1935, the war years of 1939 to 1945, and the periods of revolutionary upheavals 1947 to 1951 proved to be disastrous to the communist movement. These strategies isolated the communists from the nationalist mainstream and created an antinationalist stigma which still persists. Nationalist passions have become periodically inflamed due to events in the region and have been directed against the communists. These continued nationalist suspicions of the Communists were demonstrated by Indira Gandhi's December 1976 attack against her CPI allies and the anti-China hysteria of 1962 and 1971 which affected the CPM and the Naxalites. The same nationalist backlash would sweep the subcontinent if the Afghanistan crisis or some other regional crisis were to enable U.S.S.R. or China to penetrate the subcontinent. Coalition strategies have the result of making the Communists less vulnerable to such nationalist upheavals.

Coalition strategies also become essential because of the fluid and fragmented character of the party system, the single-member district electoral system, and the monopoly of power wielded by a single party or coalition like the Janata. Since the Indian party system is still in the development stage, opportunistic coalitions do not create the same credibility gap as they would among parties in developed political systems like Western Europe. Since all Indian parties resort to opportunistic coalition building, the communists have not been singled out for engaging in some form of unprincipled behavior. Coalition behavior is essential in the existing political environment.

Pending the outbreak of a major war on the Indian subcontinent, the unlikely collapse of the state structure, major transformation of the rural sector, or the emergence of a mass charismatic leader and the development of an effective indigenous strategy, the communist movement in India will remain a small but strategically placed force dependent upon effective coalition strategies and tactics for success and survival. Yet this very dependence on coalitions will continue to create internal problems for the movement. The need to justify coalitions in terms of a complex ideological context generates factional disputes and fragmentation. In addition there remains the persistent threat from the leftist Naxalite fringe which insists on an end to coalitions and parliamentary tactics and a resort to armed struggle. These radical movements siphon off idealistic youth and those seeking instant change and thus weaken the communist movement. They cannot, however, as has been proven constantly over the past decades, successfully conduct armed struggle against the raj.

8

Coalition Strategies and Tactics of Marxist Parties in Africa
David E. Albright

The ranks of Marxist parties in Africa have increased dramatically since the 1950s. By the late 1980s, the total of such parties had reached at least forty-nine. This figure included only those parties currently in being; it did not cover parties that had formed and then disappeared over the course of the years. Moreover, it may have overlooked some obscure underground groups.

Although the outlooks and policies of these Marxist parties vary widely, all of them have defined and continue to define coalition strategies and tactics in pursuing their political ends. No less important, there are similarities as well as differences in these strategies and tactics. The similarities derive in part from shared intellectual premises, but they also reflect common features of the situations to which the parties seek to respond. Some of the similarities, however, apply only to a limited number of parties, while others are more or less universal in character. This state of affairs renders highly complex the similarities and differences among the coalition strategies and tactics of the parties.

In light of the large number of African Marxist parties and the complex similarities and differences in their coalition strategies and tactics, presenting a coherent analysis of these phenomena is no mean task. It requires, above all, some preliminary ordering of the discussion. One viable approach involves grouping parties on the basis of like attributes of key relevance to their coalition strategies and tactics. That is what will be used here. Specifically, the chapter will examine those parties together that have the same formal legal status and that function in the same general part of Africa.

The analysis will begin, then, with a delineation of the parties to be considered and a categorization of them on the basis of their legal status and the broad area of Africa in which they exist. Examination of their coalition strategies and tactics will proceed within the framework of the categories developed. The chapter will conclude with an assessment of the prospects for continuity in the years ahead in the coalition strategies and tactics detailed.

The Marxist Parties of Africa

It is crucial to recognize at the outset that far more parties in Africa express an intention to "build socialism" in their countries than qualify as "Marxist" within the understanding of the term that informs this volume. There still exist on the continent parties that aspire to fashion some form of distinctively "African" socialism, although their ranks have thinned greatly in recent years. Other parties accept more universal conceptions of "socialism" but shy away from the essentials of Marxist teachings.

Of all the parties that as of the late 1980s claimed a desire to "construct socialism," ten enjoyed the U.S.S.R.'s blessing as communist parties;[1] thus, they clearly qualify as Marxist. They are the Party of Progress and Socialism (PPS) in Morocco, the Socialist Vanguard party (PAGS) in Algeria, the Tunisian Communist party, the Egyptian Communist party, the Sudan Communist party, the Party of Independence and Labor (PIT) in Senegal, the Socialist Working People's party (SWPP) in Nigeria, the Lesotho Communist party, the South African Communist party, and the Réunion Communist party.

Another thirty-nine parties professed to be Marxist-Leninist or Marxist at least in aspiration, and even though they did not have Moscow's imprimatur as communist parties, they deserve consideration.[2] This group consists of the Popular Movement for the Liberation of Angola—Workers' Party (MPLA-PT); the Movement for the Liberation of Sãe Tomé and Príncipe (MLSTP); the Congolese Labor party (PCT) in the People's Republic of the Congo; the Benin People's Revolutionary party (PRPB); the Patriotic League for Development (LIPAD), the Union for Communist Struggle (ULC), the Reconstructed Union for Communist Struggle (ULCR), the Voltaic Revolutionary Communist Party (PCRV), the Burkinabe Communist Group (GCB), and the Burkinabe Communist Union (UCB) in Burkina Faso; the African Party for the Independence of Cape Verde (PAICV); the African Party for the Independence of Guinea and Cape Verde (PAIGC) in Guinea-Bissau; the African Independence party (PAI), the Revolutionary Movement for the New Democracy (MRDN-AJ), the Democratic League—Labor Movement (LD-MPT), the Senegalese People's party (PPS), the Communist League of

Workers (LCT), the Socialist Organization of Workers (OST), the Union for People's Democracy (UDP), and the African Party for the Independence of the People (PAIP) in Senegal; the Socialist Union of Popular Forces (USFP) and the Organization for Democratic and Popular Action (OAD) in Morocco; the Armed Communist Organization (AC), the Revolutionary Current, the Revolutionary Progressive party (RPP), the Popular Movement, the Egyptian Communist party — January 8 (ECP-January 8), the Revolutionary Communist League (RCL), the Egyptian Communist Party — Congress Faction (ECP-CF), and the Egyptian Workers' Communist party (EWCP) in Egypt; the Workers' Party of Ethiopia (WPE); the Somali Revolutionary Socialist party (SRSP) in Somalia; the Front for the Liberation of Mozambique (Frelimo); the Congress Party for Malagasy Independence (AKFM) and the Movement for Proletarian Power (MFM) in Madagascar; the Movement for the Independence of Réunion (MIR); the Mauritian Militant Movement (MMM) and Mauritian Social Progressive Militant Movement (MMMSP) in Mauritius; and the Zimbabwe African National Union — Patriotic Front (ZANU-PF).

No other African body bases itself sufficiently on Marxist or Marxist-Leninist ideas to fit the definition of a Marxist party. Some "liberation movements" operating on the continent, to be sure, have significant Marxist elements in their ranks. Among these are the Eritrean People's Liberation Front and Tigre People's Liberation Front in Ethiopia, the Sudanese People's Liberation Movement in Sudan, the South-West African People's Organization in Namibia, and the African National Congress in South Africa. Yet these organizations thus far remain diverse in composition, lack many structural attributes of a party, and offer only vague indications of the programs they will try to implement if they gain power. Therefore, such "movements" will be omitted from the discussion here.

Of the parties that this chapter will treat, nineteen are officially proscribed in their respective states. This group includes the PAGS in Algeria; all of the nine parties in Egypt; all of the six parties in Burkina Faso; the SWPP in Nigeria; the Lesotho Communist party; and the South African Communist party. Authorities in Lesotho did "partially lift" the ban on the communist party there in late 1984 to allow it to contest elections subsequently scheduled for September 1985. But it and the other opposition parties ultimately refused to participate in the August 1985 nomination process for the elections, for Prime Minister Leabua Jonathan had rigged the process in favor of his ruling Basoto National party. Then in January 1986 the Lesotho military overthrew Jonathan and outlawed all party activity in the country.[3]

Twenty of the rest of the parties function legally within their individual states but have either no role or only a minor role in their governments. They are the PPS, USFP, and OADP in Morocco; the Sudan Communist party; the Tunisian Communist party; the nine parties in Senegal; the Réunion Communist party and MIR in Réunion; the MMM and MMMSP in Mauritius; and the AKFM and MFM in Madagascar.

The last ten parties are ruling parties. This category consists of the MPLA-PT in Angola, the MLSTP in São Tomé and Príncipe, the PCT in the People's Republic of the Congo, the PRPB in Benin, the PAICV in Cape Verde, the PAIGC in Guinea-Bissau, the WPE in Ethiopia, the SRSP in Somalia, the Frelimo in Mozambique, and the ZANU-PF in Zimbabwe. All have a monopoly of power in their countries.

Ten of the banned parties and four of the legal, nonruling parties clearly qualify as North African. This list includes the PAGS in Algeria; all nine parties in Egypt; the PPS, USFP, and OADP in Morocco; and the Tunisian Communist party. Although the now legal Sudan Communist party operates in a milieu with substantial features characteristic of sub-Saharan Africa, the setting has more in common with North Africa than with sub-Saharan Africa. The remainder of the parties unquestionably belong in a sub-Saharan African group.

Outlawed Parties in North Africa

The PAGS in Algeria and the nine Egyptian parties pursue coalition strategies and tactics influenced greatly by the illegal standing of the parties and by their North African heritage and environment. Official suppression, to begin with, imposes a need for a certain amount of secrecy about plans and activities. Too public a profile might bring on a wave of arrests and imprisonment of party members. Therefore, the coalition strategies and tactics of all these parties rely heavily upon clandestinity. In fact, the Egyptian parties aside from the Egyptian Communist party preserve such a high degree of secrecy about their outlooks and undertakings that major aspects of their coalition strategies and tactics remain obscure and not subject to analysis.

Proscription also fans hostility toward the local government, and the level of a party's hostility toward the local government has a strong impact on the party's conception of its political enemies. In common with the rest of the Marxist parties of Africa, the parties in this grouping see themselves as confronting both external and domestic enemies, but they tend to display much greater preoccupation with internal enemies, and specifically with ruling circles, than do parties that function freely in their relevant political contexts. Often, indeed, the parties in this category view internal and external enemies as virtually indistinguishable. That is, they regard ruling circles as mere agents of "imperialism," the basic external foe.

The peculiarities of the North African context strongly reinforce this focus on domestic enemies. North Africa lacks a solid tradition of democracy and tolerance of political opposition. Thus governments of the region have typically adopted measures to repress political challenges to them from any quarter, and the greater the threat that they have perceived, the harsher their steps to deal with it have tended to be. Marxist-Leninist parties have suffered some of the most severe treatment meted out to opposition organizations in the region. This sort of experience has helped to make them highly distrustful of their national governments.

But the level of that distrust differs in accordance with the precise record of official repression in individual countries. The governments of Egypt and Algeria have sought to curb local Marxist-Leninist parties more energetically and more consistently over an extended period of time than have those elsewhere in the region.[4]

An Egyptian communist party came into being in 1921, but rarely over the years since then has any communist organization in Egypt escaped proscription. Furthermore, there is a substantial tradition of outright persecution of communist party members by Egyptian rulers. In the mid-1960s, it is true, Gamal Abdel Nasser did allow individual communists to join the governing Arab Socialist Union, but he insisted that they must not have ties with any formal communist party. Furthermore, Anwar al-Sadat, Nasser's successor, adopted an essentially hostile attitude toward all local communists in the 1970s.

An Algerian Communist party emerged in 1920 as an extension of the French Communist party and eventually became a separate entity in 1936; thereafter, it operated legally under the French colonial authorities until 1955, shortly after the outbreak of the armed struggle for Algerian independence. When Algeria gained its sovereignty in 1962, the new government quickly outlawed the communist party, and it has remained suppressed ever since. Prior to the mid-1960s, Ahmed Ben Bella did permit communists to participate as individuals within the ruling National Liberation Front (FLN), but he forbade them to retain links with an organized communist party as a condition for such participation. Even this element of lenience with respect to local communists disappeared with Ben Bella's overthrow in 1965. Thereafter, the government displayed sharp antagonism toward all communists within the country.

Such lengthy histories of repression at the hands of the ruling authorities of their countries have greatly enhanced the inclinations of the

Marxist-Leninist parties in these two countries to regard their govern-ments as key enemies. The precise place that the existing local government occupies on a party's list of enemies, however, varies somewhat from case to case. Insofar as available evidence permits a judgment, all of the Egyp-tian parties seem to perceive the current local government (the Mubarak government) as their main enemy. For example, they seek the immediate ouster of that government.[5] The PAGS in Algeria believes that the Benjedid regime there has made a "swing to the right" in comparison with the previous Boumedienne regime,[6] but in PAGS eyes the policies of the Benjedid government still remain sufficiently "anti-imperialist" externally and "progressive" domestically to render it secondary to "imperialism" as an enemy. During the 1980s, for instance, the PAGS has not championed the ouster of the government. Rather, it has advocated "unity of action" of a broad spectrum of "patriotic and progressive circles," including the FLN.[7]

Another aspect of the North African setting greatly affects the rank-ing that the parties under consideration here assign to specific external enemies—regardless of whether foreign enemies be primary or secondary in a general sense. The region is predominantly Arab in character. In line with this feature of the milieu, the parties have essentially Arab member-ships, and all take staunchly pro-Arab stances in their foreign policies. Consequently, they single out Israel and those "imperialist" forces that have close ties with it as special international enemies. First and foremost among such forces, in their eyes, is the United States. For example, the pronouncements of the parties constantly lump together condemnations of "U.S. imperialism" and "Zionism."[8]

Outlaw status significantly colors a party's perceptions of who consti-tute potential allies and what specific merits they have as allies. On the domestic front it causes a party to look toward cooperation with other opponents of the government or of particular government policies; more-over, the degree of opposition that groups and individuals manifest toward the government and/or its policies provides a means of gauging the extent of feasible cooperation with them. Thus all of the parties here confine their searches for internal allies to political elements disaffected in one way or another with the government and/or its programs.

Some of the parties, to be sure, attach more weight to fashioning alliances on the domestic scene than do others. Although information is fairly sketchy, it would seem that the Egyptian Communist party is the only Egyptian party that sees the forging of such alliances as an undertak-ing of real consequence. Certainly, the rest of the Egyptian parties assume highly sectarian postures toward each other and toward the Egyptian Com-munist party. The Egyptian Communist party does eschew cooperation with its straightforwardly Marxist competitors, but it shows interest in collaboration with other opposition elements in Egypt, particularly those of a leftist character. Members of the National Progressive Unionist party (NPUP), one of several officially recognized opposition parties, afford the main focus of this interest.[9]

The PAGS in Algeria values alliances with other internal political and social forces at least as much as the Egyptian Communist party does; however, the PAGS directs its attention toward possible allies of an alternative kind. It concentrates on the radical elements in government-sanctioned bodies like the National Union of Algerian Youth and the General Union of Algerian Workers.[10]

Despite such differences in perceptions of the merits of forming alliances in the domestic political arena, all of the parties in this category have felt called upon to address one special feature of the North African setting in their calculations about internal alliances. Most inhabitants of North Africa are Muslims; furthermore, the influence of Islam and particularly of its fundamentalist interpreters on politics in the region has escalated sharply since the 1970s. Hence the parties have discerned a need to define an attitude about joint efforts with Muslims and political movements based on Islam.

None of the parties concerned here appears to reject such undertakings out of hand. As Marxist-Leninist bodies, they do regard Islam as "backward" from an ideological standpoint—as a belief system that retards the development of revolutionary consciousness among the masses. Yet insofar as it is possible to determine, all seem to grant that at least in principle Islam and political elements championing it can be "progressive" under certain circumstances. Such conditions entail the existence of a common, mutually recognized enemy—whether internal or external.

The actual relations of the parties in this category with the fundamentalist Islamic elements on their local scenes, however, have varied in the 1980s. To the extent that one can judge from available evidence, none of the Egyptian parties has collaborated actively with the Muslim Brotherhood in Egypt, but the Egyptian Communist party has hinted that it might move in this direction. After referring negatively to the "permanent contacts" of the Muslim Brothers with the government, a party communiqué issued in January 1984 went on to say that some of them do "declare for joint action" with the "progressive opposition" and especially the National Progressive Unionist party.[11]

In Algeria, the PAGS has stayed aloof from the Islamic fundamentalists there. Despite the drift to the right that it discerns in official policies since the early 1980s, it still classifies the Benjedid government as "progressive," and it has presumably wanted to avoid association with any forces that might conceivably try to overturn that government and install one of a less "progressive" nature. Above all, it has had ample demonstration of the risks that ties with Islamic fundamentalist elements might involve for itself and its already limited scope of action, for the government cracked down hard on such elements in 1982–1983 and 1985.[12]

Banned status encourages a party to see international forces that it deems to be adversaries of its local government—especially the more powerful of these—as the most desirable of allies. Such forces constitute the likeliest sources of foreign support for a proscribed party, and the stronger the forces, the more effective any support from them will probably prove to be.

All of the parties concerned here except the Revolutionary Current and RCL in Egypt seem to identify the world communist movement in general, and the U.S.S.R. in particular, as the chief external foes of their local governments and hence the logical main allies for themselves in the international arena. Such a view appears to prevail even within those avowedly Marxist-Leninist parties in Egypt to which Moscow does not accord formal recognition as communist bodies.[13]

As a Maoist group, Revolutionary Current presumably regards the world network of fellow Maoist parties as the primary outside antagonists of the Egyptian government and thus its own natural primary allies abroad, but little is known about what, if any, foreign ties the party maintains. It should be noted in this context, however, that the network of Maoist parties now lacks a patron of first-class importance because China in the 1980s has discarded many of Mao Zedong's teachings.

The RCL, similarly, probably views other Trotskyist parties around the globe as the principal foreign opponents of the Egyptian government and hence the logical candidates for its own main external allies. Yet, just as in the case of Revolutionary Current, it is not clear to what extent, if any, the RCL actually has contacts with entities outside the country.

In addition to generating standards by which the parties in this grouping rank external enemies, the Arab character of North Africa helps to shape their choices of allies abroad. As noted previously, all of the parties are basically Arab in composition, and they adopt highly pro-Arab stances in their foreign policies. Therefore, they tend to look to like-minded external forces as allies.

These forces, in the eyes of the parties at issue here, are diverse. At least the PAGS of Algeria and the Egyptian Communist party view one another as fraternal Arab organizations, and they engage in substantial interaction within the framework of the world communist movement. All of the parties under consideration apparently regard radical Arab governments and opposition movements abroad as "progressive" and fitting collaborators, even though they may have quite limited contact with these governments and movements.[14] Most important, all of the parties except the Revolutionary Current in Egypt seem to perceive the U.S.S.R. and the other members of the Soviet bloc as the chief non-Arab defenders of the Arab cause in the international arena.[15] Information at hand does not suffice to assess to which foreign entities the Revolutionary Current assigns this role.

From the standpoint of the parties in this category, of course, the international forces that they single out as their external allies do not necessarily represent ideal allies, for these allies can and sometimes do adopt positions contrary to what the parties might prefer. The U.S.S.R. is the most notorious offender in this respect. Although Soviet leaders continue to believe that communist parties will eventually come to power in states like Algeria and Egypt,[16] they contend that the U.S.S.R. has its own interests to pursue in the interim, and they often engage in friendlier relations with current governments than the communist parties in these states would like. Indeed, the parties even occasionally feel pressure from Moscow to downplay their own opposition to their local governments. For instance, the U.S.S.R. in the 1960s prodded the predecessors of the PAGS in Algeria and the Egyptian Communist party to dissolve and to instruct their members to seek admission as individuals to ruling leftist parties in the two countries.[17]

During the 1980s, Soviet attitudes toward the governments of Algeria and Egypt have differed appreciably. The U.S.S.R. has had quite amicable relations with the Benjedid government in Algeria and carried on a wide range of contacts with it.[18] Moscow has actively courted the Mubarak government in Egypt and has succeeded in restoring most of the ties that Sadat had severed in the last years before his assassination in 1981, but Soviet leaders have remained dissatisfied with the general coolness that authorities in Cairo have displayed toward the U.S.S.R.[19]

Proscribed Parties in Sub-Saharan Africa

The six parties in Burkina Faso, the SWPP in Nigeria, the Lesotho Communist party, and the South African Communist party follow coalition strategies and tactics that derive in large part from their lack of legal status and from their distinct features and experiences as sub-Saharan African entities. First of all, official outlawing of the parties in this grouping encourages them—just as it does their counterparts in North Africa—to maintain a fair degree of secrecy about their thinking and undertakings. Hence their coalition strategies and tactics have a clandestine dimension to them.

At the same time, the commitment of the parties to clandestinity is tempered by aspects of their sub-Saharan African heritage. Even though all have encountered repression on occasion, each has enjoyed significant periods as well in which it functioned without much harassment from its local government.

The South African Communist party operated legally for several decades prior to its banning in 1950. During the 1930s and 1940s it even succeeded in winning some leadership positions in the black trade union movement and a small number of seats in South Africa's legislative bodies. Among the latter were one in the national parliament, one in the provincial council of Cape Province, and a few in the city councils of Johannesburg and Cape Town.[20] Thus the party had a long record of more or less open discussion of its views and approaches before it became proscribed.

Apparently founded in 1961, the Lesotho Communist party was not formally outlawed until 1970. Furthermore, between late 1984 and early 1986, as mentioned earlier, official restrictions on it were "partially lifted." Consequently the party's leeway to carry on activities within Lesotho expanded substantially during this time.[21] Since the military takeover of the country in January 1986 and the subsequent banning of all parties, of course, that leeway has contracted once again, although it has not entirely disappeared.[22]

An antecedent of the SWPP in Nigeria, the Socialist Workers' and Farmers' Party (SWFP), came into being in 1963 and functioned in the open until the military took over the Lagos government in 1966. During that period the SWFP even set up a Patrice Lumumba Institute of Political Science in the country. After the SWPP was formed in the mid-1970s, the ruling authorities permitted it to organize its forces to try to qualify to contest Nigeria's 1979 and 1983 elections, but it failed to meet the criteria laid down by the national electoral laws to do so on both occasions. Some of its members, however, did gain key leadership posts within the officially authorized Nigerian Trade Union Congress, and they still retained these in the mid-1980s.[23]

The LIPAD, the ULCR, and the PCRV in Burkina Faso were among the key backers of Captain Thomas Sankara's initial government after he assumed power in August 1983, and several ministers in Sankara's first cabinet came from the LIPAD and the UCLR. But those from the LIPAD—by far the most numerous and influential of the lot—lost their jobs in the fall of 1984 after quarreling with the military members of the government. When Captain Blaise Compaore overthrew Sankara in October 1987, representatives from the UCB, the GCB, and the ULC acquired prominent roles in the new government.[24]

In addition, the governments of most of the states where these parties exist have rarely had sufficient strength to implement repressive policies with a great deal of efficiency. South Africa provides the major exception. Yet even there the flourishing of a multiparty system and (at least until the declaration of a nationwide state of emergency in June 1986) freedom of speech and press among the white-minority elements of the population has created conditions less inhibiting than a wholesale authoritarian environment might have.

Such factors have made all of the parties here less inclined to conceal their outlooks and plans than the outlawed parties of North Africa have been. As a result their coalition strategies and tactics are reasonably susceptible to examination. Only in the cases of the six Burkina Faso parties does significant cloudiness remain about any of the broad outlines of their strategies and tactics.

As is true with respect to the banned parties of North Africa, illegal status makes the proscribed parties of sub-Saharan Africa attach greater weight to domestic enemies than do Marxist parties that operate on the continent without formal constraints. But two facets of the sub-Saharan African setting render most of them less hostile to their local governments and more discriminating in their choices of enemies than their North African equivalents are.

First, Marxist parties have by and large come into being only fairly recently in sub-Saharan Africa. The region had produced just one such party by World War II—the Communist Party of South Africa, which was established in 1921. None of the other parties under consideration here took shape until well after the war. LIPAD's precursor, the Upper Volta section of the African Party of Independence of French West Africa, emerged in 1957, but the other five Marxist parties in Burkina Faso (formerly Upper Volta) were not organized until the 1970s (the ULCR and the PCRV) and the 1980s (the ULC, the GCB, and the UCB). The Lesotho Communist party, as noted previously, was evidently founded in 1961. Nigeria's SWPP regards itself as the lineal descendant of the Socialist Workers' and Farmers' party, which was established in 1963.

Second, sub-Saharan Africa has a substantial record of instability of governments. Of the states in which the parties in this category function, Burkina Faso and Nigeria have experienced a large number of governmental turnovers since independence—many of them the result of military intervention in politics. Nigeria has even gone through a major civil war. Lesotho had not witnessed any changes in government until the military ousted Prime Minister Leabua Jonathan in January 1986, but Jonathan had found himself under constant challenge from opposition forces since 1970, when he apparently lost the first postindependence elections yet refused to hand over power. Only the white-minority government of South Africa has shown an ability to maintain reasonably firm control over its domain across time, and even its success in quelling unrest by local non-whites has declined dramatically in the 1980s.

Because most of the parties at issue here have been around such a relatively short time, they have not had a chance to be exposed to extended periods of harassment by their local governmental authorities. Further-more, while they were officially outlawed as of the late 1980s, they had enjoyed varying degrees of freedom from governmental persecution at specific junctures in their brief histories as a result of overthrows and weaknesses of the governments of their countries. These factors have exerted striking influence on the thinking of individual parties about their enemies.

All of the Burkina Faso parties seem to view their local government as a potential enemy, yet their judgments about how significant an enemy it is have appeared to fluctuate over time in line with shifts in the nature and policies of that government.[25] If the parties have assessed the elements in power as "progressive" in foreign policy and especially in domestic affairs, they have treated external forces—namely, the "imperialist" states of the West—as their principal foes. Such was the case, for example, during the early months after Captain Thomas Sankara assumed power in 1983 and adopted a fairly radical line on both international and internal matters. If, on the other hand, the parties have determined the local ruling authorities to be "unprogressive" in character, they have fixed on it as their chief enemy. Normally, however, they have tended to see such forces as the "lackeys" of the "imperialists" and have not drawn sharp lines between external and domestic enemies.

The SWPP of Nigeria and the Lesotho Communist party delineate their enemies similarly. During the period of civilian rule in Nigeria from 1979 to 1983, the SWPP acknowledged the Shagari government's willing-ness to tolerate its existence as an "association," and the SWPP looked upon "imperialism" as the main threat to itself.[26] With the banning of all parties by the new military authorities in early 1984, the SWPP reassessed its position and focused on the military government as its chief enemy, and its perspective did not change even after Major General Ibrahim Babangida replaced Major General Muhammadu Buhari as head of the government in August 1985.[27] No doubt Babangida's announcement in July 1987 that the country's military rulers would permit the establishment of only two parties to contest the elections planned to prepare for the return to civilian rule in 1922 reinforced the SWPP's viewpoint.

Prior to Prime Minister Jonathan's launching of overtures to the communist states in the 1980s—the available evidence suggests—the Lesotho Communist party perceived his government as its primary enemy, but as ties between Maseru and the Soviet bloc increased, its attitude began to change.[28] This shift apparently accelerated when Jonathan's government adopted a less restrictive posture toward the party itself in late 1984. In any event, the party came to depict external forces, and notably "U.S. imperialism" and "South African racism," as its principal foes.[29] With the military's takeover of the country and its ensuing clampdown on party activity, however, the party's outlook seems to have reverted to that of earlier years.[30]

The South African Communist party has obviously not felt the effects of either of these general features of the sub-Saharan African context. It marked its sixty-fifth anniversary in 1986, and it had confronted severe and unremitting repression by the South African government for more than half of those years.

Therefore, the party's views about enemies display much less flexibility than do those of other parties in this category. It has consistently deemed the Pretoria government to be its chief enemy.[31] In the 1980s, to be sure, it has tended to regard "U.S. imperialism" as a key backer of that government; nevertheless, its focus has remained on the white-minority government as its main foe. The growing difficulties that the authorities in Pretoria have encountered since 1984 in trying to maintain their control over nonwhites has appeared to confirm the party's commitment to that judgment.[32]

Another feature of the sub-Saharan African milieu has a significant impact on how the parties in this grouping rank their external enemies, irrespective of whether they regard such enemies as primary or secondary. The inhabitants of the region are largely nonwhites, and all of the parties here reflect that demographic reality. In fact, only the South African Communist party has a significant body of white members.[33] Like the nonwhites of the region generally, the parties display great sensitivity to relations between nonwhites and whites, and the persistence of white-minority rule in Namibia and South Africa incenses them. As a result they all employ attitudes toward the Pretoria government as a touchstone for ordering their external enemies. In the 1980s they have identified the Reagan administration in Washington as that government's prime international defender, so it is hardly surprising that "U.S. imperialism" has stood at the top of their lists of external enemies.[34]

Proscription encourages parties in sub-Saharan Africa, just as it does parties in North Africa, to regard as potential allies all domestic opponents of their local governments and/or of the policies of those governments. Moreover, the greater dissatisfaction with the governments that these groups and individuals manifest, the more attractive they tend to appear as allies.

To be sure, the same regional peculiarities that render many of the outlawed parties of sub-Saharan Africa less hostile toward those in power in their countries than the banned parties of North Africa are toward authorities in their countries also have an impact in this context. That is, these peculiarities make the sub-Saharan African bodies more open-minded than are their North African counterparts about the possibility of cooperating with existing rulers. Indeed, as already noted, representatives of the LIPAD and ULCR in Burkina Faso even served in the cabinet of Captain Sankara for at least a time during his rule, and members of the GCB, the UCB, and the ULC became leaders and spokesmen of the Popular Front government of Captain Compaore after he displaced Sankara in 1987.

Nevertheless, all of the illegal parties in sub-Saharan Africa have displayed a substantial wariness toward the governing forces of their states. Under these circumstances, the limited willingness that these parties have evinced to consider collaboration with such forces has a short-term, tactical —rather than strategic—thrust.

Certainly, it is to opposition elements that the parties in this category have directed their attention when singling out desirable allies for the longer haul. Furthermore, such elements have been the objects of most of the wooing that parties concerned here have actually carried out—a not inconsiderable amount in all instances.

But the precise targets of courtship have differed somewhat from case to case. All of the parties in Burkina Faso except the PCRV have apparently seen some merit in collaboration with other Marxist groups. Representatives of the LIPAD and the ULCR held portfolios in the cabinet of Captain Sankara for a while after he took over the government in August 1983, and the UCB, the GCB, and the ULC all assumed important functions in the regime of Sankara's successor, Blaise Compaore. However, the LIPAD has channeled its major efforts into forging strong links with the country's trade unions. The PCRV, for its part, has expended most of its energies on building ties not only with the local trade unions but also with the national student movement.[35]

In its earlier incarnation, the Socialist Workers' and Farmers' party, the SWPP of Nigeria, tried unsuccessfully to bring about some form of cooperation with one of the key political actors on the internal scene in the mid-1960s—the United Progressive Grand Alliance. Yet the party has always focused its attempts to create alliances primarily on the state's trade unions. Here it has encountered a more favorable response than from straightforwardly political bodies.[36]

Although the Lesotho Communist party hoped, after the "partial lifting" of the ban on it in 1984, that it might become a junior partner of the ruling Basotho National party in a postelection government in 1985, Prime Minister Jonathan's rigging of the election process dashed that hope; consequently, the communist party joined with other opposition parties in refusing to participate in the elections.[37] More important, it apparently renewed its traditional emphasis on fashioning relations with trade unions.[38]

The SACP of South Africa has long endeavored to associate itself closely with the country's nonwhite elements. Prior to the late 1940s, this effort concentrated on the African National Congress (ANC). In the 1950s, after both coloreds and Asians had lost the vote, the SACP—working through a legal front called the Congress of Democrats—collaborated with the ANC, the South African Indian Congress, the South African Colored Peoples' Organization, and the South African Congress of Trade Unions in forming the Congress Alliance. But the ANC remained the main focal point of the SACP's undertakings with regard to mutual cooperation, and the ANC became even more significant in this respect after 1969, when it opened its membership to all races.[39]

As the complexity of politics among whites in South Africa has increased in the 1980s, the SACP has also perceived value in alliance with non-Marxist whites there seeking the abolition of apartheid. To be sure, the party classifies such elements as "forces for change" and distinguishes them from "revolutionary forces" like the ANC. Nonetheless, it advocates expansion of dialogue with them.[40]

One aspect of the sub-Saharan African milieu greatly affects the calculations about allies of at least most of the parties in this grouping. All except the Lesotho Communist party function in multiethnic environments, and all have had to define a posture on ethnicity and its political importance in evaluating possible allies.

This issue has been most critical for the SACP of South Africa. Although the party has accepted members from all ethnic groups for many years, it originated among whites, and whites long dominated it. Even today they play a fairly major role in its key institutions.[41] In a state in which whites constitute only about 15 percent of the population, therefore, such a party has little chance of prospering unless it aligns itself with nonwhites and their organizations. This consideration has underlain the SACP's preoccupation with bodies like the ANC.

For the six parties of Burkina Faso and the SWPP of Nigeria, the ethnicity problem has assumed a somewhat different form. Neither of the countries in which they operate contains large numbers of whites, but both—and especially Nigeria—have black populations composed of many ethnic groups. Moreover, politics in the two states still has a decidedly ethnic dimension.[42] Thus all seven parties—even though they, as ideological bodies, recruit members on the basis of intellectual commitment rather than ethnic background—often confront choices of allies that run along ethnic lines.

The responses of the parties to this kind of challenge have tended to be tactical rather than strategic in nature. That is, the parties have sought to cooperate with specific groups whenever such cooperation seemed expedient, but they have tried to avoid firm identification with any particular group. This was the approach, for example, of the forerunner of the SWPP of Nigeria in the mid-1960s when it proposed collaboration with the United Progressive Alliance—a political coalition of southerners that was dominated by the Ibos.

In sub-Saharan Africa as in North Africa, outlaw status induces parties to view as desirable external allies those international forces that the parties deem to be essentially hostile to their own local governments—especially the more powerful of these forces. The Lesotho Communist party, the SWPP of Nigeria, the SACP of South Africa, and the LIPAD of Burkina Faso see the U.S.S.R. and the other members of the Soviet bloc as the key entities that fit this bill. There is some variation, however, in the degree to which they engage in actual contacts with Moscow and its friends. The Lesotho Communist party, the SWPP, and the SACP all belong to the international communist movement, and they maintain regular ties with the U.S.S.R. and the rest of the Soviet bloc through it. While the LIPAD evinces a heavily pro-Soviet orientation, it is not clear that the party has any sort of regular links with either Moscow or its friends. The ULCR and the ULC of Burkina Faso look basically to China in the world arena, while the PCRV, the UCB, and the GCB of Burkina Faso consider themselves pro-Albanian. After Deng Xiaoping began to downplay the Maoist revolutionary model in the late 1970s, Albania proclaimed itself the fount of true Maoism, and the PCRV, the UCB, and the GCB identify themselves with Tirana for that reason.[43]

A distinctive feature of the environment of sub-Saharan Africa reinforces the inclination of most of the parties in this category to treat the Soviet bloc and particularly the U.S.S.R. as their chief external allies. As pointed out previously, all of the parties, like nonwhites in the region generally, denounce the continuation of white-minority rule in Namibia and South Africa, and they use attitudes toward the Pretoria government as a yardstick by which to determine the merits of their potential foreign allies. Among these forces, in the judgment of the parties, Moscow and its friends have proved to be the staunchest non-African proponents of majority rule throughout the continent and the harshest critics of the vestiges of racism there.[44]

Like the banned pro-Soviet parties in North Africa, of course, the ones in sub-Saharan Africa have found the U.S.S.R. something less than a perfect ally. The U.S.S.R. has its own interests in the region, and it has not hesitated to follow them when they have not fully coincided with those of the parties concerned. For instance, Moscow has vigorously courted the government of Nigeria since the civil war of the late 1960s, regardless of whether that government has adopted a repressive or a lenient attitude toward the SWPP and its predecessor.[45] In quite a different vein, Soviet leaders declined to provide economic assistance badly needed by Burkina Faso even when LIPAD representatives were in the cabinet.[46] The SACP of South Africa, too, began to experience a conflict of interests with Moscow in the mid-1980s. At least elements within the Soviet hierarchy openly expressed a distinct lack of enthusiasm about the possibility of the escalation of violence in South Africa, and they voiced doubts about the chances for, as well as the wisdom of, a quick transition to socialism in post-apartheid South Africa.[47] Nevertheless, the parties have discerned no better alternative as their main external ally than the U.S.S.R.

Militant opposition to white-minority rule in Namibia and South Africa also serves as the essential basis upon which all of the parties in this category identify other external allies. Radical African governments and bodies, especially those in the sub-Saharan region, are the principal entities that qualify in this regard. However, the extent to which the parties here deem it of merit to establish direct cooperative relations with these governments and bodies varies considerably. Within the framework of the international communist movement, the SACP of South Africa, the Lesotho Communist party, and the SWPP of Nigeria have worked not only with one another but also with other communist parties on the continent on issues of mutual concern. But the approach of all the parties to alliance with many governments and bodies thought to be worthy as collaborators has gone little beyond independent articulation of common positions.

Legal Parties in North Africa

The PPS, USFP, and OADP of Morocco; the Sudan Communist party; and the Tunisian Communist party employ coalition strategies and tactics shaped to a great extent by their standing as officially recognized parties and by the history and characteristics of the North African context in which they operate. To begin with, the right to function openly lessens the tension between a party and its local government; therefore, legal status encourages a party to downgrade internal forces in its hierarchy of enemies and to attach primary importance to external foes. Unlike most of the proscribed parties on the continent, then, all of the parties in this category —even the USFP of Morocco, which depicts itself as Marxist and not Marxist-Leninist—regard domestic enemies as secondary to external ones. The PPS of Morocco provided a good illustration of the general outlook of the group on this matter at its third national congress in March 1983. It defined its main task as preventing a foreign military presence on Moroccan territory and strengthening national independence and sovereignty.[48]

This inclination to relegate domestic foes to a subsidiary concern is bolstered by an aspect of the parties' North African heritage. As mentioned previously, North Africa has a history of authoritarian rule and of intolerance of political opposition. Although the governments of Morocco, Tunisia, and Sudan have shown less disposition to persecute local political and social elements opposed to them than have governments of other countries of the region, they have still resorted to repressive measures at times, and the parties here and/or the forces represented by them have been among the chief targets of such measures.[49]

In Morocco, an autonomous communist party emerged in 1943 and operated overtly under the French colonial regime until 1952, when it was suppressed. It reappeared as a legal entity after the country gained independence in 1956, but it soon fell afoul of the new government, which dissolved it in 1959. For the next fifteen years it experienced varying degrees of harassment by the authorities—even after it reconstituted itself as the Party of Progress and Socialism (PPS) in 1968. In 1974 the PPS won official recognition again; however, it has not totally escaped governmental crackdowns even with this status. On occasion, some of its members have been imprisoned and brought to trial for their activities, and the party's newspapers have periodically been subjected to severe censorship.[50]

The USFP came into being in 1974 as a result of a split in the National Union of Popular Forces, which had formed in 1959.[51] Although never proscribed, the USFP initially endured the same harsh treatment at the hands of the Moroccan authorities that its parent body had. The situation changed somewhat in 1977, however, with King Hassan II's increased stress on political pluralism. Since then the party has gone through cycles of official repression and leniency, during which party leaders have sometimes found themselves in jail and sometimes members of a coalition cabinet.

The OADP was founded in May 1983 by political elements dissatisfied with the amount of militancy displayed by both the USFP and the PPS. Its leader, Mohamed Bensaid, and many of its members had suffered through long periods of forced political exile in the past. Indeed, Bensaid had even been sentenced to death in absentia by the Moroccan government in the 1960s. Only in 1980 had a royal amnesty permitted political exiles like Bensaid to return to the country and resume political activity.

An autonomous Tunisian Communist party was established in 1934 by the former Tunisian Federation of the French Communist party, but the Tunisian organization was outlawed by the French colonial authorities in 1939 and was not allowed to function legally again until 1943. Thereafter, it operated above ground for nearly twenty years despite some official harassment—especially after Tunisia acquired its independence in 1956. With the uncovering of a plot against President Habib Bourguiba in late 1962, however, the party was quickly banned, and some of its leaders were arrested and imprisoned for several months. This time, the body's clandestine existence lasted for eighteen years. It finally recovered legal status in 1981.

Although Egyptian communists nurtured a Sudanese Communist party from the 1920s on, the party traces its origins as an independent body to 1946, but it was suppressed shortly afterward and compelled to function underground until the early 1950s. Permitted to resurface openly then, it remained a part of the legal political scene in the Sudan until 1958, two years after the country obtained its independence. At that time, the party's opposition to the coup of Lieutenant General Ibrahim Abbud brought about its proscription. Not until Abbud's military dictatorship was overthrown in 1964 did the party reacquire official recognition. That return to legality, however, was brief, ending after barely a year. For the next two decades the party had to carry on its activities clandestinely. To be sure, during the first year or so after radical military officers led by Gaafar Nimeiri took control in Khartoum in 1969, the new rulers did cooperate fairly closely with the communist party, even though they did not formally legalize it. Yet that cooperation ended in 1971 in the wake of an abortive coup against Nimeiri in which there was communist involvement. From then until Nimeiri's overthrow in 1985, the Sudanese government not only outlawed the party but worked assiduously to root it out from the local body politic. Nimeiri's successors finally restored official recognition to the party not long after they came to power.

In the face of such records of repression by their local governments, all of the parties in this grouping have clearly felt it wise to try to avoid outright confrontation with the authorities of their states. Such confrontation, in the eyes of the parties, could even wind up jeopardizing their ability to operate overtly.[52]

Neither their standing as legal organizations nor their reluctance to antagonize the ruling circles of their countries, of course, induces any of the parties here to exclude their local governments from their lists of enemies. This is true even of the USFP of Morocco. In agreeing to join a coalition cabinet in late 1983, for example, the head of the USFP, Abderrahim Bouabid, gave as justification the fact that one of the primary tasks of the new cabinet would be to ensure that the parliamentary elections of 1984 were not rigged.[53] The party had long maintained that the previous parliamentary elections, in 1977, had been fixed by the government.

As is the case with respect to the proscribed parties of North Africa, the Arab dimension of the North African setting strongly influences how the parties in this category rank their external enemies. All of the groups here except the Sudan Communist party have memberships almost exclusively Arab, and that of the Sudan Communist party is predominantly Arab. Thus it is hardly surprising that they all propound a highly pro-Arab line in their foreign policies. In keeping with such a line, they view Israel and its allies as their key international enemies. Among these allies, they identify the United States as the most important. Their statements, for example, typically couple condemnation of "U.S. imperialism" and "Zionism."[54] It should be noted, however, that the USFP of Morocco appears to attack the United States less often and less sharply than the other parties do.

Legal status, just as it tempers the hostility of the parties in this grouping toward their local governments, creates an atmosphere that makes possible at least limited, tactical alliances between these parties and the elements currently in power in their countries. As long as the parties do not face governmental threats to their very survival, they tend to see the ruling elements of their states as possessing both positive and negative features, and they can choose at any given time to accent the positive ones.

On occasion, all of the parties concerned here have demonstrated a willingness to align themselves with their governments, but the nature of the association deemed legitimate has differed for individual parties. Only the USFP and PPS of Morocco have proved amenable to formal cooperation with the dominant political forces in their country, and only the USFP has actually participated in "national unity" cabinets. It did so in two instances, briefly in 1977 and again in 1983–1984.[55] The rest of the parties have confined themselves basically to endorsing positions taken by their local governments.

Issues that have served as grounds for cooperation between the parties and their governments have fallen primarily within the foreign policy sphere. All of the parties have supported undertakings of their governments that the parties have felt would bolster the national independence and sovereignty of their states. The PPS of Morocco, for instance, hailed King Hassan II's rapprochement with Libya in 1983 as a necessity in light of "the serious situation prevailing in the Arab world, a divided and weakened world facing the imperialist-Zionist maneuvers."[56] In addition, the three Moroccan parties have staunchly backed the king's claims to the Western Sahara.[57]

On the domestic front, "progressive" official moves to expand the range of political forces allowed to carry on overt activities have evoked favorable responses from all of the parties. Yet the parties' assessments of the commitments of their local governments to political pluralism have varied substantially. The Tunisian Communist party and the Sudan Communist party have seemed much less convinced on this score than have the Moroccan parties.[58]

Like the banned parties of North Africa, the legal parties of the region turn fundamentally to the opponents of their local governments in search of longer-term allies within their respective countries. But there is considerable diversity among the parties in both the zeal with which they pursue domestic alliances and the kind of internal elements with which they seek to cooperate.

The USFP and the OADP of Morocco appear less preoccupied with forging domestic alliances than do the other three parties. This attitude of the USFP and the OADP stems from quite different reasons in the two cases. The USFP constitutes a significant force in its own right in the Moroccan political context. It won 35 of the 206 seats determined by direct universal suffrage in the 1984 parliamentary elections—up from 16 in 1977.[59] Cooperation with other political groups, then, is for it a useful but not essential means of furthering its interests. The OADP downplays collaboration with other political forces because of ideological considerations. It has no illusions about exercising great influence in Moroccan political life on its own for the moment (it garnered just one seat in the 1984 parliamentary balloting), but it chastises even the USFP and the PPS for what it views as their relative lack of militancy.[60] Thus it is prepared to ally itself only with radical, highly militant internal elements—elements not exactly in abundant supply in Morocco.

The three communist parties, in contrast, evidence great interest in forming alliances with opposition forces in their states. This interest derives to a major extent from a recognition of their own weakness. The PPS captured just 2 seats out of 206 in the 1984 parliamentary elections in Morocco, while the Tunisian Communist party failed to obtain even 1 out of the 125 in the 1981 parliamentary balloting in Tunisia, getting a meager 0.78 percent of the total vote. (The Tunisian party boycotted the 1986 parliamentary elections in Tunisia after the government disqualified most of the party's candidates.) In the balloting for a Constituent Assembly in the Sudan in 1986, the Sudan Communist party won only 5 of the 264 seats decided (conditions in thirty-seven constituencies in the south were so unsettled that voting could not be conducted there).[61] The parties' consciousness of their own weakness is heightened, moreover, by their awareness of the harshness with which North African governments have often dealt with local opposition groups. To counter such behavior, the parties hold, it is vital for at least some elements of the opposition to work together.[62]

With regard to specific targets of courtship, the stances of the Sudan and Tunisian communist parties are the most eclectic in nature. During the last years of the Nimeiri regime, the Sudan party called for the creation of a broad "Front of Struggle for Democracy and Salvation of the Country" that would embrace not only a variety of political parties but also trade union organizations; workers' and peasants' associations; students', women's, and young people's associations; regional organizations, especially those in the south of the country; elements of the armed forces; and influential public and political figures.[63] Despite the ouster of Nimeiri, the party's position on the subject has remained essentially unchanged. Party leaders see the task of eradicating the vestiges of the Nimeiri regime and avoiding the establishment of an Islamic republic as formidable, and they urge "the broadest possible unity" to ensure the achievement of these goals.[64]

The Tunisian party has worked assiduously since it reacquired legal status in 1981 to bring about "unity of action of the democratic forces" in the country. It has paid special heed in this effort to the Movement of Social Democrats, the Popular Unity Movement, and the Islamic Tendency Movement—the three main challengers of the ruling Destourian Socialist party. In February 1986, for instance, the Communist party cooperated with the three other parties in founding a "committee of solidarity" with the General Union of Tunisian Workers (UGTT), which had been suffering harassment by the Tunisian government.[65]

Throughout its existence the USFP has wavered between two conflicting perspectives concerning suitable collaborators on the Moroccan scene. At times it has looked leftward and essentially to the PPS for an alliance; at times it has swung to the right and especially toward such bodies as the Istiqlal, a reformist group that qualified as the leading party in the state until the 1980s and still remains a political force of consequence. To some extent, resistance to a broad opposition front by centrist and rightist parties has confronted the USFP with the necessity of choice between these two approaches, but the USFP has given plenty of signs that it welcomes the flexibility that the dual possibilities afford it to follow a course that serves its own best interests at any precise moment. As of the late 1980s the USFP appeared to have concluded that the PPS was currently the most desirable group with which to try to cooperate in the internal political arena.[66]

Since the mid-1970s, the PPS of Morocco has fixed upon the USFP as its key potential ally, and the PPS has actively sought to expand contacts and engage in collaborative undertakings with the USFP, particularly when the USFP has been responsive to overtures of this sort. In the early 1980s the two parties even held some joint meetings of their politburos. At certain junctures, it is true, the PPS has proposed formation of a broad "national front" cabinet in which it would participate, but it has always premised such proposals on the unity of the PPS and USFP.[67]

By declining to cooperate with any domestic Moroccan forces except those of a radical, militant persuasion, the OADP has greatly restricted its possible internal allies. It evidently devotes most of its attention to members of the National Union of Moroccan Students.[68]

Two features of the North African environment have visibly complicated the selection and courtship of desirable allies for many of the parties in this category. First, like their outlawed counterparts in the region, the parties here have had to take into account the overwhelmingly Muslim milieu in which they function. Specifically, they have felt compelled to set forth positions on relations with Muslims and with political movements based on Islam—especially in light of their own secularist postures as Marxist bodies. The Tunisian and Sudan communist parties have seen this undertaking as particularly important because of the existence in their countries of increasingly powerful groups with a fundamentalist Islamic outlook.

In coping with this task the parties have followed the same general tack that the proscribed North African parties have. That is, they have contended that commitment to Islam can produce either positive or negative consequences, depending on whether it stimulates "progressive," "anti-imperialist" thinking or a "reactionary," "pro-imperialist" viewpoint. If individuals and political organizations that espouse Islamic principles adopt a "progressive," "anti-imperialist" line, the argument goes on, there are suitable grounds for cooperation with them.[69]

Some of the parties in this grouping, however, have shown greater readiness in practice to collaborate with Islamic-oriented movements than have their proscribed equivalents. The Tunisian Communist party has worked actively at times in the 1980s with the Islamic Tendency Movement of Tunisia to try to achieve common ends.[70] Prior to the collapse of the Nimeiri regime in 1985, the Sudan Communist party advocated the "unity of the democratic and anti-dictatorship forces" of the state, including the Khattmiyya sect's Democratic Union and the Muslim Brotherhood, but since Nimeiri's political demise, communist leaders have excluded at least the Brotherhood from the "democratic forces" because it resists repeal of the "reactionary" legislation that Nimeiri enacted in 1983 to extend Islamic law throughout the country.[71] Only the three Moroccan parties have stood largely aloof from religious-based political bodies—no doubt in large measure because such bodies are relatively insignificant on the Moroccan political scene.[72]

Second, unlike the banned parties of North Africa, certain of the parties under consideration here have discovered that the heavily Arab character of the region injects complexities into their calculations about local forces with which they might usefully cooperate. In keeping with the basic demographics of the area, as pointed out already, all of the legal parties have a decidedly Arab cast to them—in terms of both membership and outlook. Yet Morocco and especially the Sudan have substantial ethnic minorities, and these minorities over the years have developed political organizations to articulate their interests. Although the Berber-based Popular Movement in Morocco has not confined its platform to ethnic nationalism, it has nevertheless represented Berber perspectives in the national political arena. In Sudan, Anyanya (from the 1950s into the 1970s) and the Sudanese People's Liberation Movement (in the 1980s) have derived their support from the blacks living in the southern portion of the state, and they have adopted a pronounced ethnic posture. Under circumstances of this sort, the Marxist parties in the two countries have perceived a need to formulate positions on alliances with non-Arab ethnic political groups.

The attitudes of the Marxist parties involved toward cooperation with such forces have varied appreciably. In Morocco, the OADP and PPS have essentially avoided links with the Popular Movement, although on one or two occasions the PPS has suggested the establishment of a broad "national front" cabinet that would include the Popular Movement and other rightist groups as well as itself. When the USFP has been looking to the right of the political spectrum for collaborators, it has sometimes joined with the Popular Movement in a coalition cabinet—for example, in 1977 and again in 1983–1984. But when the USFP has sought to align itself with forces to its left, it has ignored the Popular Movement. The Sudan Communist party has proved the most energetic would-be ally of non-Arab, ethnic-oriented bodies. Since 1954 it has endorsed autonomy for the southern region of the Sudan, and it has attempted to cooperate with groups committed to that end. It has been especially solicitous in the 1980s of the Sudanese People's Liberation Movement, which has rejected separatism but called for "democratization" of national life.[73]

Freedom to function openly tends to reduce the need that a party perceives for external allies in general, and particularly for external allies that evince a large measure of hostility toward its own local government, but legal standing by no means totally eliminates the desirability of such allies in the party's eyes. In fact, if a party is small and not on good terms with the ruling elements of its country, it may see great utility in collaborating with foreign foes of these ruling elements—especially the more powerful of such foes.

All of the parties in this category, because of their size and/or their strained relations with their local authorities, value cooperation with external entities that they view as adversaries of these authorities, and every one of the parties ranks the U.S.S.R. and the Soviet bloc high among such entities. The USFP of Morocco, however, does not focus as exclusively on the U.S.S.R. and the Soviet bloc in designating its top candidates for external allies as do the other parties. For instance, its list of principal external forces with which it deems collabortion is desirable embraces the French Socialist party.[74]

Furthermore, the parties differ significantly as to the kind of alliance that they envision with the U.S.S.R. The Tunisian Communist party, the Sudan Communist party, and the PPS of Morocco have long engaged in substantial interaction with the U.S.S.R. under the umbrella of the world communist movement. The USFP does not belong to the international communist movement, but it has conducted a fair amount of direct dealings with Soviet officials in the 1980s.[75] The OADP in its brief existence has seemed content with the statement of similar positions on individual issues.[76]

Just as the Arab background of North Africa has an impact on the way in which the parties here order their external enemies, it also colors their selection of allies in the international arena. Basically Arab in composition and pro-Arab in their foreign policies, the parties pay special heed to champions of the Arab cause in their quest for external allies.

The exact objects of the parties' attention in this respect are quite diverse. At least the Tunisian Communist party, the Sudan Communist party, and the PPS of Morocco treat one another as fraternal Arab bodies, and they cooperate extensively within the context of the world communist movement. All of the organizations in the grouping appear to assess radical Arab governments and opposition movements abroad as "progressive" and hence worthwhile collaborators, but their actual links with these governments and movements remain highly restricted—even in the case of the USFP, which enjoys perhaps the greatest stature outside its own state of any of the parties. Finally, every one of the parties classifies the U.S.S.R. and the other members of the Soviet bloc as the firmest non-Arab supporters of the Arabs on the international scene, and all but the OADP interact with them on at least a fairly regular basis.[77]

Like the outlawed bodies of the region, to be sure, the legal parties there do not always find the external forces that they designate as allies to be ideal ones in practice, for these forces sometimes behave in ways that run counter to the best interests of the parties. The U.S.S.R. especially does not hesitate to pursue warmer relations with the existing governments of the three countries than the parties might wish, whenever it concludes that such a step would be beneficial to it.

The 1980s have yielded clear illustrations of this Soviet propensity in the cases of Tunisia and Sudan. After the Tunisian Communist party obtained official recognition in 1981, it prodded the Tunisian authorities constantly to deepen their commitment to political pluralism, and it actually joined with other elements of the opposition in boycotting the May 1985 municipal elections and the November 1986 parliamentary elections on the grounds that the ruling party had rigged the balloting. Yet, during these same years, Moscow courted the Tunis government more intensively than it had for a long period.[78] Similarly, the U.S.S.R. in 1985–1986 failed to back the Sudan Communist party strongly in pushing the military successors of Nimeiri to live up to their promise to restore democracy in the country. Rather, Moscow adopted a fairly low profile with regard to Khartoum, in the obvious hope that the new authorities would soon expand Sudan's links with the U.S.S.R. as they had indicated that they intended to do.[79] Ultimately, it is true, Soviet leaders did not have to choose between a return to democratic rule in Sudan and a warming of relations between Sudan and the U.S.S.R., for both developments took place. Yet there was no doubt about Moscow's priorities.

Legal Parties in Sub-Saharan Africa

The nine Senegalese parties, the AKFM and MFM in Madagascar, the MMM and MMMSP in Mauritius, and the Réunion Communist party and MIR in Réunion pursue coalition strategies and tactics that flow in large measure from their freedom to operate overtly and from their sub-Saharan African heritage and environment. First, as in the case of the officially recognized parties of North Africa, legal standing reduces the hostility of the groups here toward their local governments and prompts them to rank external forces as their principal enemies. The behavior of Senegal's PIT in 1985 affords a typical illustration of the thinking of these parties on the issue. At that time, the PIT decided to focus its energies on organizing a "broad and powerful movement" designed "to frustrate the attempts at dragging the country into the aggressive machinery of the North Atlantic bloc and to prevent Senegal's transformation into a beachhead of imperialist struggle against African peoples and national liberation forces."[80] Such stress on foes abroad is especially pronounced with respect to the two parties in Réunion. Although Réunion has an appreciable degree of self-rule, the island remained an overseas department of France in the late 1980s.

This tendency to downplay the significance of internal enemies is strengthened by the sub-Saharan African backgrounds of the parties. Like the outlawed groups of the region, most of the legal parties have existed only a fairly short time, and all of them have enjoyed major periods of freedom to function openly in their countries. In fact, the vast majority of the officially recognized parties have experienced far less harassment over the years by their local authorities than have any of their banned counterparts.[81]

Of the nine Senegalese parties, only the PIT, PAI, and LD-MPT can boast much of a history. All three stem from the African Independence party founded in 1957 and subsequently proscribed by Senegalese authorities in 1960. In 1974 a number of members of this group broke away and set up the LD-MPT, which maintained an underground existence until 1981. The African Independence party's rump elements split again in the 1970s over President Leopold Sengor's offer to recognize it if it would serve as one of four legal groups representing the key postures that he envisioned in the national political spectrum—conservative, liberal, socialist, and Marxist. Those elements that make up the present PAI decided to accept the offer and obtained official recognition as the Marxist body in 1976; they have retained legal status ever since. Those elements that opted to reject the overture stayed underground until 1981, but they have functioned unfettered since then as the PIT.

The rest of the Senegalese groups emerged in the 1980s after the Dakar government lifted virtually all restrictions on party activity in 1981. None of them has ever endured a clandestine existence.

Madagascar's AKFM was established in 1948, and the MFM was formed in 1972. The former has carried on legal undertakings for the entire period since it came into being, although there have been slightly odd aspects to its status since the mid-1970s. Under the terms of Madagascar's 1975 constitution the island has just a single national party, the National Front for the Defense of the Malagasy Socialist Revolution; however, the Front contains within its ranks seven officially sanctioned groups, of which the AKFM is one. The MFM, in contrast, lost legal standing in 1976 and did not regain it until the early 1980s, when the party entered the Front. Nevertheless, the MFM appears to have avoided severe repression during the years when it was banned.

Both the MMM and the MMMSP trace their origins to the Mauritian Militant Movement set up in 1969. In the 1970s this group fell apart, with the main body continuing to be known as the MMM, and a small corps of dissidents reconstituting themselves as the MMMSP. Throughout their histories the two parties have always been able to conduct activities openly.

Of the two Réunion groups, the Communist party is the older, but it did not appear until 1959, when the island's federation of the French Communist party transformed itself into an autonomous body. The MIR grew out of the Marxist-Leninist Communist Organization of Réunion, which was founded in 1975 by a few defectors from the Communist party. Neither organization has ever suffered suppression over the years since it first took shape.

Like the legal parties of North Africa, to be sure, the parties in this category do not regard official recognition and the leeway that the ruling circles of their countries have allowed them as sufficient reason to cross these circles off their list of enemies. On the contrary, all of the groups here treat their ruling local elements basically as foes.

However, the level of antagonism that the legal parties of sub-Saharan Africa display toward their local ruling forces differs considerably. All of the groups in Senegal evince great wariness of the government of President Abdou Diouf and his Socialist party, which vastly overshadows the nine of them put together. The PIT has publicly depicted Diouf as a representative of the "neocolonists."[82] Other parties have even gone so far as to boycott elections held under the auspices of the local authorities. For example, the MRDN-AJ, UDP, PAIP, LCT, and OST all refused to participate in legislative balloting in 1983 and in municipal balloting in 1984. Although the PAI contested the 1983 elections, it joined with the preceding five groups in boycotting the 1984 voting.[83]

Both the MMM and MMMSP in Mauritius exhibit a lot of animosity toward the ruling coalition headed by Aneerood Jugnauth and his Mauritian Socialist Movement. This is particularly acute in the case of the MMM as a consequence of events of the early 1980s. In 1982 an alliance composed of the MMM and the Mauritian Socialist party won a smashing victory at the polls and took over the reins of power in the country, but disagreements soon developed within the MMM between Jugnauth, at that juncture the MMM president as well as the prime minister in the coalition government, and elements led by Paul Bérenger, the finance minister. These disputes eventually resulted in Bérenger's resignation from the cabinet and Jugnauth's expulsion from the MMM. Jugnauth responded by organizing a new party, the Mauritian Socialist Movement, and calling new elections in August 1983. For these elections he put together an alliance of several groups, with his MSM as its core, and this alliance defeated the MMM.[84]

As for the AKFM and MFM in Madagascar, the former has fairly consistently manifested greater cordiality toward the government of Admiral Didier Ratsiraka since he came to power in the mid-1970s than the latter has. Since the 1970s a representative of the AKFM has sat on Ratsiraka's Supreme Revolutionary Council, and a prominent figure in the AKFM, Giselle Rabeshala, has served in the cabinet. The MFM, in contrast, declined even to associate itself with Ratsiraka's Vanguard of the Malagasy Revolution (Arema) by participating in the National Front for the Defense of the Malagasy Socialist Revolution until the early 1980s. Then the group did consent to join the Front and even had a representative on the Supreme Revolutionary Council for a time, but by 1987 it was calling openly for a change in government—a position strongly denounced by the AKFM.[85]

The attitudes of the two parties in Réunion toward the ruling circles there are complex because the island is governed by a mix of Paris-appointed and locally elected officials. Although both parties object to a direct French political role on the island, they adopt divergent views on the merits of the local dimensions of the governmental system. Perhaps largely in light of its own substantial influence within locally run institutions, the Communist party looks upon them as a framework within which the island can win increased autonomy from France. The MIR, in contrast, sees little value in the existing institutions, for it regards them as simply the means whereby Paris seeks to forestall independence for the island, which the MIR favors.[86]

As is true with respect to the outlawed parties of sub-Saharan Africa, the essentially nonwhite character of the region has a profound impact on how the parties in this grouping order their external enemies. All of the parties here are largely nonwhite in composition, and all are highly sensitive about relations between whites and nonwhites. In this context, they strongly oppose white-minority rule in Namibia and South Africa; moreover, they use attitudes toward the Pretoria government as a key means of establishing priorities among their perceived foes abroad. In recent years they have tended to see the United States as the chief defender of that government, so they have identified it as their main external enemy.[87]

But certain other, more narrowly relevant factors also seem to enter into the precise ranking that some bodies assign to external foes that they deem of lesser importance than the United States. In Senegal, for instance, the ruling Socialist party has long maintained an affiliation with the Socialist International, and at least a number of the Marxist parties there view the Socialist International as a major external enemy. This is particularly so of the PIT.[88]

Official recognition creates possibilities for these sub-Saharan African parties, just as it does for their North African equivalents, to seek some type of limited, tactical alliance with the governing forces of their countries. Yet only a few of the groups have actually pursued such a course.

In Madagascar, the AKFM has steadfastly labored to fashion ties with the Ratsiraka regime since the 1970s, while the MFM has done so intermittently. Since the mid-1970s the AKFM has belonged to the Front for the Defense of the Malagasy Socialist Revolution, which also embraces Arema, the ruling party headed by President Ratsiraka. Moreover, as already noted, the AKFM has participated for many years in Ratsiraka's Supreme Revolutionary Council, and one of the party's top leaders has long been a government minister under Ratsiraka. Indeed, by the late 1980s the party held two cabinet posts.[89] The MFM, as pointed out previously, entered the Front for the Defense of the Malagasy Socialist Revolution in the early 1980s, and it subsequently had a representative on the Supreme Revolutionary Council for a while. By the late 1980s, however, it seemed to have abandoned efforts to woo the country's ruling forces, although it still remained a formal member of the Front.

From May 1981 to July 1984, when the communists and socialists in mainland France worked together in a coalition government, the Réunion Communist party maintained a cooperative posture toward the authorities from the metropole—especially after Paris began to devolve some of its powers to the island. The Réunion communists also joined with the local socialists to establish left-wing control of the new Regional Council that emerged out of Paris's initiatives. The withdrawal of the French communists from the national government in 1984, however, caused the Réunion Communist party to adopt a much more critical stance toward both the French authorities and its partners in the left-wing bloc in the local Regional Assembly. Soon the bloc, which had been experiencing increasing internal strife anyway, fell apart in all practical terms.[90]

In Senegal, the PIT, LD-MPT, and PPS have evinced a willingness to cooperate with the ruling elements there at least to the extent of making a multiparty system function. The PIT, in fact, has been quite explicit on the subject.[91]

Like the proscribed groups of sub-Saharan Africa, most of the legal ones of the region appear to prefer to search for allies among the opponents of their local ruling circles. Certainly they look to such quarters for potential long-term collaborators. But the enthusiasm that the parties display about constructing alliances with forces of this kind, and the specific targets of their efforts at courtship, vary substantially.

Most of the parties in Senegal have shown a fair amount of interest in finding collaborators among the domestic opposition there.[92] To a large degree they have directed their wooing at fellow Marxist groups. For instance, the LCT, LD-MPT, and UDP joined with one another in 1983 to back a common candidate in the presidential elections that year. In August 1983 the LCT, PAI, and PPS helped to found the Anti-Imperialist Action Front, and not long afterward these same three bodies assisted in setting up the Framework for United Action by the Opposition Forces, which also encompassed the LD-MPT and UDP. The LD-MPT, MRDN-AJ, OST, and UDP were among the charter members of a new, informal grouping called the Senegalese Democratic Alliance that was formed in July 1985. In February 1987 the vast majority of the nine Marxist parties signed a joint opposition communiqué vowing to coordinate their resistance to the Diouf government.

Yet many of the Marxist parties of Senegal have paid some attention to non-Marxist groups in the country as well. In the 1983 presidential election the PIT supported the candidacy of Abdoulaye Wade, head of the Senegalese Democratic party (PDS). The PDS wound up with the second largest number of parliamentary seats (8 as compared with 111 for the ruling Socialist party) in the legislative elections that took place simultaneously. The LCT, LD-MPT, and UDP endorsed Mamadou Dia, a former prime minister and the candidate of the People's Democratic Movement (MDP), in the 1983 presidential contest, and both the Anti-Imperialist Action Front and the Framework for United Action by the Opposition Forces included the MDP among its members. The Senegalese Democratic Alliance encompassed the PDS in addition to the four Marxist parties, and the PDS and some other non-Marxist groups helped to formulate the joint opposition communiqué of February 1987.

Both the AKFM and MFM in Madagascar have demonstrated some inclination to engage in mutual undertakings with the other five members of the Front for the Defense of the Malagasy Socialist Revolution aside from the ruling Arema, but the MFM has been decidedly more resolute in this regard than the AKFM. In May 1984, for example, the MFM joined with the Popular Impulse for National Unity (Vonjy), the National Movement for the Independence of Madagascar (Monima), and Socialist Monima (VSM) to call for a change in government. The essentially authoritarian and highly personalistic nature of President Ratsiraka's regime has rendered the AKFM quite cautious about joint ventures with other groups. AKFM leaders seem to believe that, by and large, they have more to lose than to gain from efforts that Ratsiraka might construe as AKFM involvement in attempts to gang up on him. Furthermore, the growing criticism of the regime's "socialist orientation" by some of the parties in the late 1980s has reduced the inherent appeal of collaboration with them.[93]

With respect to the two groups in Mauritius, the evidence at hand reveals no concern on the part of the MMMSP to fashion a cooperative relationship with any other political forces in the country, and the MMM since its founding has shown only a sporadic interest in aligning itself with other opposition political bodies. For instance, the MMM did form an alliance with the now defunct Mauritian Socialist party and the small Rodriguan People's Organization to wage the 1982 legislative elections. In fact, it even participated in a coalition government with these groups in 1982–1983. But in the legislative balloting of August 1983 the party ran independently. It did the same in the voting for municipal councils in December 1985. For the August 1987 legislative elections, however, it again entered into a coalition, this time with completely different partners than it had had in 1982. Plainly the MMM does not attach great weight to alliances or have deep convictions about the merits of particular potential allies. No doubt such views stem in substantial measure from the relative strength that the MMM has demonstrated within the Mauritian political context since the 1970s. On its own in the 1983 elections, for example, it garnered 46 percent of the total ballots and managed to obtain twenty-two of seventy seats in the new Legislative Assembly. Moreover, its candidates won a plurality of the votes in the balloting for municipal councils in 1985.[94]

The MIR in Réunion appears to eschew collaboration with all other political groups there because its demands for independence for the island put it fundamentally at odds with them, but the Réunion Communist party has quite a different perspective. Although its alliance efforts have suffered setbacks in the wake of the French Communist party's withdrawal from the coalition government in Paris in July 1984, in the 1980s it has assiduously courted local forces seeking increased autonomy from France for the island. In 1983, for instance, it worked out an agreement with the local socialists to share offices if the left won a majority of seats in the upcoming Regional Council elections. The accord also set forth terms under which other parties could cooperate with them. In July 1986 the Réunion communists in Sainte-Marie signed a protocol with the commune's Socialist and other leftist parties to prevent rightist forces from retaking control of the commune government in the wake of the March 1986 elections on the island.[95]

For most of the parties in this grouping, as for the banned parties of sub-Saharan Africa, weighing the relevance of ethnic attributes is crucial to arriving at judgments about worthwhile allies. To be sure, the parties in Réunion, where the bulk of the population has a thoroughly mixed racial ancestry, do operate in something resembling a homogeneous ethnic milieu; nevertheless, the same is not true for the other parties. Furthermore, politics in the countries where these parties function often take on a distinctly ethnic dimension. Thus the parties find it virtually impossible to select potential allies without deciding whether ethnic factors should figure in the undertaking.

The organizations concerned here offer diverse answers to the question, even though there is consensus among them on the principle that ethnicity should not enter into the recruitment of their own members. Madagascar's AKFM seems to be the most inclined to take ethnic considerations directly into account in choosing its candidates for allies. Over the years the AKFM itself has acquired a pronounced ethnic coloration, contrary to its own wishes. It draws its membership and support primarily from the Merina highlanders and has little base among the coastal tribes of the state. Therefore it has valued at least tactical association with individuals and groups of *cotier* background—notably, President Ratsiraka and his Arema.[96]

Two other parties demonstrate a willingness to cooperate with groups and elements with a clear ethnic makeup, but they do not invest a lot of energy in such collaborative efforts. The MFM of Madagascar has worked to some degree with the AKFM under the aegis of the National Front for the Defense of the Malagasy Socialist Revolution; however, the truly joint ventures of the two have been quite modest in nature. In the 1980s the PPS in Senegal has involved itself to some extent with Diola separatists in the Casamance area.[97]

The remainder of the parties shy away from links with ethnic-oriented bodies, yet their reasons for doing so vary. Although the MMM of Mauritius in the early 1980s actually entered into an alliance with the Mauritian Socialist party, a predominantly South Asian Hindu group, it now deplores what it sees as a drift back toward communal politics since 1983, and it has labored hard to expand its own backing among poor people of South Asian Hindu extraction. Parties like the LCT, LD-MPT, UDP, PAI, PIT, MRDN-AJ, and OST in Senegal have opted to associate themselves with groups lacking any particular ethnic identity. The rest of the parties have elected to stay aloof from alliances altogether.[98]

Legal status diminishes the need that the parties in this category discern for external allies, just as it does in the case of their counterparts in North Africa. Nevertheless, it does not wholly eradicate that need. As pointed out earlier, a substantial amount of tension continues to exist between many of the groups and the ruling elements in their countries. Moreover, most of the parties are small and lack much in the way of popular support. Only the MMM of Mauritius constitutes a major political force to be reckoned with in its own right. Although the alliance that the MMM headed in the August 1987 elections wound up with only 25 of the 70 seats in the Legislative Assembly, this alliance received nearly as many votes as the ruling alliance, which obtained 43 seats in the Assembly. The closest competitor of the MMM is the Réunion Communist party. This party captured 28 percent of the vote and 13 of the 45 seats in the March 1986 elections for the island's Regional Assembly. The AKFM and MFM in Madagascar both captured about 10 percent of the total ballots cast in the state's 1983 legislative elections, and this share netted them 9 and 3 seats respectively out of 137 in the Popular National Assembly. All of the other groups that have run slates in recent parliamentary elections have garnered no more than about 1 percent of the votes and obtained no seats in their national legislatures.[99] Thus the great bulk of the parties here see utility in having allies abroad—especially ones that the parties judge to be essentially hostile to the ruling circles of the countries in which they themselves function.

However, the exact entities that the parties designate as their main potential external allies differ widely—more so, in fact, than do those that the outlawed parties of the region pick. For the PIT and LD-MPT of Senegal, the AKFM of Madagascar and the Réunion Communist party, the U.S.S.R. and the Soviet bloc fit the bill. To the extent that the MMM of Mauritius seeks external allies, it too singles out the U.S.S.R. and the Soviet bloc as its top candidates. As Maoist organizations, the MMMSP of Mauritius, the MFM of Madagascar, and the MRDN-AJ of Senegal look to the international network of Maoist bodies for primary collaborators abroad, but Beijing's repudiation of many of Mao Zedong's teachings since the late 1970s has caused China itself to lose a good deal of its appeal to the parties in this regard. This consideration even induces the UDP of Senegal, another self-proclaimed Maoist group, to focus on pro-Albanian external forces. The LCT and OST of Senegal, both Trotskyist bodies, turn to the world network of Trotskyist organizations for principal allies abroad. Heading the list of possible external collaborators in the eyes of the PAI of Senegal is the Communist party of Romania. The PPS takes an avowedly independent Marxist stance. As for the other parties, their thinking about main allies abroad is not clear from available information.[100]

The kind of cooperation that the parties foresee with these external forces varies as well. Both the PIT of Senegal and the Réunion Communist party sanction formal ties with the U.S.S.R. within the framework of the world communist movement. The AKFM, too, favors a close and direct association with Moscow. For example, it has exchanged delegations with the Communist party of the Soviet Union for many years. Although the other African parties may pursue occasional contacts with the entities that they class as their chief potential collaborators abroad, they seem to perceive alliances essentially in terms of the articulation of shared perspectives.

From the standpoint of the parties in this grouping, it should be stressed, the specific forces that they target as principal external allies are not perfect choices by any means. The U.S.S.R. probably exhibits the greatest flaws of any because it discerns interests for itself that can most easily clash with those that the parties define for themselves. By and large, for instance, the U.S.S.R. sees utility in carrying on more cordial relations with France than the Réunion Communist party might prefer to do. Nonetheless, the particular entities appear to the parties to be the best options that they have at hand.

Like the proscribed parties of sub-Saharan Africa, the region's officially recognized parties use attitudes toward the white-minority government of South Africa as a key criterion for pinpointing desirable allies abroad. This factor figures prominently in the decisions that the groups make about what entities to fix upon as primary external collaborators, especially where the groups select the U.S.S.R. and the Soviet bloc. The PIT of Senegal, the Réunion Communist party, and the AKFM of Madagascar all appear to view the U.S.S.R. and the Soviet bloc as the global arena's most important champions of black-majority rule in Southern Africa.[101] Militant opposition to the Pretoria government also provides the chief grounds upon which the parties identify other worthwhile entities with which they might cooperate abroad. Here radical African regimes and organizations, particularly those in the sub-Saharan region, seem to be the predominant choices. The sort of collaboration that the parties envision with such entities, however, is by and large quite limited. Under the auspices of the world communist movement, the PIT of Senegal and the Réunion Communist party do conduct some joint undertakings with each other and with communist parties elsewhere in Africa on matters of common interest, but in most instances the parties in this classification appear content to define alliance with radical African governments and groups as merely the setting forth of like positions independently.

Ruling Parties in Sub-Saharan Africa

The MPLA-PT in Angola, the MLSTP in São Tomé and Príncipe, the PCT in the People's Republic of the Congo, the PRPB in Benin, the PAICV in Cape Verde, the PAIGC in Guinea-Bissau, the WPE in Ethiopia, the SRSP in Somalia, the Frelimo in Mozambique, and the ZANU-PF in Zimbabwe follow coalition strategies and tactics conditioned greatly by the ruling status of the parties and by the features and history of their sub-Saharan African milieu. To begin with, control of the reins of power induces all of the groups to blur distinctions between external and internal enemies and to perceive that they confront a single conspiracy headed by outside forces. As the parties see things, their rule is legitimate, and domestic challenges are unwarranted. But, the groups' argument goes on, the mere existence of their governments threatens the interests and plans of some external forces, and these forces seek to remove that threat by exerting pressure from outside and fomenting local "counterrevolution" against these governments. Therefore, the parties conclude, the major opposition to their authority comes from abroad.[102]

This sort of assessment of enemies is reinforced by the imperative that the parties feel to explain why they have not managed to avoid the domestic problems that ruling elements in sub-Saharan African countries have typically encountered since the early 1970s.[103] All of the states over which the parties preside have experienced some degree of political instability, and this has become acute at times. Furthermore, most of the states have failed to achieve significant economic growth rates or rates of increase in food production that appreciably exceed the rates of expansion of their populations. Only Congo and Cape Verde have recorded substantial economic growth per capita during the period, and only Guinea-Bissau and Benin have succeeded in keeping the rise in their food production running well ahead of additions to their populations. In fact, many of the countries have chalked up outright negative performances in both areas.[104]

The precise level of concern that individual parties evince regarding domestic enemies, however, does differ markedly. Such differences reflect the amount of active internal opposition that the parties confront. In the 1980s there have been major antigovernment insurgencies in Angola, Mozambique, Somalia, and Zimbabwe, and the regime in Ethiopia has had to contend with a number of armed struggles by separatist movements, with those in Eritrea, Tigre, and the Ogaden proving the most troublesome. Hence the parties in power in these five countries rate domestic enemies quite important. Although the other groups have all faced some type of domestic challenge to their rule, this has not taken the form of organized rebellion. Indeed, it has usually involved exile elements without much of a local base.[105] As a result, these parties do not attach nearly as much weight to internal enemies as the other five do.

Ruling status also produces great variation among the parties in the ordering of their external enemies and in the depth of their antagonism toward these discerned foes; it has even led to changes over time in one or the other regard or in both for individual parties. When a party controls its local government, it inevitably sizes up external forces in terms of whether they seem to constitute a threat to the survival of that government, which it naturally sees as a vital "national interest." Moreover, the more severe the threat that the party judges a particular entity to represent, the higher that entity will probably wind up on the party's list of its enemies abroad, and the stronger the hostility that the party is likely to manifest toward that entity. But the actual challenge that a particular entity poses — or at least the party's perception of that challenge — is not necessarily static. It can alter with the passage of time and the evolution of circumstances. In keeping with this flux, then, the entity's place on the roster of the party's external foes may shift, and/or the degree of antipathy that the party displays toward the entity may change.

Of the ten groups under consideration here, those in Ethiopia, Congo, Benin, Cape Verde, Guinea-Bissau, and São Tomé and Príncipe seem to identify "U.S. imperialism" as the only major threat from abroad to their regimes, although Ethiopia does not entirely discount Somalia's capacity to pose a challenge to it even in the 1980s. Yet these bodies do not evidence equally negative attitudes toward the United States.[106] The WPE in Ethiopia denounces the United States the most heatedly, while the PAICV in Cape Verde appears to adopt the least combative posture. Along the spectrum between these two extremes, the parties in Benin and Guinea-Bissau fall near the Cape Verde pole; those in Congo and São Tomé and Príncipe tend toward the Ethiopia one.

The groups in Angola, Mozambique, and Zimbabwe put South Africa at the top of their lists of foes abroad, and the intensity of their enmity toward South Africa is about the same, even though the Mozambique government did sign a nonaggression and good neighborliness accord with the authorities in Pretoria in 1984. At the same time, some differences do exist among the three with respect to secondary enemies. Both the MPLA-PT of Angola and the Frelimo of Mozambique clearly rank the United States just below South Africa in their assessments of external foes, but the Mozambican body views the United States as much less of a threat than does the Angolan one. To the ZANU-PF of Zimbabwe, the United States and the U.S.S.R. constitute enemies of about equal concern. Although the government of Zimbabwe deplores what it regards as U.S. intimacy with South Africa, memories linger of earlier Soviet support for the ZANU-PF's chief internal rival, the Zimbabwe African People's Union (ZAPU), and have a potent effect on the attitudes of the ZANU-PF toward Moscow.

The SRSP of Somalia is something of a maverick. It looks upon Ethiopia as its primary threat from abroad, but it sees the U.S.S.R., the principal international backer of the Addis Abeba government, as a close contestant for that designation. Such an evaluation is reinforced by the critical role that Moscow played in Somalia's defeat by Ethiopia in the Ogaden war of 1977–1978. Somalia's efforts since the mid-1980s to downplay confrontation and engage in dialogue with both Ethiopia and the U.S.S.R., it should be emphasized, stem from a shift in its tactics for dealing with them and not any revision in its basic calculations regarding them.

These judgments and outlooks of the groups about external foes reflect some modification in the groups' thinking on the subject since the late 1970s. Perhaps the most notable shift has to do with the SRSP of Somalia. No longer does the United States occupy second spot on that body's list of enemies abroad as it did as late as 1977; the U.S.S.R. has acquired that distinction. There have been other, less dramatic changes as well. For instance, the intensity of many parties' antagonism toward the United States has declined appreciably, as they have perceived a need for increased economic interaction with it. This trend has been most pronounced in the cases of Guinea-Bissau, Benin, and Mozambique.

As is true of the nonruling parties of sub-Saharan Africa, most of the ruling parties of the region pay significant heed to the attitudes of external forces toward the white-minority government of South Africa in drawing up the foregoing rosters of foes abroad. The SRSP of Somalia is the single exception. Preoccupied with its struggle with Ethiopia, it prefers to employ perspectives regarding the situation in the Horn of Africa as an alternative basis for decisions about external enemies. It should be underscored, however, that none of the parties allows its dedication to black-majority rule in Southern Africa to override the interests of its own state. That is, all of the groups to whom views of South Africa really matter temper their appraisals of foreign entities that they deem unduly sympathetic to the Pretoria government with hard-headed analysis of the benefits to their countries of having active dealings with these entities.

In common with ruling elements in the vast majority of states in sub-Saharan Africa, all ten parties in this grouping disapprove of a multiparty political system; therefore, they firmly reject the idea of domestic alliances with other formally independent political bodies—especially any cooperation that smacks of a sharing of power. At first glance, to be sure, the ZANU-PF of Zimbabwe might appear to be a deviant here. From its attainment of power in 1980 until the end of 1987, the ZANU-PF operated in a multiparty context, and it even invited representatives of the Zimbabwe African People's Union to participate in the initial government that it set up in 1980. Yet such behavior flowed essentially from force of circumstances rather than from choice. Under the terms of the constitution adopted prior to independence in 1980, the country could abolish a multiparty system before 1990 only if Parliament endorsed such a step, and Parliament, with 20 of its 100 seats reserved for whites, had to approve the measure by a 100 percent vote until 1987 or by a 70 percent vote between 1987 and 1990. From early in his rule, Prime Minister Robert Mugabe, the head of the ZANU-PF, stated repeatedly that he intended to institute a single-party state as soon as legal restrictions permitted, and he finally attained this goal in late 1987. In September 1987 Parliament ended the reservation of 20 seats for whites. The following month, elections for the vacated seats resulted in victories for all of ZANU-PF's candidates, several of whom were white. These victories gave ZANU-PF well over the 70 percent of the House seats needed to impose a one-party state, but by December 1987 Mugabe had persuaded ZAPU to amalgamate with ZANU-PF and thus bring about such a state by consent.[107]

The task of governing, however, compels the parties to pursue domestic alliances of more subtle kinds. This imperative arises from a combination of two factors.[108] First, as is typical of countries in sub-Saharan Africa, each of the states over which the parties preside is a complex entity. All except São Tomé and Príncipe, Cape Verde, and Somalia contain a number of distinct ethnic groups, and there are even some clear differences between *angolares* (descendants of a group of Africans shipwrecked off São Tomé in 1544) and *forros* (descendants of slaves and creoles) in São Tomé and Príncipe and between mulattoes and blacks in Cape Verde. Although Somalia has a highly homogeneous population from an ethnic standpoint, clans play an important role in the country. Regionalism crops up in many states as well. Often regional identifications go hand in hand with ethnic divisions, but they are also evident in countries with no strong ethnic cleavages—such as Cape Verde, São Tomé and Príncipe, and Somalia. The first two states, it should be noted, are each composed of more than one major island, and the third is made up of a couple of former colonial territories—British

Somaliland (in the north) and Italian Somaliland (in the south).

Second, the striking handicaps that the parties at issue here confronted when they became ruling entities and had to deal with states of great complexity have by no means vanished. The parties in Angola, Mozambique, Zimbabwe, São Tomé and Príncipe, Cape Verde, and Guinea-Bissau all grew out of anticolonial national liberation movements, but none of these movements had developed a constituency by the end of colonial rule that effectively bridged the major political and social divisions in its country. As of late 1975, the MPLA-PT enjoyed little support among the Bakongo and Ovimbundu elements of the Angolan population. In mid-1975 the Frelimo had significantly fewer backers among ethnic groups in the central and southern portions of Mozambique than among those in the north. The ZANU-PF lacked much in the way of links with the Ndebele people and the whites of Zimbabwe in 1980. Neither the MLSTP nor the PAICV (then a branch of the PAIGC of Guinea-Bissau) had managed to launch guerrilla warfare in São Tomé and Príncipe or Cape Verde prior to independence in 1975, and the Portuguese had maintained a tight control over political activity in both territories. Consequently, the two bodies remained largely exile organizations when they assumed power. In 1974 the PAIGC of Guinea-Bissau showed pronounced weaknesses among the diverse inhabitants of Bissau and among ethnic groups like the Fula in the northeast.

As for the parties in Congo, Benin, Somalia, and Ethiopia, they were all essentially creations of radical military elements, emerging as formal entities in 1969, 1975, 1976, and 1984 respectively, although the WPE had existed in embryo since 1979 as the Committee to Organize the Party of the Working People of Ethiopia (COPWE). Nowhere did the military elements that founded these bodies boast more than a tenuous base of support in the civilian community. Furthermore, in no instance were they broadly diversified in terms of ethnic and regional backgrounds. The elements in Benin and Congo hailed predominantly from the ethnic groups in the northern parts of their countries; those in Ethiopia, from the Amharic-speaking peoples of the central highlands; and those in Somalia, from the clans in the south—especially the Marrehaan group.

To at least some extent, then, all of the parties in this category try to build domestic coalitions within the frameworks of their own organizations. But there has, in practice, been substantial variation among them with respect to the intensity of their efforts, the general targets of their undertakings, and the precise calculus behind their labors.[109]

In the 1980s the parties in Angola, Mozambique, Zimbabwe, Ethiopia, and Somalia have displayed a much greater sense of urgency about fashioning domestic alliances than have those elsewhere. The governments controlled by these five parties have faced insurrections that have significant ties to specific local groups. In Angola, the Ovimbundu people have been the principal source of difficulties; in Mozambique, the ethnic groups in the central and southern portions of the country; in Zimbabwe, the Ndebeles; in Ethiopia, the Eritreans, the Tigreans, and, to a lesser degree, the Somalis of the Ogaden; in Somalia, the northern clans and especially the Majerteen and Isaaq groups. As a consequence of such problems, the parties have seen a strong need to forge more cooperative relations with at least elements of these groups in order to shore up their own governments. In contrast, the parties in Congo, Benin, São Tomé and Príncipe, Cape Verde, and Guinea-Bissau have not confronted armed internal threats to their regimes from any quarter. Therefore, these bodies have not attached the same importance that the others have to working out alliances on their local scenes.

Not surprisingly, the parties that emerged under military auspices in Ethiopia, Congo, Benin, and Somalia have evinced a desire to extend the span of their organizational umbrellas to a somewhat more eclectic list of domestic forces than have the other parties. These forces have included not only particular social, regional, and ethnic groups but also civilians of a wide range of stripes—especially civilians that would accept continued dominance of the parties by military elements. In Ethiopia, the WPE and its predecessor, COPWE, have paid special attention to Eritreans, Tigreans, Somalis, peasants, and urban dwellers. The PCT in Congo has devoted its energies largely to the Vili and Kongos of the south, trade unions, and students. In Benin, the PRPB has concentrated on the Fon and Yorubas in the south, trade unions, and peasants. Somalia's SRSP has focused primarily on the Isaaq and Majerteen clans, civil servants, nomads, and peasants.

The parties in Angola, Mozambique, Zimbabwe, and Guinea-Bissau have directed their concerns fundamentally to ethnic and regional groups. In Angola, the main objects of attention have been the Bakongo and particularly the Ovimbundu; in Mozambique, the ethnic elements in the state's central and southern sections; in Zimbabwe, the Ndebeles in the south; in Guinea-Bissau, the Fulas and other groups over which the Portuguese had continued to exercise control throughout the anticolonial war.

The parties in Cape Verde and São Tomé and Príncipe have paid heed principally to regional and social groups. In Cape Verde, these have consisted mostly of residents of outlying islands of the country and peasants without land; in São Tomé and Príncipe, of peasants and inhabitants of Príncipe, many of whom have resented the fact that the state's affairs have, by and large, been in the hands of São Toméans.

In seeking to draw specific internal forces into collaboration with them, the parties in Angola, Mozambique, Zimbabwe, Ethiopia, and Somalia have approached the task differently than have the other parties concerned here. These five parties have opted for alliance of a conditional sort. That is, they have refused to engage in wholesale courtship of members of the social, ethnic, or regional groups that they have targeted; instead, they have wooed just those segments of the groups willing to dissociate themselves from the organized opposition forces challenging the governments of the parties. By making this clear-cut distinction, the parties in question have clearly hoped to isolate and render impotent these organized opposition forces. Perhaps because the other five parties have not had to cope with major organized opposition to their rule for a number of years, they have seemed to view alliance in broader, more genuinely co-optive terms than the first five parties. That is, they have tended to treat all members of groups to which they have devoted special attention as inherently worthy of absorption into their ranks.

Ruling status encourages parties to single out as their main external allies entities that they believe can and will help them hold on to power.[110] The parties in this grouping, as already suggested, inevitably assign top priority in their objectives to retaining the reins of authority in their countries, and all of them discern threats of one type or another to the governments that they run. Thus the parties value highly as outside allies those forces that can and will assist them in countering these threats.

Of the ten bodies under review here, all but the SRSP of Somalia and the ZANU-PF of Zimbabwe have designated the U.S.S.R., the Soviet bloc, and Cuba as their chief collaborators abroad ever since the early days of their rule, and the eight parties have even maintained substantial contacts over the years with the ruling communist parties in these states. There are significant differences, however, in the degree to which the governments controlled by the parties actually cooperate with the U.S.S.R., the Soviet bloc, and Cuba. The regimes in Ethiopia and Angola rely heavily on these entities and carry on wide-ranging activities with them. Although the government in Mozambique has reduced its dependence on the U.S.S.R. and the Soviet bloc during the course of the 1980s, it continues to have close links with them and Cuba in many respects—especially in the military realm. The other regimes keep the U.S.S.R., the Soviet bloc, and Cuba at more of a distance while still conducting fairly extensive interaction with them.

The SRSP and the ZANU-PF have each taken an idiosyncratic position with respect to primary collaborators abroad. Until the late 1970s the SRSP deemed that the U.S.S.R., the Soviet bloc, and Cuba qualified for this role, but it then changed its mind and fixed upon the United States instead. The ZANU-PF has appeared to feel that a diverse mix of principal external allies affords it the best guarantee of staying in power. It puts the front-line state of Southern Africa at the head of its list, but in line with its assessment of South Africa as its main enemy and of the United States and the U.S.S.R. as only secondary enemies, it seems to conclude that each of the latter two countries can make meaningful contributions to the defense of the ZANU-PF government. Hence it includes both the United States and the U.S.S.R. on the list as well.

These choices of primary allies, to be sure, do not represent ideal ones from the perspectives of the individual parties. The entities involved have their own interests to further, and these interests do not always coincide with those of the states over which the parties under consideration here preside. In the 1980s, for example, the U.S.S.R. has not furnished enough military aid to the governments of Ethiopia, Mozambique, and Angola to permit them to stamp out the local armed struggles against them, and none of the governments whose parties look to the U.S.S.R. as one of their main allies abroad has received the amounts of Soviet economic assistance that it has desired. By the same token, the United States in the 1980s has not supplied the SRSP regime in Somalia with the type and quantity of military help that this regime would have liked. Nevertheless, these various forces constitute the best candidates for chief external collaborators that the parties see in the international arena.

Like the nonruling parties in sub-Saharan Africa, most ruling parties in the region employ opposition to the white-minority government in South Africa as a major basis for identifying potential foreign allies. In the cases of the eight parties that have selected the U.S.S.R., the Soviet bloc, and Cuba as their primary external collaborators, this consideration has obviously bolstered their choice, for the parties appear to regard these countries together as the most potent force on the global scene pushing for black-majority rule in Southern Africa. Far more important, this factor has served as a key criterion for all of the ruling parties except the SRSP in Somalia in picking out desirable secondary allies abroad. The nine parties and the governments that they run have displayed particular attraction to other radical groups and regimes (including one another) that have adopted a militant stance against the Pretoria government. Indeed, they have cooperated extensively with such groups and regimes in a myriad of frameworks—like the councils of the front-line states in Southern Africa, the Organization of African Unity, the United Nations, and the nonaligned movement.

Yet the precise entities that all ten parties pick as worthwhile external allies of a secondary nature and the way that the parties rank these entities in significance has more to do with the ruling status of the parties than with anything else. If a party has acquired authority in a state, as noted previously, it tends to want to hang on to that authority, and this wish in turn prompts it to evaluate possible foreign collaborators in light of their capabilities and willingness to aid it to do so. Moreover, when a party assumes power, it takes on an obligation to uphold the general interests of its country, as it perceives these interests. This duty renders a foreign entity's capacity and inclination to behave in accordance with such interests of relevance to a party's assessment of that entity's usefulness as an ally. However, the requirements to keep individual parties in power and the interests of specific states differ. As a result, the forces that a party judges of value as secondary external allies and their exact merit in its eyes can vary from context to context. In addition, any particular context can alter over the years, so a party's conclusions on these matters can shift as well.

The selections of secondary collaborators abroad by these parties at issue here have conformed to such a pattern. Since the mid-1970s both Angola and Mozambique have consistently regarded their fellow front-line states in Southern Africa as key collaborators, and in the 1980s they have expanded this classification to include the wider membership of the Southern Africa Development Coordination Conference (SADCC). In the 1980s, too, both have increasingly put emphasis on cooperation with the countries of Western Europe as both have sought to widen their economic ties abroad. Zimbabwe has stressed collaboration with fellow members of SADCC, but its actual relations have been closest with Tanzania and Mozambique. It has also looked to Great Britain and to a lesser degree China as major allies. Both Congo and Benin have long relied heavily on France, especially in the economic realm. For Congo, other Western European states like Italy and Great Britain have been of considerable consequence in the 1980s; Nigeria and to a lesser extent China have done the same for Benin. At the top of São Tomé and Príncipe's list of worthwhile secondary collaborators for a good many years has stood Angola, which maintains a military force of about 1,500 on the islands to ensure their security. Portugal and the Netherlands have always mattered signficantly as well to São Tomé and Príncipe from an economic standpoint, and France has taken on new merit in this respect in the 1980s. For Cape Verde, Portugal has continued to be an important entity with which to cooperate since the islands achieved independence, but other Western European countries have acquired growing value from the Cape Verdean viewpoint during the 1980s. Although Guinea-Bissau constituted perhaps the chief secondary ally for Cape Verde prior to the coup in Bissau in November 1980 that deposed Luiz Cabral, a

Cape Verdean by ancestry, it has ceased to do so since then. Guinea-Bissau has depended a lot on Sweden in an economic sense since the mid-1970s, and it has turned to France for similar succor in the 1980s. For political reasons, Guinea-Bissau has also seemed to value highly cooperation with Senegal and Guinea, its neighbors. Up to the early 1980s, Cape Verde, too, qualified as a major collaborator from Guinea-Bissau's perspective; however, it lost that status after the 1980 coup in Bissau. Ethiopia has assigned great weight to the countries of the European Economic Community since the 1970s because of economic considerations, but its favorites in political terms in the 1980s have been Libya and the People's Democratic Republic of Yemen. Somalia has identified Italy and Saudi Arabia as key allies for many years, and in the 1980s it has tended to place other members of the Gulf Cooperation Council aside from Saudi Arabia in this category.

Prospects

There remains the question of how lasting the coalition strategies and tactics laid out in the preceding pages will be. Clearly, the answer to this question depends largely on circumstances in the countries where the Marxist parties operate. Only rarely does any of the parties display an inflexible commitment to an abstract principle in devising its coalition strategy and tactics. The evident rejection of all domestic alliances by some of the small groups in Egypt constitutes one of the few such instances. Normally the Marxist parties of the continent tailor their coalition strategies and tactics to the precise situations that they face, as they see those situations. It is to the likely circumstances in Africa, then, that one must turn to arrive at judgments about the outlook with respect to the parties' coalition strategies and tactics.

At initial glance, conditions on the continent in the latter part of the 1980s would not seem to hold much promise of continuity in these coalition strategies and tactics for even the near future. Most of Africa—and especially the states in sub-Saharan Africa—has a long record of instability, and the 1980s have witnessed an intensification of this problem throughout the continent. Such considerations point to the probability of changes in circumstances that could spark revisions in the coalition strategies and tactics of local Marxist parties.

On closer examination, however, the prospects appear to be a lot more complex. As suggested in the previous discussion, the coalition strategies and tactics that the parties follow owe much to the legal standing of the parties and to the characteristics and backgrounds of the regions in which they function. Some of these things do promote rapid shifts in coalition strategies and tactics. For example, the experiences of many parties in sub-Saharan Africa with numerous government turnovers in their states over the short periods that they themselves have existed encourage them to alter their coalition strategies and tactics fairly frequently. Yet many of the basic factors shaping coalition strategies and tactics do not undergo change often, and some of them are not subject to modification at all. Switches in the legal status of parties, for instance, occur relatively seldom, while the Arab nature of North Africa qualifies as a permanent given. Thus, there are substantial constraints on the African scene that make for continuity in the coalition strategies and tactics of the Marxist parties. These no doubt explain the high degree of consistency apparent in the past in the coalition strategies and tactics of older groups like the Egyptian and South African Communist parties.

In sum, elements in the coalition strategies and tactics of all or most of the parties dealt with here are bound to change in the years ahead, but not many parties will feel it necessary to revise their coalition strategies and tactics drastically. Perhaps the key signal that such alterations may be in the offing in a particular case will come with a shift in a party's legal standing.

9

The Coalition Strategies and Tactics of the Indonesian Communist Party: A Prelude to Destruction
Frank Cibulka

While examining the coalition strategies and tactics of Asian Marxist parties, one must inevitably turn to the experience of the Indonesian Communist party (Partai Komunis Indonesia or PKI). Once the largest nonruling communist party in the world, and with its claimed three million members second only in size to its Chinese and Soviet counterparts, the PKI represented a mature and highly significant political movement on the international scene. Although the party, with its superb organization and its own brand of Marxist ideology, never rose from the ashes following its brutal destruction in 1965, its experience remains highly relevant. The significance is due not only to the impact that the PKI once exerted upon the world communist movement but also to the fact that, twenty years after the establishment of the "New Order," General Suharto's military regime has not yet completed the task of national integration and has been unable to provide an effective alternative to the communist vision of a solution to Indonesia's tremendous social and economic problems.

The Indonesian Communist party's chosen "road to power" after 1951 was centered in a highly complex and flexible coalition strategy which came to be known as the national united front. This largely peaceful political strategy was formulated after the assertion of power by a party faction under the leadership of D. N. Aidit, and it helped the PKI steer through the rough political waters of Sukarno's postindependence Indonesia with its heavy accent upon fervent and militant nationalism, with its political polarization and communal tensions, and with its weak and unstable parliamentary democracy and subsequent form of authoritarianism. The coalition strategy of the PKI during the years 1951 to 1965 helped to bring the Indonesian communists to the threshold of power, while a fatal deviation from it set the party up for its destruction at the hands of the military.

It is the purpose of this chapter to examine the coalition strategy and tactics of the Indonesian Communist party during the fourteen years of Aidit's leadership, which also effectively corresponded with the national united front period. Whereas the party's history prior to 1951 reveals quickly changing fortunes and unstable leadership and strategy, the Aidit period of 1951 to 1965 can be characterized as one of highly cohesive leadership and of a consistent and purposeful political strategy based on the Indonesianization of Marxist-Leninist doctrine.

The Origins of the PKI

The Communist party of Indonesia, which has the distinction of being the oldest communist party in Asia, was founded in May 1920, when the Indonesian Social-Democratic Association under the leadership of Dutch radicals and Islamic nationalists, meeting at Semarang in Java, converted their organization into the Communist Party of the Indies (Perserikaten Kommunist di India) and soon thereafter joined the Third International.[1] The structural base for the pioneering communist organization in the region was the Sarekat Islam (Islamic Association or SI), which was founded in 1912 as the first nationalist mass organization in Indonesian history. The constituent branches of Sarekat Islam were gradually infiltrated by more radical political elements, and in 1914 a Dutch communist, H. J. Sneevliet, who later served as a Comintern agent in the Far East under the pseudonym "Maring," created the "Indian Social Democratic Association," which was then converted into a communist cell.[2] The next thirty years in the history of the PKI were a curious mix of factionalism, frequent leadership and strategy changes, radical phases alternating with relatively peaceful and cooperative "united front" periods, and abortive uprisings followed by severe repression and long periods of party inactivity.

During the 1920s the party gradually came under the control of more militant elements advocating an immediate revolution. It also defied a Comintern directive to form a united anti-imperialist front with noncommunist Indonesian nationalistic organizations and to strengthen its support among the masses through the channel of communist-controlled People's Associations (Sarekat Rakjat).[3] An abortive communist revolt in Java and West Sumatra during 1926–1927 was crushed by the Dutch colonial administration. Although the PKI had only about three thousand members at the time of the uprising, thirteen thousand suspects were arrested and approximately half were either imprisoned or interned in a concentration camp in West Irian. The PKI was declared illegal and entered a long period of underground existence and relative inactivity.[4]

The PKI was reestablished only in October 1945 in the aftermath of the outbreak of the nationalistic August Revolution, although party officials later claimed that an "illegal PKI" was maintained from the end of the rebellion in 1927 until the return of the veteran communist leader Musso in 1948. Musso carried out scattered guerrilla operations and later coordinated the activities of the new legal PKI and the closely allied crypto-communist Indonesian Labor party and Socialist party.[5] During its brief resurgence of 1945–1948 the PKI was plagued by factionalism and leadership instability, but largely pursued a moderate line of collaboration with the nationalist forces. Under the leadership of the returned party veterans of the 1920s—Alimin Prawirodirdjo and Sardjono—and rejecting the militant tendencies of the Trotskyist Tan Malaka faction, the Indonesian communists backed the revolutionary nationalistic Sukarno-Sjahrir regime. The PKI was encouraged and heavily relied upon by President Sukarno when it supported the republican cabinet headed by the moderate socialist prime minister, Sutan Sjahrir, in defense of the Linggadjati Agreement between the Dutch and Indonesian governments for the establishment of the independent federal Indonesian republic.[6] The party then established a vaguely defined but politically effective united front from above called the Sajap Kiri (Left Wing), consisting of the PKI, the Socialist and Labor parties, and other organizations.[7]

The third Sjahrir cabinet was succeeded by one headed by Amir Sjarifuddin, a left-wing socialist leader and, according to his later admission, a secret PKI member. The cabinet, which remained in office from July 1947 to January 1948, also included two regular communists as ministers of state and in its brief tenure helped to increase the PKI's penetration into the political system and the military.[8] The leftist cabinet was replaced by one headed by Vice-President Mohammed Hatta, in which Sajap Kiri declined representation as junior allies.

In August 1948 the party leadership and strategy were once again altered with the return from the Soviet Union of Musso, another communist veteran associated with the militancy of the 1920s. Musso returned with instructions from Moscow and quickly assumed control over the PKI. Musso, seeking to introduce the new Zhdanov line on the international situation into the the party platform, expressed his tactics in the so-called "New Road" resolution, which represented a new, more aggressive formulation of the united front policy in accordance with Soviet wishes.

The essence of this resolution was aptly characterized by Justus Van Der Kroef:

> This outlined the Leninist principle of the multi-stage (or two-stage) revolution, stressed the Zhdanov two-camp doctrine of total confrontation of the "imperialists", described the Leninist class dynamics of the "bourgeois democratic" phase of the Indonesian struggle in terms of the appeal which had to be made to various groups of the peasantry and the middle class, and reoriented the organizational role of the party. Tactically, acceptance of the resolution meant an uncompromising fight against the Dutch and against those Indonesian politicians who might be seeking any kind of diplomatic rapprochement with them.[9]

An organizational overhaul of the party included the election of a new Politburo and the merging of the Socialist and Labor parties with the PKI, with incorporation of a large part of their membership into the communist ranks. Musso envisioned a national united front policy in which, unlike during the 1945–1948 period of Sajap Kiri, the communists would play a dominant role in order to position themselves for the subsequent seizure of power. Musso's scheme came to be known as the "Gottwald Plan" in recognition of his desire to emulate the communist coup which had just taken place in Czechoslovakia in February 1948. Musso's strategy, however, proved to be unworkable since the main political parties, namely the Masjumi (Muslim Federation) and the Indonesian Nationalist party (PNI) were unwilling to cooperate within such an arrangement. The increasing tension in the country climaxed in September 1948 in a rebellion by communist and procommunist civilians and army officers in the city of Madiun in Java. The rebellion was a premature and ill-prepared attempt to spark a communist revolution, but the PKI's top echelons, headed by Musso, though unprepared for it, felt compelled by the events to support the rebellion and proclaimed a "national front government" with Musso as its leader. The revolt was quickly put down by the Indonesian army units loyal to the Sukarno-Hatta regime. Significantly, the event resulted in the deaths of a number of top PKI Politburo members, including Musso and Sjarifuddin, and imprisonment of some thirty-six thousand PKI members and sympathizers. Only an impending attack upon the young republic by the Dutch prevented further coercive measures against the communists.[10]

The Aidit Leadership and the Concept of
the National United Front

In January 1951 the leadership of the PKI was assumed by the so-called Leninist wing (Sajap Leninis), a faction of young party officials headed by D. N. Aidit, M. H. Lukman, Njoto, and Sudisman. Aidit, who at the age of only twenty-seven years became the principal party leader, was elected to the post of first secretary.[11] A new five-man Politburo was elected, consisting of Aidit, Lukman, Njoto, Sudisman, and the aging veteran revolutionary Alimin. Aidit fairly rapidly consolidated the dominance of the Leninist wing over the party by removing the older leaders associated with the policies of Tan Ling Djie, Alimin, and Ngadiman Hardjosubroto. This group formulated the organizational strategy which came to guide the party's actions almost until its destruction in 1965–1966. This line was established at the March 1954 fifth national congress of the PKI.

Aidit had attempted to formulate the communist strategy in such a way that the application of orthodox doctrines of Marxism-Leninism would not be insensitive to the existing realities of Indonesia's social and economic situation. He found that the strategy of the national united front met this requirement. When Aidit spoke of "Indonesianizing Marxism-Leninism" in 1961, he defined it in terms of holding "fast to the principles of Marxism-Leninism and creatively determining the policy, tactics, form of struggle and form of organization of our Party on the basis of the concrete situation in our country."[12] Indeed, the form that the national united front assumed under Aidit's guidance was solidly rooted in the doctrines of Lenin and Stalin, affected by the ideological pronouncements of Mao Zedong, and yet drawing heavily from Musso's "New Road" resolution and reflecting the historical experience and the political and social environment of the PKI.

Lenin, turning his attention to national and colonial questions, emphasized that the revolution in the underdeveloped countries would have to have a bourgeois-democratic basis due to the precapitalist character of such societies.[13] Since feudalism and imperialism blocked the natural dialectical path of capitalist development, the bourgeoisie in the countries of Asia, Africa, and Latin America was obliged to wage a struggle against them as a matter of self-interest. Because the bourgeoisie as a class was too weak to alone carry out an antifeudal and anti-imperialist revolution, it needed the cooperation of the workers and peasants allied in a united front in order to complete the task. Lenin believe that, once the vanguard of the proletariat assumed the control of such movements, it could, with help from other socialist countries, pursue the socialist revolution without allowing the national bourgeoisie to establish a fully developed capitalist society first.[14] These ideas were presented in 1920 at the second congress of the Comintern, where Lenin advocated an establishment of temporary united fronts between communists and bourgeois independence movements.[15]

While Stalin also believed in the necessity of cooperation in a united front between communists and the national bourgeoisie, he adhered to the concept of a "two-stage revolution," where the socialist revolution could only come after the bourgeois-national revolution completed the break with feudalism and imperialism through a full development of capitalist society.[16]

Aidit's revolutionary theory was based on the assumption that Indonesia is still a semicolonial and semifeudal country. The definition of the semicolonial position was based upon the political realities of the unfavorable terms of the Round Table Conference agreement which ended the war with the Netherlands in 1949, and on the amount of control that foreign countries exerted over the Indonesian economy.[17] Among the main targets of the PKI revolutionary struggle were imperialism, its Indonesian compradore agents among the bourgeoisie, and feudalism.[18] Aidit, however, realized that the tactics of armed struggle could not be successfully utilized in Indonesian conditions. The two elements which favored the Chinese communists—vast hinterland and sanctuary areas capable of sustaining guerrilla warfare and the presence of a powerful adjacent ally—were lacking in Indonesia.[19] Instead, the party was forced to combine with the national bourgeoisie and other noncommunist social groups in a united front for the purpose of completing the revolutionary struggle against colonialism and feudalism. The August 1945 nationalistic revolution under the leadership of Sukarno was therefore ideologically equated with the stage of bourgeois-democratic revolution. This revolution remained unfinished and communist support was needed to complete the task. D. N. Aidit wrote after the seventh national congress of the PKI held in April, 1961:

> The democratic revolution which began in August 1945 has not been completed as yet. The following democratic sections of society are interested in carrying the revolution forward: the workers, peasants, urban petty bourgeoisie, intellectuals and the national bourgeoisie which have joined forces to form a National Front. Their interests are represented by the three political forces: the Nationalists, the religious groups and the Communists. The cooperation of these democratic parties, which we call in our country NASAKOM (NAS—Nationalists; A—religious groups; KOM

—Communists), is of paramount importance for the development of the revolution.

The reactionary forces in Indonesia are the imperialists who still preserve considerable footholds in the country, the landlords, the compradores and the bureaucratic capitalists who have strengthened their position in recent years.

The struggle between the supporters and enemies of the revolution is being waged in the economic, political, military and cultural fields. The reactionaries, who have suffered a number of setbacks, still represent a grave danger to the revolutionary gains.[20]

At the end of the first stage of the revolution would be a formation of a people's democracy "formed on the basis of the alliance of workers and peasants under the leadership of the working class." Such a government would be concerned with "not socialist but democratic reform," bringing about land reform, eliminating foreign control of the economy, guaranteeing democratic rights, and improving the living standard of the population.[21] Peaceful construction of socialism would presumably follow at a later date.

The PKI under Aidit's leadership launched its quest for power through a program which included three basic points:

1.   Creation of a "broad, mass party" with a strong organization and mixing a hierarchical democratic centralist structure with broad appeal and widespread recruitment.
2.   Pursuing a peaceful path to power through participation in the parliamentary democracy and cooperation with President Sukarno and political parties not perceived hostile to the communists.
3.   Building of a mass base through mobilization of the proletariat, seeking support among the peasantry and among sections of the bourgeoisie.

The party's commitment to the peaceful road to power was based on the Aidit leadership's conviction that armed struggle was not necessary at that point and could result in the destruction of the PKI. The party left no doubt, however, about its resolve to resort to more revolutionary tactics, should they become indispensable.

A 1958 editorial entitled "Guarding against Ideological Timidity" appeared in the party journal *Kehidupan Partai* (Party Life) and stated:

The third factor is the observation on the basis of the present balance of power in the world indicating that it is possible for certain countries to travel along the road toward Socialism gradually and in a peaceful manner. . . . Now certainly for us in

Indonesia it has been a problem of how to bring about just the right conditions that would make such a peaceful road to Socialism possible. While this allegation is very important and extremely appropriate, it can under certain specified conditions produce a disconcerting effect on certain cadres. . . . Some of our cadres are evidently forgetting that no matter how peacefully one's progress along the road toward Socialism may appear to be, the actual fact of the matter is that the road is the road of revolution and it must be conceived in terms of the principles underlying class struggle. And to this end, we must train, instruct, organize and mobilize the masses effectively and extensively into revolutionary forces.[22]

The party's policy of combining the united front strategy from above (parliamentary cooperation with noncommunist parties) with the strategy of the united front from below (building mass support among various social groups within the country) assured that it could still remain poised for militant activity by mobilizing a revolutionary base prepared through the activities of the united front from below.

One of the most prominent observers of Indonesian affairs, Justus Van Der Kroef, analyzed Aidit's strategy:

For Aidit's technique (like Mao's) within the context of the multi-stage revolutionary concept, has been essentially to employ both approaches at the same time, to seek active collaboration also in parliament and other organs of government with other "patriotic," "anti-imperialist" or "anti-feudal" organizations for the purposes of developing and completing "the national democratic" (not the Socialist) revolution—this being in effect the approach "from above"—and at the same time to build up the Communist party as such along with its front groups, aggressively insisting on "democratic liberties" which will allow the party to expand, staging campaigns to win popular support—all characteristic of the approach "from below."[23]

The skillful use of the dual strategy had, by the 1960s, brought the PKI to the threshold of power in Indonesia, yet ironically, when the deviation from the united front strategy placed the party in mortal danger in 1965, the Aidit leadership was either unwilling or unable to mobilize the highly developed network of the united front from below to its defense.

The United Front from Below

The PKI pursued the building up of its mass base first through a vast recruitment and educational campaign designed to create a large yet well-disciplined and educated revolutionary party membership. Secondly, it sought to broaden its societal support through the institution of a widely based national united front designed to draw in the country's peasantry and elements of the bourgeoisie, along with mobilizing a variety of other social groups, for example women and the youth. The PKI achieved this goal admirably through its control of a vast array of powerful front organizations.

The most immediate task facing the Aidit leadership was the expansion and invigoration of the party membership. The PKI over which Aidit assumed control in January 1951 was small, poorly organized, and severely deficient in the quality of ideological education. Aidit responded with a vigorous membership drive and began the ideological education of cadres and members. While in early 1952 the PKI only had 7,910 members and candidate members, by the end of the year its membership was up to 126,671. In March, at the time of the fifth national party congress, its membership was 165,206, and by the beginning of 1959 had increased to 1.5 million.[24] By September 1965 the PKI claimed a membership of 3 million.[25] D. N. Aidit explained in 1959:

> This led the Party to the conclusion that the recruitment of new members was necessary to enable it to carry out its tasks and win victory for the people. While participating in the Parliamentary elections, the Constituent Assembly, provincial and regional legislative bodies, the Indonesian Communists realized that a Party with a big membership would be a decisive actor in achieving victory.[26]

The party also established an Island Committee for Outer Areas in the late 1950s to facilitate the party's penetration outside of its traditional areas of influence in Java.[27]

Outside the party itself, the key source of support for the PKI was the Indonesian proletariat, which Aidit in the early 1950s estimated to count about 6 million, with only 500,000 members employed in modern industry.[28] The conditions of the Indonesian proletariat presented fertile ground for communist agitation due to the severe exploitation and poor living conditions prevalent among the country's workers. By the early 1950s the PKI gained effective control of the country's umbrella trade union federation, the Central Labor Organization of Indonesia (SOBSI), which in 1965 claimed some 3.3 million members.

The next key social group to be included in the united front strategy was the peasantry, which comprised 70 percent of Indonesia's population. In spite of the limited appeal that the PKI exerted in the Javanese countryside, Aidit declared that the agrarian revolution was essential to the completion of the people's democratic revolution in Indonesia and preached the desirability of the worker-peasant alliance. While Aidit divided the peasantry into three subclasses: rich, middle, and poor, he tried to draw the entire agrarian segment of Indonesian society into his coalition. The party gained control over the Indonesian Farmers' Front (Barisan Tani Indonesia or BTI) with its 8.5 million members and by the 1960s scored spectacular successes in its penetration into the rural areas of Java.

The third crucial component of the PKI's united front policy was the country's bourgeoisie, which Aidit, somewhat reluctantly, sought to enlist in his struggle against what he perceived as feudalism and imperialism. Aidit's analysis divided the Indonesian bourgeoisie into two groups: the comprador bourgeoisie and the national bourgeoisie. The national bourgeoisie is a petty mercantile and professional class with ambivalent political outlook, and could be drawn into cooperation with the progressive forces. The comprador bourgeoisie, on the other hand, are those sections of the bourgeois class which have an economic relationship with foreign capitalists and tend to be anticommunist in their outlook. While the comprador bourgeoisie in certain rare circumstances could become a part of the anti-imperialist struggle, its outlook was considered to be largely reactionary, and it was identified among the principal targets of the revolution.[29]

The ambivalent position of the PKI leadership toward the national bourgeoisie can be seen from an analysis by the deputy general secretary, M. Lukman:

> The wavering and double-pronged character of the national bourgeoisie is, in our opinion, explained by the fact, that on the one hand, they are oppressed by the imperialists, and on the other, they themselves exploit the working people. Their weak economic position, which naturally results in their weak political position, adds still more to their wavering attitude. Still, we are of the opinion that the vacillation inherent in the national bourgeoisie is not fatal. Provided there are strong progressive forces, plus a Party program which takes into account the interests of the national bourgeoisie, a correct style of work, and the possibility

of directing a well-aimed blow at the imperialists and their stooges at home, the national bourgeoisie can remain, or at least can be forced to remain for a long period, in the united front anti-imperialist and anti-feudal struggle.[30]

Turning to other social groups, the PKI directed a number of other front organizations, most notably the People's Youth (Pemuda Rakjat) with 2 million members and the Women's Movement (Gerwani), which claimed 1,750,000 members by 1965.[31] The party also founded and operated a number of educational and indoctrinational institutions, such as the People's University (Universitas Rakjat or UNRA) and the Institute of People's Culture (LEKRA), a nationwide mass organization of cultural workers, along with several major periodicals. It was estimated in 1965 that about a quarter of the total Indonesian population of 105 million was directly or indirectly affiliated with the PKI.[32]

In spite of the highly impressive mobilization of the population through the strategy of the united front from below, the PKI never actually fully used this resource in an all-out confrontation with its political enemies. The strength of the front organizations, no doubt, contributed to the increasingly prominent position of the Indonesian communists on the political scene during the 1960s. It may have served to temporarily restrain the hand of its enemies, especially in the military establishment, while expanding in part the closeness of the alliance between the PKI and President Sukarno.

The only case in which the PKI used its mass support and front organizations in a militant action outside of the confines of the cooperation established by the united front strategy from above was its agrarian offensive of 1963–1965. After many years of patiently building support among the peasantry, with which the party initially enjoyed only a weak line, Aidit launched what essentially amounted to a class struggle in the countryside when he authorized the PKI to lead the peasants in a campaign of unilateral actions (aksi sepihak) to enforce the land reform laws legislated by the government in 1960.[33] The campaign was initiated in late 1963 and during the next two years resulted in an increasingly polarized situation in the countryside, with violent clashes taking place, especially in east Java between the Farmers' Front supporters and the Moslem forces, which were often backed by local authorities. While the campaign did not fully achieve its goals and was scaled down by the party in 1965, it helped to coalesce political opposition at the national level against the newly militant PKI.

The United Front from Above

The Aidit leadership clearly realized that it needed to display a strong commitment to peaceful parliamentary struggle in order to minimize opposition to its campaign for mobilization of mass support. The PKI's participation in a united front cooperation from above can roughly be divided into two periods: the parliamentary alliance with the Indonesian Nationalist party (PNI) lasting from 1951 to 1959, and the special relationship with President Sukarno during the period of "Guided Democracy," 1959–1965.

The PKI's natural ally proved to be the PNI, the only major secular nationalist party in the country. The PNI was not anticommunist; it was strongly nationalistic and anti-Western, and above all, willing to cooperate with the communists in order to ensure control of the government. For the PKI such cooperation brought about respectability and freedom from repression and helped to keep out of power the parties considered to be reactionary, namely the Islamic-based Masjumi and its ally, the Indonesian Socialist party (PSI).[34] The PKI was thus able to support every Indonesian cabinet after 1951, with the sole exception of the Masjumi-led Harapah cabinet of 1955–1956.

The Indonesian communists scored the most impressive gains in the elections of 1955 and 1957. In the September 1955 parliamentary elections the PKI won fourth place, receiving 16.4 percent (or over 6 million) of the total vote. Slightly ahead of the communists were the PNI and the Moslem Masjumi and Nahdatul Ulama parties. The PKI further improved its electoral showing during the local elections in Java in 1957, when it received a 37 percent increase in its vote and eclipsed the PNI as the strongest party in Java. For all its obvious electoral strength, however, the party retained basic weaknesses in its electoral appeal due to its restricted base of support. The PKI still remained a primarily Javanese party (from where it drew 88.7 percent of its electoral support in 1955) with a secondary weaker area of influence in North and South Sumatra. The Outer Islands remained largely under the control of the Moslem-based Masjumi. The communists were much stronger in urban areas than in the countryside and had to rely primarily upon the *abangan* vote, while the more orthodox Moslem *santri* electorate presented a resistant block to communist penetration.[35] The point has been aptly made that even if the communists could have utilized the political instability of the 1956–1958 period and taken control of Java, they would have been faced with the secession of the Outer Islands.[36]

After 1955 the PKI began to draw more closely to President Sukarno, and this trend eventually resulted in the very close partnership of the 1960s. There were a number of reasons for this development. First, the communists were well aware of the crisis and the decline in importance of the parliamentary system. Secondly, Sukarno after 1955 cooled off his close association with the PNI and subsequently made a political break with his vice-president Hatta and the Masjumi party. Sukarno himself sought the PKI's support to aid him in the task of the completion of the August 1945 revolution and also to counterbalance the increasing strength of the Indonesian military. The communist party, in turn, shared Sukarno's militant nationalistic and anti-imperialist fervor and provided strong support for his adventurist foreign policy in backing his campaign for the liberation of West Irian and the confrontation with Malaysia, as well as his increasingly anti-Western position.

In July 1959, the 1945 constitution was restored with its presidential system of rule, and parliamentary democracy was extinguished in Indonesia. President Sukarno introduced his increasingly authoritarian system of "Guided Democracy," and the Aidit leadership was forced to adjust to a radically different political environment. The parliamentary road to power was firmly blocked for the PKI and the party completely shifted its united front strategy from a parliamentary alliance to an increasingly intense political marriage of convenience with the nationalistic president. It is the supreme irony that the PKI collaborated with Sukarno in dismantling a democratic parliamentary system which would, in all likelihood, have brought about a communist electoral victory and a communist-dominated government in just a few short years. An Indonesian specialist, Guy Parker, during his visit to Djakarta in late 1963 received estimates indicating that the PKI was set to win about 30 percent of the total vote, if elections were held.[37]

The parliamentary system, of course, was never effectively revived in Indonesia and the Indonesian Communist party never received its electoral opportunity. Instead, it temporarily benefited from the destruction of the party system under "Guided Democracy" since it was still allowed to operate legally on the political scene, while most other parties, including the Masjumi, were banned by Sukarno. The greatest threat to the party came in the form of increasing power of the Indonesian military, due to the escalating tension between the generals and the PKI during the 1960s. The party found itself caught in an inescapable symbiotic relationship with the president, increasingly depending upon his protection from oppression by the military while at the same time boosting his political strength and steering him into a radical foreign policy course and close ties with Beijing.

The PKI appeared to be patiently poised to claim the mantle of the leadership of the Indonesian revolution from Sukarno after his death, in part on the basis of its own increased political legitimacy within the country but, if necessary, with the aid of the revolutionary mass base created through the united front from below strategy. In spite of the restrictions imposed upon it under the "Guided Democracy," its progress on the path to power appeared to be irreversible. Yet, within a few short months during 1965–1966, the PKI, the strongest nonruling communist party in the world, essentially ceased to exist.

The Destruction of the PKI:
Aidit's Strategy Repudiated

During the final year of its existence the Indonesian Communist party aggressively pursued its quest for power. The militant posture assumed by the PKI in the course of 1965 seriously undermined its united front strategy, while its ever increasing closeness to President Sukarno appeared to have been achieved in some measure by gradual alienation from Leninist orthodoxy. The party found itself comfortable with the radical nationalism embraced by Sukarno during his final years of power and was unable to further steer his policies toward the left, both in the domestic and foreign arena. Most significantly, the party was instrumental in Sukarno's move toward a special relationship with the People's Republic of China. Sukarno's militant anti-Western policy had resulted in the country's increasing international isolation and economic weakness, while an alliance between Beijing and Jakarta appeared to be looming on the horizon. The PKI itself, while never giving up its independence within the world communist movement, after 1962 gradually abandoned its intermediate position between the Soviet and Chinese communist parties, and during the last year prior to its destruction the Aidit leadership became involved in bitter polemics with Moscow and came to embrace most of the ideological tenets of the Chinese communists.

At the same time the Aidit leadership appeared to be willing to do almost anything to retain the favor of President Sukarno and to solidify the PKI's position as his rightful heir in the leadership of the August Revolution. The party had accommodated its united front strategy to fit the context of President Sukarno's National Front, inaugurated in 1960 to serve as the main instrument for mass mobilization, superseding the military-sponsored National Front for the Liberation of West Irian.[38] The party furthermore held on steadily to the Nasakom principle (political unity of the nationalists, religious forces, and the communists) and accepted within its own platform President Sukarno's views articulated in his Political Manifesto or *Manipol* (based on Sukarno's Independence Day speech of

August 17, 1959).[39] In this speech the president set out his strategy for the completion of the Indonesian Revolution, and the PKI appeared to adapt its policies to be consistent with his guidance. Aidit's ideological flexibility and remarkable willingness to deviate from orthodox Marxist-Leninist theory in order to accommodate practical political needs can best be seen from his novel theory of a "state with two aspects," which he articulated in 1963:

> From the point of view of contradiction, the state power of the Republic of Indonesia is a contradiction between two opposing aspects: The first aspect is that which represents the interests of the people. The second aspect is that which represents the interests of the people's enemies. The first aspect is embodied in the progressive attitude and policy of President Sukarno which enjoys the support of the CPI and other sections of the people. The second aspect is embodied in the attitude and policy of the rightists and diehards; they are the old and established forces.
>
> Today the popular aspect has become the main aspect and plays a leading role in the state power of the Republic of Indonesia, meaning that it guides the course of the political development in the state power of the Republic of Indonesia.[40]

Aidit's analysis, which was remarkable in that it avoided terms of class struggle, implied that revolutionary transformation could take place in a peaceful manner in Indonesia. The dual nature of state power meant that it would not be necessary to destroy the machinery of the state, but rather it could be sufficient to strengthen its pro-people aspect and to weaken and eventually eliminate the anti-people aspect of state power.[41]

The party's post-1963 militancy in the countryside and its aggressive policy during 1965 helped to coalesce an anticommunist coalition within the country. Above all, the political aims of the PKI came to be viewed with suspicion and vehemently opposed by the military establishment, with the Murba party and Islamic forces in the rural areas actively aiding the military policies. The PKI itself, while adhering to its claims that it pursued a peaceful road to power, continued vigorous efforts to infiltrate and neutralize the powerful military institutions. The tensions between the two groups reached a climax in 1965 when the communists secured President Sukarno's approval for their proposal to arm workers and peasants through the creation of a people's militia. This new "fifth force" was ostensibly advocated for the purpose of augmenting the armed forces and police in defense against a presumed imperialistic threat associated with the campaign of confrontation with Malaysia. The PKI also seemed likely to push through the demands for "Nasakomization" of the armed forces by placing representatives of the nationalists, Muslims, and communists as political officers within the military. By mid-1965 rumors of an impending military coup, along with reports of President Sukarno's failing health, created a highly charged political atmosphere in the country.

In the early hours of October 1, 1965, six of the senior generals in the Indonesian army, including its commander General Ahamd Jani, were abducted and murdered in an attempted coup mounted by a group of air force and army personnel and led by Lieutenant Colonel Untung. The conspirators, calling themselves the September 30 Movement, claimed to have acted in order to forestall a coup d'état by the Council of Generals, and announced the formation of a Revolutionary Council to support President Sukarno's policies. Having failed to generate mass support throughout the country, the insurgency was speedily crushed by Major General Suharto, the commander of the Strategic Reserves, acting with support from the defense minister, General A. H. Nasution, who managed to escape the conspirators. The abortive coup was followed by mass arrests and execution of communists and their suspected sympathizers, with extremist Muslims aiding the army in its genocidal campaign. Estimates of the number of people killed ranged from 100,000 to 500,000.[42] The leadership of the PKI was physically liquidated, with Aidit himself arrested and summarily executed by the army in central Java on November 22. The PKI and all its affiliates were banned in March 1966, and the studying and teaching of Marxism-Leninism was formally outlawed by the Indonesian Parliament just a few months later.[43]

The extent of the PKI planning and participation in the coup attempt has remained a subject of controversy. Although the PKI officially claimed that the coup was an internal army matter, it is known that members of the party and of its front organizations participated in the coup activities as volunteers. Furthermore, an editorial in the PKI daily, *Harian Rakjat*, on October 2 expressed support for the September 30 Movement by calling it "a patriotic and revolutionary action" and appealing to the "entire people to heighten their vigilance and be ready to face all eventualities."[44] While the complete lack of preparedness of the PKI leadership and its revolutionary mass base for the consequences of the failed coup have rendered unconvincing the official army version which claims the PKI masterminded the September 30 Movement, it appears likely that Aidit and his Politburo colleagues were aware of the impending coup attempt and played at least a peripheral part in it.

The destruction of the PKI leadership was rapid. Aidit's deputies, Lukman and Njoto, were executed within a few months of his death, and by the end of 1968 only one out of the seven full members of the PKI Politburo remained alive. This was propaganda chief Jusuf Adjitorop, who has resided in Beijing since 1964. The party managed to reorganize itself temporarily in Central Java as an underground organization with Sudisman, a ranking Politburo member and a former secretary-general, serving as the chairman of the Politburo of the PKI Central Committee until his arrest in December 1966.[45] Afterwards, the new leaders of the PKI underground, including Rewang, Tjugito, and Hutabea, established a major revolutionary base in East Java near the town of Blitar. The PKI's guerrilla campaign in the area was abruptly ended in June–July 1968 with an army security operation which resulted in the capture and destruction of the South Blitar base and in the killing or capture of its principal leaders.[46] By the end of the decade, effective PKI guerrilla operations were eliminated in Java and became limited to the Outer Islands.

During 1966 and 1967 two ideological currents emerged among the remnants of the Indonesian communist movement. The underground party organization, created in Central Java under the leadership of Sudisman and calling itself the Politburo of the PKI Central Committee, was linked to a group of expatriate Indonesian communists in Beijing, who, under the leadership of Jusuf Adjitorop, constituted the Delegation of the PKI Central Committee. In addition to this pro-Chinese wing of the shattered party, another group, calling itself the Marxist-Leninist Group of the Communist Party of Indonesia, appeared in Moscow.[47] All three groups issued appraisals of the factors responsible for the party's destruction, and their criticism of the Aidit leadership amounted to repudiation of his strategy on the grounds that he adopted a revisionist approach to the quest for power. The pro-Soviet faction condemned the adventurism of the Aidit leadership in becoming involved in the September 30 Movement at the time when "there was no revolutionary situation in evidence" and "the broad masses were not prepared for armed action."[48] The Aidit leadership was condemned for deviating from the program adopted at the 1954 fifth PKI congress. Among the errors listed were an excessive reliance upon the alliance with President Sukarno, replacing class interest with policies based on nationalistic values, excessive emphasis upon the peasantry as a revolutionary class, allowing the party to be infiltrated by petty bourgeois elements and values and deviating from the Leninist party model, and overall ideological decline. The Moscow group suggested that the party should "return to the correct way of creating a national front" by above all "strengthening of the union between workers and peasants as the basic foundation of the united national front."[49]

The statements by the Sudisman guerrilla group and by Adjitorop's exile Delegation of the PKI Central Committee to a great extent reflected the sentiments contained in the criticism originating from Moscow. They repudiated Aidit's theory of "a state with two aspects" and noted the PKI's mistake in having become "bogged down in parliamentary and other forms of legal struggle" and of having "considered this to be the main form of struggle to achieve the strategic aim of the Indonesian revolution."[50] By September 1966 both of the pro-Beijing groups adopted a distinctly Maoist ideology based on the need for waging an armed agrarian revolution, thus completely breaking away from the legacy of Aidit's leadership strategy. The self-criticism adopted in January 1966 by Sudisman's pro-Chinese Politburo of the PKI Central Committee argued that "to achieve its complete victory . . . the Indonesian revolution must also follow the road of the Chinese revolution. This means that the Indonesian revolution must inevitably adopt this main form of struggle, namely the people's armed struggle against the armed counter-revolution, which, in essence, is the armed agrarian revolution of the peasants under the leadership of the proletariat."[51]

The Indonesian Communist party, which was once the largest communist party outside the U.S.S.R. and the P.R.C., has since been reduced to a few hundred members living in exile and split between pro-Moscow and pro-Beijing factions. The pro-Chinese faction counts about two hundred members and is still quietly led by Adjitorop, while the more active Moscow group is limited to roughly fifty members.[52] There were no signs of organized PKI activity in Indonesia during the 1980s, although Indonesian authorities remain on the alert for potential resurgence of the party.[53] After a lapse of more than fifteen years, former communist leaders implicated in the 1965 coup attempt were executed in the course of 1985 and 1986. Among the thirteen executed communist prisoners were Kamaruzaman, former head of the PKI secret Special Bureau, and the former leader of Indonesia's communist trade union movement, Mohammed Munir.[54] Fifteen or twenty communist activists remain under sentence of death in prison.[55]

In 1986 the military commander of Central Java disclosed the arrest there of four Indonesian communists, three of whom received military training abroad before infiltrating back into the country. In April of the same year, during a visit to West Kalimantan, the armed forces commander General Benny Murdani disclosed that communist rebels still operated in remote jungle areas along the Sabah border and that army operations in the area resulted in the arrest of several terrorists and the seizure of hundreds of guns and other arms.[56] In November 1986 General Murdani expressed the view that the main constant threat to Indonesia was communism through the remnants of the September 30 Movement of the PKI and "its latent force."[57] Currently, however, no significant communist organization is known to be existing within Indonesia, and the Suharto regime appears to be far more concerned over a national security threat originating from Islamic political violence and from an armed separatist movement in Irian Jaya.

Conclusion

The experience of the Indonesian communists typifies the difficult conditions under which Marxist parties frequently operate in the Third World. They are saddled with marketing an ideology which, within the confines of the traditional society with its complex array of religious, ethnic, tribal, and cultural values, often tends to be alien and unappealing. They operate within immature political systems which, in their instability, tend to offer both an opportunity and a mortal danger for reformist or revolutionary forces. Marxist parties in the Third World frequently find the parliamentary road to power barred by various forms of homegrown authoritarianism, while they are harassed by the formal institutions possessing a monopoly of coercive power, namely the military establishment and the police. They seek support in societies where the masses, burdened by poverty and educational deficiency and affected by the lack of means of communication, cannot easily be mobilized.

The PKI, during the nearly fifteen years of Aidit's leadership, adhered to a flexible coalition strategy in its quest for power under the difficult political conditions prevailing in Sukarno's Indonesian Republic. The party's united front strategy brought about highly contradictory results. Through its united front from above strategy the PKI obtained cooperation with the PNI, an impressive electoral showing and subsequent parliamentary representation, respectability, and ultimately a close alliance with President Sukarno. But under the Guided Democracy the communists, who championed democracy and parliamentary government, helped the president and the military to cripple other political parties and then benefited from the demise of their rivals. It was their acquiescence to Sukarno's authoritarianism that several years later made the communists vulnerable to destruction at the hands of the military. The party was able to heavily influence the domestic and foreign policies of the president, yet was unable to secure meaningful representation in the cabinet. The PKI managed to gain mass support by building up its membership to exceed three million people and by controlling many key front organizations. Yet this mass support proved to be too shallow. Furthermore, militant tendencies resulted in dangerous policies. In the end, the party was unable to defend itself in the aftermath of the failed coup. The party's impressive electoral performance during the 1950s cannot conceal the fact that the PKI remained a largely Javanese-based political force with little support in the Outer Islands. In spite of the party's gain in rural areas, the PKI never won the allegiance of large numbers of *santris* and could not escape the mistrust and hostility of the Moslem forces organized in the Masjumi party. And, perhaps most significantly, the PKI, in spite of its manipulation of nationalist sentiments, was unable to win the trust of the military establishment. The party's efforts to infiltrate and politically neutralize the armed forces were too feeble to prevent the generals from eventually liquidating the PKI.

After more than a decade of impressive gains and patient adherence to the united front strategy and to the peaceful road to power, the PKI during 1963–1965 embarked upon a much more militant course, both in regard to its agitation in the countryside and in its relation to the military. There, at the threshold of power, their militancy managed to cement a military/ Muslim coalition against the communists and, eventually, because of the PKI's adventurist participation in the September 30 Movement, resulted in the destruction of the party. For all the brilliance of Aidit's leadership, and in spite of the party's ideological creativity and flexibility, as well as sensitivity to native Indonesian conditions, the PKI failed to capture power and ultimately failed to survive as a force within the Indonesian political system. The deviation from the Marxist-Leninist united front coalition strategy in favor of a risky elite conflict,[58] proved to be a fatal mistake for the Indonesian communists. The destruction of the PKI was swift and unexpected, dramatic and tragic, leaving the world in shocked disbelief. Aidit's coalition strategy remains wrecked and repudiated and Indonesian communism so far, in vain, awaits its resurrection.

Conclusion

Trond Gilberg

The study of Marxist parties and their behavior in coalitions reveals a number of trends and patterns with major implications for politics in much of the world, over a considerable period of time. The persistence of "Marxism" as a political tendency and guide to action is one of the most important political phenomena of our century. The political flexibility exhibited by parties that call themselves Marxist has made these organizations major contenders for power in some systems, mere irritants in others; in any case, they must be understood as important political actors almost everywhere. And while their tactical flexibility has been amazing (and at times counterproductive), their dedication to long-range goals has represented another major feature of politics in our time. This, too, makes a better understanding of such parties an important task for scholarly study.

Important as Marxism has been in the political life of virtually any society over time, it is still a lesser political force than some other phenomena, chief of which is nationalism. The scholarly literature on nationalism is enormous, and there is no need to recapitulate it here; suffice it to say that *nationalism* is commonly defined as the political expression of a set of attitudes, values, and characteristics that emphasize commonality among a group of people characterized as a "nation." The commonality is based on shared characteristics which may be language, habitation on a common territory, or acceptance of a set of values, goals, and objectives which have been handed down from generation to generation. It is also possible that such feelings are based on race, religion, or ethnicity, but these characteristics are not seen as crucial elements of nationalism in the scholarly literature. Furthermore, the elements of nationalism discussed above are not the only possible ingredients, and, conversely, they are not always all present in manifestations of this enduring political phenomenon. Finally, the mix of ingredients may also vary from case to case, or in any one case it may vary over time. Nationalism, by definition, is a phenomenon that can only be studied systematically in national cases.

Despite the need to examine this phenomenon on a case by case basis, there are some aspects of nationalism that are common to all of its individual manifestations, and these characteristics make all forms of it more important than Marxism, thus helping to set the limits of Marxist power and the parameters of successful coalition activities by Marxists of all kinds. One characteristic is the ability to transcend divisions based on socioeconomic class, regional particularism, and religious differences.

The Impact of Nationalism
on Communist Strategy

Nationalism has the capability of uniting individuals who consider themselves part of the "nation" regardless of their characteristics as caused by occupation, residence, or faith. This overriding capability has been demonstrated time and time again, in most areas of the world, and under all kinds of circumstances. Thus, during the tense days preceding the outbreak of war in 1914, the Second International confidently predicted that the international organization of the proletariat would produce revolutions everywhere, sweeping away outmoded concepts of "nation" and "state" and removing the boundaries once and for all. Despite these predictions, workers flocked to the national banner and killed each other with the same kind of enthusiasm and ferocity as members of other classes. As shown in the discussion of West European Marxist parties, the main point of contention inside the Comintern in the period 1919–1923 was precisely the question of national roads to socialism and communism, as opposed to the centralized strait-jacket proposed by the CPSU and rammed through the Execution Committee of the Communist International (ECCI) in the form of the twenty-one conditions for membership.

Throughout the 1920s most of the communist parties that had been established as a result of the splits that occurred in the labor movement everywhere in Western and Northern Europe dwindled in size and became little more than mere appendages of the Soviet foreign policy-making establishment. The genuine need for leftist policy was met by socialists, social democrats, and other parties that claimed the Marxist heritage *without* subservience to Moscow. Once some of these parties came into power, their capability to deliver "goods and services" to the population made them unbeatable representatives of the political left, and the exercise of power, in turn, made these parties more aware of the complexities of their political and socioeconomic systems and the need to rule on behalf of all of the people, not merely a particular class. The communists, by contrast, seemed to have a *tactical* affiliation with their own people; they would join other parties for national causes only if it were seen as tactically expedient, or if it had been ordered by Moscow, or both. Detailed examination of actual policy-making in the West and North European communist parties reveals that there were, in fact, nationally minded individuals and groups in them, but they did not control the party apparatus. Similarly, there were parties that occasionally deviated from the path promoted by the Kremlin, but the general population had little appreciation of this fact and continued to see their local communists as lackeys of Moscow.

The notion that communists merely exhibited tactical nationalism was further strengthened by the experiences of World War II and its aftermath in Western Europe. The communists cooperated with the Nazi occupiers in the period from September 1939 to June 1941, then joined the national resistance for the duration of the war, only to help perpetuate a decisive split of the left after 1947, clearly in accordance with the policies of the Kremlin. The isolation of the communist variety of Marxism was complete in most cases by the end of the Stalin era.

The revelations at the twentieth CPSU congress in 1956 started a process that eventually led to real national communist parties, and even to a hybrid form of regional West European communism logically known as Eurocommunism. In most cases, however, this conversion to national forms was made reluctantly, or after considerable debate in each party, thus reinforcing the view of the doubters that the communists, once again, were merely "tacking against the wind," making opportunistic maneuvers. This is certainly an incorrect view in many cases, but it hardly matters if enough people believe it. In any case, genuine or not, this attempt to be "national" and "communist" at the same time could have little impact on the power structure of Western and Northern Europe because other leftist organizations were well entrenched already, preempting any move that the communists could take. What was more, the socialists and social democrats had already demonstrated their dedication to reform, redistribution of wealth, and peace through actual programs while they were in power in a number of countries. There was no need to look to the communists for this. The same applies to the various movements of the 1960s and 1970s, such as peace movements, anti-U.S. manifestations over the issue of Vietnam, and disarmament initiatives. The other, more moderate leftists were already there. Communist isolation continued.

Under these circumstances the flexibility demonstrated by the coalition tactics and strategies of the communist version of Marxism was considered mere maneuvers by most people, and certainly by the relevant political elites who controlled access to power. Thus the communists in Western and Northern Europe were unsuccessful in their policies because their programs were out of touch with political reality in the local setting, and also because they were *too* flexible in coalition maneuvering. This dual liability has yet to be overcome, and is not likely to be overcome unless the *external* circumstances of Western and Northern Europe change (e.g., "Finlandization"). That is a topic for another study.

Initially, the political environment in Eastern Europe seemed even less favorable for the success of communists, indeed all Marxists. These were peasant societies, by and large, and there was little support for any manifestation of Marxism, except in Czechoslovakia and the rump state of East Germany. Furthermore, the autocratic nature of the political order almost everywhere in the region made it possible for local authorities to persecute Marxist organizations, sometimes with rather brutal methods. There is little reason to believe that Marxists would have come to power in Eastern Europe without the overwhelming influence of the Soviet Union after World War II and the various manipulative policies that the regional hegemon produced to smooth the path for local communists. The pressing need for reform in the area would have been met by peasant parties and socialists and social democrats of a national coloration. The correlation of forces produced by Soviet influence in the region changed circumstances drastically and made it absolutely certain that the communists would be influential in some manner. This stage having been set, it was merely a question of how these elements of the left would conduct themselves in relations with other domestic political forces.

Charles Gati convincingly argues that the communists of this region differed in their approach to coalition building, because they differed among themselves about their short-range and intermediate goals. Most of the local communists were themselves confused about the conflict they experienced as they related to the internationalist order of solidarity with Moscow, on the one hand, and their values, attitudes, and feelings as Germans, Czechoslovakians, Hungarians, and so on, on the other hand. Sometimes they moved boldly, and sometimes timidly. Sharing power was often as much of an alternative as controlling it. Most of the leftists also hoped and believed that they could lead *their* country on a *national* road to socialism and communism. This was indeed one of the reasons for the relative success they enjoyed inside the coalitions they entered. By 1947, however, their mentors in the Kremlin were ready for full power, not shared authority. The East European communists followed suit, some of them reluctantly. By the time the process of Stalinist "synchronization" was over, there was no need to worry about coalitions, for contending centers of power had been eradicated. And in this process other organizations that claimed to be Marxist, such as the socialists and social democrats, had also been destroyed as a political force.

The victory of the East European communists in some systems was Pyrrhic in nature. Nationalism and its many political manifestations cannot be eradicated simply because local political elites, capitalizing on the international circumstances prevailing at the time, destroyed their competitors. Hence the East European communists, now ruling over their societies, eventually had to come to grips with their own cultures, their own circumstances, and their people. A ruling communist by definition is a *national* communist, because he or she rules over a defined territory, with a recognizable machinery of government for the exercise of political power, and with an inherited population whose values are already established and have proven remarkably resistant to communist attempts at political socialization. Soon the ruling communist realizes that he cannot "conquer" nationalism and erase it. It is better to join it and to use it to build legitimacy. This is the process that has been under way in Eastern Europe since the death of Stalin—the making of a lasting coalition with one's own people. The future of each of the systems in this region depends upon the success or failure of this, the most important coalition Marxists have entered, anywhere.

In Asia, nationalism as a political phenomenon was just as potent as elsewhere, and it had a common focus, the colonial masters. The successful Marxists in Asia were those who spearheaded the quest for independence, not those who preached social revolution and the redistribution of wealth. The economic program of Marxism did serve a useful purpose, however, because it established the Marxists as the most likely ally of the rural proletariat and the marginal farmer as well as the coolies and such industrial workers as could be found. The Marxists were freedom fighters who also demanded socioeconomic change. They were skillful coalition builders who made broad alliances with all anticolonialists and narrower ones with certain subcategories of the population, depending upon class and other characteristics. This combination was indispensable for success. Had these Marxists been internationalists rather than nationalistic in outlook, they would have been shunted aside by others who knew how to capitalize on anticolonialism. Had they been less insistent on social and economic change, others, not necessarily Marxist, would have taken their place.

This formula is clearly present in analyzing the success of the

Vietnamese Marxists (who combined elements of Marx, Lenin, and Mao, and thus cannot be called Marxist-Leninists in the strict sense of the word) and the failures of their Indian counterparts. In Indochina, the Marxists became a leading force in the quest for liberation from colonialism and then achieved power in one part of the territory, subsequently utilizing this base to conquer the other part. The Indian Marxists, on the other hand, could not compete with other nationalists who also engaged in social and economic reform, and they failed. Initial failure led to internal squabbling, factionalism, and splits, hence no real prospect for power. Coalition building in Indochina was an indispensable tool for the acquisition and maintenance of power, but in India it became mere maneuvering.

Indonesia is a hybrid case that fits neither of the two models discussed above. Indeed, it may be said that Indonesia comes closest to a case in which organizational ability and coalition-building skills account for the astonishing successes of the PKI and its subsequent bloody demise. In Indonesia there was a nationalistic movement that dominated the quest for independence, thus precluding Marxist preeminence as freedom fighters. There were other elements that shared the spotlight in demanding social and economic reform. The PKI nevertheless emerged as the largest nonruling communist party in the world. This astonishing accomplishment was built upon exceptional skills in making and maintaining coalitions. At the top, the PKI became a close supporter of the ruling party, particularly the ruling circle around President Sukarno, and this enigmatic, indeed erratic, leader personally moved much closer to the PKI line on many issues. In a system with personalized political rule this was a supremely important development which had a great deal to do with the PKI's success. The other element was coalition building at the bottom, manifested through the PKI's ability to build a strong infrastructure in the countryside, capitalizing on existing socioeconomic grievances and making alliances with elements of the local power structure.

To become as large and well organized as the PKI is risky business. On the one hand, the infrastructure is there to make a move toward full power; on the other hand, the very size of such an organization scares competitors and makes it a target for retaliation. This happened in Indonesia, with tragic consequences for the PKI. The lesson to be learned is this: Coalitions designed to capture power must lead to power, or they will be destroyed. The Indonesian experience is no doubt studied widely among ambitious Marxists.

Latin America, too, represents a good case for the notion that nationalism supersedes Marxism, and that the latter is only successful in capturing power in conjunction with the former. In Latin America outright colonialism was much less a factor than actual or perceived dominance by a regional hegemon in the setting of nominal independence. But stated as anti-Americanism, Latin American nationalism was, nevertheless, a very powerful force. There were also important forces for social, economic, and political change; one of these was Marxism in its various manifestations. As long as the local Marxists could demand *real* independence *and* reform, they were a force to be reckoned with in this diverse region.

In this context it is important to note that the Marxist-Leninists, looking to Moscow for inspiration, were not particularly successful. It was others, who combined a number of Marxist tenets with local radicalism, who led the way. Thus Castro only became a Marxist-Leninist *after* his successful quest for power, and probably in large measure because he needed the support of a protector such as the Soviet Union. Other leftist movements in contemporary Latin America (which includes Central and South America) have similar characteristics. The Chilean example also shows that there are leftist forces more radical than the communists in this region, thus further complicating the tasks of the latter when it comes to coalition building and coalition maintenance.

Nicaragua is another example of the conflict between nationalism, radicalism, and more orthodox Marxism-Leninism in this part of the world. Since the ascent to power of the *sandinistas*, the top leadership has been divided over the issue of participation by non-Marxists in the councils of power. Furthermore, the junta leaders have also debated the issue of other Marxist organizations and their relationship with the ruling circles. These debates have taken place in the context of nationalism and anti-Americanism so common to much of Central and Southern America.

The Sandinistas, having walked a fine line between ideological orthodoxy, nationalism, and limited pluralism are now confronted with yet another difficult factor of political reality, namely the demand from outside actors (particularly the United States) for greater pluralism, less dogmatism, and a wider element of public participation in the political process. The partial removal of such pluralism may be a combination of external pressures, internal proclivities on the parts of the more moderate elements in the leadership, and more tactical and temporary adjustments to serious political pressures. Whatever the specific mix, the Nicaraguan case again shows the extent to which Marxist coalition makers are tactical masters of adjustment.

It would appear, then, that Latin America is not an area where Marxists in the strict sense of the word have been successful in establishing and dominating coalitions, but rather a region in which indigenous revolutionaries have utilized elements of Marxism for their own purposes, later on becoming dependent on the Soviet Union to help maintain them in power in the political arena and propping up faltering economies which occasionally perform even worse than their predecessors. The reason why so many analysts and political decision makers consider Latin America (particularly the central area) a "Marxist" or "communist" threat is precisely this fact that local revolutionaries have become dependent upon the Soviet Union as protector and provider. Hence the threat of it is indeed real, because it is a Soviet, and not a communist or Marxist, threat.

Africa represents yet another set of circumstances, and thus another aspect of political efforts by individuals and groups that consider themselves Marxist. The main political fact of life in Africa during the last two decades was anticolonialism and the quest for independence; in this respect much of Africa resembles Asia. No party aspiring to the appellation "revolutionary" could afford to disregard this fact. And, as is the case elsewhere in the Third World, success or failure in the quest for power depends, to a large extent, upon the ability or inability of local Marxists to relate to this struggle, indeed to take charge of it. Again, this dedication to anticolonialism is coupled with a demand for significant political and socioeconomic change at home, often manifested through land reform and redistribution of land, public ownership of the means of production, and an attempt to establish rudimentary forms of political institutions and procedures utilized elsewhere under Marxist jurisdiction. This task is even more complicated in Africa than elsewhere because factors impeding nation building abound to an extent unknown elsewhere, particularly in the form of tribalism, regionalism, and ethnic particularism. In the end, the successful Marxist must continue the quest for revolution and the demand for independence, here as elsewhere in the Third World, but he must also deal with the excruciating task of overcoming the fissures of the society he has "acquired." More often than not this task becomes virtually impossible. Performance suffers, the need for outside aid deepens, and a new form of dependency develops. The old colonialism is superseded by a new form. Local revolutionaries, depending upon the Soviet Union and her allies, adopt the lingo and the trappings of Marxism. They build coalitions, they attempt to maintain them, but often these coalitions are held together by force or convenience, or both, rather than ideological affinity. These are, technically speaking, "Marxist" coalitions, but the cohesive elements are power and the need to survive, not ideological affinity. Again, the primary characteristic of these associations is that they support local leaders who have political programs that incorporate elements of Marxism in them, and they also depend heavily upon the support of the Soviet Union for their political and socioeconomic survival, much of which is ultimately dependent upon military power.

While the generalizations above hold for sub-Saharan Africa, particularly for ruling parties, they are less valid for Northern Africa. Here, the large population concentration of Arabs has created a much different political configuration in which Marxist organizations, with their alleged atheistic ideology, tend to be outlawed and in some cases persecuted. The radicalism that does exist in such societies is funneled into other political organizations, at times even a modernizing elite based on elements of the military. These elements, in conjunction with religious leaders, produce the social and economic reforms, and not the outlawed Marxists. The fact that the local leaders are nationalist and religious at the same time does not prevent them from nurturing friendly relations with the Soviet Union; and the Kremlin, pursuing Soviet state interests, looks aside even as the elites jail and sometimes execute Marxist leaders and outlaw their organizations. Under these circumstances, then, the room for coalition maneuvers is severely restricted for all individuals and groups that call themselves Marxists, and their prospects for success are likewise diminished to a considerable degree.

The evidence presented in this book is clear and unambiguous on this point: Marxism must coexist with nationalism and must learn to utilize it for the purpose of enhancing power and maintaining it if captured. If such a mutually beneficial relationship can be established between the various forms of Marxism, on the one hand, and nationalism in its many forms, on the other hand, the possibilities for coalition making, maintenance, and maneuver are enhanced. Conversely, if such a relationship is not forthcoming, Marxists have little chance of successful coalition strategies and tactics, and hence for prospects for power acquisition.

Communist Party Coexistence
with Other Universalistic Manifestations

As pointed out above, nationalism is a universalistic phenomenon with local manifestations. Much the same can be said about religion, with the exception that the unit of analysis is no longer the individual state or country, but may be much larger territorial areas (e.g., most of Southern Europe is Catholic, while a good part of Northern and Western Europe is Protestant). Furthermore, religions coexist; a country may have several religions whose doctrines, administrative infrastructures, and physical plants operate on the same territory. In any case, religion, in whatever form and denomination, is present in all societies. Marxism, in all of *its* forms, must relate to these phenomena.

The specific cases examined in this book make it abundantly clear that Marxism, ostensibly atheistic, in fact has coexisted with religious beliefs and organizations ever since this ideology appeared on the scene. Marxists have never been able to convince workers, peasants, or others to whom they have attempted to relate that religion is, indeed, the "opium of the people" and must be eradicated in order to ensure progress in the "here and now," especially in the socioeconomic and political realms. Greater success has been registered among intellectuals, but it is unclear whether this is due to the persuasiveness of the arguments or intellectuals' penchant for skepticism. In any case, religion, like nationalism, remains a major political force whose attractiveness exceeds that of Marxism and thus represents a significant obstacle to the coalition strategies and tactics of Marxist parties.

The impact of religion on political life varies greatly from area to area, even though it is always a factor everywhere. The most important political influence can be found in Muslim areas, or areas of considerable Roman Catholic strength. This has a direct impact on the policies and prospects for success facing Marxists in North Africa, the Middle East, and parts of Asia, especially the southwestern part but also Indonesia. Furthermore, Marxists have had to contend with a strong and active church and deep religious faith in parts of Eastern and Southern Europe and much of Latin America. Marxist parties in these regions have come to an understanding, however grudgingly, that there must be a form of accommodation with this potent force, which has the capability to instill political quietude or rebelliousness. Thus the ruling Marxists in Latin America have allowed the continued function of the Catholic Church in their systems. Those Marxist parties and movements that are in opposition have tried to establish a dialogue with more radical elements within the Church, particularly with exponents of liberation theology. In Southern and Eastern Europe the major communist (and other Marxist) parties have increasingly displayed a willingness to accept the notion that religion is a private affair in which no political "legislation" or doctrinaire influences are beneficial or relevant. Marxists here have attempted to form coalitions regardless of religious beliefs (or lack thereof) among potential or actual partners.

Islam has represented an even greater obstacle for the coalition strategies and tactics of Marxist parties. Most Marxist orgnizations are banned throughout the Muslim world. The fervor and universalism of Islam, particularly its Shiite version, compete with messianic tendencies in Marxism itself and propose solutions to daily problems that are often more palatable than those offered by the disciples of Marx. Thus the importance of Marxism in the Muslim world is negligible, but the influence of the Soviet

Union is of considerable importance, thus enhancing the political stature of groups that accept aspects of the leftist doctrine in their quest for social and economic change and greater independence from the West. There is a coattail effect of Soviet state power here that should not be underestimated.

Again, Indonesia is an interesting case of mass organizational capability and support for the local communist party in a population that is, to a considerable extent, Muslim. This Indonesian success depended in part upon the skills of the Marxists in understanding the socioeconomic and political reality of the village, including the religious infrastructure there. In part it stemmed from the radicalism of the nationalists themselves, who accepted (and co-opted) many of the political tenets espoused by the PKI, and allowed the communist party to function in this far-flung country with relatively few restrictions. This is clearly a case in which special local circumstances allowed a form of Marxism to function and to prosper amidst strong Muslim allegiances.

The relationship between Marxism and religion is less clear-cut in Protestant or Orthodox countries. In Protestant Europe, secularization has been under way for some time, and one would therefore expect that religion would be less of a factor in the political realm, thus removing one of the obstacles to Marxist maneuverability in coalitions or other political forms. It was therefore rather surprising to the Marxists (and the Marxist-Leninists in particular) that the twenty-one points establishing conditions for membership in the Comintern produced a serious political liability on this issue. The explanation for this seeming contradiction stems from the fact that religion and church organizations in this region have become part of the secular order, and that they therefore have legitimacy in the minds of men and women insofar as the secular system possesses this quality. After all, the churches in the area have a tradition of administering to the poor, teaching ethics and morality in the public school systems, and generally acting as one of the main providers and arbiters of the value system for elites and the general population alike. Under these circumstances the harsh definition of churches as exploiters of the poor and the masses carried little credibility. Consequently the atheist faith of doctrinal Marxism could not compete with the impact of Protestantism, even among significant elements of the working class. But at the same time Marxist parties did benefit from the relative lack of political activism of the churches as churches.

The position of Orthodoxy in relationship to Marxism was rather ambiguous. On the one hand Orthodoxy has tended to subordinate itself to secular authority in political matters; hence established communist systems in Orthodox societies benefited from this tendency, because the churches could be more easily controlled. This was certainly the case in the Slavic parts of the Soviet Union and later in countries such as Romania. On the other hand, the Orthodox Church also represented nationalism in some areas of Eastern Europe, again particularly in Romania, and this close association with the powerful fact of national consciousness produced a combination of church and state that held the peasant masses in a powerful grip, thus reducing the possibilities of political success for the Marxists and their organizations. Again, a modus vivendi with religion had to be established before Marxist parties could effectively engage in coalition politics.

The Effect of the Noncommunist Left and the Noncommunist Political Order on Communist Coalition Strategies

Since the emergence of Marxist-Leninist (or communist) parties in various areas of the world, it has become clear that this variation of Marxism is the most formidable in terms of organization, dedication, and outside support and therefore most likely to succeed in its goals and objectives. The prospects for success in communist policy, especially in coalition strategies and tactics, depend heavily upon the strength of the noncommunist (but possibly still Marxist) left and the relationship between those moderate leftist forces and the rest of the political order. This surely stands to reason. When parties other than the communists claim to be Marxist, they are in fact competing for the same political clientele, using much of the same rhetoric, claiming the same or similar ideological antecedents, and organizing the same people in similar structures. In fact the noncommunist left often has the advantage of avoiding any direct organizational association with outside centers of power, thus appearing to be more "national" and hence acceptable to more people. Furthermore, the moderate left is likely to represent more of a coalition possibility for other political parties in the domestic order, and this, in turn, may lead to earlier access to actual power and the advantages that such a position entails. This is clearly so in societies with elements of relative political consensus in the political system. Here, socialists and social democrats, occasionally retaining Marxist rhetoric in their party programs, demonstrated their adhesion to the existing system and its rules of behavior, while the Marxist-Leninists (or others to the left even of these groups) were on the fringes, or indeed outside of the parameters of the system itself. This was certainly true in much of Western and Northern Europe (but not Germany during the

Weimar Republic) even in the period between the two world wars, and definitely after World War II. This kind of competition from the pro-system, moderate left was not as evident in much of Eastern Europe, even though Czechoslovakia and Hungary approach this pattern. In Latin America there was clearly such a competitive aspect to the left, and in some cases, such as Chile, the socialists were left of the communists on many issues, but few of these elements had much impact on policy, and remained outside the autocratic political order, spending their time in fruitless ideological squabbles and competing for the same meager turf.

Africa (with the exception of South Africa, which exhibited semi-European patterns of political organization) represents a somewhat different case. In the North African political systems, socialist and other leftist ideas were often combined with nationalism and anticolonialism in a potent mixture that left little room for maneuver for other forces of the left, and particularly the Marxists. In sub-Saharan Africa, the left was weak due to the relative political and socioeconomic underdevelopment of the region, and leftism was combined with anticolonialism into a very heterogeneous package that lumped Marxists of all kinds together with other left of center elements under the control of individuals whose goal was liberation and personal power more often than it was the implementation of doctrine. The impact of Soviet, East European, and Cuban assistance for such movements and rulers eventually propelled the more leftist forces to the fore, thus enhancing the influence of self-proclaimed Marxists. In any case, there was no meaningful social democratic movement prior to independence, so competition could not come from that quarter. Thus the diffuse forms of African socialism include all kinds of elements, and the Marxist ones are only part of the much larger picture.

In Asia the existence of a noncommunist left in India (coupled with a nationalist party whose left wing already espoused radical socioeconomic reform) made Marxist prospects correspondingly dimmer in the area of coalition building and maintenance. In Indochina, Marxist elements were part of a much larger anticolonial front, and thus part of the mainstream of nationalism, with little competition from other leftist elements of the traditional kind found among socialists and social democrats elsewhere. Under such circumstances, and given outside support of various kinds, the Marxist elements (particularly the Marxist-Leninists of local hue) emerged superior because of their dedication and organizational capability. This dedication was clearly superior to anything that could be mustered by other elements of the popular front that had been formed, and it was much superior to the noncommunist elements of the South, where corruption and inefficiency reigned and the morale of the armed forces was low. Thus the Vietnamese communists combined the organizational capabilities espoused by Lenin with the military doctrine of Mao, and added the ideological dedication of both. This is a powerful combination everywhere, not just in the fluid political environment of Vietnam prior to the division of the country and in South Vietnam after that event.

In Indonesia, the PKI proved its capability of organization and doctrinal dedication at the expense of the forces on the left, but, despite its successes on this score (particularly in rural organizations) it could not supersede the nationalists in terms of popular support. Furthermore, the nationalist elements, having captured political power, retained control over the armed forces, despite certain discontented elements who sided with the communists. This, in the end, proved to be decisive. Thus Indonesia is not analogous to Indochina, but rather represents ultimate failure after spectacular successes. Vietnam, on the other hand, represents ultimate success after a prolonged period of cautious but skillful coalition building.

The problem confronted by Marxists (particularly Marxists-Leninists) in relations with the rest of the labor movement was greatest in Western and Northern Europe (and North America, which is a different case that warrants a separate study) precisely because there was a strong labor movement there in the first place, a movement which had existed for a number of decades by the time the Marxist-Leninists appeared on the scene. The movements in this geographical region had established strong organizations, mass memberships, and the beginnings of mass electoral support that had produced some tangible results. Furthermore, important elements of these movements had shown respect for the political culture in which they operated and had earned some respect, however grudging, from their political competitors. Under these circumstances the communists, true to Lenin and the Soviet-inspired doctrines of the Comintern, had little chance in democratic political systems. Since World War II, and especially after the death of Stalin, local communists have been more flexible, but it is really too late, in this area of the world, because the noncommunist left has been too successful, and the rest of the political order has been much too willing to produce reforms and engineer social change. It is hard to be a Marxist-Leninist in quest of power in the welfare state. And this brings us to the next major generalization of this study.

The Success of Coalition Strategies in Politically and Economically Unstable Societies

This is not a surprising finding, but one that is worth noting neverthe-less. Marxism, in all its manifestations, is a doctrine of protest, and some of its forms offer a detailed guide to specific political action designed to change the existing order and establishing something quite different. In political systems with considerable regime legitimacy and systemic support there are rather few prospects for antisystemic doctrines. The area of mean-ingful opposition is limited to demands for reforms inside the existing order, not drastic changes of it. In such a setting the very essence of Marxism as a revolutionary doctrine is weakened, and Marxists, like every-one else, are reduced to participating for the purpose of establishing new reforms and seeing them carried through inside this order. For this kind of political activity, however, other leftists are much better equipped, both doctrinally and in terms of political style. The area of maneuverability for Marxists (particularly Marxist-Leninists) shrinks further, and so do the coalition possibilities of the parties. Furthermore, the forces in the middle of the ideological spectrum as well as their competitors to the right of center also sponsor reform, thereby reducing viable areas of protest and challenge. The broader the consensus of systemic goals and the policies required to achieve those goals, the less the likelihood of successful Marx-ist coalition effects in the quest for power.

The consensus and legitimacy discussed above may stem from perfor-mance, procedures and structures, personal charisma or the charisma of movements and causes, or some combination thereof. In Western and Northern Europe the viability of Marxists as a political alternative has been low because of the legitimacy of the existing order based on perfor-mance. These systems simply perform well, in the sense that they provide a wide array of services for the population, maintain channels of political participation, and utilize mechanisms for elite recycling, thus producing a sense of political efficacy in the population. Bureaucratic structures are relatively efficient, and public officials are honest, thus producing trust in their performance. The political order, by and large, is not resistant to change but has rather consistently promoted it. Procedures are strictly enforced, thereby reducing the personalistic elements of politics so com-monly found in other parts of the world. Procedural legitimacy results from this approach.

It is difficult for Marxists (or other revolutionaries) to gain much headway under circumstances such as these, because the existing order in most cases has engaged in "preventative maintenance" through legislation, implementation, and bureaucratic oversight. In Western and Northern Europe, the opportunity for revolutionary successes was lost when the communists failed to utilize the turmoil and instability of the immediate post–World War I era to establish themselves as *national* revolutionaries. They became, instead, "errand boys of Moscow," unable to capitalize on a situation in which significant elements of the consensus and performance elements of the existing political order had failed. By the time greater political flexibility was allowed for communist parties, there were other competitors who knew how to utilize opportunities in their national setting, or the systems had recovered from crisis to such an extent that they once again functioned rather well, thus eliminating earlier opportunities. Marxist coalition building continued, but only for tactical gains, and with little prospect of success in the real political game, the quest for power.

In other systems and other regions different forms of legitimacy prevailed, again blocking the path to power. In much of Asia and Africa the existing order was colonial and had little legitimacy, but the leaders of the national liberation movements did, and after independence these elites emerged as the dominant political force in the countries of this region. The political order that emerged as a result of this process survived for a considerable period of time on the charismatic legitimacy of its leaders and the symbolic legitimacy of independence, thus getting a start on nation building. Under these circumstances the success or failure of the Marxist coalition strategies and tactics depended in great measure on the extent to which the emerging order was sympathetic or not. In the case of Indonesia the nationalist leadership under Sukarno was so inclined, although important elements in this camp were not. In India, there was little nationalist support for the various communist factions, and Marxist successes were therefore few and far between. In Indochina, however, the divisions among the factions of the national liberation movement allowed the communists to step forward as the champions of independence, nationalism, and systemic nation building, all wrapped up together, and this combination clearly helped them succeed in the quest for power.

In Africa the nationalism and religious fervor of the anticolonial movement in the North created mass support for the nationalist regimes but also blocked Marxist efforts. In the South, no such overriding anti-Marxist force could be found. There, success or failure depended much more on outside assistance (see below).

Latin America is different from all of the regions discussed before, and the variety of political and socioeconomic manifestations is such that generalizations become risky. Independence had been achieved early for most of the region, and this issue produced no major rallying points,

except as a cry against foreign economic dominance and political infringe-
ment of existing sovereignty. As such, nationalism became a major factor
in this region. Coupled with the widespread and broadly backed demand
for social and economic reform, the issue of greater autonomy helped fuel
anti-Americanism, thus producing a vehicle for Soviet and East European
involvement. Thus the chances for Marxists were considerably improved
in those cases where the existing political order became weakened through
corruption, poor performance, and loss of support by important institutions such as the military. In these cases the power vacuum that developed
could be filled by anti-American revolutionaries who also demanded greater
social justice and economic reform. This "package" of political demands
was co-opted by some Marxist elements and utilized for maximum effect in
coalition building.

In other areas of Latin America, political conditions were not as
favorable. The existing order, corrupt and inefficient as it may be, still
maintained control over the means of coercion, thus blocking the Marxists
and other revolutionaries. The church tended to support the existing regime,
thus further reducing the prospects for successful coalition building in the
impoverished masses, especially in the countryside. There were other organizations of the left that could compete for the allegiance of people in this
ideological model. And the existing system itself managed to institute
some reforms, however grudgingly, so that the pressure for revolution was
reduced enough for survival of the system. Thus the Marxists had fewer
opportunities for successful maneuvering in coalitions, in quest of political
power.

All of these factors were important in considerable measure. They
interacted differently in different national surroundings. Ultimately success or failure depended greatly on the nature and extent of outside support.

The Impact of Soviet, Chinese, or Cuban
Support on Marxist Coalition Efforts

The factors of internal cohesion in Marxist organizations, the ideological clarity and commitment of leaders and followers in such groups, relations with other elements of the left and the strength of these elements,
and Marxist interaction with the forces of nationalism and religion, by and
large determine the success or failure of Marxist coalition efforts, if all
other factors are held constant. In real life, however, all other factors are, of
course, not constant; in fact, as the world "shrinks" because of communications and weapons developments, outside factors become more and more

important in the domestic outcome of politics in all systems. This is especially true of the Post–World War II era, when there emerged two global powers (the United States and the Soviet Union), a potential global power (China), and a host of regional powers with new or long-standing ambitions in their immediate vicinity (e.g., Britain, France, India, Vietnam, and Cuba). These powers have the capability to influence events in neighboring countries or, in the case of the Soviet Union and the United States, extending this influence to any area in the world. Thus, depending upon the political will in Moscow or Washington, political groups in distant regions can be aided in a significant way, perhaps even a decisive way, under certain domestic circumstances. Each global power must simply assess the potential gains and liabilities of such involvement and act accordingly.

The post–World War II era can show many examples of such outside involvement in the domestic affairs of states, altering the internal balance of power in favor of one participant or another in a decisive manner. The United States helped reestablish economic prosperity in Western and Northern Europe after the war, thus giving democratic elements a chance to succeed in reconstruction and power consolidation. The United States, aided by its allies, helped turn back the tide of revolution in Portugal in the early 1970s. Japan, defeated and economically desperate, was launched on a democratic path by the occupying power, the United States. In Latin America, U.S. power has frequently been used, directly or indirectly, to shore up one domestic political element at the expense of another. In Asia, Washington (and the U.S. public) has shown insufficient will to settle political and economic disputes in its favor, and others have been more successful.

The Soviet Union has undergone a curious transformation as a foreign policy actor. In its early years, Moscow considered itself a universalist power with appeal everywhere, primarily transmitted through the Comintern. It soon became a regional power, weak at first, then much stronger as a result of World War II. Finally, at some point during the last two decades or so, the leaders in the Kremlin developed the will and the capacity to extend their power and influence over the entire globe, and this set in motion a train of events that altered the political balance in a number of countries. Already as a regional power the Soviet Union had decisively influenced events in Eastern Europe, and the Kremlin certainly had a hand in maintaining the communist regimes in China and North Vietnam (the latters' rulers benefited from Soviet aid prior to capturing power as well). In Cuba, the Soviet leaders saw an opportunity to extend their influence into the American "front yard." Subsequently, the Kremlin has become active in a number of African states and liberation movements, and this effort has been expanded by some of Moscow's loyal allies in Eastern Europe.

As communist power expanded in Asia and Central America, some communist-ruled states in these regions in turn began to act as promoters of Marxist groups and organizations in their vicinity (and in fact, even beyond). Thus China aided North Korea in a most decisive manner during the Korean War, and Beijing later helped sustain North Vietnam against France and the United States. Furthermore, the Chinese provided support in various forms for the communists in Indonesia. There are also limited Chinese efforts in Africa, particularly sub-Saharan Africa. Cuba became an "exporter" of revolutionary fervor and organized efforts in other parts of Latin America and Africa. This widening network of ruling communist elites entering in the domestic affairs of others has had a considerable impact upon the political life of the systems toward which such efforts are targeted.

This impact has been of many varieties. In Eastern Europe the Red Army occupied territory and thus could influence politics in a most decisive manner. In China and Vietnam substantial military and economic aid was provided. In Africa and Latin America economic aid and various forms of military support have been given. Compared to this, Soviet support for peace movements and some mass organizations in Western and Northern Europe became rather insignificant and incapable of altering the domestic political balance in any significant fashion.

The advantages that accrue to local Marxists from such involvement by established communist regimes are many. In a fluid political situation, assistance may tip the balance in favor of Marxist-Leninists inside broadly based coalitions, such as national liberation movements, and may indeed help propel these forces to full national power. Assistance may also help block rivals. Furthermore, Soviet, Chinese, and Cuban assistance has been instrumental in propping up regimes that consider themselves Marxist; in addition, communist economic and military aid helps maintain non-Marxist but anti-American nationalists in power, thus "denying" an area to the Americans and possibly improving the conditions for local Marxists as well (even though this second objective is strictly subordinate to the goal of Soviet, Chinese, or even Cuban *state* power enhancement).

Under all of these circumstances, then, outside influence is important for the strategies and tactics of Marxist parties and their coalition efforts. Given the global "correlation of forces," such factors are likely to remain important for the foreseeable future.

The student of Marxist coalition strategies and tactics in the future has a considerable task. First of all, he or she must examine the doctrinal variety of individuals and groups that call themselves "Marxist," so that the unit of analysis can be established with some consistency. Secondly, the analyst most certainly has to examine the interplay of "Marxism" with nationalism, religion, and the configurations of other elements on the political left in each system examined. Furthermore, he must attempt to factor in the elements of personality traits among leaders and the nature and extent of outside involvement. This is a complicated task that requires further country-by-country study. But perhaps the most important question to be asked has to do with the assumptions of the coalition strategies and tactics themselves and the way we try to study these phenomena. Up to now we have assumed that the strategies underlying Marxist coalition efforts are aimed at capturing power, and that the tactics are part of the means to get there. This is certainly consistent with the statements and acts by various groups of Marxists up to now. But can we always expect that such will be the case? Perhaps, under certain circumstances, "Marxists" would like to remain in opposition, as a "catch-all" for the discontented, not worried about the complicated and frustrating job of ruling fractious societies in which resources are always much too scarce to build effective legitimacy on the basis of performance. Under these conditions the approach to coalition building, maintenance, and termination will be different, and the measure of success or failure will change. But that is a task for future research efforts on this important topic.

Notes

2 Coalition Strategies and Tactics in Marxist Thought

I am indebted to Professor Vendulka Kaba'lakova' for her thoughtful comments on this chapter.

1. William H. Riker, *The Theory of Political Coalitions* (New Haven: Yale University Press, 1962); Riker, "The Study of Coalitions," in David L. Sills, ed., *International Encyclopedia of the Social Sciences* (New York: Macmillan, 1968), 524–29; William A. Gamson, "The Study of Coalitions," ibid., 527–34; M. Leiserson, "Game Theory and the Study of Coalition Behavior," in S. Groennings, et al., eds., *The Study of Coalition Behavior* (New York: Holt, Rinehart and Winston, 1970), 252–72; and Scott Flanagan, "Theory and Method in the Study of Coalition Formation: Toward a More General Model of Political Coalitions," *Journal of Comparative Administration*, 5, no. 3 (November 1973): 267–313. For an important modification of Riker's theory see Robert Axelrod, *Conflict of Interest: A Theory of Divergent Goals with Application to Politics* (Chicago: Markham, 1970).

2. For a critique of coalition theories see Eric C. Brown, *Coalition Theories: A Logical and Empirical Critique* (Beverly Hills: Sage Publications, 1973), and Charles R. Adrian's review of the book in *American Political Science Review*, 71, no. 4 (1977): 1612.

3. For a more comprehensive discussion see D. Easton, *The Political System* (New York: Knopf, 1953).

4. Riker, *The Theory of Political Coalitions*.

5. For my attempt to use some of Riker's generalizations, see my *Soviet Intervention in Czechoslovakia, 1968: Anatomy of a Decision* (Baltimore: Johns Hopkins University Press, 1979).

6. Vernon V. Aspaturian, "Conceptualizing Eurocommunism: Some Preliminary Observations," in V. V. Aspaturian, J. Valenta, and D. Burke, eds., *Eurocommunism between East and West* (Bloomington: Indiana University Press, 1980); Robert C. Tucker, *The Marxian Revolutionary Idea* (New York: W. W. Norton, 1969), 66–79, and Adam B. Ulam, *The Unfinished Revolution* (New York: Random House, 1960), 55.

7. See Karl Marx, "The Communist Manifesto," in *Capital, The Communist Manifesto, and Other Writings* (New York: Modern Library, 1959), 343.

8. Ibid, 342.

9. A similar revolutionary line was expressed in Marx's organizational works: *Rules and Constitution of the Communist League*, Article 1, and *Plan of Action against Democracy*.

10. *The Class Struggle in France, 1848–1850*, in *Selected Works*, (Moscow, 1962), vol. 2, p. 281.

11. Marx to Weydemeyer, March 5, 1852, in *Marx and Engels' Selected Correspondence* (New York, 1953), 86.

12. *Critique of the Gotha Program*, in the *Communist Blueprint for the Future* (New York: Dutton, 1967), 60. Marx's italics.

13. *The Communist Manifesto*, 354–55.

14. See, for example, Marx's communication with Engels in 1856 in *Selected Correspondence* (New York: International Publishers, 1942), 87 (letter dated April 16, 1856).

15. Karl Marx, *Economic and Philosophic Manuscripts of 1844* (New York: International Publishers, 1960), and Karl Marx and Friedrich Engels, *The German Ideology* (New York: International Publishers, 1947).

16. Lucio Colletti, *From Rousseau to Lenin* (New York, 1977); Bertell Ollman, *Alienation: Marx's Concept of Man in Capitalist Society* (Cambridge: Cambridge University Press, 1971); and Graeme Duncan, *Marx and Mills: Two Views of Social Conflict and Social Harmony* (Cambridge: Cambridge University Press, 1973).

17. Shlomo Avineri, *The Social and Political Thought of Karl Marx* (Cambridge: Cambridge University Press, 1968), 202–29.

18. *The Communist Manifesto*, 325–55. A similar view is expressed by Engels in his famous brochure *Principles of Communism*. Engels declared that the proletarian revolution will inaugurate "*a democratic constitution* and thereby directly or indirectly the political rule of the proletariat." See Friedrich Engels, *Principles of Communism*, in *Selected Works*, vol. 1, p. 90.

19. Karl Marx and Friedrich Engels, *Werke* (Berlin, 1956), vol. 4, p. 598.

20. George Lichtheim, *Marxism: An Historical and Critical Study* (New York: Praeger, 1961).

21. Karl Marx, "The Chartists," in *Articles on Britain* (Moscow, 1971), 119.

22. *Critique of the Gotha Program*, 18–19. Marx's italics.

23. *The First International, Minutes of the Hague Congress of 1872 with Related Documents*, Hans Gerth, ed. (Madison: University of Wisconsin Press, 1958), 269.

24. Karl Marx, *Selected Correspondence*, 334.

25. *Kritik der Sozial-demokratischen Programm—Entwurfs 1891*, *Werke*, vol. 20 (Berlin: Dietz, 1961–68).

26. Friedrich Engels' Introduction to Marx's *The Class Struggles in France*, in *Selected Works*, vol. 1, p. 129 (published shortly before Engels's death in 1895).

27. Engels in interview with *Le Figaro* (Paris), May 8, 1893, as quoted in Wolfgang Leonhard, *Three Faces of Marxism* (New York: Holt, Rinehart and Winston, 1974), 29.

28. *The Economic and Philosophic Manuscripts* were originally published in the Russian edition in 1927 and in German in 1932. In the contrary view (e.g., I. Meszaros's) it is argued that some Russian translations of *The German Ideology* accessible to Lenin included at least sections of *The Economic and Philosophical Manuscripts*.

29. V. I. Lenin, *Collected Works*, vol. 1 and vol. 25 (London: Lawrence and Wishart, 1960), 150–60, 492.

30. Ibid., vol. 25, p. 445. In my discussion I am indebted to an observation of the Austrian communist thinkers Ernst Fisher and Franz Marek in their volume *Lenin in His Own Words* (London: Penguin, 1969), 75, and personally to Marek for bringing this to my attention.

31. Lenin, *Collected Works*, vol. 23, p. 95.

32. Ibid., vol. 29, pp. 380–81.

33. Ibid., vol. 28, p. 7, and also Lenin's April thesis on *The Tasks of the Proletariat in the Present Revolution*, in *Selected Works*, vol. 2 (Moscow: International Publishers, 1951), 14.

34. Lenin, *What Is to Be Done*, in *Collected Works*, vol. 5, p. 4222 (emphasis my own).

35. The term *Otzovisty* comes from the verb *otzovat*—to recall. It describes those who

were against participating in the Duma.

36. Lenin, *Collected Works*, vol. 26, pp. 103–104, and vol. 30, pp. 491–93.

37. Ibid., 56–59.

38. Ibid., vol. 32, pp. 465, 468.

39. J. V. Stalin, *Problems of Leninism* (Moscow: Foreign Language Publishing House, 1935).

40. For a theoretical debate on the issue of coalitions and coalition building in 1919–1924, see Jane Degras, ed., *The Communist International, 1919–1943: Documents*, vol. 1, 1919–1922 (London: Oxford University Press, 1960), 66, 69, 153, 316, 341 and 414–25 in particular.

41. For theses on coalition politics adopted by the fifth Comintern congress in July 1924 and the debate on this issue in 1925–1928, see J. Degras, *The Communist International: Documents*, vol. 2, 1923–1928, pp. 151–52, 242–43, and 519–26 in particular.

42. For this debate, see J. Degras, vol. 3, 1929–1934, pp. 376–77, and vol. 4, 1934–1943, pp. 331–33.

43. For various, often contradictory, interpretations, see Gunther Nollau, *International Communism and World Revolution* (New York: Praeger, 1961), 115; Paolo Spriatno, *Storio del Partido Communista Italiano* (Turin: Guilo Einardi, 1967); J. Degras, *The Communist International*, vol. 4, p. 333; S. Carrillo, *Eurocommunism and the State* (Westport: Lawrence Hill, 1978), 113; and Daniel R. Brower, *The New Jacobins: The French Communist Party and the Popular Front* (Ithaca: Cornell University Press, 1968), 47–67.

44. The resolution of the seventh congress can be found in Jane Degras, ed., *The Communist International, 1919–1943: Documents* (London: Oxford University Press, 1965), vol. 3, pp. 355–70.

45. Santiago Carrillo, *Eurocommunism and the State* (Westport, Conn.: Lawrence Hill, 1978), esp. chap. 5.

46. Zbigniew Brzezinski, *The Soviet Bloc* (Cambridge, Mass: Harvard University Press, 1969), esp. chaps. 5 and 6.

47. A detailed analysis of the complexities of communist takeovers and the Soviet involvement in them can be found in Thomas T. Hammond, ed., *The Anatomy of Communist Takeovers* (New Haven: Yale University Press, 1975), esp. pp. 229–44 (Mackintosh), 339–68 (Lotarski), 385–98 (Ignotus), and 399–433 (Tigrid).

48. Quoted in Jane Degras, ed., *The Communist International, 1919–1943: Documents* (London: Oxford University Press, 1965), vol. 3, p. 476.

49. For an elaboration on this point, see L. Mekhlis, Y. Varga, and V. Karpinsk, eds., *The U.S.S.R. and the Capitalist Countries* (Moscow: Foreign Languages Publishing House, 1938), esp. chap. 5, "The Soviet Union—the Land of Socialism." The ideas expressed by Varga here were later on utilized by him in his discussion of Eastern Europe after World War II: see, for example, Brzezinski, *The Soviet Bloc*, 31–32.

50. Mao Tse-Tung, *People's Democratic Dictatorship* (London: Lawrence and Wishart, 1950), esp. 5–24.

51. For a detailed analysis of the entire notion of "people's democracy," see, for example, Francis J. Kase, *People's Democracy: A Contribution to the Study of the Communist Theory of State and Revolution* (Leyden, Holland: A. W. Sijthoff, 1968), esp. chaps. 1–5.

52. Jean Elleinstein, *The Stalin Phenomenon* (London: Lawrence and Wishart, 1976), esp. chap. 8.

53. For this and other criticisms, see Rosa Luxemburg, *Leninism or Marxism*, as quoted in Robert V. Daniels, ed., *A Documentary History of Communism* (New York: Vintage Books, 1962), vol. 1, pp. 163–64.

54. Ibid. See Also Luxemburg's criticism of Lenin's methods in "A Western Radical's Response to the Communists," in ibid., 160–64.

55. Carrillo, *Eurocommunism and the State*, esp. 86–91.
56. Ibid., 153–54.
57. Ibid., 102.

3   Marxists and Coalitions in Western Europe

1. For a discussion of this fundamental problem throughout the history of European communism, see David E. Albright, "An Introductory Overview," in his *Communism and Political Systems in Western Europe* (Boulder, Colo.: Westview Press, 1979), 1–43.
2. Some of these points were debated at the seventh special congress of the Soviet (or Russian) Communist party in March 1918; see, for example, *Sed'moi Ekstrennyi S'ezd(b), Mart 1918 Goda* (Moscow: Gosudarstvennoe Izdatel'stvo Politicheskoi Literatury, 1959), esp. 411–12, 443, 449–504.
3. The policy positions of this period were set forth at the first and second Comintern congresses, in *Pervyi Kongress Kominterna* (Moscow: Partiinoe Izdatel'stvo, 1933) and *Der Zweite Kongress der Kommunistischen Internationale* (Hamburg: Carl Hoym Nachf, Louis Cahnbley, 1921).
4. The thesis of the second Comintern congress reflected the organization's concern with anarcho-syndicalism in Southern Europe; see the text of the theses in Jane Degras, ed., *The Communist International, 1919–1943: Documents* (London: Oxford University Press, 1956), vol. 1, pp. 127–36.
5. These issues led to splits in a number of parties; one of the most dramatic was the development in the Norwegian Labor party (DNA), in which the majority faction under Martin Tranmael left the Comintern in November 1923. For the Comintern's position on this, see its letter to all members of the DNA, in ibid., vol. 2, pp. 58–62.
6. I have discussed this controversy in my *The Soviet Communist Party and Scandinavian Communism: The Norwegian Case* (Oslo: Universitetsforlaget, 1973), esp. chap. 2.
7. For a discussion of the Labor party approach, see O. Piatnitskii, "Zur zweiten Org-Beratung der Ki-Sektionen," *Die Kommunistische Internationale*, 2 (March 1926): 122–31.
8. On the topic of bolshevization, see D. Manuilskii, "Über die Frage der Bolshewisierung der Parteien," ibid., 2 (February 1925): 148–57.
9. Trotsky found many aspects of the Comintern's work wanting; see, for example, his critique of the draft program in his *The Third International after Lenin* (New York: Pioneer Publishers, 1957), esp. 3–10, 40–42, and 62–73.
10. See Gilberg, *The Soviet Communist Party and Scandinavian Communism*, 54–57.
11. For a discussion of the role of the Comintern as a splitter in the international movement, see Milorad M. Drachkovitch and Branko Lazitch, "The Third International," in Milorad M. Drachkovitch, ed., *The Revolutionary Internationals, 1864–1943* (Stanford, Calif.: Hoover Institution, 1966), 170–74.
12. This policy is documented in Bela Kun, *Kommunisticheskii Internatsional v Dokumentakh* (Moscow: Partiinoe Izdatel-'stvo, 1933), esp. 966–73; see also Jane Degras, *The Third International, 1919–1943*, vol. 2, pp. 423–24.
13. The very resolution of the ECCI recommending the dissolution of the Comintern smacked of such opportunism; see Degras, *The Communist International*, vol. 3, pp. 476–79.
14. The seventh congress formalized the new line; see *Seventh Congress of the Communist International* (Moscow: Foreign Languages Publishing House, 1939), 570–86.
15. An interesting (if primarily descriptive) discussion of this temporary blooming of internationalism can be found in Verle B. Johnston, *Legions of Babel: The International Brigades in the Spanish Civil War* (University Park: Pennsylvania State University Press, 1967), esp. chaps. 2, 3.

16. The disillusionment which this produced among many leftists is well described by Franz Borkenau in *The Spanish Cockpit: An Eye-Witness Account of the Political and Social Conflicts of the Spanish Civil War* (Ann Arbor: University of Michigan Press, 1963), esp. chap. 5 ("Conclusions").

17. For a vivid description of the alienation felt by many intellectuals over this policy, see Richard Crossman, ed., *The God That Failed* (New York: Bantam Books, 1965).

18. Ibid.

19. Borkenau, for example, stated that "the peculiarities of the situation only arise through the fact that Russia has in every country a party at its orders which claims to be a party of the national proletariat but in reality is completely at the orders of the Moscow Government. Moscow, it is true, proclaims a metaphysical preordained identity of the interests of every proletariat with the interests of the Moscow Government, but this is a proposition that can no longer be taken seriously" (ibid., 289–90). This was a rather widespread feeling on the left in Western Europe in the fall of 1939.

20. Hugh Seton-Watson, *From Lenin to Khrushchev* (New York: Praeger, 1963), esp. chap. 11.

21. Ibid.

22. Ibid.

23. I have summarized a great deal of literature here. Among the best comprehensive works on this subject are still Franz Borkenau, *European Communism* (London: Faber and Faber, 1953); William E. Griffith, *Communism in Europe* (2 vols.; Cambridge, Mass.: MIT Press, 1964); of newer works the best on the subject is David E. Albright, ed., *Communism and Political Systems in Western Europe*.

24. This was especially the case in France and Italy; see, for example, John C. Adams, *The Government of Republican Italy* (Boston: Houghton Mifflin, 1966), and Charles A. Micaud, *Communism and the French Left* (New York: Praeger, 1963).

25. These figures are derived from Derek W. Unwin, *Elections in Western Nations, 1945–1968* (Glasgow: University of Strathclyde, n.d.), 16–18 (Belgium); 64–66 (The Netherlands); 31–32 (France); 52–54 (Italy); 66–68 (Sweden); 24–26 (Denmark); 78–79 (Norway).

26. Derived from Zbigniew K. Brzezinski, *The Soviet Bloc* (New York: Praeger, 1961), 3–41, and *For a Lasting Peace, for a People's Democracy* (journal of the Cominform, printed in Bucharest), especially the year 1948.

27. The Furubotn-Løvlien Debate, for example, can be found in the pages of the NKP daily *Friheten*, and in special documents, e.g., Norges Kommunistiske Parti, *Partiets Konsolidering og Oppgjøret Med Det Annet Sentrum* ("The consolidation of the party and the reckoning with the second center") (Oslo: A/s Norske Forlag Ny Dag, 1950).

28. For a discussion of this period see David E. Albright, *Communism and Political Systems in Western Europe*; see also my *The Soviet Communist Party and Scandinavian Communism*, esp. 135–52.

29. On Finland, see John H. Hodgson, "Finland: The SKP and Electoral Politics," in Albright, *Communism and Political Systems in Western Europe*, 243–67.

30. I have written on Iceland in "Patterns of Nordic Communism," *Problems of Communism* 24 (May–June 1975): 20–35, and in Albright, *Communism and Political Systems in Western Europe*, 267–319.

31. An excellent analysis of contemporary radicalism in France and Italy is Sidney Tarrow, "From Cold War to Historic Compromise: Approaches to French and Italian Radicalism," in Seweryn Bialer and Sophia Sluzar, eds., *Radicalism in the Contemporary Age* (Boulder, Colo.: Westview Press, 1977), vol. 1, chap. 4.

32. Based on a great many country studies and on Albright, *Communism and Political Systems in Western Europe*.

33. *Land og Folk*, August 21, 1968.

34. Gilberg, "Sweden, Norway, Denmark, and Iceland: The Struggle between Nationalism and Internationalism," in Albright, *Communism and Political Systems in Western Europe*, 267–319.

35. Ibid.

36. Ibid.

37. E.g., Frank L. Wilson, "The French CP's Dilemma," *Problems of Communism* 27 (July–August 1978): 1–15.

38. Gilberg, "Sweden, Norway, Denmark, and Iceland," in Albright, *Communism and Political Systems in Western Europe*, 267–313.

39. Ibid.

40. Stephen Hillman, "The Italian CP: Stumbling on the Threshold?," *Problems of Communism* 27 (November–December 1978): 31–49.

41. Per Egil Hegge, "Disunited Front in Norway," *Problems of Communism* 25 (May–June 1976): 49–59.

42. This summary of the main points of Eurocommunism is based upon a volume on the subject, edited by Vernon V. Aspaturian, Jiri Valenta, and Edward Burke, entitled *Eurocommunism between East and West* (Bloomington: Indiana University Press, 1981).

43. The election results can be found in *Thjodviljinn* (Reykjavik), June 26, 27, 1978.

44. *Nordisk kontakt*, No. 16, 1979.

45. This party decision was published in *Morgunbladid* (Reykjavik), October 8, 1968.

46. Ibid., No. 10, 1980.

47. See *Thjodviljinn*, June 26, 27, 1978; see also Finis Herbert Capps, "Iceland," in Richard F. Staar, ed., *1982 Yearbook on International Communist Affairs* (Stanford, Calif.: Hoover Institution Press, 1982), 298–303.

48. Hodgson, "Finland: The SKP and Electoral Politics," in Albright, *Communism and Political Systems in Western Europe*, 243–67.

49. One of the best discussions of this is still William E. Griffith, "European Communism and the Sino-Soviet Rift," in William E. Griffith, ed., *Communism in Europe: Continuity, Change, and the Sino-Soviet Dispute* (Cambridge, Mass.: MIT Press, 1964), vol. 1, chap. 1.

50. For example, see Eric J. Einhorn, "Norway," in Staar, ed., *1982 Yearbook of International Communist Affairs*, 321–22.

51. An excellent discussion of this phenomenon is Klaus Mehnert, *Moscow and the New Left* (Berkeley and Los Angeles: University of California Press, 1977), esp. chap. 3, "The Shock of Paris."

52. The Finnish position on Afghanistan was outlined in *Nordisk Kontakt*, No. 1, 1980; the Icelandic position is described by Eric S. Einhorn in Staar, ed., *1981 Yearbook on International Communist Affairs* (Stanford, Calif.: Hoover Institution Press, 1981), 412–13.

53. The DKP position on Afghanistan was discussed by chairman Jørgen Jensen in *Berlingske Tidende* (Copenhagen), January 25, 1980. The West German communists echoed Soviet justification for the invasion; see *Unsere Zeit* (East Berlin), January 2, 1980.

54. Based on a number of sources, e.g., Richard F. Staar, ed., *1986 Yearbook on International Communist Affairs*, 463–65.

55. As usual, the Italian communists were the most ardent advocates of leftist unity and coalitions. See, for example, *L'Unita*, June 25, 1985, on the presidential elections in Italy.

56. Staar, *1986 Yearbook on International Communist Affairs*, 458–60.

57. Ibid., 547–48.

4   Communists in the Postwar All-Party Coalitions of Eastern Europe

A slightly shortened version of this chapter appeared in Charles Gati, *Hungary and the Soviet Bloc* (Durham: Duke University Press, 1986), 73–99.

1. In the *International Encyclopedia of the Social Sciences* (New York: Macmillan and the Free Press), vol. 2, pp. 524–34, William H. Riker identifies a coalition in the "broad" or "ordinary" sense as "a parliamentary or political grouping less permanent than a party or a faction or an interest group" (p. 524). William A. Gamson provides (p. 530) a far narrower definition, suggesting that a coalition means "the *joint use of resources to determine the outcome of a decision*, where a resource is some weight such that some critical quantity of it in the control of two or more parties to the decision is both necessary and sufficient to determine its outcome. Participants will be said to be using their resources jointly only if they coordinate their deployment of resources with respect to some decision. That is what is meant by saying that they have formed a coalition" (italics in the original). For a critical review of the literature on coalition theories, see Eric C. Brown, *Coalition Theories: A Logical and Empirical Critique* (Beverly Hills: Sage, 1973).

2. See Lawrence C. Dodd, *Coalitions in Parliamentary Government* (Princeton: Princeton University Press, 1976); Sven Groennings, E. W. Kelley, and Michael Leiserson, eds., *The Study of Coalition Behavior: Theoretical Perspectives and Cases from Four Continents* (New York: Holt, Rinehart and Winston, 1970).

3. The slim scholarly literature on the nature of all-party coalition formations includes Alex Vulpius, *Die Allparteienregierung* (Berlin: Metzner, 1957), and Peter H. Merkl, "Coalition Politics in West Germany," in Groennings et al., eds., *The Study of Coalition Behavior*, 13–42. Merkl's chapter provides a brief discussion of the formation of the "great" or "grand" coalition in the Federal Republic in 1966; the government had the support of 447 of the 497 deputies in the Bundestag.

4. The most widely accepted first schema was offered by Hugh Seton-Watson in his *The East European Revolution* (New York: Praeger, 1956), the second by Andrew Gyorgy of the George Washington University. I wish to thank Professor Gyorgy for making part of his course syllabus available to me.

5. Milovan Djilas, *Conversations with Stalin* (New York: Harcourt, Brace & World, 1962), 114.

6. For the purposes of this chapter, I will not treat contrary interpretations offered by the "revisionist" school of historians on the origins of the cold war.

7. For a nuanced, sophisticated study, see Vojtech Mastny, *Russia's Road to the Cold War: Diplomacy, Warfare, and the Politics of Communism, 1941–1945* (New York: Columbia University Press, 1979). For additional, highly interesting details, see also William O. McCagg, Jr., *Stalin Embattled, 1943–1948* (Detroit: Wayne State University Press, 1978). Mastny's view (p. xvii) is worth quoting (because I agree with it):

> The point at issue is Moscow's presumed "grand strategy" in 1941–1945, that is the selection and pursuit of its long-term objectives during and immediately after the war against Germany. What was the vision of the post-war world that inspired Soviet actions at that time? What were the Russian aims in east central Europe especially, the area where both world wars and also the Cold War originated? How were those aims related to the historic Russian interests there? And how did the results measure up to the expectations?
>
> A few standard assumptions have been common to Western authors of both the traditional and revisionist variety: Stalin's determination to regain the territorial acquisitions he had achieved during his pact with Hitler, his quest for a division of Europe into spheres of influence, his desire to establish dependent regimes in neighboring countries. Yet such readings of Stalin's

aspirations, though not necessarily wrong, may be misleading. *While plausible with the benefit of hindsight, they do not always conform to the contemporary evidence without important qualifications.* (Italics added.)

8. Adam Ulam, *Expansion and Coexistence* (New York: Praeger, 1968), 345.

9. For sources, further details, and analysis of these conferences, see my *Hungary and the Soviet Bloc*, 33–37. For an account of how the Communist International prepared other foreign (i.e., non-Soviet) communists for their postwar role in Eastern Europe, see Wolfgang Leonhard, *Child of the Revolution* (Chicago: Regnery, 1958), esp. chap. 5.

10. Gati, *Hungary and the Soviet Bloc*, 28.

11. As quoted in Michael Kraus, "Communist Behavior in Coalition Governments: Czechoslovakia, 1945–1948," a paper delivered at the 1978 annual AAASS convention, p. 9.

12. This paragraph is based on Lynn Etheridge Davis, *The Cold War Begins: Soviet-American Conflict over Eastern Europe* (Princeton: Princeton University Press, 1974), 72–76. On British policy, see Elisabeth Barker, *British Policy in South-East Europe in the Second World War* (London: Macmillan, 1976).

13. Davis, *The Cold War Begins*, 76. (Italics added.)

14. Barker, *British Policy in South-East Europe*, 267–68. (Italics added.)

15. For further details and analysis, see my *Hungary and the Soviet Bloc*, 28–33, and Mastny, *Russia's Road to the Cold War*, 207–12.

16. Ibid.

17. The Yalta agreements are reprinted in Diane Shaver Clemens, *Yalta* (London: Oxford University Press, 1970), 293–311.

18. Ibid., 307.

19. See Davis, *The Cold War Begins*, 335 ff., and Robert Lee Wolff, *The Balkans in Our Time* (Cambridge: Harvard University Press, 1956), 223–33 and 267–74.

20. For a fascinating account of the Beneš-Stalin discussion, see Vojtech Mastny, "The Beneš-Stalin-Molotov Conversations in December, 1943: New Documents," in *Jahrbücher für Geschichte Osteuropas*, vol. 20, 1972, pp. 367–402.

21. As quoted by Richard Hiscocks, *Poland: Bridge for the Abyss?* (London: Oxford University Press, 1963), 103.

22. *Délmagyarország* (Szeged), December 5, 1944.

23. *Izvestia* (Moscow), November 13, 1945.

24. Boris Ponomarev, "Demokraticheskie prebrazovania v osvobozhdennykh Strankh Evropy" [Democratic transformation in the liberated countries of Europe], *Bol'shevik* (Moscow), 22, no. 6 (March 1946): 121.

25. These two governments were so "broadly" based that even some of the most ardent supporters of Nazi Germany were indirectly "represented" in them. I am referring to the notorious Romanian Iron Guard and the Hungarian Arrow Cross movements, whose members were now actively recruited by and enlisted in large numbers in the Romanian and Hungarian CP's. An affidavit showing how the Hungarian CP offered exemption from prosecution for wartime criminal activity to the Arrow Cross smallfry in exchange for CP membership is in the author's possession.

26. As quoted by Paul E. Zinner, *Communist Strategy and Tactics in Czechoslovakia, 1918–1948* (New York: Praeger, 1963), 105.

27. Ibid., 104–5.

28. Seton-Watson, *East European Revolution*, 171.

29. On the politics of Eastern Europe in general and the functioning of all-party governments in particular, see sources already cited as well as Zbigniew K. Brzezinski, *The Soviet Bloc* (New York: Praeger, 1961; rev. ed.); Thomas T. Hammond, ed., *The Anatomy of Communist Takeovers* (New Haven: Yale University Press, 1975); Stephen

D. Kertesz, *The Fate of East Central Europe* (Notre Dame: University of Notre Dame Press, 1956); R. V. Burks, "Eastern Europe," in Cyril E. Black and Thomas P. Thornton, eds., *Communism and Revolution* (Princeton: Princeton University Press, 1969), 77–116. For the most important contemporary communist evaluations, see Eugen Varga, "Demokratiia novogo tipa" [Democracy of a new type], *Mirovoe Khoziaistvo i Mirovaia Politika*, March 1947, and Joseph Revai, "On the Character of a 'People's Democracy,'" *Foreign Affairs*, October 1949. (In a candid statement, Revai —speaking of the post-1944 period—observed: "The Party did not possess a unified, clarified, elaborated attitude in respect to the character of the People's Democracy and its future development.") Studies of the individual countries of Eastern Europe during the period under discussion here are too numerous to list. I should note, however, that the various tables in this study are based on them, on the works listed above, and on a brief Hungarian summary of regional developments: Emil Borsi, *Az europai nepi demokratikus forradalmak* [The European people's democratic revolutions] (Budapest: Kossuth, 1975).

30. Seton-Watson, *East European Revolution*, 169–70.
31. Ibid., 170.
32. Dodd, *Coalitions in Parliamentary Government*, 195–204.
33. Ibid., 42–43.
34. Ibid., 50.
35. Zinner, *Communist Strategy and Tactics in Czechoslovakia*, 116.
36. Hiscocks, *Poland*, 99–100.
37. This is not meant to imply that neither political differences nor personal rivalries surfaced in the communist parties. Especially in Poland and Romania, there was a clash between those who spent the war years in the Soviet Union (the "Muscovites") and the home communists. In Czechoslovakia and Hungary, too, there were early debates about the pace though not the eventual direction of the CP's approach to power. On the whole, the home communists could not understand why they should not at once establish the "dictatorship of the proletariat"; why, indeed, the parties' ultimate goals had to be postponed. With the possible exception of the "Patraşcanu affair" in Romania, however, the issue was quickly and rather easily resolved everywhere and the Muscovites' approach prevailed. Compared to the seemingly permanent feuds that characterized the noncommunist parties, then, the CP's possessed considerable internal cohesion. (I regret that, because of space limitations, I cannot further elaborate on this and some other points with respect to the fifth characteristic of the postwar all-party coalitions [as identified at the beginning of this chapter], namely, the composition, role, strategy, weaknesses, and strengths of the CP's as they entered these postwar governments for the first time.)

5   Marxists and Coalitions in Latin America

1. See Karl Marx and Friedrich Engels, *Materiales para la historia de América Latina* (Mexico City: Siglo Veintiuno, 1975), 28–32.
2. Victor Alba, *Politics and the Labor Movement in Latin America* (Stanford: Stanford University Press, 1968), 120.
3. As quoted in Enrique Dickmann, *Recuerdos de un militante socialista* (Buenos Aires: Vanguardia, 1949), 84–85.
4. From Eduardo Jaurena, ed., *Furgoni: Una vida dedicada al ideal* (Montevideo: Comisión Ejecutiva Nacional, 1950), 67–68, as quoted in Luis E. Aguilar, ed., *Marxism in Latin America* (New York: Knopf, 1968), 83.
5. Ibid., 6.
6. See the discussion of Sheldon B. Liss, *Marxist Thought in Latin America* (Berkeley and

Los Angeles: University of California Press, 1984), 23–30.

7. Miguel Jorrin and John D. Martz, *Latin-American Political Thought and Ideology* (Chapel Hill: University of North Carolina Press, 1970), 275.

8. Rollie Poppino, *International Communism in Latin America: A History of the Movement, 1917–1963* (New York: Free Press of Glencoe, 1964), 152–53.

9. The eight were Argentina, Brazil, Chile, Colombia, Cuba, Ecuador, Mexico, and Uruguay.

10. Quoted in Alba, *Labor Movement*, 123.

11. Aguilar, *Marxism*, 25.

12. "Struggles of the Communist Parties of South and Caribbean America," *Communist International*, 12, no. 10 (20 May 1935): 576.

13. *Seventh Congress of the Communist International* (Moscow: Foreign Languages Publishing House, 1939), 302, as cited by Aguilar.

14. Quoted in Robert J. Alexander, *Communism in Latin America* (New Brunswick: Rutgers University Press, 1957), 192.

15. Ibid., 279.

16. Aguilar, *Marxism*, 37.

17. Carlos Salazar Montejo, *Caducidad de una estrategia* (La Paz: Liga Socialista Revolucionaria de Bolivia, 1961), 64–65.

18. Useful accounts which have benefited from materials now available through the Freedom of Information Act include Richard H. Immerman, *The CIA in Guatemala: The Foreign Policy of Intervention* (Austin: University of Texas Press, 1982); also Stephen Kinzer and Stephen Schlesinger, *Bitter Fruit: The Untold Story of the American Coup in Guatemala* (New York: Doubleday, 1982). Also see the two-part report on Guatemala in *NACLA Report on the Americas*, 17, nos. 1 and 2 (1983).

19. Quoted by José Barbeito, *Realidad y masificación* (Caracas: Ediciones Nuevo Orden, 1965), 243, as cited in Aguilar, *Marxism*, 42.

20. For an English version of *La Guerra de Guerrillas*, see Ernesto Guevara, *Guerrilla Warfare*, trans. by J. P. Morray with prefatory note by I. F. Stone (New York: Grove Press, 1961).

21. See the discussion by Guevara in his "Cuba, excepción histórica vanguardia en la lucha anti-colonialista," *Verde Olivo*, 9 April 1961, 26.

22. Guevara, "Man and Socialist in Cuba," letter to Carlos Quijano, in John Gerassi, ed., *Venceremos! The Speeches and Writings of Ché Guevara* (New York: Macmillan, 1968), 398.

23. Liss, *Marxist Thought*, 264.

24. A student of Louis Althusser who had first visited in Havana in 1961, Debray's work was published in French in 1966. A 200,000 copy Spanish printing by Cuba appeared in January 1967. For the English source, see Régis Debray, *Revolution in the Revolution? Armed Struggle and Political Struggle*, trans. Bobbye Ortiz (New York: Grove Press, 1967), 101.

25. Ibid., 31.

26. John D. Martz, "Doctrine and Dilemmas of the Latin American 'New Left,'" *World Politics* 22, no. 2 (January 1970): 188.

27. Luis F. de la Puente Uceda, "The Peruvian Revolution," *Monthly Review*, 17, no. 6 (November 1965): 25–26.

28. John Gerassi, ed., *Revolutionary Priest: The Complete Writings and Messages of Camilo Torres* (New York: Random House, 1971), 29.

29. Liss, *Marxist Thought*, 160.

30. Jay Mallin, "Ché Guevara: Some Documentary Puzzles at the End of a Long Journey," *Journal of Inter-American Studies*, 10, no. 1 (January 1968): 83.

31. Luid E. Aguilar, "Régis Debray: Where Logic Failed," *The Reporter*, 37 (28 December 1967): 32.

32. Joint declaration of the Communist parties of Colombia and Venezuela, "Dilemma of Leadership: The Communist Party," in Aguilar, *Marxism*, 227–29.

33. Jorge Abelardo Ramos, "Los peligros del empiricismo en la revolución latinoamericana," in *La lucha por un partido revolucionario* (Buenos Aires: Ediciones Pampa y Cielo, 1964), 109.

34. Allende as quoted in Régis Debray, *The Chilean Revolution: Conversations with Allende* (New York: Vintage Books, 1971), 117.

35. See Salvador Allende, *Chile's Road to Socialism* (Baltimore: Penguin Books, 1973).

36. Liss, *Marxist Thought*, 102.

37. Allende, *Chile's Road*, 201.

38. Quoted in Cole Blasier, *The Giant's Rival: The U.S.S.R. and Latin America* (Pittsburgh: University of Pittsburgh Press, 1983), 86.

39. For a useful retrospective by a number of leading Chilean politicians, see Federico G. Gil, Ricardo Lagos, and Henry A. Landsberger, eds., *Chile at the Turning Point: Lessons of the Socialist Years, 1970–1973* (Philadelphia: ISHI, 1979).

40. Quoted in Blasier, *Giant's Rival*, 86.

41. For 1978 and the Venezuelan left, see John D. Martz, "The Minor Parties," in Howard R. Penniman, ed., *Venezuela at the Polls: The National Elections of 1978* (Washington: American Enterprise Institute, 1980), 154–71. For an early overview of the 1983 contest, see John D. Martz, "The Crisis of Venezuelan Democracy," *Current History*, 83, no. 490 (February 1984): 73–78, 89.

42. Carlos Fonseca Amador, ed., *Ideario politico de Augusto César Sandino* (Managua: Secretaria Nacional de Propaganda, FSLN, 1980).

43. John A. Booth, *The End and the Beginning: The Nicaraguan Revolution* (Boulder: Westview Press, 1982), 216.

44. David Scott Palmer, "Peru," in Jack Hopkins, ed., *Latin America and Caribbean Contemporary Record, 1981–1982* (New York: Holmes and Meier, 1983), 344–46.

45. For those addicted to such record-keeping, the IU members were the Partido Comunista Peruano (PCP), Unión Democrática Popular (UDP), Unión Nacional de la Izquierda Revolucionaria (UNIR), Partido Socialista Revolucionario (PSR), Partido Comunista Revolucionario—Clase Obrero (PCR-CO), and the Frente de Obreros, Campesinos, y Estudiantes Populares (FOCEP). The Trotskyists included the Partido Socialista de Trabajadores (PST), the Partido de Trabajadores Revolucionarios (PTR), and the Partido de Obreros Marxistas Revolucionarios (POMR).

46. Palmer, "Peru," in *Latin America and Caribbean Record, 1982–83*, 396.

47. The text appears in English translation in ibid., 403–11. The original appeared on 5 March 1983 in Lima's *El Comercio*.

48. A revised but controversial account is Mario Vargas Llosa, "Inquest in the Andes," *New York Times Magazine*, 31 July 1983.

49. *Caretas* (Lima), 20 September 1982.

50. David P. Werlich, "Peru: The Shadow of the Shining Path," *Current History*, 82, no. 490 (February 1984): 90.

51. *Washington Report on the Hemisphere*, 5, no. 2 (16 October 1984): 3.

52. Blasier, *Giant's Rival*, 95.

6   Vietnamese Communism and the Strategy of the United Front

1. Lenin's theses are printed in V. I. Lenin, *Selected Works* (English Edition, Moscow: Foreign Languages Publishing House, 1952), vol. 2, pt. 2.

2. Ho Chi Minh's conversion to Leninism is discussed in his "The Path to Leninism," contained in Ho Chi Minh, *Selected Works* (Hanoi: Foreign Languages Press, 1960–1962), vol. 4, pp. 448–50. In 1924 he presented a report on conditions in

Indochina at the fifth Comintern congress in Moscow. See Ho Chi Minh, *Selected Writings* (Hanoi: Foreign Languages Press, 1977), 24–36.

3. There are signs that his original realization of the global character of colonial oppression came through his experience at sea, where his travels took him to seaports along the Asian and African coast, as well as to Europe and the United States. For his comment about the need for communist leadership over the Asian revolution, see *Selected Writings*, 36.

4. The League and its programs have been subjected to searching analysis by Western scholars in recent years. For a penetrating study based on an exhaustive use of sources, see Huynh Kim Khanh, *Vietnamese Communism, 1925–1945* (Ithaca: Cornell University Press, 1982), 63–90.

5. The League's efforts to establish alliances with other anticolonial organizations in Vietnam are discussed in my *The Comintern and Vietnamese Communism* (Athens: Ohio University Center for International Studies, 1975), 8–10. For a more recent assessment see Khanh, *Vietnamese Communism*, 92–93. Apparently Ho had attempted to prepare for this problem while still in Moscow and had asked the Ukrainian Comintern leader, Dmitri Manuilsky, what should be done if no nationalist movement existed. Manuilsky's somewhat perfunctory reply had been to form your own. See Robert C. North and Xenia I. Eudin, *Soviet Russia and the East, 1920–1927* (Stanford: Stanford University Press, 1957), 326–28, n. 9.

6. On the class composition of the League and the training of its members, see Khanh, *Vietnamese Communism*, 64–66.

7. The turnabout had taken place at the sixth congress of the Comintern, held in the summer of 1928. See Khanh, *Vietnamese Communism*, 105–6, and Duiker, *The Comintern*, 29–30.

8. An English language version of the Party's political thesis, approved in October, is in *An Outline History of the Viet Nam Workers' Party* (Hanoi: Foreign Languages Press, 1970), 163–72. For analysis, see Khanh, *Vietnamese Communism*, 109–10, and Duiker, *The Comintern*, 18–19. Communist historians in Hanoi today are critical of the narrow class component of the ICP at that time. For example, see Tran Huy Lieu, *Les Soviets du Nghe Tinh* (Hanoi, 1960), 51–52, and Van Tao, "Tim hieu qua trinh hinh thanh va phat trien cua mat tran dan toc thong nhat Viet Nam" (Searching for the process of formation and development of the Vietnamese national united front), in *Nghien Cuu lich Su* (Historical Research), 1 (March 1959): 32; hereafter NCLS.

9. For Ho's views on the role of the peasantry in the Vietnamese revolution, see my *The Communist Road to Power in Vietnam* (Boulder: Westview Press, 1981), 21–23. Unfortunately Ho wrote sparingly on doctrinal issues, and scholars must piece together his views on the basis of flimsy evidence.

10. Duiker, *The Comintern*, 24; Khanh, *Vietnamese Communism*, 143.

11. Ironically, the ICP's only real effort to establish links with other groups was in Saigon, where Party operatives cooperated with a small Trotskyite faction. This informal alliance was broken off at the insistence of the Comintern in 1937.

12. The Party had approved a continuation of the existing front strategy at its first national congress, held in Macao in March 1935. When the results of the Comintern congress were brought to Vietnam, a Party plenum held in July 1936 made the switch.

13. Symptomatic of the Party's rising interest in the peasants was Truong Chinh's and Vo Nguyen Giap's pamphlet *The Peasant Question*, published at that time. The authors did not embrace a Maoist view of the role of the peasants in the Vietnamese revolution, but they did declare that peasants could become a reliable ally of the working class. A translation of the pamphlet by Christine Pelzer White is available as Data Paper No. 94, Southeast Asia Program, Cornell University, January 1974.

14. For Le Duan's analysis of this period, see Tran Van Dinh, ed., *This Nation and Socialism Are One: Selected Writings of Le Duan* (Chicago: Vanguard Books, 1976),

20–21.

15. The need for a cooperative effort with the revolutionary movements in Laos and Cambodia had been recognized by the Comintern in 1930. Until World War II, however, virtually no radical activity took place in either of these French protectorates. The potential role of the tribal minorities had been given cursory attention by the ICP in the 1930s. For a discussion of ICP minority policy, see Pierre Rousset, *Communisme et nationalisme vietnamien* (Editions Galilee, 1978), 201–3.

16. Tran Huy Lieu, *Lich su tam muoi nam chong Phap* (A history of eighty years of resistance against the French) (Hanoi: Van Su Dia, 1958), vol. 2, p. 70.

17. Ibid., 71. Here, of course, the ICP was emulating the experience of the CCP in China, which had decided to modify its own land program in the interest of forming a broad alliance of all anti-Japanese groups under Party leadership. Ho may have learned this lesson during a visit to Yan'an in 1938, but may also have been impressed by the results of the peasant revolt in Vietnam in 1930, when peasant radicalism had alienated the urban bourgeoisie.

18. The tension rose during the summer months, when Ho Chi Minh was in France to attend the conference at Fontainebleau. Whether his presence in Vietnam could have avoided the split is problematical.

19. For a discussion of Party policy, see Van Tao "Tim hieu moi quan he guia 'hai mat dau tranh chinh tri va quan su' va 'ba mui giap cong' trong phong trao cach mang Viet Nam" (Searching for the relationship between "two forms of struggle, political and military" and "three points of attack" in the Vietnamese revolutionary movement), NCLS, 89 (August 1966): 17–20.

20. M. N., "May net lon ve phong trao cong nhan Saigon tu 1945 den 1954" (A few major features of the workers' movement in Saigon from 1945 to 1954), NCLS, 2 (February 1967): 3–12. The author cited such factors as apathy, inappropriate slogans, French oppression, and the rise of yellow unions. For an internal Party document on the weakness of the municipal apparatus in Hanoi, see U.S. Department of State, *Working Paper on North Viet-Nam's Role in the War in South Viet-Nam* (Washington, D.C., 1968), Appendix Item No. 1.

21. The program of the new front was similar to that of its predecessors, emphasizing peace, independence, and a unity of all anticolonial groups in Vietnam.

22. For example, see Ngo Tien Chat, "Truyen thong dau tranh anh dung cua nhan dan cac dan toc Tay Bac tu sau cach mang thang tam den cuoc chong my cuu nuoc nien nay" (The tradition of heroic struggle of the peoples of the Northwest since the August Revolution to the anti-U.S. national salvation struggle today), NCLS, 95 (February 1967).

23. Edwin E. Moise, *Land Reform in China and North Vietnam* (Chapel Hill: University of North Carolina Press, 1983).

24. The formation of separate parties also reflected the rising sensitivity to Vietnamese domination among radical groups in both countries. The ICP leadership responded to the problem by introducing cosmetic changes while maintaining the substance of Party direction over the two new organizations.

25. This movement was discussed in Tran Van Giau's *Mien Nam giu vung thanh dong* (The South on the road to victory) (Hanoi: Khoa Hoc, 1964), vol. 1, pp. 86–90.

26. For a recent study of Party relations with the sects, see Jayne Werner, "Vietnamese Communism and Religious Sectarianism," in William S. Turley, ed., *Vietnamese Communism in Comparative Perspective* (Boulder: Westview Press, 1980), 107–36.

27. Ho Chi Minh, *Selected Writings*, 188.

28. For a brief discussion and sources, see my *The Communist Road*, 193–94.

29. A good example is Nguyen Huu Tho, a lawyer who became involved in protest activities against the French in Saigon during the early 1950s. He later became acting president of the Socialist Republic of Vietnam and is currently chairman of the

National Assembly. Another key figure was Huynh Tan Phat, a Saigon architect once active in the Democratic party. He is now president of the Central Committee of the Fatherland Front.

30. For a discussion of the role played by these two parties, see Douglas Pike, *Viet Cong* (Cambridge: MIT Press, 1966), 194–98.

31. One well-known exposition of this view was George McT. Kahin and John W. Lewis, *The United States in Vietnam* (New York: Dell, 1967), 119.

32. For a brief discussion and sources, see my *The Communist Road*, 107.

33. An indication of Hanoi's attitude toward the Buddhist movement appeared in the periodical *Thong Nhat* (March–June 1972). See the diary of lawyer Dinh Thao, translated in Joint Publications Research Service 57,751, Translations on North Vietnam 1924. Hereinafter JPRS.

34. A discussion of the Party's urban policy in the South, and the disappointment of some Party leaders in the results, appears in my *The Communist Road*, 252–54. Also see Gio Nom, "The Three-year Struggle of Southern Workers Reviewed," in NCLS, 112 (July 1968): 6–18. This source concedes that the effectiveness of Party work among students and within the Buddhist movement declined in 1967, but remained high among urban workers.

35. *Vietnam Documents and Research Notes* (U.S. Mission in Saigon), document no. 45 (October 1968), "The Process of Revolution and the General Uprising," 12.

36. For his background, see "Diary of Trinh Dinh Thao," cited in note 33. For further comment on the ANDPF and a short list of its members, see Huynh Van Tieng, "The Alliance of Peaceful and Democratic National Forces Crushes the Social Structure Set Up by U.S. Neocolonialism in South Vietnam," in *Cuu Quoc* (July 14, 1968), in JPRS 46,538, Translations on North Vietnam 442.

37. There is persuasive evidence from a variety of sources that recruitment efforts were less effective after 1968. For a comment, see my *The Communist Road*, 277.

38. Official sources in Hanoi claimed that the 1975 offensive included an urban uprising, but the case is a weak one.

39. For example, Truong Chinh referred to the concept of a "global united front" in a speech to the third congress of the Fatherland Front in 1971.

40. The official view in Hanoi is that leadership of the Vietnamese national liberation movement passed from the bourgeoisie to the working class with the formation of the Indochinese Communist party in 1930.

41. The term was later changed to the "Peoples' Democratic State." For a discussion of these issues, see David W. P. Elliott, "Revolutionary Re-integration: A Comparison of the Foundation of Post-Liberation Political Systems in North Vietnam and China" (Ph.D. diss., Cornell University, 1976), pt. 2, chap. 1.

42. For an extended discussion of the regime's attitude toward intellectuals, Catholics, and the national minorities, see ibid., pt. 2, chap. 1. Hanoi's effort to combine Chinese mass line techniques with Leninist reliance on the guiding role of the Party is analyzed in David W. P. Elliott, "Institutionalizing the Revolution: Vietnam's Search for a Model of Development," in William S. Turley, *Vietnamese Communism*, 199–224.

43. The best recent study of this issue is Edwin E. Moise, *Land Reform*, chap. 11.

44. Elliott, *Revolutionary*, 209–12, 223–25. Also see "Vietnamese Catholicism—1983," in *Vietnam Courier* (1-1984), for a recent view from Hanoi.

45. William S. Turley, "War and Political Change in the Democratic Republic of Vietnam," paper presented at the annual meeting of the American Political Science Association, 4 September 1975.

46. Despite such careful handling, the Party evidently encountered some difficulties in mobilizing support from the ethnic Chinese community for the war effort. See my "Ethnic Minorities and the Growth of the People's Army of Vietnam," in DeWitt C. Ellinwood and Cynthia H. Enloe, eds., *Ethnicity and the Military in Asia*, in *Journal of*

Asian Affairs, 3, no. 2 (Fall 1978): 87.

47. Significantly, according to press reports, most of those accused were also of Chinese extraction.

48. For example, see the article in *Nguoi Xay Dung* (The Builder), November 1978. Refugee accounts, however, sometimes contended that discrimination against people of middle class background was frequent. See Bruce Grant, *The Boat People: An "Age" Investigation* (Harmondsworth: Penguin, 1979), 103.

49. *Un Document du Parti Communiste Vietnamien Concernant l'Eglise Catholique*, Echange France Asie, Dossier No. 72 (February 1982).

50. Official sources today concede that many farmers in the Delta, rendered prosperous by the Saigon regime's land reform, have resisted collectivization. For a discussion, see Phan Quang, "Nguyen Van Thieu's Program of Agricultural Development and the Present Situation in Agriculture," in *Vietnam Courier* (12-1983): 14–17.

51. Whether the regime had deliberately attempted to destroy the economic power of the Chinese community in Vietnam is a controversial point. The evidence suggests that initially the program of nationalization was directed only incidentally against the overseas Chinese. Once it became obvious that many Vietnamese residents of Chinese extraction gave their primary loyalty to Beijing, the Party decided to permit, or even encourage, the departure of those Chinese hostile to the regime.

52. *Quan Doi Nhan Dan*, 26 September 1983. Also see Nguyen Vinh, "Win Victory for Socialism in the Current Struggle between the Two Paths in Our Country," in *Tap Chi Cong San* (Communist Review) (September 1983).

53. For a recent discussion of the regime's policy toward Catholics, see the article in *Vietnam Courier* cited in note 44 above. The case of Chan Tinh is discussed in an article entitled "A Collapsed Bridge," in *Far Eastern Economic Review*, March 15, 1984. The destruction of the United Buddhist Church in South Vietnam and its forcible integration into the state-supported United Buddhist Association of Vietnam, which led to the death of the prominent Buddhist monk Thich Tri Thu early in 1984 is discussed in *Indochina Journal*, 7 (June 1984): 1–4. For an overall treatment of such issues, see Ginnetta Sagan and Stephen Denney, *Violations of Human Rights in the Socialist Republic of Vietnam* (Atherton, Calif: Aurora Foundation, 1983).

53. The statement was by Nguyen Khac Vien, president of the National Academy of Sciences of the SRV. For a French translation of his public criticism of the regime, see Georges Boudarel et al., eds., *La Bureaucratie au Vietnam* (Paris: l'Harmattan, 1983), 113–19.

54. Hoang Tung, "Some Views on Thoroughly Understanding the Resolution of the Fourth Party Central Committee Plenum," in *Nhan Dan*, August 30, 1983.

55. Ibid.

7   The Coalition Strategies and Tactics of Indian Communism

1. Research for this paper was supported by the Central Fund for Research, College of the Liberal Arts, Pennsylvania State University. For accounts of the general history and development of Indian communism, see: Gene D. Overstreet and Marshall Wind-miller, *Communism in India* (Berkeley and Los Angeles: University of California Press, 1959); Victor M. Fic, *Peaceful Transition to Communism in India* (Bombay: Nachiketa Publications, 1969); Bhabani Sen Gupta, *Communism in Indian Politics* (New York: Columbia University Press, 1972) and *Communist Party of India (Marxist): Promises, Prospects, and Problems* (New Delhi: Young Asia, 1979); and Mohan Ram, *Maoism in India* (Delhi: Vikas, 1971). For a yearly summary of Communist party activities in India, see Richard F. Staar, ed., *Yearbook on International Communist Affairs* (Stanford, Calif.: Hoover Institution Press).

2. John Patrick Haithcox, *Communism and Nationalism in India; M. N. Roy and Comintern Policy, 1920–1939* (Princeton, N. J.: Princeton University Press, 1971), 21.

3. For a review of the forces leading to the fragmentation of the communist movement in India, see: Harry Gelman, "The Communist Party of India: Sino-Soviet Battleground," in A. Doak Barnett, ed., *Communist Strategies in Asia* (New York: Praeger, 1963); Mohan Ram, *Indian Communism: Split within a Split* (New Delhi: Vikas Publications, 1968); T. R. Sharma, "1964 Split in the Communist Party of India," *Modern Asian Studies*, 10, no. 3 (July 1976): 349–60; T. R. Sharma, "Indian Communist Party Split of 1964: The Role of Factionalism and Leadership Rivalry," *Studies in Comparative Communism*, 11, no. 4 (Winter 1978): 388–409; John B. Wood, "Observations on the Indian Communist Party Split," *Pacific Affairs*, 38 (Spring 1965): 47–63.

4. Walter Andersen, "India," in Richard F. Staar, ed., *Yearbook on International Communist Affairs 1980* (Stanford: Hoover Institution, 1980), 251; and Communist Party of India, *Documents of the Twelfth Congress of the Communist Party of India* (New Delhi: New Age Press, 1982), 129–30.

5. *People's Democracy*, January 14, 1979, p. 11, and Staar, ed., *Yearbook*, 1986, p. 183.

6. Asish K. Roy, "India's Third Communist Party," *Institute for Defense Studies and Analysis Journal*, 8, no. 1 (July/September 1975): 39–69; and Asish Kumar Roy, "Strategies of Maoist Movements in India and China," *Institute for Defense Studies and Analysis Journal*, 8, no. 1 (July/September 1975): 518–39.

7. For CPI membership data, see Paul R. Brass and Marcus F. Franda, eds., *Radical Politics in South Asia* (Cambridge, Mass.: MIT Press, 1973), 22; and Staar, ed., *Yearbook*, 1986, p. 183.

8. For a discussion of problems facing the communist movement in India, see the Report of the Plenum on Organization called by the Central Committee of the CPM, *People's Democracy*, January 14, 1979, pp. 1–14.

9. For a discussion of the regional support base of the communists in India, see Brass and Franda chapters 2 (Kerala), 3 (West Bengal), 5 (Andhra), and 6 (Bihar); John Wood, ed., *State Politics in Contemporary India: Crisis or Continuity* (Boulder, Colo.: Westview Press, 1984), chaps. 4 and 5; and Atul Kohli, *The State and Poverty in India: The Politics of Reform* (Cambridge: Cambridge University Press, 1987), chap. 3.

10. Bhabani Sen Gupta, "Peasant Mobilisation in West Bengal," *Perspective* (January 1978): 15–18.

11. Susanne Hoeber Rudolph and Lloyd I. Rudolph, "The Centrist Future of Indian Politics," *Asian Survey*, 22, no. 6 (June 1980): 576–79; and *In Pursuit of Lakshmi: The Political Economy of the Indian State* (Chicago: University of Chicago Press, 1987).

12. *People's Democracy*, January 14, 1979, p. 11; and Staar, ed., *Yearbook*, 1986.

13. Rudolph and Rudolph, "The Centrist Future," 585–92.

14. Ibid., 586.

15. Kathleen Gough, "Imperialism and Revolutionary Potential in South Asia," in Kathleen Gough and Hari P. Sharma, eds., *Imperialism and Revolution in South Asia* (New York: Monthly Review Press, 1973), 13; see also Donald S. Zagoria, "The Ecology of Peasant Communism in India," *American Political Science Review*, 65, no. 1 (March 1971): 144–60; and Donald S. Zagoria, "Kerala and West Bengal," *Problems of Communism*, 22 (January–February 1973): 16–27.

16. Rudolph and Rudolph, "The Centrist Future," 592–94.

17. See Myron Weiner, *India at the Polls* (Washington, D.C.: American Enterprise Institute, 1978), 67–88; and Harold Gould, "The Second Coming: The 1980 Elections in India's Hindi Belt," *Asian Survey*, 20, no. 6 (June 1980): 595–616.

18. Brass and Franda, *Radical Politics*, 45.

19. Overstreet and Windmiller, *Communism in India*, 531.

20. Gene D. Overstreet, "Leadership in the Indian Communist Party," in Richard L. Park and Irene Tinker, eds., *Leadership and Political Institutions in India* (New Delhi:

Oxford University Press, 1960), 231.

21. Haithcox, *Communism and Nationalism*, 41, 60.

22. Ibid., 129.

23. Ibid., 153.

24. Robin Jeffrey, "Matriliny, Marxism, and the Birth of the Communist Party in Kerala, 1930–1940," *Journal of Asian Studies*, 35 (November 1978): 86, Brass and Franda, *Radical Politics*, 286.

25. Haithcox, *Communism and Nationalism*, 212.

26. Ibid., 235.

27. Ibid., 234–35.

28. Brass and Franda, *Radical Politics*, 8–9.

29. M. Windmiller, "Indian Communism and the New Soviet Line," *Pacific Affairs*, 29 (December 1956): 350.

30. Marcus F. Franda, *Radical Politics in West Bengal* (Cambridge, Mass.: MIT Press, 1971), 45–52.

31. Mohan Ram, "The Communist Movement in Andhra," in Brass and Franda, *Radical Politics*, 295.

32. Ibid., 297–98.

33. Ibid., 299.

34. Brass and Franda, *Radical Politics*, 126–27.

35. Franda, *Radical Politics in West Bengal*, 54–58.

36. Mohan Ram in Brass and Franda, *Radical Politics*, 301.

37. Ibid., 309.

38. For a detailed summary of this period, see Bhabani Sen Gupta, *Communism in Indian Politics*; and Mohan Ram, *Indian Communism*.

39. For copies of documents which played a major role in party disputes up to 1956, see Democratic Research Service, Bombay, *Indian Communist Party Documents* (Bombay: Kanada Press, 1957); for later periods see *New Age* and *Party Life*, published by the CPI.

40. See Bhabani Sen Gupta, "India's Rival Communist Models," *Problems of Communism*, 22 (January–February 1973): 1–15.

41. Staar, ed., *Yearbook 1980*, 251.

42. "Indian Communist Movement Today," *Journal of Contemporary Asia*, 8, no. 4 (1978): 537, 542.

43. Francine R. Frankel, *India's Political Economy, 1947–1977* (Princeton, N.J.: Princeton University Press, 1978), 405–6.

44. Ibid., 408–9.

45. Ibid., 456.

46. Ibid., 463–64.

47. Ibid., 539.

48. For an analysis of the emergency, see Henry C. Hart, ed., *Indira Gandhi's India* (Boulder, Colo.: Westview Press, 1976).

49. *The Times of India* (Bombay), December 24, 1976.

50. For an analysis of the 1977 election, see Myron Weiner, *India at the Polls*.

51. Bhabani Sen Gupta, "Indian Politics and the Communist Party (Marxist)," *Problems of Communism*, 27 (September–October 1979): 3–4.

52. Mohan Ram and Jayanta Sarkar, "Red Star Over Bengal," *Far East Economic Review*, July 8, 1977, pp. 27–29.

53. This debate was carried on in the pages of *Mainstream* beginning in April 1977 and continuing into 1978 and 1979. The series began April 1977 with the following articles: N. G. N., "Communist Unity: Problems and Perspectives," *Mainstream*, April 28, 1977, pp. 6–8; N. K. Sarkar, "Left Unity: Problems and Perspectives," *Mainstream*, April 30, 1977, pp. 9, 30. The debate turned rapidly into a polemic between

CPI and CPM leaders. The issues in dispute were summarized by Bhabani Sen Gupta, "Left Unity Is Still a Sour (and Somewhat Faded) Dream," *Perspective*, 2, no. 1 (August 1978): 4–8.

54. See Communist Party of India (Marxist), "Political resolution, adopted at the tenth Congress of the Communist Party of India (Marxist), April 2 to April 8, 1978, Jullundur," (Communist Party of India [Marxist] , New Deli, 1978); Communist Party of India, "Political resolution: Adopted by the eleventh Congress of the Communist Party of India, Bhakna Nagar, Bhatinda, 31 March to 7 April 1978" (New Delhi: Communist Party of India, 1978).

55. See CPI Political Resolution, 21–22.

56. The polemics between the CPI and CPM were carried out openly in party journals and newspapers. See *New Age* during this period for the CPI case and *People's Democracy* for the CPM case. See also: Mohit Sen, "CPI, Congress, and Janata," *Mainstream*, April 1, 1978, pp. 6–7; Satyalpal Dang, "CPI-CPM Relations," *Mainstream*, July 22, 1978, pp. 12–14; Mohit Sen, "Namboodiripad's Gauntlet," *Mainstream*, December 9, 1978, pp. 29–30, 34.

57. See *People's Democracy*, April 16, 1978, p. 9.

58. Chandra Sen, "CPI-M Left Unity Prospects," *Mainstream*, April 21, 1978, p. 6; Satyapal Dang, "Communist Unity; The Road Ahead," *Mainstream*, June 16, 1979, pp. 15–17; Satyapal Dang, "Left Unity: New Compulsions," *Mainstream*, August 11, 1979, pp. 97–99; "A Healthy Development," *Link*, April 20, 1980, p. 14; "Left and Election," *Link*, June 1, 1980, p. 16.

59. For responses to the election results, see "The Poll Verdict," *New Age*, January 13, 1980, p. 2; and Harkishan Singh, "Election Results: Analysis and Tasks," *People's Democracy*, January 20, 1980, pp. 2–3, 10.

60. "Indian Communist Movement Today," 532–33; see also A. G. Noorani, "Rises and Falls of a CPI Leader: The Dange Letters," *Survey*, 24, no. 2 (Spring 1979): 160–74.

61. "Defeat Anti-Party Splitting Activity," *New Age*, April 20, 1980, p. 3.

62. Ibid., p. 3.

63. *The Overseas Hindustan Times*, July 5, 1980.

64. Walter Andersen, "India," in Richard F. Staar, ed., *Yearbook on International Communist Affairs 1982* (Stanford: Hoover Institution, 1982), 183–89.

65. Ibid., *Yearbook 1983*, pp. 169–74.

66. Douglas C. Makeig, "India," in Richard F. Staar, ed., *Yearbook on International Communist Affairs 1985* (Stanford: Hoover Institution, 1985), 179–86.

67. *Far Eastern Economic Review* (Hong Kong), April 24, 1986, p. 32.

68. *The Statesman* (Calcutta), July 28, 1986, p. 9, and *The Telegraph* (Calcutta), August 12, 1986, p. 9.

69. *The Patriot* (New Delhi), September 30, 1986, p. 5.

70. *The Far Eastern Economic Review* (Hong Kong), December 12, 1985, p. 32.

71. *The Far Eastern Economic Review* (Hong Kong), April 9, 1987, p. 46.

72. *The Far Eastern Economic Review* (Hong Kong), September 3, 1987, p. 36.

73. The assessment of the communist movement in India by leftist intellectuals has taken place in the context of the applicability of Eurocommunism to the Indian scene. For the critics' position, see: Pradip Bose, "Eurocommunism and India," *Mainstream*, July 22, 1978, pp. 23–26; Pradip Bose, "Communist Interactions," *Seminar-India 1978*, 233 (January 1979): 63–71; Kamal Mitra Chenoy and Anuradha Mitra Chenoy, "Eurocommunism: Its Validity and Relevance for India," *Mainstream*, August 11, 1979, pp. 15–,19; Mrinal Datta-Chaudhuri, "Democracy and Mr. Namboodiripad," *Seminar*, 233 (January 1979): 42–46.

74. For the CPI attitude toward Eurocommunism, see: Mohit Sen, "Communism and Euro-Communism," *Mainstream*, August 5, 1978, pp. 14–18, and December 9, 1978, pp. 29–30, 34; for the CPM attitude toward Eurocommunism, see E. M. S. Namboo-

diripad, "Euro-Communism and India-II," *Mainstream*, June 24, 1978, pp. 24–28; E. M. S. Namboodiripad, "Euro-Communism in India-III," *Mainstream*, July 1, 1978, pp. 17–22; E. M. S. Namboodiripad, "Once Again on Euro-Communism in India," *Mainstream*, November 11, 1978, pp. 29–32.

75. *Mainstream*, August 5, 1978, p. 18.
76. *Mainstream*, June 24, 1978, p. 28.
77. "Indian Communist Movement Today," 535–41, and *Times of India*, May 5, 1980.
78. *People's Democracy*, January 14, 1979.
79. Manindra Bhattacharjee, "Middle Class Character of Marxist Party," *Organiser*, January 28, 1979, pp. 19–20.

8   Coalition Strategies and Tactics of Marxist Parties in Africa

The views expressed in this chapter are those of the author and do not necessarily reflect those of the U.S. government or the U.S. Air Force.

1. See the annual *Yearbook on International Communist Affairs*, published by the Hoover Institution on War, Revolution, and Peace in Stanford, California. Since 1981 the "Checklist of Communist Parties" contained in each volume has also appeared, in slightly modified form, in the March–April issue of *Problems of Communism*.

2. For general information on most of these parties, see the annual *Yearbook on International Communist Affairs*; the periodic *Political Handbook of the World*, prepared under the overall editorship of Arthur S. Banks and published by McGraw-Hill in New York from 1975 to 1983 and by CSA Publications in Binghamton, N.Y., since 1984; and the annual *Africa Contemporary Record*, edited by Colin Legum and published in London by Holmes and Meier.

3. *Rand Daily Mail* (Johannesburg), October 2, 1984; London BBC World Service in English, August 13, 1985; Johannesburg SAPA in English, August 14, 1985; policy statement of the chairman of the Lesotho Military Council, Maseru Domestic Service in Sesotho, January 24, 1986.

4. See the entries for Egypt (United Arab Republic), Algeria, Sudan, Morocco, and Tunisia in Witold S. Sworakowski, *World Communism: A Handbook, 1918–1965* (Stanford: Hoover Institution Press, 1973), and the various editions of the *Yearbook on International Communist Affairs*.

5. See, by way of illustration, Michel Kamel, "What Has Changed in Egypt," *World Marxist Review*, 27 (March 1984): 60–65, and Mohamed Magdi Kamal, "Egypt and the Arab Liberation Movement," ibid., 30 (February 1987): 90–97, on the Egyptian Communist party; the reports of the Middle East News Agency on November 8, 1981, concerning the EWCP, on February 11, 1982, regarding the ECP-January 8, and on December 16, 1986, with respect to the Revolutionary Current.

6. *Le Monde*, September 27–28, 1981; Mahmoud Ben Taleb, "Safeguarding the Progressive Option," *World Marxist Review*, 27 (December 1984): 94–101; Sadek Hadjeres, "Principles, Gains, Perspectives," ibid., 29 (September 1986): 37–44.

7. See Ali Malki, "Serving the Working Class and the People of Algeria," *World Marxist Review*, 29 (March 1986): 111–13; Hadjeres, "Principles, Gains, Perspectives."

8. For a typical illustration, see the document signed by the Egyptian Communist party, the PAGS, and a number of other Soviet-recognized Arab communist parties on November 7, 1983, in *International Bulletin*, January 1984, p. 27.

9. See the communiqué issued by a plenary session of the Egyptian Communist party Central Committee in January 1984, in *African Communist*, no. 98 (Third Quarter 1984): 84–88; Kamal, "Egypt and the Arab Liberation Movement."

10. See the entries for Algeria in the editions of the *Yearbook on International Communist Affairs* for the 1980s.

11. The text of the communiqué is in *African Communist*, no. 98. See also Kamal, "Egypt and the Arab Liberation Movement."

12. On these crackdowns, see *The Economist*, April 2, 1983, pp. 56, 59; *Jeune Afrique*, October 2, 1985, pp. 42–43.

13. Long before the resumption of Egyptian-Soviet relations at the ambassadorial level in 1984, for instance, the EWCP called for an Egyptian rapprochement with the U.S.S.R. See a Middle East News Agency report of November 8, 1981.

14. See, by way of illustration, Hadjeres, "Principles, Gains, Perspectives"; Kamal, "Egypt and the Arab Liberation Movement."

15. This appears to be true of the parties that have not received Moscow's blessing as communist organizations as well as of those that have. See, for example, the Middle East News Agency report of November 8, 1981, on the EWCP.

16. For detailed analysis, see David E. Albright, *Vanguard Parties and Revolutionary Change in the Third World: The Soviet Perspective and Its Implications* (Berkeley: Institute of International Studies, University of California, forthcoming).

17. See Richard Lowenthal, *Model or Ally: The Communist Powers and the Developing Countries* (New York: Oxford University Press, 1977), chap. 4, and the entries on Algeria and Egypt in the editions of the *Yearbook of International Communist Affairs* for the late 1960s and the 1970s.

18. See the chapters on the U.S.S.R. and Africa in the annual volumes of *Africa Contemporary Record* for 1981–1986.

19. Ibid.

20. On the early history of the South African Communist party (or, as it was known prior to the 1950s, the Communist Party of South Africa), see Sheridan W. Johns, "Marxism-Leninism in a Multi-Racial Environment: The Origins and Early History of the Communist Party of South Africa, 1914–1932" (Ph.D. diss., Harvard University, 1965); Martin Legassick, *Class and Nationalism in South African Protest: The South African Communist Party and the "Native Republic," 1928–1934* (Syracuse: Syracuse University, 1973); H. J. Simons and R. E. Simons, *Class and Colour in South Africa, 1850–1950* (Harmondsworth: Penguin Books, 1969); A. Lerumo, *Fifty Fighting Years: The Communist Party of South Africa, 1921–1971* (London: Inkululeko Publications, 1971); Sworakowski, *World Communism: A Handbook, 1918–1965*, 388–94; Tom Lodge, *Black Politics in South Africa Since 1945* (London: Longman, 1983).

21. Sworakowski, *World Communism: A Handbook, 1918–1965*, 306–7; *Rand Daily Mail*, October 2, 1984.

22. See the entry for Lesotho in the *Yearbook for International Communist Affairs* for 1987.

23. See the entries for Nigeria in Sworakowski, *World Communism: A Handbook, 1918–65*, and in the relevant editions of the *Yearbook on International Communist Affairs*.

24. See *Africa Contemporary Record, 1983–1984*, B591; Howard Schissel, "Six Months into Sankara's Revolution," *Africa Report*, 29 (April 1984): 16–19; Paris AFP in English, October 29, 1984; Paris AFP in French, October 30 and November 2, 1984; *Africa Report*, 30 (January–February 1985): 37; Ernest Harsch, "A Revolution Derailed," ibid., 33 (January–February 1988): 33–39.

25. See the chapter on Burkina Faso (formerly Upper Volta) in the various editions of *Africa Contemporary Record*; Banks, *Political Handbook of the World, 1986*, 78; Schissel, "Six Months into Sankara's Revolution;" Paris AFP in French, June 2, 1987; Harsch, "A Revolution Derailed."

26. See particularly the commentaries in the journal *New Horizon*, which the party published during these years.

27. For an explication of the evolution in the SWPP's attitude on this point, see Dapo Fatogun, "A Growing Interest in Progressive Ideas," *World Marxist Review*, 28 (December 1985): 44–47.

28. Tass report from Moscow, May 4, 1982; Jeremiah Mosotho, "Lesotho: Changes in the

Alignment of Strength," *World Marxist Review*, 25 (July 1982): 59–62.

29. Mosotho, "Lesotho: Changes in the Alignment of Strength;" *Rand Daily Mail*, October 2, 1984; the entry for Lesotho in the 1985 *Yearbook on International Communist Affairs*; the report on the Lesotho party's seventh special congress of November 1984, in *African Communist*, no. 102 (Third Quarter 1985).

30. See the entry for Lesotho in the 1987 *Yearbook on International Communist Affairs*.

31. See, for example, the commentary over the years in such party publications as *The Guardian*, *New Age*, and *African Communist*. *African Communist*, now printed in the German Democratic Republic and distributed from London, has been the party's chief propaganda outlet since 1959.

32. On its appraisal of relations between the United States and the Botha government, see, for instance, *African Communist*, no. 99 (Fourth Quarter 1984), 17–30; for a post-1984 statement relevant to the ranking of enemies, see Joe Slovo, "Cracks in the Racist Power Bloc," *World Marxist Review*, 30 (June 1987): 13–21.

33. Analysts of a broad spectrum of political and policy outlooks concur that the South African Communist party does include a substantial number of whites, although it is difficult to say just how many. See, for example, *Soviet, East German, and Cuban Involvement in Fomenting Terrorism in Southern Africa*, Report Prepared for the Committee on the Judiciary, Subcommittee on Security and Terrorism, U.S. Senate, 97th Cong., 2nd sess. (Washington, D.C.: Government Printing Office, 1982); *Africa Confidential*, July 6, 1983, p. 2; Thomas G. Karis, "Revolution in the Making: Black Politics in South Africa," *Foreign Affairs*, 62, no. 2 (Winter 1983/1984): 378–406, and "South African Liberation: The Communist Factor," ibid., 65, no. 2 (Winter 1986–87): 267–87.

34. For perhaps the most elaborate but nonetheless typical statement along these lines, see that of the South African Communist party in *African Communist*, no. 99 (Fourth Quarter 1984): 17–30.

35. *Africa Contemporary Record, 1983–1984*, B591; *Africa Report*, 30 (May–June, 1985): 36–37; Harsch, "A Revolution Derailed."

36. *African Communist*, no. 21 (April–June 1965): 41; the entries on Nigeria in Sworakowski, *World Communism: A Handbook, 1918–1965*, and in various editions of the *Yearbook on International Communist Affairs*; Fatogun, "A Growing Interest in Progressive Ideas."

37. *Rand Daily Mail*, October 2, 1984; *Africa Report*, 30 (November–December 1985): 49–50.

38. On this emphasis in the past, see the entry on Lesotho in the 1980 *Yearbook on International Communist Affairs*; Mosotho, "Lesotho: Change in the Alignment of Strength." For the stress on trade unions after the military coup in Lesotho, see the entry on Lesotho in the 1987 *Yearbook on International Communist Affairs*.

39. See, for instance, Roux, *Time Longer Than Rope: A History of the Black Man's Struggle for Freedom in South Africa* (Madison: University of Wisconsin Press, 1966); Lerumo, *Fifty Fighting Years*; Karis, "Revolution in the Making" and South African Liberation;" Lodge, *Black Politics in South Africa Since 1945*; the entries on South Africa in the annual *Yearbook on International Communist Affairs*. For a concise explication from the 1980s of the SACP's attitude toward the ANC, see the statement that the party issued in response to the Pretoria government's declaration of a nationwide state of emergency in June 1986, *World Marxist Review*, 29 (September 1986): 58–59.

40. Slovo, "Cracks in the Racist Power Bloc," and the interview with Slovo in *Neues Deutschland* (East Berlin), October 24–25, 1987, set forth SACP thinking on this subject.

41. See Johns, "Marxism-Leninism in a Multi-Racial Environment;" Legassick, *Class and Nationalism in South African Protest*; Roux, *Time Longer Than Rope*; Simons and Simons, *Class and Colour in South Africa, 1850–1950*; Sworakowski, *World Commu-*

nism: A Handbook, 1918–1965, 388–94; entries on South Africa in the annual volumes of the *Yearbook on International Communist Affairs*.

42. See, for instance, the chapters on Burkino Faso (formerly Upper Volta) and Nigeria in the annual editions of *Africa Contemporary Record*; I. William Zartman, ed., *The Political Economy of Nigeria* (New York: Praeger, 1983).

43. See the entries on Lesotho, Nigeria, and South Africa in the annual volumes of the *Yearbook on International Communist Affairs*; the entries on Burkina Faso (Upper Volta) in the various editions of *Africa Contemporary Record*; Schissel, "Six Months into Sankara's Revolution;" Paris AFP in French, October 30, 1984; *Africa Report*, 30 (January– February 1985): 37, and (May–June 1985): 36–37; Harsch, "A Revolution Derailed."

44. For a forceful statement on this score by the SACP of South Africa, see the last testament of the late party chairman, Dr. Yusef Dadoo, *African Communist*, no. 98 (Third Quarter 1984): 18–19.

45. See, for example, the chapters on "The U.S.S.R. and Africa" in the annual volumes of *Africa Contemporary Record*.

46. For a reflection of official unhappiness in Burkina Faso at the Soviet position, see the editorial in *Sidwaya* (Ouagadougou), October 25, 1984.

47. See, for instance, the paper delivered by Gleb Starushenko, deputy director of the African Institute of the U.S.S.R. Academy of Sciences, at the Second Soviet-African Conference in Moscow in June 1986; *Africa Analysis*, December 1, 1986; the article by Winrich Kuhne in *Weekly Mail*, December 12–18, 1986. For a good illustration of SACP sensitivities on this matter, see *African Communist*, no. 109 (Second Quarter 1987): 79–82.

48. Tass report of the congress, March 27, 1983.

49. See, for instance, the entries for Morocco, Tunisia, and Sudan in Sworakowski, *World Communism: A Handbook, 1918–1965*; in the annual volumes of the *Yearbook on International Communist Affairs*; and in the yearly editions of *Africa Contemporary Record*. More detailed treatment of the USFP and OADP of Morocco may be found in the various volumes of the *Political Handbook of the World*; John P. Entilis, "Kingdom of Morocco," in David E. Long and Bernard Reich, eds., *The Governments and Politics of the Middle East and North Africa* (Boulder: Westview Press, 1980), 391–413; Mark A. Tressler, "Morocco: Institutional Pluralism and Monarchical Dominance," in I. William Zartman et al., *Political Elites in Arab North Africa: Morocco, Algeria, Tunisia, Libya, and Egypt* (New York: Longman, 1982), 35–91; Peter Sluglett and Marion Farouk-Sluglett, "Modern Morocco: Political Immobilism, Economic Dependence," in Richard Lawless and Allan Findlay, eds., *North Africa: Contemporary Politics and Economic Development* (New York: St. Martin's Press, 1984), 50–100; the chapter on Morocco in Richard B. Parker, *North Africa: Regional Tensions and Strategic Concerns* (New York: Praeger, for the Council on Foreign Relations, 1984); *Defense and Foreign Affairs Weekly*, May 16, 1983, p. 6, and September 24, 1984, p. 4; *Defense and Foreign Affairs Daily*, June 17, 1983; Reuters, September 15, 1984; *Jeune Afrique*, November 12, 1986.

50. For purposes of illustration, see the report by Ali Joubeili in *World Marxist Review*, 27 (August 1984): 126; *Jeune Afrique*, November 12, 1986.

51. The rump portion of the National Union of Popular Forces, also of Marxist persuasion, continued to maintain a clandestine organization through the 1970s and into the 1980s. But the available evidence suggests that by the mid-1980s it had virtually disappeared as an entity, for even highly radical elements in the Moroccan political spectrum were free to operate in an open, legal fashion. See Entilis, "Kingdom of Morocco;" Tressler, "Morocco: Institutional Pluralism and Monarchical Dominance;" Banks, *Political Handbook of the World, 1986*, 374; the chapters on Morocco in the annual volumes of *Africa Contemporary Record* since 1974; *Defense and Foreign Affairs*

Weekly, May 16, 1983, p. 86–92.

52. For an exceptionally revealing discussion reflecting calculations of this sort, see Mohammed Ibrahim Nugud (General Secretary of the Sudan Communist party), "At the Beginning of a Difficult Stage," *World Marxist Review*, 28 (September 1985): 86–92.

53. See, for instance, *Africa Contemporary Record, 1983–1984*, B48.

54. Ali Yata (General Secretary of the PPS of Morocco), "Peace: There Is No More Important Aim," *World Marxist Review*, 28 (December 1985): 20–25, affords a good illustration.

55. See, for example, Tressler, "Morocco: Institutional Pluralism and Monarchical Dominance;" the chapters on Morocco in the yearly editions of *Africa Contemporary Record*; *Keesing's Contemporary Archives*, 30 (November 1984): 33247–48, and 31 (July 1985): 33754–55.

56. Maghreb Arabe Press, Rabat, July 7, 1983.

57. See Tressler, "Morocco: Institutional Pluralism and Monarchical Dominance;" Sluglett and Farouk-Sluglett, "Modern Morocco: Political Immobilism, Economic Dependence;" the chapters on Morocco in the annual volumes of *Africa Contemporary Record; Defense and Foreign Affairs Weekly*, May 16, 1983, p. 6; *Keesing's Contemporary Archives*, 30 (November 1984): 33247–48; and commentaries in *Al-Mouharir*, *Al-Bayne*, and *Anwal*, the organs of the USFP, PPS, and OADP respectively.

58. For revealing statements by leaders of the Tunisian and Sudan parties, see Mohammed Harmel, "The Trade Union Movement Cannot Be Destroyed," *World Marxist Review*, 29 (July 1986): 75–78; Tijani Tayeb Babeqr, "Fidelity to Slogans of a Popular Rising," ibid., 29 (November 1986): 38–40.

59. Banks, *Political Handbook of the World, 1984–1985*, 347; *Defense and Foreign Affairs Weekly*, September 24, 1984, p. 4.

60. Banks, *Political Handbook of the World, 1984–1985*, 347; *Defense and Foreign Affairs Weekly*, May 16, 1983, p. 6.

61. See Banks, *Political Handbook of the World, 1986*, 374 and 559–60; the chapter on the Sudan in the *Yearbook on International Communist Affairs* for 1987; *Africa Report*, 32 (January–February 1987): 42; Yuri Potyomkin, "Tunisia: The Party After Legalization," *World Marxist Review*, 25 (November 1982): 31–37; Mohammed Ennafe, "Lofty Responsibility, a Constructive Approach," ibid., 28 (April 1985): 69–71; Nugud, "At the Beginning of a Difficult Stage;" Babeqr, "Fidelity to Slogans of a Popular Rising;" the account of the third national congress of the PPS in *International Bulletin*, June 1983.

62. See, for instance, Potyomkin, "Tunisia: The Party After Legalization;" Ennafe, "Lofty Responsibility, a Constructive Approach;" Nugud, "At the Beginning of a Difficult Stage;" Babeqr, "Fidelity to Slogans of a Popular Rising;" the report on the third national congress of the PPS; various commentaries in *Al-Bayne* during 1984.

63. By way of illustration, see Ahmed Salem, "No Longer a Dead-End, but a Pit," *World Marxist Review*, 25 (June 1982): 59; *Al-Yasar al-'Arabi* (Paris), 58 (October 1983): 12–13.

64. See Nugud, "At the Beginning of a Difficult Stage;" Babeqr, "Fidelity to Slogans of a Popular Rising."

65. *Le Monde*, February 25, 1986; *Réalités* (Tunis), February 28, 1986. For other examples of similar activities by the Tunisian Communist party, see Potyomkin, "Tunisia: The Party after Legalization;" Ennafe, "Lofty Responsibility, a Constructive Approach;" the chapters on Tunisia in the yearly editions of *Africa Contemporary Record* since 1981; *Banks, Political Handbook of the World, 1986*, 589; *Africa Report*, 30 (July–August 1985): 49–50.

66. See Tessler, "Morocco: Institutional Pluralism and Monarchical Dominance;" the chapters on Morocco in the yearly editions of *Africa Contemporary Record*; the report on the third national congress of the PPS; *Keesing's Contemporary Archives*, 30 (Novem-

ber 1984): 33247–48, and 31 (July 1985): 33754–55.

67. See the entries on Morocco in the annual volumes of the *Yearbook on International Communist Affairs* and *Africa Contemporary Record* since 1974.

68. *Defense and Foreign Affairs Weekly,* May 16, 1983, p. 6.

69. For a good reflection of such perspectives, see the interview with a member of the Tunisian Communist party's Central Committee, in *Réalités,* May 2, 1986.

70. For representative accounts of such cooperation, see Ennafe, "Lofty Responsibility, a Constructive Approach;" *Africa Report,* 30 (July–August 1985): 49–50; *Réalités,* February 28, 1986.

71. See, for instance, Izeddin Ali Amer, "US Bases Shading a Medieval Regime," *World Marxist Review,* 27 (October 1984): 103–9; Nugud, "At the Beginning of a Difficult Stage;" Babeqr, "Fidelity to Slogans of a Popular Rising;" the entries on Sudan in the annual volumes of the *Yearbook on International Communist Affairs.*

72. See Tessler, "Morocco: Institutional Pluralism and Monarchical Dominance;" the chapters on Morocco and on "The Islamic Revival" in Parker, *North Africa*; the entries on Morocco in the yearly editions of *Africa Contemporary Record* and the *Yearbook on International Communist Affairs*; *Defense and Foreign Affairs Weekly,* May 16, 1983, p. 6.

73. See Tessler, "Morocco: Institutional Pluralism and Monarchical Dominance;" the entries on Morocco and Sudan in the annual volumes of *Africa Contemporary Record* and the *Yearbook on International Communist Affairs*; *Keesing's Contemporary Archives,* 30 (November 1984): 33247–48, and 31 (July 1985): 33754–55; *Defense and Foreign Affairs Weekly,* May 16, 1983, p. 6; Godfrey Morrison, "The King's Gambit," *Africa Report,* 30 (November–December 1985): 14–18; Babeqr, "Fidelity to Slogans of a Popular Rising."

74. For a typical pronouncement reflecting the importance that the parties attach to alignment with the Soviet Union, see Yata, "Peace: There Is No More Important Aim." On the USFP, see, for example, *Africa Contemporary Record, 1981–1982,* B87.

75. In December 1983, for instance, Karen Brutents, a deputy director of the International Department of the Communist Party of the Soviet Union, met with the USFP first secretary, Abderrahim Bouabid, in Morocco, and they discussed the development of party contacts and ties. *Pravda,* December 7, 1983.

76. *Defense and Foreign Affairs Weekly,* May 16, 1983, p. 6; commentaries in *Anwal.*

77. The three communist parties have frequent contacts with Soviet and East European officials in a variety of world communist forums. For accounts of meetings between representatives of the U.S.S.R. and the USFP, see *Pravda,* May 21, 1982; December 7, 1983; July 11 and 19, 1984; and August 27, 1984.

78. On the position of the Tunisian Communist party, see Potyomkin, "Tunisia: The Party after Legalization;" Ennafe, "Lofty Responsibility, a Constructive Approach;" *Africa Report,* 30 (July–August 1985): 49–50, and 32 (January–February 1987): 42. For summaries of Soviet efforts to woo the Tunisian government, see the articles on "The USSR and Africa" in the volumes of *Africa Contemporary Record* for 1981–1986.

79. For an authoritative expression of the Sudan Communist party's viewpoint, see Nugud, "At the Beginning of a Difficult Stage." Soviet commentary on the state of affairs in the Sudan was remarkably sparse. Typical of what appeared were *Pravda,* April 15 and July 16, 1985; V. Bochkaryov, "Logical Finale," *New Times,* 17 (1985): 10–11. On the attitude of the military government toward the U.S.S.R., see, for example, the interview with General Siwar al-Dhahab in *Al-Khalij* (Al-Shirqah), April 22, 1985, pp. 1, 17.

80. *World Marxist Review,* 28 (May 1985): 89.

81. See the entries on Madagascar, Mauritius, and Senegal in the various editions of the *Political Handbook of the World*; the chapters on these three states and Réunion in the individual volumes of *Africa Contemporary Record*; the entries on Senegal and Réunion

in Sworakowski, *World Communism: A Handbook, 1918–1965,* and the various editions of the *Yearbook on International Communist Affairs;* Adele Smith Simmons, *Modern Mauritius: The Politics of Decolonization* (Bloomington: Indiana University Press, 1982); article on Mauritius by Larry W. Bowman, *Christian Science Monitor,* September 16, 1987; Virginia Thompson and Richard Adloff, *The Malagasy Republic: Madagascar Today* (Stanford: Stanford University Press, 1965); Nigel Heseltine, *Madagascar* (New York: Praeger, 1971); Gisele Rabesahala, "A Party of Patriots, of Internationalists," *World Marxist Review,* 24 (January 1981): 42–46, and "Upholding the Socialist Choice," ibid., 30 (April 1987): 43–47; *Keesing's Contemporary Archives,* 27 (June 5, 1981): 30900, and 29 (September 1983): 32382–83.

82. See, for instance, Semou Pathe Gueye, "Marxism Is Gaining Ground in Africa," *World Marxist Review,* 27 (July 1984): 94–101. For more elaborate expositions of the PIT's attitude toward the government, see Semou Pathe Gueye, "The Road Chosen By Us," ibid., 28 (April 1985): 58–63; Ibrahima Sene, "The Blind Alleys of Capitalist Orientation," ibid., 29 (September 1986): 100–105.

83. See Banks, *Political Handbook of the World, 1986,* 480–81; the chapters on Senegal in *Africa Contemporary Record* for 1982–1986.

84. See Banks, *Political Handbook of the World, 1984–1985,* 334–36; the chapters on Mauritius in *Africa Contemporary Record* for 1982–1985.

85. See the chapters on Madagascar in the volumes of *Africa Contemporary Record* since 1975; Rabesahala, "A Party of Patriots, of Internationalists" and "Upholding the Socialist Choice;" William O. Eaton, *Ethnic Rivalry in Madagascar: A Real or Imagined Threat to Stability,* DDB-2500-12-82 (Washington, D.C.: Defense Intelligence Agency, June 1982); *Africa Confidential,* January 4, 1984, pp. 4–6; Paris AFP in French, May 2, 1987; *Africa Report,* 32 (July–August 1987): 7.

86. See the entries on Réunion in the annual editions of the *Yearbook on International Communist Affairs* and *Africa Contemporary Record; Keesing's Contemporary Archives,* 27 (June 5, 1981): 30900, and 29 (September 1983): 32382–83; Lucet Langenier, "In the Midst of the Masses, in the Interest of the Masses," *World Marxist Review,* 30 (March 1987): 42–46.

87. For typical indications, see Semou Pathe Gueye, "Contrary to the Africans' Will," *World Marxist Review,* 27 (October 1984): 87–88; *Témoignages* (the daily newspaper of the Réunion Communist party), April 16 and November 4.

88. See, for example, Seydou Cissokho, "A Social Democratic 'Project' for Africa, or the Way to an Impasse," *World Marxist Review,* 26 (December 1983): 14–20; Semou Pathe Gueye, "What the Socialist International's Lima Congress Showed," ibid., 29 (November 1986): 94–101.

89. Rabesahala, "Upholding the Socialist Choice."

90. See the entries on Réunion in the editions of the *Yearbook on International Communist Affairs* and *Africa Contemporary Record* since 1981; *Keesing's Contemporary Archives,* 29 (September 1983): 32382–83.

91. Pathe Gueye, "The Road Chosen By Us," affords a good illustration.

92. The following discussion draws upon the entries on Senegal in the various editions of the *Political Handbook of the World* for the 1980s; the chapters on Senegal in the annual volumes of *Africa Contemporary Record* for the same years; *Keesing's Contemporary Archives,* 32 (January 1986): 34090; Paris AFP in French, February 13, 1987.

93. See, for instance, Rabesahala, "A Party of Patriots, of Internationalists" and "Upholding the Socialist Choice;" Paul Rabemananjara, "Socialism: The Common Aim," *World Marxist Review,* 27 (August 1984): 50–52; Noelson Razakarisoa, "Viewing the Future with Optimism," ibid., 28 (July 1985): 59–60; Eaton, *Ethnic Rivalry in Madagascar;* Paris AFP in French, May 2, 1987; *Africa Report,* 32 (July–August 1987): 7.

94. See the entries on Mauritius in the various editions of the *Political Handbook of the World* since the mid-1970s and the chapters on Mauritius in the yearly volumes of

Africa Contemporary Record for the same period; Aneerood Jugnauth, "Mauritius: The People Have Made Their Choice," *World Marxist Review*, 26 (May 1983): 70–73; *Keesing's Record of World Events*, 33 (September 1987): 35361.

95. See the entries on Réunion in the various editions of the *Yearbook on International Communist Affairs* and *Africa Contemporary Record* since the mid-1970s; *Keesing's Contemporary Archives*, 29 (September 1983): 32382–83.

96. See, for example, Heseltine, *Madagascar*, 203–4; Eaton, *Ethnic Rivalry in Madagascar*.

97. See the chapters on Madagascar and Senegal in the annual editions of *Africa Contemporary Record* since the beginning of the 1980s; *Africa Confidential*, January 4, 1984, pp. 4–6; Banks, *Political Handbook of the World, 1986*, 480; *Jeune Afrique*, April 29, 1987, pp. 20–21; Paris AFP in French, May 2, 1987.

98. See the chapters on Mauritius and Senegal in the yearly volumes of *Africa Contemporary Record* since the outset of the 1980s; *Keesing's Contemporary Archives*, 31 (January 1986): 34090; Paris AFP in French, February 13, 1987.

99. Entries and chapters on Madagascar, Mauritius, Réunion, and Senegal in Banks, *Political Handbook of the World, 1986*, and the volumes of *Africa Contemporary Record* for the 1980s; *Keesing's Record of World Events*, 32 (September 1987): 35361; article on Mauritius by Larry W. Bowman, *Christian Science Monitor*, September 16, 1987; *Témoignages*, March 18 and 22–23, 1986.

100. See the entries and chapters on Madagascar, Mauritius, Réunion, and Senegal in the various editions of the *Political Handbook of the World* and *Africa Contemporary Record* since the mid-1970s; the entries on Réunion and Senegal in the annual volumes of the *Yearbook on International Communist Affairs* since the early 1970s; *Keesing's Contemporary Archives*, 27 (June 5, 1981): 30900, and 29 (September 1983): 32382–83.

101. By the way of illustration, see commentary throughout the 1980s in *Témoignages*.

102. For a good formulation of this perspective, see part 3 of the report delivered by Mengistu Haile Mariam, secretary general of the WPE, to the first meeting of the Shengo, the new national assembly of Ethiopia, on September 9, 1987, as broadcast by Radio Addis Ababa in English to Neighboring Countries on September 9, 1987.

103. For pertinent discussion, from diverse perspectives, of the internal problems that have beset the parties, see the relevant country chapters in the yearly editions of *Africa Contemporary Record*; Michael Wolfers and Jane Bergerol, *Angola in the Frontline* (London: Zed Books, 1983); John A. Marcum, "Angola: A Quarter Century of War," *CSIS Africa Notes*, 37 (December 21, 1984); Gillian Gunn, "The Angolan Economy: A Status Report," ibid., 58 (May 30, 1986), and "Mozambique After Machel," ibid., 67 (December 29, 1986); Allen F. Isaacman and Barbara Isaacman, *Mozambique: From Colonialism to Revolution, 1900–1982* (Boulder, Colo.: Westview Press, 1983); Joseph Hanlon, *Mozambique: The Revolution Under Fire* (London: Zed Books, 1984); Mota Lopes, "The MNR: Opponents or Bandits?" *Africa Report*, 31 (January–February 1986): 67–73; Karl Maier, "Chissano's Challenge," *Africa Report*, 32 (July–August 1987): 67–69; L. Gray Cowan, "Benin Joins the Pragmatists," *CSIS Africa Notes*, 54 (February 28, 1986); Adelino Gomes, "Making Its Own Rain Fall," *Africa Report*, 31 (January–February 1986): 21–23; Howard Schissel, "Pragmatists or Partisans in Brazzaville?" ibid., 29 (January–February 1984): 55–57; Vital Balla, "Life Versus Dogma," *World Marxist Review*, 30 (August 1987): 128–31; Peter Schwab, *Ethiopia: Politics, Economics and Society* (Boulder, Colo.: Lynne Rienner Publishers, 1985); *Africa Confidential*, May 6, 1981, pp. 6–7; September 8, 1982, pp. 1–4; and November 30, 1983, pp. 6–8; *Africa Report*, 30 (July–August 1985): 46–47; Mary Kay Magistad, "On the Razor's Edge," ibid., 32 (May–June 1987): 61–64; Adelino Gomes, "Cabral's Dream," ibid., 31 (January–February 1986): 15–20; Tony Hodges, "Combating Cocoa Colonialism," ibid., 61–66; Richard Greenfield, "An Embattled Barre," ibid., 32 (May–June 1987): 65–69; Colleen Lowe Morna, "Preparing for War," ibid., 32 (January–February 1987): 55–59.

104. See U.S. Arms Control and Disarmament Agency, *World Military Expenditures and Arms Transfers, 1986* (Washington, D.C., April 1987); *FAO Monthly Bulletin of Statistics*, 10 (April 1987): 13; editions of the *Africa Review* for 1986 and 1987.

105. See the chapters on Benin, Congo, Cape Verde, Guinea-Bissau, and São Tomé and Príncipe in the annual volumes of *Africa Contemporary Record*; the entries on the same states in the various editions of the *Political Handbook of the World*; Gomes, "Making Its Own Rain Fall;" Hodges, "Combating Cocoa Colonialism;" Gomes, "Cabral's Dream;" *Africa Report*, 31 (September–October 1986): 45.

106. The most readily accessible primary sources from which to gauge the thinking of all of the parties in this category about external enemies are the monitorings of official radio broadcasts and the official press published by the U.S. Foreign Broadcast Information Service and the British Broadcasting Company. For highly useful secondary materials, see the appropriate country chapters in the yearly volumes of *Africa Contemporary Record*.

107. See the chapters on Zimbabwe in the annual editions of *Africa Contemporary Record* for the 1980s; Radio Harare Domestic Service in English, September 21, October 21 and 23, and December 22, 1987.

108. Data underlying the following analysis derive from the appropriate country chapters in George Thomas Kurian, *Encyclopedia of the Third World* (New York: Facts on File, 1978), and in the yearly volumes of *Africa Contemporary Record*; John A. Marcum, *The Angolan Revolution: Volume II, Exile Politics and Guerrilla Warfare, 1962–1976* (Cambridge: MIT Press, 1978); Thomas H. Henriksen, *Revolution and Counterrevolution: Mozambique's War of Independence, 1964–1974* (Westport, Conn.: Greenwood Press, 1983); Basil Davidson, *No Fist Is Big Enough to Hide the Sky: The Liberation of Guinea-Bissau and Cape Verde* (London: Zed Press, 1981); Tom J. Farer, *War Clouds on the Horn of Africa: A Crisis for Détente* (Washington, D.C.: Carnegie Endowment for International Peace, 1976); British Foreign and Commonwealth Office, *Ethiopia: Reality and Doctrine* (London, March 1985); Schwab, *Ethiopia: Politics, Economics and Society*; interview with Manuel Pinto da Costa by Tony Hodges, *Africa Report*, 31 (January–February 1986): 57–60; Hodges, "Combating Cocoa Colonialism;" Schissel, "Pragmatists or Partisans in Brazzaville?;" Marcum, "Angola: A Quarter Century of War;" Cowan, "Benin Joins the Pragmatists;" Maier, "Chissano's Challenge;" *Africa Confidential*, March 2, 1983, pp. 5–7, and September 7, 1983, pp. 1–4; Greenfield, "An Embattled Barre."

109. The ensuing discussion is based on information in the pertinent country chapters in Kurian, *Encyclopedia of the Third World*, and in the annual editions of *Africa Contemporary Record*; Marcum, "Angola: A Quarter Century of War;" *Africa Report*, 32 (March–April 1987): 40; Cowan, "Benin Joins the Pragmatists;" Martin Dohou Azonhiho, "Party Building Gets Priority," *World Marxist Review*, 29 (August 1986): 39–41; *Jeune Afrique*, March 4, 1987, pp. 32–33; Gomes, "Making Its Own Rain Fall;" Banks, *Political Handbook of the World, 1986*, 93; London BBC World Service in English, July 30, 1987; Jean-Pierre Thystere-Tchicaya, "From African Realities to the Socialist Ideal," *World Marxist Review*, 26 (September 1983): 62–66; Schissel, "Pragmatists or Partisans in Brazzaville?;" *Jeune Afrique*, October 21, 1987, p. 28; Yohannis Abate, "Civil-Military Relations in Ethiopia," *Armed Forces and Society*, 10 (Spring 1984): 380–400; Paul B. Henze, *Communist Ethiopia—Is It Succeeding?* P-7054 (Santa Monica: Rand, January 1985); Magistad, "On the Razor's Edge;" part 3 of Mengistu's report to the first meeting of the Shengo on September 9, 1987, as broadcast by Radio Addis Ababa in English to Neighboring Countries on September 9, 1987; Radio Addis Ababa Domestic Service in Amharic, September 18, 1987; Doha QNA in Arabic, September 20, 1987; (Clandestine) Voice of the Broad Masses of Eritrea in Tigrinya, September 23, 1987; Radio Addis Ababa in English to Neighboring Countries, October 27, 1987; Davidson, *No Fist Is Big Enough to Hide the Sky*; Gomes, "Cabral's

Dream;" Gillian Gunn, "Post Nkomati Mozambique," *CSIS Africa Notes*, 38 (January 8, 1985), and "Mozambique After Machel;" Lopes, "The MNR: Opponents or Bandits?;" *Noticías* (Maputo), June 27, 1987; Maier, "Chissano's Challenge;" interview with Manuel Pinto da Costa by Hodges; Hodges, "Combating Cocoa Colonialism;" *Africa Confidential*, May 6, 1981, pp. 6–7; September 8, 1982, pp. 1–4; March 1, 1983, pp. 5–7; July 20, 1983, pp. 3–6; September 7, 1983, pp. 1–4; and November 30, 1983, pp. 6–8; Greenfield, "An Embattled Barre;" interview with Somalia's President Mohamed Siad Barre in *Al-Tadamun* (London), May 30, 1987; Michael Clough, "Whither Zimbabwe," *CSIS Africa Notes*, 20 (November 15, 1983); Morna, "Preparing for War;" *The Financial Gazette* (Harare), September 25, 1987.

110.   The observations in note 106 regarding sources for assessing the views of the parties about external enemies apply equally to sources for determining their outlooks with respect to foreign allies.

9   The Coalition Strategies and Tactics of the Indonesian Communist Party: A Prelude to Destruction

1.   Richard V. Allen, ed., *Yearbook on International Communist Affairs 1968* (Stanford, Calif.: Hoover Institution Press, 1969), 308.
2.   George McT. Kahin, *Nationalism and Revolution in Indonesia* (Ithaca, N.Y.: Cornell University Press, 1952), 65–74.
3.   Ibid., 79.
4.   Donald Hindley, *The Communist Party of Indonesia, 1951–1963* (Berkeley and Los Angeles: University of California Press, 1964), 18.
5.   Ibid., 106.
6.   Justus M. Van Der Kroef, *The Communist Party of Indonesia* (Vancouver: University of British Columbia, 1965), 30.
7.   Ibid., 30.
8.   Hindley, *The Communist Party of Indonesia, 1951–1963*, 20.
9.   Van Der Kroef, *The Communist Party of Indonesia*, 33.
10. Hindley, *The Communist Party of Indonesia, 1951–1963*, 21.
11. Dipa Nusantara Aidit (1923–1965), who served as the PKI's principal leader from 1951 to his execution in 1965, actually held a variety of party titles without altering his leadership position. After serving as the first secretary of the Central Committee from 1951, he was named the party's secretary-general in 1953, and in 1959 became the chairman of the Central Committee of the PKI.
12. Hindley, *The Communist Party of Indonesia, 1951–1963*, 48.
13. Olle Törnquist, *Dilemmas of Third World Communism: The Destruction of the PKI in Indonesia* (London: Zed Books, 1984), 19.
14. Ibid., 19.
15. Ibid., 20
16. Ibid., 22.
17. Hindley, *The Communist Party of Indonesia, 1951–1963*, 32.
18. Ibid., 37.
19. Justus M. Van Der Kroef, "Indonesian Communism under Aidit," *Problems of Communism*, 7, no. 6 (November–December 1958): 18.
20. D. N. Aidit, "Party Building and Mass Work," *World Marxist Review*, 5, no. 9 (September 1962): 29.
21. Rex Mortimer, *Indonesian Communism under Sukarno* (Ithaca and London: Oxford University Press/Cornell University Press, 1974), 46.
22. "Guarding against Ideological Timidity," *Kehidupan Partai (Party Life)*, 9 (September 1958): 165–66 (JPRS Translation No. 2782/1960).

23. Van Der Kroef, *The Communist Party of Indonesia*, 151.
24. D. N. Aidit, "Ideological Work in the Communist Party of Indonesia," *World Marxist Review*, 2, no. 7 (July 1959): 24.
25. *The Yearbook on International Communist Affairs 1968*, 308.
26. D. N. Aidit, "Ideological Work in the Communist Party of Indonesia," *World Marxist Review*, 2, no. 7 (July 1959): 24.
27. Sudjito, "Establishing the Party in the Outer Islands and Some Important Problems it Raises," *Kehidupan Partai (Party Life)*, 7 (July 1958): 45 (JPRS Translation No. 2782/1964).
28. Hindley, *The Communist Party of Indonesia, 1951–1963*, 39.
29. Van Der Kroef, "Indonesian Communism under Aidit," *Problems of Communism*, 6, no. 7 (November–December 1958): 19–20.
30. M. Lukman, "A Correct Party Policy Guarantees a Strong United Front," *World Marxist Review*, 2, no. 8 (August 1959): 80.
31. *Yearbook on International Communist Affairs 1968*, 108.
32. Ibid., 308.
33. Mortimer, *Indonesian Communism under Sukarno*, 276–77.
34. The moderate socialist PSI under the leadership of Sjahrir was reconstituted in 1948 when the old Socialist party amalgamated with the PKI. The communists considered Sjahrir's party to be revisionist.
35. Hindley *The Communist Party of Indonesia, 1951–1963*, 222–23.
36. Ruth T. McVey, "Indonesian Communism and the Transition to Guided Democracy," in A. Doak Barnett, ed., *Communist Strategy in Asia* (New York: Praeger, 1963), 163.
37. Guy J. Parker, "Indonesia: the PKI's 'Road to Power,'" in Robert A. Scalapino, ed., *The Communist Revolution in Asia* (Englewood Cliffs, N.J.: Prentice-Hall, 1965), 267.
38. Mortimer, *Indonesian Communism under Sukarno*, 100.
39. Ibid., 95.
40. D. N. Aidit, *The Indonesian Revolution and the Immediate Tasks of the Communist Party of Indonesia* (Peking: Foreign Languages Press, 1964), 42.
41. Mortimer, *Indonesian Communism under Sukarno*, 135–37.
42. *Yearbook on International Affairs 1968*, 309.
43. Ibid., 308.
44. *Peking Review*, 7, no. 43 (October 22, 1965): 8.
45. *Yearbook on International Communist Affairs 1968*, 310.
46. Guy J. Parker, *The Rise and Fall of the Communist Party of Indonesia* (Santa Monica, Calif.: Rand Corporation, Memorandum RM-5753-PR, February 1969), 61–62.
47. *Yearbook on International Communist Affairs 1968*, 309–10 and 317.
48. Ibid., 318.
49. Ibid., 319.
50. Ibid., 310–11.
51. *People of Indonesia, Unite and Fight to Overthrow the Fascist Regime* (Peking: Foreign Languages Press, 1968), 32.
52. Richard F. Staar, ed., *Yearbook on International Communist Affairs 1984* (Stanford, Calif.: Hoover Institution Press, 1984), 226.
53. Richard F. Staar, ed., *Yearbook on International Communist Affairs 1987* (Stanford, Calif.: Hoover Institution Press, 1987), 199.
54. *Far Eastern Economic Review*, 20 (November 1986): 50.
55. *Yearbook on International Communist Affairs 1987*, 199.
56. Ibid., 199.
57. Ibid.
58. This point was made by Olle Törnquist in *Dilemmas of Third World Communism: The Destruction of the PKI in Indonesia*, 252.

Index

Abangan vote, 295. *See also* Indonesian Communist party

Abbud, Ibrahim, 256

Acción Democrática (AD), 145, 151, 158. *See also* Venezuela

Acción Popular (AC), 165, 166. *See also* Peru

Ackerman, A., 48

Action unity, 86, 90, 98. *See also* United front

Addis Abeba, 275

Adjitorop, Jusuf, 300, 301

Afghanistan, 99, 228, 236

Africa, 28, 238, 288

African Independence party (PAI), 239, 264, 265, 268, 270, 272. *See also* African Independence party

African Independence party (1957), 264. *See also* Party of Independence and Labor

Africanism, 24

African National Congress (ANC), 240, 252

African Party for the Independence of Cape Verde (PAICV), 239, 241, 273–75

African Party for the Independence of Guinea and Cape Verde (PAIGC), 239, 241, 273, 277

African Party for the Independence of the People (PAIP), 240, 265

African Party of Independence of French West Africa, 248

Agrarians, 65, 77, 82, 90, 118, 119, 122

Agrarian Reform Law of 1953, 147. *See also* Guatemala

Agrarian Union, 122. *See also* Bulgaria;

Petkov, Nikola

Aguilar, Luis, 145, 152

Aidit, D. N., 23, 284, 288–303. *See also* Indonesian Communist party

Albania, 7, 253

Algerian Communist party, 242

Alianza Popular Revolucionaria Americana (APRA), 164–66, 169. *See also* Peru

Alimin, 288. *See also* Indonesian Communist party

Allahabad high court, 224. *See also* India

Allende Gossens, Salvador, 142, 154–56, 170. *See also* Chile; Chilean Socialist Party

Alliance from above, 30. *See also* United front; United front from above

Alliance from below, 30. *See also* United front; United front from below

Alliance of National, Democratic, and Peace Forces (Lien Mien Dan Toc Dan Chu Va Hoa Binh) (ANDPF), 190–91, 196. *See also* Vietnam

All-India Communist party, 229. *See also* India; Communist Party of India

All-India Trade Union Congress, 203. *See also* India

All-party coalitions, 106–7, 119, 122, 125–26, 130

All-party governments, 107, 125

Althydubandalagid (AB), 87–88, 96–99. *See also* Iceland

Alvear, Marcelo T. de, 143

Amador, Carlos Fonseca, 161

Amharic-speaking peoples, 277. *See also* Committee to Organize the Party of the

Working People of Ethiopia
Amnesty International, 168
Amritsar, 217. *See also* India
Anarchism, 150, 164
Anarchists, 1, 12, 68, 73–75, 169, 206
Anarcho-syndicalist parties, 12
Anarcho-syndicalists, 1, 10, 68, 72–73
Andhra, 206–7, 212–17. *See also* India
Andhra Thesis, 215
Angolares, 276
Anti-Americanism, 310, 320
Anti-clerical attitude, 127
Anti-collaborationist forces, 80
Anticolonialism, 12, 20, 22, 311, 316
Anti-EEC coalition, 90, 93
Antifascism, 44, 107
Anti-feudalism, 179, 180, 291, 294
Anti-imperialism, 180, 291, 294
Anti-Imperialist Action Front, 268. *See also*
    African Independence party; Communist
    League of Workers; Party of Indepen-
    dence and Socialism
Anti-imperialist league, 177. *See also* Viet-
    nam; United front
Anti-Tito campaign, 97
Anti-Nazi forces, 70, 80, 82, 107, 112
Anti-party behavior, 65. *See also* Commu-
    nist parties; Marxist-Leninist parties
Antisocialist laws, 36. *See also* Germany
Anti-Stalin speech of 1956, 16. *See also*
    Khrushchev, Nikita Sergeevich
Anyanya, 261. *See also* Sudanese People's
    Liberation Movement
Apartheid, 252
Apparatchiki, 79, 85
Aprista, 166. *See also* Alianza Popular
    Revolucionara Americana; Peru
Arab Socialist Union, 242. *See also* Nasser,
    Gamal Abdul
Arbernz Guzmán, Jacobo, 146, 147
Argentina, 139, 143, 153
Argentine Communist party, 143. *See also*
    Argentina
Arias Sanchez, Oscar, 163
Armed Communist Organization (AC), 240
Arrow Cross, 109. *See also* Hungary
Aspaturian, Vernon, 30
Associated State of Vietnam, 183. *See also*
    Vietnam
Association for Vietnamese of Chinese Ori-
    gin, 187. *See also* Vietminh; Vietnam
Atlantic Charter, 110–11
Aufhebung des Staates, 34. *See also* Marx,

Karl; Marxism
August Revolution of 1945, 181, 188–89,
    286, 269–97. *See also* Indochinese Com-
    munist party; Vietminh; Vietnam
Austria, 129
Authoritarian political systems, 14
Avineri, Shlomo, 34
AVNOJ. 112. *See also* Yugoslavia
Axelrod, Robert, 29–30, 54
Ayacucho, 168. *See also* Peru
Azcárate, M., 54. *See also* Spanish Commu-
    nist party

Babangida, Ibrahim, 249
Bakongo, 277–78
Bakunin, Mikhail, 136
Bukuninists, 1
Balkans, 133, 129
Bandera Roja (Red Flag), 167. *See also*
    Peru
Barrantes Lingán, Alfonso, 165–67. *See also*
    Peru
Basotho National party, 240, 253
Batista, Fulgencio, 142–43, 148. *See also*
    Cuba; Castro, Fidel
Beijing, 1–2, 271, 296–98, 100, 300–301,
    322
Belaúnde Terry, Fernando, 164, 168–69.
    See also Peru
Belgium, 76, 81, 100, 129
Bella, Ahmed Ben, 242. *See also* Algerian
    Communist party
Benelux countries, 94
Beneš, Edvard, 113, 115, 119, 122, 128. *See
    also* Czechoslovakia
Bengalis, 214–15. *See also* India
Benin, 281. *See also* Benin People's Revolu-
    tionary party
Benin People's Revolutionary party (PRPB),
    239, 241, 273, 278. *See also* Benin
Benjedid government, 243–44, 246. *See
    also* Algerian Communist party
Bensaid, Mohamed, 256. *See also* Organiza-
    tion for Democratic and Popular Action
    (Morocco)
Berber, 261
Bérenger, Paul, 266. *See also* Italian Com-
    munist party
Bernstein, Eduard, 51
Betancourt, Rómulo, 157–58. *See also*
    Venezuela
Bethlen, Istvan, 109. *See also* Hungary
Bhatinda, 226, 229. *See also* Communist

Party of India
Big Three, 112
Bihar, 211–12. *See also* India
Binh, Nguyen Thi, 197. *See also* Vietnam
Blanco, Hugo, 151
Blasier, Cole, 156, 172
"Bao Dai Formula," 183. *See also* Vietnam
Bogus coalition, 108, 121, 123. *See also* Coalition
Bolivia, 145–46, 149, 152, 154
Bolshevik (journal), 119
Bolshevik model, 178
Bolshevik party, 39, 67
Bolsheviks, 39–40, 51, 67
Bolshevik takeover, 46
Bolshevization, 7, 43, 68–70, 73, 97, 137, 140
Bombay, 206, 214, 218
Borge, Tomas, 160, 163–64. *See also* Nicaragua
Borges, Alfredo Guerra, 153. *See also* Guatemala
Bouabid, Abderrahim, 257. *See also* Socialist Union of Popular Forces (Morocco)
Boumedienne, Houari, 243. *See also* Algerian Communist party; General Union of Algerian Workers; National Union of Algerian Youth; Socialist Vanguard party
Bourgeois-capitalist government, 213
Bourgeois democracy, 52–53
Bourgeois-democratic revolution, 138, 287, 288, 289
Bourgeois dictatorship, 31
Bourgeoisie, 11–12, 14, 26, 33, 60, 68–69, 72, 76, 78, 83–84, 91–92, 168, 174, 177, 181, 192, 199, 210, 213, 215, 219, 288, 292
Bourgeois-landlord class, 220
Bourgeois-landlord state, 204, 219, 230
Bourgeois-liberal groups, 11
Bourgeois national governments, 214
Bourgeois nationalism, 211
Bourgeois nationalist parties, 174, 176–78, 190, 192
Bourgeois national movements, 209, 212
Bourgeois-national revolution, 289
Bourgeois parties, 32, 42, 63–64, 74, 124, 140, 161, 169, 171, 226–27, 230
Bourgeois specialists, 194, 197
Bourgeois society, 91
Bourgeois supremacy, 31
Bourguiba, Habib, 256. *See also* Tunisian Communist party

Britain. *See* Great Britain
British, 21–22, 24, 99, 111, 113, 123
British raj, 214, 234. *See also* India
British Somaliland, 276–77
Broad coalition, 88, 90. *See also* United front
Browder, Earl, 144
Brzezinski, Zbigniew K., 89
Budapest, 109
Buddhist movement, 189–90. *See also* Vietnam
Buddhists, 182. *See also* Vietnam
Buenos Aires, 139
Buhari, Muhammadu, 249
Bukharin, Nikolai, 137–38
Bulgaria, 48, 108–9, 111, 115, 119, 121–23. *See also* Communist Party of Bulgaria
Bureaucratic bourgeoisie, 205
Burkinabe Communist Group (GCB), 239, 248, 251, 253

Cabral, Luiz, 281
Cairo, 246
Calcutta, 206, 214, 218, 231
Cambodia, 167, 179, 194, 228
Can the Bolsheviks Maintain State Power, 40. *See also* Lenin, Vladimir Ilich
Canton, China, 175, 177
Cao Dai, 180. *See also* Vietnam
Cape Province, 247
Cape Town, 247
Capitalism, 33, 68–69, 136, 145
Capitalists, 4, 32, 77, 95, 103, 288, 289
Caracas, 158
Carrillo, Santiago, 45–46, 50, 52–54. *See also* Spanish Communist party
Castillo, Jorge del, 166. *See also* Alianza Popular Revolucionaria Americana; Peru
Castro, Fidel, 136–37, 147–49, 152, 154, 157, 161, 170, 310. *See also* Cuba
Catholic Church, 11, 26, 52, 189
Catholics, 52, 152, 182, 189, 194–96, 198, 201, 312
Caudillismo, 171
CCP-Kuomintang, 177
Center of Indian Trade Unions (CITU), 205, 207. *See also* Communist Party of India-Marxist; India
Central America, 25–26, 100
Central Highlands, 185, 189, 199–200. *See also* Vietnam
Central Intelligence Agency, 147, 162

Central Labor Organization of Indonesia (SOBSI), 293. *See also* Indonesian Communist party

Cerda, Pedro Aguirre, 141–42, 154. *See also* Chile

Chamarro, Pedro Joaquin, 161. *See also* Nicaragua

Chan Tin, 200. *See also* Vietnam

Charismatic legitimacy, 319

"Chartists, The" (Marx 1852 essay), 35. *See also* Marx, Karl

Charu Mazumdar CPI (ML), 235. *See also* India; Naxalites

Checoslovaquia, el socialismo como problems, 154. *See also* Petkoff, Teodoro; Venezuela

Cheshmedzhiev, Grigor, 122. *See also* Bulgaria

Chiang Kai-shek, 21, 176

Chile, 140–42, 154–56, 316

Chilean Communist party, 156

Chilean communists, 170

"Chilean Road to Socialism," 155. *See also* Allende Gossens, Salvador

Chilean Socialist party, 154–55. *See also* Allende Gossens, Salvador

China, 7, 11, 13, 20, 89, 99, 142, 176–82, 192–94, 197, 199–200, 210, 212, 215, 221, 227, 230–36, 245, 253, 271, 281, 321–22

Chinese Communist party (CCP), 99, 176, 193

Chinese model, 20

Chinese Revolution, 59

Chinh, Truong, 195, 336 n.13. *See also* Vietnamese Communist party

Christian Democratic party, 52, 161, 172

Christian Democratic party in Italy (DC), 92

Christian Democrats, 91, 156, 159

Christian Labor party, 123, 124

Churchill, Winston, 111–112

CIA. *See* Central Intelligence Agency

Civil disobedience movement, 210

Class, 206, 305

Class coalitions, 30, 39, 43

Class cohesion, 78

Class struggle, 177

Class struggle from above and below, 49

Class Struggle in France, 1848–1850, The, 32. *See also* Marx, Karl

"Classist" approach, 197

Coalition, 9, 19, 24, 26–30, 32–33, 37, 39, 41–42, 51, 54, 56, 59–60, 68–69, 71–75, 78, 80, 83, 86, 87, 90–91,
93–94, 106–8, 118, 122, 124–25, 156, 163, 166, 170–71, 203, 221–26, 230–33, 236–37, 255, 269, 277, 298, 303–22. *See also* United front

Coalition approaches, 21. *See also* United front

Coalition building, 9, 18, 23, 26, 40, 42, 44, 51, 53, 73, 98, 148, 236, 307, 309–10, 316, 319, 322. *See also* United front

Coalition decay, 125. *See also* United front

Coalition efforts, 105, 320. *See also* United front

Coalition exploitation, 18. *See also* United front

Coalition formation, 18, 99, 133. *See also* United front

Coalition governments, 45–48, 96–97, 106–10, 113, 122, 129, 188–90, 196, 222, 267, 269. *See also* United front

Coalition governments of reconciliation, 108. *See also* United front

Coalition maintenance, 9, 301, 316, 323. *See also* United front

Coalition manipulation, 42. *See also* United front

Coalition on the left, 155. *See also* United front

Coalition partners, 30, 32–33, 130. *See also* United front

Coalition policies, 18, 23, 105. *See also* United front

Coalition politics, 24, 31, 45, 315. *See also* United front

Coalition rules, 128. *See also* United front

Coalition strategies, 9, 13, 17, 19, 26–28, 59, 62, 68–69, 72, 77, 84, 86, 88–89, 91, 102–4, 134, 173, 206, 208, 225, 227, 230, 233, 235–36, 302, 315, 318, 323. *See also* United front

Coalition strategies and tactics, 91, 93, 101–2, 201, 203, 209, 219, 233, 236, 238, 239, 241, 246–48, 263, 273, 282–85, 306–7, 312–13, 315, 319, 322–23. *See also* United front

Coalition tactics, 9, 13, 17, 19, 26–28, 42, 59, 62, 72, 76, 78, 83–84, 86–87, 89, 99, 102–4, 134, 170, 203. *See also* United front

Coalition termination, 9, 323. *See also* United front

Coalition theory, 37, 54. *See also* United front

Coalitions from above, 27, 79, 219. *See also* United front from above

Coalitions from below, 27, 79, 98. *See also* United front from below

Coalitions of national unity, 45

"Cod war," 96. *See also* Althydubandalagid; Iceland; Icelandic party

Cohn-Bendits, 98

Collaborationist phase, 75, 85

Collaborations, 16

Collective security, 74

Collectivism, 65

Collectivization, 64, 83, 86, 199

Collectivization of agriculture, 77, 86, 195

Colombia, 151–53

Colonialism, 136, 179, 310–11

Colonial regime, 21–22, 174–75, 176, 182–83, 210, 308, 319

Cominform, 48, 85–86, 144, 215

Comintern, 7, 11–13, 18, 20, 26, 41–44, 46–48, 52, 55, 67–73, 79–80, 84, 87, 97, 109, 137–40, 144, 175, 177–79, 192, 202, 209–12, 285, 289, 305, 314, 321

Comintern membership, 16

Commandantes, 162. *See also* Nicaragua

Committee for the Solidarity of Patriotic Catholics, 200. *See also* Vietnam

"Committee of solidarity," 259. *See also* Tunisian Communist party

Committee to Organize the Party of the Working People of Ethiopia (COPWE), 277–78

"Committees for national liberation," 45. *See also* Coalition governments

Committees of National Liberation, 48

Common Market (EEC), 90, 93, 98

Communism, 36, 55, 63–64, 73, 83–84, 88, 94, 103–4, 118, 148, 193, 196–97, 202, 205–6, 209, 215, 221, 233–34, 301, 305

Communists, 6, 7, 10, 12, 14, 16, 18–21, 59, 62–65, 68–69, 72–86, 88–105, 121, 124–30, 139–45, 149, 156, 158, 171–74, 185–86, 188–90, 192, 202, 205–17, 223–24, 226, 228–29, 232–36, 242, 256, 284–89, 294–308, 311, 313–318, 322

Communist coalition strategies and tactics, 84

Communist directed fronts, 193

Communist governments, 208, 217–18

Communist ideology, 235

Communist Information Bureau. *See* Cominform

Communist International, 40–41, 137. *See also* Comintern

Communist League of Workers (LCT), 239–40, 265, 268, 270, 271.

Communist Manifesto, The, 29, 31–32, 34, 36, 53. *See also* Marx, Karl

Communist Marxist party, 231. *See also* Communist Party of India-Marxist; India

Communist ministers, 121

Communist movement, 203, 206, 208–9, 221–22, 225–26, 228–37

Communist partisan forces, 112–13

Communist party/parties, 6–7, 9, 12, 15, 34, 38–41, 42–50, 54, 56, 63–73, 76, 79, 80–81, 86–87, 89, 94–95, 97–103, 106–9, 110, 115, 119, 121–30, 136, 138, 142, 144–46, 147, 150, 153–54, 155, 159, 172–74, 175–77, 180, 192, 202–3, 209–10, 222, 226, 228–31, 239, 240, 242, 246, 252, 254, 255–56, 259–60, 264, 266, 267, 272, 279, 284, 291, 305–6, 312, 314, 319

Communist Party of Algeria. *See* Algerian Communist party

Communist Party of Chile, 140, 155

Communist Party of Czechoslovakia. *See* Czechoslovak Communist party

Communist Party of Denmark. *See* Danish Communist party (DKP)

Communist Party of Finland. *See* Finnish Communist party (Suomen Kommunisti-nen Puolue) (SKP)

Communist Party of France. *See* French Communist party

Communist Party of Great Britian (CPGB), 202, 209, 215–16

Communist Party of Hungary. *See* Hungarian Communist party

Communist Party of India (CPI), 202–5, 207, 209, 211–32, 234–36

Communist Party of India-Marxist (CPM), 203–5, 208–9, 218–22, 225–32, 234–36

Communist Party of India, Marxist-Leninist (CPML), 205, 221

Communist Party of the Indies (Perserikaten Kommunist di India), 285. *See also* Indonesian Communist party

Communist Party of Indochina, 177. *See also* Vietminh; Vietnam

Communist Party of Indonesia, 285. *See also* Indonesian Communist party

Communist Party of Italy. *See* Italian Communist party

Communist Party of Nicaragua. *See* Partido Comunista de Nicaragua
Communist Party of Norway. *See* Norwegian Communist party
Communist Party of Peru. *See* Peruvian Communist party
Communist Party of Poland. *See* Polish Workers' (Communist) Party
Communist Party of Romania, 272. *See also* Romanian Communist party
Communist Party of South Africa, 248
Communist Party of the Soviet Union, 7, 9, 12, 62, 71–72, 76, 78, 80, 83, 85, 88, 94–96, 98–101, 103, 105, 272. *See also* Soviet Union
Communist Party of Spain. *See* Spanish Communist party (PCE)
Communist Party of Tunisia. *See* Tunisian Communist party
Communist Party of Venezuela. *See* Partido Comunista de Venezuela
Communist Party of Vietnam. *See* Vietnamese Communist party (VWP)
Communist patriotism, 78
Communist power, 208
Communist revolution, 220, 224
Communist society, 22
Communist Youth Group (Thanh Nien Cong San Doan), 175. *See also* Vietnam
Communist Worker's party (Kommunistische Arbeiter-Partei Deutschlands) (KAPD), 71. *See also* Germany
Compaore, Blaise, 248, 251
Comprador bourgeoisie, 197, 205, 293
Compradores, 289, 290
Compradors, 21, 24
"Comrade Gonzalo," 167. *See also* Guzmán, Abimael Reinzo
Confederación de Trabajadores de Cuba (CTC), 143. *See also* Castro, Fidel; Cuba
Congolese Labor Party (PCT), 239, 241, 273, 278
Congress Alliance, 252
Congress Forum for Socialist Action (CFSA), 223. *See also* India
Congress of Democrats, 252
Congress of Tours, 175. *See also* French Communist party
Congress party, 208. *See also* India
Congress Party for Malagasy Independence (AKFM), 240–41, 263–72
Congress Socialist party (CSP), 211. *See also* India

Conservatives, 15, 82
Constituent Assembly, 165–66, 259
Constitutional communist, 217
Contras, 162–63
Controlled coalitions, 75. *See also* United front
Cooperative coalitions, 30 *See also* United front
Coordinadora Democratica Nicaraguense, 162
Correlation of forces, 322
Council of Generals, 299. *See also* Indonesia; Indonesian Communist party
CPI-Congress alliance, 229, 235. *See also* India
CPs. *See* Communist party/parties
CPSU. *See* Communist Party of the Soviet Union
Critique of the Gotha Program, The, 32, 35. *See also* Marx, Karl
Cruz, Arturo, 162. *See also* Contras; Nicaragua
Cuba, 11, 26, 139, 142, 146, 151, 153, 157, 160, 163, 170, 172, 279–80, 321–22. *See also* Castro, Fidel
Cuban Communist party, 147
Cuban Revolution, 146–57. *See also* Castro, Fidel
Cyrankiewicz, Jozef, 128
"Czechization," 127
Czechoslovak Communist party, 126
Czechoslovak government-in-exile, 113. *See also* Beneš, Edvard
Czechoslovakia, 48–49, 53, 94, 108–9, 112–13, 119, 122–23, 126, 129, 153, 287, 307, 316
Czechoslovakians, 28, 46

Dai, Boa, 183. *See also* Vietnam
Dakar, 264
Dange, S. A., 213, 225, 235. *See also* Communist Party of India; India
Dangeism, 229, 235, 236. *See also* Communist Party of India; India
Danish Communist party (DKP), 89–90
Davis, Lynn Etheridge, 110
Debray, Regis, 150–51
Decolonialization, 24
Delegation of the PKI Central Committee, 300–301. *See also* Adjitorop, Jusuf
Democratic alliance, 142
Democratic coalitions, 48–49, 56. *See also* United front

Democratic dictatorships of workers and peasants, 49

Democratic League-Labor Movement (LD-MPT), 239, 264, 267–68, 270–71

Democratic party, 123, 181, 187. *See also* Poland

Democratic Party of South Vietnam (Dang Dan Chu Mien Nam Viet Nam), 187

Democratic Republic of Vietnam (D.R.V.), 184, 186–88, 194. *See also* Vietnam

Democratic state system, 47

Democratic Union, 261

Democratic unity, 227, 229–30. *See also* Communist Party of India-Marxist; India

Deng Xiaoping, 253

Denmark, 76, 81, 87, 89–90, 129

Deshpande, Roza, 229. *See also* All-India Communist party; India

Destourian Socialist party, 259. *See also* Tunisian Communist party

Deviationism, 16, 235

Dia, Mamadou, 268. *See also* People's Democratic Movement

Dictatorship of the proletariat, 6, 31–32, 34, 38–41, 44–45, 47–48, 51–53, 55–56, 71, 77, 83, 333 n.37

Dictatorship of the Proletariat, The, 38, 50, *See also* Lenin, Vladimir Ilich

Dictatorship of the vanguard minority party, 50

Dimitrov, Georgi, 47, 109, 119. *See also* Bulgaria; Communist Party of Bulgaria

Diouf, Abdou, 265, 268

Djie Tan Ling, 288. *See also* Indonesian Communist party

Djilas, Milovan, 108, 110. *See also* Tito, Josif Broz; Yugoslavia

Domesticism, 86, 88

Duclos, Jacques, 84. *See also* French Communist party

Dutch colonial government, 21–23,

Dutschke, Rudi, 98

Dutt, Rajani Palme, 213, 215–16. *See also* Communist Party of India; India

Easter Offensive, 191. *See also* Vietnam

East Germany, 307

Eastern Europe, 27–28

Easton, David, 29

Economic and Philosophical Manuscripts of 1844, 33, 37, 50. *See also* Marx, Karl

Edén Pastora (Comandante Cero), 160. *See also* Nicaragua

EECI. *See* Executive Committee of the Communist International

Egalitarianism, 87

Egyptian Communist party, 239, 241–43, 245–46, 283

Egyptian Communist party—Congress Faction (ECP–CF), 240

Egyptian Communist party—January 8 (ECP-January 8), 240

Egyptian Workers' Communist party (EWCP), 240

"Einen besonderen deutschen Weg zum Sozialismus," 48. *See also* Ackerman, Adolf

Electoral coalitions, 30, 42–44, 208. *See also* United front

Electoral Yennans, 228, 233. *See also* India

Elite party, 38

Elleinstein, J., 54. *See also* French Communist party

Engels, Friedrich, 1–3, 6, 26, 30–33, 35–38, 41, 43, 50–51, 53–54, 59, 62, 133, 135

England, 32, 35, 38, 61, 110–11

Enlightenment, 14, 34

Entfremdung, 34. *See also* Marx, Karl

Eritrean People's Liberation Front, 240

Eritreans, 278

Esquipulas initiative, 163. *See also* Arias, Oscar; Contras

Ethnic particularism, 311

Eurocommunism, 31, 49–51, 54–55, 88, 91, 93–95, 103–4, 154, 156, 233–34, 306

Eurocommunism and the State, 52. *See also* Carrillo, Santiago

Eurocommunist parties, 99

Eurocommunists, 30, 45, 52–56, 66

European Economic Community, 282

Executive Committee of the Communist International (EECI), 44, 67–69, 71–72, 305

Factionalism, 65, 126

Farmers' Front, 294. *See also* Indonesia; Indonesian Communist party

Farmers' Liberation Association, 187. *See also* Vietnam

Fascism, 43, 45–46, 73, 129, 140, 178–80, 211

Fascists, 18–19, 45, 64, 74–76, 78, 139, 156, 224

Fatherland Front (Mat Tran To Quoc), 185, 187, 194, 196, 200. *See also* Vietminh;

Vietnam
Fatherland front in Bulgaria, 126
Fatherland of socialism, 98
Federación Obrera de Chile (FOCH), 140.
    See also Chile; Chilean Communist party
Feudalism, 174, 215, 288–89, 293
Fidelista, 148, 153–54, 160. See also Castro,
    Fidel
Fifth Congress of the Comintern (1924),
    137. See also Comintern
"Fifth force," 298. See also Indonesia;
    Indonesian Communist party
Finland, 76, 87, 95–97, 100, 102, 104, 129
"Finlandization," 307
Finnish Communist party (SKP), 87, 97,
    100. See also Suomen Kommunistinen
    Puolue
Finnish Democratic League (SKDL), 87, 97.
    See also Suomen Kansan Demokraattinen
    Liitto (SKDL)
First Duma (1905), 40
First Indochina War, 182, 184. See also
    Vietnam
First International, 35. See also Engels,
    Friedrich; Marx, Karl
Foco tactics, 157. See also Venezuela
Fonseca, Carlos, 159. See also Nicaragua;
    Partido Socialista Nicaraguense
Four-class alliance, 197, 215. See also
    Vietnam
Four-class coalition, 213. See also Commu-
    nist Party of India; India
Fourth International, 71, 146. See also
    Trotsky, Leon
Framework for United Action by the Oppo-
    sition Forces, 268
France, 14, 33, 35–36, 38, 44, 46, 48,
    74–76, 81, 84–86, 91, 103, 129, 267,
    281–82, 321
French presence in Indochina, 179–83
French Communist party (PCF), 43, 89, 91,
    94, 99, 102–3, 175, 242, 265, 269
French Revolution (1789), 31, 34
French Revolution (1830), 31
French Socialist party, 262
Frente nacional antifranquista, 52. See also
    Carrillo, Santiago; Spanish Communist
    party
Frente Patriótica Nacional (FPN), 161. See
    also Nicaragua
Frente Sandinista de Liberación Nacional
    (FSLN), 159–63. See also Nicaragua
Front coalitions, 232. See also United front

Front for the Defense of the Malagasy
    Socialist Revolution, 266–68
Front for the Liberation of the Mozambique
    (Frelimo), 240–41, 273–74, 277
Front of Struggle for Democracy and Salva-
    tion of the Country, 259
Frugoni, Emilio, 135–36
Fuentes, Carlos, 171
Fuerzas Armadas de Liberación Nacional
    (FALN), 157–60. See also Venezuela
Furubotn, Peder, 84. See also Norway; Nor-
    wegian Communist party

Gamson, William A., 29
Gandhi, Indira, 203, 208, 222–24, 227–29,
    231–32, 236
Gandhi, Mohandas K., 202, 210, 214
Gandhi, Rajiv, 204, 208, 231–32,
Gandhi, Sanjay, 224, 229
Gandhi civil disobedience movement, 210
García Alan, 166–67. See also Alianza Pop-
    ular Revolucionaria Americana; Peru
García Marquez, Gabriel, 171
Gati, Charles, 307
General strike, 214
General suffrage, 34
General Union of Algerian Workers, 244
General Union of Tunisian Workers (UGTT),
    259
Geneva, 184
Geneva Accords, 185
Geneva Conference, 193–94
Genuine coalition, 108, 122–23. See also
    United front
Georgiev, Kimon, 122. See also Bulgaria
German Communist party (DKP), 100
German Ideology, The, 33–34, 37. See also
    Marx, Karl
German Social Democratic party, 36, 104
German-Soviet nonaggression pact (August
    1939), 74
German Workers' party (Socialist Workers'
    Party of Germany), 32
Germans communists, 40, 50
Germany, 14, 31, 33, 35–36, 38, 43, 48, 61,
    73, 75, 81, 109, 119, 210, 315
Gerö, Ernö, 109. See also Hungary; Hun-
    garian Communist party
Ghosh, Ajoy, 213, 215–16, 218. See also
    Communist Party of India; India
Giap Vo Nguyen, 336 n.13. See also
    Vietnam
Global powers, 321

"Global united front," 191. *See also* United front

Gomulka, Wladyslaw, 109, 118. *See also* Poland; Polish Workers' (Communist) party

Gottwald, Klement, 48, 109–10. *See also* Czechoslovakia; Czechoslovak Communist party

Gottwald Plan, 287

Government coalitions, 30, 42, 45. *See also* United front; United front from above

Governments of national unity, 105, 115, 117. *See also* United front; United front from above

Gramsci, Antonia, 49, 51–53

Grand coalition, 78, 80–83, 85–86. *See also* United front

Great Britain, 14, 15, 65, 74–75, 81, 94, 96, 210, 281, 321

Great October, 100, 105

Greece, 111, 129

Grol, Milan, 123

Grove, Marmaduke, 140, 142. *See also* Chile

Groza, Petru, 121, 128. *See also* Romania; Romanian Communist party

Guardia Civil, 167. *See also* Peru

Guatemala, 146–47

Guayasamin, Osvaldo, 171

Guerra Popular Prolongada (GPP), 160. *See also* Frente Sandinista de Liberacion Nacional; Nicaragua

Guerrilla warfare, 151, 215, 289

Guerrillas, 25, 151–52, 160, 181

Guevara, Ernesto "Che," 149–50, 152, 171. *See also* Castro, Fidel; Cuba

Guevarista, 153

"Guided Democracy," 295–97, 302. *See also* Indonesia; Indonesian Communist party; Sukarno

Guzmán Jacobo Arbenz. *See* Arbenz Guzmán, Jacobo

Guzmán Reinoso, Abimael, 167. *See also* "Comrade Gonzalo"

Hagberg, Hilding, 92. *See also* Sweden; Swedish Communist party

Hanoi, 181, 185, 187–93, 196–98, 200–201

Hardjosubroto, Njadiman, 288. *See also* Indonesia; Indonesian Communist party

Hargrave, Robert L., 204

Harian Rakjat, 299. *See also* Indonesian Communist party

Hatta, Mohammed, 286, 296. *See also* Indonesia

Hegemonic bloc, 52

Hegemonic coalitions, 30. *See also* United front

Hegemony, 52, 108, 234

Hermansson, Carl-Henrik, 92. *See also* Left Party of Communists of Sweden; Sweden

Hidalgo, Padre, 171

Hindi belt, 205, 207, 211–12, 233. *See also* India

Historic compromise, 52. *See also* Italy; Italian Communist party

Historic program, 161. *See also* Frente Sandinista de Liberacíon Nacional; Sandinista

Hitler, Adolf, 73, 75, 97, 109, 119, 142, 211

Hitler-Stalin pact, 75–76, 141. *See also* German-Soviet nonaggression pact (August 1939)

Hoa Hoa, 181, 198. *See also* Vietnam

Ho Chi Minh, 23, 174–76, 178–81, 191–93, 235. *See also* Vietminh; Vietnam

Holland, 35, 38

Home communists, 333 n.37

Horn of Africa, 275

Horthy, Miklos, 109–10. *See also* Hungary

Hotel Lux, 67. *See also* Comintern; Executive Committee of the Communist International

Hue, 190–91. *See also* Vietnam

Humanism, 34

Humanistic elements in Marx, 34, 49. *See also* Marx, Karl

Humbert-Droz, Jules, 137. *See also* Comintern

Hundred Flowers campaign, 194. *See also* China; Chinese Communist party

Hungarian Arrow Cross, 332 n.25

Hungarian Communist party, 118

Hungary, 46, 48, 109, 111, 115, 118–123, 126, 129, 316

Hussan II, King, 256–57

Hutabea, 300. *See also* Indonesia; Indonesian Communist party

Huynh Tan Phat, 338 n.29

Hyndman, H. M., 36

Ibáñez, Carlos, 140. *See also* Chile

Iceland, 87, 94–95, 97, 104, 129

Idealism, 150

Ideologism, 102

Il Compromisso Istorico, 92. *See also* Italy; Italian Communist party
Imperialism, 136, 140, 153, 174, 179, 180, 215, 220, 227, 241, 288–89, 293
Imperialists, 249
India, 20, 22–23, 28, 202, 205–7, 210, 215–16, 219–21, 229, 232–34, 316, 319, 321
India-China border dispute, 218
Indian communist movement, 218
Indian National Congress, 202–4, 210–11, 219, 222, 234
Indian National Trade Union Congress (INTUC), 207
Indian Social Democratic Association, 285
Indian Parliament, 203
Individualism, 65
Indochina, 22–23, 309
Indochinese Communist party (ICP), 177–84. *See also* Vietminh; Vietnam
Indonesia, 22–23, 28, 284–85, 289–90, 296, 298, 309, 314, 317
Indonesian Communist party (Partai Komunis Indonesia or PKI), 284–90, 292–303, 309, 314, 317
Indonesian communists, 284, 286, 292
Indonesian Farmers' Front (Barisan Tani Indonesia) BTI, 293
Indonesian Labor party, 286
Indonesian Nationalist party (PNI), 287, 295–96, 302
Indonesian Social-Democratic Association, 285
Indonesian Socialist party (PSI), 295
Indonesian Revolution, 298
Indonesianizing Marxism-Leninism, 288
Industrial Revolution, 14
Institute of People's Culture (LEKRA), 294. *See also* Indonesia; Indonesian Communist party
Instituto Nacional de Reforma Agraria (INRA), 147. *See also* Guatemala
Intelligentsia, 39, 219, 228
Inter-American Conferences, 145
International communism, 66–67, 89, 151, 154, 164
International communist movement, 89, 100, 145, 169, 227, 253–54. *See also* Comintern
Internationalism, 3, 17, 28, 75, 87, 104
Internationalist aspects of Marxism, 3, 62, 307–8
Irian Jaya, 302. *See also* Indonesia

Islam, 24, 244, 260, 313
Islamic Tendency Movement, 259, 261. *See also* Tunisian Communist party; Tunisian Federation
Island Committee for Outer Areas, 292, *See also* Indonesia; Indonesian Communist party
Israel, 243, 257
Italian Communist party (PCI), 52, 91–92, 94, 99, 102
Italian Marxism, 52
Italians, 24, 40, 49
Italian Somaliland, 277
Italy, 46, 48, 81, 85–86, 91, 94, 104, 129, 282
Izquierda Unida (IU), 165–66, 169–70. *See also* Peru

Jakarta, 297
Jan Mayen Island, 96
Janata, 225, 227–28, 236. *See also* India; Indian National Congress
Jani, Ahamd, 299. *See also* Indonesia
Japan, 181, 321
Java, 285, 292–95, 299–300
Johannesburg, 247
Jonathan, Leabua, 240, 249–50, 252
Joshi, P. C., 213. *See also* Communist Party of India; India
Jugnauth, Aneerood, 265–66. *See also* Mauritian Socialist Movement
Jullundur, 226. *See also* Communist Party of India-Marxist; India
Junta of National Reconstruction, 161. *See also* Frente Sandinista de Liberación nacional; Nicaragua
Justo, Juan B., 135

Kai-shek, Chiang. *See* Chiang Kai-shek
Kamaruzaman, 301. *See also* Indonesia; Indonesian Communist party
Kampuchea, 99
Katayama, Sen, 137
Kautsky, Karl, 37–38, 49–50, 53–54, 135. *See also* Marx, Karl
Keflavik, 96
Kehidupan, Partai (Party Life), 290. *See also* Indonesia; Indonesian Communist party
Kerala, 204, 206–8, 212, 217–18, 221–22, 225–29, 231–33. *See also* Communist Party of India; Communist Party of India-Marxist; India
Kerala Muslim League, 231

Khartoum, 256, 263

Khrushchev, Nikita Sergeevich, 89

Kienthal, 11

Knudsen, Martin Gunnar, 93. *See also* Norway; Norwegian Communist party

Kollontai, Alexandra, 88

Korean War, 147, 322

Košice, 113. *See also* Czechoslovakia; Czechoslovak Communist party

Kremlin, 7–8, 13, 19, 25, 59, 62, 72, 75, 94, 101, 111–12, 306–7, 312, 321

Kronstadt, 71

"Kto kogo? (Who-Whom?)," 39. *See also* Lenin, Vladimir Ilich

Kumaramangalam, Mohan, 222–23; *See also* Communist Party of India; India; Indian National Congress

Kuomintang, 176, 182, 192

Labor parties, 286–87

Labor party approach, 70

Labour party, 81, 90

Lagos, 247

Landed gentry, 180

Landless laborers, 207, 214

Land redistribution, 22, 183

Land reform, 19, 22, 83, 189

Land reform program, 183

Laos, 179, 184, 188

Larsen, Reidar, 93. *See also* Leftist Electoral Alliance; Norway; Norwegian Communist party

Latifundia, 19

Latin America, 28, 288

Latin American Organization of Solidarity (OLAS), 153

Latin American Trade Union Confederation, 139

Law for the Defense of Democracy, 142. *See also* Chile

League for the Independence of Vietnam, 179. *See also* Vietminh; Vietnam

League for the National Union of Vietnam (Lien Viet), 183. *See also* Vietminh; Vietnam

League of Oppressed Peoples of Asia (Hoi Dan Toc Bi Ap Buc The Gion), 176. *See also* Vietminh; Vietnam

Left Party of Communists of Sweden (VPK), 91, 99. *See also* Sweden; Swedish Communist party

Leftist blocs, 45

Leftist Electoral Alliance (SV), 93. *See also* Norway: Norwegian Communist party

Left-sectarian deviation, 221. *See also* Communist Party of India-Marxist; India

Left Socialist revolutionaries, 40

Left socialists, 90

Left unity, 225–26, 229

"Left-Wing" Communism: An Infantile Disorder (essay), 40–44, 48, 51. *See also* Lenin, Vladimir Ilich

Left-wing tactics, 42

Legitimacy, 308, 314, 318–19

Lenin, Vladimir Ilich, 3, 7, 15, 19, 30–31, 33, 37–48, 50–53, 55, 59, 63, 88, 135–36, 144, 153, 174–76, 198, 209–11, 235, 288–89, 309, 317

Leninism, 31, 50, 54, 105, 170, 175

Leninist four-class alliance, 179, 186. *See also* Vietminh; Vietnam

Leninist wing (Sajap Leninis), 288. *See also* Indonesia; Indonesian Communist party

Lesotho, 247

Lesotho Communist party, 239–40, 246–50, 252–54

Liberals, 90, 119

Liberation movements, 240, 322

Liberation theology, 313

Lichtheim, George, 35

Lien Viet Front, 183, 185. *See also* Vietminh; Vietnam

Liga Socialista Revolucionaria (paper), 146. *See also* Trotskyites

Lima, Peru, 165–67, 169

Linggadjati Agreement, 286. *See also* Indonesia; Sukarno

Lin Piao faction, 235

Lingán, Alfonso Barrantes. *See* Barrantes Lingán, Alfonso

Liss, Sheldon, 152, 155

Llosa, Mario Vargas, 168

Lok Sabha, 203–4, 216, 230–31, *See also* India; Indian National Congress

London, 81, 110, 113, 123

Løvlien, Emil, 84. *See also* Norway; Norwegian Communist party

Low Countries, 14

Lublin Committee, 115. *See also* Poland; Polish Communist Party

Lukman, M. H., 288, 293, 299. *See also* Indonesia; Indonesian Communist party

Lulchev, Kosta, 122. *See also* Bulgaria

Lumpenproletariat, 14

Luxemburg, 76, 129

Luxemburg, Rosa, 49–51, 53

Machado dictatorship, 139. *See also* Cuba
Machiavelli, Niccolò, 51
Maintenance of Internal Security Act
   (MISA), 224. *See also* Gandhi, Indira;
   India
Malaysia, 296, 298
Mallin, Jay, 152
Managua, 160, 163
Manipol, 297. *See also* Indonesia, Sukarno
Manuilskii, Dmitri, 47, 109
Maoism, 2, 234, 253
Maoist mod, 188
Maoists, 2, 10, 98–99, 167, 180, 192–94,
   203, 213, 216, 218, 221, 245, 253, 271
Mao Tse-tung. *See* Mao Zedong
Mao Zedong, 47, 167, 193, 215, 235, 245,
   271, 288, 291, 309, 317
Mariátegui, José Carlos, 164, 167
Marinello, Juan, 143, 148. *See also* Cuba
"Maring," 285. *See also* Sneevliet, H. J.
Marquez, Gabriel García. *See* García Mar-
   quez, Gabriel
Marti, José, 136. *See also* Cuba
Marx, Karl, 1–7, 15, 20, 24, 30–37, 59,
   62, 66, 133–36, 144, 177, 198, 309
Marxism, 1–6, 8, 12, 14–15, 17, 21, 24,
   62, 68, 75, 88, 99, 101–2, 105, 133, 136,
   144, 147, 149, 153, 157, 159, 164,
   169–70, 304–8, 310–11, 313, 315, 318,
   323
Marxism-Leninism, 2, 17–18, 20, 62, 83,
   102–3, 175, 192, 229, 233–34, 288,
   299, 310
Marxist coalition strategies and tactics, 102.
   See also Coalition; United front; United
   front from above; United front from
   below
Marxist-Leninist Communist Organization
   of Réuion, 265
Marxist-Leninist Group of the Communist
   Party of Indonesia, 300
Marxist-Leninist parties, 10–12, 99, 165,
   172, 242–43, 245
Marxist Partido Popular, 145. *See also*
   Mexico
Marxist parties, 8–12, 17–18, 62, 100, 134,
   154, 159, 170–71, 173, 238–39, 241,
   248, 261, 267–68, 282–83, 302, 304,
   305, 313, 315
Marxists-Leninists, 3, 9, 10, 12, 14–16, 54,
   80, 87, 102, 155, 157, 164, 167, 169,
   171–73, 221, 233–34, 239–40, 244, 255,
   285, 298, 303, 309–10, 314, 316–18, 322

Masjumi (Muslim Federation), 287,
   295–96, 303. *See also* Indonesia; Indonesian Communist party
"Mass-line" strategy, 189, 194, 197. *See also*
   Vietminh; Vietnam
Materialism and Empirico-Criticism (1909),
   37–38. *See also* Lenin, Vladimir Ilich
Mauritian Militant Movement (MMM),
   240–41, 263, 265–66, 269–71
Mauritian Socialist Movement (MSM), 265–
   66
Mauritian Socialist party, 266, 269–70
Mauritian Social Progressive Militant Move-
   ment (MMMSP), 240–41, 263, 265, 269,
   271
May Fourth Movement, 179. *See also* Indo-
   chinese Communist party; Vietnam
Mayorga, Silvio, 160. *See also* Frente San-
   dinista de Liberación Nacional;
   Nicaragua
Mekong delta, 181, 196, 199
Mexico, 135–37, 139, 145
Middle bourgeoisie, 213, 215
Middle class, 33, 47
Miklós, Bela Dálnoki, 121. *See also*
   Hungary
Mikolajczyk, Stanislaw, 118–19, 124, 127.
   See also Mikolajczyk's People's (Peasant)
   party; Poland
Mikolajczyk's People's (Peasant) party, 123.
   See also Poland
Mill, J. S., 34
Minh, Ho Chi. *See* Ho Chi Minh
Minimum winning status, 125. *See also*
   Coalitions
Mitterrand, François, 91, 150. *See also*
   France; French Socialist party
Modernization, 60
Monolithic control, 108
Moscow, 1–2, 25–26, 63–64, 66–67,
   73–74, 76–80, 85, 87–89, 94, 98–102,
   109–11, 113, 115, 119, 121, 126, 129,
   138–39, 146, 164, 175, 177–78, 239,
   245–46, 253–54, 263, 272, 275, 297,
   300–301, 305–7, 310, 321–22
Moslem Masjumi, 295. *See also* Indonesia;
   Indonesian Communist party
Moslems, 294, 303. *See also* Islam
Movement for Proletarian Power (MFM),
   240–41, 263–68, 270–71
Movement for the Independence of
   Réunion (MIR), 240–41, 263, 265–66,
   269

Movement for the Liberation of São Tomé and Príncipe (MLSTP), 239, 241, 273, 277

Movement of Social Democrats, 259

Movimiento Acción Popular—Marxista Leninista (MAP–MP), 162. See also Coordinadora Democratica Nicaraguense; Nicaragua

Movimento al Socialismo (MAS), 154, 158–59. See also Petkoff, Teodoro

Movimento de Izquierda Revolucionari (MIR), 151, 156–59. See also Peru

Mubarak, Hosni, 243, 246

Mugabe, Robert, 275

Munir, Mohammed, 301. See also Indonesia; Indonesian Communist party

Murba party, 298. See also Indonesia

Murdani, Benny, 301. See also Indonesia

Muscovites, 153, 167, 333 n.37

Muslims 22, 244, 260, 287, 299, 313–14. See also Islam

Musso, 286–88. See also Indonesia; Indonesian Communist party

Mussolini, Benito, 51

Mutual assistance associations, 178. See also Vietminh; Vietnam

Nagy, Ferenc, 121. See also Hungary; Hungarian Communist party

Nahdatul Ulama, 295. See also Indonesia

Namboodiripad, E. M. S., 234. See also Communist Party of India-Marxist; India

Nanking, 176

Narayan, Jayapakash, 224

NASAKOM (NAS—nationalist; A—religious groups; KOM—Communists), 289–90, 297. See also Indonesia; Indonesian Communist party

Nasakomization, 299. See also Indonesia; Indonesian Communist party

Nasser, Gamal Abdul, 242

Nasution, A. H., 299. See also Indonesia; Indonesian Communist party

National approaches, 102

National bourgeois state, 219

National bourgeoisie, 47, 180, 219, 221, 230, 289, 293–94

National coalition, 83, 182. See also United front

National collaboration, 119

National Committee, 113. See also Yugoslavia; Tito, Josif Broz

National communism, 178, 308

National Council, 127. See also Poland; Polish Communist party

National democratic front, 203, 219, 222–23, 227, 230

National democratic government, 224

National democratic state, 219

National Directorate of the FSLN, 162. See also Frente Sandinista de Liberación Nacional; Nicaragua

National emancipation, 33

National Front, 80, 289, 297

National Front for the Defense of the Malagasy Socialist Revolution, 265–66, 270

National Front for the Liberation of South Vietnam (NLF), 186–91, 197–98

National Front for the Liberation of West Irian, 297. See also Indonesia

National front cabinet, 261. See also Party of Progress and Socialism (PPS)

National front government, 287. See also Indonesia; Indonesian Communist party

National fronts, 45

National independence, 24, 27, 175–76, 179–80, 201, 220, 255

National integration, 284

National interest, 79, 180, 274

National Liaison Committee of Patriotic and Peace-Loving Catholics, 187. See also Vietnam

National liberation, 46, 180, 264

National liberation front, 184

National Liberation Front (FLN), 242–43. See also Algerian Communist party

National liberation movements, 13, 191, 213–14, 319, 322

National minorities, 182, 195

National Movement for the Independence of Madagascar (Monima), 269

National Peasants, 121, 126. See also Romania

National Progressive Unionist Party (NPUP), 244

National reconciliation, 81

National reconstruction, 79–80

National reunification, 185, 195–96

National roads to socialism and communism, 19, 307

National salvation associations (cuu quoc hoi), 181. See also Vietnam

National Union of Algerian Youth, 244

National Union of Moroccan Students, 260

National Union of Popular Forces, 255. See also Socialist Union of Popular Forces (Morocco)

National united front, 284–85, 287–88, 292
National unity, 153
National unity cabinets, 257
Nationalism, 3, 7, 12, 17, 19, 27, 74, 78–79, 86–88, 134, 177, 179, 192, 214, 219, 284, 296, 304–6, 308–10, 312, 315–16, 320, 322
Nationalist movements, 184, 202
Nationalist parties, 174
Nationalistic alliance, 183
Nationalists, 21, 84–85, 88, 172, 176, 181–82, 210–12, 218, 228, 235, 289, 297, 299, 322
Nationalization, 64, 83, 86, 97, 223; of agriculture, 86; of industry, 195; of private industry, 199
Nation building, 311, 319
Native fascism, 17
Naxalbari, 221. See also India; Naxalites
Naxalites, 205, 221, 235–37. See also India; Naxalbari
Nazi Germany, 18, 76
Nazis, 19, 75, 211, 306
Nazi-Soviet pact, 179. See also Hitler-Stalin pact; German-Soviet nonaggression pact of August 1939
Nehru, Jawaharlal, 203, 207, 210, 212–17, 219, 223
Neikov, Dimitur, 122. See also Bulgaria
Neruda, Pablo, 171
Netherlands, 76, 81, 100, 281
New Left, 72, 88, 97–99, 150–54
New Left strategy, 210. See also Comintern
New Order, 284. See also Indonesia; Suharto
New political formation, 52, 56
"New Road," 286, 288. See also Zhdanov, Andrei
Ngo Dinh Diem, 184–90. See also Vietminh; Vietnam
Nguyen Cao Ky, 190. See also Vietnam
Nguyen Huu Tho, 197. See also Vietnam
Nguyen Van Thieu, 190, 197. See also Vietnam
Nicaragua, 159, 163, 310
Nicaraguan Revolution, 159, 163–64, 171
Nigerian Trade Union Congress, 247
Nimeiri, Gaafar, 256–57, 259, 261
Nizam of Hyderabad, 214. See also India
Njoto, 288, 299. See also Indonesia; Indonesian Communist party
Noblesse oblige, 15

Nomadic peoples, 195
Nonalignment, 216
Non-Marxist left, 101
Norrbotten, 92. See also Left Party of Communists of Sweden; Sweden; Swedish Communist party
North Africa, 24
North Korea, 233, 322
North Vietnam, 23, 322
Norway, 70, 76, 81, 89–91, 93–94, 96–97, 129
Norwegian Communist party (Norges Kommunistiske Parti) (NKP), 71, 84, 89–93
Norwegian Labor party (DNA), 12, 69–71, 90, 92
Norwegian Social Democratic party, 69
Norwegian Social Democrats, 92

OAS, 147
Obbov, Alexandur, 122. See also Bulgaria
October Revolution, 40, 136
Ogaden, 278
On Coalition Government, 47. See also Mao Zedong
On Compromises (essay), 40. See also Lenin, Vladimir Ilich
One-party hegemony, 108
On the People's Democratic Dictatorship, 47. See also Mao Zedong
"Opium of the people," 313. See also Marx, Karl
Organic government, 65
Organization of African Unity, 280
Organization for Democratic and Popular Action (OADP), 240–41, 255–56, 258, 260–63
Ortega Saavedra, Daniel, 162–64
Orthodox church, 315
Orthodoxy, 102
Osobka-Morawski, 127. See also Poland
Otzovisty, 40
Outer Islands, 295, 300, 303. See also Indonesia; Indonesian Communist party
Overseas Chinese, 189, 196, 198–99, 201. See also Vietnam
Oversized coalitions, 128, 129. See also Coalition; United front
Overstreet, Gene, 209

Pakistan, 212
Palghat, 217. See also Communist Party of India
Palme, Olof, 91. See also Sweden

Palace of Pizarro, 169. *See also* Peru

Pan-Europeanism, 11

Pan-Islamic tendencies, 11

Pan-Slavism, 11

Paris, 31, 175, 266–67

Paris Commune, 32, 34, 35

Parker, Guy, 296

Parliamentarianism, 41

Parliamentary coalitions, 30, 41–43. *See also* Coalition; United front

Parliamentary democracy, 32, 45

Parochialism, 234

Participatory democracy, 17

Partido Comunista de Nicaragua (PC de N), 160–61

Partido Comunista de Venezuela (PCV), 157–59

Partido de Izquierda Revolucionaria (PIR), 145. *See also* Bolivia

Partido Guatemalteco de Trabajadores (PGT), 146–47

Partido Obrero Revolucionario (POR), 145–46. *See also* Bolivia

Partido Popular Christiano, 166. *See also* Peru

Partido Socialista Nicaraguense (PSN), 159–60, 162

Partido Socialista Popular (PSP), 148. *See also* Cuba

Party of Independence and Labor (PIT), 239, 264–65, 267–68, 270–72

Party of Progress and Socialism (PPS), 239, 241, 255–58, 260–62. *See also* Organization for Democratic and Popular Action; Socialist Union of Popular Forces

Pastora, Edén, 161–62

Pastukhov, Hristiu, 122. *See also* Bulgaria

Passivists, 85

Paternalism, 15

Patna, 231. *See also* Communist Party of India

Patrice Lumumba Institute of Political Science, 247. *See also* Socialist Workers' and Farmers' party

Patriotic Buddhist Believers' Association, 187. *See also* Vietnam

Patriotic Khmer Monks' Solidarity Association, 187. *See also* Vietnam

Patriotic League for Development (LIPAD), 239, 247–48, 251, 253–54

Patriotism, 78–79, 175

Pauperization, 14

Peace movements, 306, 322

Peaceful coexistence, 217

Peaceful transition to socialism, 217, 220

Peasant associations, 184

Peasant communism, 193

Peasant parties, 124

Peasant Question, The, 336 n.13. *See also* Marx, Karl

Peasant revolution, 157

Peasantry, 5, 33, 39, 47, 152, 174, 177, 180, 183, 192, 213–15, 219, 222, 290, 301

Peasant-worker, 151

Penetrative coalitions, 30, 43, 53. *See also* Coalition; United front; United front from below

People's Association (Sarekat Rakjat), 285, *See also* Indonesia; Indonesian Communist party

People's coalitions, 77. *See also* Coalition

People's democracy, 75, 118–19, 204, 220, 227, 230

People's democratic front, 220

People's democratic dictatorship, 193

People's Democratic Movement (MDP), 268

People's front, 16, 74

People's Liberation Armed Forces, 189. *See also* Vietminh; Vietnam

People's militia, 298. *See also* Indonesia; Indonesian Communist party

People's Party, 127. *See also* Czechoslovakia

People's Republic of China, 297

People's Revolutionary party (PRP), 187, 196. *See also* Vietminh; Vietnam

People's University (Universitas Rakjat) (UNRA), 294. *See also* Indonesia; Indonesian Communist party

People's war, 168, 188. *See also* Peru; Sendero Luminoso

People's Youth (Pemuda Rakjat), 294. *See also* Indonesia; Indonesian Communist party

Perón, Juan Domingo, 143–44. *See also* Argentina

Peru, 151–54, 164–65, 167, 169–70

Peruvian Communist party, 164–65, 167, 169

Peruvian Communist party (Shining Path), 167. *See also* Sendero Luminoso

Petkoff, Teodoro, 154

Petkov, Nikola, 122. *See also* Bulgaria; Agrarian Union

Petty bourgeois extremists, 172

Petty bourgeois nationalism, 192

Petty bourgeoisie, 27, 33, 39, 140, 153,

177, 190, 196, 213, 215, 222, 300

Pham Ngoc Thach, 181. *See also* Vietminh; Vietnam

Phan de dong minh, 177. *See also* United front; Vietnam

Phat, Huynh Tan. *See* Huynh Tan Phat

Phouma, Souvanna. *See* Souvanna Phouma

Plekhanov, Grigorii, 37

Pluralism, 65, 77, 95, 102, 162

Pluralistic democracy, 118

Pluralistic societies, 103, 107

Pol Pot, 167. *See also* Cambodia; Kampuchea

Poland, 33, 76, 99–100, 109, 112, 115, 118–19, 123–24, 129

Polish Provisional Government of National Unity, 112

Polish Social Democrats (PPS), 127–28

Polish Socialist party, 123

Polish Workers (Communist) party, 124

Political apathy, 17

Political coalitions, 30, 40, 42, 55, 119. *See also* Coalition; United front

Political efficacy, 318

Political mobilization, 65

Political pluralism, 65–66

Political socialization, 308

Politicization, 61

Polycentrism, 52, 88, 94

Popular Impulse for National Unity (Vonjy), 269

Popular democracy, 118

Popular front, 44–45, 73–75, 78, 140–44, 154, 165, 169, 178–79, 181, 251, 316

Popular Movement for the Liberation of Angola-Workers' party (MPLA–PT), 239, 241, 273–74, 277

Popular Unity Movement, 259. *See also* Tunisia; Tunisian Communist party

Populism, 151

Portugal, 81, 281, 321

Positional advantage, 126, 128, 130. *See also* Coalition

PPR, 128. *See also* Poland

Prawirodirdjo, Alimin, 286. *See also* Indonesia; Indonesian Communist party

Prado, Jorge del, 153, 165

Pretoria, 250, 266, 272, 275, 280

Problems of Leninism, 41. *See also* Stalin, Josef

Procedural legitimacy, 318

Progressive bourgeoisie, 69, 203, 222

Progressive coalition, 84–85. *See also* Coalition; United front

Progressive front, 80. *See also* United front

Proletarian consciousness, 136

Proletarian democracy, 39

Proletarian dictatorship, 39, 46, 48, 234

Proletarian hegemony, 192

Proletarian internationalism, 63, 103, 218, 234

Proletarian revolution, 40–41

The Proletarian Revolution and the Renegade Kautsky, 38. *See also* Lenin, Vladimir Ilich

Proletariat, 14, 31, 33, 35, 38–39, 43, 60, 140, 173, 175, 182, 192, 194, 213, 301

Protestantism, 312, 314

Provisional Revolutionary Government (PRG), 187, 197. *See also* Vietnam

Public ownership of the means of production, 64, 83

Putschists, 172

Quang, Thich Tri, 189–90. *See also* Vietnam

Quit Indian Movement, 211

Rabeshala, Giselle, 266. *See also* Congress Party for Malagasy Independence; Movement for Proletarian Power

Rădescu, R., 121. *See also* Romania

Radical Socialist Party (Dang Xa Hoi Cap Tien), 187. *See also* Vietminh; Vietnam

Radicalism, 87, 97

Raj, 237. *See also* India

Rákosi, M., 48, 109. *See also* Hungary; Hungarian Communist party

Ramirez, Sergio, 162

Ramos, Jorge Abelardo, 153

Ranadive, B. T., 213, 215. *See also* Communist Party of India; India

Rangel, Alberto, 151

Ratsiraka, Didier, 266–67, 269–70

Rao, C. Rajeshwar, 213, 215. *See also* Andhra; Communist Party of India; India

Ravines, Eudocio, 141. *See also* United front; Seventh Comintern Congress

Reconstructed Union for Communist Struggle (ULCR), 239, 247–48, 251, 253

Red Army, 7, 80, 96, 109, 111, 126, 322

Red River Delta, 179, 183. *See also* Vietnam

Redistribution of land, 19

Reestablish the center, 89

Reformism, 66, 102, 235

Regional Assembly, 267, 271. *See also* Reunión

Regional Council, 267, 269

Regionalism, 311

Reinoso, Abimael Guzmán. *See* Guzmán Reinoso, Abimael

Religion, 7–8, 12, 14, 15, 18, 67, 69, 121, 179, 194, 195, 198, 206, 304, 312, 314, 320, 322

Religiosity, 17

Religious beliefs, 17, 34

Religious sects, 185

Renaissance, 51

Representative of the Peoples Act (1951), 224. *See also* Gandhi, Indira; India

Republic of Indonesia, 298. *See also* Indonesia

Republic of Vietnam, 184. *See also* Vietnam

Resistance, 107

Reunión, 239–41, 263, 265–67, 269, 271–72

Reunión Communist party, 239, 241, 263, 267, 269, 271–72

Révai, Jósef, 118. *See also* Hungary; Hungarian Communist party

Revisionism, 1, 6, 98, 235

Revolution, 6, 103, 154

Revolutionaries, 20

Revolutionary class, 5

Revolutionary Communist League (RCL), 240, 245

Revolutionary Council, 299. *See also* Indonesia; Indonesian Communist party; Sukarno

Revolutionary current, 240, 245–46

Revolutionary dictatorship of the proletariat, 32, 35

Revolutionary intelligentsia, 214

Revolutionary Movement for the New Democracy (MRDN–AJ), 239, 265, 268, 270

Revolutionary party, 40

Revolutionary Progressive party (RPP), 240

Revolutionary spontaneity, 88

Revolution from above, 203, 222, 230

Revolution from below, 227, 230

Revolution in the Revolution?, 150. *See also* Debray, Regis

Rewang, 300. *See also* Indonesian Communist party

Right-wing deviationism, 69, 137

Right-wing tactics, 42

Riker, William H., 9, 29, 30, 46, 54

Rio Treaty, 145

Rivera, Diego, 171

Roca, Blas, 142, 148

Rodriguan People's Organization, 269

Rodríguez, Carlos Rafael, 148

Roman Catholic church, 313

Romania, 48, 109, 111, 115, 119, 122–23, 315

Romanians, 28, 121

Romanian Communist party, 121. *See also* Communist Party of Romania

Romanian Iron Guard, 331 n.25

Roosevelt, Franklin D., 111–12

Round Table Conference, 289. *See also* Indonesia; Netherlands

Rousseau, J. J., 34

Roy, Manabendra Nath, 137, 202. *See also* Comintern; Executive Committee of the Communist International

RPPS, 127. *See also* Osobka-Morawski; Poland

RRP, 127. *See also* Poland

Rural insurrection, 151

Rural proletariat, 33, 308

Russia, 233

Russianism, 18

Russian Revolution, 2, 11, 16, 22, 41, 62, 64, 66–67, 99, 119, 136

Russian Social Democratic party, 2, 37

Saavedra, Daniel Ortega. *See* Ortega Saavedra, Daniel

SACP of South Africa, 252, 253–54. *See also* South African Communist party

Sadat, Anwar al-, 242, 246

Saigon, 173, 181, 183, 186, 188–91, 196, 198, 200

Saigon government, 185, 191

Saint-Simon, Henri De, 135

Sajap Kiri (Left Wing), 286–87. *See also* Indonesia; Indonesian Communist party

Sanchez, Oscar Arias. *See* Arias Sanchez, Oscar

Sandinistas, 160–63, 172, 310

Sandino, Augusto César, 161, 171. *See also* Frente Sandinista de Liberación Nacional; Nicaragua

Sankara, Thomas, 247–49, 251

Santris, 303. *See also* Indonesia

Sardjono, 286. *See also* Indonesia; Indonesian Communist party

Sarekat Islam (Islamic Association or SI), 285. *See also* Indonesia; Indonesian Communist party

Satyanaryan Singh-led CPI (ML), 235
Saudi Arabia, 282
Scandinavian countries, 14, 61, 100
Second Congress of the Comintern, 136,
174. *See also* Comintern; Executive Com-
mittee of the Communist International
Second Duma (1906), 40
Second Indochina War, 184
Second International, 305
Second World War. *See* World War II
Sectarianism, 235
Sects, 183, 189, 198, 201. *See also* Vietnam
Secularization, 314
Semarang, 285. *See also* Indonesian Social-
Democratic Association
Sen, Mohit, 234. *See also* Communist Party
of India
Sendero Luminoso (Shining Path), 165,
167–69. *See also* Peru
Senegalese Democratic Alliance, 268
Senegalese Democratic party (PDS), 268
Sengalese People's party (PPS), 239,
267–68, 270–71
Sengor, Leopold, 264
September 30 Movement, 299–300, 302–3.
See also Indonesia; Indonesian Commu-
nist party
Seton-Watson, Hugh, 122–24
Seventh Comintern Congress (August 1,
1935), 44, 74, 140–41, 178, 211. *See also*
Comintern; Executive Committee of the
Communist International
SUF. 90 *See also* Norway; Norwegian Com-
munist party
Shagari government, 249. *See also* Socialist
Working People's party
Sham or bogus coalition, 121. *See also*
Coalition
Shanghai, 176
Shliapnikov, A. G., 88
Shining Path. *See* Sendero Luminoso
Sierra Maestra, 148. *See also* Castro, Fidel
Singh, Zail, 232. *See also* India
Single-member district plurality, 208
Sino-Soviet dispute, 89, 97–98. *See also*
Sino-Soviet split
Sino-Soviet split, 89, 94, 217. *See also* Sino-
Soviet dispute
Siqueiros, David Alfaro, 171
Sixth Comintern Congress (1928), 138, 210.
See also Comintern; Executive Committee
of the Communist International
Size principle, 29, 128. *See also* Coalition

Sjahrir, Sutan, 286. *See also* Indonesia;
Indonesian Communist party
Sjarifuddin, 287. *See also* Indonesia; Indo-
nesian Communist party
Skupstina, 112. *See also* Yugoslavia
Slovak Democratic party, 122. *See also*
Czechoslovakia
Slovak Democrats, 126. *See also*
Czechoslovakia
Smallholders, 15, 17, 121
Smallholders party, 115, 126. *See also*
Hungary
Sneevliet, H. J., 285. *See also* Indonesian
Communist party; "Maring"
Social democracy, 31, 37, 55
Social democratic movement, 316
Social Democratic parties, 67, 70, 76, 78
Social democratic workers, 44
Social democrats, 42, 51, 63, 68–70,
72–75, 77, 79–87, 91, 95, 97–98, 101,
104, 115, 118–19, 121–22, 126–27, 155,
305–8, 315–16
Social fascists, 72. *See also* Executive Com-
mittee of the Communist International;
Sixth Comintern Congress
Socialism, 39, 56, 69, 84, 94–95, 101,
136–37, 148–51, 153–55, 170, 173, 193,
194, 196, 199–201, 204, 221–22, 239,
254, 290–91, 305
Socialism from above, 155
Socialist commonwealth, 8
Socialist countries, 191
Socialist International, 267
Socialist Monima (VSN), 269
Socialist Organization of Workers (OST),
240, 268, 270–71
Socialist orientation, 269
Socialist parties, 42–43, 55, 78, 136, 156,
181, 187, 265, 267–68, 286–87
Socialist People's party (SF), 89–90,
92–93. *See also* Danish Communist
party; Denmark; Norway; Norwegian
Communist party
Socialist Republic of Vietnam, 196
Socialist revolution, 38–39, 49
Socialists, 2, 6, 63, 66–70, 73–74, 76, 79,
81, 83–84, 86, 91, 101, 103–4, 128, 139,
141–42, 154–55, 170, 174, 187, 200,
216, 223, 264, 267, 269, 286, 288–89,
305–8, 315–16
Socialist society, 201
Socialist state, 218
Socialist transformation, 197–98, 200

Socialist Union of Popular Forces (USFP), 240–41, 255–62
Socialist Vanguard party (PAGS), 239–46
Socialist Workers' and Farmers' party (SWFP), 247. *See also* Socialist Working Peoples' party
Socialist Working Peoples' party (SWPP), 239–40, 246–54. *See also* Socialist Workers' and Farmers' party
Societal revolution, 77
Societal transformation, 67
Somali Revolutionary Socialist party (SRSP), 240–41, 273, 275, 278–80
Somalis, 278
Somocistas, 106. *See also* Nicaragua; Somoza, Anastasio
Somoza, Anastasio, 159–61, 171. *See also* Nicaragua
South African Colored Peoples' Organization, 252
South African Communist party (SACP), 239–40, 246–47, 250, 252, 283. *See also* SACP of South Africa
South African Congress of Trade Unions, 252
South African Indian Congress, 252
South America, 25, 26
South Vietnam, 317
South Asian Hindu group, 270
Southern Africa Development Coordination Conference (SADCC), 281
South-West African Peoples Organization, 240
Souvanna Phouma, 188. *See also* Laos
Sovereignty, 78
Soviet bloc, 7, 86, 246, 250, 253, 263, 271–72, 279–80
Soviet state, 13, 97
Soviet Union, 9, 11–12, 14, 27, 45, 72, 74, 78–79, 80, 83–85, 88, 92, 94–96, 98–101, 103, 108–11, 118, 124, 126, 139, 142, 145–47, 157, 169–70, 178, 179, 210, 216, 227, 229–32, 236, 239, 245–46, 253–54, 262–63, 271–72, 279–80, 286, 301, 312–15, 321
Soviets of workers, peasants, and soldiers, 139
Spain, 24, 44, 73, 75, 81, 102, 143
Spanish Civil War, 74
Spanish Communist party (PCE), 52–53, 92, 94, 99–100
Spanish Republic, 74
Special Bureau, 301. *See also* Indonesia;

Indonesian Communist party
Specific path toward socialism, 48–49
Spontaneity, 88
Stalin, Josef, 3, 41–44, 46, 49, 73, 75, 87–89, 94, 97, 108–10, 112, 144, 153, 210–11, 288–89, 306, 308, 317
Stalin era, 87–88
Stalin School, 178
Stalinism, 45, 55, 89, 233
Staar, Richard F., 204
The State and Revolution: The Marxist Theory of State and the Tasks of the Proletarian Revolution, 38. *See also* Lenin, Vladimir Ilich
State capitalism, 98
"State with two aspects," 298. *See also* Aidit, D. N.; Indonesian Communist party
Storting (Parliament), 93. *See also* Norway
Strategic coalitions, 100. *See also* Coalition
Strategic reserves, 299. *See also* Suharto
Šubašić, Ivan, 113, 123. *See also* Yugoslavia
Sub-Saharan Africa, 24, 248, 250–51, 273, 316
Sudan Communist party, 239, 241, 255–58, 261–63. *See also* Sudanese Communist party
Sudanese People's Liberation Movement, 240, 261–62
Sudisman, 288, 300–301. *See also* Indonesia; Indonesian Communist party
Suharto, 284, 299, 302. *See also* Indonesia; Sukarno
Sukarno, 23, 284, 289–90, 294–300, 302, 319. *See also* Indonesia
Sukarno-Hatta regime, 287. *See also* Indonesia
Sumatra, 295
Suomen Kansan Demokraattinen Liitto (SKDL), 87, 97, 100. *See also* Finland; Finnish Democratic League
Suomen Kommunistinen Puolue (SKP), 87, 97, 100. *See also* Finland; Finnish Communist party
Supreme Revolutionary Council, 266–67. *See also* Congress Party for Malagasy Independence; Ratsiraka, Didier
Svenska Kommunistiska Parti (SKP), 92. *See also* Swedish Communist party
Sweden, 81, 91, 94, 97, 282
Swedish Communist party (SKP), 92. *See also* Svenska Kommunistiska Parti
Swedish Social Democratic party (SD), 91

Switzerland, 33
Symbolic legitimacy, 319
Syndicalists, 1, 12, 74–75
Szalasi, Ferenc, 109. *See also* Hungary
Szentesi Lap, 115. *See also* Hungary

Tan Malaka, 286. *See also* Indonesia; Indonesian Communist party
TASS, 76
Telengana, 213–15. *See also* India; Andhra
Teleki, Géza, 121. *See also* Hungary
Tercerista, 160–61, 163. *See also* Nicaragua; Guerra Popular Prolongada; Frente Sandinista de Liberación Nacional
Terry, Fernando Belaúnde. *See* Belaúnde Terry, Fernando
Tet Offensive, 190
Tet uprising, 191
Thach, Pham Ngoc. *See* Pham Ngoc Thach
Thao, Trinh Dinh. *See* Trinh Dinh Thao
"Thesis of the Workers' Front," 155. *See also* Allende Gossens, Salvadore
Thieu, Nguyen Van. *See* Nguyen Van Thieu
Third Duma (1907), 40
Third force, 197–98, 200. *See also* Vietnam
Third International, 137, 285. *See also* Comintern
Third International Congress of the Vietnam Workers' party, 186
Tho, Nguyen Huu. *See* Nguyen Huu Tho
Thorez, M., 48. *See also* French Communist party
Tibetan revolt, 218
Tigreans, 278
Tigre People's Liberation Front, 240
Tildy, Zoltán, 119, 121, 128. *See also* Hungary
Tin, Chan. *See* Chan Tin
Tin Sang (Saigon journal), 198. *See also* Vietnam
Tirana, 253
Tito, Josif Broz, 47, 112–13, 123
Titoism, 86, 88
Tito-Šubašić Agreement, 112, 115
Tjugito, 300. *See also* Indonesia; Indonesian Communist party
Togliatti, Palmiro, 48, 52, 94. *See also* Italian Communist party
Toledano, Vicente Lombardo, 145. *See also* Partido Popular (Mexico)
Torre, Victor Raúl Haya de la, 164

Torres, Camilo, 152, 171
Totalitarianism, 34
Trade unions, 16
Traditionalists, 101
Tranmael, Martin, 69, 70. *See also* Norway; Norwegian Communist party; Norwegian Labor party
Tribal animosity, 24
Tribal groups, 200
Tribalism, 311
Tribal minorities, 183, 185, 189, 193, 198–99
Trinh Dinh Thao, 191. *See also* Vietnam
Tripura, 204, 208, 225, 228–29, 233. *See also* Communist Party of India-Marxist; India
Trotsky, Leon, 2, 71, 153
Trotskyism, 145, 150, 170
Trotskyites, 144–46, 151, 164
Tse-tung, Mao. *See* Mao Zedong
Tucker, Robert, 30
Tunisian Communist party, 239, 241, 255–57, 259–60, 262–63
Tunisian Federation, 256
Twentieth Party Congress of the CPSU, 97, 217, 306
Twenty-one conditions, 16, 70, 136, 305. *See also* Comintern; Executive Committee of the Communist International
Twenty-sixth of July Movement, 147, 148. *See also* Castro, Fidel
Two-camp theory, 85, 86. *See also* Zhdanov, Andrei
"Two-stage" revolution, 289. *See also* Stalin, Josef

Uceda, Luis F. de la Puente (of Peru), 151
Ulam, Adam, 30, 109
Ultraleft, 221
Ultra-Leftists, 172
Undersized coalitions, 125. *See also* Coalition
"Under the blanket" sympathizers, 185, 188, 190. *See also* Vietminh; Vietnam
Unidad Popular, 155–56. *See also* Allende Gossens, Salvadore; Chile
Unilateral actions (aksi sepihak), 294. *See also* Indonesia; Indonesian Communist party
Union for Communist Struggle (ULC), 239, 248, 251, 253
Union for People's Democracy (UDP), 240, 265, 268, 270–71

Unión Revolucionaria Comunista (URC), 143. *See also* Cuba

United Buddhist Church, 200. *See also* Vietnam

United front, 69, 74, 127, 153, 173–77, 179, 184, 186, 191–94, 196, 201, 208–13, 216–17, 226, 232, 236, 285, 289, 293–96, 300–303

United front coalition, 303

United Front for the Liberation of Oppressed Races (UFLRO), 200. *See also* Vietminh; Vietnam

United front from above, 42, 69–70, 82, 176, 180, 286, 291, 294, 302

United front from below, 68–70, 82, 86, 214, 291–92, 296

United front in revolutionary way, 192

United Nations, 280

United Progressive Alliance, 253. *See also* Socialist Working Peoples' party

United Progressive Grand Alliance, 251. *See also* Socialist Working Peoples' party

United States, 26, 38, 98, 100, 107, 110–13, 135–36, 145, 147, 151, 158–59, 162, 169, 173, 188, 229, 243, 257, 267, 274–75, 280, 322

Unity of the working class, 80

Universal suffrage, 35–36, 50

Urban insurrection, 214

Urbanization, 14, 60

Urban proletariat, 5

Uruguay, 139

U.S. Advisory Committee on Postwar Foreign Policy, 110

U.S. House of Representatives, 163

U.S. imperialism, 243, 250, 257, 274

U.S.S.R. *See* Soviet Union

Utopian socialism, 135

Valencia, Luis Emiro, 151

Van Der Kroef, Justus, 287, 291

Vanguard of the Malagasy Revolution (AREMA), 266–68, 270

Vanguard of the proletariat, 7

Vanguard of the revolution, 136

Vanguard party, 192, 220–21

Vanguard role of the party, 193

Vanguard Youth Movement, 181. *See also* Pham Ngoc Thach; Vietminh; Vietnam

Varanasi, Uttar Pradesh, 230. *See also* Communist Party of India

Varga, E., 47, 49

Vaterlandslose Gesellen, 19

Vatican, 194, 198. *See also* Catholic Church

Venezuela, 145, 153–56, 158–59, 170

Videla, Gabriel González, 142

Vietminh, 181–86, 194. *See also* Vietnam

Vietminh front, 179–83

Vietnam, 20, 23, 28, 90, 98–99, 173–78, 188–89, 191–92, 198–99, 229, 233, 317, 321. *See also* Vietminh

Vietnamese Communist party (VCP), 196, 201

Vietnamese Marxists, 309

Vietnamese model, 192

Vietnamese Revolutionary Youth League (Viet Nam Cach Menh Thanh Nien Hoi), 175

Vietnam Workers' party (Dang Lao Dong Viet Nam) (VWP), 184, 187, 196

Vijayawada, Andhra Pradesh, 218, 230. *See also* Communist Party of India

Violent revolution, 31

Voltaic Revolutionary Communist party (PCRV), 239, 247, 248, 251, 253

Wade, Abdoulaye, 268. *See also* Party of Independence and Labor

War of national liberation, 150

Washington, D.C., 101, 110, 113, 321

Weimar Republic, 316

Welfare state, 104

Werner, Lars, 92. *See also* Left Party of Communists of Sweden; Sweden

West Bengal, 204, 206–8, 211–14, 216–18, 221, 225, 228–33

West German communists, 100

West Irian, 286, 296

West Kalimantan, 301

Weydemeyer, J., 32

What Is to Be Done (1902), 40. *See also* Lenin, Vladimir Ilich

Winning coalitions, 27, 29. *See also* coalition

Women's Movement (Gerwani), 294. *See also* Indonesia; Indonesian Communist party

Worker-peasant alliance, 150, 177, 182, 193, 220, 293. *See also* Coalition; United Front

Workers, 15, 17, 47, 177, 222, 290

Workers' Opposition, 71, 88. *See also* Communist Party of the Soviet Union; Kollontai, Alexandra; Shliapnikov, A. G.

Workers' Party of Ethiopia (WPE), 240–41, 273–74, 278. *See also* Eritrean People's Liberation Front; Tigre People's

Liberation Front
Working class, 214–15, 219
Working-class hegemony, 48, 51, 220
Working-class unity, 75, 82
World communism, 78
World communist movement, 204, 212,
   217, 245, 262–63, 272, 284, 297
World imperialism, 145, 174
World revolution, 67
World War I, 22, 66, 175, 210, 319
World War II, 22, 26, 45, 48, 55, 73, 77,
   84, 106, 113, 129, 140, 144, 155, 169,
   179, 248, 306, 315, 317, 321

Yalta Declaration on Liberated Europe, 113
Yennans, 208. *See also* Communist Party of
   India; Communist Party of India-
   Marxist; India
Youth Liberation Association, 187. *See also*
   Vietminh; Vietnam

Yugoslavia, 7, 86, 109, 111, 113, 115, 118,
   123–24

Zapata, Emiliano, 171
Zedong, Mao. *See* Mao Zedong
Zhdanov, Andrei, 214, 286
Zhdanov line, 286
Zhdanov "two-camp" doctrine, 287
Zimbabwe African National Union—Patri-
   otic Front (ZANU–PF), 240–41, 273,
   275–77, 279–80
Zimbabwe African People's Union (ZAPU),
   275–76, 279
Zimmerwald, 11, 66
Zinner, Paul, 126
Zinoviev, Gregorii, 3, 137
Zionism, 243, 257
Zulawski, Zygmunt, 127
Zveno (The Link), 121. *See also* Bulgaria

Contributors

David E. Albright is at present professor of national security affairs at the Air War College, Maxwell Air Force Base, Alabama. Previously he served as a research associate at the Council on Foreign Relations in New York, and he was for more than a decade on the staff of the journal *Problems of Communism*, first as associate editor and then as senior text editor. Dr. Albright has written extensively about Africa, particularly about Soviet policy toward the continent and about leftist movements there. His major works on these topics include *Communism in Africa* (Bloomington: Indiana University Press, 1980); *The U.S.S.R. and Sub-Saharan Africa in the 1980s*, Washington Paper No. 101 (New York: Praeger for the Center for Strategic and International Studies, 1983); *Soviet Policy toward Africa Revisited*, Significant Issues Series, Vol. 9, No. 6 (Washington, D.C.: Center for Strategic and International Studies, 1987). He is also the author of "East-West Tensions in Africa" in Marshall Shulman, ed., *East-West Tensions in the Third World* (New York: W. W. Norton, 1986).

Frank Cibulka is a lecturer in the Department of Political Science at the National University of Singapore. He is a specialist in Soviet/East European affairs and is currently specializing in communist movements in Southeast Asia.

William J. Duiker is professor of East Asian history at the Pennsylvania State University. A former foreign service officer stationed in Saigon in the 1960s, he has written a number of books and articles on modern China and Vietnam. Two of his most recent publications are *Vietnam since the Fall of Saigon* (Ohio University Press, 1985) and *China and Vietnam: the Roots f Conflict* (Institute of East Asian Studies, University of California, 1986).

Charles Gati is professor of political science at Union College in Schenectady, New York. He is concurrently also associated with Columbia

University's Research Institute on International Change and the Harriman Institute for Advanced Study of the Soviet Union. His latest book, *Hungary and the Soviet Bloc* (Duke University Press, 1986) was awarded the first Shulman Prize as "the outstanding book on Soviet foreign policy" published in the United States. The award was made by the American Association for the Advancement of Slavic Studies in conjunction with the Harriman Institute. In addition to several other books, Professor Gati's numerous articles appeared in such journals as *Foreign Affairs, Problems of Communism, Foreign Policy*, and elsewhere. His next book, tentatively titled *The Soviet Bloc at Century's End*, will be published in 1989. Professor Gati is a member of several professional organizations, including the Council on Foreign Relations.

Trond Gilberg is a professor of political science and head of the Political Science Department at the Pennsylvania State University. He is the associate director of the Soviet and East European Center at Penn State. He has been a visiting professor at the Christian Albrechts Universität in Kiel, West Germany, the University of Washington, the U.S. Military Academy at West Point, and the U.S. Army War College at Carlisle, Pennsylvania. His publications include two books, over two dozen book chapters, and numerous articles on communist studies, Soviet and East European politics, and the governments of Northern Europe.

Stanley A. Kochanek is professor of political science at the Pennsylvania State University. He is the author of three books: *Interest Groups and Development: Business and Politics in Pakistan*; *Business and Politics in India*; and *The Congress Party of India: The Dynamics of One-Party Democracy*; and the coauthor of *India: Government and Politics in a Developing Nation*. He has written numerous articles and book chapters on comparative politics and the politics of India and Pakistan. He is also a member of several boards of editors for major academic journals and a frequent panel participant at national and international conferences. Professor Kochanek is a member of several professional organizations, including the American Political Science Association and the Association for Asian Studies.

John D. Martz is professor of political science at the Pennsylvania State University and is the author or editor of fifteen books, his most recent publication being *The Politics of Petroleum in Ecuador* (New Brunswick: Transaction Publishers, 1987). He is editor of the forthcoming *The U.S. and Latin American Policy: Quarter-Century of Crisis and Challenge* (Lincoln: University of Nebraska Press, 1988).

Jiri Valenta is the director of the Institute for Soviet and East European Studies and professor of political science at the Graduate School of International Studies, University of Miami, Florida. He is the author or

Strain, B.R. and T.V. Armentano. 1980. Position Paper. Environmental and societal consequences of carbon dioxide induced climate change: Response of "unmanaged" ecosystems. Duke University Phytotron, Durham, N.C.

Stumm, W. and J.J. Morgan. 1981. Aquatic Chemistry. 2nd Edition. J. Wiley & Sons, New York.

Talling, J.F. 1973. The application of some electrochemical methods to the measurement of photosynthesis and respiration in fresh waters. Freshwat. Biol. 3, 355-362.

Talling, J.F. 1976. The depletion of carbon dioxide from lake water by photoplankton. J. Ecol. 64, 79-121.

Tanaka, A., K. Kawano and J. Yamaguchi. 1966. Photosynthesis, respiration, and plant type of the tropical rice plant. Int. Rice Res. Inst. Tech. Bull. 7, 46.

Thurston, J.M. 1969. The effect of liming and fertilizers on the botanical composition of permanent grassland and on the yield of hay. In Ecological Aspects of the Mineral Nutrition of Plants. Blackwell, Oxford. pp. 3-10.

Tilly, L.J. 1975. Changes in water chemistry and productivity in a reactor cooling reservoir. In Mineral Cycling, F.G. Howell, J.B. Gentry and M.H. Smith, Eds. USAEC. Tech. Info. Center, Oak Ridge, Tenn.

Tilman, D. 1980. Resources: a graphical-mechanistic approach to competition and predation. Amer. Nat. 116, 363-393.

Tognoni, R., A.H. Halevy, and S.H. Wittwer. 1967. Growth of bean and tomato plants as affected by root absorbed growth substances and atmospheric carbon dioxide. Planta 72, 43-52.

Tsuzuki, M. and S. Migachi. 1981. Effects of CO_2-concentration during growth and of ethotyzolamide on CO_2 compensation point in Chlorella. FEBS Lett. 103, 221-223.

Uchijima, Z., T. Udagawa, T. Horie and K. Kobayashi. 1967. Studies of energy and gas exchange within crop canopies. I. CO_2 environment in a corn plant canopy. J. Agric. Meteorol. (Japan) 23, 99-108.

Ultsch, G.R. and D.S. Anthony. 1973. The role of the
aquatic exchange of carbon dioxide in the ecology of
the water hyacinth (Eichhornia crassipes). Florida
Sci. 36, 16-22.

Valanne, N., E.M. Aro, and E. Rintamaki. 1982. Leaf and
chloroplast structure of two aquatic Ranunculus
species. Aquatic Bot. 12, 13-22.

Van, T.K., W.T. Haller, and G. Bowes. 1976. Comparison of
the photosynthetic characteristics of three submersed
aquatic plants. Plant Physiol. 58, 761-768.

Verduin, J. 1975. Rate of carbon dioxide transport across
air-water boundaries in lakes. Limnol. Oceanogr.
20, 1052-1053.

Weaver, C.I. and R.G. Wetzel. 1980. Carbonic anhydrase
levels and internal lacunar CO_2 concentration in
aquatic macrophytes. Aquatic Bot. 8, 173-186.

Weiler, R.G. 1974. Exchange of carbon dioxide between the
atmosphere and Lake Ontario. J. Fish. Res. Bd. Can.
31, 329-332.

Westlake, D.F. 1963. Comparisons of plant productivity.
Biol. Rev. 38, 385-425.

Westlake, D.F. 1967. Some effects of low-velocity currents
on the metabolism of aquatic macrophytes. J. Exp.
Bot. 18, 187-205.

Wetzel, R.G. 1965. Techniques and problems of primary
productivity measurements in higher aquatic plants and
periphyton. Mem. Ist. Ital. Idrobiol. 18 (Suppl.)
249-267.

Wetzel, R.G. 1969. Factors influencing photosynthesis and
excretion of dissolved organic matter by aquatic
macrophytes in hard-water lakes. Verh. Int. Ver.
Limnol. 17, 72-85

Wetzel, R.G. 1975. Limnology. Saunders, Philadelphia, 743 pp.

Wetzel, R.G. 1979. The role of the littoral zone and
detritus in lake metabolism. Erg. Limnol. Arch.
Hydrobiol. 13, 145-161.

Wetzel, R.G. 1982. Limnology. 2nd Edition. Saunders,
Philadelphia, 850 pp.

Wetzel, R.G. and B.A. Manny. 1972. Secretion of dissolved organic carbon and nitrogen by aquatic macrophytes. Verh. Int. Ver. Limnol. 18, 162-170

Wheeler, B.D. and K.E. Giller. 1982. Species richness of herbaceous fern vegetation in Broadland, Norfolk in relation to the quantity of above-ground plant material. J. Ecol. 70, 179-200.

Whittaker, R.H. 1975. Communities and Ecosystems. MacMillan Publ. Co., New York.

Winter, K. 1978. Short-term fixation of ^{14}carbon by the submerged aquatic angiosperm Potamogeton pectinatus. J. Exp. Bot. 29, 1169-1172.

Wium-Andersen, S. 1971. Photosynthetic uptake of free CO_2 by the roots of Lobelia dortmanna. Physiol. Plant 25, 245-248.

Wohler, J.R. 1966. Productivity of the duckweeds. M. Sc. Thesis, University of Pittsburgh, 69 pp.

Wong, S.C. 1979. Elevated atmospheric partial pressure of carbon dioxide and plant growth. I. Interactions of nitrogen nutrition and photosynthetic capacity in C_3 and C_4 plants. Oecologia 44, 68-74.

Wong, C. 1980. Effects of elevated partial pressure of carbon dioxide assimilation and water use efficiency in plants. In Carbon Dioxide and Climate, G.I. Pearman, Ed. Australian Academy of Science, Canberra.

Wood, K.G. 1974. Carbon dioxide diffusivity across the air-water interface. Arch. Hydrobiol. 73, 57-69.

Wood, K.G. 1977. Chemical enhancement of CO_2 flux across the air-water interface. Arch. Hydrobiol. 79, 103-110.

Wright, J.C. 1960. The limnology of Canyon Ferry Reservoir: III. Some observations on the density dependence of photosynthesis and its cause. Limnol. Oceanogra. 5, 356-361.

Yamada, N., Y. Murata, A. Osada, and J. Iyama. 1955. Photosynthesis of rice plant. II. Proc. Crop Sci. Soc. Japan, 24, 112-118.

Yoda, K., T. Kira. H. Ogawa and K. Hozumi. 1963. Self-thinning in overcrowded pure stands under cultivated and natural conditions. J. Biol. Osaka Univ. 14, 107-129.

Yoshida, S. 1973. Effects of CO_2 enrichment at different stages of panicle development on yield of rice (Oryza sativa L.). Soil Sci. Plant Nutr. 19, 311-316.

Yoshida, S. 1976. Carbon dioxide and yield of rice. In Climate and Rice, International Rice Research Institute, Los Banos, Philippines. pp. 211-221.

Yoshida, S., V. Coronel, F.T. Parao and E. de los Reyes. 1974. Soil carbon dioxide flux and rice photosynthesis. Soil Sci. Plant Nutr. 20, 381-386.

Yoshida, T. and R.R. Ancajas. 1973. Nitrogen-fixing activity in upland and flooded rice fields. Soil Sci. Soc. Amer. Proc. 37, 42-46.

co-editor of six books: *Soviet Invasion of Czechoslovakia in 1968*; *Soviet Invasion of Afghanistan*; *Eurocommunism between East and West*; *Soviet Decision Making for National Security*; *Grenada and Soviet/Cuban Policy*; and *Conflict in Nicaragua*. This chapter was written while Dr. Valenta served as a fellow at the Council on Foreign Relations at the Rockefeller Foundation in 1981–82 and he is indebted to both institutions for their support.

CO$_2$ and Plants

The Response of Plants to Rising Levels of Atmospheric Carbon Dioxide

AAAS Selected Symposia Series

 Published by Westview Press, Inc.
5500 Central Avenue, Boulder, Colorado

for the

 American Association for the Advancement of Science
1776 Massachusetts Ave., N.W., Washington, D.C.

CO$_2$ and Plants

The Response of Plants to Rising Levels of Atmospheric Carbon Dioxide

Edited by Edgar R. Lemon

AAAS Selected Symposium **84**

Copyright © 1983 by the American Association for the Advancement of Science

Published in 1983 in the United States of America by
  Westview Press, Inc.
  5500 Central Avenue
  Boulder, Colorado 80301
  Frederick A. Praeger, Publisher

Library of Congress Catalog Card Number 83-50133
ISBN 0-86531-597-3

Printed and bound in the United States of America

About the Book

This book presents information on the direct effects of increased atmospheric CO_2 on plants. The authors consider what we already know about plant responses to various CO_2 concentrations, then project what may happen at ambient levels up to 600 ppm. Formulating questions that must be answered if we are to quantify plant responses under changing conditions, they consider possible positive and negative effects of the steady increase of one of life's basic components.

Contents

About the Editor and Principal Authors........xiii

Conference Background.........................xvii

Preface.......................................xxi

1   Interpretive Summary
    Edgar R. Lemon.................................1

    Why This Book?   1
    Why Long-Term CO_2 Enrichment
       Studies?   2
    Some Concluding Remarks   4
       Carbon Metabolism,4; Physiological
       Response,4; Plant Growth and Develop-
       ment,5; Microbial Effects,5;
       Terrestrial Plant Communities,5;
       Aquatic Plant Communities,5

2   An Overview
    David M. Gates, Conference Chairman.................7

    Introduction   7
    Carbon Dioxide Concentrations   7
    General Circulation Models of
       Climate   8
    Climate Change   8
    Sources of Carbon   9
    Future CO_2 Levels   10
    Fossil Fuel Use Scenarios   10
    Non-Fossil Fuel Alternatives   11
    Plant Responses to CO_2 12
    Physiological Responses   13
    Climatology   14
    Plant Breeding   15

Seasonal CO_2 Amplitude   15
CO_2 Enrichment Studies   17
CO_2 Research Support   17
Literature Cited   18

3   Carbon Metabolism
    N. E. Tolbert, Chairman
    Israel Zelitch, Co-Chairman 21

    Panel Members   21
    Summary and Recommendations   21
    Introduction   23
    Rate of Photosynthesis   26
     Effect of CO_2 on the Reductive Photo-
     synthetic Carbon Cycle,29; Effect of
     CO_2 on the Oxidative Photosynthetic
     Carbon Cycle,33; CO_2 Fixation by C_4,
     CAM, and C_3/C_4 Intermediate Plants,37;
     Ribulose Bisphosphate Carboxylase/
     Oxygenase,40; Carbon Metabolism in
     Aquatic Plants and Algae,46; Electron
     Transport and CO_2 Fixation,48; Carbon
     Isotope Discrimination,50
    Partitioning of Substrates   51
     Sucrose and Starch,51; Acetate, Fatty
     Acids, Lipids, Hydrocarbons and Isoprene
     Polymers,53; Respiration and Nitrogen,
     Sulfur and Phosphorus,55
    Duration of CO_2 Fixation   56
    Discussion   57
    Literature Cited   61

4   Physiological Effects
    Robert W. Pearcy, Co-Chairman
    Olle Björkman, Chairman 65

    Panel Members   65
    Summary and Recommendations   65
    Introduction   66
    Response of Leaf Photosynthesis to
     Increased CO_2 Concentration   67
     The Supply Function,68; The Demand
     Function,69; Interaction with Light
     and Temperature Regimes,75; Long-
     Term Responses,77
    Responses of Stomata to Increased
     CO_2 Concentration   79
     Interaction Between Increased CO_2 and
     Other Environmental Factors on Stomatal
     Conductance,81; Effects of Stomatal

Closure on Transpiration Rate and Leaf Temperature, 83
Effects of Increased CO_2 on Water Use Efficiency 83
Effects of Increased CO_2 Concentration on Plant Water Status 87
Effects of Increased CO_2 on Utilization of Photosynthetic Products 88
Leaf Expansion, 88; Canopy Development, 89; Allocation of Photosynthetic Products, 90
Interaction of Increased CO_2 with Nutrient Supply 92
Remarks on "Limiting" Factors and Responses to Increased CO_2 95
Areas of Ignorance 96
Leaf Photosynthesis, 96; Stomatal Response and Water Use Efficiency, 97; Leaf and Canopy Growth, 97; Photosynthate Allocation, 98; Nutrient Limitations, 98
Literature Cited 98

5 Plant Growth and Development
Donald N. Baker, Chairman
Herbert Zvi Enoch, Co-Chairman 107

Panel Members 107
Summary and Recommendations 107
Introduction 109
Direct and Indirect Effects of CO_2 111
The Physiological Processes 112
Transpiration, 112; Photosynthesis and Respiration, 113; Partitioning of Photosynthate, 115; Plant Development, 115
CO_2 and Plant Dynamics 117
The Seedling, 117; The Vegetative Plant, 118; The Reproductive Plant, 122
Literature Cited 124

6 Microbial Effects
Marvin R. Lamborg, Chairman
Ralph W. F. Hardy, Co-Chairman
E. A. Paul 131

Panel Members 131
Research Recommendations and Summary 131

Global Effects   133
*Microorganisms and Photosynthesis,
133; CO_2 Concentrations in Soil and
Factors Affecting It,134; Effect of
Increased Levels of CO_2 on Solution
Equilibrium Reactions,139; CO_2 and
Soil Organic Matter Levels,140*
Estimates of the Effect of Doubling
  Atmospheric CO_2 on Soil Organic
  Matter and Biomass   143
CO_2 Production and Effects   146
*Roots,146; Fungi,146; Return of Crop
Residues to Soil,147*
CO_2 Uptake   148
*General Observations,148; Microbial
Effects,148*
Plant Microbial Associations   151
*Introduction,151; Organic Mineral-
ization-Immobilization Reactions,151;
Nitrification,154; Denitrification,
154; Nitrogen Uptake,154; Mycorrhiza,
159; Effects on Plant Pathogens,163*
Management Options   164
*Intercropping, Multiple Cropping, Green
Manures,165; Microorganism Addition,
165; New Technology Inputs,166*
Literature Cited   167

7   Terrestrial Plant Communities
    *Boyd R. Strain, Chairman
    Fakhri A. Bazzaz, Co-Chairman* 177

Panel Members   177
Summary and Recommendations   177
Introduction   180
Objectives   181
The Response of Individual Plants
  (Level 1)   182
*A Mechanistic Model,182; Details of the
Model,183; Time Dimension,187; Model
Applications to Different Functional
Types,188; Representative Biome Re-
sponses,191*
Responses of Two Interacting
  Organisms (Level 2)   195
*Plant-Plant Interactions,195; Plant-
Animal Interactions,200; Plant-
Microorganisms,201; Flowering
Phenology,201*

Responses of Whole Communities
   (Level 3)   202
Net Primary Production, 202;
Interactions with Nitrogen and
Phosphorus Supply, 204; Differential
Species Responses, 207; Species
Diversity, 209; Ecological Succession,
209; Biogeographical Effects, 210;
Interactions with Fire, 212; Inter-
action with Environment Pollutants,
213; Comparison with Lake Eutrophi-
cation, 213
Literature Cited   214

8   Aquatic Plant Communities
    Robert G. Wetzel, Chairman
    James B. Grace, Co-Chairman 223

    Panel Members   223
    Summary and Recommendations   223
    Introduction   228
    Aquatic Plants and Their Habitats, 231
    CO_2 Assimilation from Air, Water,
      and Water-Saturated Sediments   232
    Emergent, Free-Floating, and Floating-
    Leaved Macrophytes, 232; Submersed
    Macrophytes and Algae, 233
    Tentative Projections of Responses
      of Submersed Plants to Elevated
      Atmospheric CO_2 243
    Extrapolation of Controlled
      Studies to Natural Systems   244
    Rooted Emergent, Free-Floating, and
    Floating-Leaved Macrophytes, 245;
    Submersed Macrophytes, 253; Algae, 258
    Literature Cited   264

About the Editor and Principal Authors

Edgar R. Lemon *is a soil scientist formerly with the USDA Agricultural Research Service. He was professor of agronomy at Cornell, an exchange scientist to the USSR, a Guggenheim and Fulbright Fellow to Australia, a DSIR Fellow to New Zealand, and was chairman of the IBP Subcommittee on Photosynthesis and Production Processes. His interests are crop micrometeorology, carbon dioxide exchange in plant communities, and the physical environment of plants.*

Donald N. Baker *is a research agronomist and leader of the Crop Simulation Research Unit, USDA Agricultural Research Service, Mississippi State. He is involved in mathematical simulation of plant growth and in studies of photosynthesis, soil water stress, and plant responses to rising levels of carbon dioxide.*

Fakhri A. Bazzaz *is professor of botany at the University of Illinois in Urbana. His specialties include demography, physiological ecology, and plant community organization.*

Olle Björkman *is a senior scientist at the Carnegie Institute of Washington in Stanford, California, and professor of biology at Stanford University. His research on photosynthesis has involved him in issues relating to world food supplies and nutrition and the effects of carbon dioxide on plants. He is a member of the National Academy of Sciences and received the Linnaeus Prize of the Swedish Royal Physiographic Society.*

Herbert Zvi Enoch *is a senior scientist at the Agricultural Research Organization, the Volcani Center, Bet Dagan in Israel. He has worked in Denmark, England, the United States, Japan, and Israel on the influence of the environment on plant productivity. His primary interests are in growth and development, photosynthesis and carbon dioxide exchange in plants and soil, and the effect of elevated carbon dioxide on green-house crops.*

David M. Gates *is professor of botany and director of the Biological Station at the University of Michigan in Ann Arbor. A specialist in biophysical ecology, he is the author of* Energy Exchange in the Biosphere *(Harper and Row, 1962),* Atlas of Energy Budgets of Plant Leaves *(with U. N. Papian; Academic, 1971),* Man and His Environment: Climate *(Harper and Row, 1972), and* Biophysical Ecology *(Springer-Verlag, 1980).*

James B. Grace *is assistant professor in the Department of Botany and Microbiology at the University of Arkansas, Fayetteville. He has published numerous papers on the ecology of aquatic plants.*

Ralph W. F. Hardy *is director of life sciences in the Central Research and Development Department of E. I. du Pont de Nemours and Company in Wilmington, Delaware. His research has been concerned with nitrogen and carbon inputs into major crops. He edited the three volume* Treatise on Dinitrogen Fixation *series (published by Wiley in 1977 and 1979) and coauthored the monograph* Nitrogen Fixation in Bacterial and Higher Plants *(with R. C. Burns; Springer-Verlag, 1975).*

Marvin R. Lamborg *is mission manager of the Department of Enhancement of Plant Productivity at C. F. Kettering Research Laboratory in Yellow Springs, Ohio. His specialties are nitrogen-fixing symbiotic associations and the molecular biology of symbiosis. He has published on alternative (biological) fertilizer strategy for crop production.*

E. A. Paul, *professor and chair of the Department of Plant and Soil Biology at the University of California, Berkeley, has published extensively on organisms in soils and plant microbial interactions. He is coeditor of three volumes in the* Soil Biochemistry *series (with A. D. McLaren; Marcel Dekker, 1975).*

Robert W. Pearcy, *a specialist in plant physiological ecology, is associate professor of botany at the University of California, Davis. He has done research on high-tempera-ture adaptation in desert plants and on comparative physio-logical ecology of carbon-3 and carbon-4 plants.*

Boyd R. Strain *is professor of botany and director of Phytotron at Duke University. He has written extensively on photosynthesis, plant growth, and the effects of carbon dioxide on plants.*

N. E. Tolbert *is professor of biochemistry at Michigan State University in East Lansing. He has carried out an extensive research program over three decades on photosynthetic carbon metabolism, photorespiration, and peroxisomes in plants and animals. He is editor of* The Biochemistry of Plants: A Comprehensive Treatise, Vol. 1 *(Academic, 1980).*

Robert G. Wetzel *is professor of botany and adjunct professor of zoology at the W. K. Kellogg Biological Station, Michigan State University, Hickory Corners. His specialties are freshwater ecology and botanical chemical limnology, and among his many publications are* Limnology *(W. B. Saunders, 1st ed., 1975; 2nd ed., 1983),* Limnological Analyses *(with G. E. Likens; W. B. Saunders, 1979), and* To Quench Our Thirst: Present and Future Freshwater Resources of the United States *(with D. A. Francko; University of Michigan Press, 1983).*

Sylvan H. Wittwer *is director of the Michigan Agricultural Experiment Station, Michigan State University, East Lansing. His work on the effects of elevated levels of carbon dioxide on food production, in greenhouses and in the natural environment, has earned him numerous honors and awards.*

Israel Zelitch *is head of the Department of Biochemistry and Genetics and Samuel W. Johnson Distinguished Scientist at the Connecticut Agricultural Experiment Station. He has studied the physiology of leaf stomata and the biochemical and genetic regulation of photorespiration, and is the author of* Photosynthesis, Photorespiration, and Plant Productivity *(Academic, 1971).*

Conference Background

This volume had its genesis in a Workshop held at Annapolis, MD, April 2-6, 1979. The topic was the Environmental and Societal Consequences of a Rising Level of Atmospheric CO_2. That meeting was financially supported by the U.S. Department of Energy. David Burns, Director of the Climate Project of the American Association for the Advancement of Science, and David Slade, Director of the Climate Research Program of the U.S. Department of Energy, organized and convened the Workshop. The meeting was chaired by Roger Revelle. Two of the six panels in the Workshop considered the managed and unmanaged biospheres, and were chaired by myself and Boyd Strain, respectively. Participants in these two panels focused attention on the biological as well as the climatic implications of the rising level of atmospheric CO_2 (see Carbon Dioxide Research and Assessment Program publication 009, Proceedings of a Workshop, Annapolis, MD, April 2-6, 1979, National Technical Information Series, Springfield, VA).

Following the Annapolis Workshop, several papers outlining research priorities were commissioned by a joint effort of the Department of Energy and the American Association for the Advancement of Science. The research recommendations of the commissioned papers dealing with the managed and unmanaged biospheres were synthesized by myself and Charles Cooper. The synthesis formed part of a summary volume (Carbon Dioxide Research and Assessment Program publication 013, Environmental and Societal Consequences of a Possible CO_2-Induced Climate Change: A Research Agenda, Volume 1, December 1980, Roger Revelle, E. Boulding, C. Cooper, L. Lave, S. Schneider, and S. Wittwer, Editors).

It was in meetings of panel chairmen of the Annapolis

Workshop and of the working group which edited the Research
Agenda which followed, that the suggestion first appeared
as to the need for an international conference to identify
what we need to find out regarding the biological effects
on plants of a rising level of atmospheric CO_2. It was
suggested that 100-150 of the world's authorities be
assembled to specify the questions that must be addressed
for agricultural and food crops, forestry and range,
natural ecosystems, and aquatic biota.

This suggestion constituted a new direction for
carbon dioxide research sponsored by the Department of
Energy, which until then had focused almost entirely on
projected climate change. The concept of an international
conference was warmly received. The Department of
Agriculture soon came forth with an initial financial
commitment for support of the Conference. The U.S.
Department of Energy followed, and was joined by the
Environmental Protection Agency.

The American Association for the Advancement of
Science agreed to convene the Conference, and an Organizing
Committee was established, consisting of myself as
chairman, with David Burns of AAAS, David Gates of the
University of Michigan, Gerald Still of the U.S. Department
of Agriculture, Roger Dahlman of the U.S. Department of
Energy, and John Hoffmann of the Environmental Protection
Agency, as members. Additional support for the Conference,
either through a grant or contract, or through coverage of
travel costs of experts invited to attend, followed from
the Gas Research Institute, Electric Power Research
Institute, the National Science Foundation, the National
Academy of Sciences, the Weyerhaeuser Foundation, and the
U.S. Department of Agriculture.

The key to the success of the Conference was the
enthusiasm of the chairmen and co-chairmen of the six
working groups and the participating scientists. The
chairmen and co-chairmen deserve special recognition as
Principal Authors of the panel reports (Chapters 3-8 of
this book), as does the editor, Edgar R. Lemon, and the
Chairman of the Conference, David Gates. All labored hard
before, during, and after the Conference and with no
compensation other than reimbursement of expenses. No
honoraria were offered or expected.

David Burns and Pat Curlin of the AAAS staff attended
to every detail and made all arrangements, and Thomas
Ratchford, AAAS Associate Executive Officer, gave encouragement and continuing support. The Conference owes

special thanks to the U.S. Department of Agriculture's
Agricultural Research Service, which made available the
excellent facilities of the R.B. Russell Agricultural
Research Center in Athens, Georgia. Dr. David E. Zimmer,
Center Director, and Nancy Till of the Center staff,
provided outstanding support.

Among the 130 Conference participants, approximately
25 came from overseas, including six from Australia.
Special thanks are extended to John Monteith of the United
Kingdom, who was a Keynote Speaker and made a special
effort to be present for the entire Conference.

The main focus of the Conference was identification of
researchable issues relating to first order or direct
biological effects of rising atmospheric carbon dioxide on
plant productivity. But there is an inseparable linkage of
biological effects with the climate resources of sunlight,
temperature, and moisture. The two cannot be separated.

In agriculture, as well as for forests, rangelands,
ecosystems, and aquatic biota, we are concerned with both
the stability and magnitude of plant productivity.
Stability may be just as important as total production.
A lack of stability arises mainly from the impact of
environmental stresses on plants. If elevated levels of
atmospheric CO_2 can be shown to increase primary productivity (biomass and yields) and at the same time to
alleviate or partially alleviate the environmental stresses
of unfavorable light, temperature, moisture, salinity, and
air pollutants, and generally improve the climatic
resilience of plants, that is a remarkably important
phenomenon to establish. It is a phenomenon with great
implications for society and all nations.

Sylvan H. Wittwer
Chairman, Organizing Committee
Michigan State University,
East Lansing

Preface

This book represents the proceedings of a meeting held in Athens, Georgia, U.S.A., May 23–28, 1982, under the title "Rising Atmospheric Carbon Dioxide and Plant Productivity: An International Conference." The purpose of the meeting was to review what is currently known about the response of photosynthesizing plants to levels of atmospheric carbon dioxide approximately double current concentrations, and to identify needed research.

There is considerable debate about how higher levels of CO_2 may affect global climate. Nonetheless, a major task over the next decade or so is to assess the impact of possible climate change. But any valid assessment must include the direct response of plants to the extra CO_2. In this book, we identify the questions that must be answered if we are to improve our ability to predict CO_2 effects on plants, and thus on agriculture and the less-managed biosphere.

The Conference organizers established the meeting purpose, scope, and format, and appointed panel chairmen. The latter drafted working papers which were submitted to six panels of experts, each composed of 13 to 17 members. The panels discussed and extensively revised the papers during the Conference, and it is a tribute to the participants that anything was produced!

At the outset, the organizers realized that the Conference must sharply focus on how plants respond to increasing carbon dioxide, and thus avoid undue debate on other important but peripheral issues. For example, this was not a conference on the environmental plant stress problems that may arise from carbon dioxide-induced climate change, even though such stress could become the more serious issue. Rather, emphasis was given to plant interactions to more carbon dioxide over a spectrum of environmental conditions including heat, drought, wet, and cold. While there is a fine line between the two concepts -- the effects of indirect CO_2-induced stress and direct effects -- the emphasis on direct effects allowed a more thorough treatment at the plant mechanistic level. This makes this book unique and lays a firmer foundation for future research on several issues.

The Overview by David Gates summarizes his introductory speech as Conference Chairman, and also refers to the remarks of the keynote speakers. The six chapters which follow are the core of the book. No firm rules were set for the preparation of the panel reports, and it was thus the responsibility of the chairmen and their scribes to do the hard work. The reader will note obvious differences in format and style of the six chapters. These reflect the nature of the different subjects, the diversity of panel participants, and the personal interests of each chairman. I have tried to eliminate duplication -- yet leave the spice of the scientists' independent approaches. The sequence of the chapters has been altered for smoother flow, and a Summary and Recommendations section was placed at the beginning of each chapter. This placement allows the reader to grasp the essence of the chapter at the start. I have also written an Interpretive Summary, hoping to encourage the reader to dig deeper into the book as a whole.

My thanks go to all of those who made my job pleasant: the panel chairmen; David Burns, Director of the AAAS Climate Project; the scientists who participated in the panels and review process, and who worked so hard to produce a quality piece on schedule; Dr. George Thurtell, my gracious host at the University of Guelph, who arranged for the use of excellent facilities; and Mrs. Kelly Beitz, who cheerfully and conscientiously retyped the manuscripts more than once.

Edgar R. Lemon
Guelph, Ontario

1. Interpretive Summary

As editor of this volume, I have had the wonderful opportunity of studying its contents rather thoroughly. During the conference itself, there was too much "noise" to grasp the whole. Now that I can see it from a broader view, I would like to address three areas: the need for the conference and its proceedings; the need for long-term carbon dioxide enrichment studies; and, finally, a few concluding remarks.

1. <u>Why This Book?</u> We face two interrelated energy dilemmas: i) a choice between nuclear energy or fossil fuel to meet the energy needs of an increasing population; and ii) a possible change of lifestyle as we adjust to higher energy costs. In the first dilemma, nuclear energy poses risks of a sudden catastrophe, and the U.S. public currently perceives the nuclear route to be potentially dangerous; fossil fuel, however, poses risks of slow catastrophe -- environmental decay, climate change, possible crop failures, and coastal flooding. Fossil fuel is a route the public does not yet perceive as potentially dangerous.

In the second dilemma, economic and social inertia prevent a clear perception that higher energy costs for food, heat, and shelter are causing a slow decline in our standard of living and material comfort. Higher energy costs are causing a change in the lifestyle to which many of us have been accustomed. The high cost of energy is probably the root cause of current economic instability; we are struggling to devise a strategy for coping with a fundamental change in the cost of energy.

In the highly industrialized countries, food is produced by a farming system which is highly dependent on large inputs of oil and gas, and fertilizers derived from them. Changes in the price of fossil fuel inputs pose an economic threat to this system. Fossil fuels pose another kind of threat to agriculture, through slow changes in the quality of air and water, and in the likelihood of changes in climate.

In the long run, slow, incremental changes will occur -- assuming no nuclear tragedy. Society has recognized the nuclear threat; it has not yet recognized the more subtle threat posed by the continued use of fossil fuels.

This book provides a foundation for assessment of the consequences of one aspect of continued fossil fuel use: how do plants respond to more carbon dioxide in the atmosphere? What makes this book different is its focus on this subject alone -- from the level of metabolic uptake of carbon dioxide in photosynthesis, through growth and development, to competition and succession, and finally to yield. It covers not only agricultural ecosystems, but also natural land and water ecosystems under a wide spectrum of environmental conditions, such as hot and cold, wet and dry, as well as soil factors of nutrition and salinity.

We ask, in other words, what can we expect of plants growing in the natural out-of-doors over, let's say, the next 100 years? This is roughly the time it will take for the atmosphere to reach a CO_2 concentration double that of today if fossil fuel use continues to grow at present rates. This book gives some insight into that question.

2. Why Long-Term CO_2 Enrichment Studies? Every beginning biology student knows that photosynthesis will increase if you give a plant a "squirt" of CO_2 -- given enough light, nutrients, and water, and a suitable temperature. Logic tells us that if this is so, then more CO_2 in the atmosphere should mean more photosynthesis. This, in turn, should mean more yield or accumulated carbon in plants. This logic is fine for beginning biology; unfortunately, nature is not that simple.

Plant growth and yield are not controlled by photosynthesis alone. C.T. deWit speaks of an extreme example where the Dutch add CO_2 to their greenhouses to realize an earlier and bigger crop of lettuce, yet on an accumulated carbon basis, there is no difference between a CO_2 fertilized crop and an unfertilized one. The canny Dutchmen are selling more water to the housewives -- water packaged in green leaves! This example pinpoints the hazards of predicting what plants will do with more CO_2.

There is a continuing lament throughout this volume about the dearth of information on CO_2 response for other than short periods of time. There is little known about plants grown through their total growth cycle in an enriched atmosphere of CO_2, especially plants exposed to the usual stresses of outdoor life such as drought, heat or cold, or nutrient stress of low N and P.

In reading the following chapters, it becomes clear that after the initial metabolic uptake of CO_2 in photo-synthesis, there is a hierarchy of increasingly complex processes controlling the production and allocation of end-products, such as protein, starch, sugar, and fat into the various sinks that contribute to leaf expansion, root growth, fruiting, and final yield. The timing of each part of the growth cycle is also important. Little is known of what more CO_2 will do to these long-term complex growth processes or how the timing of each part of the growth cycle may be altered. If this is true for experimental plants grown under the best of conditions, it is obviously many times more difficult to predict a final outcome in competitive plant communities of either single species or mixed species at the highest level of complexity. As a general rule, however, one can argue that with increasing complexity, the initial advantages of more CO_2 in the photosynthesis process will be increasingly buffered. I have argued this point in detail elsewhere. (See Edgar Lemon, "The Land's Response to More Carbon Dioxide," in The Fate of Fossil Fuel CO in the Oceans, N.R. Anderson and A. Malahoff, Eds., Plenum, New York, 1977, pp. 97-129.)

Why has there not been more progress on long-term measurements of plants under normal growing conditions? In addition to the "innate cussedness of plants," the researcher has the usual problems of measurement, environ-mental control, and monitoring over long periods of time, say months or even years. How does the researcher simulate a natural environment, given the necessity of some kind of gas exchange chamber required for controlling the quantity of CO_2, and also required for measuring its exchange rate? How do you find a plant or a leaf that is representative and will remain representative? How do you keep the investigator from drowning in data? Where do you find the dedication and long-time leadership to guide such an effort? Remember, too, that keeping a lot of sophisticated equipment running for a long time costs a lot of money.

But that's what is required if we are to obtain credible
data on plant responses to more CO_2. Can we convince the
public that this is a genuine need?

3. Some Concluding Remarks. There is some intriguing
evidence hinting that more CO_2 in the atmosphere could be a
boon to agriculture and forestry through higher plant
yields. We know that some greenhouse crops respond well.
There is recognition that the process of photosynthetic
fixation of CO_2 -- and the likelihood that there will be
more CO_2 -- offer a potential for higher yields. The
remainder of this book discusses what we must do if we are
to realize that potential. Here I can only restate some of
the highlights of the chapters:

Carbon Metabolism. At the biochemical level, there is
the interesting question as to the purpose of photorespiration in C_3 plants, and whether it is possible for the
energy used in that process, energy which is otherwise
apparently wasted, to be channeled into useful work, either
by reducing more CO_2 or, perhaps, by metabolizing N? At
this same level of biochemical processes, can we identify
the metabolic bottlenecks which control the movement of end
products within the plant? Can we circumvent those bottlenecks and better use the end-products to improve yield?

Physiological Response. We still do not fully
understand, at the physiological level, the mechanisms
which regulate stomates. The stomates are the valves which
control gas exchange in leaves. They are exceedingly
important for any understanding of plant responses to
increased CO_2. Not only do they control CO_2 and water
vapor exchange, they are sensitive to CO_2. There is
definite good news here. Recent experiments with plants
grown continuously at higher CO_2, and subject to drought as
well, showed definite gains in water use efficiency.
Evidently the closure of stomates due to CO_2 favors the
ratio of CO_2 uptake to water vapor loss, thus holding more
water within the plant. In major crop growing areas where
drought is the norm, the prospect of using the available
precipitation more efficiently may mean fewer crop
failures. Conserving scarce water is an important plus.

There seems to be a consensus that C_3 plants will
respond more than C_4 plants to added CO_2 as far as carbon
uptake is concerned, but that C_4 plants will use water more
efficiently due to stomatal CO_2 sensitivity. There is a
hint that this mechanism may also confer more resistance to
other stresses.

Plant Growth and Development. The possibility of
earlier development of a larger leaf area looks promising.
The experimental challenge will be to channel more end-
products into fruiting or desired yield. Here, too, more
research is needed if we are to understand N nutrition and
recycling within the plant. With greater growth due to
more CO_2, the elaboration of more protein will require
more N.

Microbial Effects. The interesting chapter on soil
microbial effects addresses the problem of N transformation
in the soil and around the roots. The authors warn that
expected added litter or debris from more plant growth
could have some undesirable side effects on mineral element
availability needed to sustain growth, especially N and P.
This is, however, a research challenge that has a good
chance of success.

Terrestrial Plant Communities. At the level of
natural land ecosystems, interactions become so complex it
is quite difficult to forecast the result of more CO_2.
Plant response to more CO_2 will not be uniform. Some
species will gain a competitive advantage. Altered
patterns of competition will change population and
succession. Added litter will also create problems of
mineral nutrition, along with problems of noxious
by-products. Will various biomes overcome these problems?
Will the added CO_2 facilitate sustained growth?

Aquatic Plant Communities. Added CO_2 will cause
aquatic species many of the same problems and offer many of
the same opportunities -- with the added problems of carbon
and oxygen supply. For plants growing below the water
surface, where gas diffusion is 10^4 times slower than in
air, inorganic and organic carbon supply and O_2 supply
mechanisms are not clearly understood.

*   *   *   *

The experts who wrote the chapters that follow may not
agree with my selection of the above points for emphasis.
But if I have whetted your appetite to dig more deeply in
this volume, I've done my job!

2. An Overview

1. Introduction. The biosphere, lithosphere, hydro-
sphere, and atmosphere of the earth are in dynamic
equilibrium; each is changing and yet each sustains the
others in the sequence of naturally occurring events.
However, human activities of landscape modification,
resource exploitation, and effluent flow have reached
sufficient magnitude to perturb the global ecosystem for an
indefinite time into the future. Contaminants into the
atmosphere, which may influence climate, include dust,
aerosols, oxides of nitrogen or sulfur, complex compounds
such as freons, and carbon dioxide.

2. Carbon Dioxide Concentrations. Carefully calibrated,
detailed measurements of the atmospheric carbon dioxide
concentration were begun at the South Pole, Antarctica
early in 1957 and at Mauna Loa, Hawaii in March of 1958 as
part of the International Geophysical Year program. From
these records and other measurements begun more recently,
it is clear that atmospheric carbon dioxide concentrations
have been increasing at an annual rate exceeding 1.0 ppm
per year. Figure 1 shows the Mauna Loa record for the
period 1958 to 1982. When the measurements were begun,
the concentration was 316 ppm, while today the average
annual CO_2 concentration above Mauna Loa is 340 ppm and it
is currently increasing at 1.5 ppm per year. Measurements
made just prior to 1900 by Brown and Escombe (1905)
indicate an early-industrial level of CO_2 concentration of
about 290 ppm according to Keeling (1978). Much less
certain is the estimated pre-industrial CO_2 level which may
have been as low as 274 ppm prior to 1860 as inferred by
Stuiver (1978). The increase of atmospheric CO_2
concentration since that time may have been about 24%, and
since the turn of the century about 17%.

Neftel et al. (1982) have reported measurements of the

CO_2 concentrations in ice cores from Camp Century and North Central Greenland, and Byrd Station, Antarctica which indicate the pre-industrial value as about 280 ppm during the past 10,000 years, but about 205 ppm some 20,000 years ago.

Normally, the change in concentration of a colorless, odorless, apparently harmless simple gas in the atmospheric would be of little concern to anyone. Yet carbon dioxide has the important property, shared by all polyatomic molecules, of strongly absorbing and emitting radiation in the infrared. The earth's surface and atmosphere remain at temperature equilibrium by absorbing incoming sunlight and radiating an equal amount of infrared energy to the cosmic cold of outer space. Anything interfering with this flow of energy, from sun to earth and earth to outer space, changes the atmospheric temperature and climate. Carbon dioxide gas, by being transparent to visible light and partially opaque to the infrared, thus interferes with the earth's energy budget.

3. General Circulation Models of Climate. Climatologists Robock (1978), Agee (1980), Hansen et al. (1981), Manabe and Stouffer (1979, 1980), Manabe and Wetherald (1980), Manabe et al. (1981), Shukla and Mintz (1982), and many others have developed various General Circulation Models, GCM's, of the earth's atmosphere using computers to estimate the temperature and precipitation changes expected from increases in the CO_2 concentration, as well as changes resulting from other driving functions, such as solar activity and volcanic dust. Although idealized and simplified from the complexities of the real world, these GCM's are yielding results which have rather high levels of plausibility. The GCM's are being elaborated to include more of the physical features of the real world, such as dust, clouds, ice cover, and geography.

4. Climate Change. Climatologists, using the GCM's, estimate that with a doubling of the atmospheric CO_2 concentration, the mean temperature of the earth will increase approximately 2° C, and possibly as much as 3° C. However, temperature changes will not be uniform over the earth. Polar regions may increase by 5 or 6 degrees C and equatorial regions by less than 1° C. The present mean global temperature is approximately 15° C. For perspective as to the significance of a temperature change, it is noteworthy that the mean temperature of the northern hemisphere varied by no more than about 2° C during the last 10,000 years, including the warm altithermal period 4 to 8,000 years ago, and the "Little Ice Age" from 600 to 100 years

ago. During the Pleistocene, with glaciers covering
extensive regions of the earth, temperatures were never
more than 5° C below the present mean value.

Along with global temperature changes resulting from
an increase of the atmospheric carbon dioxide concentration, a change in the pattern of precipitation is also
predicted. A warmer world will be accompanied by increased
precipitation resulting from increased ocean evaporation
rates. However, it is predicted that certain regions of
the world will experience serious decreases in precipitation, including a large part of the central U.S., much of
Eastern Europe, and the Soviet Union. Although the
climates of Canada, Alaska, western Europe, North and East
Africa, among others, may become wetter, the dryness
predicted throughout many of the great grain belts of the
world is cause for concern.

Confidence in the GCM projections of a warmer world
and changes of temperature and precipitation is enhanced by
comparing GCM data with the real world conditions thought
to exist during the altithermal period (Kellogg and
Schware, 1981), as well as with global conditions extant
during the five warmest years versus the five coldest years
of the decades from 1925 through 1974 (Wigley et al.,
1980). The similarities of latitudinal and regional
changes is highly impressive and suggests that the world is
most likely to experience the climate changes projected.
Not only are climatologists projecting latitudinal and
seasonal increases of temperature, changes of precipitation, length of growing season, and soil moisture
content, but also reductions of the amount of sea ice, snow
cover, and ice sheets. Rising sea levels may result from
higher temperatures, and the dislocation of millions of
people living in coastal areas may slowly occur over the
next few centuries.

5. Sources of Carbon. For many years scientists have
recognized that the burning of fossil fuels, manufacturing
of cement, the plowing of prairies, and the cutting of
forests have contributed CO_2 to the atmosphere. The annual
quantities of fossil fuels consumed globally are well
documented (Baes et al., 1977). The annual growth rate
in the use of fossil fuels has averaged over 4.5% per year
throughout the period 1950 to 1973, but since then has
dropped to about 2.25% per year. In fact, during most of
the century since 1880, the average annual growth rate
remained around 4.3%, until recently. Current energy
forecasts suggest that growth rates for carbon releases
from fossil fuel burning over the next 30 to 50 years will

most likely average 2% per year or less. The current
fossil fuel release of CO_2 is estimated at about 5.3 Gt of
carbon to the atmosphere per year. By combining the
quantities of carbon released by burning fossil fuels with
the rates of accumulation in the atmosphere, one concludes
that only about 50% of the amount emitted is retained in
the atmosphere. The excess must be going to a sink,
presumably the oceans and possibly to forests.

Land use changes involving forest harvesting, grassland burning, or urbanization have contributed about 2
Gt/year of carbon. There is still a considerable amount of
uncertainty concerning this number. In fact, there is a
continuing debate as to whether terrestrial ecosystems are
a net source or a net sink for CO_2. Nevertheless, the
future concentration of atmospheric carbon dioxide is
likely to be dominated by fossil fuel releases rather than
by land use practices.

6. Future CO_2 Levels.   The earlier growth rates for the
use of fossil fuels suggested a doubling time of about 50
years for the CO_2 levels. Now, with the reduced estimated
growth rates, a doubling time of nearly 100 years is
suggested. Alvin Weinberg, speaking to the Conference,
addressed this issue. He mentioned that the world's
remaining recoverable resources of oil, gas, and coal are
estimated to contain nearly $4,130 \times 10^9$ metric tons of
carbon. If this total quantity is burned and half remains
airborne, it would increase the atmospheric carbon dioxide
concentration by about a factor of four. Since even a
doubling of the present CO_2 level is seen as troublesome
from a climate standpoint, quadrupling the amount would be
intolerable, and must be avoided. Indeed, "acceptable"
levels of CO_2 may be no more than 1.5 to 2.5 times the
present concentration, e.g. between 510 and 850 ppm. The
world's cumulative use of fossil fuels must somehow be
restricted to levels far below the total estimated
recoverable resources.

7. Fossil Fuel Use Scenarios. Many possible energy
scenarios can be projected for the use of fossil fuels.
The Council on Environmental Quality issued a report in
January 1981, entitled "Global Energy Futures and the
Carbon Dioxide Problem" which presented fossil fuel use
scenarios leading to long-term steady-state CO_2 levels
1.5, 2.0, and 3.0 times the early-industrial CO_2 level of
290 ppm, or levels of 435, 580, and 870 ppm. Two things
are particularly significant from these projections. The
first is that a rapid early burning of fossil fuels will
require drastic reductions later in order to keep the total

CO_2 level below 1.5, 2.0, or 3.0 times the early-industrial level. Fossil fuel use would have to peak in about the year 2007, 2042, or 2075 respectively. It is clear that it is going to be extremely difficult to keep the CO_2 asymptotic concentration below 500 ppm, even with corrective action. It will be less difficult to stay below 600 ppm, and relatively easy to stay below about 800 ppm.

8. <u>Non-Fossil Fuel Alternatives</u>. In order to limit the global use of fossil fuels, many conscious actions must be taken, and the earlier they are taken, the easier it will be to achieve the desired results. All reasonable effort must be made to achieve energy conservation and improved energy-use efficiency. Non-fossil fuels must be substituted for fossil fuel use wherever possible. This implies a greatly increased use of biomass, solar, nuclear, and ocean thermal energy conversion (OTEC) in the future. The time frame for remedial action is limited by the fact that it takes 18 to 20 years to plan, design, and construct a nuclear power plant, and much longer to establish the technology for an OTEC plant.

The International Institute for Applied Systems Analysis (IIASA), Austria, has recently established a careful series of energy scenarios (see IIASA, 1981). Perry and others (1982) have further elaborated on these scenarios and their implications. Together with the CEQ report (1981), one can draw the following conclusions: The population of the world is expected to increase to about 8 billion people by the year 2030. If per capita consumption of energy as a global average does not exceed 2.8 kW per person per year, compared to the current U.S. consumption of 11 kW per person per year, which represents a low growth rate scenario, then the contribution of non-fossil energy sources must reach a level within the next 35 to 50 years comparable to the present total world energy supply of 9 terawatt-years/year or 9×10^{12} Wy/y (250 quads). This would represent an average annual growth rate of the non-fossil energy sources of around 9% per year between 1980 and 2000, with a doubling time of 8 years. If this is achieved, the atmospheric carbon dioxide concentration might not exceed about 450 ppm, an "acceptable" level. If the CO_2 level is allowed to rise to 600 ppm, the annual growth rate of "replacement" non-fossil fuel for fossil fuel would be about 7% per year until the year 2000, and 3% per year until 2050. By this date the quantity of non-fossil fuel supplied must exceed 50% of today's total world energy demand. In other words, it will exceed 12.8 terawatt- years/year, or 356 quads. All of this is based on a low growth scenario -- an assumed energy demand growth

rate of 2% per year or less. If a higher growth rate
energy demand ensues, then the necessity for non-fossil
energy sources will be much greater.

From our perspective at this time, it is unlikely that
the people of the world will substitute non-fossil sources
of energy at the rate necessary to limit the ultimate
cumulative atmospheric carbon dioxide concentration to less
than about 600 ppm; a level which may be reached between
2075 and 2100. However, it is possible that global growth
rates will be even slower than now anticipated. Although
this is comforting, it does not alleviate our concern about
the CO_2-climate change issue and about our serious lack of
knowledge of the response of the biosphere to increasing
atmospheric CO_2 concentrations.

9. Plant Responses to CO_2. The decision was made that this
conference would be most useful if it assessed what is
known and not known regarding the responses of cultivated
and non-cultivated plants and ecosystems to increasing
levels of carbon dioxide, and to identify the research
needed to quantify the direct biological effects.
Consideration was to be given primarily to those effects
expected for carbon dioxide concentrations not exceeding
600 ppm.

Plants are always CO_2-limited for photosynthesis.
They respond positively to increasing CO_2 concentration,
and water use efficiency increases. There are also
negative effects among some plant physiological responses,
such as the reduction of stomatal conductance with
increasing CO_2 concentration. It is possible that lower
photosynthetic capacity will develop for plants grown at
high CO_2 concentration because of higher starch content and
decreased chlorophyll concentration in leaves. Some
experiments suggest that in addition to increasing plant
growth, higher levels of CO_2 can, to some extent,
compensate for stresses of extreme temperature and drought.
We do not know how plants will acclimate to higher
atmospheric CO_2 concentration exposures of more than one
life-cycle duration. We know that C_3, C_4, and CAM plants
each respond differently to short-term exposures at increasing levels of atmospheric CO_2 concentration. By
short-term is meant a length of time less than one life
cycle, generally minutes, hours, or even days. With a
dryer climate, will C_3 plants become more competitive with
C_4 plants? How will increasing CO_2 levels affect plant
succession? Plants are, of course, exceedingly complex.
No two plant species will respond the same, and within a
given species the responses will be different depending on

the growth conditions. Furthermore, what we expect to happen depends in part on the questions asked. If our objective is increased productivity for yield of food for humans or cattle, then the responses in which we are interested are quite different than those when we are asking ecological questions about changes in community composition, rates of succession or the movement of ecotones.

10. Physiological Responses. Paul Kramer, in addressing the meeting, put this matter somewhat differently. He asked, what has plant physiology contributed to our understanding of plant yield? "Darn little," was his answer. But the reason for this is quite simple. Plant physiologists are mainly retrospective, in that they explain "why something does what it does," but they are not predictive. One would think, a priori, that dry matter production depends on photosynthesis, but this does not seem to be exactly true. Breeding plants for high photosynthetic rates does not necessarily increase yield. Kramer asked, "What is limiting crop yield today?" The average farm yields are usually only about 25% of the maximum yields obtainable under optimum experimental conditions. Weather is the primary problem. Although the atmospheric carbon dioxide is a limiting factor, weather will be the main source of variation in yield.

Well-watered and fertilized plants in the laboratory have accelerated growth rates with CO_2 enrichment above normal levels according to Kramer (1981) and Wittwer (1980). It seems that, on the average, for .01% increase in the CO_2 concentration, growth increases about 0.9% for laboratory plants. However, for plants growing naturally, where nutrient and water supply may be limiting, plant growth would be substantially less than for laboratory-grown plants. Kramer (1981) also refers to experiments which show the largest growth response to CO_2 increase occurring in seedlings and young leaves. The response is much reduced in older leaves. Young leaves of many herbaceous plants have a higher photosynthetic capacity than do older leaves, but with the leaves of forest trees we are finding very little difference with age.

Kramer mentioned three important areas of research: 1) physiological and environmental factors affecting leaf area; 2) the amount of photosynthate which goes into marketable products; and 3) the allocation of photosynthate to root growth, leaves, stems, flowers and fruit. The last area of investigation is one of the most important in plant physiology today.

11. Climatology. One of the guidelines for this Workshop
was to avoid questions concerning plant response to climate
change, despite the fact that changes of the hydrological
cycle may have more significant impact on plant productivity than the changes of CO_2 concentration, temperature,
or light. John Monteith in his address expressed great
concern with this guideline. He pointed out that climato-
logical factors are extremely important to crop yield,
particularly the occurrence of extreme events such as
droughts, frosts, and severe storms. The length of the
growing season is a complex issue, since the growth period
sometimes gets shorter with warmer conditions, because the
plant grows faster. Monteith made the suggestion that we
are singularly ignorant of the climatology of a high-CO_2-
world, where the plants are actually grown in the field.
Records of CO_2 concentrations, as well as of temperature,
humidity, wind, and light will need to be kept at many
kinds of sites in temperate, subtropical, and tropical
areas. Some scientists disagree with Monteith as to the
efficacy of getting such detailed CO_2 climatology; this is
particularly so because of the small spatial variation of
the CO_2 concentration within the plant canopy.

John Hoffman of EPA addressed the Workshop, again
emphasizing the inseparable linkage between the biological
effects resulting from increasing CO_2 levels, with the
climatic variables of sunlight, temperature and moisture.
Elevated levels of CO_2 may not alleviate the environmental
stresses of light, temperature, moisture, or even air
pollutants.

Jennifer Huang McBeath of the University of Alaska
(Fairbanks) was particularly concerned about climatic
effects on plants since some of the greatest temperature
and precipitation changes will occur at high latitudes as
a result of increasing levels of atmospheric CO_2. What
will happen if Alaska becomes warmer? With warmer
temperature, there will be more winter precipitation and
the glaciers will advance, but if it gets too much warmer,
then the glaciers will retreat. At the moment, the
glaciers in Alaska are advancing. If the climate becomes
more moist and warmer, a number of plant pathogens will
increase. For example, spruce needle rust will get worse,
partly because it will be more successful at overwintering
on the leaves of Labrador Tea, a ubiquitous bog or wetland
plant. Many people get a rash from the spores of this
rust. Generally, there is not sufficient cover for winter
wheat to be grown successfully, but if Alaska becomes
warmer and wetter, then this condition might provide the
necessary amount of snow cover.

Notwithstanding these important ideas concerning the relationship of climate change resulting from increasing CO_2 levels, the discussions within the Workshop panels were largely focused on the direct responses of plants to CO_2. It is this emphasis which gives this volume particular significance.

12. Plant Breeding. Nicholas Frey, a scientist with Pioneer Hybrid International, presented a particularly incisive address concerning plant breeding and climate change. He pointed out that breeding, evaluation and selection of plant varieties is a continuous process which occurs while the climate is changing. A complete breeding cycle takes approximately 10 years from the time inbred development begins until a final hybrid product is identified and marketed. New hybrids emerging from the breeding programs are those best adapted to the environmental conditions at a particular site during the last three years of testing. If a significant climate change occurs over a 50 to 100 year period, that represents 5 to 10 complete breeding cycles. The entire history of hybrid corn has only included approximately 5 breeding cycles. Frey's main point throughout his talk was that the plant breeding programs already in operation automatically incorporate the responses to CO_2 concentration and changing climate at each place in the world where a particular crop is being tested.

13. Seasonal CO_2 Amplitude. C.D. Keeling was to have addressed to the workshop but could not make it at the last moment. However, he did send several manuscripts containing the latest information concerning the seasonal amplitude in the atmospheric CO_2 concentration. These results were presented at the workshop.

Bacastow et al. (1981a) report an analysis of the seasonal cycle in the Mauna Loa record and Bacastow et al. (1981b) for Canadian Weather Station P. The seasonal cycle is readily seen in Figure 1 for the Mauna Loa record. Wong and Pettit (1981) report the secular and seasonal CO_2 changes for Canadian stations at Sable Island and Alert, as well as Barrow, Alaska. The atmospheric CO_2 data show that the seasonal cycle is greatest at high northern latitudes, decreases toward the equator, almost vanishes at 14 S latitude, and is small and of opposite phase in the remainder of the Southern Hemisphere. According to these authors, the seasonal cycle must reflect both photosynthesis and respiration by the biota of the world, and may, in fact, serve as a monitor of biotic metabolism.

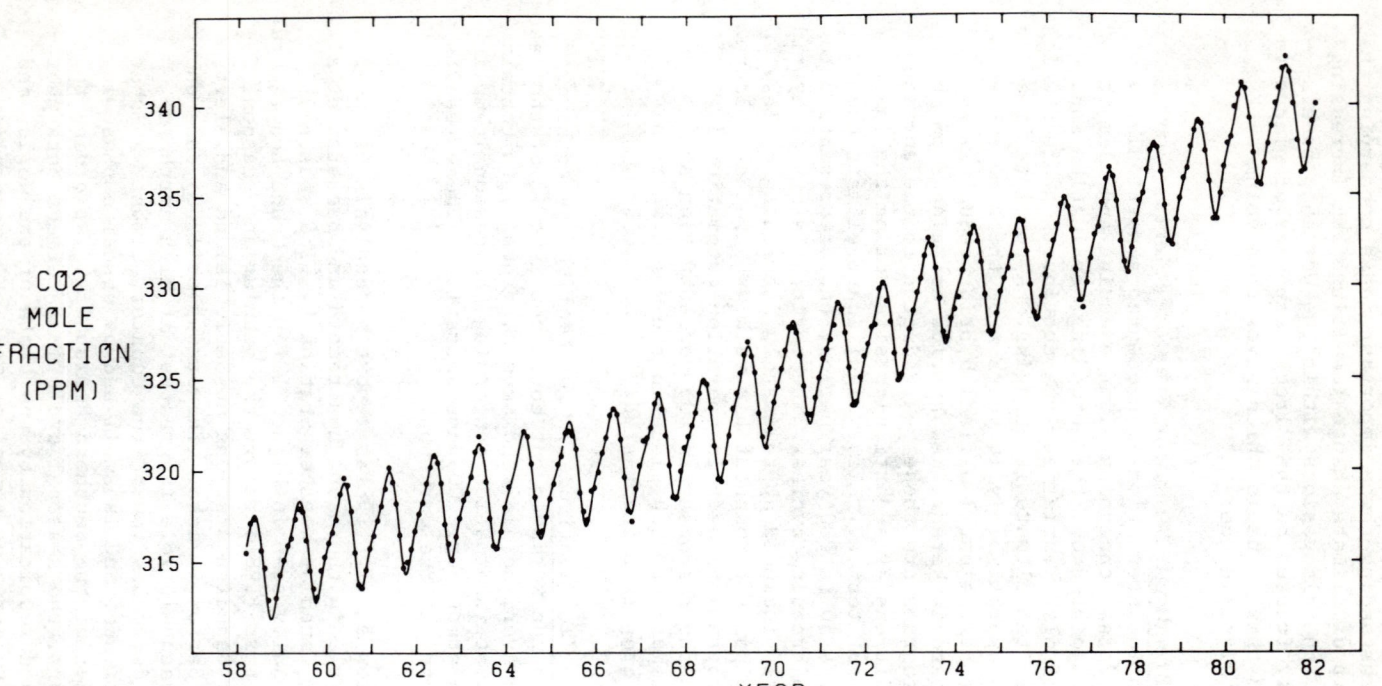

Figure 1. The atmospheric carbon dioxide concentration as monthly mean values at Mauna Loa, Hawaii, from 1958 through 1981.

The decrease in atmospheric CO_2 concentration from the spring maximum to the autumn minimum, May to early October at Mauna Loa, appears to be the difference between net ecosystem production and respiration, a difference related to photosynthesis and respiration. Although the seasonal change of ocean surface temperature will have an effect, simple numerical models of the ocean CO_2 exchange show this effect to be almost insignificant.

Careful analysis indicates that the seasonal amplitude at Mauna Loa was constant from 1959 through 1975 but appears to increase during the period 1976 through 1980. At Canadian Weather Station P the seasonal amplitude shows a large increase in 1976 which continues until 1980, but then decreases in 1980 to the 1970 to 1975 average. A small change in either net ecosystem production or respiration could produce a significant effect on the seasonal amplitude. A temporary change of climate, such as increased rainfall, could produce a change in ecosystem productivity. It is possible that the increase represents a change in yearly carbon fixation by the biota and perhaps the size of the biota itself. More data are necessary before these hypotheses can be confirmed or denied.

14. CO_2 Enrichment Studies.   H.Z. Enoch addressed the meeting on the subject of plant productivity and carbon dioxide levels. He believes the scientific community should participate in a multi-national effort to study the effects of elevated atmospheric carbon dioxide concentrations on managed and unmanaged ecosystems. He described the existence of large underground reservoirs of almost pure carbon dioxide of geological origin. This underground CO_2 could be released in a controlled manner to enrich the air surrounding a crop or stand of trees. The growth rates, water loss rates, and other physiological processes would be studied for these plants over several growing seasons while the CO_2 fertilization was continued.

Such enrichment experiments on a large scale would be expensive and difficult to undertake. Many of the underground CO_2 reservoirs are owned by oil companies who then pump the CO_2 into old oil wells to force out more petroleum. Coal gasification plants, when they go into operation, will produce massive amounts of CO_2 and this could be used for enrichment studies. Preliminary experiments being done now on a small scale may indicate whether or not large scale enrichment studies of crops and forests might be worthwhile.

15. CO_2 Research Support.   J. Phil Campbell, a former Under Secretary of the U.S. Department of Agriculture, eloquently

told the Workshop audience that no matter how good the research, nor how important it may be, unless scientists have a consensus of public opinion behind the program, the work would not be sustainable using federal money. This is indeed a matter of great concern to all who participated in this Conference.

Plants are extremely complex entities and their responses to environmental factors are many and frequently subtle. It will be no easy task to advance our under-standing of plant productivity, or plant response, to increasing carbon dioxide concentration, to a useful level within a period of time tolerable by the political process which provides the federal funding. Elements of the political system will tire of receiving perceived false alarms to rising atmospheric CO_2 levels, and at times of decreasing funds for research it will be extremely difficult to sustain support for this necessary research.

However, it is also possible to sustain support. One way of doing so is to identify well-defined and articulated research needs. That was the purpose of this Conference and is the intent of this book. Several new research ideas emerge from this effort. The reader should find the following chapters a useful review of the subject matter and they may provide a stimulus for effective research during the years ahead.

16. Literature Cited

Agee, E.M. 1980. Present climatic cooling and a proposed causative mechanism. Bull. Amer. Meteor. Soc. 61, pp. 1356-1357.

Bacastow, R.B., C.D. Keeling, and T.P. Whorf. 1981a. Seasonal amplitude in atmospheric CO_2 concentration at Mauna Loa, Hawaii, 1959-1980. Paper presented at the WMO/ICSU/UNEP Scientific Conference on Analysis and Interpretation of Atmospheric CO_2 Data, World Meteorological Organization, Geneva, Switzerland, pp. 169-176.

Bacastow, R.B., C.D. Keeling, and T.P. Whorf. 1981B. Seasonal amplitude in atmospheric CO_2 concentration at Canadian Weather Station P, 1970-1980. Paper presented at the WMO/ICSU/UNEP Scientific Conference on Analysis and Interpretation of Atmospheric CO_2 Data, World Meteorological Organization, Geneva, Switzerland, pp. 163-168.

Baes, C.F. Jr., H.E. Goeller, J.S. Olson, and R.M. Rotty. 1977. Carbon dioxide and climate: The uncontrolled experiment. Amer. Sci. 65, 310-320.

Brown, H.T. and F. Escombe. 1905. Research on some of the physiological processes of green plants with special reference to the interchange of energy between the leaf and its surroundings. Roy. Soc. London Proc. Ser. B 76, 29-111.

CEQ. 1981. Global Energy Futures and the Carbon Dioxide Problem. Washington, DC. GPO.

Hansen, J., D. Johnson, A. Lacis, S. Lebedoff, P. Lee, D. Rind and G. Russell. 1981. Climate impact of increasing atmospheric carbon dioxide. Science 213, 957-966.

IIASA. 1981. Energy Systems Program, W. Haefele, Program Leader, Energy in a finite world, Ballinger Publ. Co., Cambridge, Mass.

Keeling, C.D. 1978. Atmospheric carbon dioxide in the 19th century. Science 202, 1109.

Kellogg, W.W. and R. Schware. 1981. Climate Change and Society. Westview Press, Boulder, CO.

Kramer, P.J. 1981. Carbon dioxide concentration, photosynthesis and dry matter production. BioScience 31, 29-33.

Manabe, S. and R.J. Stouffer. 1979. A CO_2 climate sensitivity study with a mathematical model of the global climate. Nature 282, 491-493.

Manabe, S. and R.J. Stouffer. 1980. Sensitivity of a global climate model to an increase of CO_2 concentration in the atmosphere. J. Geophys. Res. 85, 5529-5554.

Manabe, S. and R.T. Wetherald. 1980. On the distribution of climatic change resulting from an increase in CO_2 content of the atmosphere. J. Atmos. Sci. 37, 99-118.

Manabe, S., R.T. Wetherald and R. Stouffer. 1981. Summer dryness due to an increase of atmosphere CO_2 concentration. Climatic Change 3, 347-386.

Neftel, A., H. Oeschger, J. Schwander, B. Stauffer, and R. Zumbrunn. 1982. Ice core sample measurements give atmospheric CO_2 content during the past 40,000 years. Nature 295, 220-223.

Perry, A.M., K.J. Araj, W. Fulkerson, D.J. Rose, M.M. Miller and R.M. Rotty. 1982. Energy supply and demand implications of CO_2. Submitted to Science.

Robock, A. 1978. Internally and externally caused climate change. J. Atmos. Sci. 35, 1111-1222.

Shukla, J. and Y. Mintz. 1982. Influence of land-surface evapotranspiration on the earth's climate. Science 215, 1498-1501.

Stuiver, M. 1978. Atmospheric carbon dioxide in the 19th century. Science 202, 1109.

Wigley, T.M.L., P.D. Jones and P.M. Kelly, 1980. Scenario for a warm, high-CO_2 world. Nature 283, 17-21.

Wittwer, S.H. 1980. Carbon dioxide and climate change: An agricultural perspective. Jour. Soil and Water Conserv. 35, 116-120.

Wong, C.S. and K.G. Pettit. 1981. Global-scale secular CO_2 trends and seasonal changes at Canadian CO_2 stations: ocean weather station P, Sable Island and Alert. Paper presented at the WMO/ICSU/UNEP Scientific Conference on Analysis and Interpretation of Atmospheric CO_2 Data. World Meteorological Organization, Geneva, Switzerland, pp. 169-176.

3. Carbon Metabolism

Panel Members: C. Black, Rapporteur, J. Bassham, H.
Brown, G. Edwards, N. Good, R.G. Edwards, S. Miyachi,
C.B. Osmond, P.K. Stumpf, D.A. Walker.

SUMMARY AND RECOMMENDATIONS

Our present knowledge of the photosynthetic process
indicates that increasing atmospheric CO_2 provides an
opportunity to increase plant productivity. Carbon
assimilation and rate of carbon flow through metabolic
pathways will increase, and will thus raise the potential
for plant growth. To realize this potential, there are
specific problems of a biochemical and physiological nature
to be addressed: 1) the initial rate and amount of CO_2
fixation, 2) the production and allocation of each product,
and 3) the duration of CO_2 fixation.

1) In the initial phase, CO_2 fixation is catalyzed by
ribulose bisphosphate carboxylase/oxygenase. The mechanisms for activation and regulation of this enzyme are
incompletely understood. This enzyme is extremely important, since it acts as a carboxylase for photosynthesis and
as an oxygenase for photorespiration.

2) The large amount of energy that is lost in photorespiration in C_3 plants at an ambient CO_2 of 340 ppm
represents an excess of energy that could be used for
reduction of CO_2 and for other growth processes such as N
metabolism. This hypothesis needs testing.

3) The energy and intermediates needed for carbon
assimilation at higher CO_2 levels seem to be limited by
photosynthetic electron transport. The details and assays
about these restrictions are not developed.

4) Limits may exist on CO_2 fixation by chloroplast envelope translocations, particularly the phosphate control of metabolic fluxes, which balance sucrose and starch synthesis.

5) How will elevated CO_2 levels modify the unique ability of C_4 and CAM plants to raise their internal CO_2 so that it does not limit their productivity? C_4 plants are less likely to respond to more CO_2 than C_3 plants.

6) There is little information about how certain photosynthetic cells that have no C_3 reductive carbon cycle will respond to more CO_2. These include stomatal guard cells, C_4 mesophyll cells, and heterocysts nitrogen-fixing cells.

7) There is a need to evaluate alternative mechanisms to concentrate CO_2 in such cells as unicellular algae.

Since increased CO_2 can increase net photosynthesis, there is a need to know the extent to which plants can use the additional products, and how they are used:

1) For example, how are the end products, starch and sucrose, as well as the secondary products of cellulose, amino acids, lipids, polymers, and phenolics -- regulated or altered at the biochemical level?

2) To what degree do N, P, and S metabolism limit or alter plant composition under higher CO_2? Will the C:N ratio be affected?

3) Will more carbohydrate from photosynthesis influence metabolic and maintenance respiration in leaves and other organs? The effect of higher CO_2 and more photosynthesis on respiratory processes has not been extensively investigated.

Finally, we know least of all, the influence of more CO_2 on the duration of photosynthesis in the life cycle of germination, growth and development, reproduction and senescence. Moreover, environmental stresses of light, water, and temperature affect the magnitude and duration of photosynthesis. The metabolic basis of these temporal changes require clarification, especially with added CO_2.

1) What are the feedback regulatory mechanisms that may limit photosynthesis at higher CO_2 and how are they regulated?

2) What is the relation between translocation and sink size on sustained higher photosynthetic rates?

3) What are the effects of more photosynthetic products and their allocation on growth and development of plants?

1. Introduction. Atmospheric carbon dioxide (CO_2) provides, through the processes of photosynthesis, all of the raw materials for biological activity on earth. The major storage products of photosynthesis are sugars, starch, proteins, and fats. These are harvested from plants and form the basis of all animal and human diets. Agriculture, the single biggest industry in the world, depends on photosynthetic metabolism for all of its products.

The present level of CO_2 in the atmosphere is a complex function of many processes, of which only one, photosynthesis, is discussed here. On a geological timescale, CO_2 has rapidly increased in the last 100 years because man is now consuming products of photosynthetic CO_2 reduction that accumulated over millions of years. The burning of fossil fuels releases CO_2 previously fixed by plants. This release is faster than the CO_2 can be absorbed by the oceans and fixed through photosynthesis by existing plant life. Plants make a major contribution to stabilizing the atmospheric CO_2 equilibrium which is presently being perturbed upward. There is general agreement that for most plants, more CO_2 can increase photosynthesis and plant growth. Changes in photosynthetic rates and plant biochemical processes may result in a species-specific increase in crop productivity, and alterations in competition among plants.

Over the last three decades research into photosynthetic carbon metabolism has clarified details of these several complex biological processes. It is now possible to integrate a wide range of biophysical, biochemical, physiological, and ecological observations which relate plant productivity to increasing CO_2 levels. This chapter reviews photosynthetic carbon metabolisms.

Photosynthetic experiments at higher CO_2 levels in greenhouses show that net photosynthetic CO_2 fixation by plants increases with additional CO_2. Evidently, photosynthetic rates and growth of plants are limited by the present ambient CO_2 (Figure 1) when other factors affecting photosynthesis (such as light, water, temperature, and nutrients) are optimal. This principle --

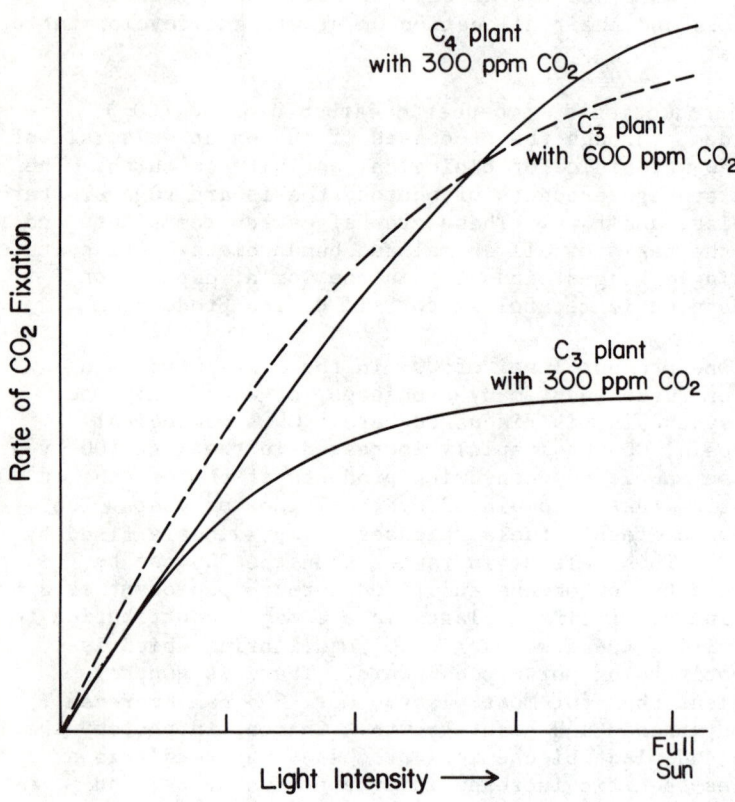

Figure 1. Schematic presentation for the approximate rate of
photosynthesis in air with increasing light intensity. The
results indicate that photosynthesis by CO_2 plants in air
saturates between 30 to 40% full sunlight intensity. For C_4
plants with the additional C_4 pathway to concentrate CO_2, the
rate of photosynthesis in air increases with light intensity
and at full light intensity is about twice that in a C3 plant.

that CO_2 limits photosyntheses -- was established by 1890. Even when the other factors are only partially limiting, as is the case most of the time, higher CO_2 still increases photosynthesis, but to a lesser extent, because only one of the limiting factors, i.e. CO_2, has been supplemented.

With insufficient ambient CO_2 in today's atmosphere limiting maximum rates of photosynthesis, C_3 plants dispose of much of the excess photosynthetic assimilatory capacity (ATP and NADPH) by photorespiration. During photorespiration, up to 50% of the CO_2 newly fixed into carbohydrate is reoxidized back to CO_2. Net photosynthesis is the sum of gross photosynthesis minus photorespiration. Altering the level of CO_2 in the chloroplast at the site of CO_2 fixation regulates this competition between photosynthesis and photorespiration. In the past, the atmospheric concentration of CO_2, perhaps as low as 250 ppm, was maintained through CO_2 removal in net photosynthesis, plus additions from geological and biological processes. Experimentally, in a closed system, C_3 plants equilibrate the CO_2 concentration to 40 to 75 ppm CO_2 without any CO_2 input from the outside. This is called the CO_2 compensation point. The CO_2 level in the closed chamber does not go to zero because CO_2 is added to the air by plants from their own photorespiration. Likewise, a balance between net photosynthesis and CO_2 generating processes maintains the atmosphere at a constant but higher CO_2 level, i.e., 340 ppm as of today. Because of the large amount of photorespiration used to consume excess energy, plants should have a sizable built-in metabolic potential for increased photosynthesis when more CO_2 becomes available. In the past century of rising atmospheric CO_2, photosynthetic rates must have increased and photorespiration rates decreased, but we have no proof of this. Nonetheless, we believe that continued increase in atmospheric CO_2 will use the excess photosynthetic potential of plants presently being wasted in photorespiration.

The established principles of photosynthetic carbon metabolism are unlikely to change with increased CO_2. However, the rate of CO_2 assimilation, its duration, and the end products should be altered by more CO_2. Changes in the balance among biochemical processes will also affect plant responses to other environmental components such as temperature, water, and light. The latter part of this chapter lists, with little discussion, those properties of carbon metabolism which are most likely to alter plant productivity under higher CO_2.

The following three sections are organized around the

biological themes: 1) the rate of CO_2 assimilation or photosynthesis; 2) the fate of assimilates or the distribution of carbon products of photosynthesis; and 3) the duration of assimilation or the effect of more CO_2 on plant growth and development.

2. Rate of Photosynthesis. Initial photosynthetic CO_2 fixation occurs via one of the three cyclic pathways (C_3, C_4, and C_4 in CAM) in specific plants. In addition, carbon accumulates in two metabolic sinks, one for sucrose and one for starch. These pathways of carbon metabolism, plus a C_2 photorespiratory pathway, coexist; combined, they represent the initial phases of carbon assimilation. The reductive photosynthetic carbon cycle of the chloroplast, or the C_3 pathway (also called the Calvin Cycle), is the primary pathway for net CO_2 fixation and reduction to sugar phosphates in all green plants and algae. The initial reaction is the fixation of CO_2 by ribulose bisphosphate carboxylase/oxygenase to form first, the three-carbon product, 3-P-glycerate. This is then reduced to sugar phosphates by subsequent reactions. From the C_3 cycle, there are two major routes for formation of carbon end products. Starch is formed and stored in the chloroplast. Triose phosphate is shuttled out of the chloroplast by a specific translocator and converted into sucrose in the cytoplasm.

Because available CO_2 generally limits photosynthesis, two additional cycles exist to cope with this limitation. In some plants, a C_4 pathway efficiently traps or stores CO_2 into the carboxyl group of four carbon acids. The C_4 pathway occurs in two variations: one in C_4 plants, the other in CAM plants. However, the C_4 pathway cannot reduce CO_2 to hexoses. This must be accomplished by the existence of a C_3 pathway in these same leaves. The addition of the C_4 cycle requires extra photosynthetic energy, and these plants are more efficient in removing CO_2 from the air when CO_2 limits the rate of photosynthesis (Figure 1). Plants with the C_4 pathway also have a better water and nitrogen use efficiency for an equivalent rate of CO_2 uptake.

In all green plants and algae there is an oxidative photosynthetic carbon cycle, or C_2 cycle (also called the glycolate pathway), that coexists with the C_3 cycle. This complex cycle is initiated in the chloroplasts by the oxygenase activity of ribulose bisphosphate carboxylase/ oxygenase, to form the C_2 compound, P-glycolate, from ribulose bisphosphate. The primary purpose of the C_2 pathway seems to be to consume excess photosynthetic assim-

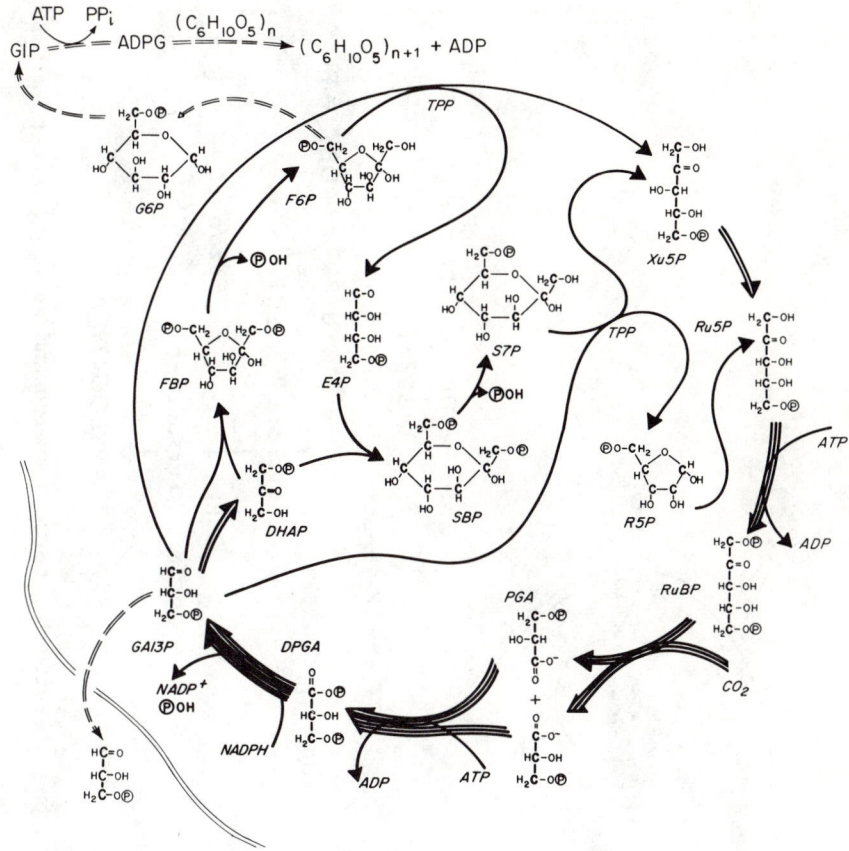

Figure 2. The reductive photosynthetic carbon cycle. The
solid lines indicate reactions of the cycle, with the number
of lines per arrow indicating the number of times each
reaction occurs for one complete turn of the cycle. In one
turn of the cycle, three molecules of CO_2 are converted to
one molecule of triose phosphate, and each reaction of the
cycle occurs at least once. The double dashed lines indicate
the principal reactions removing intermediate compounds of
the cycle for biosynthesis. After Bassham (1979).

Abbreviations: RuBP, ribulose-1,5-bisphosphate; PGA,
3-phosphoglycerate; DPGA, 1,3-diphosphoglycerate; FBP, fructose 1,6-biphosphate; F6P, fructose-6-phosphate, SBP, sedo-
heptulose 1,7-biphosphate; S7P, sedoheptulose-7-phosphate;
Xu5P, xylulose-5-phosphate; R5P, ribose-5-phosphate; Ru5P,
ribulose-5-phosphate; TPP, thiamine pyrophosphate.

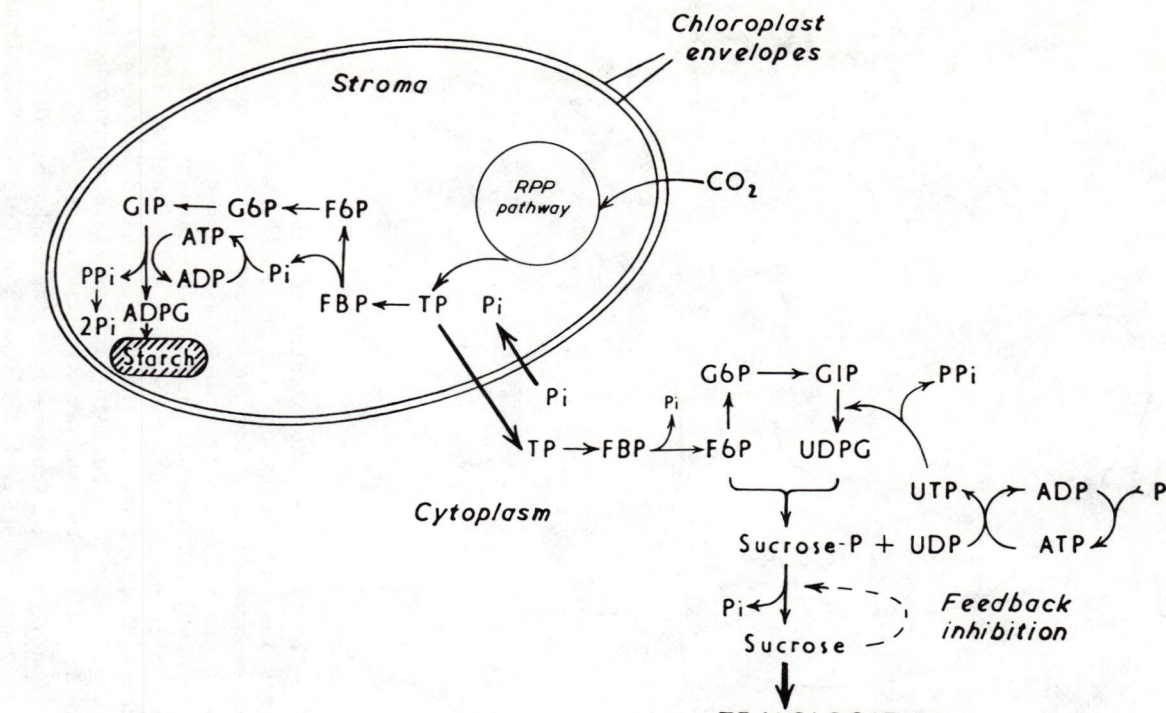

Figure 3. Metabolic pathways for carbon distribution between starch and sucrose. After Walker (1981).

ilatory power in the absence of sufficient CO_2 to saturate the C_3 cycle. Enzymatic competition between the two substrates, CO_2 and O_2, meters the flow of carbon into the C_3 versus the C_2 cycle. Since CO_2 is released in the C_2 cycle, the difference between the flow rates of these two pathways determines net photosynthetic CO_2 uptake. Increasing atmospheric CO_2 will increase the relative significance or rate of the reductive cycle over the oxidative photosynthetic carbon cycle. Although net photosynthesis should increase with more CO_2, much less is known about the duration of photosynthesis, carbon partitioning, or other metabolic consequences. The ratio of products of photosynthetic CO_2 fixation, and the activation and regulation of enzymes associated with photosynthetic carbon metabolism will probably change.

2.1 Effect of CO_2 on the Reductive Photosynthetic Carbon Cycle (C_3 cycle).

The C_3 cycle (Bassham and Calvin, 1957) is essential in all photosynthetic tissues, for it is the only pathway for reducing CO_2 to the level of sugars (Figure 2). It starts with the additon of CO_2 to the C_5 sugar phosphate, ribulose-1,5-bisphophate, to form two molecules of 3-P-glycerate. The newly incorporated CO_2 becomes the carboxyl (C_1) carbon of one of the P-glycerate molecules. In a complete cycle, in which each reaction occurs at least once, three carboxylation reactions occur with 3 CO_2 molecules and 3 ribulose-P_2 molecules, and produce 6 molecules of P-glycerate. Six P-glycerate molecules are reduced to six C_3 sugar phospate molecules or triose phosphates. The reduction of P-glycerate to triose phosphate uses ATP and NADPH produced by the light reactions and electron transport in the chloroplast thylakoids. Five out of six triose phosphate molecules are converted in the cyclic pathway to regenerate three molecules of ribulose-P_2, the CO_2 acceptors for the next turn of the cycle.

The sixth triose phosphate represents net CO_2 fixation, and is converted to starch, sucrose, or other end products of cellular photosynthetic metabolism (Figure 3). Alternatively, substantial quantities of reduced carbon can be drained from the cycle as phosphoglycolate during the process of photorespiration. This is due to the oxygenase function of the ribulose bisphosphate carboxylase. This variation is described next (2.2) as the C_2, or oxidative photosynthetic carbon cycle, for oxidation of carbon from the C_3 cycle back to CO_2.

Part of the excess triose phosphate, specifically as dihydroxyacetone phosphate, is "exported" from the chloroplasts to the cytoplasm by a specific orthophosphate/triose phosphate translocator (Heldt, 1976). The other triose phosphate, 3-P-glyceraldehyde, and to a lesser extent pentose monophosphate, can also be carried by the translocator. At the high pH (8.1) of the chloroplast stroma in the light, however, P-glycerate carries a triple negative charge and is not exported.

The rate of triose-phosphate export and counter ion movement of orthophosphate uptake into the chloroplasts appears to be controlled by the level of orthophosphate in the cytosol (Walker, 1976). This provides a link between regulation in the cytosol and regulation in the chloroplasts. Triose phosphate in the cytoplasm is the starting point for synthesis of sucrose (Figure 3), the principal reduced carbon product of photosynthetic cells. The sucrose is then transported to the sinks in the rest of the plant (Chapter 2). One effect of more CO_2 in the atmosphere may be to stimulate sucrose synthesis to a point where sucrose production is in excess of the ability of the plant to transport it, or the sinks to use it. Various types of feedback mechanisms on CO_2 fixation are then possible, whereby the rate of photosynthesis is eventually reduced, despite the increase in CO_2. Where this occurs, it may be possible by future genetic modification to alter such inhibition.

A portion of the cytosolic triose phosphate, if oxidized to 3-P-glycerate, can be utilized for energy production (NADH). This energy in the cytoplasm is used for syntheses, such as the initiation of nitrate and sulfate reduction. A portion of the triose phosphates in the cytoplasm also may be converted to other compounds, such as amino acids, or more reduced carbon compounds such as fatty acids and isoprenoid compounds. The effect of changing CO_2 levels on the extent of these biosyntheses must be linked through the phosphate shuttle from the chloroplast.

Within C_3 chloroplasts, triose phosphates not used in the regenerative part of the C_3 cycle or exported to the cytoplasm can be converted via fructose-1,6-P_2, and fructose-6-P to glucose-6-P, and hence to starch, the principal carbon storage product in the chloroplasts. The amount of starch synthesis is thought to be somewhat inversely related to the amount of triose phosphate exported and the subsequent sucrose biosynthesis. Thus, in the event of excess photosynthetic CO_2 incorporation and reduction over the needs of the plant for sucrose and other secondary products, the surplus can be stored to some degree as starch. This stored reserve can be used for respiration and syntheses at night or on cloudy days.

It is expected that stimulation of the rate of photosynthesis by increased CO_2, when sucrose formation is in excess, would lead to increased starch accumulation (Guinn and Mauney, 1980; Preiss and Levi, 1979). In extreme cases of excess CO_2, starch accumulation in the chloroplasts causes deformation of the organelle, which may be a cause of diminished photosynthetic rates. This gross "regulation" of net photosynthesis by starch deformation in chloroplasts is only one likely type of feedback regulation leading to diminished photosynthesis when high CO_2 enrichment is provided. Other possible mechanisms include actions by hormonal signals from overloaded sinks, and a chain of feedback inhibitions when sucrose is not utilized. For instance, sucrose accumulation near the photosynthetic cells could lead to accumulation of sugar phosphates in the cytosol and sequestering of phosphate as sugar phosphate, with consequent diminished levels of cytosolic orthophosphate. Since orthophosphate is exchanged from the cytosol for triose phosphate from the chloroplasts, lower orthophosphate in the cytosol could result in decreased triose phosphate export.

The flow of carbon through the reactions of photosynthetic carbon reduction in light, respiratory pathways in the dark, and from these pathways into starch, sucrose, and other products, is intricately regulated (Bassham, 1979). Within the cycle itself, the carboxylation reaction, the phosphorylation of ribulose-5-P with ATP to ribulose-P_2, the phosphatase reactions converting fructose-1,6-P_2 to fructose-6-P and sedoheptulose-1,7-P_2 to sedoheptulose-7-P, and the reaction involved in the reduction of phosphoryl-3-P-glycerate to triose phosphate with NADPH, are all activated in the light, and several are inactivated in the dark. In the light, during active photosynthesis, the ribulose-P_2 carboxylase reaction and the phosphatase reactions are rate-limiting, whereas the activation and reduction of P-glycerate to triose phosphates is highly reversible. The rate of P-glycerate reduction thus depends on substrate concentrations, especially of ATP and NADPH. But the carboxylation reaction and the conversion of triose phosphates to glucose-6-P on the way to starch synthesis are fine-tuned in terms of enzyme activity.

In general, regulated enzymes of the C_3 cycle are controlled by levels of Mg^{2+}, pH, and the reduction level of cofactors, all of which increase in the chloroplast

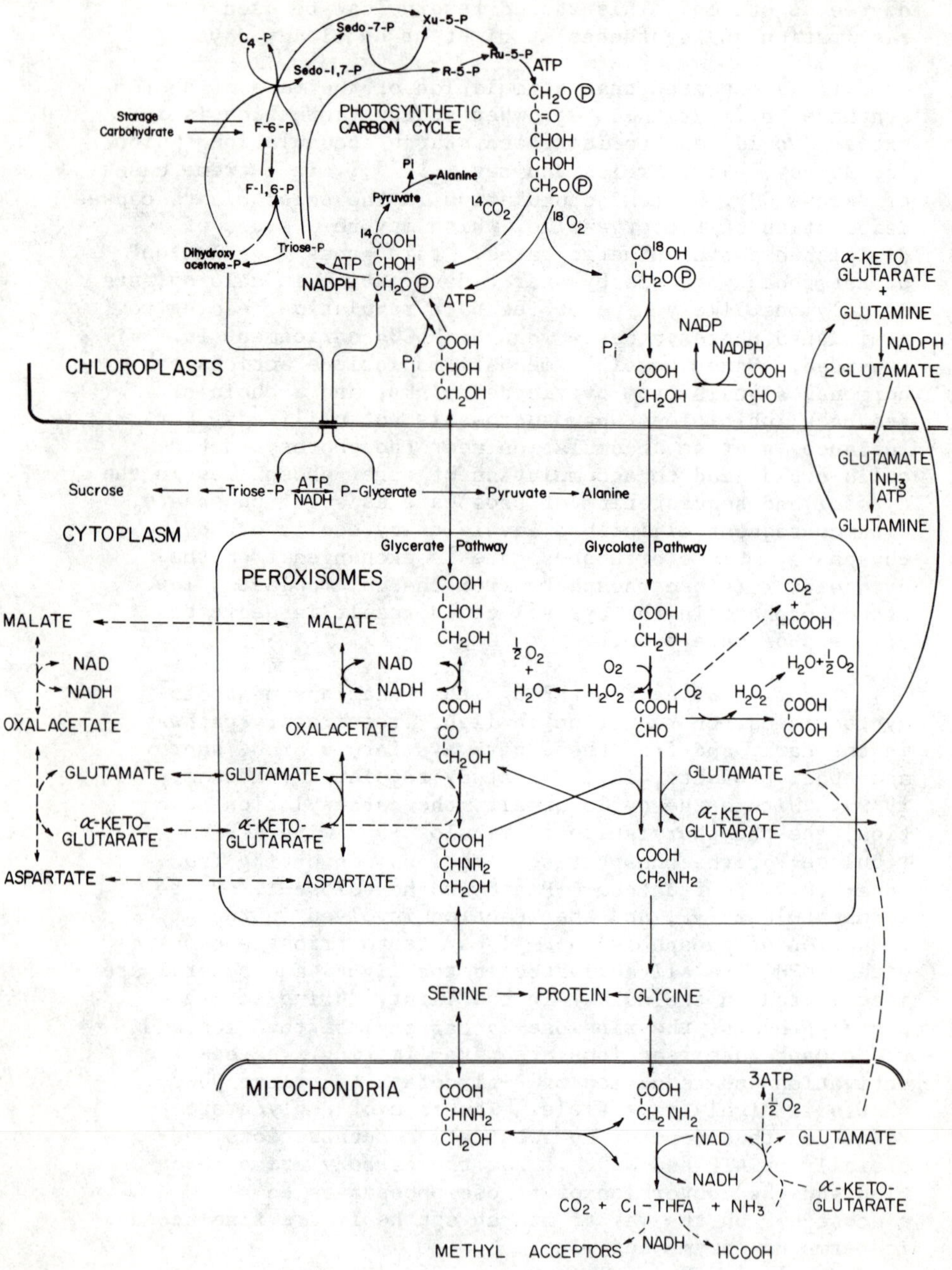

Figure 4. The C_2 oxidative photosynthetic carbon cycle for
photorespiration (from Tolbert, 1980). See text for brief
explanation of the individual parts of this cycle.

stroma in the light. The mechanisms by which the enzymes
are affected, and the extent of activity change, varies
considerably (Anderson, 1979). So far as we know, the
level of atmospheric CO_2 has no direct effect on regulating any of these enzymes, except ribulose-P_2
carboxylase/oxygenase, as discussed in section 2.4.

2.2 Effect of CO_2 on the Oxidative Photosynthetic Carbon Cycle.

Net photosynthesis is the sum of gross photosynthetic CO_2 fixation minus photorespiration. Photorespiration is the rapid oxidation of sugars recently formed by
photosynthesis back to CO_2 in the light (Zelitch, 1971 and
1975; Tolbert, 1971 and 1980). The oxidative photosynthetic carbon cycle (Figure 4) is the pathway associated
with this CO_2 evolution. The metabolic pathway for
photorespiration has also been called the "glycolate
pathway," the "C_2 pathway," or the "photorespiratory
cycle." By the C_3 reductive photosynthetic carbon cycle,
CO_2 is reduced to sugars; by the oxidative C_2
photosynthetic carbon cycle, sugars are oxidized to CO_2 in
the light.

Metabolism of glycolate accounts for CO_2 loss during
photorespiration. The mechanism of glycolate synthesis and
CO_2 production in vivo continues to be the subject of
current investigation. One well-detailed pathway involves
ribulose-P_2 carboxylase/oxygenase which is common to both
the reductive and oxidative photosynthetic carbon cycles.
The carboxylase activity with CO_2 initiates the C_3
photosynthetic reductive cycle, as described previously.
Since O_2 is present, the enzyme also catalyzes the
ribulose-P_2 oxygenase reaction which produces P-glycolate
(C_2 compound) and 3-P-glycerate (Lorimer, 1981). The C_2
compound is metabolized by the oxidative photosynthetic
carbon cycle (photorespiration) in part to CO_2.

The many steps of the photosynthetic carbon cycle
(Figure 4) seem well established, but the details, especially regulation, are subject to future investigation.
The total oxidative photosynthetic carbon cycle comprising
30 enzymatic reactions can be summarized into five different sections.

First is light-dependent glycolate biosynthesis in
the chloroplasts from the oxidation of ribulose-P_2 by the
carboxylase/oxygenase, followed by glycolate conversion in
the peroxisomes to glycine. In the mitochondria, two gly-
cines are converted to a CO_2, NH_3, a C_1-THFA derivative,
and serine. O_2 uptake occurs during ribulose-P_2 and

glycolate oxidation. This much has often been called "the glycolate pathway"; CO_2 comes primarily from glycine oxidation and O_2 uptake from ribulose-P_2 and glycolate oxidation.

Second is the interconversion between serine and P-glycerate. During photorespiration serine is converted to glycerate in the peroxisomes. Glycerate is phosphorylated by a chloroplast kinase and enters the P-glycerate pool. Third is the regeneration of ribulose-P_2, the precursor for P-glycolate. This utilizes carbon as 3-P-glycerate from several sources, and photosynthetic energy input as ATP and NADPH. This part of the oxidative cycle uses the same enzymes and is identical to the reductive photosynthetic carbon cycle except for CO_2 fixation. It is an important part of photorespiration, linking the oxidative cycle with utilization of NADPH and ATP. Fourth are malate-aspartate shuttles for energy transfer between the subcellular compartments.

Fifth are the reactions of the photorespiratory nitrogen cycle which arises primarily because the NH_3 formed during the oxidation of glycine is toxic and must not accumulate. The NH_3 (in the same quantity as CO_2) produced during glycine oxidation must be immediately refixed. Only a very small quantity of ammonia is evolved; it must be immediately refixed during photorespiration. This phenomenon is similar to the production of CO_2 from glycine oxidation, in that much of the CO_2 is also refixed, particularly in a C_4 plant. Refixation of NH_3 occurs primarily by glutamine synthetase utilizing ATP, and the glutamine is converted to glutamate in the chloroplasts by glutamate synthase, consequently using more photosynthetic assimilatory capacity (Keys et al., 1978).

The term oxidative photosynthetic carbon cycle emphasizes that in photorespiration the same reactions of the reductive carbon cycle are required to regenerate ribulose-P_2 and that they are coupled to the utilization of ATP and NADPH produced photosynthetically. Both the reductive and oxidative cycles co-exist in all C_3 cells. The ratio of activity for each is dependent on the competition between CO_2 and O_2 for the ribulose-P_2 carboxylase/oxygenase activities and will be altered by increasing atmospheric CO_2. The reductive and oxidative cycle are not independent, but combined they account for all the initial products associated with CO_2 fixation during photosynthesis in C_3 plants. Net photosynthesis is the extent to which the reductive process exceeds the oxidative process. The general term, photosynthesis carbon cycle, includes both the reductive and oxidative modes and neither cycle operates indpendently of the other. The coexistence of these two cycles is illustrated in schematic presentation in Figure 5.

Photorespiration has several functions during normal photosynthesis. It is a source of glycine and serine synthesis for protein, and for C_1 groups for all biological methylation reactions. But of greatest impotance to increasing CO_2 is the fact that the oxidative photosynthetic carbon cycle utilizes large amounts of excess photosynthetic energy as $NADPH_2$ and ATP. The photosynthetic energy must be used to reduce CO_2 or be wasted by the oxidative cycle. Thus, photorespiration represents a metabolic system for balancing photosynthetic energy production with CO_2 availability. Some of the excess photosynthetic energy that is now being wasted by photorespiration should be available for accelerated CO_2 fixation with increasing atmospheric CO_2.

Net photosynthesis is the extent to which the reductive cycle (gross photosynthesis) exceeds the oxidative cycle (photorespiration), and this is dependent on CO_2 availability for the carboxylase reactions, since O_2 for the oxygenase reaction is in constant excess. As a consequence, the distribution of CO_2 between the products of the C_3 reductive cycle (sucrose, 3-P-glycerate, starch) and the products of the C_2-photosynthetic oxidative cycle (glycolate, glycine, serine) is dependent upon the amount of CO_2 from the air that reaches the chloroplasts. Earlier experiments with C_3 plants grown in air, measured the short term (seconds or minutes) changes in distribution of CO_2 into these products as a function of large changes in CO_2 or O_2 levels. This research has been part of the basis for understanding carbon metabolism during photosynthesis and photorespiration. However, less information is available for such changes in plants actually grown for some extended time at elevated levels of CO_2. Furthermore, there are no reports on distribution among products of the reductive and oxidative cycles with the relatively small CO_2 changes we will experience in nature in the next two decades. A few reports to date have shown a decrease in the partition to products of the C_2 cycle and a rise in the C_3 products, particularly sucrose, with large increase in atmospheric CO_2 (Schnareuberger and Fock, 1976). What is not known is whether the smaller changes induced by only 10 to 100 ppm of additional CO_2 will be large enough to serve as any indicator of future changes.

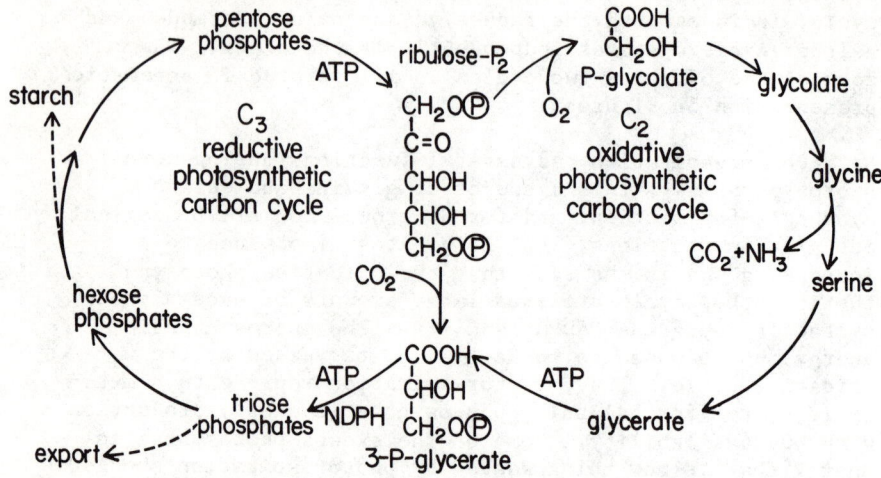

Figure 5. Schematic relationship of photosynthesis (C_3 reductive photosynthetic carbon cycle) to photorespiration (C_2 oxidative photosynthetic carbon cycle). Full details are given in Figures 2 and 4.

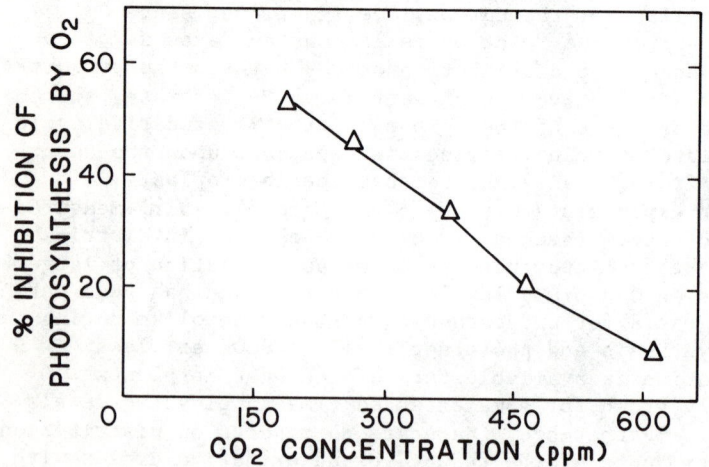

Figure 6. Inhibition of photosynthesis in potato leaves by 21% oxygen (air) at increasing CO_2 levels. This inhibition is attributed to photorespiration by the competing oxidative photosynthetic carbon cycle. From Ku et al. (1977). Increasing the CO_2 concentrations to 600 ppm reduced the O_2 inhibition of photosynthesis to about 30%.

There is also a substantial amount of literature on the effect of lowering O_2 concentrations which inhibits photorespiration in a similar way to the effect of increasing CO_2 in the presence of the constant 21% O_2 of air. If the atmospheric O_2 level is lowered to 3% or less, the oxidative photosynthetic carbon cycle is inhibited, and C_3 plants initially grow faster. This phenomenon can be expressed as percent inhibition of net photosynthesis at 21% O_2 compared to 3% O_2 (Figure 6). Photosynthesis in a C_3 plant at 340 ppm CO_2 (air) is inhibited 30 to 50% by the 21% O_2 in air. At 600 ppm CO_2 in air, inhibition decreases to around 20 to 35%. This shows that even at 600 ppm CO_2 photorespiration is still rapid and efforts to decrease it could have significant benefits.

To summarize this section, the first products of CO_2 fixation in C_3 plants vary between those of the C_3 reductive cycle and the C_2 oxidative cycle, depending on available CO_2. It is expected on the basis of past research, that C_3 plants have the inherent ability for more photosynthesis if CO_2 is increased, because of the excess capacity for CO_2 reduction which now is partially wasted in in the C_2 cycle or photorespiration.

2.3 CO_2 Fixation by C_4, CAM, and C_3/C_4 Intermediate Plants. A central feature of plants which employ the C_4 pathways of photosynthetic CO_2 assimilation is their ability to raise internal leaf CO_2 concentrations above the CO_2 levels of the surrounding air. Indeed, these plants raise their internal CO_2 so much that they nearly overcome the photosynthetically CO_2 limiting level of today's air. Two large groups of plants employ modifications of the C_4 pathway to assimilate air CO_2, namely plants termed C_4, which include corn, sugarcane, millet, and crabgrass, and plants termed CAM, which include pineapple, agave, and many cacti.

C_4 Plants. These plants have a C_4 dicarboxylic acid cycle for trapping atmospheric CO_2 in their mesophyll cells and concentrating CO_2 in bundle sheath cells (Figure 7) (Hatch, 1978; Black, 1973). The C_3 cycle (Figure 2) for ultimate sugar biosynthesis is located in the bundle sheath cells. Phosphoenolpyruvate or PEP carboxylase, which catalyzes the initial CO_2 fixation reaction in C_4 plants in mesophyll cells, is very effective (low K_m) in using the more abundant sodium bicarbonate in the cell. PEP carboxylase is not inhibited by O_2, nor does O_2 act as a substrate, so that plants in a closed system with this pathway can incorporate all of the CO_2 and bicarbonate into C_4 acids, malate and aspartate. The C_4 products of the cycle are decarboxylated (deacidified) to release the CO_2 in the

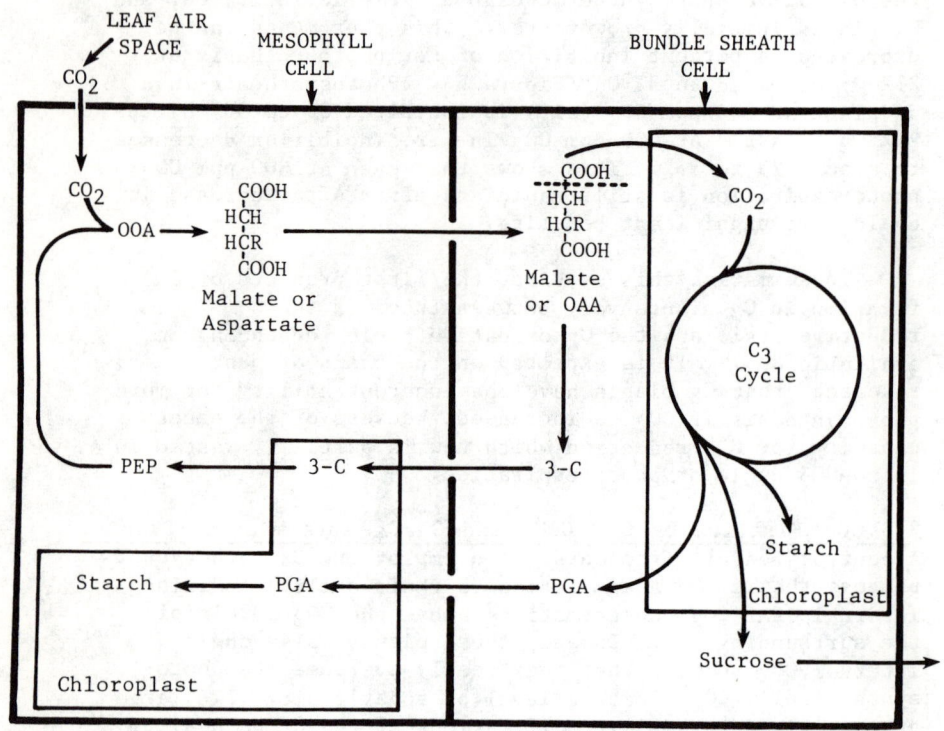

Figure 7. Reactions of the C_3 and C_4 cycles for CO_2 fixation in C_4 plants. The C_4 cycle consists of CO_2 fixation into the carboxyle group of C_4 acids in the mesophyll cells and decarboxylation of these acids in the bundle sheath cells, where the CO_2 is reduced to sugars by the C_3 cycle.

bundle sheath cells for refixation by ribulose bisphosphate carboxylase of the C_3 cycle (Figure 7). In effect, the C_4 cycle transports and concentrates CO_2 into the bundle sheath cells for reduction to sugar phosphates by the C_3 cycle. As a consequence, the C_4 plant photosynthetically and more completely removes CO_2 from air than the the C_3 plant. Since CO_2 is much less rate limiting for photosynthesis, the C_4 plant can more effectively avoid, as well, the stresses from higher temperatures and water. From this information, we project that more CO_2 will increase the primary carboxylation reaction by ribulose-P_2 carboxylase in C_3 plants, but have little effect on this reaction in C_4 plants. Nonetheless, it must be recognized that net photosynthesis is the sum of many reactions (particularly those involved in regeneration of the ribulose-P_2), therefore more CO_2 may also influence the rate and the total amount of CO_2 fixed in a C_4 plant.

The C_4 pathway of trapping CO_2 provides these plants (i.e., corn, sorghum, foxtail, crabgrass) with a competitive advantage, particularly when restricted CO_2 availability limits net photosynthesis (especially in hot, semi-arid conditions). The CO_2 concentrating mechanism allows the C_4 plant to take advantage of high light intensities; hence, further increases in atmospheric CO_2 may not benefit C_4 plants as much in some environments because of limiting light. However, under water stress or high temperature, it is likely that more CO_2 will benefit C_4 species. The capacity of photosynthesis and the photosynthetic apparatus (photochemistry and enzyme composition) needs to be determined in C_4 plants under temperature and moisture stress with higher CO_2 (See Chapter 2).

CAM Plants. Many succulent plants are capable of crassulacean acid metabolism (CAM). CAM is a sequence of photosynthetic carbon metabolism which requires most of the same biochemical steps of both the C_3 and C_4 pathways. Plants with CAM are able to fix CO_2 in the dark and store it as malic acid or other acids. In daylight, the CO_2 is then released and becomes available as an internal CO_2 source for photosynthesis. These reactions are separated temporally, but occur within the same green cell. As a result, CO_2 is fixed at night when the potential for water loss is low, yet the stomata pores can be closed during the day to reduce water loss (Ting and Gibbs, 1982).

Most CAM plants, if abundantly supplied with water, also assimilate CO_2 in the light after deacidification by processes which are analogous to C_3 plants. However, assimilation during this period may be limited by the relatively low stomatal conductance in CAM plants, and in this respect increasing CO_2 should be beneficial. Some succulent plants, which are conventional C_3 plants when adequately supplied with water, have the ability to change to a CAM type photosynthesis under water stress.

Although the growth of CAM plants can be extremely water efficient, growth is limited by the capacity for night-time storage of malic acid. An increase in atmospheric CO_2 may stimulate slightly the growth or productivity of useful CAM plants like pineapple. Studies show that under field conditions, pineapples assimilate most of their carbon in the dark, and these processes, catalyzed by PEP carboxylase, are already saturated at present levels of atmospheric CO_2 and limited by malic acid storage capacity. However, more CO_2 may increase the proportion of assimilation in the late afternoon and thereby increase the overall growth of CAM plants. No information is available on the influence of CO_2 enrichment of the day/night capacity for CO_2 fixation in CAM, the enzyme composition, or whether malate storage and partitioning of products provides limitations for growth.

C_3/C_4 Plants. A few C_3/C_4 intermediate plants are of considerable experimental potential for understanding atmospheric CO_2 effects on photosynthetic CO_2 fixation. Photosynthesis in C_3/C_4 intermediate plants is less sensitive to O_2 inhibition and has a lower compensation point than C_3 plants in air, but the biochemistry of CO_2 assimilation is poorly defined. In C_3/C_4 species, CO_2 fixation capacity may be functioning by both the C_3 and C_4 cycles simultaneously in the daytime; alternatively, there may be other biochemical means through which photorespiration is reduced in these plants. If any of these species are true biochemical intermediates, increasing CO_2 levels should favor CO_2 fixation in the C_3 mode for C_3/C_4 intermediate plants grown in air. The biochemical basis for reduced photorespiration in C_3/C_4 intermediate plants in unknown. No detailed work on the effects of changes in CO_2 concentration have been reported on photosynthesis in C_3/C_4 intermediate species. The C_3/C_4 intermediate plants theoretically offer a possibility for studying changes in products of photosynthesis induced by small changes in atmospheric CO_2 before other detectable longer-term, morphological or physiological changes are manifested.

2.4 Ribulose Bisphosphate Carboxylase/Oxygenase. This most abundant and essential enzyme exhibits both activities in all photosynthetic tissues (McFadden, 1973). Competition between the two gaseous substrates, CO_2 and

O_2, decides the extent to which carboxylation or oxygenation occurs, and this meters the flow of carbon between the reductive and oxidative modes of the photosynthetic carbon cycle (Ogren, 1977; Lorimer, 1981). Many variants of this competition exist in nature. Anaerobic photosynthetic bacteria avoid the oxygenase reaction, but its potential is always present. In air with 21% O_2, the ratio of photosynthesis to photorespiration in a C_3 plant may approach 1:1. If the CO_2 concentration is increased as in the bundle sheath cell of a C_4 plant, the relative oxygenase activity is reduced. If the O_2 level is increased or the CO_2 concentration decreased as in water stress, the oxygenase reaction increases.

In spite of voluminous literature about ribulose bisphosphate carboxylase/oxygenase (as summarized in Table 1), its regulation, activation, and reaction mechanism in the leaf are poorly understood. Complete elucidation of its properties, mechanism of regulation and biogenesis is essential for predicting plant growth responses to more CO_2. Many superlatives can be listed for this enzyme. It is the most abundant enzyme (up to 50% of the soluble chloroplast stroma protein); it is ubiquitous in photosynthetic tissue. As an A_8B_8 complex (total of 16 subunits), it is one of the largest and most complex of the enzymes. In some respects it is one of the most poorly understood enzymes. For instance, the function of the small subunits are unknown, but they may be involved in regulation. This lack of information limits progress, since the small subunit is formed from nuclear DNA, which plant breeders might be able to manipulate. Each of the eight large subunits contains one active site. The gene for the large subunit is present in chloroplasts, and since there are many (about 40) copies of this DNA per chloroplast and many chloroplasts per cell, classical genetic modification is nearly impossible at this time.

The enzyme fixes CO_2 with an extremely slow turnover rate of about 0.5 mole/sec/mole active site. The true K_m (concentration for 50% V_{max}) values of ribulose-P_2 carboxylase/oxygenase as currently known, are about 15 μM for CO_2, if measured anaerobically, and 450 μM O_2 (Figure 8). However, the apparent $K_m[CO_2]$ when measured in air levels of O_2 is about 26 μM, which is nearer the K_m value in the plant. Water saturated with air contains about 9 μM CO_2, but because of diffusion resistances in the leaf, the CO_2 level in the chloroplasts during photosynthesis has been estimated at about 5 μM CO_2. It is so low that the carboxylase in the chloroplast of a C_3 plant, if otherwise active, may only be functioning at less than 0.1 V_{max} as a

Table 1.   Properties of Ribulose Bisphosphate
Carboxylase/Oxygenase

---

1) Distribution: found in all photosynthetic plants and
algae. Comprises up to 50% of total chloroplast protein or
up to 25% of total soluble protein in leaf.

2) Molecular weight is 560,000: 8 large subunits of 54,000
each, with 1 active site; coded by chloroplast DNA; 8 small
subunits of 16,000 (with unknown function) from nuclear
DNA.

3) Activated by CO_2 (10 mM $NaHCO_3$) and $MgCl_2$ (10 mM).

4) pH optimum is 8.1 to 8.3 for both activities.

5) CO_2 and O_2 are substrates that are competitive
inhibitors.

   $K_m[CO_2]$ in air is 26 μM (910 ppm CO_2).

   $K_m[O_2]$ = 250 to 500 μM O_2.

   $K_m [Mg_{2+}]$ = 10 mM.

7) Low turnover rates = 1 mole CO_2/sec/mole of active site.

8) Enzyme has 96 SH groups, is cold labile, and heat
reactivated.

9) The substrate ribulose-P_2 at pH 8 is unstable.

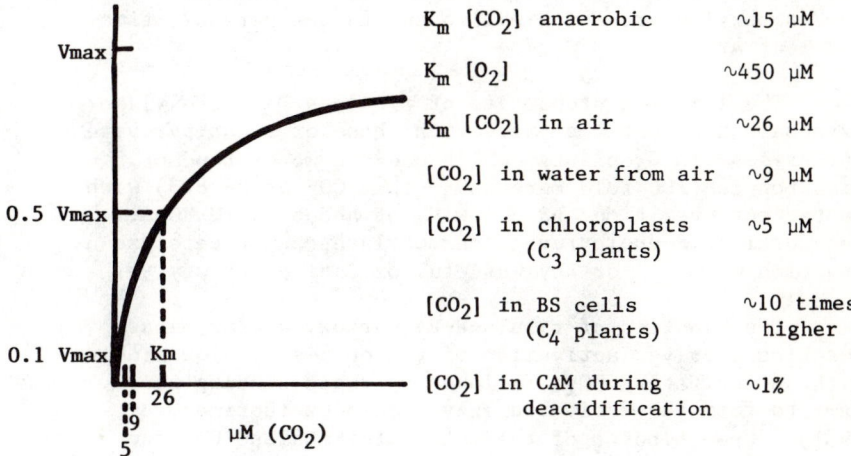

Figure 8. Properties of isolated ribulose bisphosphate carboxylase from spinach leaves. $K_{(m)}$ values are the concentration of a substrate (i.e., CO_2) in moles for half maximum velocity.

carboxylase, while the rest of its potential activity is either unused or acts in part as an oxygenase. If the atmospheric CO_2 level doubles, it would appear that excess carboxylase protein is available in the plant. In the bundle sheath cells of a C_4 plant, a 3-fold increase in CO_2 concentration by the C_4 pathway increases the carboxylase activity over the oxygenase. When considering the ribulose bisphosphate carboxylation reaction by itself, increasing atmospheric CO_2 is clearly beneficial, for with more CO_2, the carboxylase reaction will occur faster per unit time and leaf area.

The limiting properties of ribulose-P_2 carboxylase/oxygenase are to be compared with those of P-enolpyruvate carboxylase in C_4 plants, which use the more abundant bicarbonate (100 fold more HCO_3- than CO_2 at pH 8.3) with a faster turnover time and a low K_m of about 15 μM HCO_3-. In addition, P-enolpyruvate carboxylase cannot catalyze a reaction with O_2 for any wasteful oxidative pathway.

The kinetics of ribulose-P_2 carboxylase/oxygenase reaction involves activation of the enzyme by slow binding with an activating CO_2, followed by rapid binding of Mg++ to form the activated enzyme complex (Lorimer, 1981). Upon binding of the substrate ribulose-P_2, the complex can then react with either another molecule of CO_2, the substrate CO_2, or O_2. Since the three known amino acid sequences at the active site are widely distributed in the peptide map of the large subunit of the enzyme, the CO_2 activation probably involves folding of the protein to form the active site. In the intact leaf the enzyme is often only partially activated in vivo. The activated tertiary enzyme CO_2 Mg++ complex forms a quaternary complex with other molecules that bind at the active site in place of ribulose-P_2, such as 6-P-gluconate. These compounds are effectors and may be regulators of the enzyme activity, and their concentrations might be altered by CO_2 concentration.

There are indications with some plants (wheat) that the rate of CO_2 fixation is limited by CO_2 concentration and not by the regeneration of ribulose-P_2 in the light. Photosynthesis in other plants (beans) appears to have a limit on rate by ribulose-P_2 availability above ambient CO_2. Where ribulose-P_2 has been found to be high and not limiting for CO_2 fixation, it is the CO_2 level and activity for the carboxylase/oxygenase which controls the process. Limitations upon regeneration of ribulose-P_2 may reflect control by electron transport (section 2.6). It is not known what higher CO_2 will do to this balance. However, if more CO_2 induces greater activation of the ribulose-P_2 carboxylase/oxygenase, increased CO_2 fixation, above a simple mass action effect, will occur. Research about the effect of CO_2 on the carboxylase/oxygenase activity will need to be pursued vigorously.

Regulation or control of the oxygenase reaction over the carboxylase reaction has been the subject of much speculation, because it would be the way to regulate photosynthesis versus photorespiration. There is no known differential regulation by effectors, cofactors, or plant growth regulators of the carboxylase and oxygenase activities. Both activities are activated or inactivated similarly. The sole known regulation of the two activities depends upon the concentration of CO_2 and O_2, as competing substrates. Processes that regulate CO_2 concentration in the chloroplast will regulate the ratio of carboxylase to oxygenase reactions. Such factors are atmospheric CO_2 levels; size and number of the stomata openings; diffusion gradients; carbonic anhydrase to rapidly replenish the CO_2 pool from $NaHCO_3$; light intensity; and the C_4 pathway in C_4 plants to concentrate CO_2 in bundle sheath cells. The absence of any other regulatory mechanism besides the CO_2/O_2 ratio, and the ubiquitous presence of this system with both reactions in photosynthetic tissue, emphasize that both the oxidative and reductive cycles compete in all aerobic photosynthetic tissue. Further, it must be emphasized that simply doubling the CO_2 concentration does not change the competition between CO_2 and O_2 sufficiently to prevent considerable oxygenase activity at 600 or even 1000 ppm CO_2.

Recent reports indicate that the amount of ribulose bisphosphate carboxylase/oxygenase, its affinities for CO_2 and O_2, and consequently its turnover rate, vary within and between C_3 and C_4 plants. In some cases investigated to date, the amount of the enzyme in C_3 plant per unit area appears to have decreased when atmospheric CO_2 during growth was increased from current levels to 660 ppm. This change is not specific for the carboxylase/oxygenase but is accompanied by a total decrease in the photosynthetic apparatus, which is not evident if expressed as amount of carboxylase enzyme per mg chlorophyll. The present interpretation is that plants grown at higher CO_2 may have less photosynthetic apparatus relative to the rest of the leaf, which consists of other products or mass. In a sense, this finding may be similar to lower carboxylase levels in C_4 and CAM plants, where the C_4 pathway functions to increase the amount of CO_2 at the site of the carboxylase reaction. These results seem to indicate that atmospheric CO_2 levels will somehow effect the amount and activation status of ribulose-P_2 carboxylase/oxygenase. It is possible that the enzyme is not present in the C_3 leaf in excess above its need for photosynthesis.

2.5   Carbon Metabolism in Aquatic Plants and Algae.

Aquatic systems cover over two-thirds of the area of the earth, and aquatic species contribute a substantial part of the total photosynthetic activity occurring on the planet. However, except for a few species, the photosynthetic pathways and responses occurring in submersed species are largely undocumented. Thus, in reference to an increase in CO_2, it is even more difficult to draw generalized conclusions, compared to terrestrial C_3 and C_4 species (see Chapter 6).

The evidence indicates that unicellular green algae fix CO_2 via the C_3 reductive photosynthetic carbon cycle. But when grown at air levels of CO_2, they exhibit little O_2 inhibition of photosynthesis or photorespiratory CO_2 evolution, low CO_2 compensation points, and a high affinity for CO_2. These are characteristics more typical of C_4 species, yet in the unicellular algae examined so far, there is no evidence of a C_4 cycle for concentrating CO_2.

Free CO_2 from air or bicarbonate is the preferred form for photosynthesis by most submersed plants and algae. Bicarbonate ions may also be used directly as a source of inorganic carbon for photosynthesis, in addition to free CO_2, by some green and blue-green algae. These algae appear to have a CO_2 concentrating mechanism mediated by carbonic anhydrase (Badger et al., 1978; Miyachi and Shiraiwa, 1979). This state is induced by growth on low or ambient levels of CO_2. These unicellular algae can accumulate bicarbonate to levels ten-fold higher than in the medium. The internal bicarbonate pool is converted rapidly to CO_2 by the high carbonic anhydrase activity, and then the CO_2 is fixed by the C_3 cycle. There are currently two hypotheses about the mechanism of increasing CO_2 concentration in the unicellular algae. One possibility is a bicarbonate transport or pumping system, and the other is that CO_2 enters by diffusion and is converted to bicarbonate internally by carbonic anhydrase before being reconverted to CO_2 at the site of the carboxylation reaction.

Growth of unicellular algae at 1 to 5% CO_2 is many times more rapid than at air levels of CO_2. The cells grown on high CO_2 have low carbonic anhydrase and high apparent K_m (CO_2) values for photosynthesis, since they did not require the mechanism for CO_2 concentration during growth. The process for bicarbonate uptake by cells grown on air has so far been one of theoretical interest as another mechanism to concentrate CO_2 beside the C_4 cycle. There is little data on changes between unicellular algae grown on only small incremental increases in CO_2 (i.e., 340 to 600 ppm). It is also of interest to note that the function of considerable carbonic anhydrase in plant chloroplasts has not been fully appreciated. Carbonic anhydrase in chloroplasts must accelerate the conversion of bicarbonate to CO_2, as the CO_2 is removed by fixation into the C_3 cycle. However, little work has been done on this enzyme in plants grown at different levels of CO_2.

A further unusual feature of photosynthesis by unicellular algae is modifications in the C_2 cycle for photorespiration (Tolbert, 1974) which are not completely understood. These algae excrete part of the glycolate, rather than oxidize it to CO_2, and in place of the very active peroxisomal glycolate oxidase and catalase system of C_3 plants, they have only a low level of mitochondrial glycolate dehydrogenase.

Whether multicellular and macroalgae forms concentrate CO_2 similar to their unicellular counterparts is unclear. Relatively little research has been performed on them. From observations that these algae have lowered photorespiratory rates, it seems reasonable to postulate that the C_4 acids act as a source of CO_2 for the C_3 cycle in some fashion similar to C_4 plants. They cannot, however, be classified as C_4 species.

In contrast to many unicellular algae, submersed angiosperms usually have low photosynthetic rates and a very high inorganic carbon requirement to saturate photosynthesis. They possess the C_3 cycle and thus have the potential for substantial C_2 cycle photorespiration (Salvucci and Bowes, 1981; Raven, 1970; Van et al., 1976). An apparently ubiquitous characteristic is a variable CO_2 compensation point that is dependent upon prior growth conditions. Net photosynthetic rates and the affinity for CO_2 are higher when the CO_2 compensation point is low and photorespiratory CO_2 release and O_2 inhibition are decreased. However, a high CO_2 compensation point, with attendant photorespiration, appears to be the more common state, especially in temperate regions. The low CO_2 compensation point state appears to be a response to overcome adverse conditions of low CO_2 levels, high O_2, elevated temperatures, and pH that occur in densely vegetated waters during the day.

For some fresh water and marine angiosperms, current research suggests that a C_4 type system incorporating CO_2 into malate and aspartate can be induced, but exactly how this mechanism stimulates net photosynthesis is unknown. Other freshwater and marine angiosperms show no evidence of major C_4 acid production or of significant PEP carboxylase activity. For the freshwater angiosperm <u>Myriophyllum</u>, the low photorespiratory state may be mediated by a bicarbonate utilization system somewhat akin to that of unicellular green algae.

More information is needed on the pathways and responses occurring in algae divisions other than Chlorophyta, and especially those that comprise the major proportion of the phytoplankton. Because changing CO_2 levels are known to shift the photosynthetic mechanisms of many submerged species in a manner found in terrestrial plants, it is particularly important to undertake long-term growth studies at elevated CO_2 levels in the relevant physiological range to determine if any significant changes will occur. Only very high CO_2 levels (1 to 5%) have been employed in the past for the laboratory growth of algae, and these may not be relevant to the natural aquatic state. The unknown role of carbonic anhydrase is an especially crucial issue in an aquatic system where bicarbonate utilization often plays a vital role in productivity.

The sparcity of data on most aquatic species precludes drawing many inferences, but tenuous extrapolations from laboratory data would suggest that doubling the CO_2 level in the atmosphere could result in a significantly higher productivity in freshwater and marine angiosperms, but lesser increases in phytoplankton. It is likely, though, that species diversity could be drastically altered in the phytoplankton component.

2.6 Electron Transport and CO_2 Fixation. Photosynthesis involves the use of light energy to generate NADPH and ATP which, in turn, are used to reduce carbon dioxide. Depending on conditions, the rate of photosynthesis may be determined primarily, a) by the interception of light and the consequent transfer of excitation to chlorophyll, b) by the conversion of the excitation energy into electron transport with NADPH and ATP formation, or c) by reactions fixing CO_2. In considering the effects of more CO_2, we must consider direct and indirect effects on these three processes. If the added CO_2 is to be reduced, more energy from electron transport is required. Deviation of photosynthetic capacity from the oxidative C_2 cycle (Section

2.3) will probably not be sufficient, because considerable photorespiration will still occur at 600 and 900 ppm CO_2.

At usual sunlight intensities, higher CO_2 concentration results in increased photosynthesis (Figure 1). However, in a recent study (Farquhar, 1982) with plants grown in air, the rate of photosynthesis slowed and the final rate was dependent on light intensity at CO_2 concentrations not much above the present atmospheric level (340 ppm air level or 220 ppm intercellular). These results with whole plants are graphically summarized in Figure 2 of Chapter 4. The increase in CO_2 fixation did not simply conform to expectations based on the kinetics of ribulose-P_2 carboxylase/oxygenase with excess ribulose-P_2 and higher CO_2. The rate of increase seemed to be limited by light-dependent processes, presumably associated with the electron transport which provides the ATP and NADPH needed for regeneration of the ribulose-P_2. Other experiments that could be used to test this interpretation by measuring the ribulose-P_2 concentration have led to different results in different laboratories (Perchorowicz et al., 1981); thus, this question of fundamental significance in photosynthetic responses to higher CO_2 remains to be resolved.

We must also consider the effects, if any, of higher CO_2 on the disposal of the excess excitation energy present in the chlorophyll which is plentiful at all but the lowest light intensities. Does the increasing CO_2 have any effect, beneficial or otherwise, in helping protect tissues from destructive photooxidation? For instance, blocking electron transport with herbicides such as atrazine or DCMU leads to a catastrophic and rapid photodestruction of the tissues. The absence of both CO_2 and O_2 for photosynthetic carbon metabolism also causes photoinhibition. It has been proposed that the extra use of NADPH and ATP associated with photorespiration provides the necessary sink for the excitation energy at low CO_2. These hypotheses are readily confirmed in laboratory experiments with leaves (Powles et al., 1979), but evidence on how significant these processes are under ambient air conditions with ample O_2 for photorespiration is unattainable.

We also need to know if increased CO_2, which utilizes the ATP and NADPH from photosynthesis, has any effect on other reactions that also use the reducing capacity from electron transport, such as the reduction of nitrate, nitrite, and sulfate. It seems likely that competition for this reducing capacity by more CO_2 will be one factor in shifting the carbon-nitrogen balance (see Section 3.3).

Clearly, a method of continuously monitoring electron transport that is necessarily non-destructive, is needed to study the effect of higher CO_2. To the extent that the fluorescence of photosystem II chlorophyll and electron transport are inversely related, fluorescence of leaves provides such a measure. The excitation energy in the chlorophyll has four possible fates: photochemistry (= electron transport), non-radiative decay, radiative decay (= fluorescence), and spill-over of the excitation energy to the non-fluorescent photosystem I. If the properties of the last three remain constant, it is possible that fluorescence can be used to measure electron transport and the effects of CO_2 thereon. More work is needed before we can be satisfied with this conclusion.

2.7   <u>Carbon Isotope Discrimination ($\delta^{13}C$ Values)</u>. The different pathways of CO_2 fixation in land plants, based on different biochemical and physiological processes described above, lead to differences in the natural carbon isotope ratio of the photosynthetic products, and all the dry matter produced. In C_3 plants grown in normal air, the $\delta^{13}C$ value is about $-28°/oo$ relative to a standard. Against this standard, air has a $\delta^{13}C$ value of $-7°/oo$. The discrimination against $\delta^{13}C$ is largely due to the biochemical mechanism of ribulose-P_2 carboxylase, but limitations due to diffusion through partly closed stomates also contribute (O'Leary, 1981). In C_4 plants, the primary carboxylase, PEP carboxylase, shows very little discrimination. Because C_4 plants function with more tightly closed stomata, diffusional fractionations make a larger contribution to the $\delta^{13}C$ values of C_4 plants, which is in the vicinity of $-12°/oo$. In CAM plants, the $\delta^{13}C$ value varies between those of C_3 and C_4 plants, reflecting the contributions of CO_2 fixed in the dark and the light. In aquatic plants, the $\delta^{13}C$ value varies widely from -9 to $-50°/oo$. Aquatic plants are predominantly C_3 plants and this range of values reflects variations in the $\delta^{13}C$ value of carbon source in water, and the diffusional limitations of quiet boundary layers in water.

Determinations of $\delta^{13}C$ value in tissues of plants will provide a useful indicator of the changes in atmospheric CO_2 concentrations. The CO_2 added to the atmosphere following combustion of fossil fuels ($\delta^{13}C$ value about $-30°/oo$) will change the $\delta^{13}C$ value of atmospheric CO_2 by about $10°/oo$ for a doubling of CO_2 concentration (Lerman, 1975). The fractionations due to enzymic activity are unlikely to change, and there are unlikely to be large changes due to diffusional components. Thus, the $\delta^{13}C$

value of plants will become more negative in response to the more negative $\delta\,^{13}C$ value of the enriched atmosphere.

3. Partitioning of Substrates. It seems clear that higher ambient CO_2 will increase net photosynthesis in a variety of complex ways. It is essential to determine the extent and manner in which the plant uses the increased assimilated carbon. The main questions deal with how the partitioning of assimilated carbon into starch, sucrose, and secondary products is regulated at the biochemical level. Further, the increase in carbon flow should impose limitations and other implications upon nitrogen, sulphur and phosphorus metabolism.

3.1 Sucrose and Starch. The biochemical steps relating to starch and sucrose synthesis have been stated in section 2.1 (see again Figure 3). Both starch and sucrose are derived from triose phosphate. But whereas leaf starch is restricted to the chloroplast, sucrose synthesis is a cytoplasmic event (Walker, 1976 and 1981). The triose-P pools in the chloroplast and the cytoplasm are linked by the important exchange or translocator of triose-P or phosphate across the chloroplast membrane. When the concentration of phosphate in the cytoplasm is experimentally manipulated, it can be demonstrated that low external phosphate decreases total photosynthesis while increasing partitioning into starch. Each of these factors reinforces the other. Thus, when export of triose phosphate via the phosphate translocator is diminished, more substrate is made available for starch synthesis within the chloroplast stroma. These same conditions bring about high P-glycerate and low phosphate which are allosteric activators of the enzyme, adenosine diphosphate glucose pyrophosphorylase, for starch synthesis (Preiss and Levi, 1979). Conversely, active external sinks for sucrose, by favoring phosphate recycling and triose phosphate utilization in the cytoplasm, would be expected to lead to increased photosynthesis, increased export, and increased growth. While the regulation of starch biosynthesis in leaves and its relation to phosphate translocation is reasonably well defined, the regulation of sucrose syntheses is not. The effect of increased CO_2 on both systems of sucrose and starch synthesis has not yet been extensively tested.

In the dark phase, the starch is rapidly degraded to sugar phosphates, and these are used for syntheses or growth everywhere in the photosynthetic cell or the whole plant. Similarly, much of the regulation of starch degradation remains to be defined, although there is some evidence that high phosphate favors degradation, and there is little doubt that much of the carbon traffic flows through triose phosphate and the phosphate translocator. Likewise, the synthesis of other polysaccharides, particularly cellulose, is a continuous process starting with the cytoplasmic triose-P and other sugar-P pools. The direct effect of CO_2 on all these syntheses is in the amount of triose-P formed, and no indirect effects have been reported.

It seems clear that sucrose synthesis is proportional to the rate of CO_2 fixation and that, at least in some circumstances, it increases with increased CO_2. This, in itself, only indicates that sucrose can not be synthesized faster than orthophosphate can be made available, and that the ability of the chloroplast to make triose phosphate will be limited (under otherwise favorable conditions) by its ability to import phosphate and CO_2 in a ratio of 1 to 3. If the supply of phosphate does not match the increased supply of CO_2, then increased photosynthesis can only result in increased starch synthesis. In such circumstances, where the capacity for starch formation exists, starch accumulation reflects the extent to which production of assimilate exceeds utilization. Excess starch accumulation can become deleterious by physical distortions in the chloroplasts.

There is little doubt that sucrose production in the cytoplasm of photosynthesizing cells of a source leaf is strongly influenced by sink activity. There is great uncertainly about the sites for regulation of sucrose synthesis. Of the enzymes concerned, only fructose 1,6-bisphosphatase and sucrose phosphate synthetase are present at levels of activity which are as low as the rates of sucrose synthesis, and this suggests that they are possible sites of regulation. Sucrose phosphate synthetase is particularly susceptible to inhibition by uridine diphosphate, but there is evidence for direct feedback inhibition by sucrose on inhibition of these enzymes for its synthesis. Nevertheless, sucrose feeding to mature spinach leaves results in low CO_2 fixation and decreased sucrose formation; whereas sucrose feeding to young leaves of spinach and wheat stimulates sucrose formation. Obviously, increased CO_2 can lead to increased sucrose, but the extent and the manner in which this additional sucrose can be utilized may be of importance in determining which species or varieties will benefit most from the enhanced CO_2. In some species, under some conditions, the capacity for sucrose synthesis (or the ability of the sucrose synthesizing mechanism to continue to function effectively as sucrose accumulates) may be insufficient to cope with the increased potential for CO_2 fixation offered by high CO_2. Since sucrose is the starting point of a great many metabolic events and the major transport metabolite in the majority of C_3 species, there is an urgent need for further research in this and cognate areas. The latter should embrace source-sink relationships, phloem loading with sucrose, and other aspects which are further elaborated in Chapter 4.

3.2   Acetate, Fatty Acids, Lipids, Hydrocarbons and Isoprene Polymers. These many and varied hydrocarbon products from photosynthesis (Stumpf, 1980) are the most reduced products of CO_2 fixation, and the level of atmospheric CO_2 may affect these products in the leaf in two major ways. More CO_2 should result in synthesis of more of these compounds. However, the use of more of the reducing capacity of the photosynthetic apparatus to reduce increasing CO_2 to sugars may mean that less energy would be available to form these compounds. Therefore, there may be less of these compounds, and their state of reduction may be less, relative to the level of carbohydrate. At present there are no general product analyses available for plants grown at elevated CO_2 to support this hypothesis.

Fatty acid biosynthesis occurs in chloroplast of leaf cells and in proplastids in developing seeds. Fatty acids and other reduced components found in the leaf cell remain there. The interacting link between the leaf and the seed and other sinks is sucrose from the leaf. Sucrose synthesized in the leaf is translocated to developing seeds, where it is the primary source via glycolysis and mito-chondrial pyruvate decarboxylase for acetyl-CoA and energy as NADH and ATP. These components are then employed for fatty acids and other syntheses in the seed cell (Figure 9). Accordingly, the amount may increase, but the relative carbon composition of the products in the sinks (seeds and fruits) ought not be altered by increasing atmospheric CO_2, providing N, S, and P availability remain unchanged (Section 3.3). In considering the effect of increasing CO_2 on secondary carbon products, we must distinguish between products formed in the source leaf and those formed in the sinks.

In the leaf, CO_2 participates in the biosynthetic pathways for fatty acid and isoprene polymer synthesis on three major levels. The first and only level thought to be directly affected by increasing atmospheric CO_2 is the generation of more triose phosphate for the synthesis of all of these compounds. In addition, CO_2 is a product from the oxidative decarboxylation of pyruvate to acetyl-CoA.

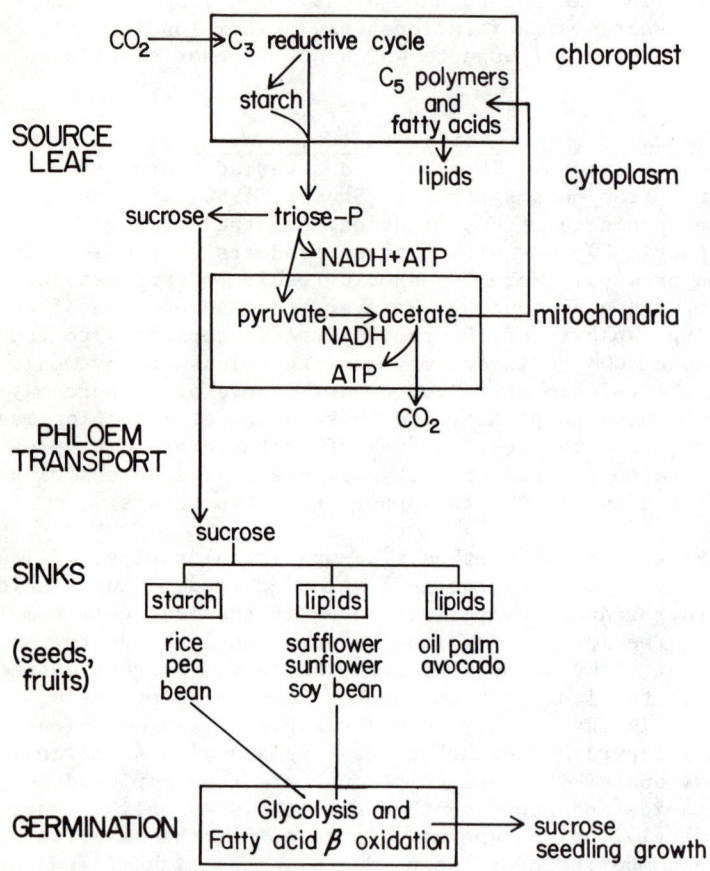

Figure 9. Relationship of photosynthetic CO_2 reduction in the aource leaf to synthesis of other carbon products in the leaf and in the sinks.

In fatty acid synthesis, CO_2 is an intermediary necessary
for malonyl–CoA synthesis, but this CO_2 is released during
subsequent steps in fatty acid synthesis.

Fatty acid or isoprene polymer synthesis involves
several subcellular compartments (Figure 9). After
triose–P formation in the chloroplast, it is converted to
pyruvate by glycolysis in the cytoplasm. Pyruvate
conversion to acetyl–CoA or acetate primarily occurs in the
mitochondria by pyruvate dehydrogenase. Some activity of
this dehydrogenase in the chloroplast is also being
investigated. Acetate return to the stroma phase of the
chloroplast is rapid, where it is reconverted to acetyl–CoA
by a synthetase. Acetyl–CoA plus bicarbonate is then
converted to malonyl–CoA before undergoing a condensation
with an acetyl–acyl carrier protein to a longer chain fatty
acid. This key reaction for fatty acid biosynthesis is
thus in competition for CO_2 with ribulose–P_2 carboxylase
of the C_3 cycle. However, in the condensation to fatty
acids, the CO_2 incorporated to form malonyl–CoA is
released, so there is no net CO_2 uptake. It is unknown,
but judged unlikely, that higher levels of atmospheric CO_2
will play a relevant role at this level in fatty acid
synthesis in leaf tissue. The remaining phases of fatty
acid synthesis terminate in the chloroplast with oleic acid
formation, and then lipid synthesis continues in the
cytoplasm and endoplasmic reticulum. Acetyl–CoA in the
chloroplast is also the precursor for mevalonate which then
flows into the synthesis of isoprene derivatives, namely,
carotenoids, isoprenes, steroids, rubber, etc.

3.3 Respiration and Nitrogen, Sulfur and Phosphorus.
Plant respiration includes utilization of the saccharide
products from photosynthesis for synthesis of all products
(acids, amino acids, sugars, etc.) necessary for growth. In
spite of much knowledge about the various metabolic respiratory pathways, little knowledge exists about the effect of
elevated CO_2 on any of the pathways or the partitioning of
carbon among them. Increased availability of substrate
saccharides for respiration should increase respiration.
Excess respiration utilizes photosynthate that might
otherwise be used for growth, and partial inhibition of
respiration by plant growth regulators has increased corn
yield in trial experiments.

The rate of respiratory activity by the tricarboxylic
acid cycle in leaf mitochondria remains uncertain during
periods of energy input from photosynthesis (Graham, 1980).
If mitochondrial respiration remains fully active in the
light, CO_2 production from this source may augment that

from photorespiration, and therefore reduce net CO_2 fixation. Some evidence suggests that leaf CO_2 compensation point increases due to respiratory CO_2 inputs when sucrose accumulates in leaves of C_3 plants. The control of these processes and their relationship to mitochondrial respiratory oxidations is unclear. It seems likely that photorespiration will decrease in response to high atmospheric CO_2, and that mitochondrial or dark respiration may increase in response to sucrose accumulation in leaves.

Increasing photosynthesis and plant growth would impose an increased demand upon nutrients or fertilizers. Nitrogen, sulfur and phosphorus limitations are of particular concern. Phosphate is essential for metabolic processes, particularly carbohydrate metabolism (Sections 2.1 and 2.4) while nitrogen and sulfur are needed for protein components. The availability of nutrients already limits plant growth, which can only increase in severity with more atmospheric CO_2. One beneficial effect of increased CO_2 will stem from stimulation of nitrogen fixation by root nodules, which can use the excess sucrose (Chapter 6). Stimulation of nitrogen fixation by the leguminous plants, however, will not alleviate nutrient stress in other crop plants and forests.

Relative changes in amino acid synthesis in plants might be a consequence of increased atmospheric CO_2. Amounts of amino acids synthesized in leaves and roots vary among species (Pate, 1980). With increasing CO_2, it is possible that less energy for nitrate reduction would be available in the leaf, and more nitrate reduction would occur in the root, due to an increased supply of sucrose. In the leaf, increase in triose-P from increased CO_2 levels could provide carbon skeletons for amino acid synthesis similarly to the increased production of fatty acids (Section 3.2), but without more nitrate reduction, amino acid and protein synthesis would be limited. Thus, with more atmospheric CO_2, the ratio of protein to carbohydrate content of leaves would decrease. Whether the amino acid composition would also change is not known.

4. **Duration of CO_2 Fixation.** The effect of more CO_2 upon plant growth and development will be related also to the duration of the increased photosynthesis. The consequences are related to the partition and fate of assimilates discussed in part 3. In the short term, the metabolic basis for these interactions involve product accumulation in leaves as a consequence of such limitations as membrane translocators or transport physiology. Feedback or other

regulation of CO_2 fixation may reduce the duration of high rates of CO_2 assimilation on a daily basis. Such limitations, mostly unknown, may affect prolonged photosynthesis at high irradiation and high temperature. In the longer term, higher CO_2 concentrations may prolong senescence so that leaves will remain photosynthetically active for longer periods. Studies on the sparing effect of CO_2 concentration on the photosynthetic apparatus and ribulose-P_2 carboxylase activity should be expedited.

The effects of increased CO_2 concentrations on the dration of CO_2 fixation may not always result in higher productivity. It may sometimes extend the growth cycle of annual crops into an unfavorable season, or may interfere with fruit development or the source-sink relationship (Chapter 3). The metabolic basis of developmental changes in the photosynthetic apparatus, and the consequence upon productivity are unknown.

Studies of C_3 plants grown in higher CO_2 concentrations for several generations so far indicate that there are no changes in the kinetic properties of ribulose-P_2 carboxylase/oxygenase or its response to effectors (Ogren, unpublished). It remains uncertain whether nitrogen-sparing and a general reduction in the photosynthetic apparatus including ribulose-P_2 carboxylase (Wong, 1980; Downton et al., 1980) is a general long-term response of C_3 plants to increasing CO_2. It is likely that changes in carbon and nitrogen allocation between proteins and lipids and between enzymes, membrane proteins, and lipids could be important, in the long term, to plant development.

The paucity of information concerning the metabolic basis and factors regulating long-term plant growth and development can only be noted in this section. As a consequence, the effects of higher CO_2 upon plant development cannot be predicted, other than from a very few experiments on whole plant growth (Chapters 6 and 7).

5. Discussion. In the complex details and regulation of photosynthetic carbon metabolism, there is no evidence to suggest that photosynthesis could increase so much that the rise in atmospheric CO_2 could be stopped. Photosynthesis plays a major role in balancing the CO_2 content of the atmosphere, and by itself photosynthesis could remove nearly all the CO_2 from the air in a few years. Even if overall photosynthesis by plants could be greatly increased, as it will to some extent with more CO_2, increased plant productivity will not prevent the

atmospheric CO_2 from rising, because the plants of today will be oxidized by man's use right back to CO_2. The CO_2 would not be put back into reservoirs equivalent to our fossil photosynthate of coal, oil, and gas. The rising atmospheric CO_2 is an environmental consequence of our excess use of fossil photosynthate which returns CO_2 to the atmosphere. The transfer of atmospheric CO_2 into the ocean reservoir of bicarbonate is apparently too slow (a century-long process) to maintain our current atmospheric balance. Neither has photosynthesis stopped the atmospheric CO_2 from rising 17% from about 290 ppm to 340 ppm in the last 100 years. And it cannot prevent further increases into the next century. But without adequate photosynthetic capacity, the CO_2 level would have zoomed upwards, more completely out of control.

Part of the excess photosynthetic reducing capacity, which is presently being wasted in an oxidative photosynthetic carbon cycle, (photorespiration), could be used instead to reduce the added CO_2. This is regulated by competition between CO_2 and O_2 for the initial reaction catalyzed by ribulose-P_2 carboxylase/oxygenase which is associated with both photosynthesis and respiration.

Research on carbon metabolism is fundamental to understanding the response of plant productivity to higher CO_2. The body of data reviewed in this chapter can be used as a background for further study, but our discussions have highlighted only major areas of uncertainty which are relevant to the response to more CO_2. Each of these can be qualified and applied to the different and less well known processes in C_4 plants and CAM plants; but for the most part, our discussion has been couched in terms of metabolism in C_3 plants. It is in the C_3 plant that we can expect up to 30-50% increase in CO_2 fixation from an increase to 600 ppm atmospheric CO_2 concentration.

The key components of carbon metabolism which are likely to limit growth, yield, and competitive ability of plants to higher CO_2 have been grouped above into three sections: rate of CO_2 assimilation; fate of the assimilates; and duration of CO_2 assimilation. Some of these components are discussed in greater detail in the other chapters, while the emphasis in this chapter has been on metabolic aspects. The importance of other aspects are also to be noted:

1) <u>Temperature and water stress.</u> Changes in atmospheric CO_2 will be accompanied by rising temperatures and increased water stress in many areas. These changes will

have complex interrelated consequences in photosynthetic
carbon metabolism (see Chapter 4). Lack of water is of
major concern, particularly as it relates to stomata
closure and lowered CO_2 diffusion into the leaf. Higher
temperatures favor photorespiration more than photosynthesis. However, rising CO_2 by itself will be
beneficial, and in the few plants tested, temperature
optimum for growth and water use efficiency are increased
by increasing CO_2 (Ku et al., 1977; Berry and Björkman,
1980). Changes in plant carbon metabolism will be the
combined effect of more CO_2, water stress, temperature
changes and nutrient limitations. At this time, there is
little data available on carbon metabolism in plants
subjected to any combinations of these changes.

2) Control of atmospheric CO_2 by photosynthesis. Atmospheric CO_2 is determined by the rate and amount of CO_2
added to the air and the amount removed by net photosynthesis and absorption by the oceans. Net photosynthesis
is determined by gross photosynthetic removal of CO_2 minus
the CO_2 added to the air by photorespiration. Gross
photosynthesis, with photorespiration, represents an
environmental protective mechanism that controls the
atmospheric CO_2 level. The two mechanisms are linked by
competition between CO_2 and O_2 as substrates for the same
initiating enzyme which acts as a ribulose-P_2 carboxylase
for photosynthesis and an oxygenase for photorespiration.
During photorespiration, part of the excess capacity for
photosynthesis is dissipated when the CO_2 level is low.
With increasing CO_2, this excess energy becomes available
for increasing net photosynthesis. Alternatively, photorespiration in theory has prevented atmospheric CO_2 from
decreasing too much. At lower CO_2 levels, photorespiration
would increase and net photosynthesis decrease. There is,
however, no geological evidence for this hypothesis,
although the principles involved have been repeatedly
demonstrated in controlled environmental plant growth
studies.

3) Plant molecular biology and plant breeding. The current
increase in atmospheric CO_2 is geologically fast or nearly
instantaneous, relative to slow environmental changes that
would permit natural adaptation and plant selection for
optimal growth at higher CO_2 levels. Consequently,
molecular biology and plant breeding techniques may have to
be used to compress into a few decades adaptive changes
that naturally would require thousands of years. Most of
our crops have been selected in recent decades for maximum
productivity at 320 to 330 ppm CO_2. Limitations from
higher CO_2, on photosynthesis and sucrose transport, must

be discovered and characterized so that the molecular biologist can proceed toward plant modifications. By accelerating all aspects of this program now, plant scientists should be able to modify existing plants in time to cope with an atmosphere of 600 ppm CO_2 or more when it arrives. It is encouraging that some research is underway on the biosynthesis and genetic properties of ribulose-P_2 carboxylase/oxygenase.

4) <u>Incremental changes in photosynthesis.</u> Changes in the distribution of $^{14}CO_2$ among the initial products of photosynthesis with increasing atmospheric CO_2 may be a sensitive biological indicator of atmospheric CO_2 concentration. The biological shifts among early products of photosynthesis that should occur with increasing atmospheric CO_2 may indicate larger changes in plant growth within the next few decades. Small incremental changes in photosynthesis should be a biological monitor of increasing atmospheric CO_2. Three research approaches might be considered: a) chlorophyll fluorescence represents unused light energy that may decrease with increasing photosynthesis from excess CO_2; b) the ratio of the stable carbon isotopes, ^{13}C to ^{12}C, in the products of photosynthesis may be altered by rising CO_2; and c) analysis of early carbon products of photosynthesis by isotopic ^{14}C and chromatographic procedures may indicate changes in product distribution from small incremental CO_2 increases.

5) <u>Experimental facilities.</u> Our panel noted that research on photosynthesis requires that plants be grown at elevated CO_2 levels with adequate controls of light, temperature, and water stress. Research facilities for growing these plants at elevated atmospheric CO_2 are needed at many institutions if the problems associated with increasing CO_2 are to be adequately investigated by the plant science community. Because competition between CO_2 and O_2 or between photosynthesis and photorespiration becomes more severe at high light intensity, growth of plants at elevated CO_2 should be in sunlight intensities experienced over a normal day schedule. Biochemical and physiological experiments require extensive laboratory facilities and a continuing program of investigation. For this reason, adequate plant material should be grown near the laboratory site. However, there was not time at this conference to extensively investigate how best to grow plants under more CO_2 for biochemical investigations. Also, plant species to be investigated were not selected. Most of our detailed biochemical research has been done on only a few plants, notably spinach leaves. Considering the wide diversity in biology, the knowledge to date about photosynthetic carbon

cycles must contain this qualifier. However, the ubiquitous and conserved properties of ribulose-P_2 carboxylase/oxygenase in photosynthetic tissues suggest that on the whole, the C_3 and C_2 cycles of photosynthetic carbon metabolism are the major or sole process for photosynthesis in both terrestrial and aquatic systems. The C_4 pathway is not an exception, but rather the C_4 cycle provides the additional ability to concentrate CO_2.

6. Literature Cited

Anderson, L.E. 1979. Interaction between photochemistry and activity of enzymes. In Encyclopedia of Plant Physiology Vol. 6, Photosynthesis II. Photosynthetic Carbon Metabolism and Related Processes, M. Gibbs and E. Latzko, Eds. Springer-Verlag, Berlin, Heidelberg, New York, pp. 271-281.

Badger, M.R., A. Kaplan and J.A. Berry. 1978. A mechanism for concentrating CO_2 in Chlamydomonas reinhardtii and variabilis and its role in photosynthetic CO_2 fixation. Carnegie Institut. Y.B. 77, 251-261.

Bassham, J.A. 1979. The reductive pentose phosphate cycle and its regulation. In Encyclopedia of Plant Physiology Vol. 6, Photosynthetic Carbon Metabolism and Related Processes, M. Gibbs and E. Latzko, Eds., Springer-Verlag, Berlin, Heidelberg, New York, pp. 1-30.

Bassham, J.A. and M. Calvin. 1957. The Path Of Carbon In Photosynthesis. Prentice Hall, Inc. Englewood Cliffs, N.J.

Berry, J. and O. Björkman. 1980. Photosynthetic response and adaptation to temperature in higher plants. Annual Rev. Plant Physiol. 31, 491-638.

Black, C. 1973. Photosynthetic carbon fixation in relation to net CO_2 uptake. Annual Rev. Plant Physiol. 24, 253-286.

Downton, W.J.S., O. Björkman, and C.S. Pike. 1980. Consequences of increased atmospheric concentration of carbon dioxide for growth and photosynthesis of high plants. In Carbon dioxide and climate: Australian research. Australian Academy of Science, Canberra, pp. 143-151.

Farquhar, G.D. and T.D. Sharkey. 1982. Stomatal conduct-

ance and photosynthesis. Annual Review Plant
Physiology 33:317:345.

Graham, D. 1980. Effect of light on dark respiration. In
Plant Biochem. Vol. 2, D.D. Davies, Ed., Academic
Press, New York, N.Y.   pp. 526-580.

Guinn, G. and J. Mauney. 1980. Analysis of CO_2 exchange
assumptions: feedback control. In Predicting
Photosynthesis for Ecosystem Models Vol. 2, J.D. Hesketh
and James W. Jones, Eds., CRC Press, Inc., Boca Raton,
Florida, pp. 1-16.

Hatch, M.D. 1978. Regulation of enzymes in C_4 photosynthesis. Current Top. Cellular Regulation 14, 1-27.

Heldt, H.W. 1976. Metabolic carriers of chloroplasts. In
Encyclyopedia of Plant Physiology, Vol. 3, Transport
in Plants III, C.R. Stocking and U. Heber, Eds.,
Springer-Verlag, London, Heidelberg, New York, pp.
137-143.

Keys, A.J., F. Bird, M.J. Connelius, P.J. Lea, R.M.
Wallsgrove, and B.J. Miflin. 1978. The photorespiratory
nitrogen cycle. Nature 275:741-743.

Ku, S.B., G.E. Edwards, and C.B. Tanner. 1977. Effects of
inhibition of photosynthesis and transpiration in
Solanum tuberosum. Plant Phsiol. 59, 868-872.

Lerman, J.C. 1975. How to interpret variations in the carbon
dioxide ratio of plants; biologic and environmental
effects.   In Environmental and Bological Control of
Photosynthesis, Ed. R. Marcelle, pp. 323-335. W.
Junk, The Hogneg.

Lorimer, G.H. 1981. The carboxylation and oxygenation of
ribulose-1,5-bisphosphate: the primary event in
photosynthesis and photorespiration. Annual Rev.
Plant Physiol. 32, 349-384.

McFadden, B. 1973. Autotrophic CO_2 assimilation and the
evolution of ribulose diphosphate carboxylase. Bact.
Rev. 37, 289-319.

Miyachi, S., and Y. Shiraiwa. 1979. Form of inorganic
carbon utilized for photosynthesis in Chlorella
vulgaris 11h cells.   Plant and Cell Physiol.
20, 341-348.

Ogren, W.L. 1977. Increasing carbon fixation by crop plants. In Fourth International Congress on Photosynthesis, G. Akoyunoglou, Ed., Balaban Int. Sci Services, Philadelphia, Pa., pp. 721-733.

O'Leary, M.H. 1981. Carbon isotope discrimination in plants. Phytochemistry 20, 553-564.

Osmond, C.B. 1981. Photorespiration and photoinhibition: some implications for the energetics of photosynthesis. Biochem. Biophysica Acta 639-77-98.

Pate, J.S. 1980. Transport and partitioning of nitrogenous solutes. Annual Rev. Plant Physiol. 31, 313-340.

Perchorowicz, J.T., D.A. Raynes, and R.G. Jensen. 1981. Light limitation of photosynthesis and activation of ribulose bisphosphate carboxylase in wheat seedlings. Proc. Natl. Acad. Sci. USA 78:2985-2989.

Powles, S.B., C.B. Osmond, and S.W. Thorne. 1979. Photoinhibition in attached leaves of C_3 plants illuminated in the absence of CO_2 and photorespiration. Plant Physiol. 64, 682-688.

Preiss, J. and C. Levi 1979. Metabolism of starch in leaves. In Encyclopedia of Plant Physiology Vol. 6, Photosynthesis II, Photosynthesis and Related Processes, M. Gibbs and E. Latzko, Eds., pp. 282-312.

Raven, J.A. 1970. Exogenous inorganic carbon sources in plant photosynthesis. Biol. Rev. 45, 167-221.

Salvucci, M.E. and G. Bowes. 1981. Induction of reduced photorespiratory activity in submersed and amphibious aquatic macrophytes. Plant Physiol. 67, 335-340.

Schnareuberger, C. and H. Fock. 1976. Interaction among organelles involved in photorespiration. Encyclopedia of Plant Physiology N.S. (eds.) U. Heber, and C.R. Stocking. New Series Vol. 3, pp. 185-134. Springer Verlag, Berlin, Heidelberg, N.Y.

Stumpf, P.K. 1980. The Biochemistry of Plants, Vol. 4, Lipids: Structure and Function. Academic Press. p. 693.

Ting, J.P. and M. Gibbs, editors. 1982. Crassulacean Acid Metabolism. American Society of Plant Physiologists.

Tolbert, N.E. 1971. Microbodies – peroxisome and glyoxysomes. Annual Rev. Plant Physiol. 22, 45–74.

Tolbert, N.E. 1974. Photorespiration. In Algae, Physiology and Biochemistry, W.D.P. Stewart, Ed., Blackwell Scientific Publications, pp. 474–504.

Tolbert, N.E. 1980. Photorespiration. In Plant Biochemistry, Vol. 2, D.D. Davies, Ed., Academic Press, pp. 488–523.

Van, T.K., W.T. Haller, and G. Bowes. 1976. Comparison of the photosynthetic characteristics of three submersed aquatic plants. Plant. Physiol. 58, 761–768.

Walker, D.A. 1976. Plastids and intracellular transport. In Encyclopedia of Plant Physiology, Vol. 3 Transport in Plants. III Intracellular Interactions and Transport Processes, C.R. Stocking and U. Heder, Eds., Springer-Verlag, Berlin, Heidelberg, New York, pp. 82–143.

Walker, D.A. 1980. Regulation of starch synthesis in leaves – the role of orthophosphate. In Physiological Aspects of Crop Productivity, Proc. of 15th Intl. Potash Inst., Bern. Pp. 195–207.

Wong, S.C. 1980. Effect of elevated partial pressure of CO_2 on rate of CO_2 assimilation and water use efficiency in plants. In Carbon dioxide and climate: Australian research. Griffin Press. pp. 159–166.

Zelitch, I. 1971. Photosynthesis, Photorespiration, and Plant Productivity. Academic Press.

Zelitch, I. 1975. Pathways of carbox fixation in green plants. Annual Rev. Biochem. 44, 123–145.

_____ *Robert W. Pearcy, Co-Chairman*
Olle Björkman, Chairman

4. Physiological Effects

Panel Members: L.H. Allen, Jr., E.W.R. Barlow,
J. R. Ehleringer, G.D. Farquhar, D.R. Geiger,
R.T. Giaquinta, R.M. Gifford, T.C. Hsiao, T.Jurik,
D.A. Phillips, K. Raschke, S.C. Wong.

SUMMARY AND RECOMMENDATIONS

We need to:

1) Elucidate the long-term effect of increased CO_2 on photosynthetic response of representative C_3, C_4, and CAM plants under different environments.

2) Determine the long term interaction of higher CO_2 with the responses of leaf photosynthesis to water, temperature, high light, and salinity stresses.

3) Determine stomatal and photosynthetic response patterns to CO_2 and light for representative plant species under long-term exposure to normal and higher CO_2 concentrations and after exposure to long-term stresses.

4) Determine how H^+ transport systems are controlled in guard cells, phloem, storage, motor, and growing cells, and elucidate the mechanism by which guard cells respond to CO_2.

5) Derive the relationships between whole canopy transpiration and responses of stomata at the single leaf level.

6) Analyze the processes accelerating leaf expansion and modifying leaf anatomy with higher CO_2.

7) Determine responses of leaf growth and canopy development to more CO_2 and elucidate the underlying processes.

8) Determine whether the distribution of photosynthetic products into major plant organs is affected by higher CO_2 concentration.

9) Determine the physiological basis of any changes in initiation, maintenance and size of major sinks due to added CO_2.

10) Elucidate the mutual interactions between growth of harvestable organs and photosynthetic activity in response to more CO_2.

11) Clarify how the incorporation of additional photosynthetic products resulting from increased CO_2 is limited by low nutrient availability, root uptake capacity, and photosynthate supply to symbiotic organisms.

1. Introduction. Photosynthesis provides all the chemical energy and the carbon compounds needed for all other growth processes. It is thus the central process governing the primary productivity of all green plants. The ultimate substrate for this process is CO_2. A wealth of experimental evidence demonstrates that the rate at which photosynthesis proceeds via the C_3 pathway found in most plants (C_3 plants) is generally strongly limited by the low CO_2 concentration in the present-day atmosphere and is further limited by the high atmospheric concentration of O_2.

Under conditions of moderate to high light intensities and temperatures, the rate of CO_2 fixation in C_3 plants, at least in the short term (minutes to days), roughly doubles with a doubling of the present atmospheric concentration. The extent of photosynthetic enhancement by CO_2 enrichment is, however, strongly dependent on other environmental conditions. Plants possessing the C_4 dicarboxylic pathway for CO_2 fixation (C_4 plants) differ from C_3 plants in the response to increased CO_2, since the C_4 pathway serves, in effect, as an internal CO_2 concentrating mechanism. In C_4 plants, photosynthesis is not inhibited by O_2, and it is only slightly limited by the present atmospheric CO_2 concentration. The vast majority of species making up the world's vegetation are C_3 plants; these include, with few exceptions, all tree species of tropical, temperate, and boreal forests. However, many important and highly productive crop species, as well as large fractions of the grassland species and shrub vegetation in the tropical, warm-temperate, and semi-arid regions of the world, are C_4 plants.

Carbon dioxide uptake and water vapor loss occur

through a common stomatal pathway, intimately linking these two processes. The ratio of CO_2 uptake to water vapor loss, or photosynthetic water use efficiency, will always increase in C_3 plants with increasing CO_2 concentration, other things being equal. This occurs because photosynthesis increases while transpiration remains unchanged; or conversely, if the stomata close slightly so that photosynthesis remains unchanged, then transpiration declines. For C_4 plants, photosynthesis will not increase much, but if stomata close slightly then water use efficiency increases. The responses of photosynthesis to more atmospheric CO_2 are thus strongly dependent on stomatal behavior. These responses have important implications for water use and productivity in agricultural systems as well as in natural ecosystems. A clear understanding of the basic mechanisms and differences in individual species is required to assess the probable effects of more atmospheric CO_2.

The expression of increased photosynthesis in added plant growth and productivity depends, of course, on many other factors, such as allocation patterns or other potential physiological limitations. Moreover, the effects of other environmental limitations, such as nutrient availability, may be influenced by the increased assimilation. Under some circumstances, growth will be unaffected, or, more likely, stimulated to an extent less than the stimulation of photosynthesis rates. However, in other cases the enhancement of photosynthesis may be amplified so that growth and productivity will be stimulated to an extent even greater than that of CO_2 uptake. At present, there are too many unknowns to reliably predict the extent to which the stimulation of photosynthesis will translate into higher plant productivity.

The objectives of this chapter are to review the current state of knowledge of the physiological effects of increased CO_2 on photosynthesis, water use efficiency, and growth of plants in diverse environments and to identify areas of ignorance.

2. Response of Leaf Photosynthesis to Increased CO_2 Concentration. The ability of leaf photosynthesis to respond to increased CO_2 concentration depends on various external and internal limits to CO_2 uptake, their dependence on CO_2 concentration, and their interactions with other environmental factors. The uptake rate depends on: firstly, the physical transport of CO_2 from the atmosphere to the carboxylation enzyme in the chloroplast, and secondly, the capacity for carboxylation. The transport and

carboxylation processes have been termed the "supply function" and the "demand function," respectively, by Raschke (1979). The components of either process can limit the rate of CO_2 uptake to a greater or lesser degree, depending on the environment and the characteristics of the leaf. Here we briefly review each step, its potential limitation to CO_2 uptake under the present CO_2 concentration, and its contribution to limiting photosynthesis as concentration increases.

2.1 The Supply Function. It is convenient to consider CO_2 uptake into the leaf in terms of a series of conductances associated with the leaf boundary layer, the stomata, the intercellular air space, the cell wall and intracellular liquid phase. The stomata provide the principal limitation to CO_2 transport into the leaf, i.e., they are responsible for the largest drop in CO_2 concentration along the diffusion path from the atmosphere to the carboxylation site.

The CO_2 concentration drop across the stomata and the boundary layer, δC, is typically 100 ppm in C_3 plants and 200 ppm in C_4 species. While this might suggest a greater stomatal limitation to photosynthesis in C_4 than in C_3 plants, in fact, the opposite is true. In C_4 plants, increases in intercellular CO_2 concentration, C_i, above normal levels of about 140 ppm cause little increase in photosynthetic rate, whereas in C_3 plants, the intercellular CO_2 concentration of about 240 ppm is still well below saturating levels. In both C_3 and C_4 plants, intercellular CO_2 concentration remains remarkably constant over a wide range of stomatal conductances, the latter caused by variation in leaf water status, leaf age, nitrogen nutrition, and growth light regime (Wong et al., 1979). This suggests that there exists a close coordination so that the supply of CO_2 to the mesophyll is adequate, yet water loss is not excessive. With changes in ambient CO_2 concentration, C_a, stomata frequently respond in a way that maintains the ratio of intercellular to ambient CO_2 concentration, C_i/C_a, at 0.6 to 0.8 in C_3 species and 0.3 to 0.5 in C_4 species. This again implies that coordination exists between the photosynthetic activity of the mesophyll and the stomatal conductances as C_a increases.

Other steps in the path usually have higher conductances than stomata. As a result, the CO_2 concentration drop across each step is less than across the stomata and, therefore, has less influence on the concentration at the carboxylation site. The boundary layer conductance, g_b, can be less than the stomatal conductance, g_s, for some

large leaves in still air, but in most cases it is likely
to be considerably higher. Thus, at moderate to higher wind
speeds, g_b, is not a major limitation to CO_2 uptake in most
species. Moreover, any changes in leaf size that might
occur at high CO_2 concentration are unlikely to alter g_b
enough to appreciably affect CO_2 uptake. The boundary
layer is, of course, also in the water vapor loss path and
is the only one in convective heat transfer, thus affecting
these processes as well.

Within the leaf, CO_2 must diffuse across the intercellular air spaces and the liquid phase from the cell
walls to the carboxylation enzyme sites within the chloroplast. Direct measurement of these conductances is not
possible, but evidence at hand suggests that neither step
imposes a significant limit to CO_2 uptake (for review, see
Farquhar and Caemmerer, 1982). Estimates of intercellular
air space conductances based on modeled systems place the
values at least four-fold greater than typical stomatal
conductances (Cooke and Rand, 1980). The maximum CO_2
concentration gradient across the intercellular air space
is probably less than 5 to 20 ppm, and is about half this
value for the average cell. However, it could be greater
in sclereophyllous leaves with tightly packed cells
(Farquhar and Caemmerer, 1982). Liquid phase conductances
have been estimated to cause a CO_2 concentration differential of between 9 to 45 ppm, depending on the assumptions
(Farquhar and Caemmerer, 1982). Consideration of the
carbon isotope discrimination ratios in leaves of C_3 plants
also suggests that the intercellular air space and liquid
phase conductances are sufficiently high to ensure that CO_2
concentrations at the carboxylation sites within the
chloroplast are appreciably higher than the compensation
point (Björkman, 1981; Farquhar et al., 1982). Changes in
leaf anatomy, particularly in the length of the palisade
mesophyll, are known to occur in response to growth at high
CO_2 (Downton et al., 1980), but are probably of little
consequence to CO_2 transport.

2.2 The Demand Function. As stated above, the supply
function is primarily determined by the stomata, with only
minor effects of other steps in the pathway. However, net
CO_2 uptake is ultimately determined by the demand function
or carboxylation reactions as well as any respiratory CO_2
evolution. There has recently been considerable success in
modelling CO_2 exchange at the whole leaf level based on
kinetics of the RuBP carboxylase-oxygenase reaction in C_3
plants (Caemmerer and Farquhar, 1981) and on the anatomy
and kinetics of PEP carboxylase and RuBP carboxylase-
oxygenase in C_4 plants (Berry and Farquhar, 1978). It is

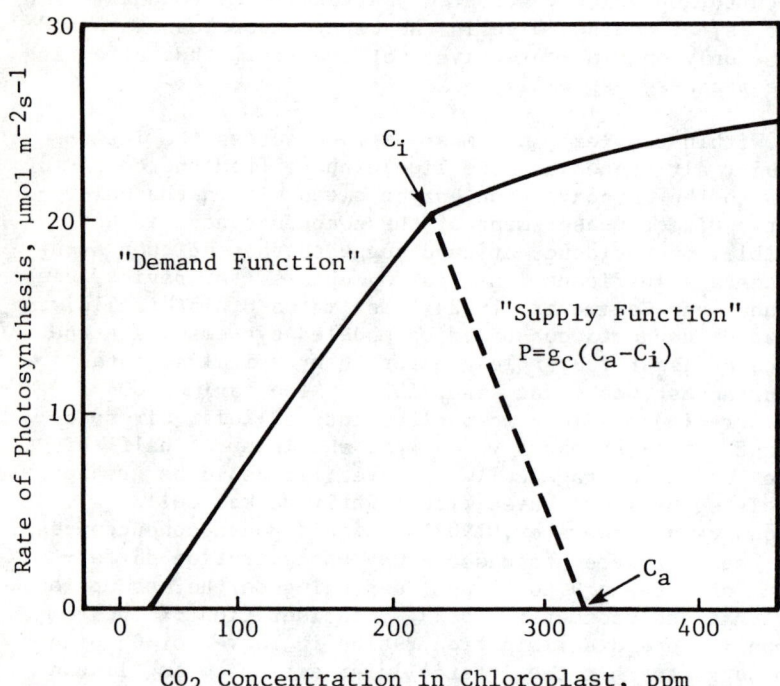

Figure 1.   General relationship between the rate of photosynthesis and CO_2 concentration in the chloroplast for a CO_3
plant.   The supply function is represented by the dashed line,
while the demand function is given by the solid line.
Redrawn from Farquhar and Sharkey (1982).

beyond the scope of this chapter (see Chapter 3) to discuss the kinetic properties of the carboxylase enzymes, so we will concentrate on the physiological properties of the demand function and its relationship to carboxylase properties.

As shown in Figure 1, the photosynthetic rate at low CO_2 concentration in the chloroplast is almost a linear function of concentration, with the slope being determined by the carboxylase activities in the leaf. At these chloroplast CO_2 concentration levels, RuBP concentrations are postulated to be saturating for RuBP carboxylase. At high CO_2 concentrations, however, RuBP regeneration may become limiting (Caemmerer and Farquhar, 1981), resulting in curvature and ultimately saturation of the curve. It is likely that at high CO_2 concentrations and consequently high photosynthetic rates, electron transport capacity and hence RuBP supply, becomes limiting, thereby reducing the concentration of RuBP.

Farquhar and Caemmerer (1982) have suggested that at moderate temperatures and light levels experienced during growth, the transition from a RuBP-saturated to a RuBP-limited state occurs at about 220–240 ppm intercellular CO_2 concentration, which is the concentration commonly observed in C_3 plants at an ambient CO_2 concentration of 340 ppm CO_2 (however, see Chapter 3). The response of many C_3 species seems to deviate from linearity at about this CO_2 concentration, although there is considerable variation in the sharpness of the transition. In other species, the transition occurs at higher CO_2 concentrations. The implication of Farquhar and Caemmerer's interpretation is that if intercellular CO_2 concentration rises with increasing ambient CO_2 concentration, then the response in many species shifts from a region where electron transport and carboxylation capacities are more or less in balance to one where electron transport is the more rate-limiting process. Moreover, the responsiveness of photosynthesis to increased CO_2 may depend on where this transition region occurs. Species differences in the transition from RuBP-saturated to RuBP-limited CO_2 uptake need to be explored in more detail before the implications of this transition for photosynthetic response to increased CO_2 are understood.

In C_3 plants, O_2 competes with CO_2 in the RuBP carboxylase reaction, reducing the carboxylation efficiency and creating a positive CO_2 compensation point. Moreover, the production of glycolate in the oxygenase reaction leads to the evolution of photorespiratory CO_2 (see Chapter 3).

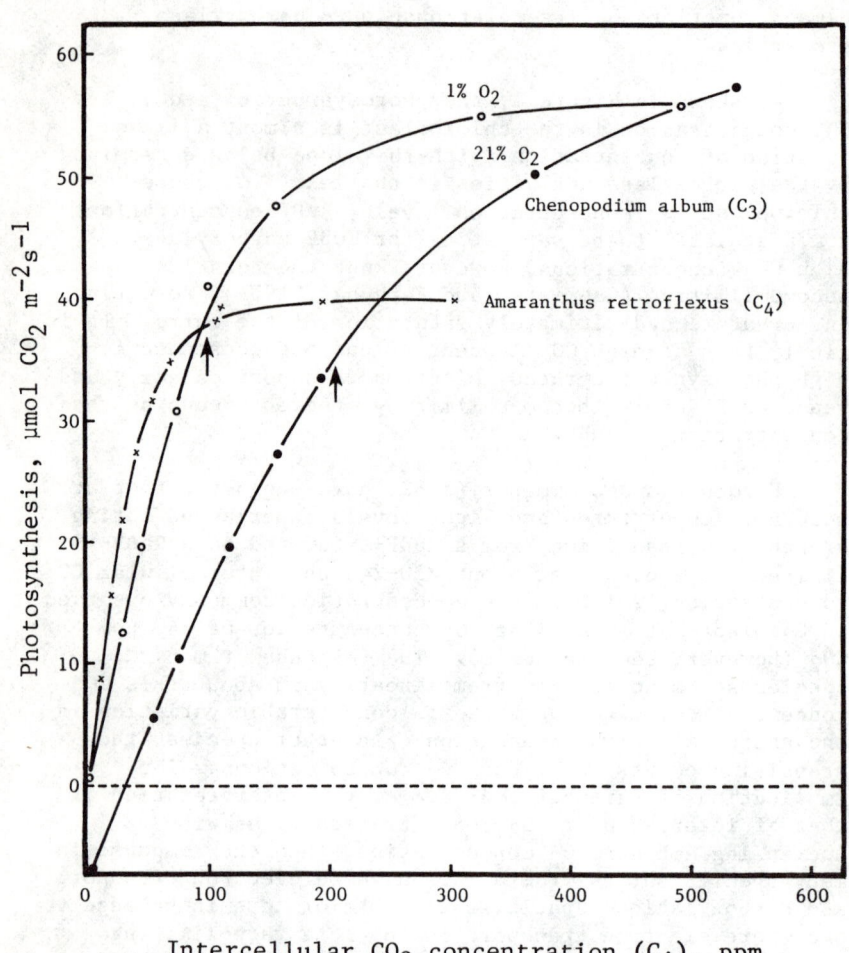

Intercellular CO_2 concentration (C_i), ppm

Figure 2. Response of photosynthesis to intercellular CO_2 in *Amaranthus retroflexus* (C_4) and *Chenopodium album* (C_3). Data from Pearcy et al. (1981) and Pearcy (unpublished).

The O_2 effect on CO_2 uptake is substantial, reducing photosynthesis by 30-40% at both light-saturating and light-limiting irradiances (Björkman, 1966; Ehleringer and Björkman, 1977). Because of its competitive nature, O_2 inhibition is strongly dependent on CO_2 concentration as shown for Chenopodium album (Figure 2). At high intercellular CO_2 concentration, the oxygen inhibition of photosynthesis is suppressed, while at low CO_2 concentrations, the inhibition is relatively greater. Thus, part of the stimulation of net photosynthesis seen in C_3 plants when CO_2 concentration is raised is due to the reduction in the O_2 inhibition.

In C_4 plants, such as Amaranthus retroflexus (Figure 2), no O_2 inhibition of photosynthesis occurs, because of an efficient CO_2 concentrating mechanism that maintains high CO_2 levels at the RuBP carboylase site within the bundle sheath cells. CO_2 entering from the intercellular air spaces is first fixed via PEP carboxylase into C_4 acids within the mesophyll cells. The C_4 acids are then transferred to the bundle sheath cells where they are decarboxylated, releasing CO_2. The 3-carbon fragment is then transferred back to the mesophyll for regeneration of PEP. The C_4 cycle operating between the mesophyll and bundle sheath cells has a high activity, and thus CO_2 concentrations are maintained at high levels within the bundle sheath. (For details, see Chapter 3.) Carboxylation efficiencies of C_4 plants are high, and CO_2 saturation occurs above 130 ppm intercellular CO_2 concentration. Since the stomata in C_4 plants regulate intercellular CO_2 concentration at or just below saturating CO_2 concentration, increases in ambient CO_2 concentration create, at the most, only a small increase in net CO_2 uptake under most conditions.

The influence of CO_2 concentration on photosynthesis in Crassulacean acid metabolism (CAM) plants is not well known. The dark CO_2 fixation characteristic of this pathway involves PEP carboxylase and fixation of CO_2 into C_4 acids. Measurements of CO_2 effects on this dark uptake was made with Kalanchoe daigremontiana, a species capable of both CAM and C_3 photosynthesis (Osmond and Björkman, 1975). These measurements revealed a dark CO_2 uptake response with a zero CO_2 compensation point, little increase in CO_2 uptake rates above 200 ppm intercellular CO_2 concentrations, and no O_2 effect on CO_2 uptake; or in in other words, a response consistent with the C_4 fixation. In contrast, CO_2 uptake in the light, which occurs in many CAM species and involves the C_3 pathway, gave a reponse to CO_2 concentration that was similar to that of C_3 photo-

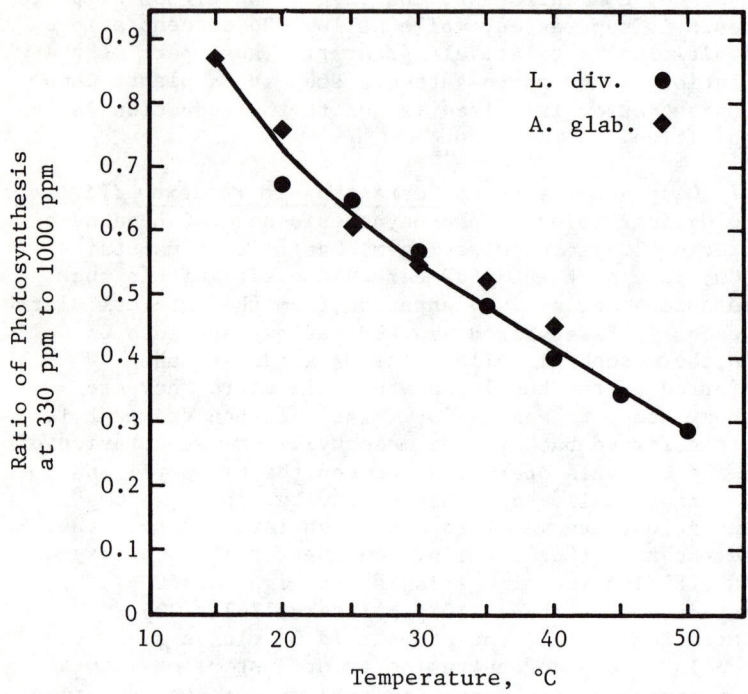

Figure 3.   The effect of temperature on the ratio of CO_2 uptake at 300 ppm to that at 1000 ppm in <u>Larrea divaricata</u> (C_3) and <u>Atriplex glabriscula</u> (C_3).   After Raison and Berry (1981).

synthesis. An increase in atmospheric CO_2 concentration from 330 to 660 ppm gave only a 10% increase in CO_2 uptake in the dark but nearly a 50% increase during the light period. Leaf conductances declined in response to increasing CO_2 concentrations in both the dark and light phases of CO_2 uptake. Thus, the enhancement of CO_2 uptake or water use efficiency in CAM species will be strongly dependent on the importance of dark (C_4) versus light (C_3) CO_2 uptake. Since this varies greatly between species and in many is strongly dependent on environmental conditions, the response of CAM to increasing CO_2 concentration is likely to be highly variable.

2.3 Interaction with Light and Temperature Regimes. Photosynthetic enhancement by increased CO_2 concentration depends strongly on other environnmental factors. For C_3 plants, the enhancement is least at low temperatures and increases continuously with increasing temperature (Figure 3). The probable cause is that the affinity of RuBP carboxylase for CO_2 declines with an increased temperature. As a result, the temperature optimum for photosynthesis is generally higher at high CO_2 than at low CO_2 concentrations. An example of this response is shown in Figure 4 for the C_3 desert shrub, Larrea divaricata. Moreover, while the temperature responses of photosynthesis in L. divaricata and Tidestromia oblongifolia, a C_4 desert shrub, are quite different at 330 ppm CO_2, they are almost indistinguishable at 1000 ppm. In contrast, the temperature responses of T. oblongifolia is not altered by increased CO_2 concentration. Shifts in the temperature responses of photosynthesis in C_3 plants could have important implications in warm environments.

The maximum absolute photosynthetic enhancement for C_3 species by CO_2 enrichment occurs at light intensities that are normally saturating for photosynthesis. However, the relative enhancement is maximal under light-limiting conditions since the light compensation point decreases with an increase in CO_2 concentration. This is because the quantum yield (efficiency of light utilization by photosynthesis) in C_3 plants increases with increasing CO_2 (Figure 5) (Ehleringer and Björkman, 1977). This quantum yield enhancement, due to a reduction of the O_2 inhibition and associated photorespiratory release, is about 40% at 30°C. In C_4 plants, the quantum yield is independent of CO_2 concentration, because of the CO_2 concentrating mechanism. At high CO_2 levels the quantum yield of C_3 plants can be considerably higher than that of C_4 plants because of the added energy cost of the C_4 concentrating mechanism. The actual difference in quantum yield between

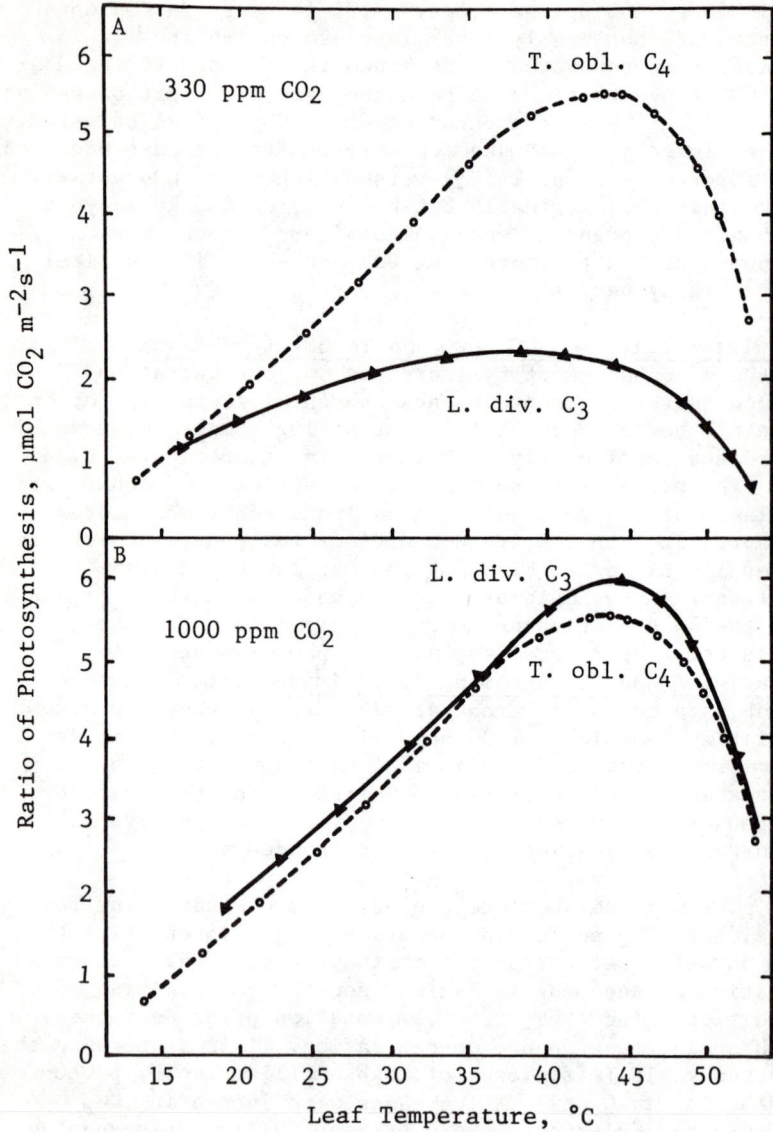

Figure 4. Temperature dependence of CO_2 uptake at (A) 330 ppm CO_2 and (B) 1000 ppm for <u>Larrea</u> <u>divaricata</u> (C_3) and <u>Tidestromia</u> <u>oblongifolia</u> (C_4). From Osmond, Björkman and Anderson (1980).

C_3 and C_4 plants may depend on the specific comparison, since there appears to be considerable variation in quantum yields among C_4 species (Robichaux and Pearcy, 1980; Ehleringer and Pearcy, unpublished observations). An increase in quantum yield means that photosynthesis of C_3 plants is stimulated in low as well as high light environments and thus in leaves at the bottom of a canopy as well as at the top. These changes in quantum yield could be important in dense canopies as well as in plants occupying shaded forest floors. In the latter, where photosynthesis is often just adequate to offset respiration much of the time, the relative effect on leaf carbon balance could be quite large.

2.4 Long-Term Responses. Short-term response studies predict a greater stimulation of photosynthesis and, consequently, growth in C_3 compared to C_4 plants under increased CO_2 concentration. However, the effects of a long-term increase in CO_2 concentration are less well known. Downton et al. (1980) found a 1.5-fold stimulation of photosynthesis in Nerium oleander, a C_3 species, when grown at 660 ppm compared to 330 ppm, but no stimulation in Tidestromia oblongifolia, a C_4 plant. Wong (1979) found a 1.5-fold increase in photosynthetic rate in cotton (C_3) grown and measured at 640 ppm, as compared to plants grown and measured at 330 ppm CO_2. In contrast, maize (C_4) in the same experiment exhibited only a 15% increase. All stimulations were, however, dependent on nitrogen nutrition. For both cotton and maize, reduced nitrate in the soil solution reduced photosynthetic rates as well as the relative stimulation caused by increased CO_2. An inhibition of photosynthesis has been reported for one C_3 species, tobacco, in which photosynthesis was lower in plants grown and measured at 1000 ppm CO_2 than in plants grown and measured at 400 ppm (Raper and Peedin, 1978). However, the leaves were grown and measured at only one-third of full sunlight, so the results are not really comparable to others.

Photosynthetic responses to CO_2 following long-term growth at high CO_2 concentration appear to be complex. In both cotton and oleander, the shapes of the CO_2 response curves were altered somewhat when the plants were grown at high CO_2. For the plants grown at high CO_2, the CO_2 response curves had a reduced slope (carboxylation efficiency) at low CO_2 and did not bend off until much higher CO_2 levels, compared with plants grown at 330 ppm ambient CO_2 concentration. These changes resulted in a 25% reduction in photosynthetic rate at 330 ppm ambient concentration in plants grown at 640 or 660 ppm, as compared with

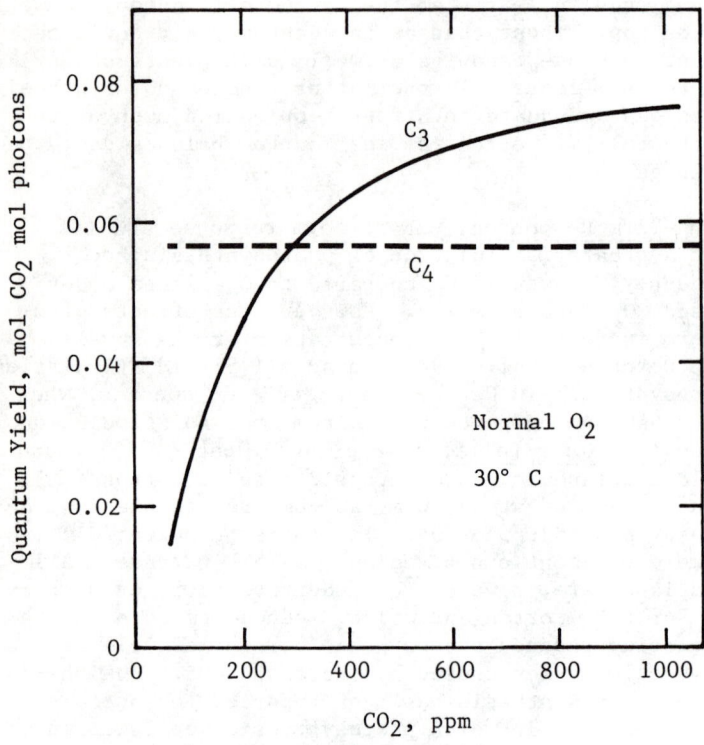

Figure 5. CO_2 dependence on quantum yield in C_3 and C_4 plants.   From Osmond, Björkman and Anderson (1980).

those grown at 330 ppm. The CO_2 concentration during growth had no effect on the photosynthetic CO_2 response curves of the C_4 species. These results might be interpreted as indicating that growth at high CO_2 concentration reduces photosynthetic capacity. However, the relevant comparison is between plants grown and measured at 330 ppm CO_2 and those grown and measured at 640 or 660 ppm CO_2. In this comparison, higher CO_2 concentration always resulted in substantially higher photosynthetic rates in the C_3 species, but much less stimulation in the C_4 species.

The lower carboxylation efficiency in the C_3 species following long-term growth at high CO_2 concentration may be explained by lower activities (and amounts) of RuBP carboxylase (Wong, 1979; Downton et al., 1980). This would tend to bring the carboxylation capacity back more in line with electron transport capacity at high intercellular CO_2 concentration, provided the latter does not also change. The reduction in photosynthetic capacity at low CO_2 concentration might be viewed as resulting from an adaptive response to high CO_2 concentration that gives higher efficiences of the component steps.

3. Responses of Stomata to Increased CO_2 Concentration. Stomata open when exposed to light but usually become narrower, i.e., stomatal conductance decreases, when the CO_2 ambient concentration in the atmosphere (C_a) increases. The closing effect of more CO_2 is smaller at high light intensities than at low intensities (Wong et al., 1978; Sharkey and Raschke, 1981). Lowering of C_a can lead to stomatal opening, even in darkness, but the width of stomatal apertures is never as great in the dark as in the light. Stomatal aperture is modified by the relative humidity of the air. Usually, stomatal apertures become narrower when the air is dry. Because increases in temperature often entail decreases in the relative humidity of the air, stomatal closure in response to decreased relative humidity counteracts the opening response to increased temperature.

Stomatal opening is the result of an accumulation of potassium salts in the guard cells. The counter-ions to K^+ are Cl^- and organic anions, mostly malate. Chloride is imported. The organic anions are produced within the guard cells after the mobilization of starch. It is not known whether expulsion of H^+ by the guard cells (in exchange for K^+) or anion transport into the vacuoles is the primary transport process involved in increasing the osmotic pressure in these cells. The increase in osmotic pressure

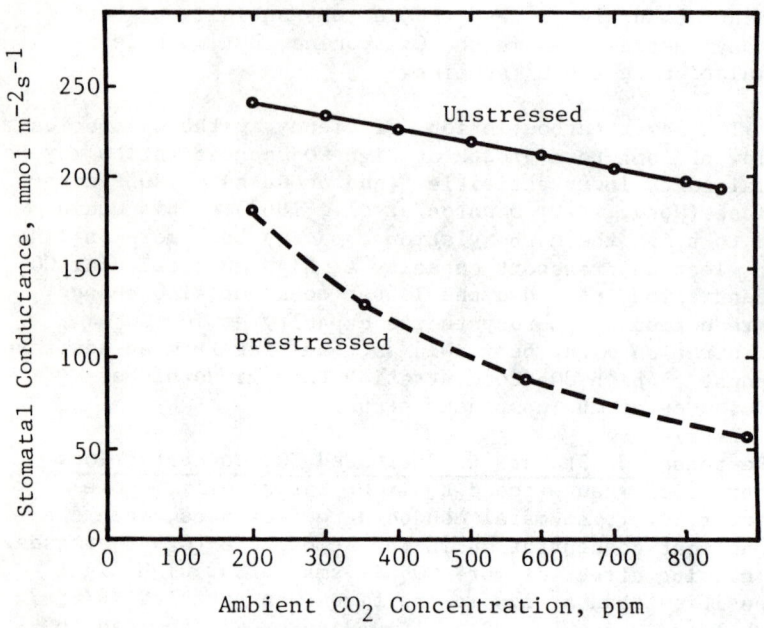

Figure 6. Response of leaf conductance to CO_2 in <u>Nerium oleander</u> (C_3) before and after water stress treatment. Data from Björkman (unpublished).

causes an increase in turgor. The guard cells swell, and the stomatal pore opens. Reversion of the processes just described leads to stomatal closure, K^+ and Cl^- are released from the guard cells and starch is reformed.

The mechanism by which the concentration of CO_2 determines whether stomata tend to open or close is unknown.

The magnitude of stomatal responses to C_a varies greatly among species. In some C_3 species, when water supply is ample, stomata respond to changes in C_a only slightly or not all (Akita and Moss, 1972; Raschke, 1975; Farquhar et al., 1978). In most C_3 and C_4 plants investigated so far, stomatal conductance changes in response to a change in C_a in such a way that the ratio of C_i to C_a remains more or less constant (Dubbe et al., 1978; Farquhar et al., 1978; Louwerse, 1980). Under stress conditions, stomata may respond to CO_2 so strongly that C_i remains nearly constant (Goudriaan and van Laar, 1978). Thus, with C_a increasing above present levels, stomata may exhibit 1) little or no response, 2) a partial closure that still allows an increased C_i but not as much as when they do not respond, or 3) a strong closing response that maintains a constant C_i. The first case results in constant transpiration but increased photosynthetic rate, whereas the third case results in constant photosynthetic rate but decreased transpiration.

3.1 Interaction Between Increased CO_2 and Other Environmental Factors on Stomatal Conductance. For the few species studied so far, increased CO_2 does not seem to alter the basic response to light and temperature, either in the short-term or following long-term growth at higher CO_2 levels (Björkman, unpublished). In contrast, low plant water potentials (drying) appear to sensitize stomata to CO_2. For example, the leaf conductances of Nerium oleander decreased more strongly in response to increased CO_2 after water stress than before stress (Figure 6).

Several lines of evidence suggest that the increased CO_2 sensitivity of stomata following water stress may be mediated by an increased level of abscissic acid (ABA). Raschke (1975) and Dubbe et al. (1978) have shown that exogenous addition of ABA greatly increases the sensitivity of stomata to CO_2 even in species such as Xanthium strumarium, which have insensitive stomata when grown under nonstressed conditions. Moreover, ABA content increases in leaves in response to water stress and other stresses such as chilling (Drake and Raschke, 1974) and waterlogging (K.

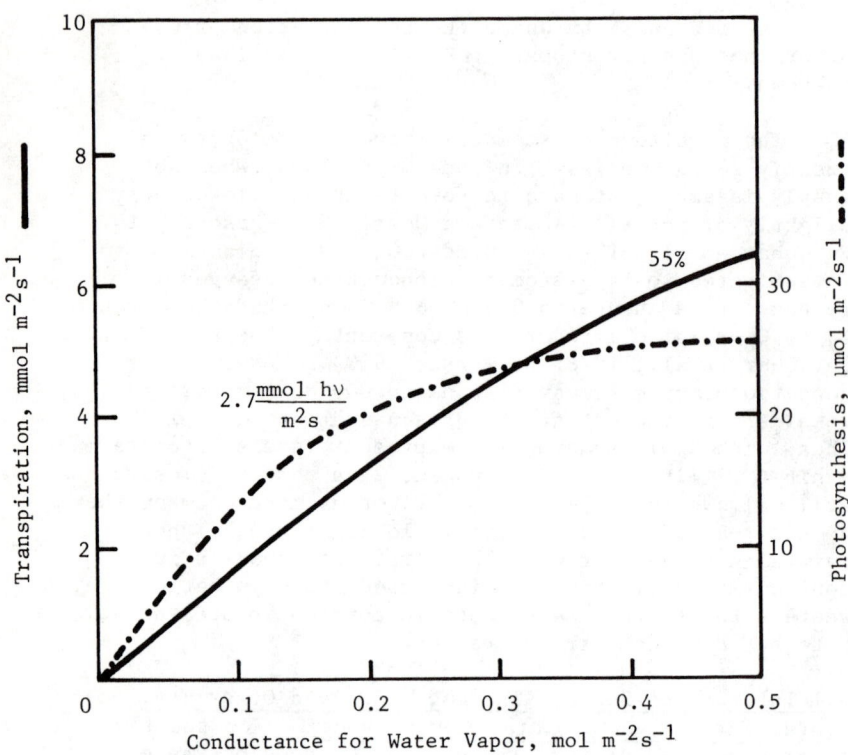

Figure 7. The dependences of transpiration and photosynthesis of CO_2 on the conductance for gases diffusing through the stomata and the boundary layer of a leaf exposed to radiation of 350 W m^{-2}, air temperature of 25°C and a relative humidity of 55%. Note the 200-fold difference in scales between transpiration and photosynthesis. After Raschke (1979).

Bradford, unpublished). However, it is not certain that increases in stomatal sensitivity to C_a are always mediated by increases in ABA levels, or that exposure to stress always leads to increased stomatal sensitivity to CO_2.

3.2 Effects of Stomatal Closure on Transpiration Rate and Leaf Temperature. As stomatal conductance decreases in response to increased CO_2, transpiration decreases in proportion, provided the leaf temperature and the relative humidity of the air remain constant. However, since a reduction in transpiration tends to increase the leaf temperature, the water vapor pressure inside the leaf increases. As a consequence, transpiration rate is not reduced in direct proportion to the reduction in stomatal conductance. Under conditions where the energy load is high and the wind speed is low, stomatal closure can lead to a considerable increase in leaf temperature. In hot environments, this temperature increase could result in heat damage to the leaves.

4. Effects of Increased CO_2 on Water Use Efficiency. For each molecule of CO_2 gained, the leaf loses several hundred molecules of water through the same diffusion path. The ratio of the CO_2 taken up in photosynthesis to the water lost in transpiration may be termed photosynthetic water use efficiency. This ratio changes during the course of a day because of changes in environmental conditions. The ratio is greatly influenced by stomatal conductance, as is illustrated in Figure 7. Water use efficiency may also be expressed in terms of the amount of biomass gained per amount of water lost over a period of time. Either expression for water use efficiency may be integrated over a whole season. Where water supply is not abundant, the seasonal growth of plants must represent some kind of compromise between the minimization of transpiration from the plant and the maximization of photosynthesis. Primary productivity is the product of the water use efficiency and the amount of water transpired, integrated over the whole growing season; in water-limited environments an increase in water use efficiency will thus be reflected in increased productivity.

At the leaf level, the direct stimulatory effects of high CO_2 concentration on photosynthesis in C_3 species increases photosynthetic water use efficiency. In contrast, if stomatal conductance, and therefore transpiration, do not change, C_4 species would not be expected to enjoy a significant boost in photosynthetic water use efficiency. Conversely, if stomatal conductance decreases in response to increases in CO_2, then transpiration would

Table 1. Response of leaf photosynthesis, leaf conductance and photosynthetic water use efficiency to growth under increased CO_2 concentrations.

	CO_2 Concentration ppm	Photosynthesis μmol m^{-2}s^{-1}	Ratio	Leaf Conductance mmol m^{-2}s^{-1}	Ratio	Water Use Efficiency mmol CO_2/mol H_2O	Ratio
Nerium oleander (C$_3$)[2]	660	35.9	1.48	200	.77	2.7	1.95
	330	24.2		261		1.4	
Gossypium Hirsutum (C$_3$)[2]	640	51.1	1.50	390	.79	6.4	1.87
	330	34.2		495		3.4	
Zea mays (C$_4$)[3]	640	65.3	1.23	260	.67	12.5	1.86
	330	53.0		390		6.7	

[1] All measurements were made at the growth CO_2 concentration, a photon flux density of 2000 μeinstein m^{-2}s^{-1} and 30 C leaf temperatures.

[2] From Downton et al. (1981). The water use efficiencies are normalized to a vapor pressure difference between the leaf and the air of 15 mbar.

[3] From Wong (1979). The water use efficiencies are normalized to a vapor pressure difference of 20 mbar.

decrease and the photosynthetic water use efficiency of both C_3 and C_4 plants would increase.

Since stomatal conductance generally declines with increasing CO_2 concentration in both C_3 and C_4 species, both will experience an increase in photosynthetic water use efficiency via reduced transpiration, and hence an increase in growth under conditions of limited water. This is shown in Table 1 for plants grown in enriched CO_2 atmospheres. For the two C_3 species, photosynthesis was stimulated by 50%, while at the same time leaf conductances declined by nearly 25%. As a consequence, photosynthetic water use efficiency nearly doubled in the enriched CO_2 atmosphere as compared to the normal atmosphere. For the C_4 species, the increase in photosynthesis was much smaller, but the conductance declined by 33% so that overall photosynthetic water use efficiency nearly doubled. Nevertheless, in a mixed community of C_3 and C_4 species, increased CO_2 concentration is likely to benefit C_3 species most, if they can take advantage of the extra available water.

Changes in photosynthetic water use efficiencies can be analyzed by considering the intercellular CO_2 concentration, since it reflects the interrelationships between photosynthetic rate and stomatal conductance. Photosynthetic water use efficiency is closely related to C_i as can be seen by dividing the equation of CO_2 transport across the epidermis of single leaves,

$$P = (C_a - C_i)\, g \qquad (1)$$

by the equation for water vapor transport

$$T = (1.6\, \delta W)\, g \qquad (2)$$

to give
$$P/T = (C_a - C_i)/(1.6\, \delta W) \qquad (3)$$

where g is the leaf conductance to CO_2, C_a and C_i are the ambient and intercellular concentrations of CO_2, respectively, and δW is the concentration difference for water vapor between the intercellular spaces and the atmosphere. The factor 1.6 is the ratio of the diffusivities of water vapor and CO_2 in air. Rearranging (3) we get:

$$P/T = \frac{C_a}{\frac{(1 - C^i/C^a)}{1.6\, \delta W}} \qquad (4)$$

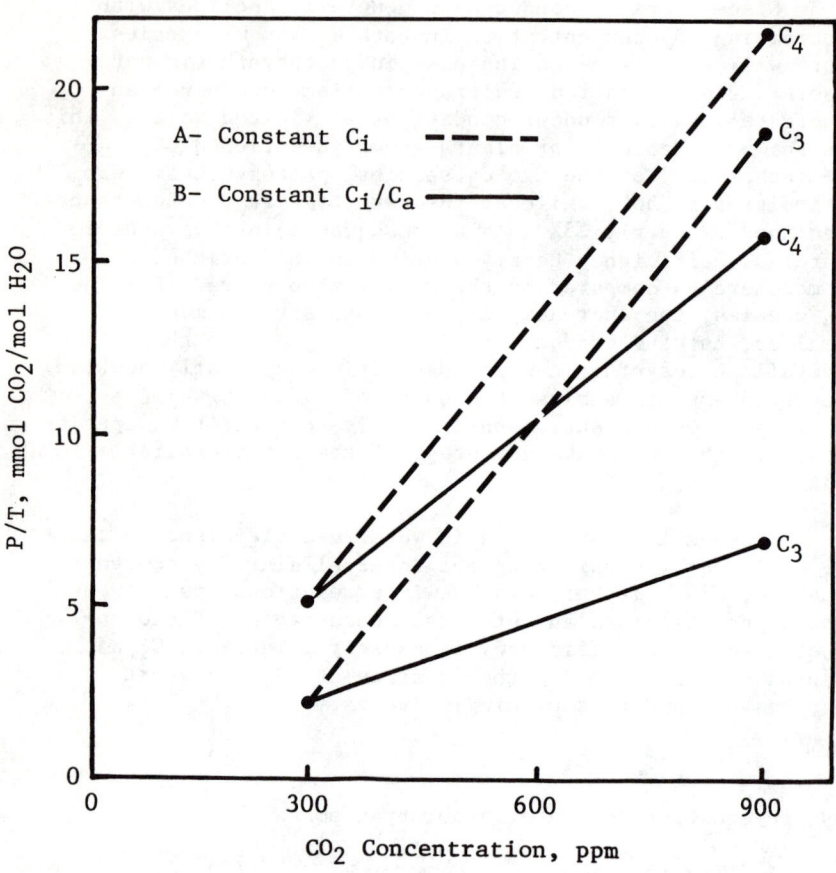

Figure 8.   Response of photosynthetic water use efficiency
(P/T) in C_3 and C_4 plants assuming (A), a constant C_i of 240
ppm in C_3 plants and 120 ppm in C_4 plants, or (B) a constant
C_i/C_a of 0.72 in C_3 plants and 0.36 in C_4 plants.   The
responses are calculated for a vapor concentration gradient
of 25 mmol mol^{-1}.

Thus, if C_i/C_a remains constant as sometimes occurs in both C_3 and C_4 species, than at constant temperature and humidity, P/T is proportional to C_a for both C_3 and C_4 species.

Since C_i/C_a is lower in C_4 species, the constant of proportionality $(1 - C_i/C_a)$ in (4) may be two or more times larger than for a C_3 species, indicating that the absolute improvement of water use efficiency of C_4 species may be even greater than that for C_3 species, even when the increase in CO_2 concentration is over the range in which C_4 photosynthesis does not respond to increased CO_2 concentration (Figure 8). If so, then under water-limited condtions the CO_2 enhancement of growth in C_4 species may be greater than in C_3 species. If instead the stomata respond to maintain C_i constant, then the photosynthetic water use efficiencies of both C_3 and C_4 plants will increase in parallel (Figure 8). The photosynthetic water use efficiency of C_4 plants will always be higher, but the relative improvement will be much greater for C_3 plants. Thus, with increasing CO_2 concentration, the photosynthetic water use efficiencies of both C_3 and C_4 species are likely to increase, but the relative improvements will depend strongly on how stomata respond and, consequently, C_i respond. This analysis also shows that environmental factors that infuence C_i/C_a will have a strong effect on the responses of photosynthetic water use efficiency to increasing CO_2 concentration, and that species differences in reponse to these factors will be important.

Predictions based on the responses to increased CO_2 at the single leaf and single plant level indicate that increased CO_2 concentration will substantially increase the amount of biomass produced per water expended. It follows that increased CO_2 concentration should substantially increase plant productivity wherever water supply exerts an important limitation to growth, and especially in arid and semiarid regions. Experimental results on the effect of increased CO_2 on water use efficiency and water-linked growth under water limited conditions in the field are still lacking, however.

5. Effects of Increased CO_2 Concentration on Plant Water Status. Increases in CO_2 may affect plant water status by several means. With reductions in stomatal conductance and in transpiration from single leaves, the gradient of water potential, ψ, driving the water flow from soil to leaves should be less, provided resistance in the soil and in the plant to liquid water flow does not change. Consequently, at any given soil water status, ψ would be raised through-

out the plant, particularly in leaves. Since organic
solutes, especially sugars of phtosynthetic origin (Acevedo
et al., 1979), constitute a major fraction of osmotic
substances in cells, increases in photosynthesis under high
CO_2 may lead to more concentrated osmotica and hence lower
(more negative) solute or osmotic potential, π, in cells.
For a given tissue ψ, lower values of π will mean higher
tissue water content or turgor.

Sionit et al. (1981a) found that wheat plants grown at
increased CO_2 concentrations had a lower leaf π than those
grown at normal CO_2 concentrations. Moreover, as water
stress developed, leaf ψ declined less steeply in the
plants grown under increased CO_2 concentrations. They
interpreted these responses as indicative of better adaptation to water stress and turgor maintenance under high
CO_2. Other studies are needed before a general assessment
of the effects of increase CO_2 on plant water status can
be made.

**6. Effects of Increased CO_2 on Utilization of Photosyn-
thetic Products.** The preceding sections show how carbon
dioxide enrichment stimulates net phtosynthetic CO_2 uptake
by leaves, reduces the rate of individual leaf transpiration rate through reduction in stomatal conductance, and
influences plant water status. The expression of these
very short-term reponses can either be amplified or
attenuated by other physiological and environmental
factors. Here we consider how leaf growth and canopy
development, and how allocation of photosynthetic products
interact and influence the translation of the leaf
photosynthetic and transpiration responses to increased
CO_2 into growth of the whole plant.

6.1 Leaf Expansion. An improved water status of a leaf
under increased CO_2 may increase the rate of leaf expansion
and ultimately the rate of canopy development. In the
short-term, the irreversible expansive growth of a leaf
cell depends on the supply of growth substrates and solute
molecules and of the absorption of enough water to maintain
the turgor pressure necessary to expand the cell. The ease
with which a cell expands at any given turgor pressure is
indicated by its gross extensibility, E_g, a coefficient
largely determined by synthesis and metabolism in the cell,
particularly that of the cell wall. The transport of water
into the cell depends on the hydraulic conductivity of the
tissue and the water potential gradient between the cell
and the xylem.

$$dV/Vdt = [E_gC/(-E_g+C)]\,|\psi\,\text{xylem}-\pi-P_{th}]$$

where dV/Vdt is the rate of cell growth, ψ xylem is the xylem water potential, V is the cell volume, P_{th} is the threshold turgor below which no cell expansion occurs, and π is the osmotic or solute potential of the expanding cell (Bradford and Hsiao, 1982). Assuming that the hydraulic conductivity, C, and threshold turgor, P_{th}, of the expanding tissue are not changed by increased CO_2, then the increased rate of cell expansion would be due to changes in E_g, and/or ψ xylem.

Since increased CO_2 concentrations probably lead to improved plant water status and an increase in ψ xylem, as well as to an increased supply of photosynthetic products, rates of leaf expansive growth should be increased.

There are no published studies of rates of leaf expansion under increased CO_2. However, mean individual leaf area and total canopy leaf area of C_3 species generally increased with increased CO_2 when other factors such as nutrients were not limiting (e.g., Wong, 1979; Sionit et. al., 1981b). In one case, leaf area index was not altered by CO_2 enrichment when wheat was grown under high light, but was enhanced under low light (Gifford, 1977). Since the leaf area index exceeded 10 under high light, it is possible that assimilate allocation was altered by dense mutual shading of leaves, and hence leaf growth was not enhanced. The response of growth to high CO_2 has been studied in only a few C_4 species. In one case (Wong, 1979), maize leaf area was not increased significantly by CO_2 enrichment, although dry matter production was enhanced slightly. In other studies, significant enhancement in leaf area was observed in maize and another C_4 species (Imai and Marata, 1978; Rogers et. al., 1980).

6.2 Canopy Development. The growth of leaves is most important in determining productivity when the canopy is incomplete and a substantial portion of the incident light is not intercepted by the plant. In this situation, canopy development and biomass accumulation are approximately exponential. That is, the rates follow first-order kinetics and are proportional to the existing canopy size or biomass. Because of this exponential behavior, any effect of CO_2 elevation on leaf growth will be compounded or amplified with time (Bradford and Hsiao, 1982), such that a small increase in the instantaneous growth rate lasting over a period of weeks will result in a much larger canopy at the end. Small changes in the partitioning of photosynthetic products between the leaves and other organs can be similarly amplified with time, as long as the canopy is substantially incomplete.

Faster canopy development in elevated CO_2 increases not only canopy CO_2 uptake, but also canopy transpiration. Nevertheless, increased CO_2 concentration should still have a beneficial effect on water use efficiency. Under water-limiting conditions where canopy closure does not occur, one can expect a diversity of responses to higher CO_2, depending on the pattern of rainfall, soil storage capacity for water, and behavior of a particular species. With agricultural species, if rainfall is light but generally well spread through the season, increases in CO_2 can be only beneficial. The size of the canopy will increase in relation to the water available for transpiration and late rains will ensure the completion of the growth cycle. However, one may speculate that if rainfall is scarce in the middle and late part of the season, and the water stored in the soil is ample for early growth but insufficient later, accelerated canopy development by increased CO_2 could prematurely exhaust the stored water.

6.3 Allocation of Photosynthetic Products. Growth depends on the export of photosynthetic products from source leaves to growing regions, "sinks," of the plants. Studies of a number of species show that export from leaf sources increases linearly with increased net CO_2 uptake produced by high light, by low oxygen and by high carbon dioxide (Servaites and Geiger, 1974; Ho, 1976). There are several processes that can control the allocation of photosynthetic products within the leaf and thus influence export from the leaf. These processes include: 1) partitioning of photosynthetic carbon between starch and sucrose; 2) the inter- and intracellular compartmentation of sucrose; and 3) the transfer of sucrose to the phloem, and loading into the sieve tubes which carry the sugar to sinks. As a consequence, the plant has several potential sites which can process the extra fixed carbon resulting from an increase in CO_2 concentration. For example, some species accumulate large amounts of starch which may be mobilized, either at night or at a later developmental stage (Ho, 1978; Allen et al., unpublished data; Giaquinta, 1980; Wong, unpublished data). Presumably, these processes will accommodate the increment of photosynthetic products with more CO_2.

Partitioning of carbon between starch and sucrose appears to be a particularly effective means of controlling carbon export from leaves. Within a daily cycle, this allocation can be influenced by photosynthetic duration and rate as well as a change in demand for products by the sinks (Silvius et al., 1979). A higher proportion of newly fixed carbon is exported from leaves that have higher photosynthesis rates under elevated CO_2. Presumably, increased export under high CO_2 results from the greater carbohydrate concentrations observed in these leaves (Ho, 1976; Allen et al., unpublished data; Geiger, unpublished data). The capacity to load sucrose into sieve tubes does not appear to exert a limitation on export from leaves since loading continues to increase even when the sucrose concentrations in the extracellular solution, from which phloem absorbs solutes, are higher than those encountered in vivo (Sononick et al., 1974). Thus, it appears that sucrose availability rather than phloem loading capacity is often the major determinant of export to growing organs.

Translocation of photosynthetic products, as well as of nutrient ions and endogenous growth regulators, is important in generating new sinks. Consequently, the development of new sinks generally accompanies enhanced photosynthetic production under higher CO_2, although the precise mechanisms are not known. If new sinks are not generated, leaf photosynthesis may decrease and the short-term photosynthetic enhancement by increased CO_2 will be reduced. The exact mechanism of this interaction between photosynthesis and sink demand is not known. A number of workers attribute the phenomenon to physically disruptive effects of starch accumulation (see Kramer, 1981, for a review) but the mechanism is probably not so direct or simple (Geiger, 1976; Hickleton and Jolliffe, 1980).

Allocation of photosynthetic products to sucrose appears to be closely regulated. Recent evidence suggests that sucrose phosphate synthetase, the enzyme that catalyzes sucrose formation in leaves, differs in regulatory properties and amount, between species that incorporate a greater percentage of new carbon into starch versus those that partition more into sucrose (Huber, 1981a, 1981b; Silvius et al., 1979). The regulation of this enzyme, for example, might be an important factor in the build-up of starch in the leaves of some species when grown under increased CO_2 concentration.

Increased CO_2 concentration generally increases both biomass and economic yield. One effect occurs simply because of greater overall size, since the harvest index (ratio of economic yield to the above ground mass of the plant) remains relatively constant (Rogers et al., unpublished; Havelka and Hardy, 1976; Gifford, 1977). For example, with wheat, enhanced yield occurs through more tillering (branching), each extra tiller eventually bearing an ear (Gifford, 1977, 1979a; Sionit et al., 1981a, 1981b), such that harvest index and individual kernel size is scarcely changed. Similarly, the high-CO_2-mediated yield increase in soybeans occurs mainly by an increase in pod and seed number, rather than seed size (Hardy and Havelka, 1976). This constancy of seed size, even under increased supply of photosynthetic carbon, suggests that sieve tube unloading or utilization within individual seeds may be limiting or controlled. Therefore, sites for short-term storage along the translocation path or in the pod wall are needed pending remobilization to the seeds (Thorne, 1979).

The timing of the increased supply of photosynthetic products is important to reproductive growth. In small grain cereals, where pre-anthesis supply is a determinant of seed number, elevated CO_2 can produce higher yields. In wheat, a higher grain yield is realized if increased supply of photosynthetic products extends from pre-anthesis through grain filling (Gifford et al., 1973; Havelka et al., 1980), whereas in soybeans the supply of photosynthetic products during seed filling appears most critical (Havelka et al., 1981).

Another effect appears to be a morphogenetic one in which the time of flower initiation or the initial rate of floral development is accelerated or decelerated by higher CO_2 (e.g. Hesketh and Hellmers, 1973; Marc and Gifford, unpublished data).

Although it is not self-evident from consideration of individual physiological processes, the composite result of these physiological responses to an increased supply of photosynthetic products is that plant parts generally increase in size to a similar relative degree. The two most important partitioning parameters for whole plants and crop stands -- root/shoot ratio and harvest index -- are scarcely affected by higher atmospheric CO_2.

7. Interaction of Increased CO_2 with Nutrient Supply. Plant responses to increasing CO_2 when other nutrients are limiting depends on the nature of those limitations and whether additional CO_2 assimilation will increase the availability of those limiting nutrients. Data relating N availability to plant growth and carbohydrate content indicate that under N-limiting conditions, stored carbohydrates accumulate (Alberda, 1965; Dorvat et al., 1972; Williams et al., 1981; Wilson, 1975). Therefore, it is doubtful that stimulating even more carbohydrates to accumulate by increasing the CO_2 assimilation rate will increase crop production in the longer term unless more nutrients become available. If additional carbon substrate is supplied, one must ask whether optimum amounts of other available mineral nutrients will be obtained by the plant.

Some data relating N assimilation and CO_2 levels are available (Hardy and Havelka, 1975; Quebedeaux et al., 1975; Sheehy et al., 1980; Williams et al., 1981, 1982), but there are no published studies on assimilation of phosphorus, sulfur, or other nutrients under various CO_2 regimes.

Ideally, one should understand the effect of increased CO_2 on rates of nutrient uptake and subsequent metabolism. In the case of soil N, however, only N concentration values have been reported from CO_2-enrichment experiments. Maize (Wong, 1979) showed little effect of increased CO_2 on N concentration, but cotton (Wong, 1979) and soybean seedlings (Williams et al., 1981) had much lower percent N values under increased CO_2. Further examination of the data obtained from cotton shows that although the leaves accumulated starch, and therefore had an altered C/N ratio, the N/leaf area ratio was unchanged by increased CO_2. The decreases in tissue N concentration under elevated CO_2 occurred in the presence of high concentrations of external N (16-24mM), and in soybean seedlings was associated with starch accumulation. Growth of Nerium oleander plants at 660 ppm as compared with 330 ppm CO_2 had no effect on the leaf protein content on a leaf weight basis but caused a significant increase on a leaf area basis. On the other hand, Atriplex triangularis plants grown under the same conditions had lower leaf protein content on both a leaf weight and a leaf area basis under 660 ppm compared to under 330 ppm CO_2 (Downton et al., 1980).

These observations suggest that in some plants, high levels of CO_2 produce an imbalance of N assimilation relative to the normal concentrations of N accumulated under ambient CO_2. The effects of such "unbalanced" growth on quality of agronomic yields and seed viability are not known, and the occurrence and possible effects of long-term "unbalanced" growth in perennial plants have not been examined.

It has been suggested that symbiotic N_2 fixation by Rhizobium bacteria in legumes is limited by the supply of photosynthetic products (Hardy and Havelka, 1975; Wilson et al., 1933). Total N content and the rate of apparent N_2 assimilation, measured as C_2H_2 reduction, increased with long-term CO_2 enrichment (Quebedeaux et al., 1975; Phillips et al., 1976). The N concentration in mature Rhizobium infected soybeans was similar under normal and elevated CO_2 conditions (Quebedeaux et al., 1975). Limitation on N_2 fixation by the supply of photosynthetic products could be associated either with a low photosynthetic rate or with inefficient transport of photosynthetic products to root nodules. Support for the first possibility comes from the fact that short-term exposure to elevated CO_2 levels (6–12 hour) increased C_2H_2-reduction rates in peas (Phillips et al., 1976) and young alfalfa plants (Sheehy et al., 1980). One interpretation is that increased amounts of photosynthetic products formed under the elevated CO_2 were translocated to root nodules where an excess N_2-fixation capacity was activated. In soybeans and older alfalfa plants, however, varying the shoot CO_2-exchange rate 800% by increasing ambient CO_2 concentration from 100 to 1200 ppm, produced little change in the maximum C_2H_2-reduction rate measured during 24 hours. These results suggest either that there is no unused N_2 fixation capacity in those plants or that the additional photosynthetic products formed under higher CO_2 were not partitioned to the root nodules.

In a more comprehensive test for unused N_2-fixation capacity in soybeans, the photosynthetic rate was increased for 10 hours with 1000 ppm CO_2 at weekly intervals for 7 weeks after planting (Williams et al., 1982). Neither root-plus-nodule respiration nor C_2H_2-reduction activity increased significantly during the treatments under increased CO_2 concentration, thus suggesting that additional photosynthetic products were not translocated immediately to the root system. Prolonging the treatment with increased CO_2 concentration had a significant effect on total root-plus-nodule respiration, and C_2H_2 reduction after 5 days, but those results reflected an increase in root nodule mass.

Reported interactions between N assimilation and CO_2 treatments must be examined carefully because many investigators have used nutrient solutions containing much higher N concentrations than the 2 mM level often measured in soil solutions. Wong (1979) published a useful study of cotton and maize grown at two levels of CO_2 with four N concentrations. Comparing the relative dry weights of plants grown at 0.6 mM N under normal and elevated CO_2 levels with those of plants grown under normal CO_2 on 12 mM N indicates that maize grown with 0.6 mM N and 330 ppm CO_2 was primarily N-limited, while cotton grown under the same conditions was limited nearly equally by the availability of NO_3^- and CO_2. With 4mM N available to both cotton and maize, increased CO_2 concentration increased relative dry weight more than with 12 mM N.

Response differences between species may be important, but plant age can also be an important factor. Growth of soybean seedlings supplied with <u>Rhizobium</u> plus zero or 2 mM N in the presence of 320 or 1000 ppm CO_2 clearly was more N-limited than C-limited when compared with plants given 16 mM N (Williams et al., 1981). In contrast, additional CO_2 given to older soybean plants during reproductive growth increased dry weight (Hardman and Brun, 1971; Hardy and Havelka, 1975) and total N, but N fertilization normally has little effect at the same developmental stage. Such observations are consistent with the concept that N availability is especially important while young plants first form a photosynthetic canopy but less important when most of the foliage has been formed. How plants maintain reasonable C/N ratios in tissue as they pass from N-limited to C-limited growth is poorly understood.

8. Remarks on "Limiting" Factors and Responses to Increased CO_2.

It seems to be a common misinterpretation of the so-called 'law of limiting factors' to assume that when the supply of other resources such as water, light, or nitrogen are suboptimal to photosynthesis and growth, increased atmospheric CO_2 will not have much effect. While the stimulation by increased CO_2 may be smaller in absolute terms, it may indeed be greater in relative terms. We have seen that more CO_2 is very likely to increase productivity in water limited environments by increasing the water use efficiency. Indeed, for wheat, at the limit where conditions were too dry to permit grain formation, higher CO_2 permitted some grain to develop, representing an infinite relative enhancement of yield (Gifford, 1979a). At limiting light levels, increased CO_2 concentration may stimulate growth relatively more than under high light conditions (Gifford, 1979). The phenomenon is known to horticulturalists as the 'mutually compensating effect' of CO_2 and light (Hopen and Ries, 1962). This beneficial effect of increased CO_2 concentration on growth at limiting light levels is caused by an increased quantum yield of net photosyntehsis (Ehleringer and Björkman, 1977).

With the possibility that increased CO_2 permits a reduction of nitrogen investment in the phtosynthetic machinery, it is not surprising that the percent stimulation of growth by increased CO_2 concentration was just as great with severely N-deficient cotton plants, compared to plants adequately supplied with nitrogen (Wong, 1979).

In conclusion, on the basis of our present limited information on basic physiological responses to higher CO_2, we can expect an enhanced plant productivity of C_3 plants in most environments. The relative enhancement is likely to be greater in warm than in cold climates. The greatest

enhancement is likely to occur in areas where productivity
is limited by water supply, and especially in the warmer
arid and semi-arid regions of the earth. In nutrient-poor
environments where productivity is primarily limited by the
availability of nitrogen, phosphorous, or other essential
nutrients, a substantial enhancement of productivity in
response to increased CO_2 would only be realized if
nutrient availability also increases. For C_4 species,
significant increases in productivity may occur only under
conditions where water supply is the primary limiting
factor.

9. Areas of Ignorance. The preceding sections of this
chapter have identified many physiological responses to
increased CO_2 concentration, both primary and secondary.
Almost all of these responses have been investigated only
in short-term experiments. In this section, we identify
key areas in which much more knowledge is required if we
are to obtain a sound basis for predicting the response of
plants to long term effects of more CO_2.

9.1 Leaf Photosynthesis. We have very limited information
on the long-term effects of increasing CO_2 on photosynthetic capacity. The number and types of wild and cultivated species investigated so far is too small to permit
any generalizations regarding differential effects among
C_3, C_4, and CAM plants in environments with contrasting
light, salinity, temperature, and water availability. More
knowledge is necessary to predict the diversity of
responses of plants to increasing CO_2 and the implications
for productivity and changes in distributional limits.

There is some evidence that increased CO_2 alleviates
the deleterious effects of high temperature and drought on
growth of C_3 species. Does increased CO_2 also protect
against other stresses such as hypersalinity and high light
levels? In view of the common symptoms associated with
many stresses, is such a protective effect of CO_2 mediated
simply through increased photosynthesis or does increased
CO_2 exert other, direct protective effects?

There is some evidence that at current CO_2 concentrations, RuBP carboxylase capacity and RuBP regeneration
capacity may be co-limiting for photosynthesis. As CO_2
concentration increases, this balance may no longer
persist. We need a better understanding of how these two
capacities change in response to increasing CO_2, and how
species or cultivars may differ in their response. This
would provide a better basis for predicting species and
varietal differences in response to increased CO_2

concentration and for genetic and other modification of
potentially rate limiting steps.

9.2 Stomatal Response and Water Use Efficiency.   There is
great variability in the stomatal responses to CO_2 among
species and within species depending on growth conditions.
We lack systematic knowledge of these responses and of the
interactions with other environmental factors such as
light, humidity, and water stress. Consequently, we cannot
make reliable predictions of the effects of a CO_2 increase
on CO_2 supply to the leaf, water use, or leaf temperature.
More knowledge would enable us to predict the guard cell
responses to increased CO_2. CO_2 may control the anion
transport system in guard cells involving active transport
of H^+. CO_2 may also directly or indirectly affect other H^+
coupled transfer mechanisms, such as phloem loading,
sucrose storage, ion uptake by roots, ion transfer causing
leaf movement, and solute transport into expanding cells.

The mechanism responsible for the observed coordination between photosynthetic capacity and stomatal conductance is unknown. More knowledge is necessary to understand
the integration of stomatal and photosynthetic responses to
increased CO_2. The mode of stomatal response to increased
CO_2 concentrations is of paramount importance since it
determines the amount of CO_2 assimilated per amount of
water transpired.

We lack the information necessary to reliably extrapolate single leaf measurements of photosynthesis and
transpiration to canopy level responses. As a consequence,
we are unble to make quantitative predictions of canopy
water use efficiency in response to increased CO_2.

9.3 Leaf and Canopy Growth.   Increased CO_2 levels can
increase the rate of leaf expansion resulting in larger
cells and larger leaves. It is not clear whether this
response is due to increased supply of photosynthetic
products, improved plant water status, or some other
factor. A mechanistic understanding of leaf expansion and
the influence of more CO_2 on plant water relations would
yield a better prediction of leaf expansion responses to
higher CO_2 in different environments.

At the canopy level, the mechanisms controlling rates
of leaf production and the total canopy expansion are
poorly understood. Under elevated CO_2, increased
photosynthesis and faster canopy growth may be accompanied
by faster total rate of water use. In many agricultural
situations, the timing of canopy growth and water use may

be critical and faster canopy growth due to elevated CO_2 may not always be desirable. We need to know how to control canopy growth rate of cropping systems to maximize yield by matching canopy development with seasonal patterns of water supply.

9.4 Photosynthate Allocation. Although available evidence suggests that the relative proportions of plant organs stay approximately constant with more CO_2, the generality of this remains to be established. To the extent that it is general, we need to know how constancy of relative allocation patterns is determined in order to better exploit the incremental growth for economic yield under CO_2 enrichment.

The timing of developmental events in crop plants is critical to economic yield. We need to know how higher CO_2 influences these events. A mechanistic understanding of these events and processes and their responses to CO_2 should lead to methods for better deployment of photosynthetic products for growth and yield.

Photosynthetic activity and product utilization by harvestable organs are integrated. Identification and appropriate manipulation of these integrated processes should lead to an increased harvest index with increasing CO_2.

9.5 Nutrient Limitations. The increased carbon gain associated with elevated atmospheric CO_2 should increase the amount of carbon relative to other essential elements in plant tissue. We do not know which elements will become most limiting as growth and photosynthesis increase in response to higher CO_2. In general, macronutrients, such as N, P, or S, could be among the first limiting factors, but micronutrient deficiencies could also be important. We should know if additional photosynthetic products will be used by the plant to increase nutrient availability through changes in the root/shoot ratio, enchancement of mycorrhizal associations, or other possible mechanisms.

10. Literature Cited

Acevedo, E., E. Fereres, T.C. Hsiao, and D.W. Henderson. 1979. Growth trends, water potential and osmotic adjustment of maize and sorghum leaves in the field. Plant Physiol. 64, 476–480.

Akita, S. and D.N. Moss. 1972. Differential stomatal response between C_3 and C_4 species to atmospheric CO_2 concentration and light. Crop Sci. 13, 234–237.

Alberda, T. 1965. The influence of temperature, light intensity and nitrate concentration on dry-matter production and chemical composition of Lolium perenne L. Neth. J. Agric. Sci. 13, 335-360.

Berry, J.A. and G.D. Farquhar. 1978. The CO_2 concentrating function of photosynthesis: A biochemical model. In D. Hall, J. Coombs and T. Goodwin, Eds., Proc. Fourth International Congress on Photosynthesis, pp. 119-131.

Berry, J.A. and J.K. Raison. 1981. Responses of macrophytes to temperature. In O.L. Lange, P.S. Nobel, C.B. Osmond, and H. Ziegler, Eds., Encyclopedia of Plant Physiology, Vol. 12A, Springer-Verlag, Berlin, pp. 277-338.

Björkman, O. 1966. The effect of oxygen concentration on photosynthesis in higher plants. Physiol. Plant 19, 618-633.

Björkman, O. 1981. Responses to different quantum flux densities. In O.L. Lange, P.S. Nobel, C.B. Osmond, and H. Ziegler, Eds., Encyclopedia of Plant Physiology New Series, Vol. 12A, Springer-Verlag, Berlin. pp. 57-107.

Bradford, K.J. and T.C. Hsiao. 1982. Physiological responses to moderate water stress. In O.L. Lange, P.S. Nobel, C.B. Osmond, and H. Ziegler, Eds., Encyclopedia of Plant Physiology, New Series, Vol. 12B, Springer-Verlag, Berlin, (in press).

Cooke, J.R. and R.H. Rand. 1980. Diffusion resistance models. In J.D. Hesketh and J.W. Jones, Eds., Predicting Photosynthesis for Ecosystem Models, Vol. 1. CRC Press, Boca Raton, Florida, pp. 93-122.

Caemmerer, S. von and G.D. Farquhar. 1981. Some relationships between the biochemistry of photosyntheisis and the gas exchange of leaves. Planta 376-387.

Davidson, R.L. 1969. Effects of soil nutrients and moisture on root/shoot ratio in Lolium perenne L. and Trifolium repens L. Ann. Bot. 33, 571-577.

Dovrat, A., B. Deinum and J.G.P. Dirven. 1972. The influence of defoliation and nitrogen on the regrowth of Rhodes grass (Chloris gayana Kunth). 2. Etiolated growth and non-structural carbohydrate, total-N and nitrate-N content. Neth. J. Agric. Sci. 20, 97-103.

Downton, W.J.S., O. Björkman and C. Pike. 1980. Consequences of increased atmospheric concentrations of carbon dioxide for growth and photosynthesis of higher plants. In G.I. Pearman, Ed., Carbon Dioxide and Climate: Australian Research. Aust. Acad. of Sci., Canberra, pp. 143-153.

Drake, B.G. and K. Raschke. 1974. Prechilling of Xanthium strumarium reduces net photosynthesis and, independently, stomatal conductance, while sensitizing the stomata to CO_2. Plant Physiol. 53, 808-812.

Dubbe, D.D., G.D. Farquhar and K. Raschke. 1978. Effect of abscissic acid on the gain of the feedback loop involving carbon dioxide and stomata. Plant Physiol. 62, 413-417.

Ehleringer, J. and O. Björkman. 1977. Quantum yields for CO_2 uptake in C_3 and C_4 plants: dependence on temperature, CO_2 and O_2 uptake. Plant Physiol. 59, 86-90.

Farquhar, G.D., D.R. Dubbe and K. Raschke. 1978. Gain of the feedback loop involving carbon dioxide and stomata. Plant Physiol. 62, 406-412.

Farquhar, G.D. and T.D. Sharkey. 1982. Stomatal conductance and photosynthesis. Ann. Rev. Plant Physiol. 33, 317-345.

Farquhar, G.D. and S. von Caemmerer. 1982. Modelling of photosynthetic response to environmental conditions. In O.L. Lange, P.S. Nobel, C.B. Osmond and H. Ziegler, Eds., Encyclopedia of Plant Physiology, New Series, Vol. 12B, (in press).

Farquhar, G.D. and M.H. O'Leary, and J.A. Berry. 1982. On the relationship between carbon isotope discrimination and the intercellular carbon dioxide concentration in leaves. Aust. J. Plant Physiol. 9, 121-137.

Geiger, D.R. 1976. Effects of translocation and assimilate demand on photosynthesis. Can. J. Bot. 54, 2337-2345.

Giaquinta, R.T. 1980. Translocation of sucrose and oligosaccharides. In J. Preiss, Ed., Biochemistry of Plants Vol. 3. Academic Press, New York, pp. 271-319.

Gifford, R.M. 1977. Growth pattern, carbon dioxide exchange and dry weight distribution in wheat growing under differing photosynthetic environments. Aust. J. Plant Physiol. 4, 99–110.

Gifford, R.M. 1979. Carbon dioxide and plant growth under water and light stress: Implications for balancing the global carbon budget. Search 10, 316–318.

Gifford, R.M. 1979b. Growth and yield of CO_2 enriched wheat under water limited conditions. Aust. J. Plant Physiol. 6, 367–368.

Gifford, R.M., P.M. Bremmer, and D.B. Jones. 1973. Assessing photosynthetic limitations to grain yield in a field crop. Aust. J. Agric. Res. 24, 297–307.

Goudriaan, J. and H.H. van Laar. 1978. Relations between leaf resistance, CO_2 concentration and CO_2 assimilation in maize, beans, lalang grass and sunflower. Photosynthetica 12, 241–249.

Hardman, L.L. and W.A. Brun. 1971. Effect of atmospheric carbon dioxide enrichment at different developmental stages on growth and yield components of soybeans. Crop Sci. 11, 886–888.

Hardy, R.W.F. and U.D. Havelka. 1975. Nitrogen fixation research: A key to world food? Science 188, 633–643.

Havelka, U.D., M.G. Boyle and R.T. Giaquinta. 1981. Total dry matter yield and starch accumulation response of soybeans to canopy CO_2 enrichment applied at different growth stage. Agronomy Abst., p. 81.

Havelka, U.D. and R.W.F. Hardy. 1976. Legume N_2 fixation as a problem in carbon nutrition. Proc. First International Symp. Nitrogen Fixation, pp. 456–475. Washington State University Press, Pullman, Washington.

Havelka, U.D., V.A. Wittenbach and R.W.F. Hardy. 1980. Effects of CO_2 enrichment on grain yield, photosynthesis, RuBPase activity and leaf senescence of field-grown Arthur wheat. Agronomy Abst.

Hesketh, J.D. and H. Hellmers. 1973. Floral initiation in four plant species growing in CO_2 enriched air. Enviro. Control in Biol. 111, 51–53.

Hicklenton, P.R. and P.A. Jolliffe. 1980. Alterations in

102   *Pearcy and Björkman*

the physiology of CO_2 exchange in tomato plants grown in CO_2-enriched atmospheres. Can. J. Bot. 58, 2181–2189.

Ho, L.C. 1976. The relationship between the rates of carbon transport and photosynthesis in tomato leaves. J. Exp. Bot. 27, 87–97.

Ho, L.C. 1978. The regulation of carbon transport and the carbon balance of mature tomato leaves. Ann. Bot. 42, 155–164.

Hopen, H.J. and S.K. Ries. 1962. The mutually compensating effect of carbon dioxide concentrations and light intensities on the growth of Cumcumis sativas L., Proc. Amer. Soc. Hort. Sci. 81, 358–364.

Huber, S.C. 1981a. Inter- and intra-specific variation in photosynthetic formation of starch and sucrose. Z. Pflanzenphysiol. 101, 49–54.

Huber, S.C. 1981b. Interspecific variation in activity and regulation of leaf sucrose phosphate synthetase. Z. Pflanzenphysiol. 192, 443–450.

Huber, S.C. 1981b. Interspecific variation in activity and regulation of leaf sucrose phosphate synthetase. Z. Pflanzenphysiol. 192, 443–450.

Hurd, R.G. 1968. Effect of carbon dioxide enrichment on the growth of young tomato plants in low light. Ann. Bot. 32, 531–542.

Imai, K. and Y. Murata. 1978. Effect of carbon dioxide concentration on growth and dry matter production of crop plants. III. Relationship between CO_2 concentration and nitrogen nutrition in some C_3 and C_4 species. Japan. J. Crop. Sci. 47, 118–123.

Kramer, P.J. 1981. Carbon dioxide concentration, photosynthesis and dry matter production. Bioscience 31, 29–33.

Louwerse, W. 1980. Effect of CO_2 concentration and irradiance on the stomatal behavior of maize, barley and sunflower plants in the field. Plant Cell and Env. 3, 391–398.

Osmond, C.B. and O. Björkman. 1975. Pathways of CO_2 fixation in the CAM plant Kalanchoe diagremontiana.

II. Effects of O_2 and CO_2 concentration on light and dark fixation. Aust. J. Plant Physiol. 2, 155-162.

Osmond, C.B., O. Bjorkman and D.J. Anderson. 1980. Physiological processes in plant ecology. Toward a synthesis with Atriplex. Springer-Verlag, Berlin. 468 p.

Pearcy, R.W., N. Tumosa, and K. Williams. 1981. Relationships between growth, photosynthesis and competitive interactions for a C_3 and a C_4 plant. Oecologia 48, 371-376.

Phillips, D.A., K.D. Newell, S.A. Hassell, and C.E. Felling. 1976. The effect of CO_2 enrichment on root nodule development and symbiotic N_2 reduction in Pisum sativum L. Amer. J. Bot. 63, 356-362.

Quebedeaux, B., U.D. Havelka, J.L. Livak and R.W. Hardy. 1975. Effect of altered pO_2 in the aerial part of soybean on symbiotic N_2 fixation. Plant Physiol. 56, 761-764.

Raper, C.D. and G.F. Peedin. 1978. Photosynthetic rate during steady-state growth as influenced by carbon dioxide concentration. Bot. Gazette 139, 147-149.

Raschke, K. 1975. Simultaneous requirement of carbon dioxide and abscissic acid for stomatal closing in Xanthium strumarium L. Planta 125, 243-259.

Raschke, K. 1979. Movements of stomata. In W. Haupt and M. E. Feinlab, Eds., Encyclopedia of Plant Physiology, New Series 7, 383-441.

Rogers, H.H., G.E. Bingham, J.D. Cure, W.W. Heck, A.S. Heagle, D.W. Israel, J.M. Smith, K.A. Surano, and J.F. Thomas. 1980. Response of vegetation to carbon dioxide, 001: Field studies of plant response to elevated carbon dioxide. Progress Report, U.S. Dept. of Energy, Carbon Dioxide Research Division, Office of Energy Research, Washington, D.C. 20555.

Robichaux, R.H. and R.W. Pearcy. 1980. Photosynthetic responses of C_3 and C_4 species from cool shaded habitats in Hawaii. Oecologia 47, 106-109.

Servaites, J.C. and D.R. Geiger. 1974. Effects of light intensity and oxygen on photosynthesis in sugarbeet. Plant Physiol. 54, 575-578.

Sharkey, T.D. and K. Raschke. 1981. Separation and measurement of direct and indirect effects of light on stomata. Plant Physiol. 68, 33-40.

Sheehy, J.E., K.A. Fishbeck, T.M. DeJong, L.E. Williams, and D.A. Phillips. 1980. Carbon exchange rates of shoots required to utilize available acetylene reduction capacity in soybean and alfalfa root nodules. Plant Physiol. 66, 101-104.

Silvius, J.E., J.N. Chatterton and D.F. Kremer, 1979. Photosynthate partitioning in soybeans at two irradiance levels. Plant Physiol. 64, 872-875.

Sionit, N., B.R. Strain, H. Hellmers and P.J. Kramer. 1981a. Effects of atmospheric CO_2 concentration and water stress on water relations of wheat. Bot. Gaz. 142, 191-196.

Sionit, N., B.R. Strain and H. Hellers. 1981b. Effects of different concentrations of atmospheric CO_2 on growth and yield components of wheat. J. Agric. Sci. 79, 335-339.

Sovonick, S.A., D.R. Geiger and R.J. Fellows. 1974. Evidence for active phloem loading in the minor veins of sugarbeet. Plant physiol. 54, 886-891.

Thorne, J.H. 1979. Assimilate redistribution from soybean pod walls during seed development. Agron. J. 71, 812-816.

Williams, L.E., T.M. DeJong and D.A. Phillips. 1981. Carbon and nitrogen limitations on soybean seedling development. Plant Physiol. 68, 1206-1209.

Williams, L.E., T.M. DeJong and D.A. Phillips. 1982. Effect of changes in shoot carbon-exchange rate on soybean root nodule activity. Plant Physiol. 69, (in press).

Wilson, J.R. 1975. Influence of temperature and nitrogen on growth, photosynthesis and accumulation of nonstructural carbohydrate in a tropical grass, Panicum maximum var. trichoglume. Neth. J. Agric. Sci. 23, 48-61.

Wilson, P.W., E.B. Fred and M.R. Salmon. 1933. Relation between carbon dioxide and elemental nitrogen assimilation in leguminous plants. Soil Science 35, 145-163.

Wong, S.C. 1979. Elevated atmospheric partial pressure of
CO$_2$ and plant growth, I. Interactions of nitrogen
nutrition and photosynthetic capacity in C$_3$ and C$_4$
plants. Oecologia 44, 68-74.

Wong, S.C., I.K. Cowan and G.D. Farquhar. 1978. Leaf
conductance in relation to assimilation in Eucalyptus
pauciflora: Influence of irradiance and partial
pressure of carbon dioxide. Plant Physiol. 62,
670-674.

Wong, S.C., I.K. Cowan and G.D. Farquhar. 1979. Stomatal
conductance correlates with photosynthetic capacity.
Nature 282, 424-426.

Donald N. Baker, Chairman
Herbert Zvi Enoch, Co-Chairman

5. Plant Growth and Development

Panel Members: B. Acock, Rapporteur, R.B. Austin, K.J.
Boote, R. Desjardins, R.R. Eddleman, N. Frey, J. Gale,
J. Goudriaan, G.H. Heichel, B.A. Kimball, P.J. Kramer,
R.S. Loomis, J.R. Mauney, N. Sionit.

SUMMARY AND RECOMMENDATIONS

The growth and development responses of most terrestrial plants to more CO_2 cannot be determined from
information available now. The patterns and levels of
stresses in the natural biosphere simply have not been
duplicated in the laboratory. Only a few species and
cultivars have been tested and there is great genetic
diversity in the primary, secondary, and tertiary
effects of CO_2 on plants. For example, there are almost
no data, anywhere, that can be used to assess what more CO_2
will do to whole mature trees (Kramer 1981). Somewhat more
is known of agricultural and horticultural crops, but not
in stressed environments.

Quantitative information on integrative and cumulative
effects can only be gained by experiment when whole plants
are grown from seed to maturity, and by mathematical simulation of whole plant growth. Both approaches are needed, the
former to gain real information on major genotypes, the
latter to provide the ability to extrapolate to the nearly
infinite number of combinations of genotypes, soils, climate
zones, weather patterns, etc.

We recommend that the following specific items be
investigated simultaneously:

1) Considerable data exist on short term leaf photosynthetic
responses to CO_2. There is a lack of agreement between

these and whole crop canopy responses under long term enrichment. Reasons for this disagreement should be
identified.

2) Experiments are needed to widen the genetic information
base on physiological process and whole plant
responses to CO_2.

3) The rules of dry matter partitioning in various species
require clarification. Mathematical tools should be used to
describe substrate source/sink imbalance effects on morphogenetic rates and organ abortion. Metabolic and hormonal
factors are important here.

4) The effects of temperature, tissue turgor, and mineral
nutrient supply on dry matter accretion should be characterized on an organ by organ basis.

5) The dynamics of seedling development relative to substrate supply should be worked out for the transition from
seed reserves to independent status under more CO_2.

6) The influence of more CO_2 on mineral nutrition is
important. Minimum N requirement for growth of each class
of organs is needed. The dynamics of storage and remobilization of N within plants should be described quantitatively.

Consequences for Agriculture: It is likely that rates of
fertilizer application will need to be increased to take
full advantage of a future CO_2-enriched atmosphere. If the
fertilizer is prohibitively expensive at that time, we may
see legumes becoming more important. Nitrogen is likely to
be the most limiting input.

It is probable that after canopy closure, high CO_2
crops will require less water. This will enable them to
grow with less rainfall or irrigation. Coupled with yield
increases, lower water use is likely to result in marked
increases in water use efficiency.

Because tubers benefit most of all from high CO_2, with
seeds a strong second, we may see changes in the types of
crops being grown. Also, because C_4 plants benefit less
from high CO_2 than C_3 plants, corn may be displaced from
its present position as the preeminent grain crop in the
United States. There are likely to be changes in the
cultivars grown to overcome problems like lodging, or the
excessive development of tillers on some winter wheat

cultivars. Dryland crops may exhaust their water supply earlier in the season due to enhanced early season growth.

Plant breeders will make adjustments to develop optimum genotypes for the new CO_2 environment. However, because the change in CO_2 concentration will be slow, they will be able to use their present methods for herbaceous plants. In trees, however, the lead time for producing a new genotype is long, and it will be necessary to start selecting trees immediately for a higher CO_2 environment.

Conclusions: A doubling of the global atmospheric CO_2 concentration will increase the rate of photosynthesis and therefore the amount of carbohydrate available for plant growth. In the absence of stresses, plant dry weight and yield will probably increase 33%. We expect that the effect of an enriched CO_2 atmosphere on crop yield under stress conditions will be much more variable, possibly ranging from some yield decrease, to very large (2-3 fold) increases. Stresses occurring during fruiting will probably be relatively more deleterious under high CO_2, although yield may not fall much below that in the present CO_2 atmosphere. High CO_2 will tend to alleviate water stress and salinity stress in many cases, but it will aggravate nitrogen stress. To be able to predict how plants in high CO_2 will react to field environments, with stresses varying in type, intensity, and timing throughout the season, we need more information on the mechanisms that control organ initiation and abortion, and dry matter partitioning. We also need to know the minimum mineral nutrient requirements for organ growth. This and other information about plant processes can be assembled and synthesized in the form of dynamic simulation models to evaluate the cumulative effects of an enriched CO_2 atmosphere on whole plant growth and development. The impact of a rising atmospheric CO_2 concentration may be significant but exceedingly variable under field conditions. The information base is at present sparse, but the experimental and mathematical technologies needed to answer our questions and perhaps allay our fears do exist.

1. Introduction. The most important societal impact of increasing atmospheric CO_2 concentration will continue to be on world food supplies. Fruits are the plant parts most often used in the development of food products. With increasing CO_2, the number of plants grown per unit of ground area, the size of each fruit, and the number of fruits per plant may change. With an atmosphere enriched

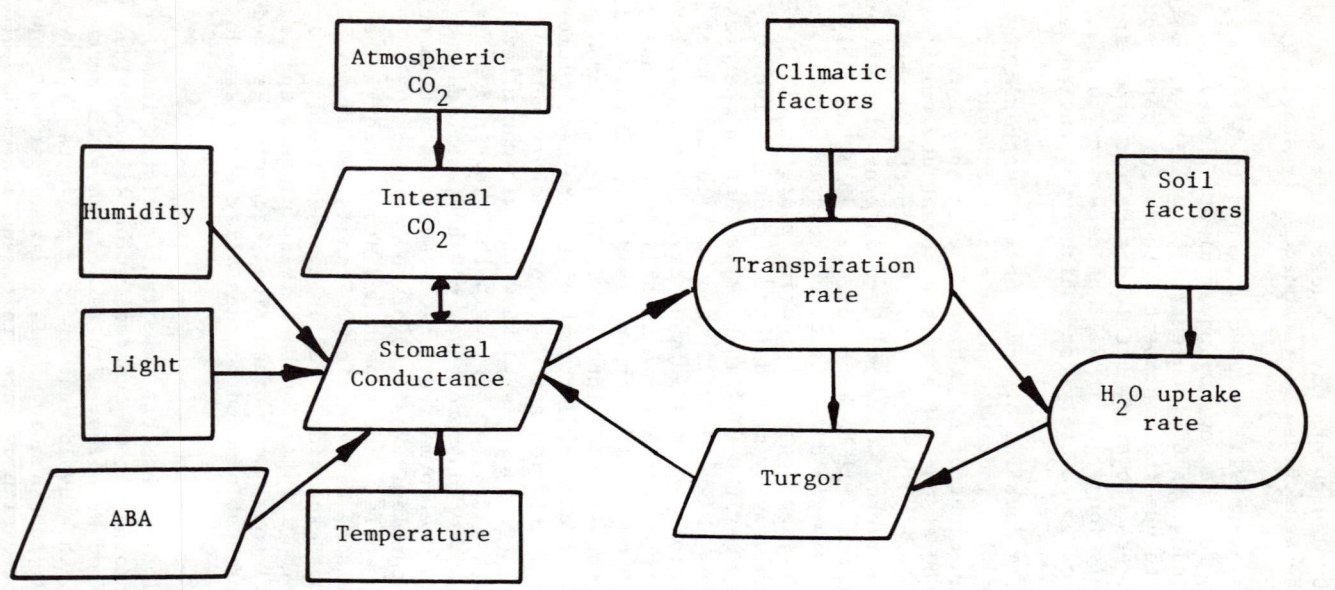

Figure 1. Major factors affecting transpiration.

in CO_2, the land may be able to support more plants with higher yields per unit land area. Many species have relatively narrow genetic limits on the size of the fruit, but enhancement of the photosynthate supplies in the plant may result in larger fruit, and the plant may be able to support more fruit. Fruit number is, by far, the most variable yield component. Plants typically initiate two to three times as many fruits as they can support. The remainder are aborted as a result of physiological stresses which may be relaxed in a higher CO_2 atmosphere. Wittwer (1978) reported dramatic yield responses in a number of fruiting crops grown in elevated CO_2 atmospheres. These yield responses are normally attributed to the high photosynthetic rates in elevated CO_2. Krizek (1979), however, noted that high photosynthetic rates alone may not be the crucial factor determining yield. He cited several studies showing that the relationship between photosyn- thetic rate and yield depends on the developmental stage during which high photosynthesis occurs. In most cases, the increased yield is associated with enhanced photosynthesis during fruiting. Peet et al. (1977) found that photosynthetic rate at pod set in dry beans was positively correlated with yield in eight of nine varieties, but they found one variety in which high seed yield was associated with very low photosynthetic rate. This variety happened to have a very high harvest index. Evans (1975), considering genetic variation in photosyn- thetic rate, commented that there was little evidence of any positive relation between photosynthetic rate and yield, nor any instance where (cultivar) selection for a greater rate of photosynthesis led to increased yield. Obviously, while yields often increase in response to atmospheric CO_2, photosynthate supply is not the only variable determining fruiting under field conditions. Clearly, any increase in photosynthetic production must be accompanied by an adequate sink capacity if it is to be beneficial. This may not always occur, since plants have very sensitive mechanisms that bring about the abortion of fruit in response to stress.

2. Direct and Indirect Effects of CO_2. Primary effects of CO_2 on photosynthesis and transpiration occur via the CO_2 concentration gradient and the CO_2 effect on stomatal aperture. There are secondary effects on organ growth as the result of enhanced turgor and substrate levels. Numerous tertiary effects occur on plant developmental rates as a result of altered carbohydrate source/sink relations, and on water uptake as a result of increased plant size. These effects are traced in Figure 1 in the following consideration of physiological processes.

3. The Physiological Processes

3.1 Transpiration. Factors affecting transpiration are identified in Figure 1. Meidner and Mansfield (1965) listed the following factors controlling stomatal behavior: light, temperature, atmospheric CO_2 concentration, leaf water status, and a number of metabolic inhibitors. In an effort to develop a theory of stomatal action, they cited literature showing that both temperature and water stress produce closing responses which are correlated with the internal CO_2 concentration of the leaf. They also suggested that metabolic inhibitors cause stomatal closure by modifying the internal CO_2 concentration, either by their effect on respiration or on photosynthesis, or both. They concluded that there is abundant evidence that light, temperature, water stress, and various inhibitors act on stomatal guard cells by their influence on the CO_2 concentration within the tissue. However, they also showed that temperature and leaf water potential have direct effects on the guard cells independent of their effects on internal CO_2 concentration. In interpreting results of such experiments it is important to remember that stomata on young leaves are not sensitive to environmental factors (Raschke, 1982). They acquire this sensitivity either in the normal course of their development, or as a result of experiencing a water stress. Raschke (1975) discussed the modulating effects of CO_2 and ABA (abcissic acid) on stomatal metabolism, noting that ABA, which increases in the leaf under water stress conditions, sensitizes stomates to CO_2. Farquhar and Sharkey (1982) have reviewed the conceptual models of the effects of environmental factors, including atmospheric CO_2 concentration, on stomatal action and rates of leaf photosynthetic CO_2 uptake.

Lange et al. (1971) and Cowan (1977) reported a direct effect of humidity on stomatal aperture.

The work of Fisher (1970) suggests substomatal CO_2 concentration is influenced by photosynthesis in the mesophyll, and that this influences the recovery of stomatal action after water stress. Several measurements of the effects of doubling CO_2 concentration on transpiration itself have been made in chambers with short-term experiments (Moss et al., 1961; Pallas, 1965; Egli et al., 1970; Akita and Moss, 1972; Carlson and Bazzaz, 1980). These workers found reductions in transpiration which ranged from 8% for wheat (Akita and Moss, 1973) to 68% for corn and sorghum (Pallas, 1965). The average reduction was about 36% for 398 observations with 14 different species. Coupled with increases in

photosynthesis, the increase in water use efficiency with
future high CO_2 concentrations could be very dramatic.
However, long-term studies are needed which follow the
effects of high CO_2 on water use, leaf area expansion, and
growth of plants through their entire life cycles.

3.2 Photosynthesis and Respiration. Factors affecting
photosynthesis and respiration are identified in Figure 2.
Carbon dioxide and water vapor exchange rates in leaves and
whole plants have been measured at various levels of
atmospheric CO_2. Gaastra (1959) presented such data for
single leaves of sugar beet, turnip, cucumber, spinach and
tomato. All of these species, except cucumber, approached
saturation at 1000 ppm CO_2. In intact maize canopies, Baker
and Lambert (1979b) showed that even at high light flux
densities, photosynthetic response curves indicate near
saturation at 600 ppm CO_2. Akita and Moss (1973) confirmed
these observations in experiments with greenhouse-grown
maize plants. However, in similar experiments with wheat,
they reported little photosynthetic response to atmospheres
enriched with CO_2 beyond 300 ppm, but they reported a very
significant decrease in transpiration up to 800 ppm CO_2. In
interpreting their wheat photosynthesis results, it is
important to note that they operated under rather low light
(about half full sun). At 1675 W/m^2, Hesketh (1963) showed
very steep CO_2 response curves up to 1000 ppm for sunflower,
maize, tobacco, and castor bean. In intact field-grown
cotton crop canopies, Baker (1965) reported linear (light
intensity dependent) photosynthetic response to CO_2 up to
600 ppm. In the same experiments, he found a very small
linear decline in transpiration with atmospheric CO_2
concentration increasing to 600 ppm. Enoch and Hurd (1977)
measured CO_2 exchange rates in spray carnation plants in
120 combinations of light flux density, CO_2 concentration,
and temperature. At the high PAR levels (450 W/m^2),
light saturation appeared to exist only at high CO_2
concentrations (up to 3100 ppm).

Egli et al. (1970) reported differing increases in
photosynthesis and decreases in transpiration with CO_2
concentration up to 600 ppm in three varieties of soybean.
Brun and Cooper (1967) presented data for soybean showing
photosynthetic responses well above 1000 ppm under bright
light. They, too, reported varietal differences.

Some photosynthate is oxidized and lost by the plant in
several metabolic processes referred to as respiration. The
portion which is associated with the photosynthesis process
is referred to as photorespiration. The rate of production
of phosphoglycolate, the photorespiratory substrate, is

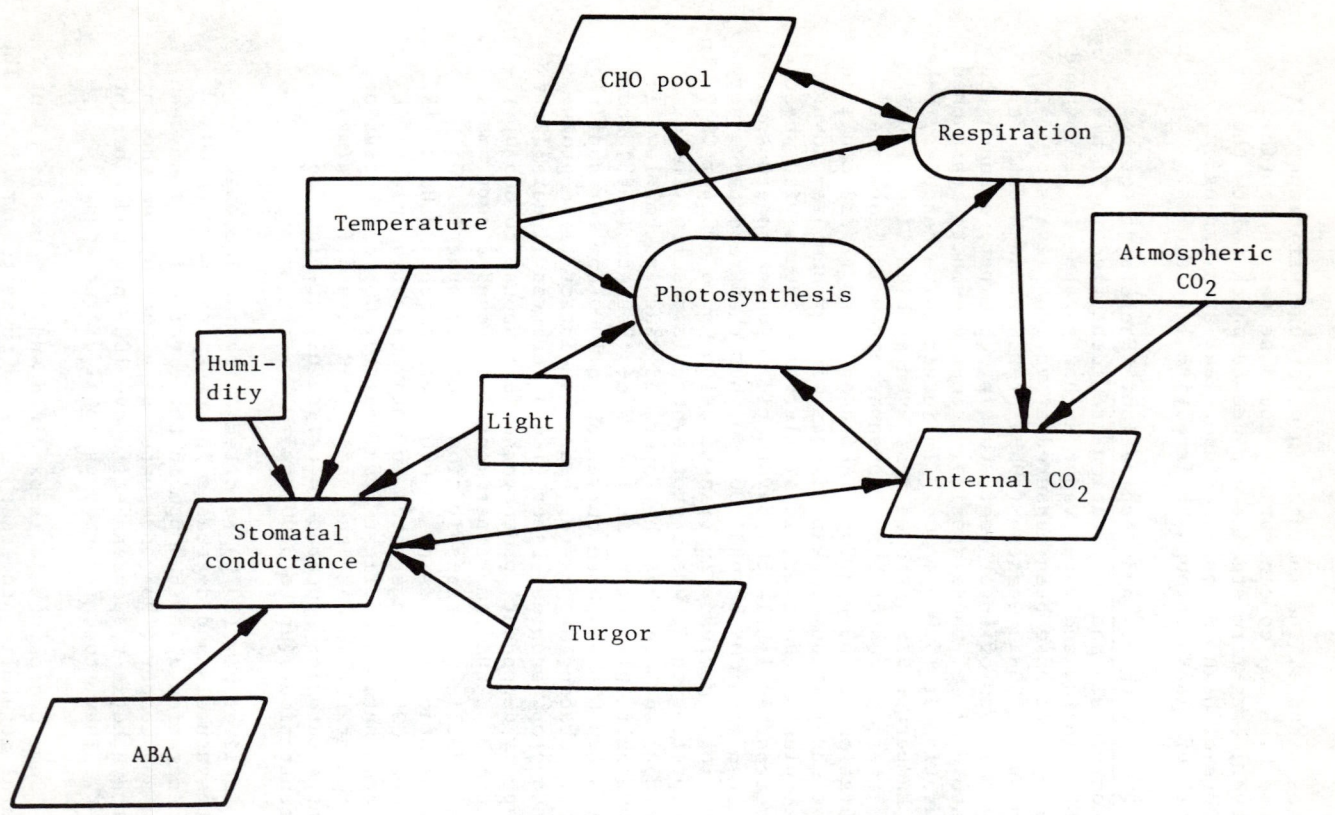

Figure 2. Major factors affecting photosynthesis and respiration.

reduced by high CO_2. Other respiratory processes appear to be needed to provide energy and building materials associated with growth (growth respiration) and with the maintenance of existing tissue (maintenance respiration) of the plants. All of these respiratory processes are temperature dependent, with a Q^{10} near 2 (Baker et al., 1972; Hurd and Enoch, 1976).

3.3 Partitioning of Photosynthate. Factors affecting organ growth are identified in Figure 3. Obviously, the variation among organs on the plant, with respect to temperature and proximity to the sources of carbohydrate, nitrogen, and water accounts for much of the variation in photosynthate partitioning. Part of the photosynthate is allocated to the growing organs. Potential organ growth depends on an adequate supply of mineral nutrients (Mauney et al., 1978; Wong, 1979) and on temperature. It also depends on organ turgor. Boyer (1970) and Meyer and Boyer (1972) have shown that different species have different "threshold" turgor levels for growth, and these turgor limits are different for cell expansion and cell division. The cell division may continue at turgor levels below which cell expansion will have ceased. These workers also showed that during turgor loss, the organ growth period will be lengthened. Thus, growth potential may accumulate during drought and it may represent a large demand on rewatering (Baker et al., 1979a). In this same paper, Baker and others have also shown that organ growth can be simulated in plant models on the basis of substrate supply. Many studies by numerous investigators have shown that organ growth is, in general, dependent on substrate supply. Thus, organ growth appears to depend on competition for photosynthate among growing points within the plant. Also, during drought, turgor differences within the plant may, for example, allow root growth when leaf growth is inhibited. In many plants, especially during the vegetative stages, photosynthate supply may exceed demand (i.e., the total sink capacity of the system). In that case, a feedback inhibition appears to develop, reducing photosynthesis (Chatterton et al., 1972; Thorne and Koller, 1974; and Clough et al., 1981).

3.4 Plant Development. Factors affecting plant development are identified in Figure 4. Developmental rate is, first of all, determined by temperature (cf. for example, Moraghan et al., 1968 and Hesketh et al., 1972). However, a tertiary effect of photosynthate supply appears in the form of delays in the developmental rate of the plant whenever there is a source/sink imbalance. Enhanced photo-

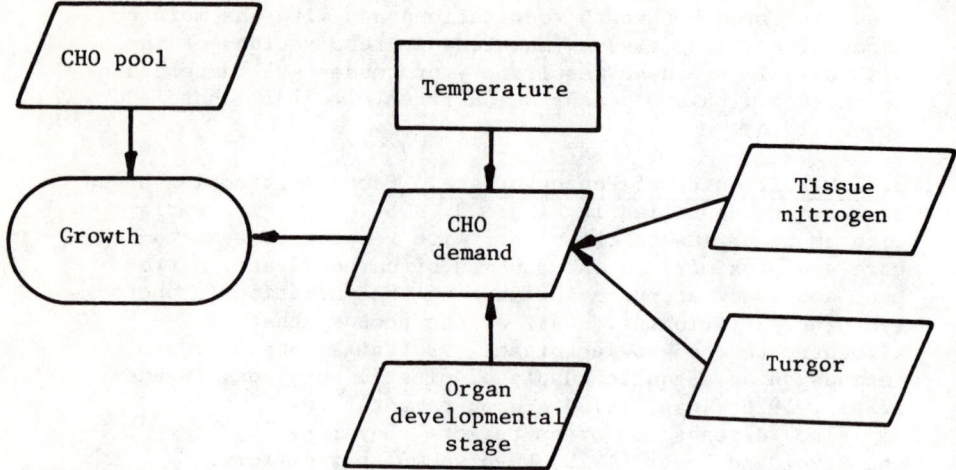

Figure 3. Major factors affecting organ growth rates.

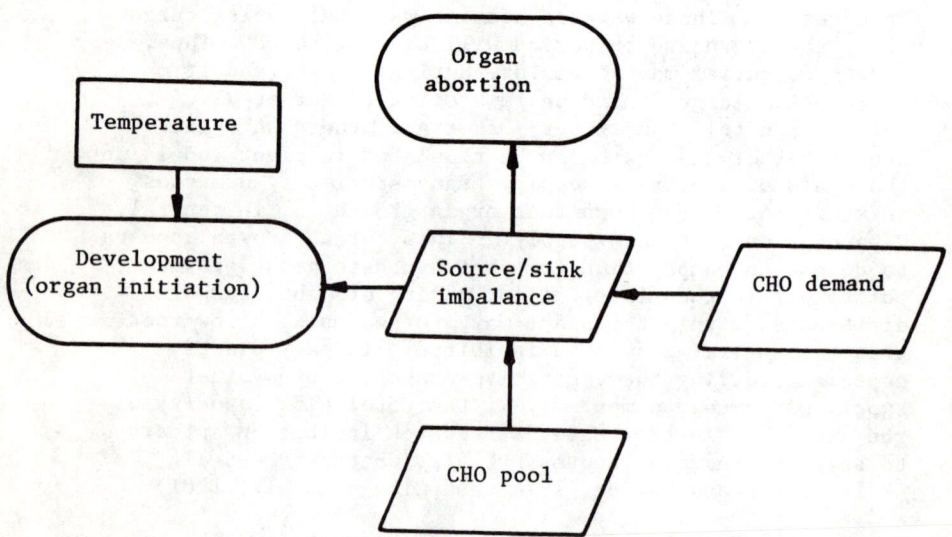

Figure 4. Major factors affecting plant development and
fruiting.

synthate production in an enriched CO_2 atmosphere will affect this balance. This effect often builds in importance, ultimately being the major determinant of plant size and yield. Thus, morphogenesis determines the size of the sink for enhanced photosynthate supplies. The metabolic stress-induced delays in morphogenesis will not be eliminated by enhanced photosynthate supplies, but they will occur later in the development of the plant. Thus, the larger plants developing in an enhanced CO_2 atmosphere may initiate and abort more fruit. While it will also probably retain more fruit, accurate generalizations about such tertiary effects cannot be made. Dynamic crop simulation models are helpful in this regard.

4. CO_2 and Plant Dynamics. Here we attempt to trace the cumulative effects of CO_2 on plant growth and yield. We will compare two plants: one grown in a "normal" atmosphere, the other grown in a "high" CO_2 atmosphere. "Normal" means approximately 340 ppm CO_2, and "high" might be, for example, 600 ppm.

4.1 The Seedling. The seedling stage covers the period from germination to the start of the expansion of the first leaf with adult form, e.g., the soybean trifoliolate. It is difficult to conceive of an elevated CO_2 atmosphere having much effect on the germinating seed in the soil. However, there is evidence that some small seeds placed on the soil surface germinate faster in high CO_2, (Heichel and Jaynes, 1974). Once the shoot has emerged, it responds to high CO_2 by initiating and expanding each leaf faster, achieving a larger leaf area (Sionit, 1982; Heichel, 1982; Mauney, 1982). This effect is not seen in all species, or even in all studies with the same species (Rogers et al., 1980).

In absolute terms, the CO_2 enhancement of seedling development is small, but a gain of as little as two days at the beginning of exponential growth can be important.

Most of the work on seedling response to CO_2 has been done with seeds grown on plants in a normal atmosphere. However, Rogers et al. (1980) found that second generation soybeans grown in high CO_2 are not affected by the CO_2 history of their parents.

In summary, some, but not all, kinds of plants grown in high CO_2 will reach the end of the seedling stage sooner and with a larger leaf area.

4.2 The Vegetative Plant

4.2.1 Organ expansion and dry weight gain. The vegetative stage is defined here as the period from the appearance of the first true leaf to the beginning of anthesis.

During the vegetative period, the high-CO_2 plant develops more and larger leaves (Mauney et al., 1978; Ford and Thorne, 1967). The leaves are thicker, often having an extra layer of palisade cells (Hofstra and Hesketh, 1975; Rogers et al., 1980). In some experiments, the increase in specific leaf weight is nearly proportional to the increases in photosynthetic rate, and leaf area is virtually unaffected by CO_2 concentration (Acock et al., 1982a). The extra weight per unit leaf area is partly in structural material and partly in stored carbohydrate (Acock and Pasternak, 1982). The added structure does not enhance the photosynthetic efficiency of the leaf, because leaves grown in high CO_2 have the same photosynthetic efficiency as leaves grown in low CO_2 when compared in the same CO_2 atmosphere (Ford and Thorne, 1967; Acock et al., 1982a).

4.2.2 Plant Development. If we define stress as anything which reduces organ growth below its theoretical maximum, then an imbalance in the source/sink relations in the plant may be thought of as a metabolic or carbohydrate stress. When a plant experiences a relaxation of this stress, it reduces morphogenetic delays that would otherwise occur, and more leaves are initiated in some plants (Baker et al., 1979c). In some cases, the vegetative period is also shortened (Sionit, 1982). Moreover, this stress relaxation suppresses apical dominance and more branches and tillers will appear (Sionit et al., 1980; Ford and Thorne, 1967; Baker, 1982a).

In short, the high CO_2 plant is larger, which means that prior to canopy closure more radiant and advective heating will occur, tending to increase water consumption, at least until the crop canopy completely shades the soil, whereupon the increased stomatal resistance decreases water use relative to the low CO_2 crop. In addition to increasing leaf dry weight, high CO_2 increases the dry weight of stems, petioles, and roots. The roots often receive a larger proportion of dry matter, which alters the root: shoot ratio (Acock et al., 1982a; Rogers et al., 1980). This may be because at 340 ppm CO_2 the discrepancy between actual and potential growth rate is larger in the root than in the top (Brouwer and deWit, 1969).

4.2.3 Water Stress. CO_2 may cause three changes in the

vegetative plant which affect water use and turgor: 1)
stomatal conductance is reduced, tending to reduce
transpiration; 2) the total evaporative surface of the
plant may be increased; and 3) a larger, more vigorous,
root system may be able to extract more soil water. 1) and
3) tend to maintain a higher turgor pressure in the larger
plant, but under dryland conditions drought may develop
earlier. There are few directly applicable data on this
point, but Gifford (1979, a, b) and Sionit et al. (1980),
using growth chambers, found that the relative yield
increase with CO_2 enrichment of water-stressed wheat was as
large or larger than that of well-watered wheat. Furthermore, the water-stressed plants in high CO_2 yielded as well
as plants without water stress in normal CO_2.

Obviously, a great deal is still to be learned about
the influence of elevated CO_2 on the growth and development of field grown plants subjected to water stress, and
more research is needed.

4.2.4 Nitrogen stress. During seedling developmemt, the
plant draws on nitrogen and other nutrients stored in the
seed. However, the vegetative plant may experience nitrogen shortage. The literature pertaining to some species
documents fairly constant minimum organ nitrogen concentrations, and it is reasonable to assume that below that
amount, growth cannot occur (Jones et al., 1974). Crop
simulation models have long been based on that assumption
(McKinion et al., 1975; Baker et al., 1976; Acock et al.,
1982b; and Baker et al., 1982). Nitrogen shortage may
reduce the amount of protein in leaves, and especially
those proteins (such as RuBP carboxylase) involved in
photosynthesis. It may also reduce stomatal aperture and
root water permeability (Radin, 1981; Radin and Ackerson,
1981; and Radin and Boyer, 1982). Thus, nitrogen stress
could reduce growth directly, or indirectly via an effect
on carbohydrate supply to the organ, or via a reduction in
organ turgor. Of these possibilities, the latter two are
most likely to limit plant response to CO_2 under
well-watered conditions, but very little research has been
done in this important area.

It has often been observed for many species that
nitrogen stress will disproportionately restrict leaf
growth. The reduction in carbon utilization by leaves may
result in carbohydrate storage. Since leaf area growth is
usually matched to nitrogen supply, leaf enzyme content may
not limit individual leaf photosynthesis. Leaf nitrogen
content can be halved without much effect on photosynthesis. Also, in extremis, plants extract nitrogen from

the lower, senescing, leaves and use it to supply upper
expanding leaves, so that those leaves fixing most of the
carbon suffer the least nitrogen stress. However, during
the reproduction stage, when the upper leaves in the canopy
are mature and senescing, and their nitrogen is being
extracted and moved into fruit, leaf nitrogen content
commonly limits photosynthesis. Thus, a nitrogen stress
during leaf growth will rarely limit the photosynthetic
response to CO_2 on a leaf area basis. However, if leaf
growth and light capture are restricted, canopy phytosynthesis may be reduced. During seed fill, nitrogen stress
can limit photosynthesis on a leaf eara basis so much that
the seeds will not be completely filled (Egli et al., 1978).

Over a very large part of the world's land surface,
nitrogen limits plant growth. Although Sionit (1982)
working with non-nodulating soybeans, has shown that CO_2
may partially offset the yield effect of nitrogen shortage,
it will almost certainly be necessary to add more fertilizer nitrogen to crops to take full advantage of the
increased CO_2 (Baker and Lambert, 1979b). The additional
nitrogen needed by plants in high CO_2 will probably be
proportionately less than the increase in plant dry weight
because the carbon/nitrogen ratio is lower in such plants.
The change in this ratio is propbably entirely due to the
change in specific leaf area discussed earlier. In
addition to nitrogen, it is likely that other nutrients will
become limiting as atmospheric CO_2 increases.

4.2.5 Saline Stress. Under irrigated agriculture, salts
often accumulate to toxic levels. The effect of elevated
CO_2 in increasing salt tolerance was reported by Enoch et
al. (1973). They were able to grow tomato plants in a 1.3
percent salt solution. One effect of a mild salinity
stress is to increase the maintenance respiration rate,
probably because the plant must expend energy to exclude
(or remove) salt from its tissues. Another effect is to
decrease stomatal conductance and photosynthetic rate.
Both effects reduce substrate supply and growth. High CO_2
partially alleviates salinity stress by enabling the plant
to fix more carbon and increase its carbohydrate supply.
In this way, high CO_2 will enable plants to grow faster in
mildly saline conditions and it will permit survival under
more severe salinity conditions. Alternatively, where
soil salinity is increasing, it will be possible to crop
the land longer than would be possible without increased
CO_2.

4.2.6 Starch Accumulation and Photosynthesis Suppression.
From the above, it is clear that several kinds of stress

tend to reduce growth rate, but have little direct effect
on photosynthesis, resulting in the accumulation of photosynthate in plants. This is especially noticeable in
plants grown in high CO_2. This accumulation of starch
(Cave et al., 1981) or sugar often has the indirect effect
of reducing photosynthesis (Mauney et al., 1979; Hofstra
and Hesketh, 1975). However, no cause and effect relationship has ever been established, although large starch
grains may, in some instances, physically disrupt the grana
of the chloroplasts. The mechanism connecting carbohydrate
accumulation and the reduction of photosynthetic rate is
not known, but it can be viewed teleologically as a
mechanism for balancing carbon fixation and use.

4.2.7 Partitioning of Photosynthate. Stresses often seem
to affect one type of organ more than another, and dry
matter is preferentially partitioned to certain parts of
the plant. We have only vague ideas about the mechanism
controlling this partitioning. In general, we observe that
dry matter accumulation is fastest in those organs nearest
the supply of material that is in deficit (Boote, 1976).
For example, during water stress, the roots grow faster
than other organs. Once again, the mechanism appears to be
one for balancing the supply of and demand for materials
needed by the whole plant for balanced growth. The
enhanced root growth tends to alleviate the water stress.
Referring to this control of partitioning, plant physiologists frequently discuss the maintenance of a functional
balance between organs. Although the interpretation given
here is teleological, it seems reasonable, and we are
probably safe in using this idea to predict how plants will
respond to a stress in high CO_2. In those instances where
growth of the organ nearest to the material in short supply
will enable the plant to obtain more of that material, high
CO_2 will tend to alleviate that stress. However, the idea
is not very useful quantitatively, and we need further
research and testable hypotheses about the control
mechanism involved in partitioning.

4.2.8 Leaf Senescence. High CO_2 probably has little direct
effect on leaf senescence. Leaves on wheat plants grown in
high CO_2 have been seen to senesce three to four days
earlier, probably because they were initiated earlier
(Sionit et al., 1981). Hardy and Havelka (1975) reported
delayed senescence in soybeans, probably because the high
CO_2 enabled nodules to fix nitrogen faster, delaying
extraction of nitrogen from the leaves. A delay in leaf
senescence will increase fruit yield in those cases where
the length of the fruit growth period would otherwise be
limiting.

4.3 The Reproductive Plant. At anthesis, the high CO_2 crop will be heavier. In the absence of stresses, Kimball (1982) has reported that a doubling of atmospheric CO_2 will result in approximately a forty percent increase in plant dry weight. The plant will have a larger leaf area, a much larger root system, and it will probably contain more stored carbohydrate.

At anthesis, stress begins to develop rapidly in the plant grown in normal CO_2 because it initiates many more fruits than it can supply with substrate for growth (Frey, 1981). Typically, this stress builds exponentially in time, and many of the fruits are aborted. Also, if the plant is indeterminate in its growth habit, delays in further development will build, resulting in a sigmoid growth curve. The biochemical basis for these delays and the abortion of such large numbers of fruit is unknown. However, much can be learned from the use of CO_2 as a variable in controlled environments.

In monoecious plants like cucumber, fruit number depends on the number of female flowers. High CO_2 can alter the sex ratio to give more female flowers in cucumber (Enoch et al., 1976). This occurs because high CO_2 encourages branching and there are more female flowers on the branches than on the mainstem. In fertile soils, carbohydrate supply is likely to be the most limiting factor for fruit development and growth. Thus, the plant in high CO_2, in the absence of other stresses, will bear more fruit because of its larger carbohydrate supply. Its enhanced capacity results from the direct effect of the CO_2 concentration on the diffusion into the leaf, and, in open canopies or isolated plants, because of the indirect effect of the CO_2-induced larger vegetative structure which captures more light.

There is an age window in the development of a fruit. During this period the fruit is vulnerable to abortion. The level of source/sink imbalance at which fruits begin to be aborted is reached somewhat later by the high CO_2 plant than by the low CO_2 plant, and more fruit are enabled to pass through this developmental period without being aborted.

As the load of fruits which are beyond the age of vulnerability builds, the plant increasingly partitions carbohydrate and nutrients to fruit at the expense of growth or even maintenance of the vegetative parts. In terms of continued life of the plant, this has a devastating effect. It reduces water and nutrient uptake by the roots and enhances the rate of leaf senescence, which manifests itself as a decline in photosynthetic efficiency. An unstable feedback effect is set up and the plant self-destructs. In the high CO_2 plant, all of this is delayed, and more and larger fruit are produced. In determinate plants, the substrate supply has already been taken into account, and the plant will have enough photosynthate to grow those fruits. In the event that the plant has fewer fruit than it can supply, e.g. in the case where stresses are relaxed during the fruiting period, the fruit growth rate will not be enhanced by high CO_2 (Egli and Leggett, 1976).

Sionit et al. (1982) have published some data on the effects of stress on four species of annual plants. Obviously, much more research in this area is needed. Considering the myriad patterns of stresses of different types which occur in nature, we can probably hope to answer these questions only with the use of simulation models.

Stress may reduce fruit growth, and some variation in fruit size occurs. Low temperature stress also causes reduction in growth rates. The high CO_2 plant exposed to these conditions will yield somewhat more than the low CO_2 plant (Beckford et al., 1981).

In numerous greenhouse and growth chamber experiments, CO_2 enrichment increased yields of leaves 42 percent; fruit 23 percent; seeds 47 percent; and tubers 64 percent (Kimball, 1982). While these experiments were done in CO_2 enriched atmospheres, the CO_2 was not controlled at specific concentrations. The relatively few experiments with controlled CO_2 concentrations indicate that a doubling of CO_2 concentration will probably increase leaf and seed yields by 45% and fruit yield by 19%, but no data are available for root or tuber crops (Kimball, 1982). However, in agronomic crops, metabolic stresses may change very little because of the use of denser plantings. In this case, the yield increase would result from a larger number of plants and fruit per unit and area. It would occur with little or no change in partitioning within the the plant. Stresses occuring during the vegetative stage have less effect on yield, except in leaf crops. The greatest yield reduction comes from stresses in early seedfill. However, the plant grown in high CO_2 is generally more robust. It has greater reserves to carry it through stress or to counteract stress.

5. Literature Cited

Acock, B., and D. Pasternak. 1982. pers. comm.

Acock, B., D.N. Baker, V.R. Reddy, J.M. McKinion, F.D. Whisler, D. del Castillo and H.F. Hodges. 1982a. Soybean responses to CO_2: Measurement and simulation. In series Response of Vegetation to Carbon Dioxide, Dept. of Energy and Dept. of Agriculture.

Acock, B., V.R. Reddy, F.D. Whisler, D.N. Baker, J.M. McKinion, H.F. Hodges, and K.J. Boote, 1982b. The soybean crop simulator GLYCIM. In series: Response of Vegetation to Carbon Dioxide. Dept. of Energy and Dept. of Agriculture.

Akita, S. and D.N. Moss. 1972. Differential stomatal response between C_3 and C_4 species to atmosphere CO_2 concentrate and light. Crop Science 12, 789-793.

Akita, S. and D.N. Moss. 1973. Photosynthetic responses to CO_2 and light by maize and wheat leaves adjusted for constant stomatal apertures. Crop Sci. 13 (2), 234-237.

Baker, D.N. 1965. Effects of certain environmental factors on net assimilation in cotton. Crop Sci. 5, 53-56.

Baker, D.N., J.D. Hesketh, and W.G. Duncan. 1972. The simulation of growth and yield in cotton: I. Gross photosynthesis, respiration and growth. Crop Sci. 12, 431-435.

Baker, D.N., J.R. Lambert, C.J. Phene, and J.M. McKinion. 1976. GOSSYM: A simulator of cotton crop dynamics. In Computers Applied to the Management of Large-Scale Agricultural Enterprises. Proc. U.S.-U.S.S.R. Seminar, Moscow, Riga, Kishiniev, pp. 100-133.

Baker, D.N., J.A. Landivar, and J.R. Lambert. 1979a. Model simulation of fruiting. Proc. Cotton Production Research Conf. Phoenix, AZ., pp. 261-263.

Baker, D.N., and J.R. Lambert. 1979b. The analysis of crop responses to enhanced atmospheric CO_2 levels. In Report of the AAAS-DOE Workshop on Environmental and Societal Consequences of a Possible CO_2-Induced Climate Change, Annapolis, MD, April 2-6, 1979.

Baker, D.N., J.A. Landivar, F.D. Whisler and V.R. Reddy. 1979c. Plant responses to environmental conditions and modeling plant development. Weather and Agr. Symp., Kansas City, MO., pp. 69-135.

Baker, D.N., J.M. McKinion and J.R. Lambert. 1982. GOSSYM: A simulator of cotton crop growth and yield. S.C. Agr. Exp. Sta. Bull. In press. 270 pp.

Baker, D.N. 1982. pers. comm.

Beckford, H.A., N. Sionit and N.D. Camper. 1981. An investigation in the mineral nutrition of okra. Res. Bull. 16. South Carolina State College.

Boote, K.J. 1976. Root:shoot relationships. Proc. Soil and Crop Soc. of Fla. 36, 15-23.

Boyer, J.S. 1970. Leaf enlargement and metabolic rates in corn, soybean and sunflower at various leaf water potentials. Plant Physiol. 46, 233-235.

Brouwer, R., and C.T. de Wit. 1969. A simulation model of plant growth with special attention to root growth and its consequences. In Root Growth: Proc. 15th Easter School in Agric. Sci., Univ. Nottingham. pp. 224-244.

Brun, W.A., and R.L. Cooper. 1967. Effects of light intensity and carbon dioxide concentration on photosynthetic rate of soybean. Crop Sci. 7 (5), 451-454.

Carlson, R.W., and F.A. Bazzaz. 1980. The effects of elevated CO_2 concentrations on growth, photosynthesis, transpiration, and water use efficiency of plants. In Environmental Climatic Impact of Coal Utilization, J. Singhjag and A. Deepek, Eds., Academic Press, New York. pp. 609-623.

Cave, G., L.C. Tolley and B.R. Strain. 1981. Effect of CO_2 enrichment on chlorophyll content and starch grain structure in Trifolium subterraneum leaves. Physiol. Plant. 51, 171-174.

Chatterton, N.J., G.E. Carlson, W.E. Hungerford and P.R. Lee. 1972. Effect of tillering and cool nights on photosynthesis and chloroplast starch in Pangola. Crop Sci. 12, 206-208.

Clough, J.M., M.M. Peet and P.J. Kramer. 1981. Effects of high atmospheric CO_2 and sink size on rate of photosynthesis of soybean cultivars. Plant Physiol. 67, 1007-1010.

Cowan, J.R. Stomatal behavior and environment. 1977. In Advances in Botanical Research, Vol. 4. Academic Press, pp. 117-227.

Egli, D.B., J.W. Pendleton and D.B. Peters. 1970. Photosynthetic rate of three soybean communities as related to carbon dioxide levels and solar radiaton. Agron. J. 62 (3), 411-414.

Egli, D.B. and J.E. Leggett. 1976. Rate of dry matter accumulation in soybean seed with varying source-sink ratios. Agron. J. 68, 371-374.

Egli, D. B., J. E. Leggett and W. G. Duncan. 1978. Influence of nitrogen stress on leaf senescence and nitrogen redistribution in soybeans. Agron. J. 70, 43-47.

Enoch, H.Z., N. Zielsli, Y. Biran, A.H. Halevy, M. Schwartz, B. Kessler and D. Shimshi. 1973. Principles of CO_2 nutrition research. Acta. Hort. 32, 97-118.

Enoch, H.Z., J. Rylski and M. Spigelman. 1976. CO_2 enrichment of strawberry and cucumber plants grown in unheated greenhouses in Israel. Scientia Horticulturae 5, 33-41.

Enoch, H.Z., and R.G. Hurd. 1977. Effect of light intensity, carbon dioxide concentration and leaf temperature on gas exchange of spray carnation plants. J. Exp. Bot. 28, 84-95.

Evans, L.T. 1975. The physiological basis of crop yield. In Crop Physiology, Cambridge University Press, pp. 327-355.

Farquhar, G.D., and T.D. Sharkey. 1982. Stomatal conductance and photosynthesis. Ann. Rev. Plant Physiol. 33, 317-345.

Fisher, R.A. 1970. After-effect of water stress on stomatal opening potential. J. of Exp. Botany 21 (64), 386-404.

Ford, M.A., and G.N. Thorne. 1967. Effect of CO_2

concentration on growth of sugar-beet, barley, kale and maize. Ann. Bot. 31, 629–644.

Frey, N.M. 1981. Dry matter accumulation in kernels of maize. Crop Sci. 21, 118–122.

Gaastra. P. 1959. Photosynthesis of crop plants as influenced by light, carbon dioxide, temperature and stomatal diffusion resistance. Meded. Landbouwhogesch, Wageningen 59, 1–68.

Gifford, R.M. 1979a. Carbon dioxide and plant growth under water and light stress: Implications for balancing the global carbon budget. Search 10, 316–318.

Gifford, R.M. 1979b. Growth and yield of CO_2 enriched wheat under water-limited conditions. Aust. J. Plant Physiol. 6, 367–378.

Hardy, R.W.F., and U.D. Havelka. 1975. Photosynthate as a major factor limiting N_2 fixation by field grown legumes with emphasis on soybeans. In Symbiotic Nitrogen Fixation in Plants, R.S. Nutman, Ed., Cambridge University Press. London.

Heichel, G.H., and R.A. Jaynes. 1974. Stimulating emergence and growth of Kalmia genotypes with carbon dioxide. Hortscience 9, 60–62.

Heichel, G.H. 1982. Pers. comm.

Hesketh, J.D. 1963. Limitations to photosynthesis responsible for differences among species. Crop Sci. 3(6), 493–496.

Hesketh, J. D., D. N. Baker and W. G. Duncan. 1972. Simulation of growth and yield in cotton: II. Environmental control of morphogenesis. Crop Sci. 12, 436–439.

Hofstra, G., and J.D. Hesketh. 1975. The effects of temperature and CO_2 enrichment on photosynthesis in soybean. In Environmental and Biological Control of Photosynthesis, pp. 61–70.

Hurd, R.G.,and H.Z. Enoch. 1976. Effect of night temperature on photosynthesis, transpiration and growth of spray carnations. J. Exp. Bot. 27, 695–703.

Jones, J.W., J.D. Hesketh, E.J. Kamprath and H.D. Bowen.

1974. Development of a nitrogen balance for cotton growth models: A first approximation. Crop Sci. 14, 541–546.

Kimball, B.A. 1982. Carbon dioxide and agricultural yield. An assemblage and analysis of 430 prior observations. WCL Report 11. U.S. Water Conservation Lab., Phoenix, AZ.

Kramer, P.J. 1981. Carbon dioxide concentration, photosynthesis and dry matter production. Biosci. 31, 29–33.

Krizek, D.T. 1979. Carbon dioxide enrichment. In Cotton Physiology - A Treatise, Section I, Flowering, Fruiting and Cutout. Cotton Production Res. Confs. Proc. pp. 283–290.

Lange, O.L., R. Losch, E.D. Schulze and L. Kappen. 1971. Responses of stomata to changes in humidity. Planta 100, 76–86.

Mauney, J.R., K.E. Fry and G. Guinn. 1978. Relationship of photosynthetic rate to growth and fruiting of cotton, soybean, sorghum and sunflower. Crop Sci. 18, 259–263.

Mauney, J.R., G. Guinn, K.E. Fry and J.D. Hesketh. 1979. Correlation of photosynthetic carbon dioxide uptake and carbohydrate accumulation in cotton, soybean, sunflower and sorghum. Photosynthetica 13, 260–266.

Mauney, J.R. 1982. pers. comm.

McKinion, J.M, D. N. Baker, J.D. Hesketh and J.W.Jones. 1975. SIMCOTT II: A simulation of cotton growth and yield. In Computer Simulation of a Cotton Production System User's Manual. ARS-S-52. pp. 27–82.

Meidner, H. and T.A. Mansfield. 1965. Stomatal responses to illumination. Biol. Rev. 40, 483–509.

Meyer, R.F., and J.S. Boyer. 1972. Sensibility of cell division and elongation to low water potentials in soybean hypolcotyls. Planta 108, 77–87.

Moraghan, B.J., J.D. Hesketh and A. Low. 1968. Effects of temperature and photoperiod on floral initiation among strains of cotton. Cotton Growing Rev. 45, 91–100.

Moss, D.N., R.B. Musgrave and E.R. Lemon. 1961. Photosynthesis under field conditions. III. Some effects of light, carbon dioxide, temperature and soil moisture on photosynthesis, respiration and transpiration of corn. Crop Science 1, 83-87.

Pallas, J.E. Jr. 1965. Transpiration and stomatal opening with changes in carbon dioxide content of the air. Science 147, 171-173.

Peet, M.M., A. Bravdo, D.H. Wallace and J.L. Ozbun. 1977. Photosynthesis, stomatal resistance, and enzyme activities in relation to yield of field-grown dry bean varieties. Crop Sci. 17, 287-292.

Radin, J.W. 1981. Water relations of cotton plants under nitrogen deficiency. IV. Leaf senescence during drought and its relation to stomatal closure. Physiol. Plant. 51, 145-149.

Radin, J.W. and R.C. Ackerson. 1981. Water relations of cotton plants under nitrogen deficiency. III. Stomatal conductance, photosynthesis and abscissic acid accumulation. Plant Physiol. 67, 115-119.

Radin, J.W. and J.S. Boyer. 1982. Control of leaf expansion by nitrogen nutrition in sunflower plants. Plant Physiol. 69, 771-775.

Raschke, K. 1975. Stomatal action. Ann. Rev. Plant Physiol. 26, 309-340.

Raschke, K. 1982. pers. comm.

Rogers, H.H., G.E. Bingham, J.D. Cure, W.W. Heck, A.J. Heagle, D.W. Israel, J.M. Smith, K.A. Surano and J.F. Thomas. 1980. Field studies of plant responses to elevated carbon dioxide levels. In series: Response of Vegetation to Carbon Dioxide. Dept. of Energy and Dept. of Agr.

Schwartz, M. and J. Gale. 1981. Maintenance respiration and carbon balance of plants at low levels of sodium chloride salinity. Jour. of Exp. Bot. 32, 933-941.

Sionit, N., H. Hellmers and B.R. Strain. 1980. Growth and yield of wheat under CO_2 enrichment and water stress. Crop Sci. 20, 687-690.

Sionit, N., B.R. Strain and H. Hellmers. 1981. Effects of

different concentrations of atmospheric CO_2 on growth yield components of wheat. J. Agric. Sci. 79, 335–339.

Sionit, N. 1982. pers. comm.

Sionit, N., H. Hellmers and B.R. Strain. 1982. Interaction of atmospheric CO_2 enrichment and irradiance on plant growth. Agron. J. in press.

Thorne, J.H. and H.R. Koller. 1974. Influence of assimilate demand on photosynthesis, diffusive resistances, translocation, and carbohydrate levels of soybean leaves. Plant Physiol. 54, 201–207.

Wittwer, S.H. 1978. Carbon dioxide fertilization of crop plants. In Crop Physiology, U.S. Gupta, Ed. Oxford and IBH Publishing Co., New Delhi.

Wong, S.C. 1979. Elevated atmospheric partial pressure of CO_2 and plant growth. Oecologica 44, 66–74.

Marvin R. Lamborg, Chairman
Ralph W. F. Hardy, Co-Chairman
E. A. Paul

6. Microbial Effects

Panel Members: G. Bethlenfalvey, Peter Dart, C.L. Luh,
R.J. Luxmoore, Barbara Mazur, J.H. McBeath, Yaacov Okon,
W.H. Patrick, Jr., W.J. Payne, G.A. Peters, T. St. John.

RESEARCH RECOMMENDATIONS AND SUMMARY

The recommendations for microbiological research needs
are based on the following general scenario: a) increased
atmospheric CO_2 will increase crop productivities by 10-40%,
depending on crop and geographic area, which in turn will
increase biomass and soil organic matter by 5-40%; b)
additional root-derived materials and crop residue in the
soil will increase soil microbial activities, producing a
greater flux in most major cycles and possibly some changes
in pool sizes of -10% to +30%; c) these effects will
increase biological N_2 fixation, and the increased demand
for N will place significant limitations on phosphorus and
other mineral nutrients; d) no significant changes will
occur in soil O_2 or CO_2.

1) Quantification of the key soil components, processes and structure, as a function of increased atmospheric
CO_2, is essential. Components and processes to be measured
includes mycorrhiza, nitrogen fixation, biomass production,
mineralization-immobilization, nitrification, denitrification, organic matter, available phosphorus and other
nutrients, soil CO_2 and O_2, and soil structure. These
determinations should be carried out in the key agricultural
and forest ecosystems of the tropical and temperate zones.
Information should also be collected on microbial
mobilization of limiting nutrients and on the sensitivity
of mobilization to atmospheric CO_2. Organisms of note are
those involved in N_2 fixation, nitrification, and
denitrification, as well as mycorrhiza. Rhizosphere
changes will probably precede those in the root-free zone.

131

Some of these measurements will of necessity be long term, perhaps 5-10 years.

2) Soil limitations should be defined in terms of N, P, and other nutrients. The N_2-fixing organisms and mycorrhiza are especially important to study. The latter can scavenge P and perhaps other limiting nutrients in unfertilized areas, and there is insufficient information on them. Development of inoculants composed of nitrogen-fixing organisms, and especially mycorrhiza, are essential.

3) Minimum tillage is suggested as a large-scale operating model resembling the conditions of soils which may occur under elevated CO_2.

4) On the assumption that additonal P and N will be needed to obtain crop production increases from elevated atmospheric CO_2, alternative economical sources of N and P should be developed with emphasis on biological systems.

5) Among the questions to be addresed are: Is there a significant increase in the amount of N_2O released to the atmosphere? Are soil-borne plant diseases increased or decreased? What is the effect of possible decreased litter quality?

6) The rapid rate of technological change, especially in molecular genetics, dictates the need to develop scenarios for the impact of increased CO_2 based on the use of futuristic rather than current technologies. The recently established molecular biology and recombinant DNA technologies should be applied to increase the beneficial interaction of soil microbes and plants. In this way, the postulated nitrogen, phosphorus, and nutrient limitations may be reduced, and the requirement for multiple interacting organisms may be eliminated.

Summary

The postulated doubling of atmospheric CO_2 is not likely to have a direct effect on soil microbial activity because during the growing season, the concentration of CO_2 in the soil atmosphere is already ten to fifty times higher than existing atmospheric CO_2. Based on all available experimental information, it is estimated that a doubling of atmospheric CO_2 will cause an increase in primary productivity of ten to forty percent, depending on locale. The increase in biomass will, in turn, produce a limitation of available soil nutrients, especially nitrogen and phosphorus. Increased organic carbon together with nitrogen and/or phosphorus limitation will result in a preferential increase in nitrogen fixation and mycorrhizal activities as the expedient means for supplying required nutrients to sustain the predicted increase in primary productivity. Therefore, increased emphasis should be placed on fundamental research related to soil microbiology with special reference to nitrogen-fixing, nitrifying and denitrifying bacteria, and to the mycorrhizal fungi.

1. Global Effects. The biogeochemical cycle of carbon which integrates aerial, soil, and aquatic activities constitutes the basic mechanism for the production of renewable resources such as food, fiber, and fuel, and for the removal of organic detritus through mineralization. Man is increasingly affecting the carbon cycle by burning fossil fuels, by intensifying agriculture and forestry, and by destroying segments of the earth's plant cover. Soil microorganisms are an important determinant in defining the extent to which plants can respond to the increased level of atmospheric CO_2. Because the concentration of CO_2 in the soil is already an order of magnitude higher than the atmospheric concentration, soil microbes are unlikely to be affected by the anticipated atmospheric change. They will, however, be affected by the primary plant response, increased CO_2 fixation and increased biomass. Predicting the response of soil microbes to this secondary extent was the charge given to the "Microbial Inputs" group. The major conclusion of the group's discussions is that soil microorganisms will provide the major source of nutrients required by plants in response to the increased atmospheric CO_2. The extent of the plant response will be dictated by the soil activities. Increased knowledge of the soil changes may enable beneficial management for improved plant productivity under increased atmospheric CO_2. A summary of our knowledge and postulated changes in the various soil activities and recommendations for future research follows.

1.1 Microorganisms and Photosynthesis. At first glance, bacterial and cyanobacterial photosynthesis may not loom as large in cultivated and non-cultivated ecosystems as green plant photosynthesis, but the contributions of microbes to carbon fixation cannot be ignored (Karagouni and Slater, 1978). Microbial CO_2 fixation is reviewed in this chapter (see Section 3). Nitrogen fixation, the second most significant source of energy potential and nutrients for plants (Hardy and Havelka, 1975), is tied both directly and indirectly to photosynthesis. The photosynthetic prokaryotes which form the base of many food chains also fix nitrogen. In addition, the photosynthate generated by legumes and many other plants contributes the energy and electrons used by the nodule-forming and associative heterotrophic bacteria that fix nitrogen.

Carbon dioxide, a product of both aerobic and anaerobic metabolism, is important not only because it completes the carbon cycle but also because of its direct influence on microbial growth. Chemoautotrophic and photoautotrophic microorganisms must have CO_2, as it is their sole carbonaceous nutrient. CO_2 is stimulatory to, and often required by, many heterotrophs. Frequently growth will not proceed in its absence. Yet high levels can be toxic.

1.2 CO_2 Concentrations in Soil and Factors Affecting It.
The CO_2 concentration in soil is much higher than that in the atmosphere because of the continued generation of CO_2 by biological processes. General soil levels under aerobic conditions usually approximate 3,000 ppm where active microbial or plant growth occurs. Under waterlogged conditions, soil CO_2 levels of 10,000–30,000 ppm are usually considered to be the average. All measurements of CO_2 are made on the air in the macropores between soil aggregates. The actual microsite could be much higher; however, because respiring roots and microorganisms are usually on the outside of aggregates in larger pores, the inside of aggregates probably do not generate large amounts of CO_2.

The movement of CO_2 from reactive sites follows the general laws of gaseous diffusion (Fick's law). The diffusion rates of gases are linearly related to the concentrations in the air, the soil depth, and the diffusion constant in soil. The solubility of gases in the water phase depends on the type of gas, the temperature, the salt concentration, and their partial pressure in the atmosphere. CO_2 has a diffusion constant in air similar to O_2 and N_2 (0.2 cm^2 sec^{-1}). The relative diffusion constant of all gases in water is lower by a factor of 10^{-4}. Because CO^2 can become ionized, it has a much higher solubility in water than O^2 (0.9 cm /liter vs. 0.031 cm^3/liter for oxygen at $10°C$ and 760 mm of mercury).

As concluded from Fick's law, the diffusion rate across water films will control O_2 and CO_2 content relative to the fluxes associated with O_2 use and CO_2 production in soil. Calculations based on the diffusion coefficients and solubilities of CO_2 and O_2 in water indicate that CO_2 should move away from the respiring root 23 times more quickly than O_2 will move in (Greenwood, 1970). Thus, under normal circumstances O_2 will become limiting before growth of plant roots and microorganisms is inhibited by an excess of CO_2 (Garrett, 1981). This could change, however, if a proliferation of microbial, fungal, and other plant material raises the below-ground concentration of CO_2 above 100,000 ppm by elevating $HCO3^-$ concentrations to the range known to inhibit fungal metabolism (see Section 5.6) (Griffin, 1972).

The soil volume is approximately half solid and half pore space. The water content of the pore space controls the proportion of soil air, with an average medium textured soil having approximately 25% air space (one half of the pores are water filled). The proportion of pore space may increase with increased organic matter (Russell, 1973). Any associated increase in total porosity would be expected to increase the gas diffusion coefficient, favoring rapid gas exchange.

During the growing season, the CO_2 concentration in soil is usually much higher than that of the atmosphere because of the generation of CO_2 by biological processes. On the average, the CO_2 concentration of the soil atmosphere varies from 10 to 50 times higher than the atmospheric CO_2. The seasonal change is the most important variable. Temperature has a major influence on plant productivity and litter decomposition rates. Moisture, while having the same effect as temperature, also has a major influence, in that CO_2 concentrations can become very high when major pore spaces are filled during or immediately after rainfall or irrigation. Table 1 shows the range of CO_2 concentrations in a North American grassland during the growing season. Diffusion during the winter had equalized soil CO_2 levels at various depths. Initiation of plant growth increased CO_2 at the surface, with two rainfall events in June and July resulting in CO_2 concentrations above 10,000 ppm occurring in the surface layers. As the winter approached, surface layers had less CO_2 due to decreased plant growth and microbial activity. The CO_2 content at lower depths could have been due to slow diffusion rates or continued microbial activity in soils that were still relatively warm during this time of the year.

The position of the water table is a major factor controlling CO_2 in the soil profile. In contrast to the data shown in Table 1, the highest CO_2 concentrations in Figure 1 occurred adjacent to the water table. The high gradient between 35 and 60 cm, illustrated in Figure 1 is

Table 1. CO_2 concentrations in a native grassland during the growing season (from de Jong, et al., 1974).

Soil depth (cm)	CO_2 ppm (x 10^2)					
	May 24	June 6	July 6	Aug. 5	Sept. 9	Oct. 10
15	15	109	161	33	10	3
30	12	41	123	73	9	4
45	10	14	40	92	6	4
90	10	13	30	23	14	33
150	7	18	24	30	38	29

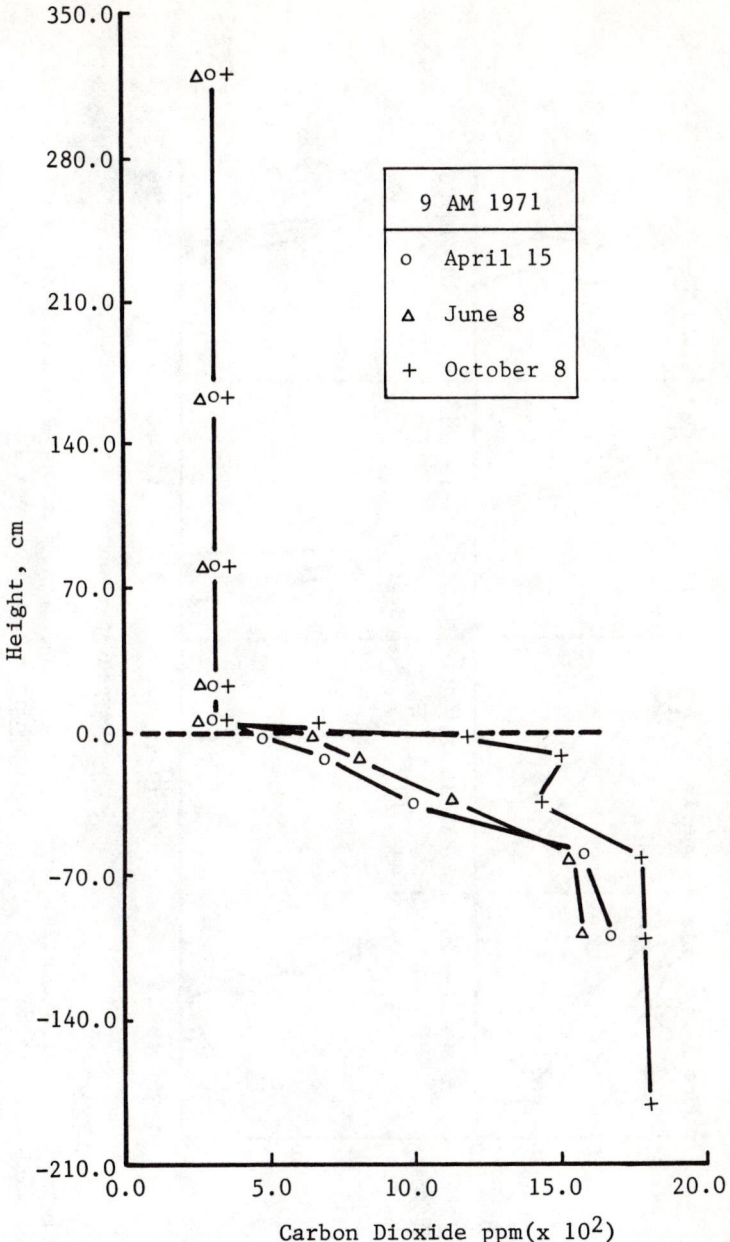

Figure 1. Representative profiles of carbon dioxide concentration above the ground-water table on three selected dates. From Schwartz and Bazzaz (1977).

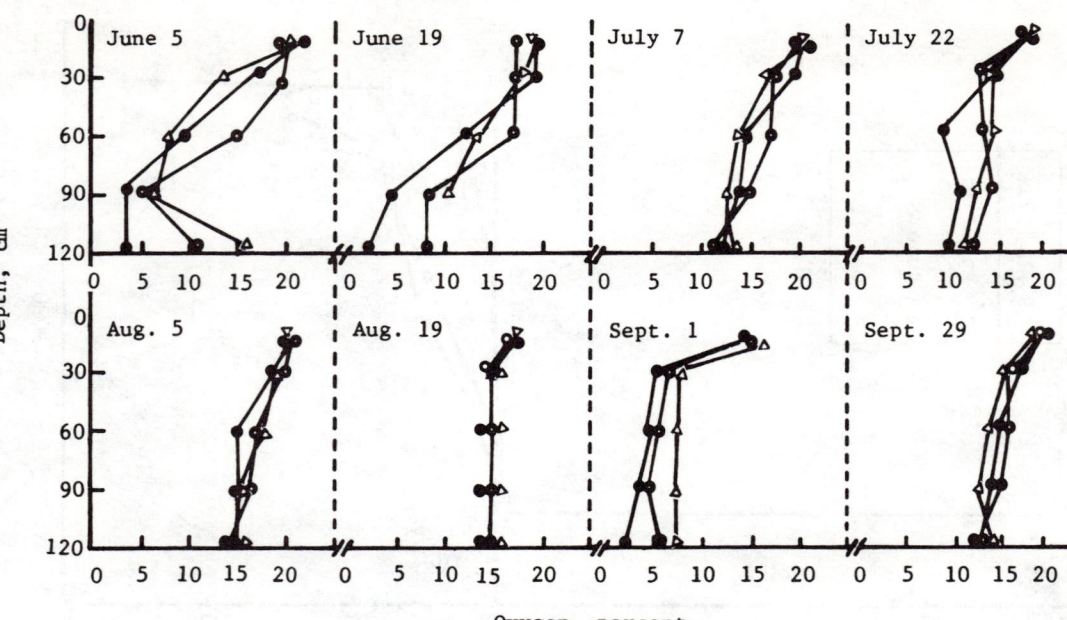

Figure 2. Oxygen content during the growing season in three replicated profiles in soil planted to cotton (Gossypium hirsutum L.). From Patrick (1977).

related to clay content and vegetative growth resulting from the development of root structures.

On a macro basis, O_2 curves are generally reciprocal to the CO_2 curves, justifying the assumption that O_2 is consumed in the production of CO_2. But the agreement is not absolute and the discrepancies are considerably beyond the limit of experimental error. Oxygen content of Louisiana soils were low in the sub-soil of silty clay loam growing cotton early in the spring, but increased as the season progressed. Heavy rains between the 19 August and 1 September samplings interfered with oxygen exchange in soil and caused a temporary decrease in oxygen content (Figure 2).

Roots are the major contributors to total soil respiration, with an average of 20 to 50% of the total soil respiration being attributed to roots and the closely associated microflora (Johnen, 1974; DeJong and Paul, 1979). Similar values are obtained for forests as for agricultural sites (Reichle et al., 1973; Coleman, 1973).

In summary, soil CO_2 under aerobic conditions approximate 3000 ppm where active microbial or plant growth is occurring. Under waterlogged conditions, CO_2 levels of 10,000 to 30,000 ppm are usually considered to be an average that plant roots and microorganisms are exposed to. No significant change in soil microbial activity is likely as a direct result of the projected increase in atmospheric CO_2, since soil CO_2 is always several orders of magnitude higher than ambient CO_2. In wetland soils that are marginally aerated, increased plant residue decomposition resulting from higher plant production may further restrict aeration and cause a shift toward microbial activity which uses electron acceptors other than O_2. This should affect sensitive microbial reactions such as denitrification, and possibly result in the production of some inhibitory metabolites as well as decrease the decay of plant residues.

1.3 Effect of Increased Levels of CO_2 on Solution Equilibrium Reactions.

The carbonate system is comprised of gaseous CO_2, dissolved CO_2, carbonic acid (H_2CO_3), bicarbonate (HCO_3^-), carbonate ($CO_3^=$), and carbonate-containing materials. The equilibrium concentrations of minerals containing Ca, P, Fe, Mn, Cd, Cu, and Pb are affected by CO_2 partial pressures. The $CaSO_4.2H_2O$ (gypsum)–$CaCo_3$ (calcite) equilibrium is operative in many dry land soils. The solubility of calcite is decreased as CO_2 pressures increase. At 340 ppm CO_2 in the atmosphere, calcium sulfate and calcium carbonate coexist at pH 7.8. Increasing the CO_2 concentration lowers the pH at which the two minerals can coexist. Similarly, the equilibrium between dolomite [$MgCa(CO_3)_2$] and calcite ($CaCO_3$) is shifted to dolomite by increasing CO_2. It has recently been postulated that the formation of calcium carbonates could provide a sink for increased CO_2 because the inorganic carbonates are in equilibrium with atmospheric CO_2, provided that exchangeable calcium and complexes such as gypsum are available in the soil. In flooded soils, the siderite ($FeCO_3$)-CO_2 equilibrium has a major buffering effect on soil CO_2 levels.

Because carbonate minerals tend to be relatively insoluble, an increased CO_2 concentration generally leads to decreases in the solute concentrations of cations such as iron and copper, and heavy metals such as lead and cadmium. The inorganic chemistry of phosphate, however, is complex; increased pH and increased CO_2 result in greater solubility of certain phosphate minerals. A 10-fold increase in CO_2 was said by Lindsay (1979) to shift the solubility line of octacalcium phosphate upward by 1.3 log units $H_2PO_4^=$.

Calculations show that CO_2 at 600 ppm in equilibrium with rain water would decrease the pH 0.15 unit. The buffering capacity of soil, and the great range in normal soil and sediment, however, are more important than the effects of increased CO_2 in the atmosphere. It has generally been supposed that roots excrete H^+ to the soil system and render nutrients available. It is now believed that when plants utilize NO_3^-, the absorption of more anions than cations results in an excretion of HCO_3^-. This yields an increase in pH. Roots growing on NH_4^+ and N_2-fixing organisms should cause a pH drop surrounding the roots. There are, however, other effects, and higher HCO_3^- concentrations are said to increase root hair density (Nye and Tinker, 1977).

1.4 CO_2 and Soil Organic Matter Levels. Erosion plays a major role in the amount of humus in both cultivated and forested soils. The majority of organic materials are usually deposited near their source. Sediments are slowly decomposed. Addition of nutrients to sediments, rivers and oceans can cause increases in eutrophication and a net sequestering of C. Eroded sites present new landscapes and soil organic matter formation occurs rapidly. This has been shown in the revegetation of mine spoils, where the general rise in soil organic matter averages approximately 400 kg/ha/yr over the first 50 years of revegetation.

Climatic alterations due to a "greenhouse effect" could have major influences on soil organic matter levels. Peat lands, taiga forests and sub-alpine tundra exposed to warmer temperatures would have both greater productivity and greater diversity. The amount of potential agricultural land that could be exploited in the northern hemisphere is limited by terrain and by endogenous nutrients. It is known, however, that transformation of northern forested land to agricultural land, and formation of sod Podzolic soils will increase soil organic matter levels.

Soil organic matter comprises approximately 1700 x 10^{15} g of C on a global basis. This is three times the level found in the atmosphere or in the land biota. Movements of C in and out of this source, therefore, can have major impacts on the global CO_2 levels (Bolin et al., 1979). Soil organic matter also plays a major role in soil properties and nutrient dynamics and will be vital to the future response of plants and microorganisms to increased CO_2 levels.

Predictive models of man's influence on soil organic matter (Jenkinson and Rayner, 1977; van Veen and Paul, 1981) have been developed which mimic the effect of past management practices and predict possible future levels. This has been possible since soil humus is composed of a number of constituents which are acted on by a large but generally inactive microbial population. The general concept that soils of the tropics have lower humus levels than those of temperate areas has been disproved (Sanchez et al., 1982a,b). Chemical analyses have shown that all soils have similar components and carbon dating has demonstrated that half of the soil humus is comprised of recalcitrant fractions with mean turnover times of at least 1000 years (van Veen and Paul, 1981).

In aerobic environments, the level of plant C addition has a limited effect on soil humus contents at low plant C/N ratios. Organic matter is stabilized by the reaction of phenol and lignin with inorganic and organic N. The content of these aromatic fractions, their reaction with inorganic particles, and their aggregation leads to long-term stabilization. Green manuring with N-rich legume can have major impacts on the N economy of soil and can relieve much of the fossil fuel requirement for the production of nitrogen fertilizer. Green manures will not, however, lead to major increases in soil organic matter levels unless other management techniques are also incorporated.

Table 2. Effect of Gradual Doubling of Atmospheric CO_2 on Plant Residues, Soil Organic Matter, and Soil Biomass

	Upland Temperate Zone				Upland Tropics				Wetlands		
	Agri. Total	Culti- vated	Forest	Grass- land	Agri. Legume	C_4 Plants	Grass- land	Forest	Paddy	Other*	Tundra
I. Plant matter	1.3	1.25	1.2	1.35	1.4	1.2	1.3	1.10	1.4	1.3	1.3
Soil organic matter	1.1	1.05	1.2	1.2	1.1	1.05	1.15	1.05	1.1	1.4	1.4
Soil nutrients remaining											
N	1.1	1.05	1.1	1.2	1.1	1.05	1.15	1.05	1.1	1.2	1.3
P	0.95	----	.95	.95	----	----	1.0	0.9	0.95	1.1	0.9
Micronutrients		----	.95	.95	----	----	1.0	0.9	0.95	1.0	0.9
Microorganisms		1.05	1.5	1.5	1.1	1.05	1.1	1.05	1.1	1.5	1.00
II. Present soil-C (10^{15}g)	73		210	147			197	90		313-300	30
Estimated new levels (10^{15}g)	80		252	176			226	94		?	42

Area and soil C levels from Bolin et al., 1979.

Values in Part I are ratios of predicted versus present values.

*Includes swamps, marshes and peat bogs.

Crop breeding has been selecting for plants with low C/N ratios, low root production, and low phenolic contents. However, in contrast to maize, cotton which has a high C/N ratio, can yield increased humus levels when grown over a 20-30 year period (Lal and Kang, 1982). The organic matter model of van Veen and Paul (1981) demonstrated that straw incorporation over a 50-year period could result in a stabilization of soil humus levels that were 5-10% higher than those where straw had not been incorporated.

2. Estimates of the Effect of Doubling Atmospheric CO_2 on Soil Organic Matter and Biomass. The carbonaceous substrates drive soil microbiological processes ranging from mineralization-immobilization, through nitrogen fixation, to denitrification. An understanding of these effects has to be based on estimates of the changes in available carbon attributable to plant residue additions, to exudates and other root derivatives. Table 2 shows the estimates of some of these variables for a number of representative plant community types. Those estimates for productivity are generally lower than values given by Rogers et al. (1980), Idso (1981), and Idso and Kimball (1982). Idso and Kimball (1982) have recently reviewed the literature on the effects of CO_2 on the yield of crops. Of the 355 separate samples exposed to CO_2 for extended periods, the enrichment increased yields up to 28%. Goudriaan and Atjay (1979) concluded that, in the field, plant production is usually limited by shortages of water and nutrients. Mulching with plant residues has increased both plant yields (Goswami and Suri, 1982) and nitrogen fixation in soybeans (Shivashankar et al., 1976), although the extent to which this is due to CO_2 or to indirect effects on soil temperature and water evaporation is not known. Water and temperature were not considered as limiting factors in calculating productivity in Table 2. This can in part be rationalized by the fact that new moisture and temperature regimes will merely represent a displacement of these zones from their present locations. To simplify comparisons, values are given as a ratio of present levels. Thus, a value of 1.25 for plant matter represents a 25% increase in plant productivity from present 1982 levels.

This possible displacement of agricultural crops or ecosystems to different parts of the world would require slow adjustments in associated soil organic matter levels. The 100 year time frame involved probably means that this is possible for agricultural crops. However, forested areas and wetlands such as peats cannot as easily be transposed to other portions of the globe without producing major dislocations on the source-sink relationships. The possible utilization of peat lands for agricultural crops after attendant drainage, would result in significant increases in atmospheric CO_2 and major mineralization of sulfur, nitrogen and phosphorus.

Soil organic matter levels are estimated to respond only slightly to increased productivity. This is in agreement with the results of long term nutrient application trials and in model predictions such as those of van Veen and Paul (1981). It also takes into account that green manures raise soil fertility, but not long term soil organic matter levels.

Phosphorus and nitrogen availability will be major limiting factors for both crop production and soil organic matter stabilization. The increases in productivity shown in Table 2 would require a major input of fertilizers for agricultural lands. In natural ecosystems where fertilization is not feasible, limitations of N, P and trace elements will limit plant adaptation to increased CO_2.

The good response of legumes to CO_2 was considered in the estimates for cultivated and tropical dryland and for legume and grassland systems. Rice is also known to respond well. Temperate cultivation includes a mixture of legumes and less responsive C_4 crops which should have an intermediate increase in plant productivity. Tropical C_4 crops are predicted to respond poorly, since some of these grasses have low nutritive value and grow in soils which are both deficient in P and contain toxic levels of Al.

Tropical and temperate forests contain a large initial biomass of nonphotosynthetic tissue so that only a modest increase in biomass is predicted as the result of increased atmospheric CO_2. These areas sequester nutrients in biomass. Therefore, increased growth will result in major nutrient stress causing increased C:N ratios of the substrate and lowering of decomposition rates due to changes in plant type and composition. For example, beech leaves (Fagus grundifolia) with a lignin content of 24%, have a half-life in litter of nine years, while the half-life for ash leaves (Fraxinus americana) which have 12% lignin, is 1.4 years (Mellilo et al., 1982). Many temperate forests have a small proportion of nutrients tied up in the phytomass.

Kimmins et al. (1979) and Swank and Waide (1980) summarized studies of thirteen forest sites. The data show that 10.3% (std. dev. 2.9%) of the nitrogen, and for seven sites 21.0% (std. dev. 19.2%) of the phosphorus was associated with the vegetation (roots included). The total system nutrient levels included the soil chemical content to a depth of 1 m or less. Sufficient nutrient capital exists within many temperate forests for a growth response to elevated CO_2 if mechanisms for increasing nutrient availability exist. One possible mechanism of increasing phosphorus supply to trees may result from increased oxalate excretion by mycorrhizal symbionts. Graustein et al. (1977) have demonstrated oxalate release by mycorrhizae, and have outlined feasible reactions by which oxalate could increase phosphate concentration in soil solution. The possibility of increased phosphorus, nitrogen (Section 5.5), and water supply (Section 5.6.4) led Luxmoore (1981) to hypothesize an increase in phytomass and nutrient retention of forests with an increase in atmospheric CO_2. This contrasts with other assessments (Goudriaan and Atjay, 1979; Kramer, 1981) which suggest that existing water and nutrient limits on growth may continue to limit plant response to increased CO_2.

The projected yield increases and organic matter production will require major nutrient transfers from both increased N fixation and from mining of presently insoluble P forms. For example, temperate forests would require a conversion of one-third of their present inorganic P to biomass and soil organic matter for the above production figures to be attained. Mycorrhizal effects and biological N_2 fixation will have to be even more significant than at present; mycorrhizal activity will probably be the major limiting factor in nutrient mobilization.

These data show that microbial soil populations will be exposed to significantly more available substrate. Most of the newly produced organic matter is more easily mineralized than preexisting biomass after the initial immobilization has been overcome. This will result in bursts of microbial activity. Thus, the large initial size of the current soil biomass in all studied ecosystems, together with increased activity, precludes major changes in biomass. Pulses of microbial growth will cause larger short term fluctuations in biomass and nutrient turnover than the steady state levels indicated in Table 2. The estimates for increased soil organic matter levels include changes in management, such as zero tillage. Residue handling problems, toxic intermediates, and the use of more of the plant residue for biofuels could alter these calculations.

The estimated new equilibrium levels for soil organic

matter were obtained by multiplying estimates for present
levels of soil carbon by the expected increase reached
after the soils have attained new steady state levels. The
estimates for carbon in peat and swamplands varies from 300
x 10^{15} g (Atjay et al., 1979) to 900 x 10^{15} g (Bolin et
al., 1979). This represents the largest carbon reservoir,
which has been built up over many years. The method used
for calculating new equilibrium levels cannot be applied to
these soils. The present productivity of these wetlands is
estimated at 4 x 10^{15} g C yr^{-1} out of a total of 63 x 1
10^{15} g C yr^{-1}. The proportion that is stabilized in the
ecosystem is difficult to estimate, but it is much higher
than that for upland sites, indicating that these sites
will continue to be sinks for fixed C as long as climatic
changes do not materially dislocate the lowland areas from
present sites.

3. CO_2 Production and Effects

3.1 Roots. Any increased root growth that may occur under
elevated atmospheric CO_2 will increase the oxygen demand
for root respiration. Root proliferation will be favored
in zones with adequate aeration. However, at very high
root densities the oxygen supply to roots may limit
respiration. Generally, excess CO_2 will not limit root
respiration as much as O_2 deficiency. Also, the apparent
length of the diffusion path in the liquid phase
surrounding roots is more often a factor limiting normal
root respiration than is the gaseous composition of soil
pores (Grable, 1966). This factor could become more
significant at elevated CO_2 if soil water films tend to be
thicker as a result of a slower rate of plant water use.
In fine textured soils and marginally wet soil areas, root
growth may be limited by oxygen supply, and responses to
increased atmospheric CO_2 may not be expected in these
areas.

3.2 Fungi. Changes in the soil atmosphere affect fungal
growth. Soil fungi are relatively insensitive to
reductions in O_2 concentrations to about 4% in the gas
phase. At lower concentrations of O_2, there are some
marked differences among species, and nearly all fungal
growth rates decline at 1% O_2 (Griffin, 1972). In the
presence of 21% O_2, CO_2 has little effect on the growth
rate of most fungi until CO_2 exceeds 10,000 ppm (Smith and
Griffin, 1971). Within the soil, increased partial
pressures of CO_2 are always associated with a reduced
partial pressure of O_2. Therefore, enhanced fungal growth
in gas mixtures containing more CO_2 and less O_2 than the

atmosphere may not be unusual (Griffin, 1972). However, when the CO_2/O_2 ratio exceeds unity, significant changes in the mycoflora occur (Macauley and Griffin, 1969). A significant alteration of the soil atmosphere due to both increased root respiration and to degradation of more soil organic matter could therefore produce unforeseeable changes in the soil mycoflora.

Vesicular Arbuscular Mycorrhiza (VAM) Fungi. These organ-isms may represent up to 20% of the dry weight of the fungus-root association in some plants (Bethlenfalvay et al., 1982), and total respiration rates in mycorrhizal roots may be twice those in roots not colonized by VAM fungi. If these high respiration rates were to raise the concentration of bicarbonate ion in the soil solution, it could conceivably inhibit VAM fungal growth. Should this be the case, P limitation might lead to diminished symbiotic N_2 fixation. It could also indirectly diminish associative N_2 fixation by decreasing plant growth and root exudation (see Section 5).

3.3 Return of Crop Residues to Soil. With increased above-ground biomass production levels, there will be a greater return of crop residues to the soil, particularly in minimum tillage situations, where straw is not burned. Straw residues of temperate cereals such as wheat can influence development of subsequent crops adversely if there is insufficient time for the residues to be decom-posed by microbes. Early in the breakdown process organic acids can accumulate in cool temperate climates, which can inhibit cereal seed germination (Lynch, 1978). To obviate this effect will require attention to such agronomic details as the time and depth of planting of the subsequent crop.

In tropical environments a product of sorghum residue breakdown can severely inhibit the growth of a subsequent crop. Polyphenolic compounds are implicated, and their toxic effect can be ameliorated by allowing a longer period for microbial breakdown of the residues before planting a subsequent crop. It is possible that inoculation of the soil with bacteria can hasten this process.

In semi-arid tropical environments, the growth of annual crops in soils with low nitrogen content may be enhanced by the addition of relatively small amounts (5 t/ha) of organic matter to the soil in the form of farmyard manure. The reason for the beneficial effect does not appear to be the extra supply of plant nutrients. Such plant growth responses suggest that processes which increase the rate of return of plant residues to the soil can have beneficial effects on subsequent crop growth.

4. CO_2 Uptake

4.1 General Observations. A relatively comprehensive assessment of the effect of CO_2 concentration factors, though somewhat outdated and preceding recognition of C_4, is found in the chapter from "Photosynthesis, Vol. II, Part 1" by Rabinowitch (1951). Additional good discussions are found in "Prediction and Measurement of Photosynthetic Activity" (Denmead and Lemon, 1970). While no attempt will be made to address this aspect in detail, several points will be made. Given a doubling in atmospheric CO_2, plant biomass can be expected to increase, although for this to occur, more combined nitrogen may be required. It is also possible that more root exudation will occur. This could stimulate microbial growth in the root zone, especially in tropical and subtropical soils where carbon sources are likely to be limiting.

4.2 Microbial Effects. As the principal and ultimate degraders of carbonaceous plant and animal litter, detritus, and ejecta, heterotrophic bacteria and fungi would be affected indirectly by increased CO_2 by having more oxidizable or fermentable substrate to deal with and more CO_2 to assimilate. Further, if the mean temperature rises as a consequence of CO_2 accumulation, rates of heterotrophic respiratory and fermentative activity may be expected to rise significantly. It will be important to know whether successions of microbial species in various habitats change from indirect influences such as greater carbon availability and higher temperatures.

The K_M for cell free fixation of CO_2 by the autotrophic nitrifying bacteria Nitrobacter has been calculated to be 5.9×10^{-3} M with respect to bicarbonate ion. At pH 7.6 and 30°, a CO_2 of approximately 1 vol % is required to produce this HCO_3^- concentration (Kiesow et al., 1972). The intercellular CO_2 of Nitrobacter equilibrated with air was found by the above authors to be 1.2 vol %, indicating that the CO_2 within the cells is substantially higher than the partial pressure of CO_2 in the atmosphere. It is generally considered that the requirement for CO_2 of autotrophic bacteria such as nitrifiers is met when biologically produced CO_2 in the soil must diffuse through approximately one inch of soil. Soil CO_2 levels are normally not thought to have a

direct effect on nitrification and, subsequently,
denitrification.

The increased CO_2 resulting from the microbial
degradation of soil organic matter of a rewetted rice soil
has been reported to result in a flush of green algae and a
depression of the cyanobacteria (Rogers and Kulasooria,
1980). Cyanobacteria, however, have a competitive
advantage over green algae at the alkaline pH often found
in flooded fields during high photosynthetic periods. The
decreased light intensities and N levels associated with the
latter periods of rice growth also favor cyanobacteria growth.

Nitrogen-fixing cyanobacteria (blue-green algae)
appear to have a ubiquitous distribution on earth. In the
free-living state, this distribution seems to be most
influenced by the pH of the milieu in which the algae grow.
Generally, they are inhibited by acid conditions where the
pH is less than pH 5.5-6.0, but particular forms apparently
have adapted to more acid conditions. Their considerable
growth and nitrogen-fixing activity in estuarine, marine,
and inland lake environments is dealt with in Chapter 6.
They are also well adapted to growing on the soil surface
over a very wide range of environments in forests, on beach
and river sands, pastures, and arable fields in both
temperate and tropical environments.

Cyanobacteria are often numerous enough to develop a
soil crust, usually in association with green algae. The
balance between green algae and cyanobacteria in these soil
niches is influenced by light intensity with the cyanobacteria favored at the low-light intensity associated with
greater plant canopy closure. Cyanobacteria are also
favored by lower soil mineral nitrogen levels, and possibly
by the CO_2 levels in the atmosphere surrounding the algae.
Temperature and soil moisture conditions, and climatic
factors indirectly influenced by atmospheric CO_2 concentrations, are also likely to influence the growth of cyanobacteria on the soil surface. Cyanobacteria seem to be
adapted to higher soil temperatures and, because they
produce resistant spores, to periodic wetting and drying
phases. The latter is a situation likely to increase in
some parts of the earth as part of the CO_2-induced climatic
changes. Thus cyanobacteria distribution is likely to be
only modestly affected by increases in atmospheric CO_2,
although their occurrence on soils receiving little or no
nitrogen fertilizer may increase.

The nitrogen-fixing activity of these cyanobacteria

can have a significant influence on the nitrogen economy of
their habitat. In desert and tundra soils they appear to
be a major current source of nitrogen input to soil. In
agricultural lands, they occur as soil crusts under annual
crops in both temperate and tropical regions, and in rice
they float freely in the paddy water, as well as encrusting
the basal parts of the rice stems. They also occur in
pastures receiving little or no N fertilizer, but their
extent is very much influenced by the canopy development of
the associated plant species. In certain situations, such
as tropical sorghum and grass fields (Dart and Wani, 1982),
the nitrogen-fixing activity can be high, with estimates of
up to 25 Kg N/ha/season. On the Broadbalk long-term wheat
experiment started in 1843, this amount of N would be
sufficient to provide all the nitrogen input necessary to
produce the crop. In tropical soils, the cyanobacterial
nitrogen fixation seems to be mainly limited by surface
soil moisture, and can be reduced to negligible levels
within three days of rain or irrigation because of soil
drying.

Cyanobacteria also occur in symbiotic association with
higher plants, such as mosses, ferns, cycads, and
angiosperms, where their nitrogen fixation contributes
significantly to plant growth. One particular association,
that between the floating fern Azolla, and the cyanobacterium, Anabaena azollae, has particular significance in
wet land rice cultivation, and in fresh water ponds, in
both tropical and temperate environments (Moore, 1969;
Peters and Calvert, 1982).

Considering surface soil microbes, specifically
free-living photosynthetic prokaryotes and lichens, it is
necessary to appreciate that CO_2 concentration at the
soil-atmosphere interface is influenced to some extent by
the biota itself (see Section 1 and 2). It should also be
noted that a number of cyanobacteria and unicellular green
algae (eukaryotes) which exhibit C_3 photosynthesis, exhibit
very low CO_2 compensation points and/or no O_2 inhibition of
photosynthesis (Bidwell, 1977; Lloyd et al, 1977) because
they possess a CO_2 concentrating mechanism when grown under
current ambient CO_2 (Berry et al., 1976). This mechanism is
not present at elevated pCO_2 partial pressures (Kaplin et
al, 1982) and it is probable that in organisms possessing
it there will be little effect from increasing CO_2. Higher
CO_2 levels may favor those cyanobacteria and other algae
which lack such a mechanism. Photoheterotrophic growth
and/or heterotrophic growth of such organisms might be
stimulated in nature through an increase in soil organic
matter.

5. Plant Microbial Associations

5.1 Introduction. Microorganism populations are stimulated many fold in the vicinity of plant roots as a result of the release of root derived substances as exudates and as a result of the decay of root cap and cortical cells. Bacteria live within root tissues and in specialized root structures such as nodules. This microbial population has a direct effect on plant growth through its production of plant growth promoters and inhibitors, through their competition for plant nutrients (immobilization), and through their release of nutrients by breakdown of dead cells (mineralization). Certain bacteria, such as Azospirillum, can enhance nutrient uptake by crop plants by a mechanism that is currently not clear. The activity of rhizosphere microorganisms will be enhanced by the larger photosynthetic activity of plants at higher CO_2 which will release a greater supply of microbial substrates through the roots. Current evidence suggests that the microbial population will be qualitatively similar, and that the results of their enhanced activity will be, in general, beneficial for plant growth.

Although more CO_2 is likely to initially increase immobilization of nutrients into microbial biomass, their subsequent turnover through mineralization should favor enhanced nutrient supply under maintenance fertilization regimes. If nutrients are not supplied as fertilizer, then immobilization of nutrients is likely to reduce plant growth, even though plant adaptation features, such as reduced concentration of nutrients per unit of dry matter, will work towards maintaining plant growth rates. Increased plant growth will lead to an increased demand for plant nutrients such as P and S. The reduced levels of combined nitrogen in the rhizosphere will favor nitrogen-fixing bacteria.

Root associated bacteria can also modify the pH of the immediate root environment, thereby affecting the solubility of certain plant nutrients. For pastures in South-East Australia dominated by annual clover plants, one of the consequences of nitrogen fixation by the root nodules has been a gradual lowering of soil pH to values which may limit continued reinfection and nodulation by Rhizobium. With enhanced N_2 fixation rates predicted as atmospheric CO_2 rises, this problem could be exacerbated, requiring new management techniques to maintain the pasture

5.2 Organic Mineralization-Immobilization Reactions. The mineralization of nutrients in the geocycle of elements can

occur by specific enzymes elaborated during periods of
nutrient deficiencies. It is known that phosphatases and
sulfatases are produced under such conditions. Amidases
are known to occur, but it is generally considered that N
accumulates in the NH_4^+ form only when microorganisms
mineralize more NH_4^+ as a byproduct than is required for
microbial growth.

The current mineralization—immobilization rates of
nutrients such as N, S and P occur at two to three times
the net rates measured by crop uptake or nutrient
accumulation under fallow conditions. The microbial
biomass accounts for 2-5% of the soil carbon and 3-8% of
the N of surface soils (Jenkinson and Ladd, 1980).
Microbial products with fairly rapid turnover rates
comprise an equal fraction. Management of the biomass
and their metabolites through residue management and
timing of cultivation and of fertilizer application could
result in a major decrease in the nitrogen that is lost
from most soil systems. Immobilization should occur
during periods of maximum crop growth. Even a 10%
reduction in the high levels of nitrogen loss, usually
associated with crop growth, would have a major impact on
fertilizer requirements and on nutrient availability.

Increased plant productivity will increase the amounts
of carbon entering the organic pool, first as live biomass
and later as soil organic matter. We have estimated
earlier the soil organic matter build-up from the input of
more live biomass. The large anticipated increase in total
biomass will produce a considerably lower increase in
organic matter.

The increased mineralization of plant material will
increase heterotrophic microbial activity. An increased
demand for the mineral nutrients needed for microbial
decomposition that are not contained in plant material will
further stress the soil resources of nitrogen, phosphorus,
potassium and other essential minerals. The increased
requirement for nitrogen can be partially met by increased
fixation of atmospheric N_2, but the increased requirement
for other nutrients will necessarily be met by either soil
resources, in an unfertilized ecosystem, or by both soil
and fertilizer sources in agricultural systems. Table 2
predicts some depletion in the soil reservoir of these
nutrients. The decreased availability of these plant
nutrients will exert a limiting effect on plant production.

The higher rate of biomass production should stimulate
biological nitrogen fixation, since a widening of the C:N

ratio of the soil stimulates N_2 fixation by both
free-living organisms and N_2-fixing organisms. The
widening ratios may also encourage increased migration of
legumes into grassland. It is unlikely, however, that
enough nitrogen will be fixed to maintain the soil C:N
ratio and some slight, but permanent, increase in the
soil C:N ratio can be predicted to accompany increasing
biomass.

For wetlands and poorly aerated uplands, the higher
demand for oxygen resulting from increased plant production
will cause increased accumulation of plant material, as
peat in the wetlands or as increased soil organic matter in
the poorly aerated uplands. This organic matter will have
a high C:N ratio because of its limited decomposition. The
absolute amounts of carbon, nitrogen, sulfur, and other
mineral nutrients tied up in this organic material will
significantly increase.

A similar effect will occur in those upland areas
where the additional plant biomass is difficult to decom-
pose because of its content of inhibitory compounds such as
lignins and tannins. This condition will exist in some
forests and will result in a higher organic matter
accumulation and a wider C:N ratio.

Incomplete oxidation of plant material, especially
under conditions of limited soil aeration, will produce
organic acids, such as acetate, propionate and butyrate,
which are toxic or inhibitory to some biological processes.
It is safe to predict an increased concentration of these
compounds in oxygen deficient systems. Under current
atmospheric CO_2, residues of crop plants such as sorghums
and millets produce high amounts of such compounds and the
crops must therefore be grown in rotation to avoid such
inhibitory effects (Dart, personal communication).

Under seriously limited aeration, the mineralization
of increased amounts of biomass produces reduced sulfur
compounds such as hydrogen sulfide (H_2S), dimethyl sulfide,
and methyl mercaptans which are toxic to both microorganisms and higher plants. Ecosystems that are marginally
aerated may be adversely affected by an increased oxygen
demand.

Less sulfur and phosphorus will be available under
conditions of increased biomass production and the
consequent increase in the organic matter pool dilutes what
may be an already limited supply. Except for the input of
additional sulfur from atmospheric fallout and sulfur and

phosphorus fertilizers, plants are limited to the existing soil supplies.

5.3 Nitrification. With available moisture and oxygen, and the simultaneously increased availability of CO_2 and NH_3 from mineralization, nitrification by autotrophic bacteria in the surface layer of soil will be stimulated. Nitrite and nitrate, the intermediate and the final products of nitrification, may still serve as plant nutrients, but the nitrogen in these oxidized forms is vulnerable to loss through leaching and/or denitrification by subsurface bacteria. In addition, if oxygen becomes limiting during nitrification so that only the ammonia-oxidizing bacteria function, toxic levels of nitrite may result. Finally, an adventitious result of nitrification is the release of as yet unpredictable amounts of nitric and nitrous oxide (Lipschultz et al., 1981). More NO and N_2O is liberated by denitrifying than by nitrifying organisms. Nitrous oxide moves into the earth's atmosphere and may erode the stratospheric ozone layer. There is currently an equilibrium between loss and replacement of ozone. Increased rate of nitrogen oxide release might decrease the protection afforded by ozone, and increase the penetration of ultraviolet radiation.

5.4 Denitrification. Denitrifying bacteria are widely distributed in the soil. In an anaerobic environment, these organisms convert nitrate and nitrite to NO, N_2O and N_2. Populations are greatest in the zone reaching from just below the surface to a depth of 15 to 30 cm. Penetration of this zone by nitrate and nitrite added as fertilizer or generated at or near the surface, coupled with increased availability of soil organic matter, will result in increased rates of release of N_2 and a loss of a significant plant nutrient. Smaller but significant quantities of NO and N_2O relative to N_2 will also be released (McKenney et al., 1982) and added as the major source to the stratospheric load described in the previous section.

5.5 Nitrogen Uptake. Of the essential elements limiting plant growth, N is frequently in notoriously short supply (Subba Rao, 1977). Thus, if CO_2 availability were removed as a limiting factor, increased reliance on N_2 fixation as a source of N would occur. A stimulation of N_2 fixation as a result of atmospheric CO_2 fertilization has been observed (Havelka and Hardy, 1976). This would shift the floristic composition of the vegetation toward legumes and non-legumes capable of symbiotic N_2 fixation (Newton et al., 1977). Plants and bacteria mutually benefiting from associative N_2 fixation (Vose and Ruschel, 1981) would also flourish.

5.5.1 Symbiotic N_2 Fixation

<u>5.5.1.1 Effects of Higher Atmospheric CO_2 Levels</u>. The major effects of CO_2 enrichment are probably via indirect effects on the symbiotic organisms. Nitrogen-fixing organisms such as <u>Rhizobium</u> and <u>Frankia</u> have major requirements for energy provided as plant photosynthate. They in turn are the major organisms contributing N_2 to agricultural and natural ecosystems, respectively. Highly productive systems cannot be achieved or maintained until a large stock of organic matter is built up during a number of years of N_2 fixation. Early experiments with low light levels and with defoliation indicated that these treatments greatly affected the root-associated symbionts. Quantitative data concerning the effects of CO_2 concentrations are limited. Mulder and van Veen (1960) observed an increase in N_2 fixation when hydroponic culture solution was aerated with 40×10^3 ppm CO_2.

Hardy and Havelka's field experiment (1975) showed that over a nine-week period plants grown with supplemental CO_2 reduced five times as much C_2H_2 and had a greater mass of root nodules than untreated controls. Senescence of the N_2-enriched plants had significantly more nodules than untreated controls. Senescence of the N_2-fixing system was delayed. The work by Phillips et al. (1976) indicated that CO_2-enriched plants had significantly more nodules than the controls. However, CO_2 enrichment had no effect on the number of nodules which developed per unit dry weight of a pea plant and a linear regression existed between the number of root nodules and the dry weight of pea plants. They concluded that CO_2 enrichment resulted in an integrated growth of the entire plant with no special promotion of nodule growth, while Hardy and Havelka (1975) and Rogers et al. (1980) showed preferential fixation of N_2 vs. use of fixed N by CO_2 enrichment.

<u>5.5.1.2 Partitioning of Photosynthates</u>. Nitrogen fixation is a highly energy-intensive process and represents a significant sink for photosynthate (Phillips, 1980). Minchin and Pate (1973), in their classic study of C partitioning in nodulated legumes, found that approximately 10% of the fresh assimilate is used as a substrate for nitrogenase. This figure was later confirmed by Kucey and Paul (1982) in mycorrhizal hosts. Increased N input into the symbiotic association by the microsymbiont in turn stimulates plant growth and photosynthesis. The resulting

autocatalytic cycle (Bethlenfalvay et al., 1978) may
finally be limited by other factors.

5.5.1.3 Productivity. Two major effects on root and soil
processes will be produced by increased plant productivity.
Water and minerals will become even more limiting to
plants. This is especially true for nitrogen, because it
is frequently the most limiting nutrient, and nitrogen from
the mineralization of soil organic nitrogen will not
increase as rapidly as demand for crop production. Thus, the
need for fertilizer will increase more rapidly than
increases in productivity. This will also be expected for
nitrogen-fixing crops such as soybeans.

Thus, nitrogen fixation may increase faster than
productivity, due to the limited ability of the soil to
supply additional nitrogen. Associative and free-living
nitrogen fixers may be stimulated in the same way, but the
effect may be less since they are more dependent on soil
nitrogen concentration rather than plant demand. Mulching,
and increased soil organic matter content, expected to
occur under minimum tillage practices, may also have a
significant effect on N_2 fixation.

5.5.1.4 CO_2 Concentration in the Rhizosphere. The effects
of below-ground CO_2 may be different for host and endophyte. Low concentration of soil CO_2 may be necessary for
optimal root growth, and higher concentrations can be
inhibitory, with peas being inhibited at CO_2 concentrations
as low as 15,000 ppm. At 65,000 ppm of CO_2, beans and
sunflowers are strongly inhibited, while barley and oats
are not (Stolwijk and Thimann, 1957). Under somewhat
different experimental conditions, 80,000 ppm CO_2 was
moderately inhibitory to both peas and barley (Geisler,
1967).

Removal of CO_2 from air is inhibitory to both the
nodulation of legumes and the growth of rhizobia in culture
(Mulder and van Veen, 1960; Lowe and Evans, 1962). The
effect of elevated CO_2 concentration is less clear. It has
been reported that nitrogenase activity, measured by
acetylene reduction, is not measurably different at 0 and
30,000 ppm CO_2 in pea and soybean nodules (Mahon, 1979;
Coker and Schubert, 1981). But in alders, 30,000 ppm CO_2
inhibits nitrogenase activity 20% (Winship and Tjepkema,
1982), while no consistent effect is found in soybean
nodules (Coker and Schubert, 1981). In peas, the
respiration of nodulated root systems is substantially
inhibited by 30,000 ppm CO_2, but this is apparently due to

inhibition of root respiration rather than to nodule respiration (Mahon, 1979).

Increased CO_2 could lead to more productive rhizobia/ legume associations. In legumes, high concentrations of CO_2 can increase root and nodule growth due to PEP-carboxylase catalyzed carbon fixation. The fixed carbon serves as a carbon skeleton for nitrogen fixation, and as an energy-producing metabolic intermediate. CO_2 at sufficiently high concentrations can be toxic to plant roots, but good growth occurs even at 240,000 ppm CO_2, and thus increased atmospheric CO_2 should not be a significant factor.

5.5.2 Nodulated Non-Legumes. Frankia, an actinomycete, nodulates a relatively diverse group of wood dicotyledonous plants including Alnus, Myrica gale, Shepherdia and Casuarina. These N-fixing symbiotic associations are a significant source of combined N in various ecosystems. Since the plants are C_3, it is anticipated that an increase in atmospheric CO_2 will increase rates of photosynthesis and photosynthate for the nodule endophyte. This may enhance total N_2 fixation and N input from these associations.

5.5.3 Nitrogen-fixing associations. Nitrogen-fixing bacteria occur in the rhizosphere of many plants, particularly in the tropics (Dart and Day, 1975; Neyra and Dobereiner, 1977). Nitrogen balance studies for soil-grown plants in pots containing measured amounts of combined nitrogen, show that such bacteria may supply nitrogen for plant growth. Studies with $^{15}N_2$ for sorghum, sugar cane, Paspalum notatum, Digitaria decumbans and Setaria italica confirmed that biologically fixed nitrogen was transferred to the plant tops (DePolli et al., unpublished; Wani, Day and Dart, unpublished).

More than 50 plant species from both temperate and tropical environments, including agriculturally important crops such as sorghum, pearl millet, setaria, maize, rice, and wheat are known to stimulate nitrogenase activity in their rhizospheres as measured by acetylene reduction assays. For rice, sorghum, millet, setaria and Paspalum notatum, there appears to be genotypic differences in activity between lines (Dart and Wani, 1982).

The Broadbalk wilderness experiment at Rothamsted, started in 1888, suggests that nitrogen fixation associated with the roots of several weed species resulted in the build up of soil organic matter, calculated to be 40 kg N/ha/yr from fixation (Jenkinson and Rayner, 1977).

Other N balance field experiments in Brazil and India
suggest that biological nitrogen fixation contributes
significantly to the plant nitrogen economy. In India a
cross between Pennisetum purpureum and P. americanum
produced 136 tonnes/ha above ground dry matter in a low
fertility alfisol soil. The crop removed 1185 kg N/ha in
30 months, without addition of N fertilizer.

This nitrogen-fixing activity also plays an important
part in the nitrogen economy of estuarine communities and
for Spartina alterniflora in salt marshes, appears to
provide most of their nitrogen requirement (Buresh et al.,
1980). Nitrogen-fixing activity is generally stimulated by
high photosynthetic activity and by high soil moisture
(Dart and Wani, 1982). Both of these are likely to be
enhanced by higher atmospheric CO_2.

If the C to N ratio of the extra plant tissue derived
from increased photosynthetic activity does not change,
then this will create a greater demand for nitrogen, which
must be supplied either by fertilizer or by increased
nitrogen fixation.

5.5.3.1 Inoculation responses. Many different types of
nitrogen-fixing bacteria have been isolated from the
rhizosphere. Some, such as Azotobacter and Azospirillum,
can also influence plant growth by other means (Okon,
1982), perhaps by production of plant growth promoters and
by enrichment of mineral uptake. It is, however, difficult
to quantify the contribution of each process following
inoculation of plants with N_2-fixing bacteria.

Inoculation with N_2-fixing bacteria has increased the
yield of nitrogen and dry matter of a variety of cereal
crops in both pot and field experiements in Israel, India,
and Brazil (Okon, 1982; Dart and Wani, 1982; Boddey and
Dobereiner, 1982). Plants inoculated with Azospirillum
form associations with roots of cereals and forage grasses
which significantly increase mineral uptake (N, P and K) by
the roots and also contribute fixed nitrogen to the plant,
mainly during flowering (Okon, 1982). Significant
increases in yields were obtained in Azospirillum inoculated fields that received an intermediate level of
nitrogen fertilization at planting. Effects of this type
(N_2 fixation, enhancement of mineral uptake) associated
with rhizosphere bacteria such as Azospirillum, will be
further enhanced by the higher rate of root surface
activity resulting from higher photosynthate supply to the
roots. Furthermore, if the root respiration rates
increase, there may be a selection for bacteria that adapt

and are more efficient under microaerobic conditions, such as Azospirillum.

It is not clear if rhizosphere bacteria are specially active with C_4 plants compared with C_3 plants. Some promising Azospirillum isolates have been obtained from the roots of weeds. It will be important to know if high CO_2 will enhance weed growth more than that of crops. To exploit the potential of root associations with bacteria in agricultural systems will require careful management of any fertilizer additions to obtain maximum benefit under 600 ppm CO_2.

5.5.4 Azolla. Azolla is a floating aquatic fern which contains a cyanobacterium, Anabaena azolla, as a symbiont. Both partners are photosynthetic, and the cyanobacterium can provide the association with its total N requirement. Azolla is a C_3 plant with Calvin cycle intermediates, an O_2 inhibition of photosynthesis and an O_2 dependent CO_2 compensation point. Under optimized laboratory conditions these associations have been shown to double their biomass in 1.6 to 2.0 days and to contain 5-6% N on a dry weight basis. Under good field conditions, doubling times are on the order of 3-5 days with 4-5% N on a dry weight basis. These associations provide an alternative N source for rice. While both rice and Azolla may be expected to respond to CO_2 enrichment of the atmosphere, rice will require additional combined nitrogen if quality is maintained and yields enhanced. Azolla-Anabaena associations may play a significant role in meeting this additional N requirement for rice, and perhaps for other aquatic crops, such as taro.

5.6 Mycorrhiza. Mycorrhizae are symbiotic associations between the host-plant root and a mycorrhizal fungus. The fungi are generally referred to as ecto- or endomycorrhiza. These fungi belong to different classes of the Eumycota. Ectomycorrhizae (ECM) generally colonize woody plant species and are important in forest ecology. Endomycor- rhizal fungi are mostly categorized as "vesicular- arbuscular" because of their distinctive morphological characteristics. This latter category colonizes practi- cally all native and agricultural plant species except species belonging to the orders Caryophyllales, Polygonales, and Capparales (Gerdemann, 1968). Ectomycorrhizae are generally biotrophic, but often can be grown in pure culture. Vesicular-arbuscular mycorrhizal (VAM) fungi are obligate biotrophs. They lack host specificity, and some species are world-wide in distribution.

5.6.1 Inoculum. Vesicular-arbuscular mycorrhizal fungi
have not yet been cultured under axenic conditions in the
absence of a host plant, in spite of considerable research
efforts in several laboratories. Efforts are being made to
produce VAM fungi for large-scale inoculation by soil
culture (J. Menge, personal communication) and by a
nutrient-film technique (Rothamsted Report, 1981).

Some data are available which indicate that certain
host-endophyte combinations are more effective than others,
in spite of a general lack of host specificity. The
effectiveness of VAM fungi appears to be more affected by
soil characteristics than by compatibility with any
specific host plant (Mosse, 1975).

Inoculation of field crops with VAM fungi may be
successful when native soil populations are sparse or
consist of relatively ineffective species (Hayman, 1974).
Yield or plant growth increases resulting from field
inoculations have been reported by Black and Tinker (1977).
Inoculation of cowpea with Rhizobium and chopped roots of
a mycorrhizal native grass was carried out in a Brazilian
oxisol by S.M. LaTorraca and T.V. St. John (unpublished
data). Yield of VAM plants in five fertilization
treatments were up to twice those of controls that received
sterilized grass roots and live Rhizobium.

Field inoculations of ectomycorrhizal fungi already
play an important role in establishment of exotic forest
species and reclamation of mine spoils and other unfavorable sites (Marx and Krupa, 1978). Thus, techniques
already exist that would allow new ectomycorrhizal fungi to
be introduced as needed to deal with changing conditions
brought about by increasing atmospheric CO_2.

5.6.2 Development. Effects of CO_2 on aerial portions
of the plant (increased photosynthesis) can be expected to
favorably influence the mycorrhizal symbiosis (Hayman,
1974). Competition for carbohydrates by the symbiosis
under limiting light intensity was shown to result in
growth depression of the host plant (Bethlenfalvay et al.,
1982b). The development of host and VAM endophyte appear
to be interrelated ontogenetically with source-sink
relationships as a controlling factor (Bethlenfalvay et
al., 1982a, 1982b). A possible increase in world mean
temperature might influence fungal physiology (Furlan and
Fortin, 1973; Hayman, 1974). Spore germination, infection,
proliferation and sporulation of mycorrhizal fungi all
depend on favorable environmental conditions. Some
environmental factors to which VAM fungi are particularly

sensitive are pH, temperature, and excess water (Mosse et al., 1981).

The presence of decomposing soil organic particles stimulates the proliferation of VAM extra-matrical mycelium (St. John et al., submitted). Since soil hyphae are able to initiate new VAM infection points (Powell, 1976), the presence of increased soil organic matter may encourage more rapid spread of VAM. The direct effects of CO_2 on mycorrhizae have not been studied.

Saif (1981) examined the effect of oxygen concentration on mycorrhizal infection and plant growth response. He found that plants responded better to VAM at CO_2 concentrations of 12 and 16% than at 21%. His artificial atmosphere did not contain even the normal ambient amount of CO_2. His techniques could be used to study CO_2 effects, and work at Rothamsted Experiment Station has apparently shown VAM infection to respond favorably to small increases in CO_2 concentration (B. Mosse, personal communication).

ECM fungi have been studied only slightly more than VAM fungi. Telson et al. (1980) reported that the difference in growth of mycorrhizal and non-mycorrhizal <u>Pinus</u> <u>sylvestris</u> was greater under conditions of higher CO_2 concentration. The growth of the mycorrhizal fungus <u>Pisolithus</u> <u>tinctorius</u> in pure culture was improved by higher than normal CO_2 concentrations.

Read and Armstrong (1972) showed that formation of the mantle of ECM in certain conifers is dependent on transport of oxygen through roots. They noted that oxygen can be very deficient in coniferous humus layers and suggested that mycorrhizal function in the humus environment is dependent on diffusion of O_2 from host roots. If they are correct, ECM establishment and function may be essentially independent of ambient CO_2 levels in nature.

Destruction of native vegetation, the main consumer of CO_2, sometimes has the additional effect of the modification or destruction of mycorrhizal inocula (Reeves et al., 1979). Successional vegetation or agricultural and ornamental species subsequently occupying the site may be strongly influenced by the lack of inocula (Janos, 1980). One consequence is likely to be reduced production on that site, and therefore O_2 production and CO_2 consumption.

<u>5.6.3 Effect on Plant Growth</u>. Most of the P present in mineral soils is precipitated as the aluminum or iron

salt in acid soils and as the calcium salt in alkaline
soils (Focht and Martin, 1979). Only a small fraction of
the total P present in a soil may be available to plants.
As a result, P is one of the major factors which limit
plant growth under natural and cultural conditons.
Mycorrhizal fungi may significantly increase the uptake of
P and other relatively immobile nutrients, such as Zn and
Cu, by their host plants (Hayman, 1978). The mechanism for
this phenomenon is a thorough permeation of the soil volume
availabe to the host by the extra-matrical fungal mycelium,
which can reach soil microsites not exploited by the host
alone (Tinker, 1978). In addition, mycorrhizae release
oxylate which, in turn, causes the release of some
additional nutrients from soil minerals (Graustein et al.,
1977).

5.6.4 Effect on Water Uptake. The effect of mycorrhizal fungi on plants when waƚer is the major limiting
factor may be significant, but is not well known (Trappe,
1981). While few crop plants will survive when soil water
potential is below -15 x 10^5 Pa (Hall et al., 1979), many
fungi and bacteria will thrive at values far below this
(Focht and Martin, 1979). Of particular interest in this
respect are VAM, which appear to be common in desert plants
(Trappe, 1981; Bethlenfalvay, unpublished data).
Modification of plant water status by VAM may result in
increased rates of photosynthesis under intermittent
drought conditions, thus providing a better sink for CO_2.
The mechanism of enhanced water uptake by mycorrhiza is
controversial. Higher rates of P uptake and the improved
nutritional status of mycorrhizal plants have been
implicated as the causal factors (Safir et al., 1972).
More recent work, some of which was reviewed by Hardie and
Leyton (1981), suggests that VAM may help plants acquire
soil water not available to uninfected plants.

5.6.5 Respiratory Cost. Mycorrhizae growth could be
limited by high soil CO_2 concentrations. VAM may represent
up to 20% of the dry weight of the fungus-root association
(Bethlenfalvay et al., 1982d). As respiration by fungi is
2 to 4 times higher than that of vascular plant tissue, and
as CO_2 evolution by mycorrhizae is probably enhanced by
infection respiration (Cooke, 1977), total respiration
rates in mycorrhizae may be up to twice as high as in roots
not colonized by VAM fungi. Increases in above-ground
biomass may therefore be translated into below-ground
respiration rates considerably higher than those found in
experimentation with nonmycorrhizal plants under controlled
conditions.

5.6.6 Effect on N_2 fixation. There are close linkages
between organic C and N accumulation in mature soils and P
contents in the original parent materials. Microbial
growth processes are the principal arena for the adjustment
of N supply to the supply of P (Cole and Heil, 1981). The
availability of P is crucial to N_2 fixation, a process
which has a many-fold higher requirement of P than does
the host plant (Mosse, 1976). Thus the availability of P
is a factor which may determine the rate at which N_2
fixation will be able to accommodate the increased N
requirements of plants growing at a higher CO_2
concentration. Increased uptake of P by mycorrhizal fungi
has been shown to enhance symbiotic N_2 fixation
(Bethlenfalvay and Yoder, 1981) and associative N_2 fixation
(Bagyaraj and Menge, 1978). These processes may therefore
occupy a key position in modifying and controlling the flux
of P and N to plants experiencing enhanced growth due to
CO_2 fertilization.

5.7 Effects on Plant Pathogens

5.7.1 Fungus. Elevation of CO_2 concentration in the
atmosphere and in soil may affect fungal development.
Fungal species such as Sclerotinia minor and Phytophthora
infestans are quite sensitive to CO_2. Species like
Penicillium nigricans, Cochliobolus sativus and many
species of Fusarium are quite tolerant of high CO_2. A
rapid increase in CO_2 may have an adverse effect on some of
the fungi, and changes in the compostion of the fungal
community would be expected. This phenomenon might be
observed in soil pores and microsites which contain a high
concentration of entrapped CO_2 gas. However, given the
adaptative capabilities of microorganisms, a gradual
increase of CO_2 concentration over a long period of time
may cause little overall change to the species present,
and/or their growth.

Extremely high CO_2 concentrations (200,000 ppm or
more) inhibit the hyphal growth of fungi, but sporulation
and development of fruiting bodies (morphogenesis) seems to
be much more sensitive to CO_2. In mushrooms, for instance,
production can be improved by manipulating CO_2. At a high
CO_2, the pathogenicity of Rhizoctonia solani and
Sclerotium rolfsii is reduced. High CO_2 can also
reduce losses by inhibiting the growth of fruit-rotting
fungi on fruits and vegetables.

5.7.2 Bacteria and other plant pathogens. Effects of
doubling the CO_2 in the atmosphere on the growth and
community composition of plant pathogenic bacteria may be

important because bacteria can survive from season to season by living in decaying plant tissues. Hence, the return of extra plant residues to soil may increase the population of pathogens as well as useful organisms.

For other plant pathogens -- virus, mycoplasma, rickettsia, etc. -- that are closely associated with the host system, little direct effect can be expected from increased CO_2 in the atmosphere.

6. Management Options

Direct effects of increased CO_2 levels are not considered to be of major significance on microbial soil activity. This conclusion is based on the assumption that soil CO_2 will not be significantly increased by a doubling of atmospheric CO_2. Photosynthetic microorganisms on the soil surface will be unaffected by increased CO_2 because they already possess a CO_2 pumping system.

Indirect effects of increased atmospheric CO_2 as the result of increased plant productivity will strongly affect microbial soil activity which in turn will control the extent of the crop productivity that is realized. Management of the soil system including the application of existing and yet to be developed technologies will be key to the degree of crop productivity that is realized. Furthermore, some of these technologies, such as minimum tillage, provide models to study the impact of increased crop production.

Techniques such as minimum tillage greatly reduce erosion and the requirements of energy for cultivation. They increase the potential for crop growth and for stabilization of soil organic matter (Phillips et al., 1980). The plant cover and absence of physical disturbance produces a 2°-6°C drop in soil temperature, while soil moisture and aggregate stability are maintained. Minimum tillage in the U.S. is projected to increase from 2.2 Mha in 1974 to 62 Mha, or 45% of the total U.S. cropland, by 2000. At Sydney, Montana, minimum tillage maintained soil organic matter at the level of a virgin grassland site, while conventional tillage reduced organic matter content by 20%. The nitrogen requirement, at least in the short term, is increased, possibly due to increased immobilization and/or losses due to denitrification. Phosphate requirements in minimum tillage may parallel those of nitrogen.

The 1,600 - 2,000 Mha of potentially available land in

the tropics that is subject to rapid decomposition rates
and erosion may benefit from minimum tillage. At present, 60%
of this area is devoted to shifting cultivation. Management and maintenance of soil organic matter levels are
essential for erosion control, water penetration, buffering
against acidification, blocking P absorbing sites, and as a
nutrient reservoir. An organic matter increase of 625
kg/ha for annual pastures and 1150 for perennial pastures
has been observed in Australia. Bush fallow produces
similar increases. Residue mulch - minimum tillage has
maintained tropical soil and temperate organic matter
levels 20% above those under conventional tillage.

6.2 Intercropping, Multiple Cropping, Green Manures.
The use of legumes for intercropping, multiple cropping or
as green manures is a management option for nitrogen
provision. Combination of hairy vetch in minimum tillage
maize production is an example. Hairy vetch grown during
the winter periods in Kentucky and other southern states
not only decreases soil erosion and weed growth, but has
the potential for supplying 100-200 kg N/ha to the
following corn crop. The use of a herbicide at the time of
maize growth and the perennial nature of hairy vetch
enables the cycle vetch-maize-vetch.

6.3 Microorganism Addition. Phosphorus limitation
and aluminum toxicity inhibit plant growth in a vast area
of tropical savanna such as the cerrado of Brazil (Sanchez
et al., 1982a). Mycorrhizal fungi, as discussed earlier,
have the potential to cause major increases in P uptake
under tropical conditions of both upland and lowland crops
(Islam et al., 1980; Tinker, 1982). Mycorrhizal
inoculation coupled with their increased activity from
increased crop production will impact positively on these
large areas. Systems for production and inoculation with
preferred mycorrhizal strains are needed. Mycorrhizal
research is needed to provide management options for P
input.

After phosphorus, nitrogen is probably the most
important nutrient for increased crop productivity by
increased CO_2. Several management options exist. In the
case of legumes, inoculation with the most effective
N-fixing microbe will continue to be most important. The
criteria for strain selection are ability to successfully
compete with ineffective indigenous rhizobia, ability to
nodulate the host plant, and ability to efficiently convert
N_2 to ammonia. Similar approaches are being used with
Frankia for the non-legume N_2-fixing trees. Other options
exist for other crops. The Azolla-Anabaena association is

being evaluated as an intercrop with paddy-grown rice. Some management changes may be needed to optimize nitrogen input by this system, since in the presence of elevated CO_2 the canopy may close earlier than it does now. The associative N_2-fixing systems such as between cerial grains and Azospirillum have been shown to definitely increase crop yield in at least a few locations (see Section 5.5.3). Azospirillum inoculation may evolve as a management option for increasing nitrogen input.

6.4 New Technology Inputs. Manipulation of genetic materials of both host and microbial symbionts has great potential to provide new options for increased productivity. The rate of scientific advances in molecular genetics has been great relative to the modest rate of increase in atmospheric CO_2. It is thus reasonably safe to assume that this evolving technology will obviate many of the limitations of existing technologies.

A discussion of possible relevant molecular genetic inputs follows. The time required for most of these technological advances is longer than many have suggested, but the advances within the next 25 years should be great. Molecular genetic manipulations of the N_2 fixation system pose some of the most difficult challenges in agriculture because of the high multiplicity of the genes and because of the sensitivity of nitrogenase to O_2.

With the above qualifications, the potentials for genetic manipulation in N_2 fixation and denitrification will be considerable. Genetic studies have defined many of the nitrogen fixation genes in blue-green algae, in free-living organisms, and in Rhizobium, and the genes responsible for nodulation are similarly being characterized. Improved versions of these genes will be developed and transferred among strains. Rhizobium which most efficiently fix nitrogen may be transformed to become the more effective nodulators, and, reciprocally, strains which dominate in the field may be the recipients of improved nitrogen fixation genes. Nodulation genes could also be transferred among Rhizobium strains in order to alter their host specificity. Alternatively, nitrogen fixation genes could be moved into mycorrhiza or perhaps even plants.

Following parallel lines of experimentation, nodulation and association genes could be transferred to associative bacteria. Identification of the plant genes necessary for these interactions will allow new plant hosts to be developed through genetic transfer of the plant symbiosis genes. Of particular interest in this regard would be both transferring symbiosis genes to crop plants such as corn and wheat, and transferring stem nodulation genes from peanuts, Sesbania, or Aeschynemene to new hosts. Stem nodules might be less susceptible to soil nitrate/ammonia inhibition and might be more able to take advantage of more CO_2.

The problem of denitrification may similarly yield to genetic solutions. The genes that produce N_2O uptake enzymes could be altered to increase their affinities for N_2O. They could then scavenge N_2O and reduce it before its escape to the atmosphere.

Finally, opportunities will arise to create strains with novel synthetic enzymes. Hybrid genes are now being created by splicing segments of different genes together, and we can expect that novel nitrogenase genes will also be formed through gene synthesis and gene splicing. Such constructions should yield nitrogen-fixing enzymes that bear little resemblance to the present enzymes. One purpose for generating such modified enzymes would be to fix nitrogen to products other than ammonia. Many more such opportunities to create novel enzymes will undoubtedly present themselves. These technologies will greatly expand the management options in the coming decades.

9. Literature Cited

Atjay, G.L., P. Ketner and P. Duvigneaud. 1979. Terrestrial primary production and phytomass. In Scope 13, The Global Carbon Cycle, B. Bolin, E.T. Degens, S. Kempe and P. Ketner, Eds., John Wiley and Sons, New York, pp. 129-181.

Bagyaraj, D.J. and J.A. Menge. 1978. Interaction between a VA mycorrhiza and Azotobacter and their effects on rhizosphere microflora and plant growth. New Phytol. 80, 567-573.

Bauer, A. and A.L. Black. 1981. Soil carbon, nitrogen and bulk density comparisons in two crop plant tillage systems after 25 years and in virgin grasslands. Soil Sci. Sco. Am. J. 45, 1166-1170.

Berry, J., J. Boynton, A. Kaplan, and M. Badger. 1976. Growth and photosynthesis of Chlamydomonas reinhardii as a function of CO_2 concentration. Carnegie Institute Year Book. 75, 423-432

Bethlenfalvay, G.J. S.S. Abu-Shakra, and D.A.

Phillips, 1978. Interdependence of nitrogen
and photosynthesis in Pisum Sativum L. II.
Host plant response to nitrogen fixation by
Rhizobium strains. Plant Physiol. 62, 131-133.

Bethlenfalvay, G.J. and J.F. Yoder. 1981. The Glycine-
Glomus-Rhizobium symbiosis. Physiol. Plant. 52,
141-145.

Bethlenfalvay, G.J., M.S. Brown, and R.S. Pacovsky. 1982a.
Relationships between host and endophyte development
in mycorrhizal soybeans. New Phytol. 90, 537-543.

Bethlenfalvay, G.J., R.S. Pacovsky, M.S. Brown, and G.
Fuller. 1982b. Mycotrophic growth and mutualistic
development of host plant and fungal endophyte in an
endomycorrhizal symbiosis. Plant Soil (in press).

Bethlenfalvay, G.J., R.S. Pacovsky, H.M. Bayne, and A.
Stafford. 1982c. Interactions between N_2 fixation
mycorrhizal colonization and host plant growth in the
Phaseolus-Rhizobium-Glomus symbiosis. Plant Physiol.
(in press).

Bethlenfalvay, G.J., R.S. Pacovsky, and M.S. Brown. 1982d.
Parasitic and mutualistic associations between a
mycorrhizal fungus and soybean: development of the
endophyte. Phytopathology. 72, 894-897.

Bidwell, R.G.S. 1977. Photosynthesis and light and dark
respiration in fresh water algae. Can. J. Bot.
55, 809-818.

Black, R.L.B. and P.B. Tinker. 1977. Interaction between
effects of vesicular-arbuscular mycorrhiza and
fertilizer phosphorus on yields of potatoes in the
field. Nature 267, 510-511.

Boddey, R.M. and G. Dobereiner. 1982. Association of
Azospirillum: Other diazotrophs with tropical
Gramineae. 12th Intl. Congress of Soil Science. New
Delhi, India, Feb. 8-16, 1982. Symposia Papers pp.
23-47.

Bolin, B., E.T. Degen, S. Kempe and P. Ketner, Eds. 1979.
The Global Carbon Cycle. John Wiley and Sons, New
York.

Buresch, P.J., M.E Casselman and W.H. Patrick, Jr. 1980.

Nitrogen fixation in flooded soil systems, a review. Adv. Agron. 33, 149-192.

Coker, G.T. and K. Schubert. 1981. Carbon dioxide fixation in soybean roots and nodules. Plant Physiol. 67, 691-696.

Cole, C. V. and R. D. Heil. 1981. Phosphorus effect on terrestrial nitrogen cycling. In F. E. Clark and T. Rosswell, Eds, Terrestrial N-Cycles Ecological Bulletin. Vol. 3. Stockholm, pp. 363-374.

Coleman, D.C. 1973. Compartmental analysis of "total soil respiration": an exploratory study. Oikos 24, 361-366.

Cooke, R. 1977. The Biology of Symbiotic Fungi. John Wiley and Sons, London.

Dart, P.J. and J.M. Day. 1975. In Non-symbiotic Nitrogen Fixation, N. Walker, Ed. John Wiley and Sons, New York, pp. 225-252.

Dart, P.J. and S.D. Wani. 1982. Nonsymbiotic nitrogen fixation and soil fertility. In The Tropics Trans. 12th Intl. Congress of Soil Science 1, 3-27.

de Jong, E. and E.A. Paul. 1979. The composition of the soil atomsphere and its relationship to soil aeration and respiration. In Encyclopedia of Earth Science Series. Vol. VI. Soil Science and Applied Geology. O.W. Finkle, Jr., Ed. Reinhold Book Corp., New York.

de Jong, E., H.J.V. Schappert and K.B. MacDonald. 1974. Carbon dioxide evolution from virgin and cultivated soil as affected by management practices and climate. Canadian J. Soil Sci. 54, 299-307.

Denmead, O.T. and E.R. Lemon. 1970. Prediction and measurement of photosynthetic activity. Wageningen Center for Agricultural Publishing and Documentation, pp. 149-164 and 199-205.

De-Polli, H., M. Eiichi and J. Dobereiner. 1977. Confirmation of nitrogen fixation in two tropical grasses by molecular nitrogen 15 incorporation. Soil Biol. Biochem. 9, 119-123.

Dreyfus, B.L. and J.R. Dommergue. 1981. Nitrogen fixing nodules induced by Rhizobium on the stem of tropical legume Sesbania rostrata. FEMS Lett. 10, 313-317.

Focht, D.D. and J.P. Martin. 1979. Microbiological and biochemical aspects of semi-arid agricultural soils. In Agriculture in Semi-Arid Environments, A.E. Hall, G.H. Cannel and H.W. Lawton, Eds. Springer-Verlag, Berlin, pp. 119-147.

Furlan, V. and J.A. Fortin. 1973. Formation of endomycorrhizae by Endogone calospora on Allium cepa under three temperature regimes. Nat. Can. 100, 467-477.

Garrett, S.D. 1981. Soil Fungi and Soil Fertility. Pergamon Press, Oxford.

Geisler, G. 1967. Interactive effects of CO_2 and O_2 in soil on root and top growth of barley and peas. Plant Physiol. 42, 305-307.

Gerdemann, J.W. 1968. Vesicular-arbuscular mycorrhiza and plant growth. Ann. Rev. Phytopathol. 6, 397-418.

Goswami, K. and V.K. Suri. 1982. Carbon fertilization: Influence of simulated field soil respiration on soybean crop. Proc. 12th ISSS Congress, Delhi.

Goudriaan, J. and G.L. Ajtay. 1979. The possible effects of increased CO_2 on photosynthesis. In The Global Carbon Cycle, B. Bolin, E.T. Degens, S. Kempe and P. Ketner, Eds. John Wiley and Sons, New York, pp. 237-250.

Grable, A.R. 1966. Soil aeration and plant growth. Adv. Agron. 18, 57-106.

Graustein, W.C., K. Cromack and P. Sollins. 1977. Calcium oxalate: Occurrence in soils and effect on nutrient and geochemical cycles. Science. 198, 1252-1254.

Greenwood, D.J. 1970. Distribution of carbon dioxide in the aqueous phase of aerobic soils. J. Soil Sci. 21, 314-329.

Griffin, D.M. 1972. Ecology of Soil Fungi. Syracuse Univ. Press., Syracuse, N.Y.

Hall, A.E., K.W. Foster and J.G. Waines. 1979. Crop adaptation to semi-arid environments. In Agriculture in Semi-Arid Environments, A.E. Hall, G.H. Cannell and H.W. Lawton, Eds. Springer-Verlag, Berlin, pp. 148-179.

Hardie, K. and L. Leyton. 1981. The influence of vesicular-arbuscular mycorrhiza on growth and water relations of red clover. I. In phosphate deficient soil. New Phytol. 89, 599-608.

Hardy, R.W.F. and U.D. Havelka. 1975. Photosynthate as a major factor limiting N$_2$ fixation by field grown legumes with emphasis on soybeans. In Symbiotic Nitrogen Fixation in Plants, R.S. Nutman, Ed., Cambridge University Press, London, pp. 421-439.

Havelka, U.D. and R.W.F. Hardy. 1976. Legume N$_2$ fixation as a problem in carbon nutrition. In Nitrogen Fixation, W.E. Newton and C.J. Nyman, Eds., Vol. 2., Washington State Univ. Press, pp. 456-475.

Hayman, D.S. 1974. Plant growth responses to vesicular-arbuscular mycorrhiza. VI. Effect of light and temperature. New Phytol. 73, 71-80.

Idso, S.B. 1981. Carbon dioxide - an alternative view. New Scientist 92, 444-446.

Idso, S.B. and B.A. Kimball. 1982. Man, carbon dioxide, climate and food: A global perspective. Symposium on Plant Production Under Drought Conditions. Tulsa, OK.

Islam, R., A. Ayanaba and F.E. Sander. 1980. Response of cowpea (Vigna unguiculata) to inoculation with VA mycorrhizal fungi and to rock phosphate fertilization in some unsterilized Nigerian soils. Plant and Soil 54, 107-117.

Janos, D.P. 1980. Mycorrhizae influence tropical succession. Biotropica 12 (Supplement), 56-64.

Jenkinson, D.S. and J.H. Rayner. 1977. The turnover of soil organic matter in some of the Rothamsted classical experiments. Soil Sci. 123, 298.

Jenkinson, D.S. and J.W. Ladd. 1980. In Soil Biochemistry, Vol. 5, E.A. Paul and J.W. Ladd, Eds., Marcel Dekker, New York.

Johnen, B.G. 1974. Bildung, Menge und Umsetzung von Pflanzenwurzein im Boden. Agrikulturchemischen Institut der Rheinishchen Friedrich-Wilhelms-Universitat, Bonn.

Kaplan, A., D. Zenvirth, L. Reinhold and J.A. Berry. 1982.

Involvement of a primary electrogenic pump in the mechanism for HCO_3^- uptake by the cyanobacterium Anabaena variablis. Plant Physiol. 69, 978–982.

Karagouni, A.D. and J.H. Slater. 1978. Growth of the blue-green alga Anacystis nidulans during washout from light- and carbon dioxide-limited chemostats. FEMS Microbiol. Lett. 4, 295–299.

Kimmins, J.P., J. de Catanzaro and D. Binkley. 1979. Tabular summary of data from the literature on the biogeochemistry of temperate forest ecoystems. ENFOR Project P-8 Report, Faculty of Forestry, Univ. of British Columbia, Vancouver, British Columbia, p. 104.

Kramer, P.J. 1981. Carbon dioxide concentration, photosynthesis, and dry matter production. BioScience 31, 29–33.

Kucey, R.M.N. and E.A. Paul. 1982. Carbon flow, photosynthesis and N_2 fixation in mycorrhizal and nodulated faba beans (Vicea faba L.). Soil Biol. Biochem., in press.

Lal, R. and B.T. Kang. 1982. Management of organic matter in soils of the tropics and subtropics. Proc. 12th ISSS Congress, Delhi. 1, 152.

Lindsay, W.L. 1979. Chemical Equilibria in Soil. John Wiley and Sons, New York.

Lipschultz, F., O.C. Zafiriou, S.C. Wofsy, M.B. McElroy, F.W. Valoris and S.W. Watson. 1981. Production of NO and N_2O by soil nitrifying bacteria. Nature 294, 641–643.

Lloyd, N.D.H., D.J. Canvin and D.A. Culver. 1977. Photosynthesis and photorespiration in algae. Plant Physiol. 59, 936–940.

Lowe, R.H. and H.J. Evans. 1962. Soil Science 94, 351–356.

Luxmoore, R.J. 1981. CO_2 and phytomass. BioScience 31, 626.

Lynch, J.N. 1978. Productivity and phytotoxicity of acetic acid in anaerobic soil and plant residues. Soil Biol. Biochem. 10, 131–135.

Macauley, B.J. and D.M. Griffin. 1969. Effects of carbon dioxide and oxygen on the activity of some soil fungi. Trans. Brit. Mycol. Soc. 53, 53–62.

Mahon, J.D. 1979. Plant Physiol. 63, 892-897.

Marx, D.H. and S.V. Krupa. 1978. Mycorrhizae. A. Ectomy-corrhizae. In Interactions between Non-pathogenic Soil Microorganisms and Plants. Y.R. Dommergues and S.V. Krupa, Eds. Elsivier Scientific Publishing Co., Amsterdam, pp. 373-400.

McKenney, D.J., K.F. Shuttleworth, J.R. Vriesacker and W.I. Findlay. 1982. Production and loss of nitric oxide from denitrification in anaerobic Brookston clay. Appl. Environ. Microbiol. 43, 534-541.

Melillo, J.N., J.D. Aber and J.F. Muratore. 1982. Nitrogen and lignin control of hardwood leaf litter decomposition dynamics ecology (in press).

Minchin, F.R. and J.S. Pate. 1973. The carbon balance of a legume and the functional economy of its nodules. J. Exp. Bot. 24, 259-271.

Moore, A.W. 1969. Azolla: biology and agronomic significance. Bot. Rev. 35, 17-34.

Mosse, B. 1975. Specificity in VA mycorrhizas. In Endomycorrhizas, F.E. Sanders, B. Mosse and P.B. Tinker, Eds., Academic Press, London. pp. 469-484.

Mosse, B. 1976. The role of mycorrhiza in legume nutrition on marginal soils. In Exploiting the Legume-Rhizobium Symbiosis in Tropical Agriculture, J.M. Vincent, A.S. Whitney and J. Vose, Eds., Coll. Trop. Agri. Misc. Publ. 145. Univ. Hawaii, pp. 275-292.

Mosse, B., D.P. Stribley and F. Le Tacon. 1981. Ecology of mycorrhizae and mycorrhizal fungi. Advances in Microbial Ecology 5, 137-210.

Mulder, E.G. and W.L. van Veen. 1960. The influence of carbon dioxide on symbiotic nitrogen fixation. Plant and Soil 13, 265-278.

Newton, W., J.R. Postgate, and C. Rodriguez-Barrueco. 1977. Recent Developments in Nitrogen Fixation. Academic Press, London.

Neyra, C.A. and J. Dobreiner. 1977. Nitrogen fixation in grasses. Adv. Agron. 29, 1028.

Nye, P.H. and P.B. Tinker. 1977. Solute movement in the

soil-root system. University of California Press,
Berkeley.

Okon, Y. 1982. Azospirillum: Physiological properties,
mode of association with roots and its application
for the benefit of cereal and forage grass crops.
Special volume on Nitrogen Fixation. Israel Journal
of Botany, in press.

Patrick, W.H. 1977. Oxygen content of soil air by a field
method. Soil Sci. Soc. Am. J. 41, 651-652.

Payne, W.J. 1981. Denitrification. Wiley-Interscience, New
York.

Peters, G.A. and H.E. Calvert. 1982. The Azolla-Anabaena
Symbiosis, Chapter in Algal Symbiosis: A Continuum
of Interaction Strategies. Sponsored by the
Phytological Society of America, Cambridge
University Press (in press).

Phillips, D.A., K.D. Newell, S.A. Hassell, and C.E.
Felling. 1976. The effect of CO_2 enrichment on root
nodule development and symbiotic N_2 reduction in
Pisum sativan L. Amer. J. Bot. 63, 356-362.

Phillips, R.E., R.E. Blevins, G.W. Thomas, W.W. Frye and
S.G. Phillips. 1980. No tillage agriculture. Science
208, 1108-1113.

Phillips, D.A. 1980. Efficiency of nitrogen fixation in
legumes. Ann. Rev. Plant Physiol. 31, 29-49.

Powell, C.L.I. 1976. Development of mycorrhizal infections
from Endogone spores and infected root segments.
Trans. Brit. Mycol. Soc. 66, 439-445.

Rabinowitch, E.I. 1951. Photosynthesis, Vol.
II, Part I.   Interscience Publishers Inc.,
New York, p. 886.

Read, D.J. and W. Armstrong. 1972. A relationship between
oxygen transport and the formation of the ectotrophic
mycorrhizal sheath in conifer seedlings. New Phytol.
71, 49-53.

Reeves, F.B., D. Wagner, T. Moorman and J. Kiel. 1979.
The role of endomycorrhizae in revegetation practices
in the semi-arid West. I. A comparison of incidence
of mycorrhizae in severely disturbed vs. natural
environments. Am. J. Bot. 66, 6-13.

Reichle, D.E., B.E. Dinger, N.T. Edwards, W.F. Harris and P. Sollins. 1973. Carbon flow and storage in a forest ecosystem. In G.M. Woodwell and E.V. Pecan Eds., Proc. of the Symposium in Biology, Upton, New York.

Rogers, P.A. and S.A. Kulasooriya. 1980. Blue-green algae and rice. The International Rice Research Institute, Los Banos, Laguna, Phillipines.

Rogers, H.H., G.E. Bingham, J.D. Cure, W.W. Heck, A.S. Heagle, D.W. Israel, J.M. Smith, K.A. Surano, and J.F. Thomas. 1980. Response of vegetation to carbon dioxide. U.S. Department of Energy and U.S. Department of Agriculture Joint Publication.

Russell, E.W. 1973. Soil conditions and plant growth. 10th ed. Longmans, London, Chapter 18.

Safir, G., J.S. Boyer and J.W. Gerdemann. 1972. Nutrient status and mycorrhizal enhancement of water transport in soybean. Plant Physiol. 49, 700-703.

Saif, S.R. 1981. The influence of soil aeration on the efficiency of vesicular-arbuscular mycorrhizae. I. Effect of soil oxygen on the growth and mineral uptake of Eupatorim odoratum L. innoculated with Glomus macrocarpus. New Phytol. 88, 649-659.

Sanchez, P.A., D.E. Bandy, J.F. Villachica and J.J. Nicholaides. 1982a. Amazon basin soils: Management for continuous crop production. Science 216, 821-827.

Sanchez, P.A., M.P. Gichuru and L.B. Katz. 1982b. Organic matter in major soils of the tropical and temperate regions. Proc. 12th ISSS Congress, Delhi. 1, 99.

Schwartz, D.M. and F.A. Bazzaz. 1973. In situ measurements of carbon dioxide gradients in a soil-plant-atmosphere system. Oecologia 12, 161-167.

Shivashankar, K., K. Vlassak and J. Livens. 1976. A comparison of the effect of straw incorporation and carbon dioxide enrichment on the growth, nitrogen fixation and yield of soybeans. J. Agric. Sci. 87, 81-85.

Smith, A.M. and D.M. Griffin. 1971. Oxygen and the ecology of Armillariella elegans Heim. Austr. J. Biol. Sci. 24, 231-262.

176 *Lamborg et al.*

Stewart, W.D.P. 1975. <u>Nitrogen fixation by free-living organisms</u>. Cambridge Univ. Press.

Stolwijk, J.A. and K.V. Thimann. 1957. On the uptake of carbon dioxide and bicarbonate by roots, and its influence on growth. <u>Plant Physiol.</u> 32, 513–520.

Subba Rao, N.S. 1977. Nitrogen deficiency as a world-wide problem. In <u>A Treatise on Nitrogen Fixation</u>, R.W.F. Hardy and A.H. Gibson, Eds. John Wiley and Sons, New York, pp. 3–32.

Swank, W.T. and J.B. Waide. 1980. Interpretations of nutrient cycling research in a management context: Evaluating potential effects of alternative management strategies on site productivity. In <u>Forests: Fresh Perspectives from Ecosystem Analysis</u>, R.W. Waring, Ed. Oregon State University Press, Corvallis, pp. 137–158.

Telson, M., I.A. Leone and F.B. Flower. 1980. The role of an ectomycorrhizal fungus <u>Pisolthus tinctorius</u> in the survival and growth of scots pine subjected to landfill conditions. (Abstr.) <u>Phytopathology</u> 70, 470.

Tinker, P.B. 1978. Effects of vesicular-arbuscular mycorrhizae on plant nutrition and plant growth. <u>Physiol. Veg.</u> 16, 743–751.

Tinker, P.B. 1982. Mycorrhizas: The present position. In <u>Whither Soil Research. Trans. 12th Intl Congress of Soil Science</u>. New Delhi. 5, 140–166.

Trappe, J.M. 1981. Mycorrhizae and productivity of arid and semi-arid rangelands. In <u>Advances in Food Producing Systems for Arid and Semi-Arid Lands</u>. Acad. Press, London, pp. 581–599.

van Veen, J.A. and E.A. Paul. 1981. Organic carbon dynamics in grassland soils. I. Background information and computer simulation. <u>Can. J. Soil Sci.</u> 61, 185–201.

Vose, P.B. and A.P. Ruschel. 1981. <u>Associative N_2 fixation, Vols. 1 and 2</u>. CRC Press, Boca Raton.

Winship, L.J. and J.D. Tjepkema. 1982. <u>Plant Physiol.</u> (accepted).

Boyd R. Strain, Chairman
Fakhri A. Bazzaz, Co-Chairman

7. Terrestrial Plant Communities

Panel Members: W.D. Billings, J. Detling, J.P. Grime,
P. Grubb, O.L. Loucks, J. Melillo, H.A. Mooney, W.C. Oechel,
D. Overdieck, D. Patterson, W. Reiners, H. Rogers,
M. Rutter, P. Vitousek, D. West.

SUMMARY AND RECOMMENDATIONS

Unfortunately, almost no measurements of long term CO_2 enrichment have been made at the community level. Indeed, very few long-term studies have been made of single plant responses either. Thus, any predictions made today are highly speculative. Since plant communities are composed of individual plants interacting to abiotic and biotic factors of their habitat over time, differences in individual responses to more CO_2 will dictate new community structure. Cumulative interactions can be expected to operate through many reproductive generations. Expected climate changes will also interact with direct CO_2 effects to produce added control on the dynamics of terrestial vegetation. The climate changes could be favorable or adverse. A predicted increase in net primary productivity of individual crops may not mean an increased productivity of lightly or unmanaged ecosystems. An initial increase in productivity may cause limited N and P availability in moderately infertile sites. If so, more land will revert to lightly managed or unmanaged ecosystems. A decrease in forage quality (i.e., C/N ratio) in lightly managed but heavily grazed savannas and grasslands can be expected. Rotations of intensely managed forests may be shortened and fertilizers may be required to sustain yield.

There has been little research focused on the direct influence of higher levels of CO_2 on plant communities. Two experiments are now under way with natural systems, and five with simplified mixtures of two or more competing

species. To speed up understanding in this field, two
approaches should begin simultaneously:

1) Models can give early insight to the sensitivity of
various plant controls. We therefore suggest the development of mechanistic plant models detailed enough to follow
responses through many life cycles, and including the
processes of establishment, growth, reproduction, and
survival.

2) Experimental work is required to provide data of
the accuracy needed for each hierarchical level: a) single
plant physiological mechanisms; b) two or few species
competition; c) long-term multiple species interactions in
natural-like environments.

Conclusions:

1) Species and subspecies of plants will respond
directly but differentially to increasing CO_2 in ways that
are described in detail in Chapters 3, 4, and 5 of this
book.

2) There are many interactions between vascular plants
and microbes that will cause indirect effects of CO_2
enrichment on plants as described by the panel on microbial
effects (Chapter 6).

3) Since the ecological structure of plant communities is established by individual plants interacting with
the abiotic and biotic environment of their habitat
through time, the differential rates and nature of responses of species and subspecies to continuously increasing
CO_2 will cause changes in the ecological structure of plant
communities.

4) The predicted increase in net primary productivity
of individual plants and crops may not necessarily mean
increased net ecosystem productivity in lightly or unmanaged ecosystems. This means that the β-factor for global
biotic growth described in Bacastow and Keeling (1973) may
be small or zero in most natural ecosystems.

5) Any effects of elevated CO_2 on climate which do
occur will interact with direct CO_2 effects to produce
additional important controls on the dynamics of terrestrial vegetation. Some of the CO_2 climate interactions
will be positive and some will be negative on plant
communities.

6) An increase in carbon fixation may ultimately decrease the availability of nitrogen and phosphorus in moderately infertile sites. If so, more land area will revert to lightly managed or unmanaged ecosystems where available N and P limit plant growth.

7) An increase in the quantity, but a decrease in the quality (e.g., C/N ratio), of forage available in the lightly managed but heavily grazed savannas and grasslands can be expected.

8) The length of harvesting rotations in intensively managed forests may be decreased. Sustained increased yields will require nutrient additions (fertilization) of these systems.

9) The more rapid completion of plant life cycles will affect coevolved relationships between and among plants, animals, and microbes. It is currently not possible to predict the outcome of these interactions as they operate through many reproductive generations.

10) Unfortunately, few measurements of long term CO_2 enrichment have been made at the community level. Indeed, few appropriate long term measurements have been made of individual plant responses either. Thus, any predictions made today are highly speculative.

Research Recommendations: Little research has been done on the direct effects of more CO_2 on terrestrial plant communities. Two projects are underway (Billings on arctic tundra microcosm cores and Oechel on tussock tundra plots). Approximately five projects (Overdieck, Patterson, Bazzaz, Wong, and rumored work at Oregon State University) are underway with simplified mixtures of 2 or a few competing species. Only Billings et al. (1982) have published results. Some autecologically oriented research projects have been completed or are underway, but they must be carefully interpreted to be useful in questions of plant community response. Because of the dearth of information, we wish to limit our research recommendations to generalities only.

1) Develop mechanistic plant response models with enough detail to analyze plant response through several life cycles. The models should include those features diagrammed in Figure 1 of this chapter. Four or five biome types should be included as indicated in Figure 2, and several functional types from each biome addressed as outlined in Figure 3.

2) Use these models to critically analyze the mechanism of carbon dioxide effects on plant establishment, growth, reproduction, and survival.

3) Use the results of the work above to select experimental projects to acquire data for the models to improve their predictions.

4) Select research approaches which will provide data of the accuracy and level of complexity needed. Hierarchical levels appropriate are: 1) single plant, to develop necessary physiological mechanisms, 2) two or few species interactions, to study interference and competition responses, and 3) long term studies of multiple species interactions in complex environments, to study ecological controls operating through time.

5) Initiate long term studies in representative ecosystems to validate the models and detect possible CO_2 effects on plant communities. The Long Term Ecological Research program of the National Science Foundation offers excellent facilities and opportunity for the meeting of this objective in the United States.

1. Introduction. An ecological approach to the analysis and prediction of direct effects of enhanced atmospheric CO_2 is essential from three general points of view:

First, it is believed that CO_2 enrichment will have positive effects on world agroecosystems, leading to more primary productivity. While short term physiological data underlie and justify this expectation, there is still uncertainty about the reality of such increases. The uncertainty is, in part, related to the complexity of longer term ecological linkages that constrain productivity even in relatively simple agronomic systems. Thus, an ecological analysis of the interacting effects of nutrients, weeds, and pests is needed to substantiate realistic expectations of higher yields.

Secondly, an ecological analysis is critical to alerting us to possible disequilibria created in semi-natural ecosystems such as range lands and managed forests, and in wildlands such as arctic tundra and tropical forests. The more complex arrays of interactions in generally more diverse natural systems often gives rise to disruptive interactions following environmental change. One modern-day example is desertification in North Africa. Droughts persisting over decades, interacting with excessive grazing, are causing changes in ecological structure. The Sahara Desert is expanding southward (Cloudsley-Thompson, 1974). Presumably, other environmental changes can cause similar results if they prevail over long enough time. Higher CO_2 can have such an effect if the atmospheric enrichment prevails for many decades or centuries.

A third justification for an ecological analysis concerns the global carbon cycle itself. At present, there is a question about the changing mass balance of global carbon as carbon from fossil fuel is redistributed among various sinks. The debate revolves around whether or not terrestrial ecosystems are a net source or sink of atmospheric CO_2 (Bolin et al., 1979). Part of the debate rests on whether enhanced CO_2 will, in itself, make terrestrial ecosystems a net carbon sink (Bolin, 1977; Woodwell, et al., 1978). Energy policy and scientific decisions are at stake.

2. Objectives. A major objective of this chapter is to design the most efficient and direct approach to predict effects of elevated atmospheric CO_2 on terrestrial ecosystems of the world. This approach focuses on the vegetation (plant cover) of land surfaces. This focus is dictated by the dominant role plants play in carbon flux and storage. Vegetation is regarded here as a dynamic entity, changing in physiognomy, floristic composition, population structure and other attributes over a range of temporal and spatial scales. The frequency of disturbance, whether in annual crop systems or long-lived forests, and in resultant change via succession or replacement, is an explicit part of the vegetation concept.

The analysis of plant responses to elevated CO_2 is organized around a three-level approach, from the most simple in terms of interactions, to the most complex.

The first level concerns predictive models for individual plants. Interactions of single plant species with more CO_2 and other environmental variables are emphasized. This approach is largely autecological and physiological, in which life cycle processes are ultimately generalized for sets of functionally differentiated plant types.

The second level concentrates on plant-plant interaction. At complex hierarchical levels, additional interactions occur among a limited number of organisms. Predicted behavior from autecological investigation should provide generalizations about behavior in plant competi-

tion, plant-animal, plant-microorganism, and other direct
interactions. This hierarchical level includes intra-
population interactions.

The third level takes up more complex assemblages.
The goal here stresses predictive capability and
understanding of the interactions of aggregations of
populations (communities) with the entire biota, plus
interacting abiotic components (ecosystems). At this last
level, complex control loops, positive and negative
feedbacks between biotic and abiotic components, and
aggregated properties such as net primary productivity, are
addressed. This level evolves from the mechanisms and
generalizations established by the individual plant and the
plant-plant investigations, and from consideration of the
mechanisms unique to this final hierarchical level of
organization.

3. The Response of Individual Plants (Level 1)

3.1 A Mechanistic Model. The impact of more CO_2 on plant
growth and community interactions is difficult to assess
because of the diverse pathways carbon can take within the
plant and the community, as well as the tight coupling of
carbon flow to water and nutrient fluxes. A powerful way
to conceptualize these interactions is through models.
Here we present a model for a single plant to represent
plant-plant competitive interactions. Further, the single
plant model is a building block toward a more comprehensive
ecosystem view. As presented, the model indicates the flow
of carbon into the plant and its allocation to various live
plant parts, and then into dead parts. An important
feature of this model is the indication of controls, not
only on the timing and amounts of allocation, but also on
certain plant structure properties such as carbon/nitrogen
ratios and stem lengths, which have implications in
plant-plant, plant-animal and plant-decomposer interactions. The variables, processes, and controls included
in this model represent our best ideas about how biotic and
abiotic factors interact to control plant growth and
development. Such a model can address questions of
potential interactions between two or more species in the
same habitat, once important physiological and morphological parameters are known. Thus, the model can lead to
predicting competitive interactions among species differing
in responses to CO_2, temperature, light, water, etc. If,
however, validation experiments fail to substantiate model
predictions, modification of the model structure or
parameter estimates will be necessary. Of course this will
lead to a better understanding of community function.

Interseasonal biomass dynamics are considered as functions of light, water, soil and air temperature, nutrient content, leaf age, CO_2, and time. The model Figure 1) interrelates photosynthesis, carbon partitioning to vegetative and reproductive plant parts, maintenance and growth respiration, root material, export, litter quality, leaf duration, and transfers between living and dead biomass. Quantitative data are needed to make this model work. Such models now exist, in part [Detling et al., 1979; MEDECS (Jacobson et al., 1981); ARTUS (Miller et al., 1976); Miller (unpublished); and others].

3.2 Details of the Model

3.2.1 Photosynthesis. Controls on photosynthetic rate include leaf conductance of CO_2, temperature, light, CO_2 concentration, and carbohydrate content of leaves and roots. In turn, leaf conductance is a function of light, CO_2 levels, humidity, and leaf water potential.

Generally, these processes are understood for short periods, i.e., minutes to hours, for a few species; but we do not understand those interactions for the great majority of plant types, including many crop plants, for longer periods. Plant photosynthetic rates, then, are dependent on photosynthesis rate and leaf conductance, and thus on the total nonstructural carbohydrate (TNC) pool and water use efficiency (see Figure 1).

3.2.2 Photosynthate Allocation. Carbohydrates move to other parts of the plant from the TNC pool. Plant productivity is controlled, in large part, by the allocation patterns. A particular allocation pattern is controlled by a combination of environmental and genetic factors. Allocation time schedules vary among species as well. Although photosynthesis and respiration are important to overall carbon balance, net primary productivity rests heavily upon partitioning of carbo-hydrates into developing new leaf surface area (Mooney, 1972). Allocation patterns may be more important to primary production than are photosynthetic rates (see e.g., Oechel et al., 1981; Bigger and Oechel, 1982).

Carbon allocation is controlled by such factors as temperature, light, daylength, water, nutrients, carbo-hydrate levels, and plant age. For example, when nutrients and water are limiting, there is a proportionately larger allocation of TNC to roots or other below ground structures. When TNC is low, there is relatively more allocated to leaf and stem. Environmental and physio-

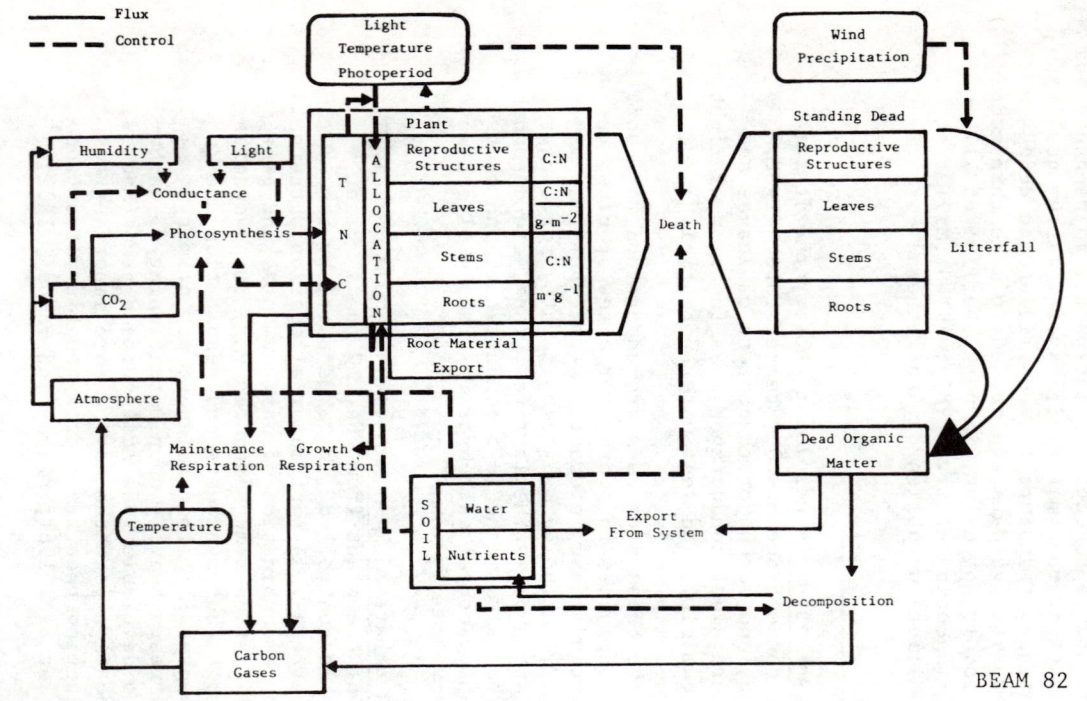

Figure 1. Conceptual model showing interrelationships in photosynthesis and carbon allocation in a plant as it is affected by atmospheric CO_2 concentration. Carbon transfer following tissue death and decomposition is also shown. Control points for carbon movement are indicated by dotted lines and carbon flux is indicated by solid lines.

logical stresses, in many cases, trigger a shift in allocation to flowers, fruits, and seeds.

The carbon-nitrogen ratio, C/N, is critical to carbon allocation in plant tissue. The higher the C/N ratio which may be expected as a result of elevated CO_2, the lower the tissue quality for herbivores and decomposers -- i.e., less protein. Other organic compounds also produced can affect consumption by animals and decomposition processes. Organic chemicals likely to inhibit herbivore feeding and decomposition including lignins, phenolics, and terpines. Carbon allocation within plant tissue is expected to be especially sensitive to changes in the relative availabilities of TNC and nutrients, driven by more CO_2.

The C/N ratio is also partially controlled by aridity. For example, sclerophyllous leaves of arid-land plants usually have higher C/N ratios than do leaves of mesophytic plants. Likewise, within a given species, C/N ratios are generally higher in leaves of plants growing in xeric habitats than in those from more mesic locations.

3.2.3 Respiration. Respiration is the main sink for carbohydrates in plants. For example, in the chaparral, 2/3 of the photosynthate fixed is used for respiration and 1/3 goes to plant net primary production (Oechel and Lawrence, unpublished). In our model, both growth and maintenance respiration are considered. Growth respiration represents the energy and carbon losses associated with synthesis of plant tissues from carbon precursors, usually carbohydrate. In general, growth respiration is about 30% of that for new tissue production (Penning deVries, 1975). Maintenance respiration is a function of temperature, with the rate of respiration often doubling with a 10° C increase in temperature. However, the respiration rate may increase up to 7 fold for a 10° C. increase in temperature. Protein turnover is a main source of CO_2 in maintenance respiration; the level of maintenance respiration is therefore highly dependent on plant protein comment.

Through the control of carbohydrate levels on growth rate, TNC levels will affect growth respiration rates, but are not expected to affect the rates of maintenance respiration (McKree, 1970).

3.2.4 Root Exudation. Root exudation, rich in carbohydrate and exported to symbionts, is critical in supporting nitrogen-fixing symbionts and mychorrhizae. Leakage of carbohydrates from the roots can be the chief carbon supply to fungal and bacterial populations in the

rhizosphere. Root exudation tends to increase when
carbohydrate levels within the plant are high.

3.2.5 Death of Plant Parts. Since total carbon gain and
loss in plants depends on the size of the constituent
living parts, it is necessary to know death rates of these
parts over a growing season. Superimposed upon a geneti-
cally-fixed maximum potential life span are a host of
environmental factors which influence death rates of
various parts. Certainly environmental extremes, such as a
hard frost or severe drought early in the growing season,
may kill young leaves. The onset of leaf senescence in the
fall may be triggered by a combination of lower temperatures, reduced photoperiod, and changes in light quality.
Similarly, leaf death in some species of drought-deciduous
shrubs is initiated by drought-photoperiod interactions
(Mooney, pers. comm.). Root death, particularly that of
the fine roots, parallels periodic soil droughts. In fact,
fine root biomass may turn over several times in a single
season in some arid and semi-arid environments as a result
of successive dessication cycles (Parton et al., 1978).

3.2.6 Litterfall. Transfer of dead plant parts to litter
is quite predictable for some systems. For example, most
leaves of deciduous trees and shrubs fall in a relatively
short time after the onset of senescence. The rate at
which dead branches fall from the same trees is less
predictable. Wind, degree of decomposition, and frequency
and intensity of ice storms, are among the factors
affecting this fall. Environmental control on rates of
transfer of standing dead plants to litter in grasslands is
more poorly understood, but is potentially important in
controlling carbon flow.

In dense temperate grasslands dominated by perennial
grasses, such standing dead material may interfere with
light interception by live leaves, especially early in the
growing season (Detling et al., 1979). Therefore, growth
rate and subsequent productivity can be significantly
reduced. In grasslands, litterfall is controlled in part
by factors such as rainfall intensity, wind velocity, and
snow load. Whether plants growing in elevated CO_2 will be
more highly lignified and hence less readily converted to
litter is not known.

3.2.7 Decomposition. Decomposition rates are critical to
storage or release of carbon and to nutrient availability,
cycling and retention capacity, water holding capacity, and
to soil temperature and heat flux.

In addition to control by environmental and senescence
factors, decomposition rates are controlled in large part
by the carbon/nitrogen ratio and by the composition of
recalcitrant or noxious organic chemicals. The chemicals
include lignins, phenolics, and terpines.

One of the major effects of elevated CO_2 may be
mediated through the action of litter composition on
decomposition rates, and hence on nutrient availability and
other ecosystem properties, such as soil organic matter
content.

Decomposition rates are not expected to show direct
response to elevated CO_2. Therefore, in the short term,
photosynthetic rates may increase in response to increasing
CO_2 levels while dark respiration and decomposer systems do
not immediately respond (Oechel, unpublished).

3.3 Time Dimension. Plant communities develop from various
plant populations interacting through time. This interaction is biotic, e.g., the organisms directly affecting
each other by interference and competition, and abiotic,
e.g., the individual plants responding to physiochemcial
factors and in turn modifying those factors. Given
sufficient time or a relatively stable environment, a
relatively stable vegetation will develop. Environmental
change will affect the ecological balance and changes will
occur in the vegetation. The degree and nature of
vegetation change is dependent on which environmental
factors change, and the rate of change (Odum, 1971).

The interaction of organisms and environment is a
dynamic process. Plants adapt to the environmental
complex, and then maintain a predictable behavior as they
mature through a "normal" season (Detling et al., 1979).
Predictability is derived from first-principles models of
physiological response (Tenhunen et al., 1977) or from
simulation models developed more empirically through time
(Reynolds et al., 1980). Both of these approaches to the
prediction of the direct effects of CO_2 on plants require
information from long-term experiments on plants. Adequate
understanding of the possible effects of a long-term
increase in carbon dioxide concentration is hindered by the
lack of information from long-term experiments with CO_2
enrichment. Most experimental evidence on the direct
effects of CO_2 on plants has come from plants first grown
at prevailing CO_2 levels. These plants are then subjected
to sudden increases in atmospheric CO_2 and tested in
relatively short-term measurements of net photosynthesis,
stomatal conductance, transpiration, or growth (Strain

and Sionit, 1982). This has been particularly true for native species. Almost no data have been published on native plants grown from germination to reproductive maturity under enriched CO_2 atmospheres. Research underway at the University of Illinois, Duke University, the University of Osnabruck, West Germany, and San Diego State University, is the first generation of ecological studies on native species grown at high CO_2 throughout their life cycles. Preliminary data from these studies indicate that the responses of plants grown for entire life cycles in high CO_2 concentrations cannot be adequately predicted from short-term experiments subjected to suddenly increasing CO_2 (see Section 3.4 below).

3.4 Model Applications to Different Functional Types. The vast numbers of plant species which exist in the world can be grouped into various functional types. Each group represents plants with a certain degree of commonality in ecological requirements and responses. For example, annual weeds generally have high photosynthetic capacities, high leaf turnover, high reproductive outputs, and short life spans. A more complete system of classification of functional types is discussed in later sections.

In assessing the effects of elevated CO_2 on plant growth and allocation, it is important to consider specific functional types. This is clear from preceding chapters in this book which consider differential responses of C_3 versus C_4 plants to more CO_2. Other examples are for plants from certain habitats with stomata which are insensitive to CO_2. The different types represent plants with different intrinsic allocation patterns and turnover rates of plant parts. These patterns have evolved in response to the resource limitations of their habitats.

It is not known specifically how all of the different functional types would respond to elevated CO_2, but various scenarios can be envisioned. For example, plants from high nutrient habitats with fast growth rates would probably have even higher leaf turnover rates and this would impact on community nutrient relations.

The implications of differential responses of different plant types to CO_2 to competitive relations are discussed later. The point to be made here is that each species will respond somewhat differently to CO_2 enrichment just as they would to nutrient enrichment. These differential responses have implications at the community level. Obviously we cannot study the potential responses of all species; however, we can study the responses of representatives of the various functional types so that we will be able to make generalized predictions of the impact of CO_2 enrichment on community processes.

Modelling experiments designed to study the direct effects of changing levels of atmospheric CO_2, must adhere to the same rigors of any other examination of plant/ nutrient relationships. Thus, any credible plan to provide information on ecosystem response to changes in CO_2 must necessarily consider interactive effects with other nutrients and environmental parameters, as well as differential responses among species.

Competitive interactions among species frequently mask growth-rate changes observed for single species. Evidence for this differential and somewhat counter-intuitive response has been shown by Botkin et al. (1973) and West et al. (1980). In these simulation studies, individual trees in a forest stand did not show changes in growth that were consistent with variable growth-change parameters assigned to individual species.

Essentially nothing is known regarding the response of woody plants to increased CO_2 levels, and information is especially lacking regarding forest tree response to realistically projected levels of CO_2 concentrations in the atmosphere. Based upon available physiological data and projected increases in CO_2, ecosystem response to changing CO_2 levels will likely be subtle. Empirical information necessary to document and/or predict this response will be obtained slowly and with difficulty. Forest growth models (Botkin et al., 1973; Shugart and West, 1977) could provide insight to the subtle changes in ecosystem behavior as CO_2 slowly increases. In such models, water, light, and nutrient availability could be integrated into the calculation of the yearly diameter increment of each tree. The availability of each of these resources would integrate a wide variety of simulated processes.

System-level models have been shown to be valuable, not only as a predictive tool, but also as a mechanism for clarifying research needs. Through simultaneous examination of many complex variables, models can show areas in which data are needed, and more clearly define frequently unsuspected effects of variable interactions. Ecosystem models, correctly built in a stepwise progression of leaf to tree to stand-level considerations, have the capability of clarifying feedback mechanisms that need emphasis for laboratory and field investigations. Future physiological, glasshouse, and field experiments should be designed to

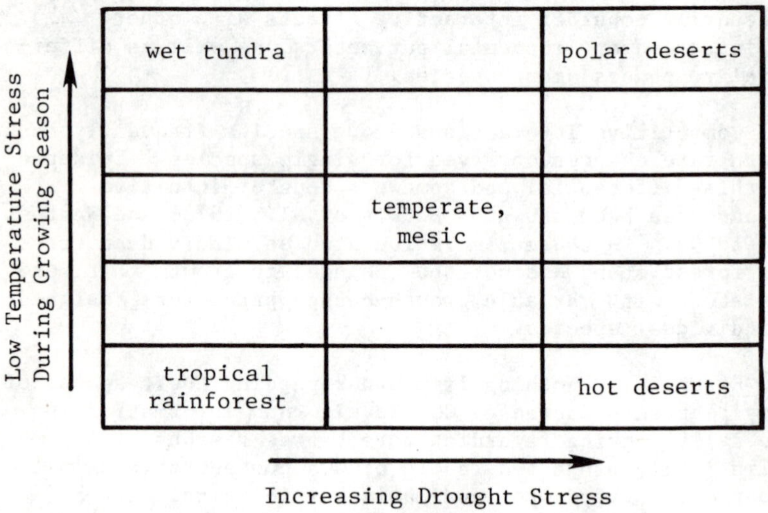

Figure 2. An environmental gradient matrix upon which the major terrestrial biomes of the world may be placed to represent extremes and functional relationships.

obtain data amenable to existing models in use for tree and
stand-level simulations.

3.5 Representative Biome Responses. It is possible to
extrapolate the single-plant model to the vegetation of the
biosphere by making certain assumptions. The first is that
processes, pools, and controls will be essentially the same
for a large community type or biome, as for a single plant.
However, the rate and quantities will vary with environment
and species diversity.

It is not possible, in a single chapter of a book, to
cover the complex matrix of the earth's principal biomes.
We will consider only five biomes, as shown in Figure 2, in
which the two axes represent gradients of drought stress
and low temperature stress during the growing season. Of
the five biomes shown, four represent extremes in environmental and species diversity; these are tropical rainforest,
wet arctic tundra, hot desert, and polar cold desert.
The fifth, temperate region tall grassland, represents a
biomes amenable to being converted to crop ecosystems.

Along the temperature axis, a continuously warm, wet
climate, has, in the past, been occupied by tropical
rainforests of various kinds. Here, the dominants are
large trees, but most of the plant species are of smaller
size (e.g., epiphytes, vines, and herbaceous plants).
These are limited by low light (shade), and low or rapid
nutrient turnover. Root systems are generally shallow and
quickly recycle nutrients that are made available by rapid
decomposition by fungi and bacteria. Photosynthesis also
captures a great deal of carbon dioxide, including that
released in decomposition. Much of the nutrient pool and
the carbon pool are tied up in plant structures (stems,
leaves, etc.) rather than in the soils. The annual rate of
primary productivity is high (Bazzaz and Pickett, 1980).

At the other end of the latitudinal temperature gradient from the tropical rainforest is the wet arctic tundra.
Instead of a continual growing season and equal-length
days, the tundra is unfrozen for only a few weeks. During
this short season, the sun is continually above the horizon
in a cold "summer." Species diversity is very low, less
than 1% that of the rainforest. Most of the dominant
plants are non-woody grasses and sedges. All have the C_3
pathway. Most of the phytomass is below ground in roots
and rhizomes. This can amount to about 75 to 90% of the
total biomass of the system. The soil thaws only to a few
decimeters. Below this annual depth of thaw, lies perma-
nently frozen ground (permafrost) or white ice-wedges and

ice-lenses insulated by peat. Nutrients are low and
limiting, decomposition is very slow, and carbon-rich peat
accumulates at present low temperatures. The wet tundra is
a carbon dioxide sink at the present time (Billings et al.,
1982). The carbon budget of the wet tundra at Point
Barrow, Alaska, is fairly well-known (see diagrammatic
figures in Billings, 1978; and Brown et al., 1980).

Not all of the arctic is wet tundra. As one
approaches the northern limits of land, there are extensive
polar deserts that are not only dry, but underlain with
permafrost. As the great ice caps melt, more such desert
comes into existence. Species diversity is extremely low.
Again, as in the tundra, most of the plant material lies
below ground in the soil layer that thaws only slightly in
midsummer. At present, it seems likely that this desert is
neither a source nor a sink for carbon dioxide.

At the extreme end of the drought axis in the tropics
are the hot, barren deserts such as parts of the Sahara,
Australia, Peru, and even parts of the American Southwest.
Species diversity can be almost zero, but under conditions
of some "winter" or "summer" rain, a fair amount of plant
diversity and a variety of life-forms can exist. Such an
example is the Sonoran Desert of Arizona and northwestern
Mexico. Here, carbon dioxide is captured by annual plants
(for a short time during the year), perennial herbs,
shrubs, and succulent plants (cacti and/or euphorbias). The
photosynthetic mechanisms in the Sonoran Desert are represented by C_3, C_4, and CAM plants, the latter being mostly
cacti. These tropical deserts may have almost no organic
carbon in the most barren places, to small amounts in those
that receive some rain. Decomposition of organic matter is
slow, in direct proportion to the degree and length of
drought. In most ecological ways, tropical hot deserts are
the opposites of wet arctic tundras.

As an average biome between four extremes, lies the
original tall-grass prairie of the American Midwest. Under
the present climate, these grasslands represent the ultimate in productivity of herbaceous plants in undisturbed
systems. There is a fairly high amount of species diversity in which the dominant tall grasses and dicots are
represented by plants with either C_3 or C_4 photosynthetic
mechanisms. The soil is generally deep, and with considerable carbon content. Root systems are also diverse, and
range from deep to shallow. Decomposition varies with the
climatic gradients within the biome; at times in the past,
it has been slow, with the accumulation of nutrient-rich
organic matter, but it may be faster today. At present,

most of the original vegetation of this biome is gone. It has been replaced by managed agroecosystems. It is one of the most highly productive regions on earth. A knowledge of the biological, climatic, carbon, and nutrient relationships of the original tallgrass prairie could act as a guidepost in understanding what might happen in these crop ecosystems under increasing atmospheric carbon dioxide.

It is our opinion that the direct effects of CO_2 will increase the rate of net primary productivity only slightly in old, closed vegetation of forest, tundra, or prairie, because other factors will soon become limiting. However, carbon dioxide could have a greater and possibly significant effect on increasing productivity in young, successional vegetation, or in some agroecosystems.

Measurements of species responses to increased CO_2 have been mainly in the form of short-term controlled environment experiments with crop plants, forage grasses, and arable weeds. If full value is to be obtained from this approach, it is necessary to expand the range of plants under investigation to include species of contrasted ecology from each major terrestrial biome.

There is also a need for studies in which comparisons of response to elevated CO_2 are made between species drawn from the same plant community. Here a careful selection of communities is necessary to ensure that information relating to CO_2 responses can be complemented by existing data on the germination, growth characteristics, and field ecology of the component species.

The most compelling argument for care in the selection of species relates to the need to minimize the effort required to achieve reliable generalizations concerning the relationships between habitat, species characteristics and responsiveness to rising CO_2. On theoretical grounds and from experimental studies, there is reason to expect that some differential responses will coincide with differences in photosynthetic pathway. It would be unfortunate, however, if preoccupation with C_3 and C_4 plants allowed other important sources of variation in CO_2 responses to remain undetected. With this problem in mind, the following principles are suggested as a guide to the selection of species for controlled environment studies of response to CO_2 enrichment.

1) Selection should permit comparison of the responses of plants representing types of ecological specialization within each major terrestrial biome (tundra, temperate, tropical, and arid zones).

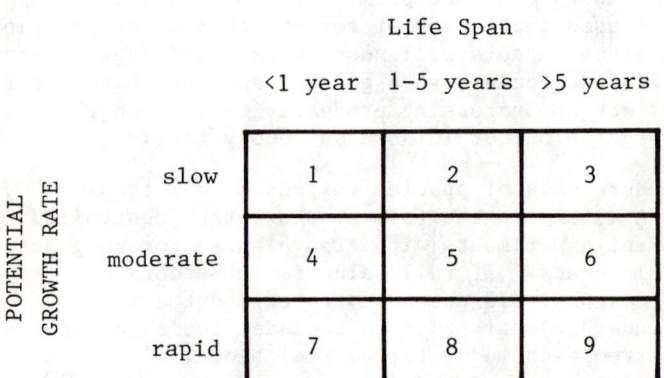

Figure 3. Matrix for the selection of species in controlled environment studies of response to CO_2 enrichment. When applied to certain categories, not all cells of the matrix will be occupied. For example, dedicuous trees and shrubs would not be expected to occur in cells 1, 4, and 7.

2) Within-biome comparisons should include species known to differ in their responses to other factors, such as soil fertility, drought, shade, and defoliation.

3) Comparisons should be made between species of different life history, potential growth-rate, and successional status, but exploiting the same geographical area.

4) Additional criteria for selection (e.g., photosynthetic pathways) should be used, but these should not have priority over 1 and 2.

5) The number of species selected for study should be restricted in order to allow adequate measurement of growth, and, where possible, reproduction.

One method of ensuring that CO_2 response data are relevant to community and ecosystem processes and provide a basis for generalization, is to select species by reference to a classification of functional plant types (Grime, 1974, 1979). In its simplest form, this scheme can be represented as a matrix (Figure 3) in which species are classified with respect to life history and potential growth rate. The matrix can guide the selection of species within each biome, within habitat types (arable, pasture, wetland, forest), within life forms or taxa (deciduous trees and shrubs, conifers, herbs and ferns, bryophytes and lichens) and within photosynthetic types (C_3, C_4, and CAM). Selection on this basis is the minimum requirement for effective use of data from single species response studies.

4. Responses of Two Interacting Organisms   (Level 2)

4.1 Plant-Plant Interactions

4.1.1 Available data. The following discussion concerns only the growth phase when vegetative and flowering plants are competing for resources. Here we do not allow for any effects on other stages of the life cycle that could be important in the field situation (e.g., germination) or the cumulative effects of changes in the quality of plant residues (see Section 4.1.2).

The available results are summarized in Table 1. They can be interpreted with some confidence in terms of general findings on plant-plant competition set out in the next section concerned with relative sensitivity to increases in C and N supply, seed size, and growth rate.

Table 1.   Results of experiments with increased CO_2 on mixtures of plant species

Plant Types	Growing Conditions	Findings	References
C_3 grass (rye-grass, Lolium perenne) and C_3 legume (white clover, Trofolium repens) planted in 1:1 mixture.	Micro-glasshouses, 275 and 547 ppm CO_2 (averages) by day; garden soil; harvest 4 and 8 weeks after germination.	(1) At low CO_2, the taller-growing plant (rye-grass) was clearly the superior competitor. (2) At high CO_2, the proportion of legume in the mixture (by above-ground dry-weight) increased from 0.12 to 0.26.	D. Overdieck (Unpublished)
C_3 crop (wheat, Triticum aestivum) and C_4 crop (Japanese millet, Echinochloa frumentacea) planted mixtures	Larger greenhouse; 340 and 680 mmp CO_2 sterilized sandy soil with 2 levels of added NO_3 and 2 light levels; harvest 6 weeks after germination.	(1) At low CO_2, high light, and high N the large-sseded plant (wheat) was the superior competitor, despite its CO_3 metabolism. (2) At high CO_2, with high light and high or low N, the proportion of the C_4 plant in mixture was reduced. (3) At low light, there was no growth enhancement with extra CO_2.	S.C. Wong (Unpublished)
C_3 crop (soybean, Glycine max) with C_3 weed (Abutilon theophrasti) or C_4 weed (Amaranthus retroflexus) planted in 1:1 mixture.	Chambers within a glasshouse; 300 and 600 ppm CO_2; rooting medium; harvested 8 weeks after germination.	(1) At low CO_2, the C_4 weed depressed the yield of the crop more than the C_3 weed did. (2) At high CO_2, the C_3 weed had the greater depressive effect.	F.A. Bazzaz (Unpublished)

In further experiments, where different concentrations of CO_2 were used with mixtures of 4-6 species (Bazzaz, unpublished), and the supply of light, water, and mineral nutrients was varied, it was found that species differed in whether they increased more in response to added CO_2 or more in response to increased light, water, or mineral nutrients. For two-species mixtures, results could be forecast from results of experiments of the two species grown alone.

4.1.2 Relevant general findings on plant-plant inter-relations. The key characteristics that determine which of two interacting species (or two genotypes within a species) can reduce the yield of another in mixture have been clearly established in numerous experiments summarized by de Wit (1961) and Harper (1977).

For annuals in the growth phase, key characteristics are:

1) Mass and energy content of seed and embryo.

2) Temporal pattern of growth (phenology).

3) Relative growth rate (RGR -- amount of new material produced per mean amount of material per unit time).

4) Root characteristics (branching pattern, root-hair length, uptake rates per unit area).

5) Canopy structure (especially height at which leaf blades are held).

6) Access to extra sources of mineral nutrients, e.g. nitrogen-fixing root-nodules.

Item 6 is especially important in mixtures of legumes and non-legumes, and is highly relevant to the issue of increased CO_2, since legumes may be limited more by C than by N on a moderately fertile soil, while non-legumes such as grass may be relatively more limited by N than by C.

For perennials, the key characteristics are the same, except that the starting capital each year is composed of perennating organs rather than seeds. Another potentially important feature of a closed community of perennials is that competition above ground may be as important as competition below ground from the beginning of the growing season, whereas in an open community of annuals, competition below ground is certainly the more important at first.

All of the six characteristics listed must be considered because an advantage in one aspect may compensate for a disadvantage in another. In particular, it is important to realize that the plant with the higher yield when grown alone will not necessarily be the superior competitor. For example, in the present atmosphere, a C_4 plant may lose to a C_3 plant if the latter has much larger seed, as in Wong's unpublished experiments on Japanese millet versus wheat (see Table 1).

In short-term experiments, an increased concentration of CO_2 may conceivably alter any of the six characteristics listed, but will have its primary effect on RGR, and in that way tip the balance between species. This is true in the case of experiments in which mineral nutrients have been added or different temperatures have been used. While the available evidence suggests that the competitive balance will be changed by extra CO_2 in most pairs of species, it may not always be so. In one case, the yield of mixtures of two grass species with similar RGR was much increased with the addition of nitrogen, but the balance between the species was unchanged.

A major point to be established is whether or not the competitor benefitting in a mixture from CO_2 enrichment can be forecast from the responses of the two species grown alone. In the case of adding mineral nutrients rather than CO_2, the effects in mixture can be forecast from the effects on single species, at least where the species used have substantially different responses (Mahmoud and Grime, 1976).

Under field conditions, taken over the whole annual cycle, relative abundances of two species are determined to a significant extent by differences between species in the numbers of seeds produced per plant, survival of seeds and requirements for germination and establishment, and not just by the competitive balance between established plants. The balance between any two co-existing annuals generally varies greatly from year to year, apparently as a result of weather and predators, and therefore any effects of more CO_2 on competitive balance might become apparent only after several years.

Also important under field conditions is the quality of plant residues. It is established that crop residues may contribute substantial amounts of phenolic acids and other allelochemics to agricultural soils (Chou and Patrick, 1976; Cochran et al., 1977; Guenzi and McCalla, 1966). It is widely believed that allelochemics have major effects on plant development in the field (Rice, 1974). If more CO_2 does increase phenolics in plants, and allelochemics effects are indeed important, there may be significantly enhanced allelochemic effects in both crops and unmanaged vegetation.

In the case of perennials, cumulative effects may occur through greater buildup of perennating organs in certain species, or through increased accumulation of litter. The extra litter may accumulate simply through increased production or partly through being richer in phenolics and more slowly decayed. Short-lived species that need bare ground for establishment, and lower-growing species, are known to be lost from perennial grasslands when extra litter accumulated because of addition of nutrients or cessation of grazing (Harper, 1977).

4.1.3 Weed/Crop interactions. Weeds are among the most damaging of all crop pests. They compete directly with crops for the same limited environmental resources upon which plant growth depends. In the United States, annual losses in crop yield and quality combined with the costs of weed control exceed $18 billion.

Most of the world's food crops have the C_3 photosynthetic pathway; 12 of the 14 most important crop species are C_3 plants (Harlan, 1975). On the other hand, of the world's 18 worst weeds, 14 have the C_4 photosynthetic pathway (Patterson, 1982). Conversely, many major weeds which compete with the few C_4 plants that are important food crops, are C_3 plants. For example, 19 of the 38 major weeds in corn in the United States are C_3 plants (USDA, 1972).

It is generally accepted that C_3 and C_4 plants respond differently to CO_2 enrichment. In most studies in which the growth of C_3 and C_4 plants have been compared, high levels of CO_2 stimulate the growth of C_3 plants more than that of C_4 plants (Patterson and Flint, 1980; see also Chapters 3 and 4). These differential responses to CO_2 enrichment may be expected to influence weed/crop competition in a high-CO_2 world. Increases in global atmospheric CO_2 may increase the impact of C_3 weeds in C_4 crops and decrease the impact of C_4 weeds in C_3 crops (Patterson and Flint, 1980). For example, in controlled-environment experiments, increasing the CO_2 concentration from 350 to 600 or 1000 ppm, increased the growth of the C_3 weed, velvetleaf, relative to growth of the C_4 crop, corn. In contrast, the growth of the C_4 weed, itchgrass, was decreased relative to that of the C_3 crop, soybean, at 1000 ppm (Patterson and Flint, 1980).

Of course, other environmental factors may limit plant responses of CO_2 enrichment. However, Patterson and Flint (1980) reported that even under low nutrient conditions which reduced total plant growth by as much as 60%, the growth-enhancing effects of CO_2 enrichment were not eliminated. Soybean and two leguminous weeds responded differentially to CO_2 enrichment to the extent that weed/crop ratios for significant growth parameters were altered. Thus, increases in the global atmospheric CO_2 concentration probably will influence weed/crop interactions. However, the relative responses of weeds and crops will vary according to species, photosynthetic pathway, growth habit, seed size, and many other parameters.

4.2 Plant-Animal Interactions. Conclusions about the response of herbivory to CO_2 increases are difficult to make because herbivores vary greatly in size and characteristics between ecosystems. Frequently, however, rates of herbivory are limited by the quality of available food rather than by its quantity (Franklin, 1970). In such situations, increases in organic production would not be expected to directly influence the rates of food uptake by herbivores unless these increases were very large.

Changes in the chemical and to a lesser extent physical quality of leaves, stems and roots may favor certain herbivore species at the expense of others, and thus alter the community composition of first order consumers. These changes, in turn, could affect both the producers upon which the herbivores depend, and the higher order consumers which feed upon the herbivores. Unfortunately, there are few data available to test these hypotheses.

Herbivore wastes play an important role in the intra-system recycling of plant nutrients by increasing availability of certain nutrients for plant absorption (Kitzell et al., 1979). Thus, changes in herbivore community composition might alter the chemical composition of wastes, thereby changing availability of nutrients to the producers. Since plant growth is dependent upon the amount of available nutrients rather than the total supply in the soil, herbivores can exert a greater control on nutrient absorption by primary producers than is suggested by their density of biomass. Little is known, however, about how changes in herbivore community composition affect nutrient cycling, but given the strong influence which insect outbreaks can exert upon forest growth (Brown et al., 1979), effects could be significant. Research is needed which examines herbivore consumption and nutrient availability interactions under the influence of more CO_2. There is a special need to examine the conditions which promote insect outbreaks often associated with the occurrence of other stresses such as climatic anomalies (U.S. Environmental Protection Agency, 1977; Bromenshenk, 1978).

4.3 Plant-Microorganisms (see Chapter 6). We are not aware of any direct studies on the effect of increasing atmospheric CO_2 on disease organisms or mycorrhiza. It is established that symbiotic nitrogen-fixation in root nodules is increased (Finn and Brun, 1982), and it is likely that parasymbiotic nitrogen-fixation will be increased if there is increased linkage of carbohydrates for the roots. Many plant-microorganism interactions associated with increased plant productivity have been described (Marshall, 1977). Therefore, we would expect increased carbohydrate production to affect soil microorganism activity.

In the long term, the most marked changes may arise from a slower and less complete decay of the dead plant remains if these prove to contain lower concentrations of N and P, and higher concentrations of phenolics. A slower rate of decay would involve a slower rate of release of major nutrient ions (nitrate, phosphate) and a gradual reduction in the fertility of the soil. It is also established that the phenolics leached from plant parts before their death can inhibit microbial activity, and in this way nutrient release below the surface layers of the soil may also be inhibited.

4.4 Flowering Phenology. Experiments with three annual species (Bazzaz, unpublished) have shown that flowering phenology was also influenced by higher CO_2, but, again, species differed in their response. While in Abutilon theophrasti rate of development (days-to-flowering) was insensitive to CO_2, Datura stramonium was affected. In the latter species, the plants grown at 450 and 600 ppm CO_2 flowered several days earlier than those at 300 ppm. In four populations of Phlox drummondii, higher CO_2 changed the time to first flowering, time of maximum flower production, and the time of maximum flower display in most populations. However, there were significant differences in the response of those populations to more CO_2.

1) Shift in flowering phenology and asynchrony with pollinators leads to differential seed production.

2) Shift in fruiting phenology may result in asynchrony with seed dispersers.

3) Shift in growth phenology change aparancy and availability to herbivores, e.g., the East African plains (McNaughton, 1979).

4) Shift in phenology may alter susceptibility to pathogens and other pests.

5.   Responses of Whole Communities   (Level 3)

The previous sections outlined two levels of scientific inquiry needed to understand the response of whole plant communities to higher CO_2. These are, first, the conceptual and quantitative response of individual species to increased CO_2, recognizing the varied adaptation among these plants to CO_2 uptake and water loss; and second, the quantitative response relation (predictive, insofar as possible) resulting from competition between two species in the presence of higher CO_2 concentrations.

The following sections therefore deal with multiple species or whole community response that now need evaluation prior to or during the projected increase in CO_2. Insofar as possible, a general research approach will be described recognizing, however, that substantial results from work on the single species or two species system still are needed before a significant research potential is realized.

5.1 Net Primary Production. As discussed above (Figure 1), elevated atmospheric carbon dioxide will initially increase the rate of net carbon fixation (photosynthesis minus dark respiration) in most plants, even those limited by light, water, or nutrients. Since net primary production (NPP) is simply the sum of the net carbon fixation by all of the individuals in a plant community, the initial effect of elevated CO_2 will be to increase NPP in most plant communities. This increase in NPP could be limited or reversed by nutrient availability, herbivory, or successional dynamics as discussed below. However, even without such effects, a critical question is the extent to which the increase in NPP will lead to a substantial increase in plant biomass. Alternatively, increased NPP could simply increase the rate of turnover of leaves or roots without changing plant biomass.

There will be no single or simple answer to this
question. In part, the relative importance of growth and
turnover will depend on nutrient availability, herbivory,
and the stage of succession (see later sections of this
Chapter). In general, though, where communities are
exploiting un- or under-utilized resources, elevated CO_2
would lead to increased biomass as observed in open top
field chambers (Rogers, 1980). In established
communities with adequate water and nutrients, however,
leaf area may be sufficient to intercept most incoming
light, and most of the soil may be within the influence
of roots or mycorrhizae. Additional photosynthate
could be allocated to wood (in forests or shrublands),
or it could lead to more rapid replacement of leaves or
roots. Evidence from fertile tropical forests suggests
that, in fact, relatively more photosynthate is
allocated to leaf production and turnover than to wood
production under those conditions (Jordan, 1982).

The increased water use efficiency resulting from
elevated CO_2 might increase the leaf area that could be
supported on water-limited sites. The greatest increases in
biomass (of both leaves and support tissue) might be expected
in such circumstances.

If turnover increased more than plant biomass, what
would be the direct consequences of increased plant litter
production? If decomposition rates did not change, the
amount of surface litter and soil organic matter would
increase. The increase in surface litter could be
predicted from existing models (Meetemeyer et al., 1982),
except that any increase in surface litter would increase
the probability of fires (see later sections of this
Chapter). More work would be required to predict changes
in soils.

Any increase in surface litter accumulation could have
substantial impacts on a variety of plant communities.
Surface litter accumulations prevent the germination and/or
establishment of many species by physical effects (Sydes and
Grime, 1981a, b), decreasing surface soil temperatures and
possibly allelochemical effects (Rice, 1974).

These observations as to possible responses in net
primary production by whole communities represent hypotheses
likely to be formulated more precisely as results from single
plant and selected field chamber studies become available.
Ultimately, however, these questions must be answered under
field conditions.

The problem of how to detect and document the first effects of higher CO_2 on plant communities in the field was examined thoroughly at a conference in 1981 (MacCracken and Moses, 1982), and several of the recomendations of that report are worth repeating here:

1) Establishment of a network of seven field ecological monitoring stations at high latitudes, to be coordinated with LTER sites in the conterminous U.S.

2) Expand ecological monitoring in temperature and northern zones to include:

   a. community and population variables
   b. physiology variables
   c. nutrient cycles alteration
   d. terrestrial species composition variation
   e. carbon storage by ecosystem type

3) Develop models of CO_2, temperature and pollutant effects in temperate and tundra ecosystems, in order to integrate results of field measurements and experiments.

5.2 Interactions with Nitrogen and Phosphorus Supply. Increased NPP could lead to either an increase in plant nutrient uptake or increased plant C/N or C/P ratios (or some intermediate). The first would occur if nutrients were available in excess of plant requirements or if increased plant TNC caused increased nutrient uptake. Ways that TNC could be allocated to increase nutrient uptake include increased root and/or mycorrhizal production, symbiotic nitrogen fixation, and phosphatase production and release.

An increase in nutrient uptake and nutrient circulation may occur in many sites. It may be the predominant response in areas where nutrient availability is not high -- for example, lowland tropical forests on volcanic soils (Vitousek et al., 1982). The well-demonstrated N and/or P deficiencies in many, perhaps most, unfertilized plant communities demonstrate that nutrient uptake often cannot be incresed in response to plant demand, however. Consequently, we expect that C/N and/or C/P ratios in plant communities will increase as atmospheric CO_2 increases. Thus areas of moderately infertile soils will become strongly nutrient-limited, and areas where moderate nutrient deficiencies occur will expand.

The consequences of elevated C/N or C/P ratio depend in part on the form of the "excess" carbon. Some studies report

very large amounts of TNC (mostly starch) in CO_2-enriched
plants (Cave et al., 1981; Wulff and Strain, 1982) or
low-nutrient plants (Brown et al., 1980). Other studies
have shown that much of the "excess" carbon in plants with
high C/N or C/P ratios in structural and polyphenolic
compounds (Loveless, 1962; Lamb, 1975) and that plants of the
same species grown with high nutrient availability have much
lower amounts of polyphenols.

The increase of C/N ratios and possible increase in
structural and phenolic compounds could have substantial
effects on herbivory. Many herbivores require relatively
high nitrogen concentraions in their food to survive, and
their growth rate may be reduced at intermediate nitrogen
concentrations (Mattson, 1980). This includes domestic
animals as well as pests; "protein starvation" in cattle is a
problem.

In addition, both structural and phenolic compounds can
deter grazers. This difference can be a consequence of
physical protection, reduced digestibility, or toxic effects;
polyphenols may have been selected in part for their
importance in reducing grazing. On the other hand, the
production of nitrogen-rich secondary compounds such as
alkaloids, which are also important in reducing herbivory,
may be reduced by high C/N ratios in plants.

Increased C/N and/or C/P ratios and increased structural phenolic compound production could also have important
effects on decomposers, and consequently profound effects on
nutrient cycling and plant growth. Litter produced by
plants with elevated C/N and C/P ratios will also have
elevated ratios; if nutrient reabsorption from senescing
leaves is greater in low-nutrient plants (H.G. Miller et
al., 1976), then CO_2 enrichment will cause greatly increased
C to nutrient ratios in litter. Litter with high C/N and/or
C/P ratios causes decomposers to be relatively nutrient
limited (Melillo, unpublished). This is expressed through
nutrient immobilization in their biomass and microbial
nutrient uptake from soil. Decomposers therefore release
nutrients to available pools more slowly and even compete
with plants for available nutrients. The presence of
elevated levels of structural and phenolic compounds can
further slow decomposition (Melillo et al., 1982), leading
to the accumulation of surface litter, the suppression of
seedling establishment, and a further reduction in nutrient
release through decomposition. Immobilization and slower
decomposition lead to reduced nutrient availability to the
plants, which in turn causes further increases in the C/N or
C/P ratios in plants. This positive feedback system

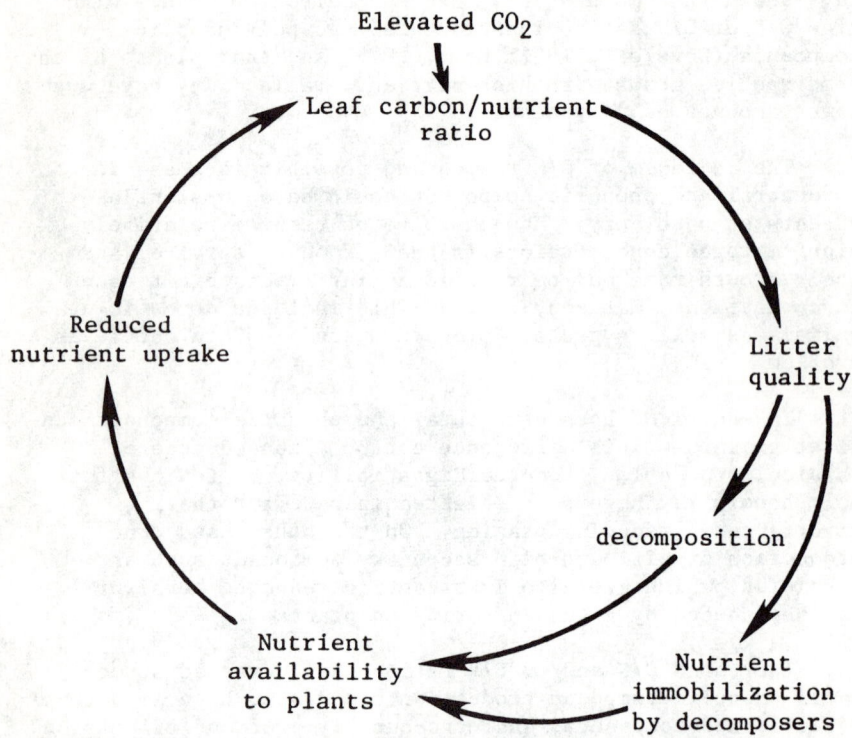

Figure 4. Expected consequences of elevated CO_2 on litter quality and nutrient availability in natural ecosystems. Elevated CO_2 is assumed to increase the C/N and C/P ratios of leaves but not directly affect nutrient availability. The increased C/nutrient ratios reduce litter quality (both directly and by increasing the relative amounts of structural and phenolic C), decrease decomposition, increase the competitive ability of microbes for soil nutrient availability, and cause a further increase in the C/N and C/P ratios of leaves. Similar dynamics probably occur for roots and root litter, though adequate data are not now available.

can maintain high ratios and low nutrient availability; its influence has been observed for nitrogen in a variety of natural and fertilized systems (Lamb, 1975; H.G. Miller et al., 1976; Vitousek et al., 1982).

The reduction in nutrient availability will cause reduced nutrient uptake and eventually reduced NPP, and it will reduce the possibility of substantial nutrient losses following disturbance (Vitousek et al., 1982). These positive feedbacks will eventually be balanced by decreased growth rate (NPP) and litter production, or they will be reset by a disturbance such as fire (see later sections of this Chapter).

Although much is known about the quantitative inter-actions among these components for natural systems, analysis and documentation of enhanced constraints on the system from increased CO_2 uptake will require the most sophisticated use of advanced modelling capabilities and data from field study sites. Taken together, however, the hypotheses appear to be testable and the questions as to nutrient interactions answerable within a decade or so.

5.3 Differential Species Responses. Differential species growth and changes in other aspects of the plants' response (e.g., water use efficiency and phenology) would likely result in shifts, extensions, or contractions in the range of habitat a species may use, and perhaps to extensions of its geographical range as well. The compensation of elevated CO_2 concentrations for high temperature (Kriedemann et al., 1976) and low temperature (Sionit et al., 1981) strongly suggests that this might occur to species in natural communities. The consequences of differential habitat and range changes would be difficult to predict, but have implications for community composition, species density, and the patterns of evolutionary interactions between species populations. In any given area of the landscape, we may observe changes in community characteristics resulting from a) addition of new species by migration and range extension, b) deletion of species by migration out of the community, and c) changes in competitive interactions between the remaining species and genotype, and the invading ones. Thus it would be difficult at this time to predict whether species density will increase, decrease, or remain unchanged.

It is now well established that elevated CO_2 concen-tration will increase photosynthesis, growth, and water use

efficiency in many plant species (see Chapters 4 and 5). It
also is established that species within a given community
will individually respond differently to higher CO_2
concentrations (Carlson and Bazzaz, 1980). Based on
theoretical consideration and some experimental evidence
concerning the effect of community structure on variation in
soil, moisture, and nutrients (Pickett and Bazzaz, 1978;
Parrish and Bazzaz, 1982; Bazzaz and Grubb, unpublished), we
can predict that increased CO_2 concentrations will influence
community organization through changes in competitive
relationships between species, and indirectly by differential changes of phenology. These changes will have
effects on other components of the ecosystem including
pollinators, dispersers, herbivores, etc., which in turn
influence community organization through other feedback
control loops.

It is possible that because of these differential
effects of CO_2 in the species biology, competitive
interactions in communities will alter and their structure
and function will be modified. Based on data available on
the response of species mixtures to the addition of
environmental resources (e.g., nutrients), it may be
predicted that species density, and perhaps genotypic density
in communities, will decline with CO_2 increase. Bazzaz and
coworkers (unpublished), who carried out competition
experiments with an assemblage of plant species at elevated
CO_2 concentrations and different levels of soil moisture,
nutrients, and light, showed the following results:

1) Total community production increased significantly
at elevated CO_2 concentrations, but only when nutrients were
not severely limiting. The increase in production was also
more pronounced at high moisture levels.

2) Elevated CO_2 concentrations caused a change in the
biomass hierarchy and a shift in dominance of the species.
These effects were more pronounced under high moisture,
nutrients, and light. In low light, community production
was higher at 450 ppm CO_2 than at either 300 or 600 ppm.

3) There were significant CO_2 effects on shoot biomass
in only one of six species under four nutrient levels. However, mean seed biomass changed significantly in three of
the six species examined.

4) Production of flowers and seeds were increased in
several species at 450 and low light and at 600 ppm for
several species, some of which did not reproduce when grown
under low light and 300 ppm. CO_2 concentration did not

influence the flowering and fruiting of plants grown under ample light. Thus elevated CO_2 concentrations seem to compensate for reduced light. Survivorship under low light intensity was also enhanced by elevated CO_2, especially in Polygonum pennsylvanicum and Abutilon theophrasti.

5.4 Species Diversity. It is difficult to predict the overall effects of elevated CO_2 on species diversity, especially because the mechanisms controlling its components (species richness, the number of species per unit area, and equitability, the distribution of abundance among species) are not thoroughly understood. Some of these mechanisms are known, however, and they may be affected by elevated CO_2.

5.5 Ecological Succession. The effects of elevated CO_2 will be modified depending on the successional status of plant communities, and elevated CO_2 can in turn affect the rate of succession. CO_2 will have its greatest effect on primary production and especially biomass accumulation early in secondary succession (the development of plant communities on sites influenced by previous occupancy). Immediately after disturbance, defined as the removal or destruction of biomass (Grime, 1979), light, water, and nutrient availability are relatively high and plants are exploiting largely unutilized resources (Bormann and Likens, 1979). Moreover, the plants which occupy such sites are selected for dispersal (or persistent seeds) and rapid growth; they store less nutrient or energy than plants adapted to later succession (Bazzaz, 1979; Grime, 1977). Early successional plants are more likely to allocate any additional photosynthate to growth, and more likely to have the nutrient levels allowing it.

More rapid growth early in secondary succession, however, will hasten the time at which the canopy is closed, soil water is largely transpired, and nutrient availability is no longer in excess of plant uptake. In fact, both leaf area (Marks, 1974) and nutrient uptake may reach maxima shortly after canopy closure; the resource competition among individuals can be more intense. Increased photosynthesis will probably not be reflected in increased growth during this time, and interactions with nitrogen and phosphorus may become more important. Still later in succession, net nutrient uptake is less and growth effects are perhaps more likely.

The general pattern is one of an increased rate of succession, with CO_2-responsive communities in early succession changing more rapidly into much less responsive later successional communities. Forest fertilization similarly increases the rate but does not change the course or the final state of forest plantation development. CO_2 may have a similar effect, although it should be noted that CO_2 would represent a chronic low-level addition, unlike forest fertilization. Additionally, CO_2 additions would make a forest more rather than less nutrient-limited, and would thus alter root-shoot ratios and the character and thickness of the litter layer.

If CO_2 does speed succession, it would lead to a number of other consequences. More rapid growth early in succession would cause a greater mean biomass over a landscape. Disturbed sites would be open habitats for a shorter period of time, and a smaller group of species might disperse where suitable sites for germination were still available (Grubb, 1977). Early successional tree species that must reach a certain age to reproduce might fail to do so. On the other hand, many disturbances (both natural and human caused) which initiate secondary succession are dependent on the state of a community, and the return frequency of such disturbance (logging, fire, insect outbreaks, even the consequences of windstorms) may be shortened.

The discussion above only applies to secondary succession. The effects of elevated CO_2 on primary succession (the development of vegetation on previously unoccupied sites) will probably be less. The elevated CO_2 may increase soil and rock weathering early in primary succession. More importantly, symbiotic nitrogen fixation, which is early in most primary successions (Walker and Syers, 1976) could be increased.

5.6 Biogeographical Effects. Climate changes and CO_2 enrichment significantly influence ecosystem dynamics at the species and community level. Since biotic communities are composed of species adapted to the local environment, shifts in environment can be expected to differentially affect the adaptive capacity of local species, and possibly create new species assemblages. Many cases of species migration and replacement in plant and animal communities are known, ranging from the sequence of successional communities which follow farmland abandonment, to the migration of species and entire communities following movement of continental glaciers.

Species differ widely in their capacity to adjust to environmental change. Both phenotypic and genotypic plasticity are important. Organisms adapted to disturbed conditions, and those with broad distribution ranges, are often the most plastic, and therefore most likely to adapt to environment shifts. Species adapted to habitats characterized by high seasonality or episodic frequencies of natural events (storms, fires) are more likely to adjust to change than those found in more constant and predictable environments.

Migration rates of species are largely determined by the type of locomotor structures in animals and the type of propagule structure in plants. If climate changes are very small or gradual, many species may migrate along with preferred climate conditions, or simply make in situ adjustments. But large or rapid climate changes, such as are predicted for high latitudes, could extend beyond the adaptive limits of some species and lead eventually to extinction. Similar events could result from sudden, drastic shifts in precipitation patterns.

Existing biotic communities are composed of species populations which are connected by a web of interspecific relationships that have evolved over thousands or millions of years. If entire communities or all the species except for a few minor ones migrate, these community interactions may be preserved. In the highly disturbed and man-influenced global ecosystem, however, it is doubtful that intact ecosystems can survive by migration. Unfortunately, we presently do not understand the role of many species in communities, and rare species, about which we often know least, may be more sensitive to rapid environmental change.

If a species complex breaks down because certain species lag behind others in adjusting to change, the assemblages of species that do adjust may not function efficiently as a community because too little time has elapsed for evolutionary and population adjustments to occur. Instead, instabilities may develop like those associated with the invasion of natural communities by non-indigenous species.

Natural ecosystems must not be regarded solely as static carbon pools which release or absorb CO_2 in response to outside driving forces. The metabolism of unmanaged ecosystems depends heavily on interspecific adjustments and species adaptations subject to genetic selection. Part of the energy initially fixed by primary producers is channelled into maintaining mechanisms for survival in the midst of competition for limited resources, and for adaptation to slowly changing environmental conditions. If rising CO_2 disturbs these mechanisms, wildlife, recreation, water resources values, and other ecological benefits which we

obtain from unmanaged ecosystems, can be expected to
diminish.

5.7 Interactions with Fire.   As an ecological factor,
intense fires rapidly convert organic matter back into
oxides of carbon, sulfur, and nitrogen, thereby shortening
the usual lag time that characterizes the decomposition
phase of the carbon cycle. Burning also improves the availability of most nutrients (e.g., phosphorus, and nitrogen).
This is highly variable, however (Raison, 1979). Wildfires
occur in many ecosystems and are probably a primary factor
in determining the vegetation structure and composition of
systems such as tropical savannas and temperate and tropical
grasslands, shrublands, and woodlands. Many fires are pur-
posely set by man in order to clear forests or increase forage.

The role of fires in the world carbon cycle is uncertain, but estimates suggest that it is significant. Recent
estimates of the release of carbon by fire place the gross
release at around 6×10^{15} g C yr^{-1} and the net release
between 0.6 and 1.5×10^{15} g C yr^{-1} (Wong, 1978, 1979).
More recently, Seiler and Crutzen (1980) calculated a gross
annual burning rate of $2-4 \times 10^{15}$ g C yr^{-1} of which 0.5 to
1.7×10^{15} g C yr^{-1} is sequestered as charcoal.

When fires burn in peat bogs or in other ecosystems
with low decomposition rates, some carbon is released which
had been sequestered for periods in the range of 10^2 to
10^4 years. This adds to the net accumulation of carbon in
the atmosphere within the time period of interest to man.
Decreasing precipitation patterns and increasing temperature
are likely to increase the probability of fire, with greatest consequences for carbon storage in northern latitudes
where large carbon storage is found in detritus, peat, and
humus. Increases in fire frequency can be expected in any
ecosystem subject to temperature increases and precipitation
decline. Therefore, accelerated global transfer rates of
carbon from slowly exchanging carbon pools to the atmospheric pool would be expected.

Systems where productivity is expected to increase with
increasing CO_2 levels and where fire frequency is associated
with accumulating biomass and standing dead material may
show particular increases in fire frequency with rising
CO_2. The chaparral may be one example of such a system.

The magnitude of probable increases in fire frequency
would be very difficult to predict and efforts to do so may
not be warranted. But research questions which should be
addressed include: 1) What are the implications of more

frequent fires of various types for carbon sequestering in major vegetation types throughout the world especially in the tropics and in peat areas? 2) What is the relationship between fire type, fuel quality, and rates of carbon oxidation? For example, coarse woody debris may release only a small fraction of its carbon stock in many forests (Fahnestock, 1979; Seiler and Crutzen, 1980). The fraction varies according to fire type (crown or ground fire), fire intensity, time of year, and type of litter.

5.8 Interaction with Environment Pollutants, e.g., SO_2. Concurrent with increasing atmospheric CO_2 concentration, SO_2, NO_x, O_3, and other air pollutants are affecting plants. To examine possible interactions between atmospheric gases, six annual species (three C_3 and three C_4) were grown at either 300, 600, or 1200 ppm CO_2 and under 0.0 and 0.25 ppm fumigation with SO_2. Fumigation with SO_2 caused reduced growth of the C_3 species at 300 ppm CO_2, but not at the higher concentrations. Fumigation with SO_2 reduced growth of the C_4 species at ambient CO_2 concentrations and the reverse seems to be true at high CO_2 concentrations. The reduction of photosynthesis and growth of soybean plants caused by SO_2 was mitigated by high CO_2. These high concentrations caused a decrease in both stomatal and residual conductances and depressed the amounts of CO_2 absorbed by the leaves (Carlson, 1982). Thus, more CO_2 modified the detrimental effects of SO_2 and provided some protection from the toxic gas.

5.9 Comparison with Lake Eutrophication. It has been suggested that the increase in CO_2 represents an enrichment of global ecosystems analogous to the eutrophication of aquatic ecosystems. On its surface, the parallel is appealing -- it illustrates that increased growth can have negative (decreased diversity, loss of a resource) as well as positive consequences. A brief view of our understanding of lake eutrophication may be revealing, however.

In the late 1960's there was a substantial controversy over whether CO_2 or phosphorus caused lake eutrophication. Short-term measurements clearly demonstrated that CO_2 fixation in low-alkalinity lakes was increased by added CO_2, while P additions had little or no effect. Whole lake experiments, however, showed that even in the lowest alkalinity lakes, the eutrophication process was driven by P additions (Schindler et al., 1973). While CO_2 additions stimulated photosynthesis, algae cells could not divide without P. Only additions of P allowed the populated increase necessary to convert a clear lake to a green lake. Where P is available, enhanced CO_2 level should merely

accelerate the increase to the same final level without
increasing standing crop within a growing season.

Terrestrial ecosystems are different in several ways.
Many (especially in the temperate zone) have sufficient P,
and N can be added by N fixation. The limitation on these
systems would be the kinetics of phosphorus conversion to
available forms. N and P fertilization of temperate zone
crops and some forests would allow growth to occur in
response to elevated CO_2. Structural tissue is low in N
and P, and terrestrial plants can produce that, while
unicellular algae cannot. Finally, terrestrial plants can
store large amounts of organic carbon without continuing
cell divisions.

In many terrestrial systems primary productivity is
limited by available moisture. Increasing water use
efficiency (see chapters 3, 4, and 5) should increase
productivity per unit of rainfall. Semi-arid and desert
areas in particular may show sizable increase in standing
crop and productivity under elevated CO_2.

Accordingly, we can expect some biomass growth in
terrestrial plants as a consequence of CO_2 enrichment.
Growth, however, will still often be nutrient limited, and
if CO_2 interacts with N and P as outlined in Figure 4, its
net effect will be to make many natural and managed
terrestrial communities progressively more oligotrophic.

6. Literature Cited

Bacastow, R. and C.D. Keeling. 1973. Atmospheric carbon
    dioxide and radiocarbon in the natural carbon cycle.
    II. Changes from AD 1700 to 2070 as deduced from a
    geochemical model. In Carbon and the Biosphere, G.
    Woodwell and E. Pecan, Eds., U.S. Atomic Energy
    Commission, Washington, D.C. pp. 86–134.

Bazzaz, F.A. 1979. The physiological ecology of plant
    succession. Ann. Rev. Ecol. Syst. 10, 351–371.

Bazzaz, F.A. and S.T.A. Pickett. 1980. Physiological
    ecology of tropical succession: a comparative review.
    Ann. Rev. Ecol. Sys. 11, 287–310.

Bigger, A. and W.C. Oechel. 1982. Nutrient effect on
    maximum photosynthesis in Arctic plants. Holarctic
    Ecol. 5, 158–163.

Billings, W.D. 1978. Plants and the Ecosystem. 3rd ed.

Wadsworth Publ. Co., Belmont, Calif. 177 pp. (see p. 96).

Billings, W.D., J.D. Luken, D.A. Mortensen, and K.M. Peterson. 1982. Artic tundra: a source or sink for atmospheric carbon dioxide in a changing environment? Oecologia 53: 7-11.

Bolin, B. 1977. Changes of land biota and their importance for the carbon cycle. Science 196, 613-615.

Bolin, B., E.T. Degens, P. Duzigeneaud and S. Kempe. 1979. The global biogeochemical carbon cycle p. 1-56. In Bolin, B., E.T. Degens, S. Keple, and P. Ketner, Eds., The global carbon cycle. SCOPE 13. John Wiley and Sons, Chichester.

Bormann, F.H. and G.E. Likens. 1979. Pattern and process in a forested ecosystem. Springer-Verlag, New York.

Botkin, D.B., J.F. Jonak, and J.R. Wallis. 1973. Estimating the effects of carbon fertilization on forest composition by ecosystem simulation. In Carbon in the Biosphere, G.M. Woodwell and E.V. Pecan, Eds., Conf.-720510, U.S. National Tech.Inform. Ser., Springfield, VA.

Bromenshenk, J.J. 1978. Investigations of the impact of coal-fired power plant emissions upon insects: Entomological studies in the vicinity of Colstrip, Montana. In The Bioenvironmental Impact of a Coal-fired Power Plant. Third Interim Report, Colstrip, Montana. U.S. EPA Ecological Research Series. EPA 600/3-778-021. pp. 140-212 and 473-507.

Brown, J., P.C. Miller, L.L. Treszen, and F.L. Burnnell. 1980. An arctic ecosystem: the coastal tundra at Barrow Alaska. US/IBP Synthesis Series 12. Dowden, Hutchinson, and Ross, Inc. Stroudsburg, PA, 571 pp.

Brown, J.H., Jr., D.B. Haliwell, and W.P. Gould. 1979. Gypsy moth defoliation: impact on Rhode Island forests. J. For. 7, 30-32.

Carlson, R.W. 1982. The effect of SO$_2$ on photosynthesis and leaf resistance at varying concentration of CO$_2$. Environmental Pollution (in press).

Carlson, R.W. and F.A. Bazzaz. 1980. The effects of elevated CO$_2$ concentrations on growth, photosynthesis, transpiration, and water use efficiency of plants. J.J. Singh and A. Deepak, Eds., in Environmental and Climatic Impact of Coal Utilization, Academic Press, New York.

Carlson, R.W. and F.A. Bazzaz. 1982. Photosynthetic and growth response to fumigation with SO_2 at elevated CO_2 for C_3 and C_4 plants. Oecologia 59: 50–54.

Cave, G., L. Tolley, and B.R. Strain. 1981. The effect of carbon dioxide enrichment on chlorophyll content, starch content and starch grain structure in Trifolium subterraneum leaves. Physiol. Planta. 51, 171–174.

Chou, C.H. and T.A. Patrick. 1976. Identification and phytotoxic activity of compounds produced during decomposition of corn and rye residues in soil. J. Chem. Ecol. 2, 369–387.

Cloudsley-Thompson, J.L. 1974. The expanding Sahara. Environmental Conservation 1, 5–13.

Cochran, V.L., L.F. Elliot, and R.I. Papendick. 1977. The production of phytotoxins from surface crop residues. J. Soil Sci. Soc. Am. 41, 903–908.

Detling, J.K., W.J. Parton, and H.W. Hunt. 1979. A simulation model of Boutelova gracilis biomass dynamics on the North American shortgrass prairie. Oecologia 38, 167–191.

Fahnestock, G.R. 1979. Carbon input to the atmosphere from forest fires. Science 204, 209–210.

Finn, G.A., and W.A. Brun. 1982. Effect of atmospheric CO_2 enrichment on growth, nonstructural carbohydrate content, and root-nodule activity in soybean. Plant Physiol. 69, 327–331.

Franklin, R.T. 1970. Insect influences on the forest canopy, pp. 86–99, in D.E. Riechle, Ed., Analysis of Temperate Forest Ecosystems. Springer-Verlag, New York. 304 pp.

Gosz, J.R., G.E. Likens, and F.H. Bormann. 1973. Nutrient release from decomposing leaf and branch litter in the Hubbard Brook forest, New Hampshire. Ecol. Monog. 43, 173–191.

Grime, J.P. 1973. Competitive exclusion in herbaceous vegetation. Nature 242, 344-347.

Grime, J.P. 1974. Vegetation by reference to strategies. Nature, pp. 26-31.

Grime, J.P. 1977. Evidence for the existence of three primary strategies in plants and its relevance to ecological and evolutionary theory. Am. Nat. 111, 1169-1194.

Grime, J.P. 1979. Plant strategies: vegetation and vegetation processes. John Wiley, London.

Grubb, P.J. 1977. Control of forest growth and distribution on wet tropical mountains with special reference to mineral nutrition. Ann. Rev. Ecol. Sysm., 8, 83-107.

Guenzi, W.D., and T.M. McCalla. 1966. Phytotoxic substances extracted from soil. Proc. Soil Sci. Soc. Am. 30, 214-216.

Harlan, J.R. 1975. Crops and Man. Amer. Soc. Agronomy. Madison, Wisc. USA.

Harper, J.L. 1977. Population Biology of Plants. London, Academic. 892 pp.

Heinselman, M.L. 1981. Fire and succession in the conifer forests of Northern North American. In D.C. West, H.H. Shugart, and D.B. Botkin, Eds., Forest succession. Springer-Verlag, New York. 517 pp.

Herrer, J.R. Gosz, and J.M. Melillo. Interactions of biogeochemical cycles in forest ecosystems. In Bolin, B. and R. Cook. Interactions of biogeochemical cycles, SCOPE Report (in press).

Huston, M. 1979. A general hypotheses of species diversity. Am. Nat. 113, 81-101.

Jacobson, J.S. 1982. Economic impacts of air pollutants: a summary. Jour. Air Poll. Cont. Assoc., 32, 144-145.

Jacobson, M.B., W.A. Stoner, and S.P. Richards. 1981. Models of plant and soil processor change 11. In P.C. Miller, Ed. Resources use by chaparral and matoral: A comparison of vegative function in two Modelterania ecosystems. Springer Verlag, New York. 465 pp.

Jordan, C.F. 1982. The nutrient balance of an Amazonian forest. Ecology 63, 647-654.

Kitzell, J.F., R.Z. O'Neill, D. Webb, G.A. Gallepp, S.M. Barttell, J.R. Koonze, and B.S. Ausmus. 1979. Consumer regulations of nutrient cycling. BioScience 29, 28-43.

Kriedemann, P.E., R.J. Sward, and W.J.S. Downton. 1976. Vine response to carbon dioxide enrichment during heat therapy. Aust. J. Pl. Physiol. 3, 605-618.

Lamb, D. 1975. Patterns of nitrogen mineralization in the forest floor of stands of Pinus radiata on different soils. J. Ecol. 63, 615-625.

Loveless, A.R. 1962. Further evidence to support a nutritional interpretation of sclerophylly. Ann. Bot. 104, 551-561.

MacCracken, M.C. and H. Moses. 1981. The first detection of carbon dioxide effects: Workshop Summary. Proc. of the First Detection of Carbon Dioxide Effects Workshop, Harpers Ferry, W.V. DoE, CO_2 Effects Program, Washington, D.C.

McKree, K.J. 1970. An equation for the rate of respiration in white clover plants grown under controlled conditions. In Prediction and Measurements of Photosynthetic Productivity. pp. 221-229. Wagingen, PUDOC.

McNaughton, S.J. 1979. Grazing as an optimization process: grass-ungulate relationship in the Serengeti. Amer. Nature 113, 691-703.

Mahmoud, A. and Grime, J.P. 1976. Analysis of competitive ability in three perennial grasses. New Phytologist 77, 431-435.

Marks, P.L. 1974. The role of pincherry (Prunus pennsylvanica L.) in the maintenance of stability in Northern hardwood ecosystems. Ecol. Monog. 44, 73-88.

Marshall, J.K.. Ed. 1977. The belowground ecosystem: A synthesis plant associate processes. Range Science Dept., Science Series No. 26, Colorado State Univ., Fort Collins, 351 pp.

Mattson, W.J. 1980. Herbivory in relation to plant nitrogen content. Ann. Rev. Ecol. Sys. 11, 119-161.

Meetemeyer, V., E.O. Box, and R. Thompson. 1982. World patterns and amounts of terrestrial plant litter production. BioScience 32, 125-128.

Melillo, J.M., J.D. Aber, and J.F. Murature. 1982. Nitrogen and lignin control of hardwood leaf litter decomposition dynamic. Ecology 63, 621-626.

Miller, H.G., J.M. Cooper and J.D. Miller. 1976. Effects of nitrogen supply on nutrients in litter fall and crown leaching in a stand of Corsican pine. J. Appl. Ecol. 13, 233-248.

Miller, P.C., W.A. Stoner, and L.L. Tieszen. 1976. A model of stad. photo for the wet meadow at Barrow, Alaska. Ecol. 57, 411-430.

Mooney, H.A. 1972. The carbon balance of plants. Ann. Rev. Ecol. Sys. 3, 315-346.

Odum, E.P. 1971. Fundamentals of Ecology. W.B. Saunders Co., Philadelphia. 574 pp.

Oechel, W.W., W. Lowell and W. Jarrell. 1981. Nutrient and environmental controls in carbon dioxide flux in Mediterranean shrubs from Calif., in N.S. Margaris and H.A. Mooney, Eds., Component of productivity of Mediterranean climate regions: Basic and Applied Aspects, Dr. W. Junk Publ. The Hague. 279 pp.

Parrish, J.A.D. and F.A. Bazzaz. 1982. Competitive inter-actions in plant communities of different successional ages. Ecology 63, 314-320.

Parton W.J., J.S. Singh and D.C. Coleman. 1978. A model of production and turnover of roots in shortgrass prairie. J. Appl. Ecol. 15, 515-542.

Patterson, D.T. 1982. Effects of light and temperature on weed/crop growth and competition. Pp. 407-420; in Hatfield, J.L. and I.J. Thomason, Eds., Biometeorology in Integrated Pest Management. Academic Press, New York.

Patterson, D.T. and E.P. Flint. 1980. Potential effects of global atmospheric CO_2 enrichment on the growth and competitiveness of C_3 and C_4 weed and crop plants. Weed Science 28, 71-75.

Penning de Vries, F.W.T. 1975. Use of assimilates in higher
plants, in J.P. Cooper, Ed., Photosynthesis and
Productivity in Different Environments. Cambridge
Univ. Press, Cambridge. 715 pp.

Pickett, S.T.A. and F.A. Bazzaz. 1978. Organization of an
assemblage of early successional species on a soil
moisture gradient. Ecology 59, 1248–1255.

Raison, R.J. 1979. Modification of the soil environment by
vegetation fire with particular reference to nitrogen
transformation. Review Plant and Soil 51, 73–108.

Reynolds, J.F., B.R. Strain, G.L. Cunningham, and K.R.
Knoerr. 1980. Predicting primary productivity for
forest and desert ecosystem models, In J.D. Hesketh
and J.W. Jones, Eds., Predicting photosynthesis for
ecosystem models. Vol. II. CRC Press, Boca Raton, FL.
279 pp.

Rice, E. 1974. Allelopathy. Academic Press. New York. 368 pp.

Rogers, H. 1980. Field studies of plant responses to
elevated carbon dioxide levels. DOE Progress Rept. 001
(1980). CO_2 Res. Div., Office of Energy Research,
Washington, D.C. 20545.

Seiler, W. and P.J. Crutzen. 1980. Estimates of gross and
net fluxes of carbon between the biosphere and the
atmosphere from burning biomass. Climatic Change 2,
207–247.

Shugart, H.H. and J.M. Hett. Succession: similarities of
species turnover rates. Science 180, 1379–1381.

Shugart, H.H. and D.C. West. 1977. Development of an
Appalachian deciduous forest succession model and its
application to assessment of the impact of the Chestnut
Blight. J. Environ. Management. 5, 161–179.

Sionit, N., B.R. Strain, and H.A. Beckford. 1981. Environmental controls on the growth and yield of okra. I.
Effects of temperature and of CO_2 enrichment at cool
temperature. Crop Sci. 21, 885–888.

Solomon, A.M., D.C. West, and J.A. Solomon. 1981. Simulating
the role of climate change and species immigration in
forest succession. In D.C. West, H.H. Shugart, and
D.B. Botkin, Eds., Forest Succession. Springer-Verlag,
New York. 517 pp.

Strain, B.R. and N. Sionit. 1982. Direct effects of carbon dioxide on plants: a bibliography. Dept. of Botany, Duke Univ., Durham, NC 27706. 66 pp.

Sydes, C. and J.P. Grime. 1981a. Effects of tree leaf litter on herbaceous vegetation in the deciduous woodland. I. Field investigations. Journal of Ecology 69, 237-248.

Sydes, C. and J.P. Grime. 1981b. Effects of tree leaf litter on herbaceous vegetation in the deciduous woodland. II. Field investigations. Journal of Ecology 69, 249-262.

Tenhunen, J.D., J.A. Weber, C.H. Filipek, and D.M. Gates. 1977. Development of a photosynthesis model with emphasis on ecological applications. III. Carbon dioxide and oxygen dependencies. Oecologia 30, 189-207.

USDA. 1972. Extent and cost of weed control with herbicides and an evaluation of important weeds, 1968. U.S. Dept. Agric. ARS-H-1. Washington, D.C.

U.S. Environmental Protection Agency. 1977. Photochemical air pollution effects on a mixed conifer forest ecosystem -- a progress report. Ecological Research Services, EPA-600/3-77-104.

Vitousek, P.M., J.R. Gosz, C.C. Grier, J.M. Melillo, and W.A. Reiners. 1982. A comparative analysis of potential nitrification and nitrate mobility in forest ecosystems. Ecological Monographs 52, 155-177.

Walker, T.W. and J.K. Syers. 1976. The fate of phosphorus during pedogenesis. Geoderma 15, 1-19.

West, D.C., S.B. McLaughlin and H.H. Shugart. 1980. Simulated forest responses to chronic air pollution stress. J. Environ. Qual. 9, 43-49.

Wit, C.T. de. 1961. Space relationships within populations of one or more species, in Mechanisms in Biological Competition (Sym. Soc. Exp. Biological Competition, No. 15), F.L. Milthorpe, Ed., pp. 314-329. Cambridge.

Wong, C.S. 1978. Atmosphere input of carbon dioxide from burning wood. Science 200, 197-199.

Wong, C.S. 1979. Carbon input to the atmosphere from forest fires. Science 204, 210.

Woodwell, G.M., R.H. Whittaker, W.A. Reinevz, G.E. Likens, C.C. Delwiche, and D.B. Botkin. 1978. The biota and the world carbon budget. Science 199, 141-146.

Wulff, R.A. and B.R. Strain, 1982. Effects of CO_2 enrichment on growth and photosynthesis in Desmodium paniculatum, Can. J. Bot. 60, 1084-1091.

_____ *Robert G. Wetzel, Chairman*
James B. Grace, Co-Chairman

8. Aquatic Plant Communities

Panel Members: E.A.D. Allen, J.W. Barko, Sven Beer,
G. Bowes, M. Bristow, Charles C. Coutant, B.G. Drake,
J.E. Hobbie, Osmund Holm-Hansen, Hidde B.A. Prins,
J.H. Peverley.

SUMMARY AND RECOMMENDATIONS

1) This report evaluates the expected responses of
aquatic plants to elevated concentrations of atmospheric
CO_2. We include aquatic plants with emergent foliage, as
well as submersed macrophytes and microscopic algae. We
consider both freshwater and marine plants. We review
known effects of inorganic carbon on aquatic plants,
project the possible effects of a doubling in atmospheric
CO_2 on aquatic plants, and discuss needed research on this
problem.

2) Plants with emergent foliage obtain most of their
CO_2 from the atmosphere. Emergent aquatic macrophytes are
largely similar to terrestrial plants in their physiology
and, therefore, are expected to respond similarly to
elevated CO_2.

3) Submersed plants are exposed to a variety of exogenous forms of inorganic carbon because of the formation and
dissociation of carbonic acid. All submersed plants can
utilize dissolved CO_2, many can utilize HCO_3^- ions, and
it is likely that none can utilize $CO_3^=$ ions.

4) Submersed plants have a wide array of important
morphological and physiological adaptations to facilitate
carbon uptake in the aqueous environment. Nonetheless, for
many plants, especially the vascular plants and macroalgae,

223

the slow diffusion of inorganic carbon in water poses a
major limitation to carbon uptake and metabolism.

5) We conclude that the probability of increased
growth responses of aquatic plants is as follows: Emergent
aquatic angiosperms > submersed vascular plants and
macroalgae > attached microalgae > freshwater phytoplankton
> marine phytoplankton.

6) Emergent vascular plants of saline and freshwater
habitats are commonly exposed to conditions conducive to
CO_2 limitation. Field experiments for rice and water
hyacinth under cultivated and nutrient-rich conditions have
demonstrated substantial increases in plant growth from
enrichments of CO_2. However, no comparable field data
exist for non-cultivated aquatic plants.

7) Submersed vascular plants and macroalgae require
high levels of CO_2 to saturate photosynthesis and,
particularly in fresh waters, are commonly CO_2-limited
under natural conditions. Although the ability of some of
these plants to assimilate bicarbonate from the water is
very important, most plants require free CO_2 to achieve
maximal rates of photosynthesis. The principal limitation
to carbon uptake is the high external resistance to the
diffusion of inorganic carbon into these submersed plants
because of the slow rate of diffusion of inorganic carbon
in water.

8) Microalgae are likely to be less limited by
inorganic carbon than are submersed vascular plants because
of an increased ability to utilize bicarbonate and a higher
surface-to-volume ratio. Although not conclusively
demonstrated, freshwater phytoplankton will generally
exhibit only small increases in photosynthetic production
in response to elevated inorganic carbon supply because of
mineral nutrient (P, N) limitations. However, shifts in
species composition of freshwater algae are likely. Marine
phytoplankton are not likely to respond to elevated
inorganic carbon under most conditions because of strong
mineral nutrient limitations and the abundance of
bicarbonate.

9) Quantitative predictions of change for natural
populations are extremely difficult to make with much
confidence. However, we project increases in photosynthetic production from doubled atmospheric CO_2 to be

near zero for marine phytoplankton and approximately 25% for emergent and submersed freshwater plant communities.

10) For those systems that increase photosynthetic production in response to elevated inorganic carbon, decreases in species diversity are possible. Existing emergent and submersed aquatic plant communities, however, are already low in diversity compared to most terrestrial communities. Insufficient information exists to permit predictions about specific changes in species composition.

11) If the production of emergent plant litter is increased, more sediment organic matter accumulation would be expected for wetlands and lakes. Because of the slow rates of emergent plant litter decomposition and nutrient release, a greater quantity of mineral nutrients would be tied up in an unavailable form. If increased productivity is to be maintained, microbial enhancement of nutrient supplies will be required.

12) Soluble organic degradation products of lignin and cellulose from emergent plants can normally suppress the metabolism of submersed angiosperms and lake phytoplankton. Suppression occurs by means of nutrient sequestering and reduced nutrient recycling. As a result, if CO_2 enrichment causes increased growth of emergent wetland plants, this may result in long-term acceleration of sedimentation and filling of lake basins. These effects, accelerating lake succession and altering the ecosystem, could overwhelm direct responses to increased CO_2 by submersed photosynthetic productivity.

13) At present, our information about both the physiological responses of aquatic plants and their operation within the context of the ecosystem is woefully inadequate for quantitative predictions about CO_2 effects. Much work needs to be done on whole-system responses and the underlying mechanisms in order to refine our projections.

Research Recommendations

The supply of inorganic carbon affects, directly or indirectly, to some degree, most processes within aquatic ecosystems. Variety of habitat requires that studies cover a broad range of conditions. Experiments, especially field studies, should focus on basic mechanisms so as to facilitate extrapolation to other conditions. We recognize

three broad categories of aquatic plant communities: a)
emergent plant communities, b) submersed angiosperms and
macroalgae, and c) freshwater algae. (This report does not
deal extensively with marine algae because we believe the
open sea has an abundance of bicarbonate and is so nutrient
deficient that increasing CO_2 will not materially affect
photosynthesis or productivity.)

There are few long-term studies of CO_2 enrichment on
any aquatic communities. Our recommendations are therefore, with some notable exceptions, similar in many
respects to those of the preceding chapters.

1) We need to initiate long-term studies of CO_2
enrichment in order to clarify issues such as basic carbon
metabolism, mineral nutrition, growth response, competition,
and population dynamics.

2) Some aquatic plants live partly out of the water.
The supply of inorganic and organic carbon is important to
those plants and organs growing below the water surface
where gas diffusion is 10^4 times slower than in air.
Thus, O_2 supply to the roots growing in sediments is also
important. Mechanisms of C and O_2 supply and plant
adaptations are not clearly understood.

3) If more CO_2 causes greater plant productivity,
then problems of added litter, N fixation, nutrient
sequestering, and noxious byproducts come into play. How
do these problems affect sustained growth and plant
population change?

To answer these questions, we recommend experiments
of long-term exposure of enclosed systems to elevated CO_2
under field conditions.

These studies should focus on a number of processes
simultaneously and will require an interdisciplinary
approach. Processes found important should be investigated
in more detail by coupling field studies with laboratory
analyses.

Emergent Plant Communities

Important processes include:

a) The response of carbon metabolism to elevated CO_2
and its interaction with various enviornmental factors,
especially minearl nutrition.

b) Whole plant responses to elevated CO_2 and inter-action with environmental conditions.

c) Oxygen transport to the roots and rhizosphere, and the metabolic activation of roots in relation to oxygen, mineral nutrients, and salinity stress. Work should couple effects of carbon metabolism on root growth and metabolism with rhizosphere activities and nitrogen fixation.

d) Differential species responses should be coupled with studies of population dynamics and competition so as to determine community responses.

These analyses are particularly important in relation to ecosystem processes because of the differential effects of species on production, decomposition, and mineral cycling.

Submersed Angiosperms and Macroalgae

1) We need to investigate long-term exposure of enclosed systems to elevated CO_2 and HCO_3 in shallow waters under field conditions. Simultaneous examination of a number of processes would require an interdisciplinary approach. Processes found to be most important should be studied further under more controlled conditions.

2) Examination of inorganic carbon transport in littoral systems with emphasis on water circulation and the diffusion of CO_2/HCO_3-.

3) Processes of major importance include:

a) The effects of increasing CO_2 and HCO_3- on carbon metabolism and a coupling of these processes with mineral nutrition.

b) Growth responses of plants to CO_2 and HCO_3- variations under a variety of conditions.

c) Inorganic carbon supplied by sediments or from the atmosphere. Studies should utilize plants of various growth forms.

d) Oxygen transport to the roots and rhizosphere, and the metabolic activities of roots in relation to oxygen, mineral nutrients, and salinity. Also, the effects of carbohydrate allocation on subterranean processes, including nitrogen fixation.

e) Population and community responses should be studied within the context of habitat fertility and chemistry with emphasis on differential species responses.

f) The interrelationships between submersed macrophytes and their epiphytes. Differential responses of the two components to elevated inorganic carbon as a function of pH, alkalinity, and nutrient supply.

Freshwater Algae

1) We need to investigate long-term exposures of mixed species systems under controlled and seminatural conditions to enriched CO_2 availability. Emphasis should be placed on using systems of various degrees of complexity in order to encompass dynamics of populations, turbulent mixing and grazing.

2) We also need comparative studies of carbon metabolism coupled with mineral nutrition.

3) The interaction between dissolved organic matter, bacteria and phytoplankton for algae of contrasting physiology. Objectives would be to determine the effect of species composition changes on mineral cycling processes in the water column.

4) Growth responses of green, blue-green, and diatom algae under various nutrient regimes. Investigations should be coupled with studies of population dynamics and settling processes.

5) The effects of inorganic carbon on the chemical composition of algae.

6) The response of zooplankton grazing to changes in species composition, cell size, and chemical composition.

1. Introduction. Water covers three-fourths of the world's surface. Although productivity per unit area in the submersed environment is relatively low, the total global yield is large. In contrast, emergent aquatic plants inhabit a smaller area, but are among the most productive. Aquatic plant systems have an enormous impact on human society. Rice, often cultivated as an emergent aquatic plant, feeds more people than any other crop. Many other aquatic plants are of major human concern because of their involvement in fisheries, wildlife, water resources, and other uses.

Evaluating the effects of more atmospheric CO_2 on the physiology, ecology, and productivity of aquatic plants is in some ways more difficult than in terrestrial plants. Several factors contribute to this difficulty. First, aquatic plants include a diverse assemblage of plants: a) microscopic algae (both procaryotic and eucaryotic) that are attached to substrata or freely floating; b) macro-algae; and c) higher plants (together referred to as "macrophytes") that are adapted to submersed, floating, and emergent habits. For example, increasing atmospheric CO_2 will affect aquatic plants in an aerial environment quite differently than plants that obtain a portion or all their inorganic carbon from the water. Secondly, as gaseous CO_2 is absorbed and dissolved in water, it enters the carbonate system, and forms HCO_3^- and $CO_3^=$, the final concentrations of which are influenced by many properties of the water solution itself. Lastly, relatively little is known of the physiology and ecology of aquatic plants in comparison to terrestrial plants.

Virtually none of the critical experiments have yet been made to determine the long-term effects of higher CO_2 in aquatic plants under field conditions. Given that the significance of increasing CO_2 has only been appreciated in recent years, it is not surprising that our knowledge is so limited. For these reasons, we are as concerned with identifying knowledge gaps as we are with reviewing existing information. Therefore, a general discussion of research recommendations is included in the paper.

Because of the diversity of plants and their habitats, we briefly discuss the major groups and associated terminology before addressing specific aspects of their physiology and ecology related to CO_2 availability. Our discussion places less emphasis on marine phytoplankton than on either freshwater aquatic plants or marine macrophytes since, as we shall argue later, marine phytoplankton are not likely to respond in a major way to more atmospheric CO_2. Freshwater plants inhabit a spectrum of waters from very soft waters, in which inorganic CO_2 availability is influenced by atmospheric sources, to very bicarbonate-rich hard waters in which atmospheric sources are a relatively minor portion of total inorganic carbon. Most marine habitats belong in the latter category. In addition, most emergent aquatic plants that possess C_3 metabolism, upon which atmospheric CO_2 enrichment could have significant direct physiological and indirect community effects, are primarily from freshwater habitats.

Table 1.   Extent and productivity of aquatic ecosystems.

	Area (10^6 km^2)	Average Productivity (mg/ha/y)
Lakes and Streams	2[a]	
Phytoplankton		2[d]
Submersed Macrophytes		10[d]
Marshes and Swamps	2[a]	
Herbaceous Emergent Macrophytes		55[d]
Cultivated Paddy Rice	1.4[b]	15[b]
Salt Marshes		30[d]
Oceans	361[c]	
Phytoplankton		2[d]
Algal beds, Reefs, and Estuaries	2[a]	30[d]

[a]Lieth, 1975; these values do not include cultivated systems.
[b]Murata, 1976.
[c]Whittaker, 1974.
[d]Westlake, 1963.

1.1 Aquatic Plants and Their Habitats. Aquatic plants
are found in a variety of habitats and are usually grouped
according to their size and modes of attachment (or lack of
it) to substrata. By far the largest number of aquatic
plant species consist of microscopic algae of freely-
floating habit (phytoplankton) or attached to both living
and non-living substrata. The macroalgae, which are
primarily sessile, are poorly represented in fresh waters,
but form the main component of coastal marine environments.
Although salinity has marked effects on many physiological
functions of vascular and non-vascular plants, primary
characteristics of CO_2 assimilation and photosynthetic
physiology are similar in these plants.

Vascular aquatic plants can be separated into four major
groups based on growth forms:

a) Emergent angiosperms are rooted in water-saturated or
submersed soils from the point at which the water table is
about 0.5 m below the soil surface to the point where the
sediment is covered with ca. 1.5 m of water. Emergent
macrophytes are primarily rhizomatous or cormous perennials.
Many species may exist as (usually sterile) submersed forms;
all produce aerial reproductive organs.

b) Floating-leaved rooted angiosperms are primarily
angiosperms that occur attached to sediments at water
depths from about 0.5 to 3 m. Submersed leaves precede or
accompany the floating leaves. Floating leaves are on
long, flexible petioles, or on short petioles from long
ascending stems.

c) Submersed angiosperms occur only to about 10 m depth in
fresh waters. Certain species of the few marine
angiosperms (seagrasses) occur to at least 30 m depths in
clear waters.

d) Freely floating macrophytes include an extremely diverse
assemblage of plants that live within or upon the water.
Freely floating macrophytes range from large plants with
rosettes of aerial and/or floating leaves to minute
surface-floating or submersed plants with few or no roots.

From the viewpoint of primary productivity, aquatic
plant communities may be grouped into seven categories
(Table 1). Some communities, such as freshwater marshes,
are among the most productive biotic systems known. For
comparison, temperate forest productivity is about 15 Mg
ha^{-1} yr^{-1}. However, the total global area of these

highly productive emergent aquatic systems is relatively small and they fix only about 2% of the total terrestrial productivity (Lieth, 1975). Most of the aquatic production occurs in the open ocean where photosynthesis per unit of area is low but area is large. Despite the low proportion of total global primary production, the aquatic communities provide a significant part of man's food supply; rice feeds millions of persons and fisheries produce vital protein.

2. CO_2 Assimilation from Air, Water, and Water-Saturated Sediments

2.1 Emergent, Free-Floating, and Floating-Leaved Macrophytes.

Atmospheric CO_2 is clearly the dominant source of inorganic carbon among emergent, floating-leaved (rooted), and freely-floating macrophytes. A few species of freely-floating angiosperms (e.g., some duckweeds, Lemna) utilize both atmospheric and aqueous carbon sources (Wohler, 1966; Wetzel and Manny, 1972; Ultsch and Anthony, 1973). Heterophyllous aquatic angiosperms are presumably similarly adapted to assimilate both atmospheric CO_2 and aqueous inorganic carbon sources. Short-term CO_2 enhancement (500 to 1000 ppm) has been shown to increase photosynthetic rates of three species of floating duckweeds (Loats et al., 1981).

There are at least three potential sources of CO_2 for plants with emergent foliage; sediment CO_2 absorbed directly by roots, sediment-derived CO_2 released into the canopy, and CO_2 which comes into the canopy from the above atmosphere. Studies with rice (Oryza sativa L.) have shown that most of the CO_2 fixed is derived from the atmosphere, with sediment-derived CO_2 supplying 0 to 12% of the carbon for net production. Direct absorption of CO_2 by the roots is 1 to 2% (Murata et al., 1957; Mitsui and Kurihara, 1962; Tanaka et al., 1966; Yoshida et al., 1974). It is not clear at present if rhizomatous species have similarly low root uptake. Where the sediment is in direct contact with the atmosphere, sediment derived CO_2 may be important to photosynthesis (Moss et al., 1961; Monteith et al., 1964). However, under wet conditions, the diffusion of CO_2 from the soil to the atmosphere is strongly inhibited.

Evidence suggests that the physiological processes in emergent foliage of aquatic plants are the same as in terrestrial plants. Most emergent species possess C_3 metabolism, and under conditions of high light and temperature these species exhibit high levels of photorespiration (Jones and Milburn, 1978; Filbin, 1980). Studies by McNaughton (1966, 1969) and McNaughton and Fullem (1969)

present evidence that Typha latifolia possesses C_3 carbon
metabolism, despite its high rates of photosynthesis and
relatively low rates of photorespiration. C_4 species
often found in freshwater habitats include Cyperus
esculentus, C. papyrus, Echinochloa crus-galli, Panicum
spp., and Zizaniopsis miliacea. In contrast to freshwater
marshes, C_4 species Spartina alterniflora, S. patens, S.
townsendii, and Distichlis spicata often dominate salt
marshes.

2.2 Submersed Macrophytes and Algae

2.2.1 Inorganic Carbon System in Natural Waters.
CO_2 is very soluble in water and obeys normal solubility
laws. When water is in equilibrium with air, dissolved
free CO_2 is approximately 10 μmol. Dissolved CO_2
hydrates to carbonic acid (H_2CO_3) at a concentration which
is very low (1/40th of free CO_2). H_2CO_3 rapidly
dissociates to HCO_3-. The final concentrations are
governed by the partial pressure of CO_2, temperature, pH,
and ionic strength of the water solution. Concentrations
of all forms of inorganic carbon can be predicted by
solubility and dissociation equations for any concentration of atmospheric CO_2 by assuming equilibrium between the
atmosphere and water. Increasing atmospheric CO_2 causes a
linear increase in dissolved CO_2. This increase will in
turn generally result in an increase in HCO_3 concentration. However, the increase is not as great as, nor is it
linearly proportional to, the CO_2 increase because of a
simultaneous reduction of pH (Figure 1). For example, a
doubling of atmospheric CO_2 will result in a reduction of
0.28 pH units of seawater under equilibrium conditions
(Stumm and Morgan, 1981).

Both oceanic and many fresh waters are close to equilibrium with atmospheric CO_2 much of the time. In the
marine habitat, the inorganic carbon pool contains about
2.5 mM C, largely as HCO_3-, a concentration twice that of
the atmosphere. In fresh waters, the total inorganic
carbon is much more variable (50 μM to 10 mM); pH is more
variable because of differing alkalinity and high photosynthetic carbon demands in freshwater ecosystems. Free
CO_2 (dissolved) is predominant in water at pH 5 and below,
while above ph 9.5, $CO_3=$ is quantitatively significant.
Between pH 7 and 10, HCO_3- predominates.

The magnitude of CO_2 exchange between the ambient air
and some fresh waters cannot be determined by partial
pressure differences alone. Many lakes with surface waters
near neutrality are slightly supersaturated with CO_2

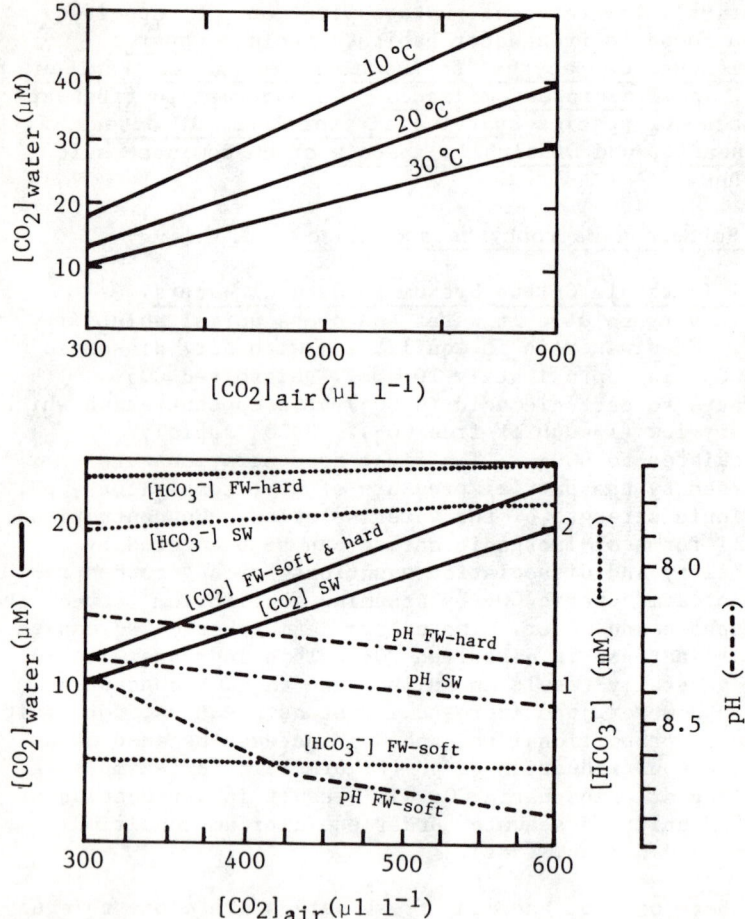

Figure 1. <u>Upper:</u> Free dissolved CO_2 concentrations in fresh water as a function of increasing atmospheric CO_2 concentrations at air equilibrium and various temperatures (μl 1^{-1}=ppm).
<u>Lower:</u> Effects of increasing atmospheric CO_2 concentrations on the carbonate system in three water types at 20°C and alkalinity values of (a) soft fresh water, 0.5 meq/l; (b) hard fresh water, 2.47 meq/l; and (c) seawater, 2.47 meq/l.

relative to the air. Alkaline bicarbonate lakes containing
large amounts of HCO_3^- and $CO_3^=$, are not in equilibrium
with the air, and a net efflux of CO_2 to the atmosphere can
occur throughout much or all of the year (e.g., Otsuki and
Wetzel, 1974).

In more productive waters, consumption of CO_2 by
phytoplanktonic algae can create a flux of atmospheric CO_2
into the water (Weiler, 1974; Emerson 1975) as dissolved CO_2
concentrations decline and photosynthetically-induced
concentrations of carbonate increase (Wood, 1974, 1977;
Talling, 1976).

The amount of excess CO_2 required to maintain stability
of bicarbonate in solution increases rapidly as the
bicarbonate increases. If a solution of bicarbonate (in
calcium-rich hard waters) in equilibrium with CO_2, H_2CO_3,
and $CO_3^=$ loses a portion of the CO_2 required to maintain the
equilibrium (e.g., CO_2 assimilated photosynthetically), the
pH and carbonate concentration may rise to a level exceeding
the solubility of $CaCO_3$. Calcium carbonate will precipi-
tate (as marl) until equilibrium is reestablished. Excess
CO_2 that is required to maintain large amounts of HCO_3^- in
solution can also be lost to the atmosphere by photosynthetic removal, resulting in massive precipitation of
$CaCO_3$.

2.2.2 Carbon Assimilation by Algae and Submersed
Macrophytes. Algae and submersed aquatic macrophytes
require an abundant and readily available source of carbon
for high sustained rates of growth. Abundant physiological
evidence indicates that free CO_2 is the form of inorganic
carbon most readily utilized by many algae and submersed
vascular plants. Many algae and submersed macrophytes,
particularly the mosses and pteridophytes, utilize only
free CO_2 (Bain and Proctor, 1980). Other algae and aquatic
vascular plants can utilize bicarbonate ions as an
exogenous carbon source when free CO_2 is very low and HCO_3^-
is abundant. There is little conclusive evidence that
algae or higher aquatic plants assimilate $CO_3^=$ directly as a
carbon source. A comprehensive review of the subject is
given by Raven (1970, 1981; cf. also Allen and Spence,
1981).

In some cases of high photosynthetic demand, the
resupply of CO_2 from the carbonate species can be rate
limiting. Below a pH of 8.5, the theoretical dissociation
kinetics of the CO_2-HCO_3^- -$CO_3^=$ complex, derived from pure
solutions, agree very well with the concentrations of the
ionic species found in natural waters (Talling, 1973). Above

pH 8.5, however, the total inorganic carbon dioxide concentrations fall considerably below values calculated on the basis of the apparent dissociation constants K_1' and K_2' of carbonic acid, as derived from measurements of alkalinity. Although the explanation for this phenomenon is not completely clear, it appears to be related to the presence of a noncarbonate, nonhydroxide alkalinity component arising from ionized silicate (Talling, 1973).

Direct assimilation of bicarbonate ions is variable among planktonic algae, macroalgae, and submersed angiosperms (Raven, 1970; Allen and Spence, 1981). Bicarbonate utilization is an active process that includes the dehydration of HCO_3^- and is coupled to a stochiometric excretion of hydroxyl ions. Although carbonic anhydrase activity is found in submersed plants, its activity is generally lower than that found in both terrestrial plants and in unicellular algae (Weaver and Wetzel, 1980). In marine angiosperms that utilize HCO_3^-, carbonic anhydrase activity is apparently too low to contribute significantly to photosynthesis (Beer et al., 1980).

Since the affinity for HCO_3^- ions is lower than for CO_2, a higher concentration of HCO_3^- ions is required to saturate photosynthesis. The maximal rates of photosynthesis in HCO_3^- solutions are one-third to one-half those obtained at saturating concentrations of dissolved CO_2 in both freshwater and marine algae and submersed angiosperms (Lucas, 1975; Beer et al., 1977; Lucas et al., 1978; Kadono, 1980; Allen and Spence, 1981).

Equilibrium concentrations of dissolved CO_2, particularly in alkaline hardwater lakes with a pH $>$ 8.5, are inadequate to saturate photosynthesis in submersed plants. When waters become more productive, and in densely populated littoral zones of less productive lakes, pH is rapidly altered by metabolism on a diurnal basis (pH ranges from a low of 6 to a high of 10 or more in 24 hours), reducing carbon fixation or bicarbonate assimilation. Under stagnant conditions common to heavily colonized littoral zones of lakes, the shift to bicarbonate metabolism, as well as the increased pH, is often associated with severe reduction in CO_2.

Among planktonic diatoms, for example, successive CO_2 enrichments induced a three- to five-fold increase in algal biomass over that of unenriched controls (Jaworski et al., 1981). A certain degree of cellular adaptation occurred with successive generations exposed to CO_2 reductions. Inorganic carbon limitations could be

counterbalanced by reducing the pH without any additions
of total inorganic carbon; this increases the relative
proportion of free CO_2. This effect often is observed
under culture conditions.

In addition to potential direct effects of higher CO_2
on algal photosynthesis, the relative abundance of other
exogenous carbon sources (HCO_3-) can influence phytoplankton species composition and population succession
(Paerl and Ustach, 1982; Jaworski et al., 1981). Inorganic
carbon depletion in the photic zone of nutrient-enriched
lakes can occur and result in increased sinking rates of
diatoms (lacking buoyancy control). The diatoms can be
subsequently replaced by buoyant, bloom-forming blue-green
algae. Buoyancy in blue-green algae apparently facilitates
inorganic carbon assimilation, by bringing algae closer to
the surface and thus enhancing productivity (e.g., Booker
and Walsby, 1981).

Morphological adaptations among submersed leaves,
stems, and some petioles include thin leaves (1 to 3 cell
layers), reduced cuticle development, extreme reduction or
elimination of mesophyll, and dense distribution of
chloroplasts in epidermal cells. These adaptations all
increase utilization and exchange of gases. Massive
intercellular gas spaces in leaves, stems, and petioles
facilitate rapid internal diffusion.

Photosynthesis limitation by slow diffusion of CO_2 in
water has received much attention, especially related to the
alternate utilization of bicarbonate ions. Rate-limiting
steps in the flux of CO_2 from the air to metabolic pathways
of cells vary widely among aquatic environments depending
upon differences in water chemistry, physical mixing, and
rates of CO_2 utilization. CO_2 exchange between the air and
water surface can be quantified using the "stagnant film"
model or more complex models (cf. review of Danckwerts,
1970; Broecker, 1974). Transfer rates depend upon the CO_2
gradient between the air and surface water, turbulent mixing
of both air and water at the interface, function of wind
speed controlling both air and water boundary layer thick-
nesses (and thus the transfer coefficients), and chemical
enhancement by reaction of CO_2 with water and OH- ions (cf.
Wood, 1974 for transfer coefficients from several sources).
Transfer coefficients in well-stirred systems probably vary
from 0.01 cm s^{-1} in lakes with high winds and whitecaps to
less than 0.001 cm s^{-1} on calm days (Verduin, 1975). The
flux of CO_2 from the air may be too slow to support
potential CO_2 demands by aquatic plants in nutrient-rich
lakes. Production can be restricted by slow air-water

transfer in softwater lakes, whereas bicarbonate sources may sustain productivity in hardwater situations. It is probable that with increased CO_2 in air, algal photosynthesis will not be accelerated in nutrient-limited fresh waters, but may be enhanced in nutrient-rich lakes.

In large submerged angiosperms and algae, the diffusion path is long (up to 50 μm), through the cells of the thallus or leaf, to which must be added another boundary layer of about 100 μm of unstirred water at the cellular surfaces; further, diffusion rates through the larger cells are much slower than among microalgae (Steemann Neilsen, 1947; Raven, 1970; Smith and Walker, 1980). Low velocity currents in the bulk fluid increase photosynthesis among submersed angiosperms by reducing the stagnant boundary layer, thus decreasing diffusion path lengths (e.g., Barth, 1957; Westlake, 1967).

Stagnant layers around plant cells (algae) and tissues (macrophytes) clearly limit the assimilation of both CO_2 and HCO_3^- during photosynthesis (Browse et al., 1979; Smith and Walker, 1980; Black et al., 1981; Prins et al, 1982a, 1982b). Internal diffusive resistance is much less than resistance associated with the stagnant boundary layer at the air-water interface. Internal resistance apparently accounts for only a small fraction (- 5%) of total resistance to CO_2 assimilation in several species of <u>Potamogeton</u>. Turbulence reduces the thickness of the stagnant boundary layer and can promote photosynthesis at fixed levels of available carbon in aqueous systems (Westlake, 1967). However, a residual boundary layer (ca. 10 μm thick) parallel to the plant surface remains even when plants are exposed to water movements or when planktonic algae sink. Mass transport across this residual layer is by molecular diffusion. Diffusion of CO_2 and HCO_3^- through these stagnant layers is an important rate-limiting process both to availability of CO_2 and to membrane transport of HCO_3^- ions. Mucilage sheaths surrounding algal cells, especially among blue-green algae, can further reduce the uptake rates of inorganic carbon (Chang, 1980). A doubling of the pCO_2 will double the rate of carbon transport.

Bicarbonate ions as a carbon source supplementary to carbon dioxide has been demonstrated in a number of studies. Space does not permit detailed discussion of the results of all of these studies. Utilization of HCO_3^- under natural conditions has been reported for a number of freshwater and marine angiosperms (e.g., Raven, 1970; Beer et al., 1977, 1979; Helder and Zanstra, 1977; Lucas et al., 1978; Browse et al., 1979; Allen and Spence, 1981; Beer and Wetzel,

1981; Prins et al., 1980, 1982a, 1982b, 1982c), while other
species were found to utilize mainly CO_2 (Wetzel, 1969;
Brown et al., 1974; Van et al., 1976; Moeller, 1978;
Winter, 1978; Kadono, 1980). In algae, especially larger
macroalgae, the ability to utilize bicarbonate ions in
photosynthesis is widespread, but not universal. The
extensive work on this subject among mosses and angiosperms
by Steemann Nielsen (1944, 1947), Ruttner (1947, 1948,
1960), and others (e.g., Bain and Proctor, 1980; Raven and
Beardall, 1981) has shown that certain freshwater red algae
and all assayed genera of freshwater submersed mosses
utilize primary free CO_2. These latter plants are
restricted almost always to soft waters of relatively low
pH, or to streams in which CO_2 concentrations are
relatively higher. In two reported cases, the levels were
2.8×10^{-4} M free CO^2, which is 20 times the concentration
in air (Bristow, 1969; Browse et al., 1977).

In summary, evidence indicates that, among the
diversity of concentrations and states of inorganic carbon
in fresh and marine waters, there exists a large number of
cases where free CO_2, even in equilibrium with the
atmosphere, may be inadequate to sustained high levels of
photosynthesis (see especially Talling, 1976; Jaworski, et
al., 1981). In other cases, free CO_2 may be inadequate as
a result of slow diffusion rates and chemical losses from
the system. Possession of an affinity for bicarbonate is a
distinct adaptive advantage in most submersed plants.

2.2.3 Aeration in submersed tissues. The size of internal
lacunal systems is highly variable among species, but is
extensive and constitutes a major portion (often exceeding
70 per cent) of the total plant volume. The lacunae are
gas-filled. Even if the plant is damaged, the lacunal
spaces do not flood because a number of lateral plates and
watertight diaphragms, permeable to gases, interrupt the
lacunae at intervals (Arber, 1920; Schulthorpe, 1967).
Although experimental evidence is very meager, it is known
that much of the oxygen produced during photosynthesis and
retained in the lacunal system can diffuse from the leaves
through the petioles and stems to underground root and
rhizome systems where respiration demands are high.

The gases within the intercellular lacunae of submersed
angiosperms diffuse along gas partial pressure gradients.
In floating-leaved plants (e.g., the yellow water lily
Nuphar), however, evidence indicates that the internal gas
spaces function as a pressurized flow-through system
(Dacey, 1981). Ambient air enters the youngest emergent
leaves against a small gas pressure gradient as a result of

physical processes driven by gradients in temperature and water vapor between the atmosphere and the lacunae. The lacunal gas spaces are continuous through young emergent leaves, petioles, rhizomes, and petioles of the older emergent leaves. The older leaves vent the elevated pressure generated by the younger leaves. The resulting flow-through ventilation system accelerates both the rate of oxygen supply from the atmosphere to the root tissue, and the rate of CO_2 and methane (Dacey and Klug, 1979) transport from the roots to the atmosphere.

The movement of oxygen (from the atmosphere in emergent and floating-leaved plants or from sites of oxygen production in submersed plants) to roots is essential to prevent the accumulation of toxic metabolic end products (e.g., ethanol produced during glycolysis). Wetland and submersed plants often increase the volume of the lacunal gas system when sediments become more reducing (e.g., Katayama, 1961; Armstrong, 1978; Penhale and Wetzel, 1982). In addition, a number of aquatic plants have developed metabolic adaptations to anaerobic conditions. Diverse non-toxic endproducts (malate, shikimic acid) can be produced during glycolysis (Crawford, 1978; Penhale and Wetzel, 1982; Sale and Wetzel, 1982), or ethanol can be released to the environment (Bertani et al., 1980).

There is no question that the evolution of an extensive internal lacunal gas system in submersed angiosperms constitutes interrelated morphological adaptations to (a) enhanced efficiency of carbon fixation, (b) flexibility to withstand water movements, (c) positive buoyancy and positioning of leaves towards greater available light, and (d) an efficient transport system for oxygen diffusion to roots and rhizomes.

2.2.4 Metabolism in submersed plants. Submersed vascular plants are exposed to more variable concentrations of dissolved oxygen and CO_2 than are emergent aquatic or terrestrial plants. Light availability is generally lower, and temperature is less variable than in the terrestrial environment. Furthermore, submersed and freshwater emergent aquatic plants are never subjected to the water stress to which terrestrial C_4 plants of arid environments have become adapted. The slower diffusion of CO_2 in water and the presence of massive internal gas lacunae can slow loss of CO_2 from submersed angiosperms and facilitate refixation of respired and photorespired CO_2 (Carr, 1969; Hough and Wetzel, 1972; Hough, 1974; Sondergaard, 1979; Sondergaard and Wetzel, 1980). In softwater lakes, concentrations of total inorganic carbon in the water are very low; certain soft-water submersed angiosperms utilize CO_2 of the sediment interstitial water to supplement CO_2 assimilated from the water (Wium-Andersen, 1971; Sondergaard and Sand-Jansen, 1979). Uptake of CO_2 by root tissue for photosynthetic fixation by submersed plants of hardwater lakes, where concentrations of inorganic carbon were high, could not be demonstrated (Beer and Wetzel, 1981).

In contrast to a relatively constant CO_2 compensation point for a given terrestrial species, values for submersed angiosperms appear to be quite variable, depending on prior growth conditions (Helder et al., 1974; Brown et al., 1974; Van et al., 1976; Lloyd et al., 1977; Hough and Wetzel, 1978; Bowes et al., 1979; Salvucci and Bowes, 1981; Barko and Smart, 1981). Values are similar to those for certain unicellular algae (Tsuzuki and Miyachi, 1981). The CO_2 compensation point is important as an indicator of the photosynthesis/photorespiration ratio. High values suggest significant photorespiration.

Photoperiod and temperature conditions of summer may decrease the CO_2 compensation point, whereas winter-like conditions may increase it (Salvucci and Bowes, 1981). Correlated with these observations, photorespiration in Scirpus subterminalis is relatively low in summer and increases in winter (Hough, 1974). Similarly, photorespiration and dark respiration are ten-fold greater in fall compared to summer as the annual submergent Najas enters senescence (Hough, 1974). For Hydrilla and Myriophyllum, a low CO_2 compensation point is associated with higher rates of net photosynthesis (or an increased affinity for CO_2), decreased rates of photorespiration, and reduced oxygen inhibition of photosynthesis (Holiday and Bowes, 1980; Salvucci and Bowes, 1981). With a high CO_2 compensation point, the reverse is true.

Preliminary evidence indicates that changes in the CO_2 compensation point may be related to the CO_2 concentration in the environment. For Hydrilla, low CO_2 levels (100 ppm gas phase) induced a low CO_2 compensation point, whereas high levels (2,000 ppm gas phase) restored a high value (Salvucci and Bowes, 1981).

Conditions conducive to accelerated photorespiration and reduced net photosynthesis can develop in the littoral zone, particularly among dense submersed plant populations with little turbulence (Wetzel, 1965, 1975; Goulder, 1980;

Table 2: A: Equilibrium concentrations of CO_2 amd HCO_3^- in water under 300 and 600 μl 1^{-1} (ppm) of atmospheric CO_2. B: Projections of potential photosynthetic responses by submersed plants to a doubling of atmospheric $[CO_2]$. C: Projections of productivity responses of various aquatic plant communities to a doubling of atmospheric $[CO_2]$ under field conditions (see text for explanation).

A: CO_2 System	Aqueous $[CO_2]$		Aqueous $[HCO_3^-]$	
	330 μl i^{-1} in atm.	600 μl 1^{-1} in atm.	300 μl 1^{-1} in atm.	600 μl 1^{-1} in atm.
Marine	∿10 μM	∿ 20 μM	∿ 2.5 mM	Slight increase
Fresh water, soft	∿10 μM	∿ 20 μM	∿ 0.5 mM	Very slight increase
Fresh water, hard	∿ 10 μM	∿ 20 μM	∿ 2.5 mM	Slight increase

B: Potential Photosynthetic Responses (Submersed)

	μ moles O_2 . mg chl^{-1} . h^{-1}		
	Present Rates[a]	Δ Rates, Projected[a]	Maximal Rates[a,b]
Marine:			
Angiosperms	3-50	2x	70-120
Macroalgae	1-8	1-2x	?
Phytoplankton	100-300	1x	100-300
Fresh Water:			
Macrophytes (Algae, Angiosperms)	5-20	2x	50-80
Phytoplankton	25-100	1-1.5x	100-400

C: Probable Community Responses

	Increase from Present Levels
Marine: Submersed	
Angiosperms	1.2x
Macroalgae	1.2x
Phytoplankton	1.0x
Freshwater: Submersed	
Macrophytes (Angiosperms; algae)	1.25x
Phytoplankton	1.1x
Emergent Macrophytes	
Saltmarsh	1.1x
Freshwater	1.25x

[a] Under light saturation and well-stirred conditions.

[b] At CO_2 and HCO_3^- saturation of photosynthesis.

Hough, 1974). Many studies suggest that photorespiration increases through the day as dissolved oxygen increases from photosynthesis, temperature increases, and CO_2 availability decreases (Wetzel, 1975, 1982).

Evidence indicates that freshwater and marine submersed angiosperms possess the C_3 photosynthetic pathway (Hough and Wetzel, 1977; Winter, 1978; Browse et al., 1979; Valanne, et al., 1982; critically discussed in Beer and Wetzel, 1981, 1982a, 1982b), and thus there is a potential for photo-respiratory CO_2 loss. A number of marine and freshwater species also exhibit C_4 acid formation, particularly malate, in the light (Beer et al., 1980; Browse et al., 1980; Holiday and Bowes, 1980; Kremer, 1981; Beer and Wetzel, 1982b; Helder and Harmelen, 1982). It has been suggested that these acids function to balance excess cation uptake, or as an anapleurotic source of compounds for the TCA cycle or amino acid synthesis (Browse et al., 1980). In Hydrilla, production and turnover of malate in the light undoubtedly contributes to its inducible low photorespiratory state (Holiday and Bowes, 1980). However, malate may also accumulate in the dark for subsequent decarboxylation and refixation of CO_2 in the light analogous to that in terrestrial CAM plants (Keeley, 1981, 1982; Beer and Wetzel, 1981).

Some species, such as Myriophyllum spicatum (Salvucci and Bowes, 1981) and certain seagrasses (Beer and Waisel, 1979; Beer et al., 1980) possess low rates of photo-respiration, yet exhibit no evidence of C_4 acid metabolism. It is possible that an inducible bicarbonate utilization mechanism in these species demonstrated for unicellular green algae.

Efficient internal recycling of respired CO_2, utilization of bicarbonate, and augmentation of exogenous inorganic CO_2 by decarboxylation of malate are all mechanisms by which certain submersed species adapt to limited CO_2.

3. Tentative Projections of Responses of Submersed Plants to Elevated Atmospheric CO_2. In Table 2 we project the photosynthetic responses of various groups of submersed plants to increases in atmospheric CO_2 in soft and hard freshwaters and in seawater. These projections are based on photosynthetic rates of single plant species obtained in the laboratory under light saturation and well-stirred conditions. Thus, these projections are best thought of as photosynthetic potentials.

Submersed plants suffer from more severe diffusion limits than do terrestrial species because of the surrounding water medium. Among some groups, however, HCO_3^- utilization can partially offset this limitation. Phytoplankton can combine an effective HCO_3^- use with high surface area to volume ratios. Thus phytoplankton have relatively high photosynthetic rates, approaching inorganic carbon saturation. Consequently, little increase in photosynthesis is expected by a doubling of the atmospheric, and thus aqueous, free CO_2 concentration.

In contrast, photosynthetic rates of submersed plants are relatively low. Many species of marine angiosperms are HCO_3^- but not CO_2 saturated. Hence, increases in free CO_2 in the marine environment should increase photosynthesis in plants. Photosynthesis of freshwater angiosperms is below HCO_3^- or CO_2 saturation in most waters. Thus a doubling of the CO_2 concentration should increase photosynthesis since free CO_2 is more readily assimilated than bicarbonate. If short-term photosynthetic measurements can be extrapolated to field productivity, the submersed plants and macroalgae would be expected to increase relative to the microalgae.

Part C of Table 2 presents approximate values for increases in productivity expected under field conditions. The basis for these values is more fully developed later. Marine and freshwater phytoplankton estimates are derived from both field and laboratory studies. Projections for emergent and submersed angiosperms and macroalgae were estimated from very limited field evidence and should be interpreted with caution.

4. Extrapolation of Controlled Studies to Natural Systems. This section addresses the question, "What are the ecological consequences of physiological and whole-plant responses to enrichments of CO_2?" Current knowledge and existing data are insufficient to predict the responses of aquatic plant communities and ecosystems to levels of atmospheric CO_2 in the range of 400-600 ppm. Despite our uncertainty, we can extrapolate from known effects of CO_2 enrichment on whole-plants to response under field conditions. All of these extrapolations must be viewed with considerable caution since they are extended from physiological studies under controlled conditions, often in monocultures with good water and nutrient supply. The nature of the response under varying field conditions is considered following the discussion of potential effects of CO_2 enrichment.

4.1 Rooted Emergent, Free-Floating, and Floating-Leaved Macrophytes

4.1.1 The Variety of Whole-Plant Responses.
There are few studies of CO_2 enrichment on rooted emergent, free-floating, and floating-leaved macrophytes (hereafter referred to simply as "plants with emergent foliage"). In many ways plants with emergent foliage are physiologically similar to terrestrial plants, especially in above-ground processes. As discussed earlier, there are many important exceptions to such a generalization because of the aquatic existence of lower plant parts. Nonetheless, the same observed whole-plant responses of many terrestrial plants might be expected in aquatic plants with emergent foliage. A select list of plant responses, derived largely from terrestrial plants, are presented in Table 3 (cf. also Chapters 2, 3, and 5).

When considering Table 3, it is important to keep in mind that most of the reported effects of CO_2 enrichment on plants are derived from short-term experiments. For example, in recent studies where plants were grown under higher levels of CO_2 from the time of germination, several developmental changes occurred which acted to offset the initial response of photosynthesis to elevated CO_2 levels; i.e., decreased levels of RuBP carboxylase (Downton et al., 1980; Wong, 1980).

Most short term studies indicate that CO_2 enrichment will increase biomass production (cf. Table 3 and other chapters in this volume). Those plants that are likely to benefit most are C_3 plants with a high CO_2 compensation point and which are water stressed (for example, plants in seasonally dry habitats, and salt marsh plants under certain conditions). Because of the interaction between CO_2 and high light, especially in C_3 plants (Gaastra, 1963), plants in high light habitats will be more responsive to CO_2 than shaded plants due in part to suppressed photorespiration. However, even under light-limited conditions, more CO_2 can cause proportional increases in net photosynthesis.

Temperature and higher levels of CO_2 interact to affect photosynthesis as well. Evidence suggests that the temperature optimum for net photosynthesis is extended into higher temperature ranges at elevated CO_2; this effect is greater among C_3 than C_4 plants. Also, the tolerance of at least some plants to low (Sionit et al., 1981) or high temperatures (Kriedemann et al., 1976) is increased with more CO_2. Such effects, as well as species differences in

Table 3. Whole-plant responses of emergent aquatic and terrestrial plants
to CO_2 enrichment [taken largely from Strain and Armentano
(1980) and Chapters 2, 3 and 5 in this volume].

A. Increased Plant Growth:

   1. Enhanced water use efficiency

   2. Enhanced nitrogen fixation

   3. Enhanced root growth

   4. Enhanced mycorrhizal development

   5. Increased light saturation

   6. Increases resistance to temperature extremes

   7. Decreased photorespiration

   8. Increased temperature optimum in C_3 plants

B. Altered Growth Form:

   1. Reduced apical dominance

   2. Increased sexual reproduction

   3. Leaf area increase

   4. Leaf weight/area increase

   5. Decreased chlorophyll content

   6. Root/shoot increase

C. Altered Timing of Event:

   1. Induction of seed germination

   2. Delay of leaf senescence

   3. Plant maturation accelerated

---

degree of response, should influence geographical distribution of species.

In terrestrial plants there is also interaction between response to CO_2 and N metabolism. Wong (1979) concluded that growth response to increased CO_2 is largely independent of available N levels. For cotton, a C_3 plant, percent growth increase at higher CO_2 was constant under both high and low levels of available N. Decreased N per unit of leaf area at high CO_2 was associated with reduced levels of RuBP carboxylase in the leaves. In contrast, corn -- a C_4 plant -- did not benefit from elevated CO_2 under low N conditions. There is no similar information for aquatic vascular plants. Further, no information is available for other mineral elements.

Vesicular-arbuscular mycorrhizae develop under non-waterlogged conditions in some emergent aquatic and semi-aquatic species including rice (Clarke and Mosse, 1981). Only a few species have microbial N fixers associated with their roots (Glyceria, Oryza, Spartins, Typha) and emergent leaves or fronds (Eichhornia and Salvinia). In some cases, N fixation by these associations may make a significant contribution to the N economy of the plant (Bristow, 1974; Casselman et al., 1981; Buresh et al., 1980; Patriquin and Keddy, 1978; Yoshida and Ancajas, 1973). Paddy rice can derive substantial amounts of combined N through fixation by the blue-green algae symbiont of Azolla growing in the field (Peters and Calvert, 1982).

Alterations in plant growth form are expected from increased CO_2. As plants increase in size, their patterns of growth may shift dramatically (Harper, 1977). Increased allocation of biomass to sexual and vegetative modes of reproduction are commonly reported with increasing plant biomass (cf. Grace and Wetzel, 1981a, 1981b, 1982a, 1982b). Realistically, however, since plants do not grow in isolation in either natural or agricultural situations, plant density may act to alter the responses of individual plants to increased CO_2. Experiments summarized by Harper (1977) show that because of the effects of soil fertility on plant density, low productivity conditions can favor larger biomass of individual plants. The effects of density on plant form and reproduction will be considered further in a later section. Reduced apical dominance and change in leaf area alter plant form with more CO_2. Increases in the proportion of roots from elevated CO_2 have been reported for terrestrial species (Tognoni et al., 1967). However, other studies have failed to show this

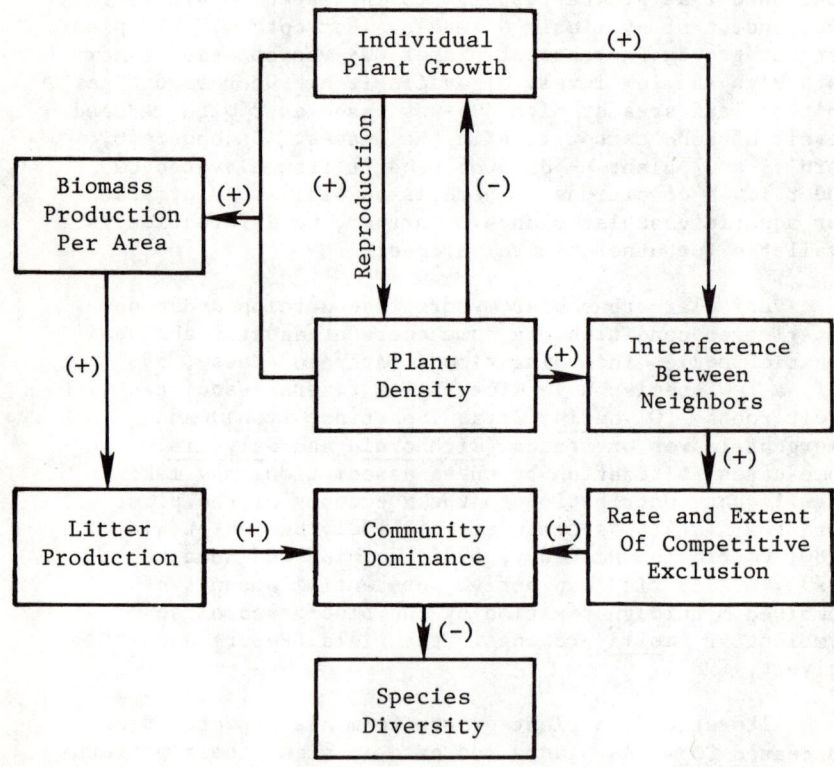

Figure 2.   Some population and community responses of emergent aquatic angiosperms to increased plant productivity. Limited evidence indicates that these community responses are applicable to submersed angiosperms as well.

(Gifford, 1979). It seems likely that other environmental factors such as mineral nutrient availability would affect the proportion of root responses. If added CO_2 induces mineral nutrient limitation, then the proportion of roots would be more likely to increase than if mineral nutrients were not limiting.

Timing of life cycle events would be altered if growth is speeded up. For isolated plants, increased growth rate can lead to more rapid maturation (Hand and Cockshull, 1975). For herbaceous plants, increased growth rate can lead to increased rates of both leaf production and senesence (Noble et al., 1979). However, CO_2 enrichment has been reported to delay leaf senescence (Strain and Armentano, 1980). What this effect would be in the field if more rapid growth leads to increased leaf area, is unknown. Elevated CO_2 may not slow leaf senescence in dense canopies, but such counterposing effects should be examined further.

4.1.2 Population and community consequences of whole-plant responses. A wide range of effects at the population and community levels are to be expected with increased plant productivity. It is important to keep in mind that most of these effects are derived from studies under controlled mineral nutrition and light intensity.

One of the better established relationships in terrestrial plant ecology is that increased plant productivity leads to enhanced sexual and vegetative reproduction (Harper, 1977). This relationship applies to emergent aquatic plants as well (Grace and Wetzel, 1981a). Increasing plant density inhibits individual plant growth as available resources per individual decline. Non-clonal plants will self-thin according to the $-3/2$ Thinning Law of Yoda et al. (1963), which determines the relationship between plant size and density. For clonal plants, thinning is greatly reduced (Hutchings, 1979; Dickerman and Wetzel, 1982), but in either case the yield per unit area is simply the product of density and average plant size. As individual plant growth is increased, biomass production will increase but average plant size and density may not be predictable.

One consequence of increased productivity is intensified competition (Figure 2). Direct tests of this "paradox of enrichment" come from field fertilization studies (Thurston, 1969) in which dominance is increased and species richness is decreased as biomass production increases, presumably by competitive exclusion. Indirect support for this relationship is provided by the model of Grime (1979) and quantitative comparisons of Al-Mufti et al. (1977). It appears that in addition to the importance of direct (exploitative) competition in increasing community dominance, accumulation of persistent litter is also important.

Emergent aquatic communities are notoriously low in species richness (Hutchinson, 1975) compared to terrestrial plant communities. In particular, the dominance of emergent wetlands areas by one or two species is a common characteristic of these habitats. Recent work has shown that the species richness of certain wetlands is negatively correlated with the quantity of above-ground plant material (Wheeler and Giller, 1982). In more productive habitats low diversity could well act to limit both reductions in species diversity and changes in species composition.

Differential species responses to CO_2 enrichment will arise from differential photosynthetic responses. C_4 metabolism occurs among both salt marsh (e.g., Spartina) and freshwater (e.g., tropical papyrus) emergent plants, but is most common among salt marsh species. Evidence clearly indicates that C_3 plants are more likely to respond positively to elevated CO_2 while responses by C_4 plants will be less. Thus, more CO_2 will favor C_3 plants in competition with C_4 plants and could shift species distribution in salt water marshes. Still more complications arise from CO_2 influence on growth form. For example, more roots could alter the nature of competition, thus altering competitive success (for terrestrial plants, see Snaydon, 1971).

Perhaps the most consistent effect of elevated CO_2 on terrestrial plants is an improved water balance (Downtown et al., 1980; Wong, 1980). Aquatic plants with emergent foliage typically possess high rates of transpiration (Sculthorpe, 1967; Hutchinson, 1975). In wetlands where aquatic communities intergrade into terrestrial communities, it is possible that decreased transpiration and improved water use efficiency may permit aquatic communities to extend into slightly more terrestrial habitats. For terrestrial species at the wetland interface it seems unlikely that elevated CO_2 will enhance their tolerance to waterlogged soils. If water balance is improved for wetland species at their boundary with terrestrial plants, we might expect the hydrophyte competitive ability to be improved and their landward boundary extended. Improved relations would also be important for those plants, both freshwater and saline, which are subject to periodic exposure by daily or seasonal water level fluctuations.

A variety of the reported effects of elevated CO_2 on plants could act to alter the timing of events in emergent aquatic communities. The seeds of terrestrial species show a variety of responses to increased CO_2 (Mayer and Poljakoff-Mayber, 1975). Because of the resistance by water to diffusive gas exchange, aquatic plant seeds are usually exposed to high levels of CO_2 at the sediment surface. Thus, it is not surprising that elevated CO_2 is not considered to be a key factor in regulating seed germination (Sculthorpe, 1967).

The principal effect of elevated CO_2 on the timing of events is likely to be an accelerated rate of maturation in plants whose growth rate is increased. Faster maturation of species could provide a competitive advantage for the earlier germinating species, especially if senescence is delayed. Strain and Armentano (1980) suggested in their review of the effects of increased atmospheric CO_2 on unmanaged ecosystems that earlier flowering could cause a disruption of the normal synchrony between plants and their pollinators. Most emergent aquatic plants are wind pollinated (Sculthorpe, 1967). Nonetheless, even for those species whose timing of flowering is not regulated by photoperiod and are likely to flower earlier, normal yearly variations in the timing of flowering suggest that synchrony between flowering and specific pollinators is not highly critical. Such generalizations, however, deserve further study.

Most studies of CO_2 effects have dealt with crop species which have been selected for high productivity. On the other hand, some evidence exists that species adapted for living in stressful environments possess a low inherent growth rate and a low degree of responsiveness to limiting factors (Grime, 1979, Chapin, 1980). Such species are able to survive unfavorable conditions by possessing low metabolic maintenance costs and by extending use of captured resources by means of slow growth rates. In habitats in which elevated CO_2 enhance the acquisition of a primary limiting resource (for example nitrogen in salt marshes), we would expect "competitive" species of higher productivity to become more abundant. However, in sites where elevated CO_2 did not enhance the acquisition of the primary limiting resource (perhaps certain conditions of extreme phosphorus limitation), we would expect plants that were not responsive to elevated CO_2 to be favored since excess growth could deplete the plants' phosphorus supplies.

4.1.3 Likely Responses to Elevated CO_2 Under Natural Conditions. Here we are concerned with responses in the range of 400 to 600 ppm. The effect of CO_2 levels on growth and yield in rice have been studied under field as well as greenhouse conditions. Yoshida and others have used plastic enclosures in the field to investigate yield responses to CO_2 (Matsushima et al., 1961; Cock and Yoshida, 1973; Yoshida, 1973, 1976). Various factors, especially temperature, can affect the optimal level of CO_2 (Yamada et al., 1955; Akita et al., 1969). In a review of the subject, Yoshida (1976) concluded that available data suggest an optimum CO_2 concentration for growth and yield between 1,500 and 2,000 ppm. Exposure of rice to 1,200 ppm under greenhouse conditions produced a 45% increase in yield in the interior of the stand and a 189% increase at the border (Riley and Hodges, 1969). Lack of ventilation was shown to be the cause of the observed depression in the interior. Growth responses at 600 ppm would be considerably lower.

Emergent aquatic communities are some of the most productive systems in the world (Lieth, 1975). Certainly not all wetlands are highly productive, however, particularly those in cold climates. However, they are typically more productive than terrestrial communities under similar climate where there is a lack of water. Studies for water hyacinth have shown carbon limitation under field conditions (Wittwer, personal communication).

Work by Uchijima et al. (1967) showed that for corn, CO_2 depletion in the canopy was positively related to the leaf area index and negatively related to wind speed. We would expect that this relationship would generally be valid for emergent aquatic plants and that those sites sufficiently fertile to support high leaf areas will be those most likely to be CO_2 limited. However, it is possible that dense canopies will reduce the ability of rice to respond to elevated CO_2 due to air stagnation.

We would expect rice paddy culture conditions to be nearly optimal except for a CO_2 limitation and thus show a positive response to elevated CO_2. Therefore, the increases in biomass production of rice when exposed to optimal CO_2 would probably define the upper limit of the response expected.

The vast majority of freshwater emergent species are C_3 and would be expected to respond to elevated CO_2. Further, freshwater marshes are commonly N limited (cf. Grace and Wetzel, 1981a) and, based on whole-plant responses,

would be expected to show increased productivity despite N
limitation. If the litter produced by these plants is high
in C/N ratios, it is possible that decomposition and therefore mineral nutrient regeneration will be slowed,
resulting in nutrient immobilization. Increased rates of N
supply from mineralization or N fixation will be required
to prevent reduced site productivity. Although N fixation
is not uncommon in these systems, it is questionable
whether the rates are high enough to compensate for the
increased demand.

In contrast to freshwater marshes, some of the most
abundant salt marsh species are C_4. These species are
usually associated with the most saline habitats, but do
occur intermixed with C_3 species in less saline areas.
Abundant evidence suggests that these systems are limited
by available N because of inhibition of ammonia uptake at
high salinity (Morris, 1980). Enrichment by CO_2 would be
expected to favor the C_3 plants and to permit their
extension into areas currently occupied by C_4 species.

4.2 Submersed Macrophytes

4.2.1 Whole-Plant Response.
Much of the preceding
discussion of emergent whole-plant responses to elevated
CO_2 could apply to submersed plants but research in this
area has lagged. The high CO_2 requirements for net
photosynthesis by submersed aquatic plants, as well as
various mechanisms of increasing CO_2 acquisition and
retention, have been reviewed earlier in this paper. Also,
increased light utilization and decreased photorespiration
have been found to occur at elevated levels of inorganic
carbon. Therefore, as among emergent and terrestrial
plants, we would expect submersed plants which responded to
elevated atmospheric CO_2 to have increased growth rates,
especially under conditions which favor photorespiration.

Effects of elevated inorganic carbon on the growth
forms of submersed plants have not been demonstrated except
for the work of Bristow (1969), who utilized concentrations
much higher than those considered in this paper. Under low
nutrient conditions, increased CO_2 fixation could lead to
increases in the proportion of root biomass. Also, in
those rare cases where mycorrhiza are associated with
submersed plants (Sondergaard and Laegaard, 1977), mineral
nutrient uptake could be enhanced.

Under some circumstances, N supply is enhanced by N
fixers (largely bacteria and blue-green algae) associated
with the roots of submersed macrophytes (Simms, 1976;

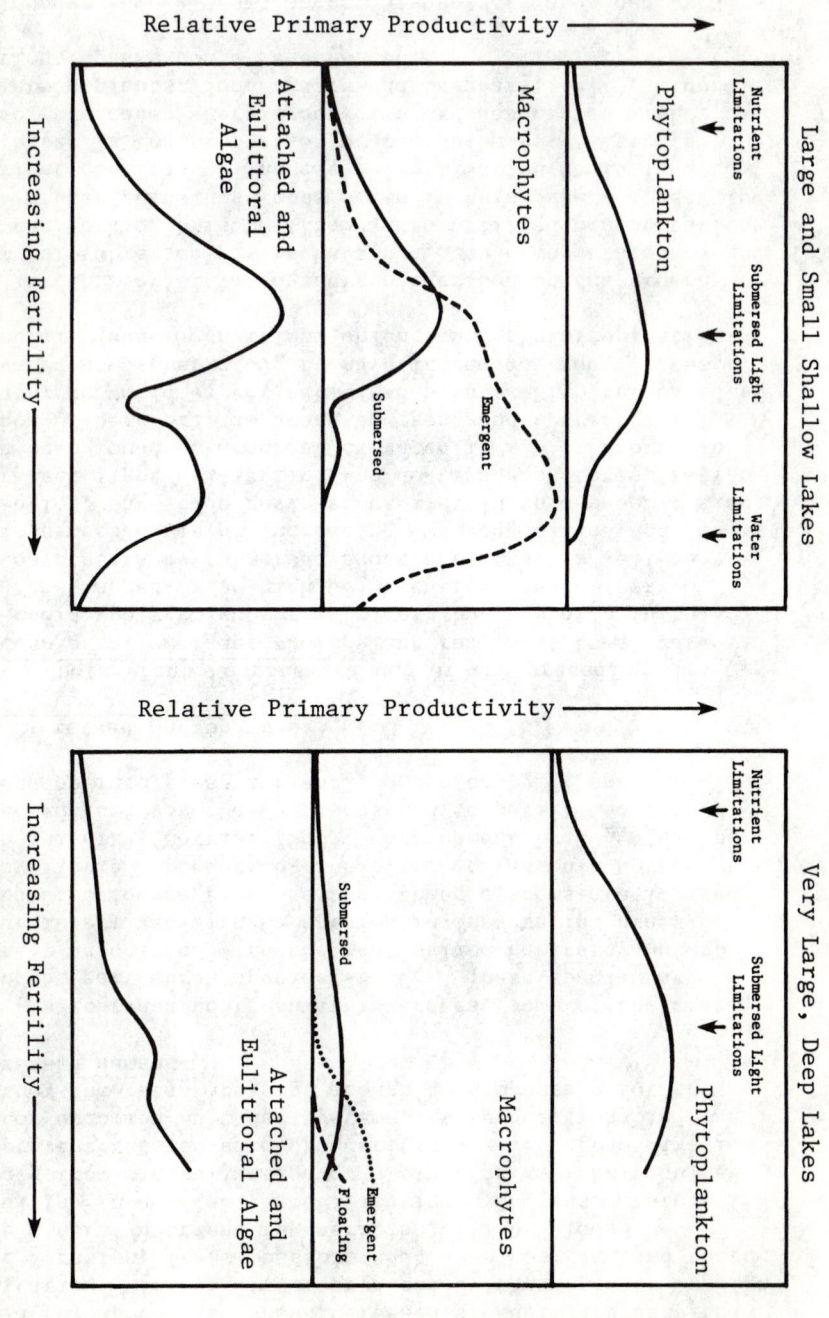

Figure 3. Generalized relationships of total primary productivity versus mineral loading from external and internal sources and lake fertility. Wetzel (1979).

Finke and Seeley, 1978; Blotnick et al., 1980). Because
of the often greater importance of N as a growth-limiting
nutrient in highly productive aquatic ecosystems, increased
N supply by these mechanisms may be necessary to accomodate
photosynthetic gains resulting from more atmospheric
CO_2.

4.2.2 Population and Community Consequences of Whole-Plant Responses.

In considering the effect of increased
plant production on population and community processes, we
should keep in mind that most of our information comes from
studies of nutrient enrichment or temperature increases.
Most of the processes outlined in Figure 2 for emergents
should apply to submersed plants with the possible
exception of litter effects, which have not been noted for
submersed plants. Unfortunately, few data exist with which
to confirm the processes for submersed plants in Figure 2.

Many, but not all, species of submersed vascular
plants are capable of assimilating bicarbonate as well as
CO_2. Hutchinson (1975) has shown that the ability to
utilize bicarbonate is associated with species which occur
in waters of high alkalinity. Under these conditions,
plants which supplement CO_2 uptake with bicarbonate will be
less affected by free CO_2 depletion. Thus, elevated levels
of CO_2 dissolved in the water would favor those species
that utilize only free CO_2.

Associated with increases in site fertility are a
number of changes in macrophyte communities (Lind and
Cottam, 1969; Hutchinson, 1975; Wetzel, 1975, 1982; Crowder
et al., 1977). Figure 3 represents the general relationships of primary productivity of phytoplankton, macrophytes
and attached algae for shallow and deep lakes as site
fertility increases (Wetzel, 1979). These major shifts
would not be expected as a short-term direct effect of CO_2
enrichment but, as discussed later, long-term effects could
act to accelerate the process of increasing site fertility.
Slight changes in site productivity of the magnitude
conceivable for CO_2 effects are associated with shifts in
the species composition and growth form of submersed
macrophytes.

Macrophytes of infertile habitats are more commonly of
the rostulate form with a high proportion of roots (e.g.
Lobelia dortmanna) (e.g. Crowder et al., 1977). These
macrophytes are likely to obtain most of their mineral
nutrients (as well as, in some cases, organic carbon) from
the sediments (Sondergaard and Sand-Jensen, 1979). As
nutrient loadings to the water column increase, there is an

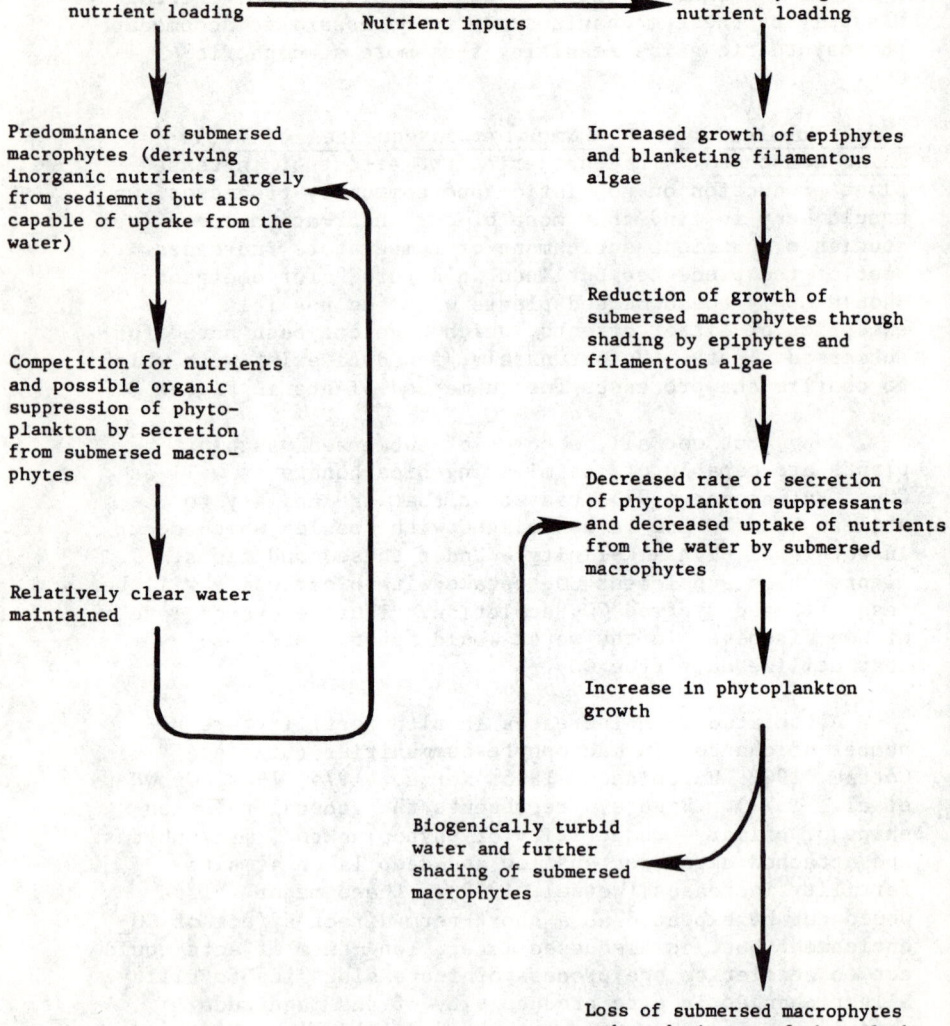

Figure 4.   Hypothesized mechanisms of submersed macrophyte decline as mineral nutrient loading of lakes increases. Modified from Phillips et al. (1978).

increasing frequency of plants of more elongated vittate form (e.g., Myriophyllum).

As inferred from Figure 3 there are a number of interactions between submersed macrophytes, their epiphytes, and planktonic algae. Phillips et al. (1978) have postulated a series of interactions whereby the growth of epiphytes leads to a decline in the submersed macrophyte populations when lakes are fertilized (Figure 4). Evidence for the validity of this model is accumulating (Sand-Jensen and Sondergaard, 1981; Rogers and Breen, 1981; Losee and Wetzel, 1982), and competitive interactions between macrophytes and epiphytes have been shown (Wetzel, 1975, 1982). Carbon limitations may occur for epiphytic algae under fertile conditions (McIntire and Phinney, 1965) and it has been clearly shown that epiphytes can fix a significant quantity of carbon which would otherwise be available to macrophytes (Allen, 1971; Penhale, 1977; Sand-Jensen, 1977). However at present, the model in Figure 4 is largely untested.

If our general projections are correct about how macrophytes, epiphytes, and phytoplankton will respond to elevated atmospheric CO_2, we would expect macrophyte growth to be enhanced the most, epiphytic algae somewhat less, and phytoplankton the least. This pattern of response would act to offset somewhat the effects of increased mineral nutrients.

4.2.3 Likely Responses to Elevated CO_2 Under Natural Conditions.

Available evidence indicates that the inorganic carbon supply is limiting for the growth of submersed macrophytes. Table 2 suggests that photosynthetic rates are normally limited by inorganic carbon for both marine and freshwater plants. Mineral nutrient limitation may have a significant effect on the ability of these systems to respond, but little is known about the interaction between the uptake of phosphorus, nitrogen, sulfur, and other elements and CO_2 responses.

Two habitat characteristics are important to the supply of atmospheric CO_2 to the leaf surface: the diffusion path from the water-air interface and the degree of turbulent mixing. In addition, the proximity of a plant's leaves to respiratory sources of CO_2 in the system, e.g. sediments, makes it possible for atmospheric impacts to be less important.

Dense canopy formation at the water surface is associated with high surface temperatures and low light penetration to depth (Dale and Gillespie, 1977; Barko and Smart, 1981). Because canopy formation can have detrimental effects on water use, the influence of CO_2 on canopy formation should be studied.

4.3 Algae

4.3.1 The Variety of Algal Responses. The effects on algae of increased atmospheric CO_2 are likely to be confined to effects on net photosynthesis similar, at least metabolically, to those cited earlier. The greatest response will be found under conditions of high light, high dissolved oxygen, high temperature and high available nutrients (Lewin, 1962; Fogg, 1975; Stewart, 1974). Based on projections in Table 2, increased inorganic carbon may increase photosynthesis a little, but it is likely saturation will rapidly occur.

4.3.2 Population and Community Consequences of Algal Responses. Evidence from a variety of sources suggests that sometimes algae can be carbon limited (Wright, 1960; King, 1970; Schindler and Fee, 1973). We have already mentioned that limited invasion of CO_2 into the water from the atmosphere and downward movement by turbulent mixing may result in conditions where inorganic carbon in the water column is inadequate to meet potential algal photosynthesis within other chemical and physical constraints. Enhanced algal production and standing crops in surface water have a number of effects on the depth distribution of algae. Increased production of surface water phytoplankton results in higher surface concentration of algae, reduced light penetration, and reduction in the depth of the photic zone. Such a shift in the distribution of algae results in a shift in the proportion of algae exposed to the warmer near-surface temperatures and high dissolved oxygen concentrations. Plankton productivity per unit surface area may not increase under these conditions regardless of nutrient loading (Tilly, 1975).

Another potential effect of elevated inorganic carbon is a shift in species composition. Shapiro (1973) reported that additions of CO_2, along with additions of nitrogen and phosphorus, resulted in a rapid shift from blue-green algal dominance to green algal dominance. It has been postulated that blue-green algae have inorganic carbon uptake kinetics which are more effective at low levels of available inorganic carbon and at high pH (Shapiro, 1973). Kalff and Knoechel (1978) argue that shifts in species composition are associated with site productivity, but that most shifts are not consistent enough to be predictable. Further, they argue that the observed dominance of blue-green algae at high cell densities might be a result of lower rates of settling rather than superior uptake kinetics or productivity. Much more needs to be done on this problem.

The relationship between community productivity and phytoplankton diversity is not fully established (Kalff and Knoechel, 1978). If species coexistence is being affected by the intensity of competition, reduced species diversity is predictable due to competitive exclusion at high levels of community productivity (Tilman, 1980).

In addition to changes in species composition, several major changes in the phytoplankton community are associated with increasing community productivity (Wetzel, 1975, 1982; Kalff and Knoechel, 1978). As community productivity increases, there is typically an increase in the proportion of net plankton and a concomitant decrease in the proportion of nannoplankton. At the same time, specific productivity may not change as rates of biomass turnover decline. The primary factors driving these changes appear to be related to selective grazing of nannoplankton by zooplankton and the differential settling rates of the net plankton. These effects should occur regardless of whether mineral nutrients or elevated levels of inorganic carbon lead to increased community productivity.

4.3.3 The Likely Responses of Phytoplankton. Much of the literature dealing with CO_2 enrichment on freshwater phytoplankton has been stimulated by the controversy over the relative roles of C, N, and P in lake eutrophication (cf. Likens, 1972). While not all investigators would agree, there is a fair consensus of opinion among limnologists that inorganic carbon supplies in most lakes are sufficient to sustain very high standing crops of phytoplankton (Schindler, 1971). Evidence from several sources suggest that carbon limitation of photosynthetic rates commonly occur during midday in nutritionally-enriched aquatic ecosystems (e.g., Schindler and Fee, 1973). However, additions of inorganic carbon to these systems do not increase biomass, which suggests that even in the situation where midday carbon limitation occurs, it is unlikely that elevated atmospheric CO_2 will have a major effect on algal biomass. Nonetheless, shifts in species composition would be expected. Marine phytoplankton are even less likely to respond to elevated atmospheric CO_2 because of the high amounts of available bicarbonate and strong nutrient restrictions on photosynthetic productivity.

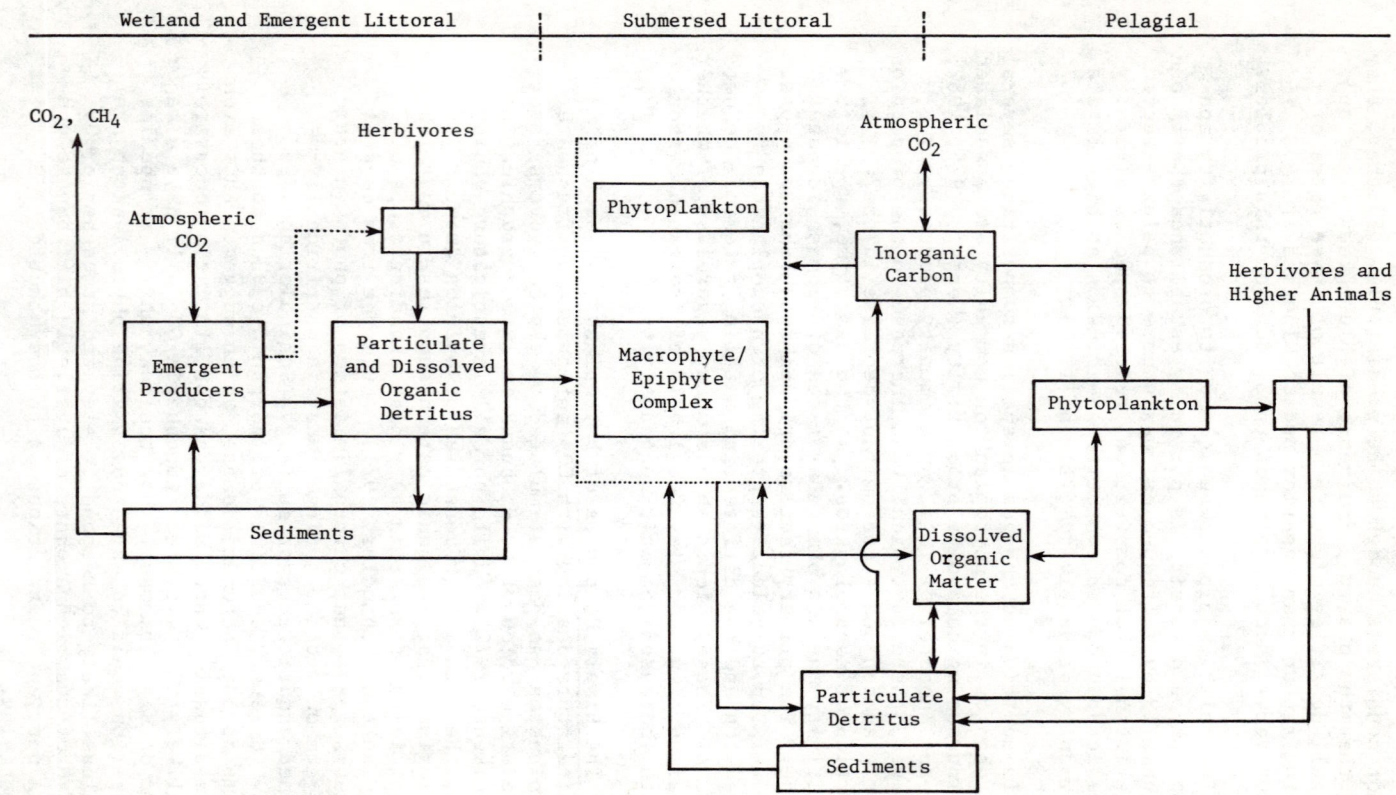

Figure 5.   Generalized model of carbon movements in aquatic ecosystems.

4.3.4 Ecosystem Structure and Function: General Effects.
The details of ecosystem structure and function are far
too complex to consider in detail in this brief paper.
However, Figure 5 represents a simple model to facilitate
further consideration. Only the most major components and
processes are illustrated. Figure 5 is arranged so as to
emphasize the interactions between emergent, submersed and
pelagial communities. Inputs of both particulate and
dissolved organic and inorganic compounds from emergent
plants link the submersed littoral and pelagial communities
to the emergent community by a complex system of metabolic
processes (Wetzel, 1975, 1979, 1982). Because of the
impacts of emergent communities on submersed littoral and
pelagial communities, the effects of elevated CO_2 levels on
emergent communities can have a major, indirect impact on
the other components of aquatic ecosystems (Wetzel, 1979).

Most freshwater ecosystems of the world are small and
relatively shallow, and the vast majority of lakes and
ponds are surrounded by extensive wetlands and littoral
areas. The dominating emergent macrophytes of these areas
are extremely productive, being several orders of magnitude
more productive than photosynthesis production within the
water per se. The chemical composition of emergent
macrophyte litter is very much more resistant to
decomposition than that of submersed macrophytes and
contains appreciably less available nitrogen than the less
productive floating-leaved and submersed macrophytes and
algae. Furthermore, because of the typically high carbon
to nitrogen ratio and high lignin content of detritus
introduced into sediments from these emergent plants,
interstitial ammonia-nitrogen concentrations may be reduced
by microbial decomposition, thereby further lowering
nitrogen availability (e.g., Ponnamperuma, 1972). These
emergent plants load the lake ecosystem with increasingly
greater inputs of resistant dissolved and particulate
organic matter (Figure 6). Accumulations of this coarse
particulate organic mater (POM) in dense mats in the
littoral sediments, and transport of fine POM to deeper
sediments, encourages the development of highly reducing
conditions and the accumulation of end products of
anaerobic metabolism (e.g., H_2S, fatty acids). The result
is a slow rate of decomposition and an acceleration of
sediment accumulation.

Other more subtle, but nonetheless significant,
interactions of organic compounds of emergent macrophytic
origin can lead to accelerated rates of sediment
accumulation (Figure 6). A number of humic derivatives of
lignified and cellulosic tissue can (a) condense to form

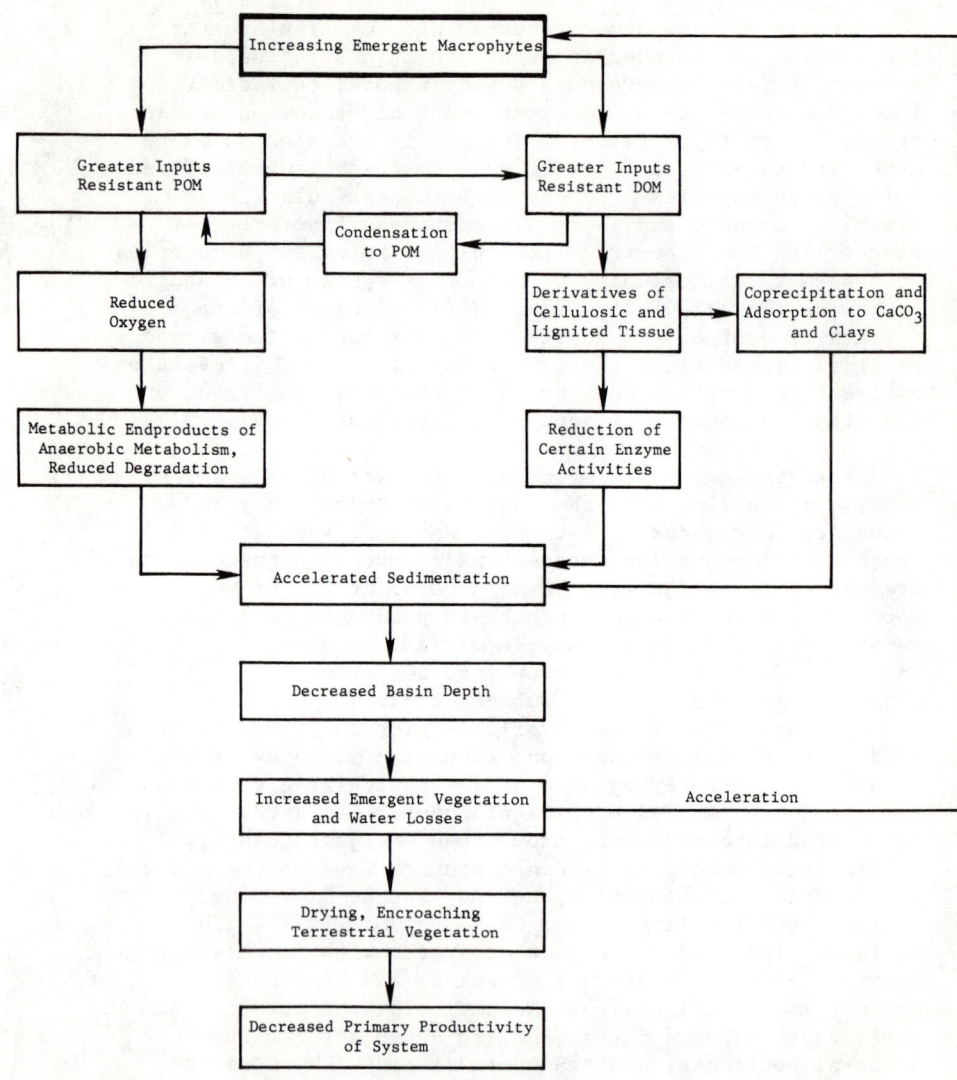

Figure 6.   Relationships of increasing loading of relatively resistant organic matter from dominating emergent littoral and wetland flora to that of controls of decomposition rates, sedimentation (= sediment accumulation), acceleration of emergent macrophyte development, and the ontogeny of lake ecosystems.   POM and DOM = particulate and dissolved organic matter, respectively.   From Wetzel (1979).

polymers and eventually shift from the dissolved to participate phases (e.g., Chen and Schnitzer, 1976), and (b) adsorb on $CaCO_3$ or clay particles, or be coprecipitated with nucleating $CaCO_3$ (e.g., Otsuki and Wetzel, 1973) as photosynthetically mediated precipitation occurs (Mickle and Wetzel, 1978). There is further evidence that (c) certain derivatives of lignified tissue, especially of the fulvic acid group, irreversibly bind with enzymes, such as phosphotase, and cause a reduction in enzymatic activity (e.g., Cunningham and Wetzel, 1978). This mechanism is likely accentuated under conditions of anaerobic decomposition and high loading of emergent macrophytic tissue and would lead to further accelerated sedimentation.

This reduced rate of decay and increased sedimentation, often at prodigious rates, leads to rapid filling and reduction in basin depth. These morphometric changes lead in turn to increased habitat for further expansion of emergent macrophytes so that the cyclic relationship to reduced decomposition and increased sedimentation is self-augmenting. With increased development of emergent vegetation, rates of water loss increase by means of intensive evapotranspiration. As the basin gradually fills and water losses from evapotranspiration exceed inputs, water becomes limiting to the emergent macroflora. Encroachment by terrestrial flora leads to marked reduction in the total primary productivity of the former lake-wetland system. The rate of this ecosystem successional process can be accelerated by any process, such as atmospheric CO_2 enrichment, that enhances emergent macrophyte productivity.

In considering ecosystem processes, it is important to keep in mind the overriding importance of climate in regulating rates of production and decomposition. The balance between production and decomposition, i.e., net ecosystem storage, is determined by many factors other than climate. Nonetheless, climate plays a vital role in determining the geographic distribution of, for example, wetland types. Peat accumulation in tundra ponds and in bogs is strongly a function of prevailing patterns of temperature and precipitation (Wetzel, 1975). These relationships take on special importance when considering climate changes, such as those projected from elevated levels of CO_2 (Manabe and Stouffer, 1979). Shifts in the patterns of precipitation and temperature could cause a wide array of changes in net ecosystem productivity. Of special concern, however, is the possibility that many existing peat deposits might dry out due to shifts in rainfall. The amount of carbon stored in peat bogs is very large relative to the total quantity in the atmosphere. Therefore, the interaction between ecosystem processes and climate is of major importance not only in determining the response of plants to increasing carbon dioxide levels, but also in determining the effect of plants on the atmospheric content of CO_2 itself.

5. Literature Cited

Akita, S., A. Miyasaka, and Y. Murata. 1969. Studies on the difference of photosynthesis among species. 1. Differences in the response of photosynthesis among species in normal oxygen concentration as influenced by some environmental factors. Proc. Crop Sci. Soc. Japan 38, 507-524.

Allen, E.D. and D.H.N. Spence. 1981. The differential ability of aquatic plants to utilize the inorganic carbon supply in fresh waters. New Phytol. 87, 269-283.

Allen, H.L. 1971. Primary productivity, chemoorganotrophy, and nutritional interactions of epiphytic algae and bacteria on macrophytes in the littoral of a lake. Ecol. Monogr. 41, 97-125.

Al-Mufti, M.M., C.L. Wall, S.B. Furness, J.P. Grime and S.R. Band. 1977. A quantitative analysis of plant phenology and dominance in herbaceous vegetation. J. Ecol. 65, 759-791.

Arber, A. 1920. Water Plants: A Study of Aquatic Angiosperms. Cambridge University Press, Cambridge, 436 pp.

Armstrong, W. 1978. Root aeration in the wetland condition. In Plant Life in Anaerobic Environments, D.C. Hook and R.M.M. Crawford, Eds. Ann Arbor Science Publishers Inc., Ann Arbor, Michigan. pp. 269-297.

Bain, J.T. and M.C.F. Proctor. 1980. The requirement of aquatic bryophytes for free CO_2 as an inorganic carbon source: Some experimental evidence. New Phytol. 86, 393-400.

Barko, J.W. and R.M. Smart. 1981. Comparative influences of light and temperature on the growth and metabolism of selected submersed freshwater macrophytes. Ecol. Monogr. 51, 219-235.

Barth, H. 1957. Aufnahme und Abgabe von CO_2 und O_2 bei submersen Wasserpflanzen. Gewässer Abwässer 4 (17/18), 18-81.

Beer, S. and Y. Waisel. 1979. Some photosynthetic carbon fixation properties of seagrasses. Aquatic Bot. 7, 129-138.

Beer, S. and R.G. Wetzel. 1981. Photosynthetic carbon metabolism in the submerged aquatic angiosperm Scirpus subgerminalis. Plant Sci. Lett. 21, 199-207.

Beer, S. and R.G. Wetzel. 1982a. Photosynthesis in submersed macrophytes of a temperate lake. Plant Physiol. 70, 488-492.

Beer, S. and R.G. Wetzel. 1982b. Photosynthetic carbon fixation pathways in Zostera and three Florida seagrasses. Aquatic Bot. 13, 141-146.

Beer, S., A. Eshel, and Y. Waisel. 1977. Carbon metabolism in seagreasses. I. The utilization of exogenous inorganic carbon species in photosynthesis. J. Exp. Bot. 28, 1180-1189.

Beer, S., A. Shomer-Ilan and Y. Waisel. 1980. Carbon metabolism in seagrasses. II. Patterns of photosynthetic CO_2 incorporation. J. Exp. Bot. 31, 1019-1026.

Bertani, A., I. Brambilla and F. Menegus. 1980. Effect of anaerobiosis on rice seedlings: Growth, metabolic rate, and fate of fermentation productions. J. Exp. Bot. 31, 325-331.

Black, M.A., S.C. Maberly and D.H.N. Spence. 1981. Resistances to carbon dioxide fixation in four submerged freshwater macrophytes. New Phytol. 89, 557-568.

Blotnick, J.R., J. Rho and H.B. Gunner. 1980. Ecological characteristics of the rhizosphere microflora of Myriophyllum heterophyllum. J. Environ. Qual. 9, 207-210.

Booker, M.J. and A.E. Walsby. 1981. Bloom formation and stratification by a planktonic blue-green algae in an experimental water column. Br. Phycol. J. 16, 411-421.

Bowes, G., A.S. Holaday and W.T. Haller. 1979. Seasonal

variation in the biomass, tuber density, and photosynthetic metabolism of Hydrilla in three Florida lakes. J. Aquat. Plant Manage. 17, 61–65.

Bristow, J.M. 1969. The effects of carbon dioxide on the growth and development of amphibious plants. Can J. Bot. 47, 1803–1807.

Bristow, J.M. 1974. Nitrogen fixation in the rhizosphere of freshwater angiosperms. Can. J. Bot. 52, 217–221.

Broecker, W.S. 1974. Chemical Oceanography. Harcourt, Brace, Jovanovich, New York.

Brown, J.M.A., F.I. Dromgoole, M.W. Towsey and J. Browse. 1974. Photosynthesis and photorespiration in aquatic macrophytes. In Mechanisms of Regulation of Plant Growth, R.L. Bieleski, A.R. Ferguson, and M.M. Cresswell, Eds. Bull. 12, Royal Soc. New Zealand, Wellington, pp. 243–249.

Browse, J.A., F.I. Dromgoole, and J.M.A. Brown. 1977. Photosynthesis in the aquatic macrophyte Egeria densa. I. ^{14}C fixation at natural CO_2 concentrations. Aust. J. Plant Physiol. 4, 169–176.

Browse, J.A., J.M.A. Brown, and F.I. Dromgoole. 1979. Photosynthesis in the aquatic macrophyte Egeria densa. II. Effects of inorganic carbon conditions on ^{14}C fixation. Aust. J. Plant Physiol. 6, 1–9.

Browse, J.A., J.M.A. Brown, and F.I. Dromgoole. 1980. Malate synthesis and metabolism during photosynthesis in Egeria densa Planch. Aquatic Bot. 8, 295–305.

Buresh, R.J., M.E. Casselman, and W.H. Patrick, Jr. 1980. Nitrogen fixation in flooded soil systems, a review. Adv. Agron. 33, 149–192.

Carr, J.L. 1969. The primary productivity and physiology of Ceratophyllum demersum. II. Micro primary productivity, pH, and the P/R ratio. Austral. J. Mar. Freshwat. Res. 20, 127–142.

Casselman, M.E., W.H. Patrick, and R.D. Delaune, 1981. Nitrogen fixation in a Gulf Coast (Louisiana, USA) salt marsh. Soil Sci. Soc. Amer. J. 45, 51–56.

Chang, T.P. 1980. Mucilage sheath as a barrier to carbon

uptake in a cyanophyte, Oscillatoria rubescens D.C. Arch. Hydrobiol. 88, 128-133.

Chapin, F.S. 1980. The mineral nutrition of wild plants. Ann. Rev. Ecol. Syst. 11, 233-260.

Chen, Y. and M. Schnitzer. 1976. Scanning electron microscopy of a humic acid and of a fulvic acid and its metal and clay complexes. Soil Sci. Soc. Amer. J. 40, 682-686.

Clark, C. and B. Mosse. 1981. Plant growth responses to vesicular-arbuscular mycorrhizae. New Phytol. 87, 695-704.

Cock, J.H. and S. Yoshida. 1973. Changing sink and source relations in rice (Oryza sativa L.) using carbon dioxide enrichment in the field. Soil Sci. Plant Nutr. 19, 229-234.

Crawford, R.M.M. 1978. Metabolic adaptations to anoxia. In Plant Life in Anaerobic Environments, D.C. Hook and and R.M.M. Crawford, Eds. Ann Arbor Science Publ. Inc., Ann Arbor, Michigan. pp. 119-136.

Crowder, A.A., J.M. Bristow, M.R. King, and S. Vanderkloet. 1977. The aquatic macrophytes of some lakes in southeastern Ontario. Naturaliste Can. 104, 457-464.

Cunningham, H.W. and R.G. Wetzel. 1978. Fulvic acid interferences on ATP determinations in sediments. Limnol. Oceanogr. 23, 166-173.

Dacey, J.W.H. 1981. Presssurized ventilation in the yellow waterlily. Ecology 62, 1137-1147.

Dacey, J.W.H. and M.J. Klug. 1979. Methane efflux from lake sediments through water lilies. Science 203, 1253-1255.

Dale, H.M. and T.J. Gillespie. 1977. The influence of submersed aquatic plants on temperature gradients in shallow water bodies. Can. J. Bot. 55, 2216-2225.

Danckwerts, P.V. 1970. Gas-liquid Reactions. McGraw Hill, New York.

Dickerman, J.A. and R.G. Wetzel. 1982. The pattern and process of clonal growth in a Typha latifolia population. Ecol. Mongr. (submitted).

Downton, W.J.S., O. Björkman and C. Pike. 1980. Consequences of increased atomospheric concentrations of carbon dioxide for growth and photosynthesis of higher plants. In Carbon Dioxide and Climate, G.I. Pearman, Ed. Australian Academy of Science, Canberra.

Drake, B.G. and M. Read. 1981. Carbon dioxide assimilation, photosynthetic efficiency, and respiration of a Chesapeake Bay salt marsh. J. Ecol. 69, 405–423.

Emerson, S. 1975. Chemically enhanced CO_2 gas exchange in a eutrophic lake: A general model. Limno. Oceanogr. 20, 743–753.

Filbin, G.J. 1980. Photosynthesis, photorespiration and primary productivity in floating, floating leaved and emergent aquatic plants. Ph.D. Dissertation, Wayne State Univ., Detroit.

Finke, L.R. and H.W. Seeley. 1978. Nitrogen fixation (acetylene reduction) by epiphytes of freshwater macrophytes. Appl. Environ. Microbiol. 36, 129–138.

Fogg, G.E. 1975. Algae Cultures and Phytoplankton Ecology. 2nd Edition. Univ. Wisc. Press, Madison.

Gaastra, P. 1963. Climatic control of photosynthesis and respiration. In Environmental Control of Plant Growth, L.T. Evans, Ed. Academic Press, New York. pp. 113–140.

Gifford, R.M. 1979. Growth and yield of carbon dioxide enriched wheat under water-limited condition. Aust. J. Pl. Physiol. 6, 367–378.

Goldman, J.C. 1973. Carbon dioxide and pH: Effect on species succession of algae. Science 183, 306–307.

Goulder, R. 1980. Day-time variations in the rates of production by two natural communities of submerged freshwater macrophytes. J. Ecol. 58, 521–528.

Grace, J.B. and R.G. Wetzel. 1981a. Phenotypic and genotypic components of growth and production in Typha latifolia: Experimental studies in marshes of differing successional maturity. Ecology. 62, 789–801.

Grace, J.B. and R.G. Wetzel. 1981b. Habitat partitioning

and competitive displacement in cattails (Typha): Experimental field studies. Amer. Nat. 118, 463-474.

Grace, J.B. and R.G. Wetzel. 1982a. Niche differentiation between two plant species: Typha latifolia and Typha angustifolia. Can. J. Bot. 60, 46-57.

Grace, J.G. and R.G. Wetzel. 1982b. Variations in growth and reproduction within two rhizomatous plant species: Typha latifolia and Typha angustifolia. Oecologia (in press).

Grime, J.P. 1979. Plant Strategies and Vegetation Processes. John Wiley and Sons, New York.

Hand, D.W. and K.E. Cockshull. 1975. Roses I: The effects of CO_2 enrichment on winter bloom production. J. Hort. Sci. 50, 183-192.

Harper, J.L. 1977. Population Biology of Plants. Academic Press, New York.

Helder, R.J. and M.V. Harmelen. 1982. Carbon assimilation pattern in the submerged leaves of the aquatic angiosperm Vallisneria spiralis L. Acta Bot. Neerlandica. In press.

Helder, R.J. and P.E. Zanstra. 1977. Changes of the pH at the upper and lower surface of bicarbonate assimilating leaves of Potamogeton lucens L. Proc. Koninklijke Nedderl. Akad. Wetenschappen, Ser. C., Biol. Med. Sci. 80, 421-436.

Helder, R.J., H.B.A. Prins and J. Schuurmans. 1974. Photorespiration in leaves of Vallisneria spiralis. Proc. Koninklijke Nederl. Akad. Wetenscahppen, Ser. C. Biol. Med. Sci. 77, 338-344.

Helder, R.J., J. Boerman and P.E. Zanstra. 1980. Uptake pattern of carbon dioxide and bicarbonate by leaves of Potamogeton lucens L, Proc. Koninklijke Nederl. Akad. Wetenschappen, Ser. C., Biol. Med. Sci. 83, 151-166.

Holiday, A.S. and G. Bowes. 1980. C_4 acid metabolism and dark CO_2 fixation in a submersed aquatic macrophyte (Hydrilla verticillata). Plant Physiol. 65, 331-335.

Hough, R.A. 1974. Photorespiration and productivity in submersed aquatic vascular plants. Limnol. Oceanogr. 19, 912-927.

Hough, R.A. and R.G. Wetzel. 1972. A ^{14}C-assay for photorespiration in aquatic plants. Plant Physiol. 4, 987-990.

Hough, R.A. and R.G. Wetzel. 1977. Photosynthetic pathways of some aquatic plants. Aquatic Bot. 3, 297-303.

Hough, R.A. and R.G. Wetzel. 1978. Photorespiration and CO_2 compensation point in Najas flexilis. Limnol. Oceanogr. 23, 719-724.

Hutchings, M.J. 1979. Weight-density relationships in ramet populations of clonal perennial herbs, with special reference to the -3/2 power law. J. Ecol. 67, 21-33.

Hutchinson, G.E. 1975. A Treatise on Limnology. Vol. 3. Limnological Botany. John Wiley and Sons, New York.

Jaworski, G.H.M., J.F. Talling and S.I. Heaney. 1981. The influence of carbon dioxide-depletion on growth and sinking rate of two planktonic diatoms in culture. Br. Phycol. J. 16, 395-410.

Jones, M.B. and R.T. Milburn. 1978. Photosynthesis in papyrus (Cyperus papyrus L.). Photosynthetica 12, 197-199.

Kadono, Y. 1980. Photosynthetic carbon sources in some Potamogeton species. Bot. Mag. Tokyo 93, 185-193.

Kalff, J. and R. Knoechel. 1978. Phytoplankton and their dynamics in oligotrophic and eutrophic lakes. Ann. Rev. Ecol. Syst. 9, 475-495.

Katayama, T. 1961. Studies on the intercellular spaces in rice. Crop Sci. Soc. Japan Proc. 29, 229-233.

Keeley, J.E. 1981. Isoetes howellii: A submerged aquatic CAM plant? Amer. J. Bot. 68, 420-424.

Keeley, J.E. 1982. Distribution of diurnal acid metabolism in the genus Isoetes. Amer. J. Bot. (in press).

King, D. 1970. The role of carbon in eutrophication. Jour. Water Poll. Cont. Fed. 42, 2035-2051.

Kremer, B.P. 1981. Aspects of carbon metabolism in marine macroalgae. Oceanogr. Mar. Biol. Ann. Rev. 19, 41-94.

Kriedemann, P.E., R.J. Sward and W.J.S. Downton. 1976.

Vine response to carbon dioxide enrichment during heat therapy. Austr. J. Plant Physiol. 3, 605-618.

Lewin, R.A., Ed. 1962. Physiology and Biochemistry of Algae. Academic Press, New York.

Lieth, H. 1975. Primary production of the major vegetation units of the world. In Primary Productivity of the Biosphere, H. Lieth and R.H. Whittaker, Eds. Springer-Verlag, New York. pp. 203-215.

Likens, G.E., Ed. 1972. Nutrients and Eutrophication: The Limiting-Nutrient Controversy. Special Symposium, Amer. Soc. Limnol. Oceanogr. 1.

Lind, C.T. and G. Cottam. 1969. The submerged aquatics of University Bay: A study in eutrophication. Amer. Midl. Nat. 81, 353-369.

Lloyd, N.D.H., D.T. Canvin and J.M. Bristow. 1977. Photosynthesis and photorespiration in submerged aquatic vascular plants. Can. J. Bot. 55, 3001-3005.

Loats, K.V., R. Noble and B. Takemoto. 1981. Photosynthesis under low-level SO_2 and CO_2 conditions in three duckweed species. Bot. Gaz. 142, 305-310.

Losee, R.F. and R.G. Wetzel. 1982. Epiphytic shading: Characterization and effects on submersed macrophyte growth. Hydrobiol. Stud. 8, (in press).

Lucas, W.J. 1975. Photosynthetic fixation of [14]carbon by internodal cells of Chara corallina. J. Exp. Bot. 26, 331-346.

Lucas, W.J., M.T. Tyree and A. Petrov. 1978. Characterization of photosynthetic [14]carbon assimilation by Potamogeton lucens L. J. Exp. Bot. 29, 1409-1421.

Manabe, S. and R. Stouffer. 1979. Study of climate impact of CO_2 increase with a mathematical model of global climate. Nature 282, 491-493.

Matsushima, S., G. Wada, T. Tanaka and T. Okabe. 1961. Analysis of developmental factors determining yield and yield prediction in lowland rice. LVII. Effects of different concentrations of carbon dioxide in the air in different growth stages on the grain yield, yield constitutional factors, and the chemical composition of rice plants. Proc. Crop Sci. Soc. Japan 29, 29-30.

Mayer, A.M. and A. Poljakoff-Mayber. 1975. The Germination of Seeds. Pergamon, New York.

McIntire, C.D. and H.K. Phinney. 1965. Laboratory studies of periphyton production and community metabolism in lotic environments. Ecol. Monogr. 35, 237-258.

McNaughton, S.J. 1966. Ecotype function in the Typha community-type. Ecol. Monogr. 36, 297-325.

McNaughton, S.J. 1969. Genetic and environmental control of glycolic acid oxidase activity in ecotypic populations of Typha latifolia. Amer. J. Bot. 56, 37-41.

McNaughton, S.J. and L.W. Fullem. 1969. Photosynthesis and photorespiration in Typha latifolia. Plant Physiol. 45, 703-707.

Mickle, A.M. and R.G. Wetzel. 1978a. Effectiveness of submersed angiosperm-epiphyte complexes on exchange of nutrients and organic carbon in littoral sytems. I. Inorganic nutrients. Aquatic Bot. 4, 303-316.

Mickle, A.M. and R.G. Wetzel. 1978b. Effectiveness of submersed angiosperm-epiphyte complexes on exchange of nutrients and organic carbon in littoral systems. II. Dissolved organic carbon. Aquatic Bot. 4, 317-329.

Mitsui, S. and K. Kurihara. 1962. On the utilization of carbon in fertilizers through rice roots under pot experimental conditions. Soil Sci. Plant Nutr. 8, 226-233.

Moeller, R.E. 1978. Carbon-uptake by the submerged hydrophyte Utricularia purpurea. Aquatic Bot. 5, 209-216.

Monteith, J.L., G. Szeic and K. Yabuki. 1964. Crop phytosynthesis and the flux of carbon dioxide below the canopy. J. Appl. Ecol. 1, 321-337.

Morris, J.T. 1980. The nitrogen uptake kinetics of Spartina alterniflora in culture. Ecology 61, 1114-1121.

Moss, D.N., R.B. Musgrave and E.R. Lemon. 1961. Photosynthesis under field conditions. III. Some effects of light, carbon dioxide, temperature, and soil moisture on photosynthesis, respiration and transpiration of corn. Crop. Sci. 1, 83-87.

Murata, Y. 1976. Productivity of rice in different climatic regions of Japan. In Climate and Rice, International Rice Research Institute, Los Banos, Philippines.

Murata, Y., A. Osada and J. Iyama. 1957. Physiological roles of carbon dioxide in plants. Agric. Hortic. 32, 11-14.

Noble, J.C., A.D. Bell and J.L. Harper. 1979. The population biology of plants with clonal growth. I. The morphology and structural demography of Carex arenaria. J. Ecol. 67, 983-1008.

Osmond, C.B., O. Björkman and D.J. Anderson. 1980. Physiological Processes in Plant Ecology. Springer-Verlag, Berlin.

Otsuki, A. and R.G. Wetzel. 1973. Interaction of yellow organic acids with calcium carbonate in freshwater. Limnol. Oceanogr. 18, 490-493.

Otsuki, A. and R.G. Wetzel. 1974. Calcium and total alkalinity budgets and calcium carbonate precipitation of a small hard-water lake. Arch. Hydrobiol. 73, 14-30.

Paerl, H.W. and J.F. Ustach. 1982. Blue-green algal scums: An explanation for their occurrence during freshwater blooms. Limnol. Oceanogr. 28, 212-271.

Patriquin, D.G. and C. Keddy. 1978. Nitrogenase activitiy (acetylene reduction) in a Nova Scotian salt marsh: Its association with angiosperms and the influence of some edaphic factors. Aquatic Bot. 4, 227-244.

Penhale, P.A. 1977. Macrophyte-epiphyte biomass and productivity in an eelgrass (Zostera marina L.) community. J. exp. Biol. Ecol. 26, 211-224.

Penhale, P.A. and R.G. Wetzel. 1982. Structural and functional adaptations of eelgrass (Zostera marina L.) to the anaerobic sediment environment. Can. J. Bot. (in press).

Peters, G.A. and H.E. Calvert. 1982. The Azolla-Anabaena azollae symbiosis. In Algal Symbioses: A Continuum of

Interacting Strategies, L.J. Goff, Ed. Cambridge
Univ. Press, Cambridge, (in press).

Phillips, G.L., D. Eminson and B. Moss. 1978. A mechanism
to account for macrophyte decline in progressively
eutrophicated freshwaters. Aquat. Bot. 4, 103-126.

Ponnamperuma, F.N. 1972. The chemistry of submerged soils.
Adv. Agron. 24, 29-95.

Prins, H.B.A. and R. Walsarie-Woff. 1974. Photorespiration
in leaves of Vallisneria spiralis. The effect of
oxygen on the carbon dioxide compensation point. Proc.
Akad. van Wetensc. Amsterdam (Ser. C). 77, 239-245.

Prins, H.B.A., J.F.H. Snel, R.J. Helder and P.E. Zanstra.
1980. Photosynthetic HCO_3^- utilization and OH-
excretion in aquatic angiosperms. Light-induced pH
changes at the leaf surface. Plant Physiol. 66,
818-822.

Prins, H.B.A., J.F.H. Snel and P.E. Zanstra. 1982a. The
mechanism of bicarbonate utilization. In Studies on
Aquatic Vascular Plants, J.J. Symoens, S.S. Hooper and
P. Compere, Eds., Royal Bot. Soc. Belgium, Brussels.
pp. 120-126.

Prins, H.B.A., J. O'Brien and P.E. Zanstra. 1982b.
Bicarbonate utilization in aquatic angiosperms, pH and
CO_2 concentration at the leaf surface. In Studies on
Aquatic Vascular Plants, J.J. Symoens, S.S. Hooper and
P. Compere, Eds. Royal Bot. Soc. Belgium, Brussels.
pp. 112-119.

Prins, H.B.A., J.F.H. Snel, P.E. Zanstra and R.J. Helder.
1982c. The mechanism of bicarbonate assimilation by
the polar leaves of Potamogeton and Elodea.
CO_2 concentration at the leaf surface.
Plant, Cell Environment, (in press).

Raven, J.A. 1970. Exogenous inorganic carbon sources in
plant photosynthesis. Biol. Rev. 45, 167-221.

Raven, J.A. 1981. Nutritional strategies of submerged
benthic plants: The acquisition of C, N and P by
rhizophytes and haptophytes. New Phytol. 83, 1-30.

Raven, J.A. and J. Beardall. 1981. Carbon dioxide as the
exogenous inorganic carbon source for Batrachospermum
and Lemanea. Br. Phycol. J. 16, 165-175.

Riley, J.J. and C.N. Hodges. 1969. Plant response to carbon dioxide enrichment - a function of microenvironment. Presented at the Southwestern and Rocky Mountain Division, American Association for the Advancement of Science. Colorado Springs, Colorado.

Rogers, K.H. and C.M. Breen. 1981. Effects of epiphyton on Potamogeton crispus L. leaves. Microbial Ecol. 7, 351-363.

Ruttner, F. 1947. Zur Frage der Karbonatassimiliation der Wasserpflanzen. I. Die beiden Haupttypen der Kohlenstoffaufnahme. Öst. Bot. Z. 94, 265-294.

Ruttner, F. 1948. Zur Frage der Karbonatassimilation der Wasserpflanze II. Das Verhalten von Elodea canadensis Und Fontinalis antipyretica in Lösungen von Natrium - bzw. Kaliumbikarbonat. Öst. Bot. Z. 95, 265-294.

Ruttner, F. 1960. Über die Kohlenstoffaufnahme bei Algen aus der Rhodophyceen-Gattung Batrachospermum. Schweiz Z. Hydrol. 22, 280-291.

Sale, P.J.M. and R.G. Wetzel. 1982. Growth and metabolism of Typha species in relation to cutting treatments. Aquatic Bot., (in press).

Salvucci, M.E. and G. Bowes. 1981. Induction of reduced photorespiratory activity in submersed and amphibious aquatic macrophytes. Plant Physiol. 67, 335-340.

Sand-Jensen, K. 1977. Effect of epiphytes on eelgrass photosynthesis. Aquatic Bot. 3, 55-63.

Sand-Jensen, K. and M. Sondergaard. 1981. Phytoplankton and epiphyte development and their shading effect on submerged macrophytes in lakes of different nutrient status. Int. Rev. ges. Hydrobiol. 66, 529-552.

Schindler, D.W. 1971. Carbon, nitrogen and phosphorus and the eutrophication of freshwater lakes. J. Phycol. 7, 321-329.

Schindler, D.W. and E.J. Fee. 1973. Diurnal variation of dissolved inorganic carbon and its use in estimating primary production and CO_2 invasion in Lake 227. J. Fish Res. Board Can. 30, 1501-1510.

Sculthorpe, C.D. 1967. The Biology of Aquatic Vascular Plants. St. Martin's Press, New York, 610 pp.

Shapiro, J. 1973. Blue-green algae: Why they become dominant. Science 182, 382–384.

Simms, K. 1976. A seasonal study of associated nitrogen fixation in the rhizosphere of Najas flexilis. M. Sc. Thesis, Queen's Univ., Kingston, Ontario. 53 pp.

Sionit, N., B.R. Strain and H.A. Beckford. 1981. Environmental controls on the growth and yield of okra. I. Effects of temperature and of CO_2 enrichment at cool temperature. Crop Sci. 21, 885–888.

Smith, F.A. and N.A. Walker. 1980. Photosynthesis by aquatic plants: Efects of unstirred layers in relation to the assimilation of CO_2 and HCO_3^- and to carbon isotopic discrimination. New Phytol. 86, 245–259.

Snaydon, R.W. 1971. An analysis of competion between plants of Trifolium repens L. populations collected from contrasting soils. J. Appl. Ecol. 8, 687–697.

Sondergaard, M. 1979. Light and dark respiration and the effect of the lacunal system on refixation of CO_2 in submerged aquatic plants. Aquatic Bot. 6, 269–283.

Sondergaard, M. and S. Laegaard. 1977. Vesicular-arbuscular mycorrhiza in some aquatic vascular plants. Nature 268, 232–233.

Sondergaard, M. and K. Sand-Jensen. 1979. Carbon uptake by leaves and roots of Littorella uniflora L. Aschers. Aquatic Bot. 6, 1–12.

Sondergaard, M. and R.G. Wetzel. 1980. Photorespiration and internal recycling of CO_2 in the submersed angiosperm Scirpus subterminalis. Can. J. Bot. 58, 591–5989.

Steemann Nielsen, E. 1944. Dependence of freshwater plants on quantity of carbon dioxide and hydrogen ion concentration. Dansk Bot. Ark. 11, 1–25.

Steemann Nielsen, E. 1947. Photosynthesis of aquatic plants with special reference to the carbon sources. Dansk Bot. Ark. 12, 5–71.

Stewart, W.D.P., Ed. 1974. Algal Physiology and Biochemistry. Univ. Calif. Press, Berkeley.